An Introduction to the Old Testament Prophetic Books

AN
INTRODUCTION
TO THE
OLD TESTAMENT
PROPHETIC
BOOKS

C. Hassell Bullock

MOODY PRESS
CHICAGO

Library of Congress Cataloging-in-Publication Data

Bullock, C. Hassell.
   An introduction to the Old Testament prophetic books.

   Bibliography; p.
   Includes index.
   1. Bible. O.T. Prophets—Criticism, interpretation,
etc. I. Title.
BS1505.2.B85   1986   224'.06   85-29862
ISBN 0-8024-4142-4

1 2 3 4 5 6 7 Printing/BC/Year 90 89 88 87 86

Printed in the United States of America

To my father and mother,
Erbie L. and Agnes C. Bullock

CONTENTS

Preface 9

1. Introduction 11

Part One
The Prophets of the Neo-Assyrian Period

2. Jonah: Preface to the Prophets 41
3. Amos: Call for Moral Obedience 55
4. Hosea: A Prophet's Dilemma 84
5. Micah: Judgment, Hope, and Promise 103
6. Isaiah: Prophet Par Excellence 125

Part Two
The Prophets of the Neo-Babylonian Period

7. Zephaniah: Profile of a People 165
8. Habakkuk: Prophet of Transition 174
9. Jeremiah: Prophet to the Nations 185
10. Nahum: The Reality of Judgment 215
11. Ezekiel: The Merging of Two Spheres 227
12. Obadiah: Edom's Day of the Lord 254
13. Lamentations: Reflections of the Soul 263

Part Three
The Prophets of the Persian Period

14. Daniel: Witness in Babylonia 279
15. Haggai: The Temple and the Future 301
16. Zechariah: Prophet of the New Kingdom 310
17. Joel: The Day of Decision 324
18. Malachi: Prophet of Covenant Love 335

Abbreviations in Bibliography 344
Bibliography 346
Index of Subjects and Persons 381
Index of Authors 385
Index of Scripture 389

PREFACE

"To be a prophet," said Abraham Heschel, "is both a distinction and an affliction."[1] Writing a book about them is hardly otherwise. The deep satisfaction of studying the words of some of history's most profound spokesmen is indescribable. But so is the deep anguish of the message they delivered to their ancient audience with its application for the modern world. Their call to righteousness, their summons to fasten social structures to the character of an ethical God, and their insistent proclamation that the Lord's patience would not endure forever, even though in the end sin could not outdo His grace or undo His love—those were emphatic precepts that the prophets iterated and reiterated to their world, precepts that still have not lost their potent relevance.

The satisfaction of learning from others who have pored over the prophetic oracles along with the anguish of trying to represent them fairly and to learn from their erudition as well as their theological anomalies are part of the mixed package of writing a book on the prophets. Their erudition has taught me far more than their anomalies, and to my teachers who have instructed me both from the lectern and the published page, I am inexpressibly grateful. I hope they can find gratification in the positive features of this book while letting the responsibility for its contraventions rest squarely on my shoulders.

Our technological distance from the age of the prophets is almost a measureless chasm. From ancient writing methods to the modern computer is an expanse that can hardly be appreciated even by those who have been liberated from pen and page to the efficiences of word processing. Yet God forbid that we should make the mistake of assuming that efficiency and technology have removed us also from the demands of the prophets' God, who comprehends the broad time expanse that technology has made so wide. At this point I gratefully acknowledge those who have assisted me in writing the manuscript until my own computer skills matured. Mrs. Jane Marston typed portions of the manuscript from my rough copy, and Mrs. Mary Lou McCurdy put portions of it into the computer. Their technical skills and their personal friendship have given a dimension to the manuscript that only I can readily discern but from

1. Abraham J. Heschel, *The Prophets*, 2 vols. (New York: Harper & Row, 1962), 1:17–18.

which the reader will also unconsciously profit. Then there have been my graduate assistants who have contributed to the growth of this book at various levels, Henry Sun and James Coleman. Their help has freed me to concentrate on the task of research and writing. Another person who deserves far more thanks than a line of text can provide is my friend and former student, Don Patrick, who did the footwork for the bibliography. Members of my family also merit much thanks for their patience with me. My wife, Rhonda, has at times felt that her husband and the computer were synonymous, and my children, Scott and Becky, have often wished that their father would allow them more computer time for their playful moods. Finally, I am heartily grateful to the Board of Trustees of Wheaton College for a sabbatical leave in the fall of 1984, when much of this work was accomplished.

A notable part of the distinction of writing this book has been that I have done it as an offering of thanksgiving for my parents, Erbie L. and Agnes C. Bullock, whose love for God and faithfulness to His church and their family of six children have indelibly recorded their names in the roster of those "of whom the world was not worthy."

The value of the Hebrew prophets has been assessed and weighed by three millennia of history, and thankfully they, being dead, yet speak. The distinction and the affliction are still part of their legacy. If writing this book brings the minutest participation in that legacy, even if it be overweighted more with affliction than distinction, and if the God whose will the prophets sought to proclaim has been glorified, the effort expended has been well worthwhile.

1

INTRODUCTION

THE PLAN OF THE BOOK

THE FOCUS of this study is the latter prophets, as they are known in the Jewish canon, or the major and minor prophets, as they have come to be called in the Christian canon.

The plan of this book is to follow a historical line through the literary prophets, to the degree that it is visible to modern scholarship. Of course, all scholars do not agree on such fundamental issues as the date, authorship, and literary integrity of the books and their component parts. Those matters will be discussed in some detail in the chapters that follow. My attempt to line the prophets and their books up on a time line rather than treating them in the canonical order carries an element of risk, but it seems worth the venture in order to see the cultural, theological, and historical interrelationships that existed among the canonical prophets. This perspective is not easily appreciated by either the beginner in prophetic studies or the advanced student who concentrates on the prophets book by book and never sees the broad picture, with the individual prophets in their historical and theological niches.

Though the prophets were not given to quoting one another by name, they did draw upon each other, some more than others. Once that dependence is recognized, a new view of the prophetic movement emerges. They were not lone individualists who knew nothing and cared nothing for what others who bore the name "prophet" had said. Rather they saw themselves in a line of succession and were aware of the tradition they had received from their predecessors.

The prophets spoke to Israel in times of crisis. In fact, historical and moral crisis, if the list of canonical prophets is any indication, called them forth. Had there been no crisis, there would have been little need for the prophets. When the list of literary prophets is posted, it will be noted that they are clustered around critical historical events or eras.

The historical continuum of Israel's history from the eighth to the fifth centuries B.C. can be sketched, even if roughly, in the literary prophets. Three centers, corresponding to the three international eras, bring them into sharp focus. Or, it might as accurately be said that the literary prophets bring three historical centers into sharp focus.

The first category includes those of the *Neo-Assyrian* period, whose attention fell upon the circumstances leading up to and the conditions following the fall of the Northern Kingdom (Israel) in 722 B.C. The constellation of prophets who assessed the moral and theological climate that led to the end of Israel was constituted by Amos, Hosea, Micah, and Isaiah. In varying ways but with sympathetic insight, they saw the end of Israel and its implications for Judah. The critical nature of this era had much to do with the preservation of the prophetic oracles as sacred literature. Although Jonah was not preoccupied with that event and obviously belongs on the periphery of this era, it might be said that the judgment he reluctantly saw submerged in Yahweh's compassionate nature re-emerged in the era of this prophetic constellation.

The second group of prophets is composed of those of the *Neo-Babylonian* era, whose focus marked out the attendant circumstances and succeeding conditions of the fall of the Southern Kingdom (Judah) in 586 B.C. At the end of the Assyrian period, when the shifting lines of international domination blurred and then cleared again with the rise of the Chaldean-inspired Babylonian empire, some of the most powerful and discerning voices of history addressed the developing crisis. Zephaniah, Jeremiah, Habakkuk, Nahum, Ezekiel, and Obadiah contributed their distinctive insights to their contemporaries and delivered their message from the Lord to Judah. The tragic model of Israel and her adamant persistence in idolatry was like a dark, foreboding cloud that settled over Judah. With the passing of time historical memory faded; the tragedy of 722 diminished as a moral example, and Judah stood on the same treacherous precipice as had her sister Israel. This group of prophets, with irresistible compulsion, tried to coax Judah away from the edge of the abyss and announced the bad news of what would happen if she did not move back into the safety zone of covenantal observance. Yet thankfully the news was not all bad, for the fall of Jerusalem, at a certain point as inevitable as Samaria's fall, carried a message of hope that Judah would miraculously revive.

After the Exile, during the *Persian* period, the third group of prophets built upon that hope. They set forth Yahweh's new order as Babylonian austerity passed into Persian indulgence. With a new landlord Judah's fortunes, partly smothered in the long exile but kept alive by religious enthusiasts, took a turn for the better. The decree of Cyrus in 538 B.C. marked the beginning of that era. The first faint flurry of hope might even be traced to the release of Jehoiachin from prison after the death of Nebuchadnezzar in 562 B.C. Daniel, Haggai, Zechariah, Joel, and Malachi in their respective ways articulated the hope and implicated the changing conditions of the first hundred years of postexilic life in Judah. The ebbing tide of history had fallen to its lowest mark in the fall of Jerusalem, a disaster once popularly thought to be impossible. The rise of Cyrus after the Exile represented the incoming tide of Judean history.

THE PRELIMINARY STAGES

The roots of prophecy are deeply imbedded in Israel's history and in the culture of the ancient Near East. From patriarchal times eminent leaders gave guidance to the people of God. The patriarchal mode of leadership transcribed in a later era into the charismatic guidance of Moses and Joshua and the judges. When such leaders led Israel, the need for prophets was minimal, although the prophetic phenomenon was known even during those eras (Num. 11:24–30; Deut. 18:15–22). However, from the closing phase of the period of the judges to the end of the biblical period as it is recorded in the Old Testament (OT), the word of the prophet is one of the most distinctive traits of Israelite culture and religion.

Four terms were applied to individuals, both men and women, who demonstrated prophetic traits: "man of God" ('*îsh hā-elōhîm*), "seer" (*rō'eh*), "visionary" (*hōzeh*), and "prophet" (*nābî'*). The word "diviner" or "soothsayer" (*qōsēm*) is used of those who practiced formal divination, perhaps using lots or other methods of discerning the will of the deity, but that term was not applied to those prophets who receive legitimate sanction in the OT. The terms "seer" and "visionary" (*rō'eh* and *hōzeh*) are descriptive of the individual's experience, the first emphasizing the extraordinary insight that came to the prophets, and the second the method of reception by means of visions or dreams. The terms "seer" and "man of God" are both attested in the case of Samuel (1 Sam. 9:9), the former term being the older of the two. The implication of the phrase "man of God" is that the person was possessed by God for special service. In the transition period between the nonliterary (those whose words have not been preserved in books that carry their names) and literary prophets (those whose words have been preserved in written form under their respective names), little distinction can be detected between the terms "man of God" and "prophet" (*nābî'*).[1] With the dawn of literary prophecy, however, the Hebrew term *nābî'* became the common name for the prophet. Some scholars believe the word came into disrepute in the time of Amos, inciting him to protest the allegation that he was a *nābî'*. His protestation, however, was more likely provoked by the motives that the priest Amaziah attributed to his ministry in Bethel—that he was there to earn his bread. The reply of Amos in which he explains his real occupation supports that interpretation (Amos 7:14–15).

A bygone generation of scholars deprecated the predictive or "foretelling"

---

1. T. J. Meek, *Hebrew Origins*, p. 147, cites *nābî'* as coming from a common Akkadian root, not found in Hebrew, meaning "to speak," thus "speaker." William F. Albright disagrees with that etymology and relates it to the Akkadian word *nabu* ("to call"), thus "one who is called (by God)" (*From the Stone Age to Christianity*, p. 303). Klaus Koch's interpretation of the term as referring to one who is "entrusted with a message" is very close to that explanation (*The Prophets*, 1:16).

element in the prophets in favor of the "forthtelling" role.[2] The Septuagint (LXX) translation of the word *nābî'* as *prophētēs* (one who speaks for, in behalf of) has been cited as evidence that the prophets were "forthtellers" rather than "foretellers." Yet that word is quite a general term, and does not capture the entire function of the *nābî'* in itself. Although it can accurately be said that the prophets were basically preachers, that is, that they spoke to their own times and situations, interpreting current events of history in light of God's will for Israel, the predictive element was a distinctive part of their message (Amos 3:7). Subtract that and, as Alfred Guillaume has said, they would become preachers and not prophets.[3]

ORIGINS OF PROPHECY

The origins of Hebrew prophecy have been variously traced to Canaanite, Egyptian, and Arabic sources, but more recently attention has shifted to Mesopotamia, especially the ancient city of Mari,[4] for enlightenment on the phenomenon of Hebrew prophecy. The Mari texts, dating from the first half of the second millennium B.C., are particularly interesting in their exposure of a group of prophets, both men and women, who practiced intuitive divination. That is, they were not practitioners in the standard techniques of divination but were dependent upon inspiration for their oracles, much in the same way as the Hebrew prophets.[5] Found in administrative records, their oracles were short and limited to materials relating to the reign of King Zimrilim. As a consequence of the nature of those texts and their direct relation to the royal court, we do not get as full a picture of the Mari prophets as we do of the Hebrew prophets. Further, the documents of Mari were most likely preserved within the royal court, whereas those of the Hebrew literary prophets were for the most part preserved apart from the court, thus exercising a kind of independence from the kings.

The evidence is still insufficient to draw any confident conclusion regarding the origins of Hebrew prophecy. The one thing that can be said confidently is that prophecy, like temple and sacrifice, was a general phenomenon in the ancient world of the Bible. The attempt to trace its origins to any one culture outside of Israel is no more possible than it would be to trace Mari or Canaanite prophecy to its derivation. So far as the OT generally and the prophets

---

2. E.g., Meek, *Hebrew Origins*, p. 148.
3. Alfred Guillaume, *Prophecy and Divination*, pp. 111–12.
4. See John H. Hayes, "Prophetism at Mari and Old Testament Parallels," pp. 397–409; William L. Moran, "New Evidence from Mari on the History of Prophecy," pp. 15–56; John F. Craghan, "Mari and Its Prophets: The Contributions of Mari to the Understanding of Biblical Prophecy," pp. 32–55; Abraham Malamat, "Prophecy in the Mari Documents," pp. 74–84; "Prophetic Revelations in New Documents from Mari and the Bible," pp. 207–27.
5. Malamat, "Prophetic Revelations," p. 208.

particularly were concerned, prophecy had its origins in the call of Yahweh. Through the prophets He revealed His will for Israel and spoke His Word of judgment and salvation. To be sure, it was not a unique phenomenon. Yet although the study of parallels may produce useful results, the question of origins remains unanswered. The best and most illuminating sources for understanding Hebrew prophecy are found in the OT itself.

NONLITERARY PROPHECY

Running parallel to literary prophecy in its earlier phase was the preliterary or nonliterary prophetic movement, so called because it did not leave a literary legacy, except as it impinged upon the history and fortunes of the monarchy (as found in Samuel, Kings, and Chronicles). Judging from OT literature, the prophets did not become a significant factor in religious history until the rise of the monarchy. Samuel was both a transitional and foundational figure in that process. The records of nonliterary prophecy are not entirely lost to us, for they are interwoven into the histories of Israel as they are told in the books of Samuel, Kings, Chronicles, Ezra, and Nehemiah.

In fact, the author of Kings viewed the prophetic movement as the only hope of reformation in the Northern Kingdom, particularly in view of the religious apostasy and moral corruption of the northern monarchy for which Jeroboam I established the determining and insurmountable precedent. The religious reforms that were instigated in the north were the direct result of such courageous prophets as Elijah and Elisha. But in the view of the writer of Kings, virtually no reforming elements originated with the northern kings themselves. In stark contrast, the religious and social reforms in the Southern Kingdom, ruled by the Davidic dynasty whose beginnings and continued existence were tied directly to prophetic authority, originated with the kings. That is especially evident in the religious revivals initiated by Asa, Jehoshaphat, Hezekiah, and Josiah. The only literary prophets mentioned by the author of the book of Kings are Jonah and Isaiah. Thus not even honorable mention of the majority of the literary prophets is part of the plan of that writer. That silence is an enigma. Its explanation, however, is probably to be found in the purpose of the book, especially its deep respect for the legitimacy of the Davidic dynasty, which came into being through the instrumentality of the prophets, particularly Samuel and Nathan. The author's main interest lay in the Judean monarchy and its internal power to survive and revive. Perhaps the author wrote his history as a record of hope that David's house would rise again. The release of Jehoiachin from prison, with which the book ends, implies that hope.

The main sources of our knowledge about the nonliterary prophets, the books of Samuel and Kings, disclose the public life of those individuals. But like their literary successors (sometimes called the classical prophets), they had their private lives too. They maintained private domiciles, where they were on occasion consulted (1 Kings 14:4; also 13:18). However, their understudies, the "sons of the prophets," maintained some kind of communal existence. We see them involved in a unified effort to move their residence to the Jordan River during the time of Elisha (2 Kings 6:1–7). Yet, in light of 2 Kings 4:1 it seems safe to assume that they led a life with the ingredients of that of a private citizen. Here the wife of one of the sons of the prophets appeals to Elisha on behalf of her two children, whom her dead husband's creditor threatens to enslave.

Some evidence points to the receipt of fees for prophetic services. That was certainly true of the court prophets, and in some cases it may have been true of others. In 1 Samuel 9:8 Saul's servant had money to pay for the services of Samuel to locate the asses of Kish. So also Jeroboam sent a gift by his wife when she went to inquire of Ahijah (1 Kings 14:3). Such a practice was even known by Ben-hadad of Syria, for he sent Elisha a gift by Hazael when he wanted to know whether he would recover from his sickness (2 Kings 8:8). Yet we should also note that these prophets could not be manipulated by remuneration. Elisha refused to accept the gift that Namaan brought him when he requested healing of his leprosy (2 Kings 5:16),[6] and his servant Gehazi was struck with leprosy when he accepted the gift (vv. 24–27).

The psychological orientation of the nonliterary prophets reveals that they sometimes had ecstatic experiences, especially in association with the bands of prophets (1 Sam. 10:5–13). They were given to dreams, visions, ecstasy, and divining. The word of Yahweh to Micaiah ben Imlah took the form of a vision (1 Kings 22:13–23), and Yahweh's word to Nathan regarding the construction of the Temple was described as "in accordance with all these words and all this vision" (2 Sam. 7:17). The visions often occurred at night.[7]

Generally these prophets were not concerned with moral issues as such, except as they had a direct bearing upon the destiny and welfare of Israel. So although they spoke to individuals rather than the nation, their fundamental concern was national destiny. In that sense the literary or classical prophets were truly their spiritual successors. The nonliterary prophets were a kind of conscience to the king, admonishing him to faithfulness to Yahweh. There was no set pattern of consultation. Kings called on prophets, and prophets called on kings.

---

6. Norman H. Snaith, *The First and Second Books of Kings*, 3:210, evaluates the gift at about eighty thousand dollars.
7. To Samuel (1 Sam. 15:16); to Solomon, although he was not a prophet (2 Chron. 1:7, 7:12); to Nathan (2 Sam. 7:4; 1 Chron. 17:3).

THE PROPHETS AND THEIR CULTURE

We cannot ignore the basic fact that the prophets found their legitimacy and valid credentials first of all in Yahweh's call. The prophetic call is the frontispiece of several of the prophetic books (Hosea, Jeremiah, Ezekiel), and Amos and Isaiah record their calls later in the collection of their oracles (Amos 7; Isa. 6). The book of Jonah is a treatise on the call and execution of the prophetic office. Even where the prophetic call is never formally recorded, it is nevertheless imbedded in the books in the form of the reception formulas, which fix the prophet's word as the Word of the Lord ("Thus says the Lord" and others). The importance of Yahweh's call of the prophet cannot be exaggerated. Even when a record of the formal call has not survived among a given prophet's oracles, we must nevertheless assume that his audience was somehow assured of his credentials.

It has been said that history makes the man, and that was true with the prophets. Of course, the man also makes history, and that was true of the prophets as well. Which perspective was more important is impossible to determine. They are complementary perspectives. I will discuss four of the forces working within the culture that shaped the prophets and was shaped by them: historical events, the monarchy, idolatry, and social oppression.

OF HISTORY AND PROPHETS

History was intimate with the prophets, an intimacy that partially stemmed from their deep relationship to the Lord of history. Yahweh had entered into the historical process to protect His vital interests in the world He created. Israel was at once the end and means of His actions, and the prophets were the witnesses of His vital concerns. Unlike the nature religion of Canaan, Yahweh's revelation came through historical events. The prophets were patrons of that conviction, and their insistent preaching, even if it did not turn the nation to repentance, fortified the faith against the naturalism of the Baal cult. In the long run they preserved this vital element, which has been passed on to Judaism and Christianity.

Vying for the helm of Israel's spiritual craft, the prophets frequently positioned themselves against the power structures of priesthood and monarchy. They attempted to steer Israel through the narrow straits of political uncertainty and moral inexactitude. One only wonders what horrible thing might have happened to Israel that did not in fact happen—perish the thought!—if the prophets had not guided the nation through much historical change.

Assyria, buzzing like a swarm of bees, alighted upon Israel in the eighth century and left the Northern Kingdom stunned beyond recovery and the Southern Kingdom put on notice that her future hinged only on the contingency of spiritual change. That was the message of history as read by the eighth-century prophets. The two groups that stood to benefit most from the disaster of 722 B.C., the Jerusalem priests and Judean kings, still were not the major initiators of change that evoked God's mercy. Hezekiah's reform that followed this catastrophe, it might be admitted, temporarily staved off a like disaster for Judah. But his despicable son, Manasseh, reversed his father's policies and put the nation in jeopardy again. Yet the prophets were stabilizers of national destiny, or so they sought to be. They were present and speaking when kings clammed up and shut their eyes to the signs of the times. Perhaps we should not overrate the prophets' objectivity, because they had their special interests. But life viewed through Yahweh's covenantal demands was, from a theological point of view, as objective as one could be. So the prophets spoke not theirs but Yahweh's Word. They were in line for no political advantage and sought no permanent institutional power. Through divine revelation they foresaw the crisis of 722 B.C. and sought to steer the survivors through it. Amos announced the awful day and its unavoidable consequences, "as when a man flees from a lion,/ And a bear meets him" (Amos 5:19). Hosea, caught between divine judgment and incomparable love, declared the severance of Israel's covenantal status but reaffirmed the hope of a future with Yahweh.

The Babylonians, the greedy successors of international dominance, played their role against Judah as meticulously as Assyria had done against Israel. Zephaniah, standing in the position that Amos had occupied in the Assyrian era, announced the Day of the Lord for Judah, and proponents of that message were found also in Jeremiah, Habakkuk, and Ezekiel. With their unstoppable army the Babylonians marched against Judah. Pawns of Yahweh's wrath and instruments of His irresistible power, in 586 those pagans reiterated the disaster of 722 on a more southerly latitude and again proved that the prophets were justified in their spiritual discernment.

Yet the hope that had from the beginning of literary prophecy been irrepressible began to take a more distinct form in the message of Ezekiel and later in the visions of Daniel and Zechariah and the oracles of Haggai, Joel, and Malachi. Now that the Day of the Lord had come for Judah as well as for Israel, when would its counterpart arrive for the nations and the unadulterated blessings of the new order be showered upon the Lord's remnant? The question was renewed and the answer formulated afresh in the postexilic era when Cyrus, the Lord's shepherd, aroused new hopes that the anticipated era of restoration had dawned. Indeed it had, but not to the extent that Isaiah had described it. In fact, the horrible thought of the Day of the Lord was reintroduced by Joel to remind the reforming nation that moral demands were still part of God's program for Israel and that judgment always loomed when moral obedience and cultic purity were not observed. The Persian era was one of hope.

The prophets were pawns of no power structures and represented no vested interests—except the irresistible power of God and the vital interests that He had vested in Israel through the Sinai covenant. "The Lord took me from following the flock" (Amos 7:15), and "The Lord God has spoken!/Who can but prophesy?" (Amos 3:8*b*). These were the trademarks of that irresistible force that moved the prophets. "Then in my heart it becomes like a burning fire/Shut up in my bones; And I am weary of holding it in,/And I cannot endure it" (Jer. 20:9) was Jeremiah's expression of the same inner compulsion. His reluctance that preceded his response was the reversal of Isaiah's response that preceded his reluctance: "Here am I. Send me!" and "Lord, how long?" (Isa. 6:8, 11).

No figure was out of the prophets' speaking range. Amos's words reached to the defiant ears of King Jeroboam, Isaiah's challenge to the impious Ahaz, and Jeremiah's words of doom to the impervious Jehoiakim. Even the kings of foreign nations, at least theoretically, came within earshot of the prophets' oracles.

The symbolic actions of the prophets were a sign of their involvement in the historical process. Isaiah's naked promenade, Hosea's marriage to a harlot, Jeremiah's wearing of an ox's yoke, and Ezekiel's extended repose, all fall in that category. The prophets could no more extricate themselves from history than the Lord Himself could. They blended into the brocade. Just how effective they were in turning the course of history is a matter of debate. Certainly they did not achieve the goal of bringing Israel to repentance and thus averting the national disasters of 722 and 586. But in the long range of history they were proved right and their opponents wrong. History became their vindicator.

The prophets' interest in the future grew out of deep theological conviction. They believed the ideal for society was laid down in covenantal legislation of the past. Justice and righteousness, which the law prescribed as the pillars of a theocratic society, were to be the order of every age. The present found its anchorage and preshadowing in the past. As has been observed, psychologically and terminologically the OT has its face to the past and its back to the future. Society should perpetually reflect the ideals set forth in the law, a law that was itself imparted by the prophet Moses: "But by a prophet the Lord brought Israel from Egypt, and by a prophet he was kept" (Hos. 12:13). In Hosea's view, law and prophecy were forever united in Moses. Rejection of the law was tantamount to rejection of prophecy, and so exactly did he see the prophets as representatives of the covenantal position that the opposite could also be said—rejection of prophecy signaled rejection of the law. Yet it was the quality of that legislation, not its quantity, that Israel had rejected; "Though I wrote for him ten thousand precepts of My law, they are regarded as a strange thing" (Hos. 8:12).

The detached relationship to the law, exhibited in a continuous chain of legal violation and moral transgression, was Jeremiah's concern when he analyzed his society and predicted the day when the law would be written on tablets of flesh rather than tablets of stone (Jer. 31:31–34). Therefore, when society deviated from the covenantal norm, the prophets called Israel back to it and anticipated a reformed order in the future.

Their corrective program called for the establishment of justice up and down the social ladder, especially to widows and orphans and the socially oppressed. Through a reformation of the legal system, corrupted by greed and bribery, a new order of justice could come. That was not bare social reform divested of religious underpinnings. The prophets had no such concept. The new age would begin with the reforming forces of moral change in the present and climax with the dramatic new day of peace, justice, righteousness, and holiness, with Israelite political and religious domination of the world. Repentance, which the prophets demanded in unalloyed genuineness, could effect a drastic turn in Israel's fortunes and redirect the forces of history for the shaping of the new order. That order would be geographically located in this world with Jerusalem as the religious center. To her the nations would turn in order to acquire a knowledge of the Lord.

Not historians in the technical sense, the prophets' interest in future events was tied to the concerns of the present. It is erroneous to assume, as was done by an earlier generation of scholars, that the predictive element was extraneous to prophetic preaching. On the contrary, the future was a vital part of prophetic theology. Yet repentance did not occur in broad enough proportions to alter Yahweh's plans for judgment. Therefore, judgment was unavoidable. It was both punitive and rehabilitative. In the absence of general repentance, the prophets expected divine intervention on a scale like that of the Exodus to put the society back in order. The new day would come no less as a result of God's self-initiated action than the deliverance from Egypt. Thus, although built upon the present order, the future would be drastically different from it.

Furthermore, the prophetic future was both immediate and remote. The depth of their view is not readily discernible because the prophets merged the present and future so unpretentiously in their descriptions of time. The line of division is faint, and hermeneutically the time elements of the prophetic books, that is, whether a statement applies to the past, present, or future, is a critical issue. It is my opinion that there was a remote future involved in prophetic eschatology. Thus statements with future implications did not always involve events just around the next bend in the road. When that future had come to pass, it would definitely have similarities to the present order.

The trophy of prophetic preaching was not the decline and fall of the Israelite and Judean states. That was a message they reluctantly proclaimed; they hoped against hope that it would not happen. Rather their triumph was the survival of the people of God in the exile and the restoration of the Judean state in the postexilic period. Whereas the Assyrian and Babylonian disasters proved their message of woe to be well founded, the turn of events in the Persian era proved their message of weal also to be motivated in the divine will. Most of the pre-exilic prophets had a major interest in the era of restoration.

OF KINGS AND PROPHETS

Within Israelite society the strongest power structure with which the prophets had to deal was the monarchy, first of the United Kingdom (Saul, David, and Solomon) and then of the separate monarchies of Israel and Judah.

The kingship came into being through the intermediate agency of the prophet Samuel (1 Sam. 8); Saul, the nation's first king, participated in the ecstatic practices of the prophets of his day (1 Sam. 10:1–13). The importance of Samuel as a transition figure is strongly emphasized in the first book of Samuel, and his precedent-setting role of making the kingly office responsive to the prophet should be noted well. The model can be seen in the reign of David with Nathan's transmission of Yahweh's master plan for building the Temple (2 Sam. 7) and his aggressive role in putting Solomon on the throne (1 Kings 1:22–48).

Amid the uncertainties that marked the end of Solomon's reign, Ahijah of Shiloh fanned the fire of secession and offered Jeroboam a five-sixths share of tribal loyalty (1 Kings 11:29–40). When civil war threatened to deepen the schism after Solomon's death, Shemaiah, the man of God, sued for peace and averted Rehoboam's plans for war against the north (12:21–24).

Jeroboam's religious apostasy, centralized in Dan and Bethel, brought the anonymous man of God from Judah to announce that a Judean king would bring an end to the apostate priesthood (1 Kings 13:1–10).

The interaction of prophets and kings in the preliterary stage came to a climax in the relations between Elijah and Elisha and the Israelite kings. Especially did Elijah's zealous ministry for Yahwism concentrate upon restoring national loyalty to the ancient God of Israel. With unprecedented success against Baalism, aided by the reform movement of the Rechabite Jehonadab (2 Kings 10:15–17), Elijah dealt a devastating blow to the alliance between the northern monarchy and Baalism. Sadly, however, it did not endure.

It has been proposed that the prophets after the division of the kingdom, at least down to the eighth century, were proponents of national reunion.[8] That element was likely an integral part of their platform, but their interests were broader than that. They were basically religious, calling for the purge of pagan elements from the national religion. They were politically inclined but religiously motivated. The two were paired.

The role of the preliterary prophets in national emergencies is indisputable,

8. Edward Robertson. "The Role of the Early Hebrew Prophet," pp. 412–31.

but we should reiterate that their motive was basically religious. Samuel, architect of a new age and government, recalled Yahweh's miraculous deliverance from Egypt and His ensuing care. He asserted the principle that faithfulness to Yahweh's commandment was the path to national prosperity (1 Sam. 12:6–17). As already noted, Elijah's theological diplomacy called for the same platform (1 Kings 18:18). It should be no surprise, therefore, that the first of the classical prophets, Amos, Hosea, Micah, and Isaiah, were intensely interested in the monarchy. Amaziah of the Bethel priesthood sized up Amos's message as conspiracy against Jeroboam II (Amos 7:10). Hosea condemned the northern monarchy as illegitimate (Hos. 8:4), and Micah envisioned the rise of a future ruler from the unpretentious town of Bethlehem (Mic. 5:2). Isaiah, among those prophets, was most directly involved with the monarchy. He personally challenged Ahaz to ask a sign of Yahweh (Isa. 7:3–17) and was chief prophetic counsel to Hezekiah (36–39).

Yet it should be noted, as will be developed further in the discussion on Jonah, that with the literary prophets the addressees of the divine oracles were less frequently kings and more often the population at large. It is very likely that the prophets carried their message directly to the people in the hope that they would repent and instigate national reform. That strategy was logical in view of the failure of the monarchy to instigate lasting reform. As noted above, the author of Kings saw the Judean monarchy as a source of religious reform, but at the same time the monarchy, particularly as represented by Manasseh, was the cause of the fall of the state. In its hands was the power to turn the nation toward good or evil.

OF GODS AND PROPHETS

The books of Kings and the majority opinion of the literary prophets are in agreement that the fall of the Judean state was a result of idolatry in its various forms. After Hezekiah's courageous reforms that turned Judah in a divergent direction from the recently fallen Israelite state, his son Manasseh's reversal of the reforms inalterably determined the fate of the nation (2 Kings 21:10–16; 23:26–27; 24:3–4).

Especially was the prophetic opposition strong against the form of idolatry known as *Baalism,* a fertility cult that the Israelites found deeply rooted in the native culture of Canaan at the time of the settlement. The alleged suzerainty of the god Baal over the land of Canaan came into conflict with prophetic belief that Yahweh was Lord of the land. The prophets were keenly aware that He had brought the Israelites out of Egypt and caused them to inherit the Promised Land. The Exodus and the conquest were lodged in prophetic memory and belonged to that same line of tradition that gloried in the rise of Nazirites and prophets as Yahweh's agents (Amos 2:9–12).

Both the prophetic view and that of Kings were grounded in the Mosaic understanding of the sovereignty of the Lord and His demand for exclusive worship (Ex. 20:3–6; Deut. 5:7–10). In fact, the fundamental problem with idolatry was its defiance of God's sovereign rule over His world. Isaiah, for example, emphasized the Creator's right to rule the world and to demand honor from His creatures (Isa. 40:12–31).

The worship of idols violated another critical principle in OT religion. It disregarded the ethical undergirdings of Yahwism. Basic human relationships, defined and guarded in the Pentateuch, were broken down in the Baal cult. The boundaries that secured family ties, especially sexual regulations, were erased by the fertility rites performed in the pagan sanctuaries. The ethical demands of justice and righteousness, with their implications for the court of law and the marketplace, lost their tenacity within Baalism. Its fundamental moral assumptions were in contradiction to those of prophetic persuasion. Idolatry summed up all that was wrong with Israel. Somewhere in its mystic anatomy was a cavity where every sin had its fullest expression and found its perfect lair.

It is generally recognized that the Exile cured Judah of her idolatry.[9] A painful cure, to be sure, the deep soul reflection that caused the covenant people to abandon paganism as a religious option was one of the monumental accomplishments of the prophets. In addition to predicting the catastrophe, they offered the monotheistic explanation that originated in the Sinai revelation.

The popular religion set forth in the Pentateuch was basically a priestly religion. It did not develop in the Exile, as the Wellhausen school has propagandized. (Julius Wellhausen's formalization of critical thinking on the Pentateuch, known as the documentary hypothesis, advanced the idea that four distinct documents—J, E, D, and P—went into the final composition of the Pentateuch in the post-exilic era. In his view, the prophets were strongly influential in shaping OT religion that had its crowning expression in the Pentateuch.) The relationship of the prophets to it has been explained as a creative role. That we can readily affirm, for the prophets were not mere reflectors of an ancient theology. With creative insight they proclaimed the Word of God. Among their theological developments was the eschatology that described Israel's future as the renewal of historical events, such as the Exodus, wilderness, and conquest. Yet their role was not genetic in the sense that they created OT religion. Although it is legitimate to speak of prophetic religion, it should be remembered that its base rested upon Mosaic foundations. The monotheism of Mosaism moved the prophets to announce judgment and salvation oracles within the context of the faith. Whether they formally engaged the curse-blessing literary form for their oracles is an arguable point. However, the curse-blessing motif was inscribed on the prophetic mind, and the assumption

9. See Yehezkel Kaufmann, *The Babylonian Captivity and Deutero-Isaiah*, p. 16.

that the people of God accepted that theological premise is clear, for the literary prophets did not try to prove the premise. When announcing judgment, the justification they gave was the sins of the nation. They did not need to explain that sin deserved judgment. That was popularly assumed. Even when the false security of the eighth century had grown up around the concept of election, the prophets found compelling warrant within the ancient faith to base security upon the contingency of moral obedience (Deut. 28). The point is that prophetic monotheism and its opposition to idolatry was not an innovation of the eighth and subsequent centuries. Its roots were anchored deeply in convenantal theology of the Mosaic era.

OF SOCIAL OPPRESSION AND PROPHETS

The Israelite settlement in Canaan and the gradual assimilation of Canaanite civilization created a social problem for the fledgling nation, that of a new class. As the tribal organization and the collective solidarity that went with it began to dissolve, the individual and his interests became more evident. The right to hold private property and the practice of amassing wealth were both recognized and practiced by the Hebrews in Canaan. Thus we have the basis for class distinction between the rich and the poor.[10]

The Israelite monarchy played no small part in deepening class distinctions. David left a kingdom that stretched from the Euphrates River to the Mediterranean Sea and from Dan to Beersheba (1 Kings 5:4–5). With Egypt and Assyria at a low political ebb, Israel was at peace. Thus the people could develop their agricultural or pastoral production. Julian Morgenstern suggests that that was the period when Israel began producing more than her people utilized for their own needs. Such commodities could be bartered for things the people did not themselves produce. The merchant interest would explain the motives of David's and Solomon's friendly relations with the Phoenicians (cf., e.g., 1 Kings 5).[11]

Yet not all of the people enjoyed the same prosperity. Cities became more important as business and cultural centers of exchange. A definite class interest began to assert itself. The rich became richer and the poor became poorer. A society that only two or three centuries earlier had been seminomadic with, ideally at least, no class distinctions among its citizens now accommodated the wealthy and the poor. And as is generally the case, the economic differences gave rise to social distinctions that bred corruption, oppression, and injustice. Samuel warned Israel that the monarchy would introduce alarming social change (1 Sam. 8:11–18). The thought of an aristocracy was most distasteful to Samuel.

10. J. Lindblom, *Prophecy in Ancient Israel*, p. 347.
11. Julian Morgenstern, *Amos Studies*, 1:186.

The prophets were not social reformers. They were theological reformers, for their basic motivation was generated within their commitment to the fundamental laws of God. Their reaction against the developing social order can be seen as early as Elijah and his defense of Naboth against Ahab and Jezebel (1 Kings 21). The king as chief guarantor of justice to his people was a common understanding in the ancient Near East. Yet he had taken on the reverse role. Having no channel of authority except Yahweh's Word, the prophets stepped forth to defend the oppressed, the widow, the orphan, the poor, and the resident alien. Assuming a role that otherwise belonged to the king, they provided a third-party defense. Their concern emanated from Yahweh's own compassionate nature (Deut. 15:11; 24:14–15; Ex. 22:21–27) and the responsibility of each citizen to dispense justice (Mic. 6:8). Abraham Heschel has stated that justice was important to the prophets because it was God's stake in human life.[12] It is in man-to-man relations that the life of God is expressed, and it is between man and man that the reputation of God is at its greatest risk.

The poor did not in any sense constitute a party or a social class in the modern sense of the word; nor is there any evidence that the prophets were members of that class in whose behalf they spoke. Further, there is no indication that the poor had asked for a spokesman; but the prophets arose to their defense as a consequence of the call from a God whose nature demanded justice. They bore no hatred of their society; rather they wanted to see the social decay reversed and devotion to Yahweh restored. That social concern, which was keenest among the pre-exilic prophets, was an index to covenant loyalty. At some point the prophets believed that the ills of the society could be cured in part by a reversal of social behavior, particularly by caring for and ensuring justice to the poor. Security was to be found in making others secure—"Here is rest, give rest to the weary" (Isa. 28:12a). No less fittingly Isaiah verbalized the prophets' experience of bitter rejection—"but they would not listen" (28:12b).

As a third party the prophets stepped forth unbidden by anyone, except Yahweh and their own sense of justice, and interceded for those who had no intercessor. Nowhere was the decay of the society better registered than in the neglect of the indigent poor, and nowhere was the true nature of Israel's God more faithfully conveyed than in the words of the prophets for the disadvantaged and oppressed. The most fatal consequence of poverty was to be without defense, and where the king and officials, either because of apathy or inaccessibility, stepped out of their expected role, the prophets stepped in. They saw justice as the golden thread that bound Yahweh's society together in wholeness.

12. Abraham J. Heschel, *The Prophets*, 1:198.

THE CULTURE AND ITS PROPHETS

Culture has a way of producing its own religious forms and expressions. The literary prophets and their predecessors were affected by their culture, but their credentials were issued by Yahweh Himself. Yet already in the preliterary period the culture, especially the Canaanite cultic strand of it, had produced a strain of prophets that greatly influenced royal policy. We see them operating in force in the court of Ahab in the middle of the ninth century (1 Kings 22), and it was against their kind that Elijah contended on Mt. Carmel (1 Kings 18). To what degree the counter-profession of prophets in the literary period owed its origin to the Baal prophets is impossible to determine. However, by the time of the eighth century there had come into being a profession of prophets, usually called "false prophets," who operated in parallel order to the literary prophets. Whether they ever produced a literature is not known, but if they did, it would not likely have survived, for eventually the events of history proved their message to be false. Thus we only know them through the eyes of their principal critics, the literary prophets. Judging from the attention that Micah, Jeremiah, and Ezekiel gave them, they made up quite an influential movement. Perhaps more than any other profession of their day, they represented the popular religion. In fact, their origin may partly be attributed to the popular beliefs of the people. They filled a popular need to hear a word of direction from God. Thus the people, including the leaders, consulted them and paid them for their services. One of the claims made against them was that they were mercenary (Mic. 3:5, 11; Jer. 6:13; 8:10).

Speaking in the name of Yahweh was the critical feature of prophetic speech. Yet many spoke in that name, and many spoke presumptuously. The issue was really what security the public had against these devious spokesmen. Deuteronomy adds another test to that one—that if the prophet's word came to pass, he was a true prophet (Deut. 18:22). The unfolding reality of the prophetic word was a test that had to be performed in the laboratory of human experience, sometimes requiring long periods of time. Therefore, that was little security against the deceitful words of the false prophets. Thomas Overholt, recognizing that there were no absolute criteria which the public could draw upon to test the prophetic word, points to Jeremiah's conflict with false prophets in chapters 27–29 and submits that valid judgments could be made about their genuineness. Hananiah in particular ignored the historical situation when he predicted that the exile would last only two years (Jer. 28).[13] H. B. Huffmon takes note of the problem and concludes that "only internal and subjective confessional criteria can distinguish true and false prophecy."[14] During Jeremiah's ministry, for exam-

---

13. Thomas W. Overholt, "Jeremiah 27-29: the Question of False Prophecy," pp. 241–49.
14. Herbert B. Huffmon, "The Origins of Prophecy," in *Magnalia Dei: The Mighty Acts of God*, p. 184.

ple, the false prophets cried, "Peace," while the true ones declared there was no peace (Jer. 8:11; 23:17/6:14; Ezek. 13:2–10). The false said sword and famine would not be in the land, while the true said the false prophets themselves would be their victims along with the people they had misled (Jer. 14:15). The false said Judah would not serve the king of Babylon, and the true countered their message with a prediction of exile (Jer. 27:9–14; 28:11/27:4, 6–7). The false prophets predicted that the vessels of the Lord's house would be shortly brought from Babylon, and the true said the rest of the vessels still in the Temple would be carried to Babylon (Jer. 27:16/27:19–22). Operating by point/counterpoint, gradually a certain platform became clear for the false prophets as well as the true. The public, depending upon its given disposition, could appeal to that body of formulations. Thus the subjective and internal nature of the matter produced a set of external criteria for judgment.

Yet, although we recognize that certain cases were dependent upon very subjective standards, there seems to have been a more objective criterion, which the literary prophets applied in other cases: the life of the prophet, whether he lived in accord with the demands of Yahweh. The widespread use of formal divination by the false prophets may both explain their popular appeal and constitute one of the marks by which they were identified as false. The Deuteronomic law forbade the use of divination (Deut. 18:10, 14), and that practice played no part in the ministry of the literary prophets. The means by which the false prophets divined God's will is not explained. The use of lots, which was a priestly method of determining the divine, could have been one of them, but that is by no means certain. Yet the technical term for divination (*qsm*) occurs frequently in reference to the false prophets. From what we know of those methods, they would have provided the client with almost immediate results, not leaving him to wait it out. Evidently their technicians derived a comfortable living from public use of their services. Frequent use of dreams and visions is also mentioned. The picture we are given is that of men and women who received their word largely by those three methods—divination, dreams, and visions. Although the literary prophets did receive visions and had dreams, they were much more dependent upon the direct communication of Yahweh's Word. Jeremiah said the false prophets' dreams were like straw compared to the true prophets' oracles, which were like wheat (Jer. 23:28).

So the culture produced its own prophets. Their ears were cocked to what the people wanted to hear; and whatever the current trend happened to be, they offered the popular wares. Judging from the literature, the law of supply and demand worked well for them.

PRESERVATION AND VINDICATION: THE SHAPING OF THE PROPHETIC LITERATURE

With the rise of modern biblical criticism the prophetic books have come under a scrutiny that has both illumined and eclipsed our understanding of their message. The vast body of literature on the prophets has shown them to be first of all religious spokesmen in their own world and to their own times. That view is certainly correct, but not to the exclusion of their theological relevance for the future of Israel and the world. Unfortunately modern critical methodology has not consistently set the stage for greater confidence in the integrity of the biblical prophets and the authenticity of their oracles and writings. The ongoing and asymmetric editing of the prophetic materials in the biblical period, as suggested by some modern approaches to this literature, is at best hypothetical. Much remains to be discovered about the literary process, and that inquiry must take place not only in a literary context but in a theological one as well. At the risk of over-simplification, we must ask whether the prophetic commitment to ethical behavior and moral principles does not itself cast light on the extent to which succeeding prophets could and would alter the oracles and message of a prior prophet.

A DESCRIPTION OF THE LITERATURE

The books of the prophets are for the most part collections of various kinds of utterances made on different occasions and called forth by varying circumstances. As a rule, the ancient compilers of these books did not have the same reverence for chronology that a modern collector might have. They were far more interested in getting a message across. Thus a book like Jeremiah cannot be read consecutively with any chronological appreciation unless the reader takes that fact into account. The prophets of the Assyrian period had very little interest in chronology. Basically the superscription to the book provided the major time clues, and many scholars are of the opinion that they were editorial. If that is true, the editor was quite well aware of the period of the prophet's ministry; "editorial" is not a euphemism for inaccuracy. With the Babylonian period, however, we see a heightening interest in chronology. It first becomes evident in the prophecies of Jeremiah and then becomes a more general method of recording prophecies in Ezekiel, Daniel, Haggai, and Zechariah. Yet that developing interest in dating oracles still did not become the principal criterion for their arrangement in the final collected editions.

The contents of the prophetic books fall into five literary classifications: oracles, visions, poetry, biographical narrative, and autobiographical narrative. Those categories are condensed by Claus Westermann to three (accounts, prophetic speeches, and prayers) and by Geo Widengren to four (oracles, poetry, autobiographical prose, and biographical prose),[15] and one will encounter other variations in the literature on the prophets.

Prophetic oracles. These are commonly introduced by "Thus says the

---

15. Claus Westermann, *Basic Forms of Prophetic Speech*, pp. 90, 136.

Lord,'' ''The Word of the Lord was to (the prophet),'' or a similar messenger formula verifying the message as Yahweh's Word to the prophet. These oracles, which make up the major part of the prophetic books, generally contain a word of judgment against Israel or Judah or a comforting message of salvation. In addition to oracles addressed to the nation, there are a few oracles directed to individuals. Westermann has observed that in the books of Kings the judgment oracles are without exception pronounced against individuals rather than the nation as a whole. It is in the literary or classical prophets that we first encounter judgment oracles against the nation.[16] In view of the fact that the judgment speeches arise out of social situations that represented violations of the old law, it is not surprising that eventually the prophets came to pronounce judgment against the nation rather than individuals. It is Yahweh's legal proceedings against an erring people, and perhaps the judgment speeches are best understood against the backdrop of legal proceedings in the court of law.[17]

The fact that oracles of judgment are often punctuated by words of salvation for Israel should not be surprising. Israel's understanding of her relationship to Yahweh had from earliest times included an eminent word of grace. Prophetic theology was based upon the ancient revelation of God in the lives of the patriarchs and His special revelation at Sinai, and the element of divine grace was part of those revelations. As prophetic theology took form and eschatology acquired its detail, the word of salvation was an integral part of it. Hosea testified to that as early as the middle of the eighth century. Having doomed Israel by cancelling the Mosaic covenant with her (Hos. 1:9), he followed it with words of restoration under the patriarchal covenant, which he may have considered to be the primary and unconditional covenant. Moreover, the Mari documents, which contain both oracles of judgment and salvation, have confirmed the existence of salvation and judgment prophets alongside each other. In Israel a single prophet normally incorporated both theological aspects into his preaching. Thus the older inclination of scholarship to exclude words of comfort and salvation from some of the prophetic books (Amos, for example) failed to take into account the broader base of prophetic theology.

In addition to oracles against Israel and Judah, there are numerous oracles against foreign nations, often gathered together in special collections in the prophetic books (Isa. 13–23; Jer. 46–51; Ezek. 25–32; Amos 1:3–2:3; Zeph. 2:5–15). Some of those oracles were occasioned by historical circumstances. The nation addressed had turned against Israel and created a situation that caused the prophet to address the nation with words of judgment. Other national oracles, however, arose from the general eschatology espoused and preached by the prophets. No particular historical occasion prompted the

16. Geo. Widengren, *Literary and Psychological Aspects of the Hebrew Prophets*, p. 86.
17. Claus Westermann, *Basic Forms of Prophetic Speech*, p. 127.

oracle, but the general relationship of Israel to the Gentile world, and especially the Gentile world to the God of Israel and His law, occasioned the oracle. It was not because the prophet hated the foreign nation that he spoke, but because Yahweh would not tolerate evil. Zephaniah may provide the best illustration of that kind of national oracle.

One problem with the national oracles as with other oracles that involve prediction is that many scholars believe there is no genuine prediction, only "prediction" after the event (*vaticinium ex eventu*). That is the problem with some of the oracles in Zephaniah, for example, 2:4–15. To solve that problem Hyatt rules the superscription of Zephaniah invalid and opts for a date during the time of Jehoiakim.[18] Yet a better solution is to be found in the rather well-developed eschatology of the prophets that was current in Zephaniah's time. As indicated above, it was out of their eschatological and theological understanding that the prophets issued their oracles against the nations. Thus they were not occasioned by specific historical occasions.

Were the oracles ever delivered to the Gentile nations with which they were concerned? Generally scholars answer that question negatively.[19] It has been suggested that the oracles functioned more as comfort to Israel than judgment against the foreign nation.[20] That function cannot be denied, but still the explanation is far too simple. In the case of Amos, for example, the foreign oracles led to a denunciation of Israel too. So comfort was hardly one of their purposes.[21] Two passages in Jeremiah may suggest that sometimes (even though it may have been the exception) the oracles were transmitted to the rulers of the foreign nations. When foreign envoys had gathered in Jerusalem for consultations with Zedekiah, Yahweh instructed Jeremiah to make thongs and yoke-bars and send them to the kings of Edom, Moab, Ammon, Tyre, and Sidon with a warning about plotting against the king of Babylon (Jer. 27). In a second but quite different incidence Jeremiah sent one of his prophecies to be read by the Euphrates River and then cast into it (51:59–64). In that case the king of Babylon could hardly be expected to hear the oracle. It was enough to pronounce it against him. However, delivery of the oracle on Babylonian soil seems to carry some significance.

Very few words of salvation are found in the oracles against the nations, although words of salvation assurance for Israel are frequently interspersed in them. We will discuss the reason for the absence of salvation promises elsewhere (see chap. 12).

Visions. Visions constituted another experience and literary form, although a

18. J.P. Hyatt, "The Date and Background of Zephaniah," pp. 25-29.
19. E.g., John W. Wevers, *Ezekiel*, pp. 25–26; Moshe Greenberg, *Ezekiel 1–20, A New Translation with Introduction and Commentary*, p. 17.
20. E.g., A. Weiser, *The Old Testament: Its Formation and Development*, p. 249.
21. John D. W. Watts, *Obadiah, A Critical Exegetical Commentary*, p. 22.

minor one. Among the nonliterary prophets, Micaiah's vision during Ahab's reign gives evidence that the form was an old one (1 Kings 22:17–23). Its earliest occurrence in the literary prophets was brief and contained a terse message for the prophet or his audience. Sometimes the prophet was merely a spectator (as with Amos), whereas in other cases he was a participant in the action of the vision (as with Isaiah, Ezekiel, and Zechariah). As a rule the accounts are related in autobiographical form. In the later period the presence of an interpreter was also a feature. Amos records five visions (7:1–3, 4–6, 7–9; 8:1–3; 9:1–4), even though they are not specifically called "visions" (the verbal form does occur in 1:1). Isaiah and Jeremiah both received their call in visions (Isa. 6. Jer. 1), and the popularity of the visionary form in the Babylonian and Persian periods is attested in Ezekiel (1; 8–11:4; 37; 40–48), Daniel (7–12), and Zechariah (1:7–6:15). Judging from the polemic against the false prophets, the visionary experience was also very common among those prophets who did not receive canonical sanction.

Poetry. As has been recognized since Robert Lowth's famous work on Hebrew poetry, much of the prophetic materials are written in poetic style. However, what I mean by this category is those compositions that are poetic and do not fall in the category of oracles, such as doxologies (e.g., Amos 4:13; 5:8–9; 9:5–6), short sayings (e.g., Ezek. 18:2), and prayers (e.g., Amos 7:2*b*, 5; Isa. 6:11*a*, and Jeremiah's prayers).

Autobiographical narrative. This literary form shows how important the individual prophets believed their words and experiences to be. The very fact that they recorded them points up their personal assessment of the gravity of their call and ministry. By the personal nature of the form, it follows that it is written in the first person. The call narratives generally fall into this category (e.g., Hos. 3, Isa. 6, Jer. 1).

Biographical narrative. This is the record about the prophet composed in prose style. Isaiah 37–39 and the biographical narratives of Jeremiah (26–29) and 32–45) are among the fine illustrations of this literary component. If autobiographical prose was a clue to the prophet's own assessment of the value of his work, this form may be evidence of the value of the prophet's work in the eyes of those who were closely associated with him.

All these five components have a place in the larger collections of the prophetic works. Therefore, when we talk about prophetic literature, we must think in terms of all these literary forms rather than oracles only. Whereas the oracles are the center of attention on the canvas, the other forms fill out the literary picture of the activity and words of the prophets.

THE FORMATION OF THE LITERATURE

When we have spoken of the literary forms, we have still only detailed the literature as it has reached us. The actual process by which the forms have taken shape and assumed written status is a much more complicated and elusive matter. It involves recording, collecting, preserving, and diffusing the literature.

Before proceeding further, we should speak about the motivation behind the formation of the literature. The most important motivational factor was the nature of the Word of the Lord. The prophets understood how serious was the will of God, and they knew that man could not survive without it, much less flourish. When Yahweh had spoken, who could keep from prophesying (Amos 3:8; Jer. 20:9)? God's Word would outlast nature (Isa. 40:8), and whatever the Lord sent it out to do, it would accomplish without fail (45:23; 55:11). Given that understanding of the eternal significance of the divine Word, we should expect the prophets to commit their words to writing.

A second motivational factor was the need that the prophet be vindicated. This can be seen in two dimensions. First of all, from the earliest period of the prophetic movement there was a general concern for the legitimacy of the prophet. As we have already noted, a popular and lucrative profession of prophets offered its verbal products to the highest bidder. Moreover, such prophets operated alongside the true prophets, making public differentiation most difficult. The fear of having one's words disqualified ran high among the prophets. So the value of committing their words to written form so that they might pass the test of time and experience was of much importance to them. It is also widely recognized that in the ancient Near East a messenger customarily carried his message in written form. In addition to delivering it orally, it could be verified against the written document. Further, with the passing of the age in which prophets spoke mainly to kings and officials and their oracles were preserved in the court annals as at Mari (see also 2 Kings 8:4–6), the need arose for private initiative in the matter.

The second dimension of vindication was the prophets' future predictions and the need for history to verify their accuracy. That may be involved in Yahweh's command to Isaiah to write the words "Belonging to Maher-shalal-hash-baz" on a large tablet (Isa. 8:1). There would later be evidence that Ahaz had indeed heard the words of Isaiah. Perhaps also that motive is involved in Isaiah's sealing his teaching among his disciples (8:16). It was definitely the concern of Habakkuk (2:2–3), and Daniel (12:4), and Jeremiah (28:5–9); Deuteronomy (18:20–22) also emphasized the test. If the prediction came true, the prophet was exonerated of any false pretenses.

The prophet's role in the formation process included the activities of speaking, writing, and dictating. No more proof is needed than is found on the face of the prophetic literature to establish the prophets as speakers. Not even the most radical critic would deny that. However, not as much consensus can be found on the matter of the prophets as writers. However, the general use of writing in the period of literary prophecy and the references to writing within the books themselves bolster the idea that the oral and written stages of the literature were simultaneous. Against the Scandinavian school which has urged the primary status of oral transmissions,[22] a good case has been made by Widengren for the simultaneous functions of speaking and writing.[23] Evidence that the prophets could and did write can be found in several texts (Isa. 8:1, 16; 30:8; Jer. 36:2; 51:60; Ezek. 2:9–10; 43:11–12; Hab. 2:2). In the case of Jeremiah, he dictated some of his words to his scribe and friend Baruch, who wrote them down and read them to the intended audience (Jer. 36). However, it should be pointed out that the occasion was one on which Jeremiah was physically hindered from going to the Temple to deliver his words. On another occasion he personally wrote the prophecy against Babylon (51:60).

The evidence that others were involved in the writing and transmission of the prophets' words is more difficult to collect. Gehazi, Elisha's servant, transmitted stories about his master (2 Kings 8:4–6). The warrant for assuming that the prophets had disciples is based in part upon the practice among the nonliterary prophets and in part upon the reference to "disciples" in Isaiah 8:16. But the extent to which those devotees assisted their masters is impossible to determine. There is also some evidence in Jeremiah 26 that the elders of the nation had a part in transmitting, whether orally or in written form, the prophetic words, for they came to Jeremiah's defense with the words of Micah (Jer. 26:17–18).

It should not be underemphasized that the prophet himself was the major means of retrieval of his words. As has been observed, after about two decades Jeremiah dictated many of his prophecies to Baruch, and when Jehoiakim had burned the scroll, he added still more words to the second edition. He obviously remembered his prophecies well and was capable of recalling them. The transmission process, therefore, began with the prophet himself, a fact that is attested also by Isa. 8:16, Ezek. 43:11, Dan. 12:4, and Hab. 2:2.[24]

I am in agreement with Widengren that it is wrong to build too great a contrast between the oral and written stages of prophecy.[25] The two aspects of the process were taking place at the same time. A further word of prudence regarding oral transmission may be mentioned: it carried a heavy baggage of inaccuracies.[26]

In summary, the prophets committed many of their words to writing, among them oracles, poetry, and autobiographical narratives. Whereas the time lapse between speaking and writing was in some cases brief, in others it may have been as long as a decade or two. But the prophet remembered his words and could recall them. The written (and not the oral) form was the principal form of

---

22. See Eduard Nielsen, *Oral Tradition.*
23. Widengren, p. 56.
24. Ibid., pp. 77–78.
25. Ibid., pg. 56.
26. Ibid., pp. 32–33.

the prophetic materials. When oral transmission did occur, it sometimes could be checked against a written document. When it could not, other controls over accuracy included the prophet himself, or his associates, and perhaps even the people who had heard him.

It is quite possible that some of the prophets lived long enough to collect their own oracles and give their books their final form. The ministries of Isaiah, Jeremiah, and Ezekiel were long enough that they could recognize the need to put their prophecies in basic form for preservation. In other cases, however, the task of editing must have fallen to their close associates or disciples. But it is unlikely that more than a generation intervened between the life of the prophet and the final edition of his book. That is not to deny that minor editorial changes have occurred in the transmission of the documents, but generally those were of little import. In view of the data available to us, the extensive editing presupposed by modern scholarship, particularly the tradition criticism, is incredible. The books in the forms as we have them are reliable sources of the prophets' words and activities.

CANONIZATION OF THE PROPHETS

The question of canonization involves the degree of authority attributed to the prophetic oracles and books by the ancient Israelite community. To what degree were the prophets' words considered authoritative, and thus their writings? Moreover, at what point in time were the Latter Prophets collected into an authoritative corpus?

The authority of the prophetic word could hardly be a doubtful issue after the fall of Samaria in 722 B.C., for that event verified the prophets Amos, Hosea, Micah, and Isaiah as accurate both in their perception of Israel's spiritual problem and its disruptive consequences. Whereas Isaiah and Micah continued to speak beyond that crisis, Amos and Hosea had been definitely vindicated by it. The authoritative status of their word was transferred quite naturally to their literature, whether or not it dealt specifically with the end of the Northern Kingdom.

The predictive accuracy of the prophets, however, was only one factor that helped them to achieve canonical status. Another factor, and perhaps a more important one, was their loyalty to the covenant religion with its emphatic insistence upon obedience to the ethical demands of Yahweh. In that respect the prophets were on dead center. Regardless of the popular opposition they encountered from those who did not want to hear their words, the element of Israelite society that preserved their message was in agreement with their loyalty to the covenant demands. The circles within which the preservation of the prophetic oracles became a reality naturally exerted an influence in the direction of canonical authority. Israel's elders and the prophetic order with its adherents were most likely responsible for maintaining the momentum of the canonical process in the pre-exilic period. In the year 609 the elders of Judah came to Jeremiah's defense by citing Micah's message that Jerusalem would be destroyed (Jer. 26:16–19). By that time Micah's oracles carried the weight of authority, which is especially evident in the fact that his prophecy was so negative but was nevertheless preserved and viewed as a precedent for Jeremiah's oracles of destruction. By the last half of the seventh century the eighth-century prophets had achieved the equivalent to what we call canonical authority. Zephaniah's use of Amos's concept of the Day of the Lord is further evidence of that. Therefore, the prophets of the Neo-Babylonian period had a powerful precedent to build upon.

The Exile, like the fall of Samaria, again vindicated the word of the prophets who foresaw the impending crisis and called Judah to repentance. By the end of that critical period Daniel had at his disposal certain "books," among them Jeremiah, in which he searched to see how long the Exile would last (Dan. 9:2). He even perceived that the Lord had set His laws before Israel through His servants the prophets (Dan. 9:10). The violation of those laws had resulted in the Exile, just as Moses had warned. Zechariah shared that view and declared that calamity came because Israel disregarded Yahweh's words and statutes, which His servants the prophets had delivered to them (Zech. 1:2–6). The prophetic message and literature were by that time as much a part of the life of Israel as the law of Moses. The prophets had put forward the demands of the covenant laws. That agreement with Mosaic religion went a long way to assist the prophetic word in achieving canonical status.

With the alliance between the priestly and prophetic circles in the early post-exilic era, especially represented by Haggai, Zechariah, and Malachi, a collection of the pre-exilic or "former" prophets (Zech. 1:4) existed and exerted an authoritative force in the community. The question of canonical authority for prophetic literature had been settled, and the prophetic word was a vital part of Israelite life. The post-exilic prophets probably found life a bit easier vis-a-vis their society than did the pre-exilic prophets. The element of popular opposition that looms quite prominently in the pre-exilic literature is in low profile in the post-exilic prophets. Their authority as Yahweh's spokesmen was unquestionable. Therefore, it may be assumed that the time lapse between a post-exilic prophet's oracles and their canonical status was no more than the time between the speaking and writing of the oracles, barring any theological contradictions between the message itself and covenant religion. The canonical process was much swifter. Thus the oracles of Haggai, Zechariah, Joel, and Malachi likely carried canonical authority within their lifetimes.

So by the middle of the fifth century the prophetic corpus was complete. That does not necessarily mean that all of the books were fixed in their present form by that time. The fluidity of the text is implied by the different order of certain books in the Greek version, notably Jeremiah. However, it should be recognized that the history of the Greek text tradition is a separate tradition from the Hebrew. Consequently we ought to be cautious not to extrapolate and attribute a similar fluidity to the Hebrew text of the prophets. At the same time, however, we ought not rule out a minimal amount of textual additions of genuine but independently circulating oracles. Yet due to the general acceptance of the prophets as canonical in the post-exilic era and the familiarity with the material within the community and its circles of custodians (such as the prophets, priests, and elders), wholesale revamping of prophetic books is not very likely.

THE PROPHETS OF THE NEO-ASSYRIAN PERIOD

JONAH
AMOS
HOSEA
ISAIAH
MICAH

THE NEO-ASSYRIAN PERIOD AND THE PROPHETS

JUST AS THE JEHU DYNASTY of the kingdom of Israel was coming to an end, an Assyrian resurgence was taking shape in the East. Following almost half a century of weakness in Assyrian politics, a usurper, Tiglath-pileser III, gained the throne. The time was politically advantageous for Assyria but most inopportune for Israel and Judah. Both of those nations had enjoyed a long period of prosperity and relative peace from pesty neighbors. The long reigns of Jeroboam II in Israel (793–753) and of Uzziah in Judah (792–740) had created luxury and ease for many and spawned poverty and injustice for numerous others. Assyrian weakness had allowed the two countries to focus their attention on their home turf without the economic and emotional drain that war always caused. However, the century-long Jehu dynasty in Israel ended within a year of the death of Jeroboam II, and a time of insecurity set in. In Judah the long-term reign of Uzziah terminated a decade after Jeroboam's passing, and although the Davidic dynasty in the south gave a greater sense of stability to Judah than Israel enjoyed, the spiritual and social problems in Judah were similar to Israel's.

Tiglath-pileser III was an aggressive king, and soon after stabilizing his rule in the East he turned his attention westward. The ministries of the prophets Amos, Hosea, Micah, and Isaiah all dealt at some time with the Assyrian crisis, first posed by Tiglath-pileser and then by his successors, Shalmaneser V (726–722), Sargon II (721–705), and Sennacherib (704–681). The prophecy of Isaiah in particular and that of Hosea and Micah more generally reflect the five Assyrian invasions of Syria-Palestine.

Tiglath-pileser's first campaign to the West occurred in 743–738 and is more difficult to identify in the eighth-century prophetic oracles than the following invasions. It is the subject, however, of 2 Kings 15:19–20. At that time King Menahem of Israel paid the Assyrian monarch the exorbitant tribute of 1,000 talents of silver. In his second major invasion, provoked by the alliance of Syria and Israel against the Assyrians, Tiglath-pileser dealt a fatal blow to Damascus, the capital of Syria, and captured the Galilean tribes of Israel, thus depriving Samaria of her buffer zone in the north. When Rezin of

Syria and Pekah of Israel tried to force Judah into their anti-Assyrian coalition, Isaiah challenged Ahaz to ask from the Lord a sign that his enemies would not succeed. Although rejected by Ahaz, this alternative was the occasion for the "Immanuel" prophecy of Isaiah 7. The cost to Judah for overtuning Assyria for help was her independence, for after the Assyrians obliged Ahaz, Judah was virtually a puppet state in the Assyrian axis.

The third major Assyrian campaign with which the eighth-century prophets interacted was conducted by Shalmaneser V in 725–722 and resulted in the fall of Samaria in 722 B.C. Amos, Hosea, Micah, and Isaiah predicted this awful tragedy. Probably more than any other event of this century, the fall of Samaria vindicated the prophets in the eyes of Israel. The reputation of the prophets was raised to a new plane of authority and respect. The memory of this event would henceforth turn listeners from an unheeding disposition to an uncanny discomfort when the prophets talked about judgment and disaster.

The fourth Assyrian invasion was led by Sargon II in response to an uprising instigated by the city of Ashdod. Isaiah opposed Judah's participation in this rebellion and symbolized the Assyrian devastation of Egypt and Ethiopia by walking naked and barefoot for three years (Isa. 20).

The final invasion was the well-publicized campaign of Sennacherib against Hezekiah in 701 (Isa. 36–37; 2 Kings 18:13–19:37; Mic. 4:6–13). The Assyrian defeat was a great victory for Hezekiah's orthodoxy; yet the Assyrian influence by no means ended at that point. It was sustained for almost a century longer. Although the prophets had much more to say than pronouncements about the political perils of their time, they can only be understood within the political context of their age.

2

JONAH: PREFACE TO THE PROPHETS

PREFACING A STUDY of the prophets with the book of Jonah may at first seem inappropriate. A book around which so much controversy has revolved in modern biblical scholarship could cast a veil over the entire study at the start. However, my aim is to introduce the study of the prophets, a task whose proportions are stagging to scholar and student alike. The choice of Jonah, rather than the more standard introduction that begins with Amos, is dictated by three considerations: the early date assigned to Jonah by the writer of Kings (2 Kings 14:25), the book's emphasis upon the prophetic career, and the transitional nature of Jonah's prophecy from the pre-classical to the classical model.

JONAH AS INTRODUCTORY TO THE PROPHETS

THE REFERENCE IN THE BOOK OF KINGS

First, laying aside for the moment the question of the date of composition of Jonah, the reference by the author of Kings to his prophecy in the reign of Jeroboam (793/92–753 B.C.) fixes his activity in the first half of the eighth century and prior to this king's expansionist success. Even in view of the exilic date for the book of Kings, few scholars today would question the identity of the subject of this book with the "Jonah, the son of Amittai, the prophet, who was of Gath-hepher" in Kings. Even the summary of his message, that Jeroboam would restore the border of Israel "from the entrance of Hamath as far as the Sea of the Arabah," is no surprise, for we might have guessed from the tone of the book of Jonah that he had strong nationalist leanings. We may recognize that fact without simultaneously accepting the view that the purpose of the book was to countermand those convictions.

It may not be possible to determine conclusively whether Amos preceded Jeroboam's territorial expansion, but the luxury and leisure of Israelite society as Amos described it points, it would seem, more toward the post-expansionist period than the years prior to it (Amos 4:1; 6:1, 4–7). The sense of security that characterized the era in which Amos spoke (6:1, "Woe . . . to those who feel secure in the mountain of Samaria") further suggests the post-expansionist period. Moreover, it is obvious from Amos 5:18–20 that something had occurred that inflated Israel's false anticipation of the "Day of the Lord" as a time of victory and success. Perhaps it had been the prophecy of Jonah regarding Jeroboam, or maybe even the military triumphs themselves that had evoked Amos's rebuke. In any event, there was undeniably a bloated sense of security in Jeroboam's Israel when Amos delivered his threatening prophecies in the king's sanctuary. That is in no way to put Amos in opposition to Jonah, for Jonah may not have been responsible for any negative implications that developed in the Northern Kingdom as a result of his prophecy. In fact, the editorial comment in 2 Kings 14:26 seems to be the explanation for Yahweh's favorable treatment of Jeroboam, even though the author had already written that "he did evil in the sight of the Lord" (v. 24). Divine mercy, which looms so large in the book of Jonah, is seen to have been the result of God's grace in Israel as it was also in Nineveh. When the writer of Kings continued his editorial statement, that "the Lord had not said that He would blot out the name of Israel from under heaven, so he saved them by the hand of Jeroboam the son of Joash" (v. 27, RSV), he made that remark in reference to the Exile that he later reported, the Exile that Amos among the prophets first predicted. If we are correct to read the verb (with RSV) in v. 27 as a pluperfect ("had not said"—at that time), then the writer may well have had in mind Amos's prophecy in which the prediction was clearly made. That is, after He showed mercy through the military advances of Jeroboam, then He announced (by Amos) that He would destroy Israel,[1] thus putting Amos after the prophecy of Jonah.

THE CAREER OF A PROPHET EXEMPLIFIED IN JONAH

The second consideration that prompts me to use Jonah as a foreword to the prophets is that the book concentrates on the career of a prophet. Whereas a number of secondary themes can be identified, the major theme of the book is really the story of Jonah the prophet, not the repentance of Nineveh or the narrow nationalism of Israel. Yahweh called Jonah, detailed his mission, and sent him to fulfill it. Any intermediate detour on the prophet's part was just that—intermediate—because the sovereign Lord of the world would have obedience and nothing less. Every prophet whom Yahweh called subsequently had Jonah's model before him, and the compelling power of God could not be resisted. The inner tension was undeniable. Amos, for example, felt that the Lord "took" him from following the sheep (Amos 7:15). In this sense Jonah is a macrocosm of the prophetic career. None could be more traumatic, more demanding, more frustrating.

---

1. The same verb ("to blot out") is used in 2 Kings 21:13 to describe the destruction of Jerusalem, and it is interesting that that devastation is compared to the destruction of Samaria.

JONAH AS TRANSITIONAL

Third, Jonah makes a helpful prologue to the classical prophets because he was a transition prophet, representing the shift from the preclassical model that we have in Elijah and Elisha to that of Amos, Hosea, Micah, and Isaiah. The preclassical prophets addressed their message to the king and his court, whereas the classical prophets addressed all levels of the society. J. Holladay has proposed that this shift took place as a result of the Assyrian crisis. The Assyrians, whose blossoming new empire began at the end of Jeroboam's reign with the rise of Tiglath-pileser III, instituted a policy of torture and wholesale deportation of conquered peoples. Such action swung the attention from king to commoner. So Holladay theorizes that the result of this shift in political policy was paralleled by a change in the function of the prophet, who had formerly addressed the king and his officials. Now the prophet had to speak to everyone.[2] Yet Holladay's explanation for that change of prophetic focus from king to people is only a partial reason, belonging to a web of causes, not the least of which was God's determination to call His people back to Him.

Further, the preclassical prophets, when announcing judgment, do not appear to have preached a message of repentance. Yehezkel Kaufmann has made the observation that the earliest biblical stories, the Flood, tower of Babel, and the overthrow of Sodom, give no place to repentance. God may repent (Gen. 6:6), but punishment is not staved off by human repentance. Even David's repentance of adultery did not avert punishment (2 Sam. 12), and Ahab's repentance only delayed it (1 Kings 21:27–29). The book of Jonah brings forward the concept that repentance may avert divine punishment.[3] And in Jonah the repentance of Nineveh triggered divine repentance (3:10). The classical prophets, with few exceptions, capitalized on that principle. John Walton has insightfully applied that observation to Jonah and has proposed that the book focuses on the changes that took place between preclassical and classical prophecy, "It is the mechanism by which the age of classical prophecy is introduced."[4]

In summary, the book of Jonah represents prophetic activity that precedes even Amos, providing a model of Yahweh's sovereign control over the prophet and his message, and lays a plank for moving from the preclassical to the classical era of prophecy. The date of composition of the book is another question to be dealt with below, but the historical setting and the nature of the prophetic ministry captured in its intriguing story provide a fitting preface to our study of the classical prophets. Obviously the editor of the prophetic corpus was working with other criteria for his arrangement of the prophets. However,

---

2. J. Holladay, "Assyrian Statecraft and the Prophets of Israel," pp. 29–51.
3. Yehezkel Kaufmann, *The Religion of Israel*, pp. 284–85.
4. John Walton, *Jonah, Bible Study Commentary*, p. 73.

we have chosen to follow a chronological sequence to the degree that it is determinable, and by beginning with Jonah we have chosen both chronology and theology as justification.

JONAH THE MAN

Little personal information is known about Jonah. Both Jonah 1:1 and 2 Kings 14:25 identify him as the son of Amittai, and Kings gives the further information that he was from Gath-hepher, a town in lower Galilee about three miles northeast of Nazareth in the ancient tribal claim of Zebulon. The character lines in the book are well drawn, and we feel that we know Jonah quite well when the story concludes. He had a mind of his own. Even when he knew he had lost the war, he still waged his personal battle (4:1–11). The book is short on oracular material (only 3:4*b*), and the psalm of chapter 2, although not an oracle, reveals one side of the prophet's disposition, balanced precariously against another side drawn out in chapter 4. We need not view that as editorial shaping of the literature. It was a very human reaction that Jonah should be thankful for his own deliverance but resentful about Nineveh's.[5]

THE NATURE OF THE LITERATURE

THEORIES OF INTERPRETATION

Three major schools of thought exist regarding the literature type of the book of Jonah, with variations within each of the schools. The types are allegory, parable, and history.

Allegory. The OT has several examples of allegory.[6] All of them are rather brief and contain clear evidence that they are allegories. Those who propound this interpretation of Jonah make the point that his name means "dove," a word that later (much later!) became the symbol for Israel.[7] So Jonah becomes the figure to represent Israel, and the fish becomes the world power (Babylon) that swallowed up Israel. Nineveh would be the symbol of the conversion of the Gentiles, and Jonah's subsequent complaint the theological objection to their inclusion in the covenant.[8] However, no OT allegory is written so

---

5. B. S. Childs, *Introduction to the Old Testament as Scripture*, pp. 423–24, advocates that the psalm of chap. 2 was inserted to put chap. 4 in a new light. But see my discussion of the psalm pp. 50.
6. OT allegories are: Eccles. 12:3–5; Jer. 25:15–29; Ezek. 17:3–10; 19:2–9; 24:3–5; Zech. 11:4–17.
7. G. Ch. Aalders, *The Problem of the Book of Jonah*, p. 26, correctly disqualifies Ps. 74:19, Hos. 7:11, and 11:11.
8. G. A. Smith espoused this interpretation in his commentary on Jonah, *The Book of the Twelve Prophets*, pp. 491–541. Another kind of allegorical interpretation is given by Sheldon H. Blank, *Understanding the Prophets*, pp. 129–38.

straightforwardly as historical narrative as is Jonah. T. T. Perowne comments that the setting of the book "is too exact, too detailed, too closely in accordance with facts, to be in keeping with the allegory itself."[9]

Parable. In current scholarship this is the prevailing opinion. G. Ch. Aalders gives two characteristics of the OT parable: (1) simplicity, treating one central subject, and (2) an accompanying interpretation. Yet Jonah is a compound story and has no interpretation.[10] The exponents of this position stress the didactic nature of the book. It exposes the narrowness of nationalism, or teaches the universalism of God, or some other worthy idea. Objections to this interpretive method are the length of the story in contrast to the shorter form of the parable and the inclusion of miracle elements, which do not occur in other ancient Near Eastern parallels.[11]

History. Until modern times the book was generally viewed as a historical account of the prophet Jonah. Christians appealed to the use Jesus made of the story in Matthew 12:39–41 and Luke 11:29–30. C. F. Keil has pointed out that as narrative the book of Jonah is similar in content and form to the history of Elijah and Elisha (1 Kings 17–19; 2 Kings 2:4–6).[12] G. A. Smith remarked that "the peculiarity of the Book of Jonah is not the presence of narrative, but the apparent absence of all prophetic discourse."[13] We have already observed that the only semblance of prophetic oracles is 3:4b, "Yet forty days and Nineveh will be overthrown." The double call (1:2; 3:2) as well as the dialogue between Jonah and God (4:2–11) also fall within natural categories of prophetic material, even though they are not oracles per se. Nevertheless, Smith's observation does raise the question of why Jonah is included among the prophets. Yet the ancient arrangement of the Jewish canon into Former and Latter Prophets (Joshua-Kings and Isaiah-the Twelve Prophets) was dependent, especially in the Former Prophets, upon the prophetic character of persons involved rather than prophetic oracles.[14] On that score there should be no problem with Jonah's qualifications.

We can unhesitatingly agree that the book is different from the other books among the Latter Prophets. Yet when placed alongside the Elijah/Elisha materials in Kings we recognize that Jonah was written with the same kind of motive in mind. That is, it was written as a refined theological treatise on the life and activity of an ancient prophet. The writer has skillfully analyzed and utilized

9. T. T. Perowne, *Obadiah and Jonah*, p. 49. See also the objections of R. K. Harrison, *Introduction to the Old Testament*, p. 912.
10. Aalders, pp. 15–17. His list of OT parables is the following: Judg. 9:8–15; 2 Sam. 12:1–4; 14:6–7; 1 Kings 20:39–40; 2 Kings 14:9.
11. Donald J. Wiseman, "Jonah's Nineveh," p. 32.
12. C. F. Keil, *The Twelve Minor Prophets*, 1:380.
13. Smith, 2:493.
14. Ibid., pp. 493–94.

the activities of Jonah to elevate the theological motifs that his prophetic ministry illustrated, so that theology and history are artistically interwoven. The motifs of the book illustrate the author's theological interests: the sovereignty of God over individuals, nations, and nature, the inclusion of Gentiles to divine grace, and the grief of the Almighty over His erring creatures. It is an illustration of a prophet's career that has been written in contemplative retrospect. The literary character of the book takes us a step beyond the literary nature of Hosea 1 and 3. As in Hosea's marriage, the prophetic actions have been maximized, illuminating them and interpreting their theological significance by means of Hosea's oracles, especially those in chapters 2 and 4–14. Perhaps Jonah's prophetic oracles had not survived except in summary form (3:4*b* and 2 Kings 14:25), so the story line itself, as so often in the Kings material, became the means of interpretation.

Regarding Jesus' use of the book (Matt. 12:39–41; Luke 11:29–30), His reference to the repentance of the Ninevites and, even more compellingly, to the queen of the South, whose existence and embassy are verified in 1 Kings 10:1–10, certainly indicates His belief that Jonah was historical. If the reference to the Ninevites is taken to be merely illustrative and not historical, then we have a confusing mixture of non-historical and historical material in the same analogy. Further, the condemnation of Jesus' generation is far less effective if the repentance of the Ninevites is non-historical. There is little question that Jesus believed His references to be historically valid.

PROBLEMS OF HISTORICITY

Some of the problems that have been cited as obstructions to historicity fall into two areas: those relating to Nineveh, and the miracles in the story.

Nineveh. The book calls Nineveh "the great city" (1:2; 3:2; 4:11; and a variant form in 3:3), a phrase that may have a theological implication, that is, great in God's estimation.[15] Actually the only possible reference to the size of the city occurs in 3:3, "a three day's walk." In 3:4 Jonah is said to have begun to go through the city "one day's walk," implying that the term "walk" (*mahalāch*) referred to distance. Yet A. H. Layard's excavations of the site of Nineveh in 1843 revealed a much smaller area. Subsequently attention was turned to the circumference of the city walls that were enlarged by Sennacherib from 9,300 cubits to 12,515, giving a distance of about seven and a half miles.[16] Yet a three-days' journey could easily be forty-five to sixty miles. So a strict reference to the size of the city is not likely.

---

15. The Hebrew phrase in 3:3*b* is literally "a great city to God." The medieval commentator David Kimchi compared it to a similar use of *El*, the shorter form of God, in Pss. 36:7 (English v. 6) and 80:11 (English v. 10), suggesting that that was a way to form the superlative. Yet the examples in Psalms lack the preposition, which may suggest that we ought to render it quite literally here.
16. Wiseman, p. 37.

It has been proposed that "a three day's walk" may refer to the size of the administrative district, composed of Asshur, Calah (Nimrud), and Dur-Sharruken (Khorsabad). All three of those were occupied within the period between 850 and 614 B.C., and all were within one to three days' walk of each other.[17] That solution makes good sense.

Another proposal is that the phrase refers to the size of the project. Jonah's task, which included preaching to the citizens (3:5) and perhaps also an official visit to the king,[18] thus required three days to complete. It is conceivable that he could have delivered the bad news to all of Nineveh's citizens in a period of three days, stopping at the main gates (Nineveh had over a dozen), the temple courts, and perhaps the king's palace.[19]

Related also to the questions surrounding the city of Nineveh is the population, said to be "more than 120,000 persons who do not know the difference between their right and left hand" (4:11). D. J. Wiseman cites a text discovered at Calah (Nimrud) that King Asshur-nasir-apli II, at the opening of his new city in 865 B.C., entertained 69,574 guests in a period of ten days.[20] Those probably came from Calah as well as neighboring cities, but if we are dealing with the administrative district rather than Nineveh by itself, then 120,000 people is a plausible figure.

The term "king of Nineveh" (3:6) has caused problems for interpreters on two counts. First, in Jonah's day Nineveh does not seem to have been the principal royal residence. Shalmaneser I had a palace there from 1265 to 1236 B.C. In the tenth century the city served as the capital, and again from the reign of Sennacherib (about 700 B.C.) it was the capital city, but in the early eighth century it does not seem to have been the capital. Nineveh was finally destroyed by the Medes and Babylonians in 612 B.C. Even though the city was not the capital, if the king had a palace there, as Shalmaneser I had, that would solve the problem. Unfortunately, we have no such information, but the objection hardly seems substantive enough to disqualify the term as historically valid.

The second problem with the phrase, in the opinion of some scholars, is that the king of the empire is called "king of Nineveh." Yet there are other

17. Ibid., pp. 38–39. Wiseman seems to favor this proposal.
18. It is clear that Jonah preached to the citizens of Nineveh, and they repented (3:5). If we take "the word" in 3:6 to be Jonah's word, which he now announced to the king, then he also spoke directly to the king. However, it may be that the king issued his decree only upon the report ("the word") of the general revival among the citizens. It would seem more likely that a prophet who caused such a stir in the city would have at some point made a diplomatic visit to the king's palace.
19. Walton, p. 39, advances this proposal, finding a cue in Neh. 2:6. He points out that in other instances where a three day journey is mentioned, a different term is used (Gen. 30:36; Ex. 3:18; 5:3; Num. 10:33).
20. Wiseman, pp. 40–41.

instances of this in the OT. Ahab was called "king of Samaria" (1 Kings 21:1) and Benhadad of Syria "king of Damascus" (2 Chron. 24:23). Some interpreters have opted to understand "king" in the sense of a lesser official such as governor.[21] In any event the difficulty of retaining the standard meaning of "king" does not seem insurmountable.

Miracles. In this respect the book of Jonah (unlike most of the classical prophets) again has interesting similarities to the Elijah/Elisha stories, in which a number of miracles are recorded. However those similarities may be, the miracles have been a stumbling block in the way of historicity for some scholars. We need not, however, belabor the point. It comes down to the simple question of whether or not miracles are possible. Yet if one wishes to pursue the matter further, the secondary literature on Jonah provides evidence that a few people in modern times have been swallowed by the sperm whale and survived.[22] Moreover, the nocturnal growth of the plant (4:6), sometimes identified as the castor-oil plant,[23] is another miracle that need not be explained by naturalistic means. Both are introduced by "the Lord appointed," a formula that signals divine action. They are presented as miracles, and any amount of explaining will fail to convince the skeptical that God could and would do them.

In summary, the narrative texture of the book, in which very little of the authentic oracles of Jonah has survived, tends to draw attention to the well-told story and its meaning rather than the historical and cultural data, although such data are definitely included. The book is a refined account of a prophetic career written for its theological value. Yet the author has not abused history in order to communicate that theology. The objections raised against the historicity of the book, though sometimes substantive in nature, are not sufficient to disqualify it as historical.

THE PSALM AND THE STRUCTURE OF THE NARRATIVE

The narrative is structured along the story line. The action of the book is fast and compressed. The narrative is not heavy with details; therefore the reader may move through it smoothly and as quickly as the rapid succession of events requires. The dialogue perfectly supports the action and the action the dialogue. That is, the action is as important, if not more important, than the dialogue. The statements are brief, the questions to the point, and the answers give only essentials. Other than the psalm in chapter 2, the most sustained statements (which are still brief) are balanced against one another, the one being Jonah's

---

21. E.g., Walton, pp. 68–69.
22. See G. Macloskie, "How to Test the Story of Jonah," pp. 334–38; Ambrose John Wilson, "The Sign of the Prophet Jonah," pp. 630–42.
23. Harrison, p. 910.

complaint (4:2–3) and the other God's rebuke of the prophet (4:10–11). The first defends Jonah's actions ("That is why I made haste to flee to Tarshish," RSV), whereas the second defends God's ("Should I not have compassion on Nineveh?").

The book is broken down into five parts. The criteria that determine the sections are the word of the Lord to Jonah (1:1; 3:1) and Jonah's prayers (2:1; 4:2). The threads of the message are tied together in the final dialogue between God and Jonah (4:5–11). It was not a Joban submission with Jonah repenting in dust and ashes, but it was nevertheless a triumph of God's will over the prophet's. The reader is left hanging on to the rhetorical question at the end, but it is rhetorical only in a formal sense because the answer has already been given in the Lord's mercy on Nineveh. Indeed, Jonah had admitted against his own obstinate judgment that Yahweh was that kind of God (4:2). It was a forced resolution that showed the prophet's will vanquished by divine mercy. The basic outline may be diagrammed as follows:

THE DICHOTOMY: THE LORD'S WILL OR JONAH'S

The Lord's Word to Jonah 1:1—	Jonah's Thanksgiving 2:1—
The Lord's Second Word to Jonah 3:1—	Jonah's Lament 4:2—

Resolution:
Final Dialogue between God and Jonah—4:6–11

The action of the story is initiated by Yahweh's first word to Jonah (1:1–17). When the action has reached a climax, then Jonah offers his prayer of thanksgiving, with his deliverance following (2:1–10). The Lord's Word to Jonah the second time initiates the second cycle of action, which climaxes in another act of divine mercy, the deliverance of Nineveh from judgment (3:1–10; compare 2:10, Yahweh's first act of mercy). The second cycle of events brought Jonah to prayer a second time (4:1–4). Yahweh's question, "Do you have good reason to be angry?" (4:4) breaks off the dialogue (such as it was). The closing section creates a new situation wherein Jonah repeats his request to die (4:8; cf. 4:3), and God repeats His question (4:9), which gets a response this time, opening up the closing dialogue. The threads are tied together in the exchange, "You had compassion on the plant for which you did not work . . . And should I not have compassion on Nineveh . . ." (4:10–11). Finally the essence of the narrative is laid out—Is it your way or mine, Jonah? Is it you or

God? You pitied the plant that you did not make, and you don't think I should pity Nineveh (that I did make)?

The psalm in 2:2–9 is similar in language and subject to the psalms of thanksgiving in the Psalter (compare Pss. 5:7; 18:6; 31:22; 42:7; 120:1; 142:3; 143:4). Three lines of interpretation have been followed: (1) literal—Jonah actually prayed the prayer while still in the fish's belly; (2) figurative—the writer describes deliverance from some mortal danger he has faced, and the metaphors for drowning are figures for that danger; (3) allegorical—the psalm refers to the Babylonian Exile.[24]

The theory has been advanced that the psalm has been interpolated after 2:1 where it does not fit. It would be better after 2:10, that is, after Jonah had been regurgitated. The observation that the psalm does not speak specifically of Jonah's experience in the fish's belly is valid enough. But, as Aalders keenly speculates, a later editor would have precisely written in the actual circumstances so the psalm would fit the situation perfectly.[25] Even though the prayer is a psalm of thanksgiving for help received, from Jonah's viewpoint of faith he was already saved when he was swallowed up by the fish. The psalm fills out the prophet's personality profile, grateful for divine mercy when it came his way, but resentful when it turned toward Nineveh.

PURPOSE OF THE BOOK

B. S. Childs is right when he says the purpose of the book is the "most crucial and perplexing problem of the book."[26] Views on purpose have ranged widely. Smith summed it up as God's care and provision of His Word to the Gentiles,[27] and a more recent, and attractive, proposal is that it affirms the possibility of repentance for man, and where this occurs, God may avert the disaster that the prophet had announced.[28]

In my discussion above I have offered the thesis that the book of Jonah introduces the classical prophets well, because he was a transition figure between preclassical and classical prophecy. By that, however, I do not mean that the author wrote the book for that purpose. It serves that function for our study of prophecy, even though it need not have been the author's purpose for writing. He set out to tell his own story (if Jonah authored it) or the story of the eighth-century prophet whose reputation was at best one of reluctant obedience to the prophetic call. That, however, in no way disqualified him as God's

---

24. Hinckley G. Mitchell, John Merlin Powis Smith, and Julius A. Bewer, *A Critical and Exegetical Commentary on Haggai, Zechariah, Malachi and Jonah*, p. 24.

25. Aalders, p. 23.

26. Childs, p. 419.

27. Smith, 2:501.

28. R. E. Clements, "The Purpose of the Book of Jonah," pp. 16–28; Walton, p. 73.

prophet. It is quite possible that prophets in subsequent generations saw their own reluctance vis-a-vis God's sovereign will illustrated in Jonah's experience. We suggest that the purpose of the book, therefore, is to affirm God's irresistible will in His world. That world extends beyond the borders of Israel, includes the elements of nature, and centers itself on the word and actions of His prophets. There are, of course, minor developments of that theme woven into the story. Yet the purpose must be located in the story itself, and Yahweh's sovereign will effected through His prophet is the most obvious element.

DATE OF COMPOSITION

The ministry of the historical Jonah (to keep distinct the date of his ministry and the date the book was written) is generally placed within one of two time frames, either that of the Assyrian king Adad-nirari III (810–783 B.C.) or the reign of Asshur-dan III (771–754 B.C.). It is assumed that the kind of international exchange represented in the book could only have taken place during a time of Assyrian weakness. The brief note in 2 Kings 14:25 dates Jonah in Jeroboam's reign, but that overlapped both of those Assyrian kings' reigns. Some kind of revival occurred during the rule of Adad-nirari III, but its purpose was to concentrate worship upon the god Nabu (Nebo). That could hardly have been the revival that followed Jonah's preaching. The reign of Asshur-dan III was a particularly troubled time in Assyria, with the solar eclipse of June 15, 763, and a famine that began in 765 and continued to or recurred in 759. Perhaps when Jonah arrived in Nineveh, the ominous eclipse and famine had already ripened the city for repentance.[29]

The book could have been composed any time between the middle of the eighth century and the canonization of the Twelve Prophets by the end of the fifth century. A good number of scholars date the writing of the book some time between the Exile and the era of Ezra-Nehemiah, and Julius A. Bewer even puts it somewhere between 400 and 200 B.C.[30] The late date is based upon the tension between universalism and nationalism in the book, but Kaufmann has convincingly demonstrated that universalism was an early phenomenon in Israel, and the kind that is found in Jonah belonged to that of the preclassical prophets. They did not foresee the nations giving up idolatry as did the classical prophets. In Kaufmann's view that demands a date as early as the dynasty of Jehu, that is, the time period in which the book of Kings places him.[31]

It is likely that there were circulating in preclassical times collections about the prophets, just as their works circulated in the classical period. The Elijah/

---

29. Wiseman, pp. 44–51.
30. Bewer, p. 13.
31. Kaufmann, pp. 282–83.

Elisha collection, to which we have compared the book of Jonah, may have been among those materials the writer of Kings had at his disposal. Sellin and Fohrer's comment that Jonah was not extant by 600 B.C. because Kings did not use it is unjustified.[32] The narrative would hardly have fit his theological scheme, so we would not expect him to use it even if he had it at his disposal.

The presence of Aramaisms[33] in the text has become a weak argument for an exilic or post-exilic date as the study of ancient Semitic languages has progressed. Aramaic was the language of correspondence in early times, and the book of Kings verifies that that was true as early as the reign of Sennacherib (2 Kings 18:26).

The book of Jonah could have been composed as early as the middle of the eighth century. There are no compelling reasons that it could not have been. Yet it is also possible that it may have come into existence in its present form at a later time, but before or soon after the fall of Samaria and the dispersion of the northern tribes. The story has a northern air about it, almost a pride in this prophet who undertook a mission to one of Assyria's major cities and preached the bad news. The fact that Yahweh spared Nineveh upon her repentance was a faithful witness to His sovereign control over that foreign power.

There is no way we can determine who might have written the book. The narrative is in the third person, with only Jonah's words in the first person. The prophet himself could have been the author. Certainly he composed the psalm. Yet it is not necessary to insist that the book was written by Jonah. Whoever the writer was, he was a skilled author. His Hebrew is smooth and simple, and his literary ability to tell a story is unsurpassed by any other author in the Old Testament.

THE MESSAGE OF THE BOOK

We have already made the point that Jonah provides a bridge between preclassical and classical prophecy. It has something old, something new. With his face to the era of preclassical prophecy, Jonah preached judgment but not repentance. Further, as in the stories of Elijah and Elisha, miracles figure prominently in the book. With his face to the era of classical prophecy, Jonah proclaimed his message to the citizens of Nineveh rather than just to the officials (3:4–5). Moreover, he presented motifs that found prominence in the preaching of the prophets of the eighth century and onward. Among them was the idea that repentance may divert God's wrath—though this theme was forced upon Jonah rather than preached by him. The sovereignty of God over the gods, over man and nature, and over Assyria is another

---

32. Ernst Sellin and Georg Fohrer, *Introduction to the Old Testament*, p. 441.
33. Keil lists them, 1:381; Smith also has a list of grammatical and lexicographical concerns, 2:497, nn. 2 and 3.

thread woven into the fabric of the narrative. Further, the relationship of the prophet to God and the irrevocability of the prophetic call figure eminently in the book.

GOD AND THE GODS

The polemic against the pagan gods does not come up to the syllogistic argument of Isaiah. Rather it operates on the same level as the contest Elijah conducted on Mt. Carmel. "Then you call on the name of your god, and I will call on the name of the Lord, and the God who answers by fire, He is God" (1 Kings 18:24). Though not put in quite the same terms, the effect was the same. When the Lord who made the sea and dry land (1:9) calmed the storm, the sailors feared Him greatly and offered sacrifice and made vows (1:16). The "each to his own" theology practiced by the men aboard ship had no effect on the sea that Yahweh had made (1:5). The deity who could control nature was Jonah's God.

YAHWEH SOVEREIGN OVER MEN AND NATURE

The real hero of the story is the Lord God. He dominates the action in the narrative: the Lord hurled a great wind on the sea (1:4); the Lord appointed a great fish to swallow Jonah (1:17); the Lord commanded the fish (2:10); God relented concerning the calamity (3:10); the Lord God appointed a plant (4:6); God appointed a worm (4:7); God appointed a scorching east wind (4:8). His control of the world extended to nature, to prophets, and to pagans. He was sovereign in judgment and even in mercy. "He did not do it" was Yahweh's "cancelled" stamped across His decree of judgment (3:10).

WHOSE SERVANT?

It is interesting that the writer of Kings calls Jonah the Lord's "servant" as well as "prophet." Evidently the prophet had a considerably longer career than is represented here and by the brief note in 2 Kings 14:25. We really have no other basis on which to evaluate Jonah's role as servant except the book that bears his name. And the question here is, "Whose servant was he?"

Although we have no basis for quibbling with the author of Kings, in the book of Jonah this prophet is rather self-serving. His flight from the presence of the Lord (1:3, 10) was a flight toward his own ego. Our author in the beginning leaves us with only the bare fact that "Jonah rose up to flee to Tarshish from the presence of the Lord" (1:3), providing no explanation. Not until God repented of the calamity He had declared upon Nineveh did Jonah offer an explanation for his elopement: "Was not this what I said while I was still in my own country? Therefore, in order to forestall this I fled to Tarshish, for I knew that Thou art a gracious and compassionate God, slow to anger and abundant in lovingkindness, and one who relents concerning calamity'' (4:2). Jonah knew God well, knew Him too well for his own comfort. Although this was a very real theological struggle for him, his pity, which at some point ought to mature and turn toward Nineveh, turned upon himself. Angry over God's mercy on Nineveh and happy about the plant that shaded him, the scorching east wind and hot Near Eastern sun brought his self-pity to the surface.[34] A plant and a city of 120,000 people, how do they compare? A prophet called to preach to Nineveh and the God who made the city, how do they compare?

In this book at least, Jonah was the Lord's servant only because he could not say no to God. The call of God was irrevocable. A servant can have his own mind, and he may turn his attention to what he wishes God had said rather than what He in fact has declared; but God's call to prophesy will arrest him wherever he is and compel him to obedience. Yes, even the self-seeking servant is God's servant, for he cannot say no to God. He can flee to Tarshish, but God will take the defiant letters of his no and twist them into his obedient yes.

OUTLINE OF JONAH

    I.   The Lord's First Word to Jonah (1:1–17)
         A.   Jonah's Call and Flight (1:1–3)
         B.   His Plans Complicated (1:4–10)
         C.   The Miraculous Calm (1:11–16)
         D.   Judgment on Jonah (1:17)
   II.   Jonah's Response to Divine Mercy (2:1–10)
         A.   His Prayer (2:1–9)
         B.   His Deliverance (2:10)
  III.   The Lord's Second Word to Jonah (3:1–9)
         A.   Jonah's Second Call and Mission (3:1–4)
         B.   Nineveh's Response to the Prophet (3:5–9)
  IV.   Jonah's Response to Divine Mercy (3:10—4:5)
         A.   His Prayer and God's Response (4:1–4)
         B.   Waiting for Judgment (4:5)
   V.   Final Dialogue Between God and Jonah (4:6–11)

---

34. See Sheldon H. Blank's article, '' 'Doest Thou Well to be Angry?' A Study in Self Pity.''

3

AMOS: CALL FOR MORAL OBEDIENCE

THE PROPHET FROM TEKOA found, as did his eighth-century contemporaries Hosea and Micah, that being a prophet was not an easy or well-appreciated occupation. Hailing from the little town of Tekoa about six miles south of Bethlehem in the Judean hills, Amos made his entrance into the kingdom of Israel with a message of judgment. Yet it would be inaccurate to say that he was exclusively a prophet of judgment, for he, perhaps to a lesser degree than Hosea, bore witness to Yahweh's grace and mercy. His voice was not a welcome sound in the sanctuary of Bethel, but he was aware of the irresistible compulsion that brought him there even though his audience may have had no appreciation for that driving force. Amos was called from his pastoral occupation to one of the flourishing urban centers made infamous by Jeroboam I. His hometown was among the cities that Jeroboam's Judean rival, Rehoboam, fortified to provide his kingdom with a defensive chain of fortresses (2 Chron. 11:6). It was in that region also that Jehoshaphat defeated the Ammonites, Moabites, and Edomites (2 Chron. 20:20–30), three peoples that interestingly enough fell under Amos's indictment.

With Amos, Hebrew prophecy reached a new plateau.[1] The moral character of Hebrew religion was incorporated into the fabric of his prophecies. That was not an entirely new phenomenon, for Nathan had expected ethical, or at least compassionate, behavior from David (2 Sam. 12), and Elijah had condemned the illegal seizure of Naboth's vineyard (1 Kings 21). But no prophet before Amos, with the exception of Moses, had linked the welfare and survival of the nation to the moral obedience of the people. Moses had in fact warned the fledgling nation that national welfare and moral or covenantal faithfulness were vitally linked (Deut. 28). Amos applied that theological principle to the Northern Kingdom and set a standard for his successors.

AMOS THE MAN

This Judean prophet, so easily moved to righteous indignation, had his beginnings among the shepherds (*nōqedîm*) from Tekoa. The word *nōqedîm* occurs in the OT only one other time (as a singular form), to describe the king of

---

1. See discussion of non-literary prophecy, pp. 15–17.

Moab who dealt in sheep (2 Kings 3:4). The word is reputed to be a cognate of the Arabic *nakkad*, which is a breed of short-legged sheep producing very fine wool. The Septuagint translator of 2 Kings 3:4 evidently did not know the meaning of *nōqēd*, for he simply transliterated it. There the plural of that form (*nakkarim*) is used. In 7:14 Amos uses another unique word (*bôqēr*) to describe his occupation, and generally the two words are taken synonymously, some scholars even suggesting, without textual warrant, that (*bôqēr*) should be emended to *nōqēd*. The Targum (Aramaic translation) recognized the two terms to be synonymous and rendered them with the same term "master of the flocks." The reference to "the flock" in 7:15 would suggest the association of *bôqēr* with sheep. Whereas some scholars have understood *nōqēd* in 2 Kings 3:4 as "sheep breeder," Arvid S. Kapelrud has associated that word with the Mesopotamian temple herds. Working under the supervisors of the herds were several *naqidu*, who were sometimes temple officials and responsible for the temple cows and sheep. Thus he proposes that Amos was such an official.[2] Although that is an interesting proposal and would certainly make him a cult figure, the evidence for it is not easily gathered. In fact, there is a serious question whether Amos had any cultic associations other than those that any eighth-century Judean layman would have had. Although he had a vision of the Lord standing beside the altar, which was probably the altar of the Jerusalem Temple (9:1), there is little firm evidence in the book that he was a cultic functionary or a prophet associated with the cult. We may concede that some prophets were closely linked to the Jerusalem cult, but that seems to have been the exception rather than the rule. Perhaps some modern scholars have been overly enthusiastic in their effort to find cultic associations in the prophetic materials, just as others of a bygone era overemphasized the cleavage between prophet and cult. The most that we can say confidently from the biblical evidence is that Amos was a sheep-herder. That is borne out by the association in 7:15: "But the Lord took me from following the flock. . . ."

In addition to being a shepherd, Amos also refers to himself with the term *bôlēs* to describe some part in the growing of sycamore figs. That fruit was produced by an evergreen tree that reached a maximum height of forty feet. The fruit was smaller than the common fig, had a sweet taste, and had to be pinched or pierced about four days before harvesting so that it would ripen.[3] The Septuagint rendered the Hebrew participle *knizōn*, which means "nipping" or "pricking." Evidently Amos was a pincher or piercer of those figs. King David appointed a special supervisor for the sycamore fig industry (1 Chron. 27:28), suggesting its importance to the national economy.

Because the high elevation of Tekoa was unsuitable for sycamore figs, some

---

2. Arvid S. Kapelrud, *Central Ideas in Amos*, p. 6.
3. Harold N. Moldenke and Alma L. Moldenke, *Plants of the Bible*, pp. 106–8.

commentators have suggested that Amos was not a native of Tekoa. The rabbinic tradition located Tekoa in the tribal claim of Asher (e.g., Ibn Ezra and David Kimchi on Amos 1:1). Yet it is probable that Amaziah considered Judea to be the prophet's home (7:12). Most likely those involved in the sycamore trade traveled to the shephelah (which seems to be the suggestion of the Targum on 7:14 as well as 1 Chron. 27:28) or down toward the Dead Sea, where the climatic conditions were more favorable for the fruit.

The ancestry of Amos is not mentioned at all, some commentators interpreting that to mean that his family was well known and there was no need to mention his father,[4] others hearing from the silence a word about the poor class from which Amos sprang. We simply do not know how to interpret the absence of family names in the superscription. It is the case also in other prophetic books (e.g., Micah and Malachi). One thing for certain, however, is that when Amos stepped forth in the sanctuary at Bethel to proclaim a word of judgment upon Israel, he made his authority clear enough—"The Lord took me . . . and the Lord said to me, 'Go prophesy' '' (7:15).

The question of Amos's relation to the cult has already arisen and deserves further consideration. On the one hand, this prophet declares the Lord's word on the matter:

> I hate, I reject your festivals,
> Nor do I delight in your solemn assemblies.
> Even though you offer up to Me
> burnt offerings and your grain offerings,
> I will not accept them;
> And I will not even look at the peace offerings
> of your fatlings.
> Take away from Me the noise of your songs;
> I will not even listen to the sound
> of your harps.
> But let justice roll down like waters
> And righteousness like an ever-flowing stream.
> Did you present Me with sacrifices
> and grain offerings in the wilderness for
> forty years, O house of Israel?
> (5:21–25)

Yehezkel Kaufmann has advanced the opinion that Amos did not reject the cult unconditionally. That would have been a rejection of the tradition upon which 5:25 itself is based. Rather, says Kaufmann, Amos rejected the cult in favor of morality.[5]

4. E.g., Kapelrud, p. 5.
5. Yehezkel Kaufmann, *The Religion of Israel*, p. 365.

On the other hand, in his fifth vision Amos saw the Lord standing beside the altar (9:1). Kapelrud, adopting a cultic interpretation of Amos, cites 5:4 and 6 and interprets the imperative "seek" in a cultic sense, that is, to seek an oracle from the priest or prophet. Perhaps Amos was instructing the Israelites to "seek" the Lord in Jerusalem.[6] John D. W. Watts also argues for a formal relationship to the cult and cites the prophet's mention of major sanctuaries, Gilgal (4:4; 5:5), Carmel (1:2; 9:3), Beersheba (5;5; 8:14), and Dan (8:14), as well as his knowledge of cult functions (1:2; 2:14; 4:4–5; 5:5; 5:21–23, 25; 8:10) and cult abuses (2:7–8, 12; 5:26; 7:9; 8:14). In fact, queries Watts, was it possible to perform the function of a prophet without being related to the cult in some way? His somewhat ambiguous answer is that if Amos did function within the cult he did so as one who preserved the right relations to the covenant as Yahweh's spokesman, as a preacher of repentance, and as intercessor for his people.[7]

Yet there is no reason a layman could not perform all of those functions apart from the cult without any official relationship to it other than that of a lay worshiper. We should not at all be surprised that the prophets knew a great deal about the cult, for they were covenantally involved with it even if they were not functionaries in it. We may, therefore, assume that they knew parts of the liturgy, and even liturgical compositions within the prophetic material can hardly prove the case for cultic associations.

Moreover, it is difficult to see how the prophets, whose message presupposes the Mosaic covenant, could so easily abandon an institution established by that legislation. As is evident, we cannot accept the Wellhausen developmental and evolutionary scheme of Old Testament religion. Of course, a developmental approach is in some respects justifiable, but the inverted pyramid of ideas and institutions popularized in the last century of biblical scholarship is a bit simplistic and overtaxes the archaeological and literary evidence. It seems much more likely that the prophets intervened to reveal the ethical intent of the sacrificial system. It was designed to ensure and promote Israel's basic relationship to Yahweh. Walter Brueggeman has correctly assessed the prophetic protest against sacrifice and cultic worship as protests "against worship which had ceased to edify covenant, against rites which did not serve the dialogue of Word and answer, against a liturgy which did not function as a legitimate vehicle for relation between the speaker of the Word and the creature of the Word. The cult the prophets denounced had ceased to be a genuinely Israelite form of worship."[8]

Although it would be ill-advised to say there were no cult prophets in this era, the evidence that Amos was one is quite meager.

6. Kapelrud, pp. 36–37.
7. John D. W. Watts, *Vision and Prophecy in Amos*, pp. 18–20.
8. Walter Brueggeman, *Tradition for Crisis: A Study in Hosea*, p. 98.

DATE OF HIS ACTIVITY

Dating Amos at first would seem to be an easy task. The superscription (1:1) provides three bits of evidence. His ministry occurred during the reigns of Uzziah of Judah and Jeroboam of Israel and two years before the earthquake. We know from 2 Kings 14 that the reigns of Uzziah (Azariah) and Jeroboam had a rather long overlap. Edwin R. Thiele gives 782–753 B.C. as the regnal years of Jeroboam as sole ruler of Israel and 767–740 as the reign of Uzziah as sole ruler in Judah.[9] Using that system the ministry of Amos had to occur sometime between 767 and 753 B.C., within a span of sixteen years at the most. If we knew the date of the earthquake, which was still remembered in the days of Zecharaiah (520–518 B.C., Zech. 14:5), then we could date Amos's ministry with no difficulty. Unfortunately we can only guess.

Another bit of corroborative, though not definitive, evidence is supplied by 2 Kings 14:25. The prophet Jonah had predicted, and Jeroboam had accomplished, the reenstatement of Israel's borders from "the entrance of Hamath as far as the Sea of the Arabah." Disappointingly, we cannot determine at what point in Jeroboam's reign that territorial expansion was completed. Evidently, however, the indicting and threatening prophecy of Amos 6:14 presupposes its completion:

> "For behold, I am going to raise up a nation
>   against you,
> O house of Israel," declares the Lord God of hosts,
> "And they will afflict you from the entrance of Hamath
> To the brook of the Arabah."

Although we cannot be dogmatic at this point, the fact that Amos does not mention the Assyrians at all might, against the opinion of Richard S. Cripps,[10] indicate a date before the rise of Tiglath-pileser III (744 B.C.). We may suggest that the bloated self-confidence of Israel during the ministry of Amos could fit into most any period of the overlapping reigns of Jeroboam and Uzziah, if indeed the territorial expansion of Israel had been completed by 767, a fact we cannot ascertain. William Rainey Harper seems to be on safer ground by suggesting a range of years, 765–750 B.C. (using a lower chronology than Thiele).[11] Hans Walter Wolff has dated Amos's activity about 760,[12] whereas the latter years of Jeroboam's reign are selected by R. K. Harrison[13] (750),

9. Edwin R. Thiele, *A Chronology of the Hebrew Kings*, p. 75.
10. Richard S. Cripps, *A Critical and Exegetical Commentary on the Book of Amos*, xxiii, 36.
11. William Rainey Harper, *A Critical and Exegetical Commentary on Amos and Hosea*, p. 5.
12. Hans Walter Wolff, *Joel and Amos*, p. 90.
13. R. K. Harrison, *Introduction to the Old Testament*, p. 884.

Watts[14] (c. 752), and Julian Morgenstern[15] (752 or 751). Certainly Morgenstern's proposal of the fall equinox of 752 or 751 involves more specificity than can be justified from the book itself.

Perhaps Amos 8:9 is a prediction of the solar eclipse that occurred in 763 B.C., according to Assyrian records. If that is the case, then his prophecy occurred sometime between 767 and 763, if we assume a relatively short period of prophetic activity. Admittedly, however, Amos could be employing metaphorical language, but we know that ancients did pay close attention to natural catastrophes as the voice of God. It is interesting that in 8:8 Amos seems to speak of an anticipated earthquake, following that up in 8:9 with the prediction of a solar eclipse. If the two occurred in proximity to one another, they would provide a double confirmation of Amos's prophecy. The Assyrian weakness during that period would contribute more heavily to the growing sense of security and ease that marked the reign of Jeroboam II. Arguing with our own thesis, we might wonder why Amos mentioned only the earthquake in 1:1 if the solar eclipse had also been a major confirming factor. The eventualities of the data are so tentative that we might settle back on safer ground and broaden the range of possibilities to that suggested earlier, the co-regency of Jeroboam and Uzziah (767–753).

Morgenstern's thesis that Amos only prophesied on the one occasion, delivering his message in about thirty minutes,[16] has the appeal of novelty, but it is hard to believe that so influential a prophet would have had no greater prophetic involvement. In fact, the allegation of the priest Amaziah, that Amos had conspired against Jeroboam (7:10), implies time for Amos to have spoken more than once, and the interchange between the two men as well as the message dispatched to the king (not to mention a reply) would suggest a longer period of time, perhaps weeks or even months.

THE LITERARY NATURE AND PLAN OF THE BOOK

About half the book of Amos is composed of the oracles against the nations (1:3–2:16) and the five visions (7:1–9; 8:1–9:10), plus their appendixes. Those

---

14. Watts, pp. 34–35, proposes that on the New Year's festival of 752 B.C. Amos reported his first two visions and added the third, followed by a repetition of the three visions and the addition of the fourth on the same day in 751, and concluded by a repetition of the first four with the addition of the fifth in 750, the last being delivered in Bethel. Thus the "two years before the earthquake" of 1:1 would date his appearance at Bethel rather than his initial activity as a prophet.

15. Julian Morgenstern, "Amos Studies I," p. 140, takes Jotham's accession as co-regent with his father Uzziah (750 or 749) as the cutoff date, the co-regency being necessitated by the leprosy of Uzziah (2 Kings 15:5). Thus the "two years before the earthquake" would push the date back to 752 or 751. Harrison evidently follows the same line of reasoning. However, there still seems to be little reason to push the date so far to the end of Jeroboam's reign, except that the Assyrian crisis perhaps was appearing more and more viable.

16. Morgenstern, pp. 26–27.

two segments occupy a prominent place in the literary plan, which has led some scholars to advance the thesis that the book has two literary centers, the oracles and the visions, and that the rest of the prophecy has clustered around those two collections. Arthur Weiser, for instance, proposes that the two collections circulated independently for a time, and that the oracles in chapters 1–6 (originally concluded with 7:10–17) were prefixed to the visions, already actualized by events, in an effort to preserve the oracles.[17] Hughell E. W. Fosbroke speaks of "floating oracles" among the admirers of Amos that were written down to form the first collection of the sayings of Amos. The visions were, in his estimation, probably written or dictated later by Amos when the delay in the destruction that he predicted prompted him to record them for the day when his message would be vindicated by history.[18] Even though such a scheme correctly recognizes the centrality of the oracles and visions, it may also introduce much disparity into the various parts of the book. Moreover, as Harrison argues, the integration of the oracles and visions to obtain a wholistic picture of Amos's ministry is necessary. In fact, already in the first vision (7:1–3) Amos entreated Yahweh for mercy upon Israel, for whom he had already predicted disaster in the oracle of 2:6–16.[19]

Harper's analysis of the book divides the material into three parts: oracles (1:3–2:16), sermons (3:1–6:14), and visions (7:1–9:8b). Within those three main sections are numerous secondary passages that did not originate with Amos. In addition to them, 1:1–2 and 9:8c–15 are by later hands.[20] The analysis of Sellin/Fohrer is similar in that they view the books as being composed of many short sayings and reports of visions spoken in isolation. According to their assessment, 1:3–2:16 is the only large unit of oral proclamation, with 7:10–17 the only other longer sections.[21] Eissfeldt, whom Fohrer follows, counts twenty-five individual sayings in those passages outside of the oracles and visions.[22]

A much more coherent literary plan is detected by S. R. Driver, who sees a thematic development through it. Chapters 1–2 introduce the theme of the book, judgment upon Israel, chapters 3–6 argue against the privileged guarantee of safety that the Israelites believed they enjoyed, and chapters 7–9 reinforce that theme of divine judgment.[23] Keil's analysis follows the same thematic criterion and falls into the same three parts.[24] Although modern criticism of the book has often paid little attention to a synthetic theme and instead has

---

17. Arthur Weiser, *The Old Testament: Its Formation and Development*, pp. 243–44.
18. Hughell E. W. Fosbroke, *The Book of Amos*, pp. 771–72.
19. Harrison, p. 891.
20. See chart in Harper, p. cxxxii.
21. Ernst Sellin, and Georg Fohrer, *Introduction to the Old Testament*, p. 434.
22. Otto Eissfeldt, *The Old Testament, An Introduction*, p. 400.
23. S. R. Driver, *An Introduction to the Literature of the Old Testament*, pp. 314–16.
24. C. F. Keil, *The Twelve Minor Prophets*, pp. 237–38.

accentuated the disjunctive nature of much of the material, the thematic criterion remains a logical approach to understanding the prophets generally and
Amos particularly.

The assumption of Hermann Gunkel's form-critical method, that short sayings
constituted the basic building blocks of the prophetic writings, is highly questionable. Whereas most modern scholars would not accede to the thesis in that
form, at least for practical purposes many of them do underwrite it as a basic
working hypothesis. However, if Amos had anything to do with the composition of his own book, a proposition we shall consider further, it is highly
unlikely that he would have given his book the stamp of disarray that many
commentators believe they see there. The phrase "two years before the earthquake" suggests that Amos gave his prophecies their present literary form after
the earthquake that he predicted (8:8) had confirmed him a true prophet. His
intent was obviously to present his oracles and visions that had conveyed the
message of destruction in order to vindicate himself and all prophets—"Surely
the Lord God does nothing unless He reveals His secret counsel to His servants
the prophets" (3:7).

It might very well be that at that time Amos added the message of restoration
(9:11–15), which would be most appropriate in the face of the catastrophe, as
well as encouraging Israel in anticipation of the future captivity he had earlier
predicted (5:27; 9:4). Now they could be even more confident that he had not
been speaking amiss. We have no way of knowing whether Amos personally
delivered any additional oracles in the Northern Kingdom after the earthquake
ratified his prophetic credentials; but we can be sure that the thunderous words
of judgment and the ensuing encounter with Amaziah the priest had not been
forgotten. If the prophet himself had not made believers out of some of the
Northern citizens, the earthquake did. And those whose ears had been opened
to the voice of God, whether by prophetic proclamation or natural calamity,
would be glad to listen to Amos's words again and review his forebodings,
whether they should be delivered by him personally or his appointee.

We may theorize consequently that the book received its present form two
years after his ministry in Bethel. The final plan of the book (1) details his
oracles and visions delivered in the north two years prior, (2) recognizes the
confirmation of his prophecy by the earthquake, and (3) offers hope in anticipation of the impending storm yet to occur at the hands of the unnamed Assyrians.
Thus the published form of the book in its entirety reviewed how Amos had
accurately foretold what had actually happened, and it reminded Israel that
there was more to come.

It is most probable that the bulk of the oracles and visions had already been
committed to writing before the final edition of the book. In addition to the
work of arranging and editing, Amos or a disciple added 1:1 and perhaps also
1:2, the latter a reminder to the near-pagans of the Northern Kingdom that the

prophet speaks for Yahweh from Jerusalem, and His Word has a devastating effect on the extremities ("the summit of Carmel") of His land. No defiant priest need threaten with expulsion the prophet who speaks in the name of that God.

THE ORACLES AGAINST THE NATIONS (1:3–2:16)

FORM

Eight oracles against the nations begin the main body of the book, climaxing with the oracle against Israel. A standard form, with only slight variations, is shared by the first seven oracles, whereas the eighth departs considerably from it. Five items characterize this oracular form: (1) the introductory formula, "Thus says the Lord"; (2) a terse formulaic statement of Yahweh's irrevocable judgment, "For three transgressions of [city or state] and for four I will not revoke its punishment"; (3) the indictment proper, introduced by the Hebrew preposition *'al* ("because") and an infinitive with the subject suffix ("they threshed"), followed by the details of the crimes; (4) a statement of the punishment introduced by the formula "So I will send fire upon [object of punishment] and it will consume the citadels of" (absent from the Israel oracle, and the Ammonite oracle has the variation "So I will kindle a fire," rather than "send fire"); (5) the concluding formula, "Says the Lord" (missing in the Tyre, Edom, and Moab oracles, and in the Gaza oracle it has the form "Says the Lord God," whereas in the Israel oracle its form is "Declares the Lord" or "Oracle of the Lord").

Aage Bentzen has argued that the form of these oracles is that of the Egyptian cultic execration text.[25] Those were texts written on pottery vessels and contained the names of people and places the priest or worshiper wished to curse. Then the priest would break the vessel in a ritual of sympathetic magic to bring about the desired curse upon the person or place named. Wolff, on the other hand, has argued persuasively against that thesis, pointing out the difference in literary form (execration texts are just lists of names) and other divergences from the form of the Amos oracles.[26] John H. Hayes, considering the general nature and *Sitz-im-Leben* of the oracles, has proposed that their origin is to be sought in speeches made against enemies before battle. The giving of such oracles, in his judgment, was primarily a prophetic function. Eventually the form was adapted in the cultic liturgy, very likely the setting that most influenced Amos.[27] That hypothesis, however ingenious, does not

---

25. Aage Bentzen, "The Ritual Background of Amos 1:2–2:16, pp. 85–99. See also ANET, pp. 328–29 for a translation of some of these texts.
26. Wolff, pp. 144–46.
27. John H. Hayes, "The Usage of Oracles Against Foreign Nations in Ancient Israel," pp. 81–92.

Oracles Against the Nations

	Damascus (1:3–5)	Gaza (1:6–8)	Tyre (1:9–10)	Edom (1:11–12)	Ammon (1–13:15)	Moab (2:1–3)	Judah (2:4–5)	Israel (2:6–16)
1. Introductory formula: "Thus says the Lord"	------	------	------	------	------	------	------	------
2. Yahweh's irrevocable judgment: "For three transgressions of . . . and for four I will not revoke its punishment."	------	------	------	------	------	------	------	------
3. Indictment proper: "Because they/he . . ." + details	------	------	------	------	------	------	------	------
4. Punishment: "So I will send fire upon . . . And it will consume the citadels of . . . (her citadels)" + other details	------	------	------	------	"So I will kindle a fire" (v. 14)	------	------	"Behold, I am weighted down beneath you" (v. 13)
5. Concluding formula: "Says the Lord"	------	"Says the Lord God"	//////	//////	------	------	//////	"Declares the Lord" (Oracle of the Lord)

------ = repeated
////// = does not occur

satisfactorily explain the oracles of Amos. As John Barton has observed, the similarity between Amos 1–2 and other prophetic oracles against the nations is not very great.[28]

If any benefit is to be derived from identifying the origin of the form of these oracles in ancient Israelite society, Wolff's insistence that they are associated with the "messenger speech" does most justice to their form and function in Amos. Wolff's hypothesis results from an examination of speeches made by diplomatic messengers in the ancient Near East, both biblical and non-biblical.[29] We might surmise that if Amos was searching for a literary form in which to couch his message of judgment against the nations, that would have served very well.

In view of the irresolute nature of the question of form, we must agree with R. E. Clements's conclusion, also followed by Barton, that the oracles are a distinctive genre of their own and draw from many aspects of Israelite life.[30]

The Amos oracles have generally been grouped into three categories based upon form and content: (1) oracles against Damascus, Gaza, Ammon, and Moab; (2) oracles against Tyre, Edom, and Judah; and (3) oracle against Israel. The first group shares an identical form and content, whereas the second shares the trait that the punishment (element no. 4) is apocopated, ending with "So I will send fire upon . . . and it will consume the citadels of . . ." (or "her citadels"). Further, those three oracles do not contain the concluding formula, "Says the Lord." The content of the Judah oracle is different from Tyre and Edom. The latter two are indicted for wartime atrocities, whereas Judah is only condemned for religious apostasy. But the reason for that is not hard to find. The Judah oracle is a transition oracle, providing the hinge between condemnation of Israel's neighbors for military crimes and condemnation of Israel for her social crimes and religious apostasy. Because the oracle against Israel is the climax, Amos is more explicit about the sins of Israel, whereas he only mentions Judah's sins in general. His purpose was to indict Israel, not Judah. So Judah slips by with the bare mention of her general backsliding nature, whereas Israel receives a caustic rebuke in the most explicit detail.

The oracles, except for that against Israel, are brief and to the point. They have an arresting psychological force about them, preempting the agreement of the audience. But once the auditors have been quite won over to the prophet's assessment of their neighbors, then Amos turns the tables and judges them according to the same standards. It was a trap door, and once inside, the door closed hopelessly behind them.

The conclusion of Wolff and the majority of modern scholars that the oracles

28. John Barton, *Amos's Oracles Against the Nations: A Study of Amos 1.3–2.5*, p. 10.
29. Wolff, pp. 135–48.
30. R. E. Clements, *Prophecy and Tradition*, p. 72; Barton, p. 15.

of the second group (Tyre, Edom, and Judah) are later additions is not as "inescapable" as he claims.[31] To coerce Amos into agreement with modern form-critical analysis does injustice to the literary ingenuity of this prophet, requiring of him a uniformity of style that is pleasing to the literary analyst but that may misrepresent the literary sensitivities and psychological frame of mind of an eighth-century prophet. By the same method we might feel compelled to deny the Israel oracle to Amos as well. In fact, in form and content it is the most divergent of them all. But if we are willing to allow Amos the excellence of literary skill to which the book as a whole testifies, the oracle against Israel gives evidence of the prophet's literary versatility.

PURPOSE

The oracles against the nations obviously had a cumulative effect, whose sum was the absolutely inescapable judgment of Israel. Driver says it well: "As none of these will escape retribution for having broken the common and universally regarded dictates of morality, so Israel, for similar or greater sins (2:6–8), aggravated, indeed, in its case by ingratitude (vv. 9–12), will not be exempt from the same law of righteous government."[32]

More generally, however, the oracles against the nations pose a problem for the interpreter. What was the need to speak of or to nations that could not hear and consequently could not respond to the prophet's warning or word of judgment, whether in repentence (cf. Jonah 3:4–10) or self-defense? Probably no single answer to that question is possible, but in the case of the Amos oracles, there seems to have been no external purpose involved. That is, Amos had no motive that might benefit the nations outside of Israel. His purpose was aimed solely at Israel. The foreign nations are illustrations of Yahweh's irrevocable judgment. In fact, the oracles, as with numerous other foreign oracles, do not contain a direct address to the nations but speak of them in the third person. Those oracles that address a foreign nation directly (cf. Isa. 18:1–7; Jer. 49:7–22; Ezek. 27:3–36; 28:2–19, and others) may constitute a different aspect of the problem. Does the prophet expect a response? If so, how does the nation hear the word of the prophet? With the exception of Jonah among the writing prophets, none seems to have spoken to the nations on location.

The idea of sympathetic magic is not very convincing, because the Old Testament generally is adverse to the use of magic and sorcery. Perhaps the matter may be put to rest for our purposes by suggesting that the prophets, because they did not call upon the nations to repent, did not expect a response from them. The accountability for the execution of judgment was left with

31. Wolff, p. 140; also Barton, p. 24; Sellin, p. 436; Eissfeldt, p. 400; Fosbroke, p. 774, etc.
32. Driver, p. 314.

God, as is clearly the case in Amos. The prophets were not manipulative in the exercise of their function against the nations. Even though foreigners did not enjoy the covenant privileges and responsibilities, they nevertheless had a knowledge, though indistinct, of the ethical demands of Yahweh.[33] The nations, therefore, were accountable, not because they had heard the voice of God through the law and prophets, but simply because they had heard His voice through nature and social convention, what has come to be called natural revelation. Whereas Israel had a distinctly unique relationship to Yahweh ("You only have I chosen among all the families of the earth," 3:2*a*), the foreign nations had not been left devoid of some relationship to Him either:

> Are you not as the sons of Ethiopia to Me,
> O sons of Israel? declares the Lord.
> Have I not brought up Israel from the land of
> Egypt,
> And the Philistines from Caphtor and the Arameans
> from Kir?
>
> (9:7)

TIME SPAN

The general view is that the time period in which the numerous and sundry atrocities were committed was approximately the century before Amos, around 850 to 753 B.C. Keith N. Schoville's analysis leads him to opt for the period around 841, especially because Amos's time was relatively stable.[34] Norman K. Gottwald, following Kaufmann, dates the atrocities in the fifty or seventy-five years before Amos, identifying the events of the Damascus oracle as the attacks of Hazael against Transjordan during the reigns of Jehu and Jehoahaz between 837 and 805 (2 Kings 13:1–9, 22, 25). The "covenant of brotherhood" in the oracle against Tyre might be dated during the purge of the Omri dynasty by Jehu in 841; although, if that be true, the reference is probably to retaliatory measures by Tyre after the murder of Jezebel.[35] Barton, in his helpful analysis, more or less follows the recent or near-recent position taken

---

33. Kapelrud, p. 68, correctly makes this observation. But when he looks for the reason that underlay Amos's assumption that the nations knew this common ethical law, he proposes that in the eighth century B.C. Yahweh and El were so completely amalgamated that one name could be substituted for the other. That, he advocates, is in fact the source of Amos's universalism seen in 9:7 (pp. 42–47). Although we can allow for natural revelation, that may be an overstatement of the case, despite the religious syncretism in the Northern Kingdom. Universalism, as we shall see from Isaiah, was also a feature of the religion of Judah during this century and ought not to be traced to pagan elements.
34. Keith N. Schoville, "A Note on the Oracles of Amos Against Gaza, Tyre, and Edom," pp. 55–63, esp. p. 61.
35. Norman K. Gottwald, *All the Kingdoms of the Earth*, pp. 104–5.

by Wolff.[36] Even though recent events would seem to affect Amos and his audience more acutely, we must keep in mind that those were traditional enemies of Israel. So just the mention of the names, whether the crimes were recent or a century past, might accomplish the effect Amos intended.

ADDITIONAL ORACLES (3:1–6:14)

Five proclamations follow the oracles against the state of affairs in the Northern Kingdom and expand the indictment of the Israel oracle. The first three are introduced by "Hear this word!" and are addressed to the Israelites generally (3:1), the women of Samaria (4:1), and the house of Israel (5:1) respectively. In the first oracle (3:1–15) Amos indicted the whole of Israel for abusing the privileged relationship that they had with Yahweh. Israel's Exodus from Egypt carried with it responsibility, which they had not accepted. So the Lord would punish them for all their iniquities (3:2). Just as the visions are interrupted with Amos's account of his call (7:10–17), in like manner the oracles against the nations are followed by a biographical defense of his prophetic involvement (3:3–8). Things do not just happen. There is a cause-effect pattern evident in nature and history. By a series of rhetorical questions that require a negative answer, the prophet moves toward his climax: "A lion has roared! Who will not fear? The Lord God has spoken! Who can but prophesy?" (3:8).

The second oracle (4:1–13) addressed the women of Samaria who were a part of the oppressive machinery of that society. To be such an evil time, one might think that religion was at a low ebb, but that was not so. The people enjoyed being religious and were good at it:

> "Offer a thank offering also from that which
>   is leavened,
> And proclaim freewill offerings, make them known.
> For so you love to do, you sons of Israel,"
> Declares the Lord God.
>
>   (4:5)

But tragically their religion did not get beyond the shrines where they worshipped. The last part of the proclamation (vv. 6–12) builds a case for obedience and faithfulness out of Yahweh's unrelenting attention to Israel and her needs, and in view of the ungrateful response, the Lord vows judgment and commands Israel to prepare to meet her God (v. 12). Judgment is certain. Now Israel must get ready for its dreadful arrival. This is not a call to repentance. It is a pronouncement of doom.

---

36. Barton, chap. 4; Wolff, pp. 150–51.

The third oracle (5:1–17), addressed to the "house of Israel," begins with a lamentation (v. 2) over the doom that Amos has pronounced upon Israel. There is no evidence that Amos lived to see the fall of Israel in 722, so this lament is in anticipation of it. But no sooner had he said the last rites at the graveside than he summoned this people to seek the Lord and live (5:4, 6, 14). The future was contingent upon Israel's response to the summons—"Perhaps the Lord God of hosts may be gracious to the remnant of Joseph" (v. 15). If judgment came, for there was no effort to stave it off, the wailing and lamentation would be like the mourning of the Egyptians for their only sons, because the Lord would again pass through their midst (vv. 16–17).

The last two proclamations are introduced by the exclamation "woe" (NASB "alas" in 5:18). The fourth (5:18–27) pronounces woe upon impenitent Israel and ends with the prediction of exile beyond Damascus. Interestingly there were those in Amos's audience who were eagerly awaiting the "day of the Lord," for they expected a day that would signal victory for Israel and defeat for her enemies. But Amos inverted that concept and declared that it would be a day of darkness from which no one could escape (5:18). They may have evaded dangerous perils before and acquired a false security in the process, but the Lord had sufficient auxiliary systems to accomplish His plans and execute judgment. It would come when they thought they were safe at last:

> As when a man flees from a lion,
> And a bear meets him,
> Or goes home, leans his hand against the wall
> And a snake bites him.
>
> (v. 19)

The fifth oracle (6:1–14) was addressed to the political leaders of Judah and Samaria who had been lulled into a sense of false security by their wealth and success. Their real sin was that "they have not grieved over the ruin of Joseph" (v. 6). The reference in verse 2 to Calneh and Hamath, which did not fall to the Assyrians until around 738 B.C., and to Gath, which fell to Assyria around 734, has led some scholars to suggest a later date for this oracle. Wolff assigns it to Amos, but he sees a reinterpretation during the time when those cities fell.[37] J. A. Motyer regards the reference as an indication of their affluence rather than their fate, and he translates "better" as "better off."[38] Just as the first woe-oracle ended with a prediction of exile, this one concludes with a reference to the nation that will inflict the fatal wound upon Israel.

---

37. Wolff, p. 274.
38. J. A. Motyer, *The Day of the Lion*, p. 141.

THE VISIONS AND APPENDIXES (7:1–9:15)

THE FIVE VISIONS

The five visions stand alongside the oracles against the nations as one of two major literary centers to which the other materials of the book are attached. That does not mean that the words of Amos outside those two centers are not important. On the contrary, they provide a fuller account of the nature of Amos's preaching. With the exception of the Israel oracle, we would not know Amos as a preacher of social righteousness were it not for those additional words. The visions, although revealing much about Amos's prophetic experience, do not detail the religious and social sins of Israel. It is quite probable that Amos took the two collections and enlarged them with other oracles and words to underwrite and justify the broad terms of judgment declared in the national oracles and visions. In fact, we can see that function discharged by the materials interwoven into the visions.

Form. In literary form the visions proper fall into two pairs and a single vision. Visions 1 and 2 are a literary pair as are also visions 3 and 4, whereas vision 5 stands alone. The first four visions are introduced by "Thus the Lord God showed me," with a variant in the third ("Thus He showed me," 7:7), whereas vision 5 begins with "I saw the Lord" (9:1). Vision 1 (7:1–3) reports a locust plague in the spring that was destroying the crop. The prophet interceded for Israel: "Lord God, please pardon! How can Jacob stand, for he is small?" (7:2). The Lord's response to the prophet's prayer follows. Then the vision concludes with the voice of Yahweh: " 'It shall not be,' said the Lord" (v. 3*b*). Vision 2 (7:4–6) exhibits the same form. The Lord showed Amos a consuming fire that threatened to devour the great deep and the land. A second time Amos interceded: "Lord God, please stop! How can Jacob stand, for he is small?" (v. 5). The same statement of the Lord's relenting response follows, and the conclusion parallels that of vision 1: " 'This too shall not be,' said the Lord God" (v. 6).

The second pair of visions employs symbolism to communicate their message. Further, they were written as a dialogue between Yahweh and Amos. There is no prophetic intercession but only the dreadful verdict: "I will spare them no longer" (7:8; 8:2). Each of the visions appends an additional word of judgment, in vision 3 judgment upon the sanctuaries and the house of Jehoboam (7:9) and in vision 4 upon the palaces (8:3). In vision 3 (7:7–9) Amos saw the Lord standing by a wall with a plumbline in His hand, whereupon He questioned Amos about the identity of the object He had shown him. The purpose of the question-answer pattern in vision 4 was evidently to provide the sound for the word play on "summer" that follows ("summer" = *qayits*, "end" = *qēts*, both words using the same consonants). Following Yahweh's question is

ANALYSIS OF VISIONS

	Vision 1 (7:1–3)	*Vision 2 (7:4–6)*
1. Introductory formula	Thus the Lord God showed me,	Thus the Lord God showed me,
2. Optical content	and behold, He was forming a locust-swarm (v.1)	and behold, the Lord God was calling to contend with them by fire (v. 4)
3. Prophet's intercession	And it came about, when it had finished eating the vegetation of the land, that I said, [lit. "and I said"] "Lord God, please pardon! How can Jacob stand, for he is small?" (v. 2)	Then I said, [lit. "and I said"] "Lord God, please stop! How can Jacob stand, for he is small?" (v. 5)
4. Yahweh's response	The Lord changed His mind about this. "It shall not be," said the Lord (v. 3).	The Lord changed His mind about this. "This too shall not be," said the Lord God (v.6).

	Vision 3 (7:7–9)	Vision 4 (8:1–3)
1. Introductory formula	Thus He showed me,	Thus the Lord God showed me,
2. Optical content	and behold, the Lord was standing (v. 7)	and behold, a basket of summer fruit (v.1)
3. Dialogue	And the Lord said to me, "What do you see, Amos?" And I said, "A plumb line."	And He said, "What do you see, Amos?" And I said, "A basket of summer fruit."
4. Interpretation	Then the Lord said, "Behold, I am about to put a plumb line in the midst of My people Israel."	Then the Lord said to me, "The end has come."
5. Irrevocable verdict	'I will spare them no longer' (v. 8)	'I will spare them no longer' (v. 2).
6. Concluding judgment	"The high places of Isaac will be desolated" (v. 9).	"The songs of the palace will turn to wailing." (v. 3).

	Vision 5 (9:1–4)
1. Introductory formula	I saw the Lord (v. 1*a*)
2. Yahweh's command	"Smite the capitals . . . and break them" (v. 1*b–c*)
3. Yahweh's judgment	"Then I will slay the rest of them" (vv. 1*d*–4*a*)
4. Concluding verdict	"And I will set My eyes against them for evil and not for good" (v. 4*b*)

+ appendix 9:5–15

Amos's answer and then Yahweh's interpretation of the object that Amos identified. Concluding both visions, as already noted, is the Lord's avowal that He will spare them no longer, perhaps a reference to His mercy extended to Israel when Amos pleaded for His forebearance in the first two visions (7:2–3, 5–6).

We should also note that visions 3, 4, and 5 have long appendixes. After vision 3 the appendix takes the form of the encounter between Amaziah, the priest of Bethel, and Amos (7:10–17). The form of the appendix to vision 4 is that of an oracle prefaced by "Hear this" (8:4–8), followed by three doomsday oracles (8:9–10, 11–12, 13–14), each using the eschatological language of the day of the Lord ("And it will come about in that day," v.9; "Behold, days are coming," v.11; "In that day," v.13). To vision 5 is attached an appendix (9:5–15) that includes a hymnic interlude lauding Yahweh as Controller of the earth (9:5–6), a restatement of the coming judgment upon Israel (9:7–10), and two statements (9:11–12, 13–15) describing the eschatological future, both using eschatological language ("In that day," v.11; "Behold, days are coming," v. 13).

Vision 5 opens differently from the first four. Amos "saw the Lord standing beside the altar" (v.1). There is no dialogue here as in visions 3 and 4, only the Lord's command to smite the capitals of the sanctuary. The message of the vision is the same as that of 5:18–20—there will be no escape when judgment falls!

The critical discussion of the visions has been rather extensive. Morgenstern, observing that the announcement of the end came in 8:2, would move vision 3 to follow 7:6, giving the pattern of two intercessions that brought no results among the people, only a respite for Israel, and finally the announcement of the end. He suggests, therefore, that the first four visions (in the order of 1, 2, 4, 3) were the preparation for Amos's ministry. Vision 1 is dated in the spring, vision 2 in midsummer when the summer produce had ripened, vision 4 only three or four weeks after that, and vision 3 at the end of summer, just before the annual harvest festival. Vision 5 then came while Amos was in Bethel on the occasion of the harvest or New Year's festival, after he had finished his prophetic address and denounced Amaziah.[39] Watts also puts vision 5 at the end of Amos's ministry, proposing that he reported them over a succession of three harvest or New Year's festivals.[40]

Although in general Morgenstern's timetable for the visions is plausible, the rearrangement is not necessary, particularly because both visions 3 and 4 are quite foreboding in their declaration that the Lord would no longer spare Israel (7:8; 8:2). Moreover, the pronouncement in vision 4 that the end had come would understandably provoke Amaziah to deliver his pungent denunciation of Amos. Evidently Amos was present in Bethel during a major festival, perhaps that which had been instituted by Jeroboam I on the fifteenth day of the eighth

---

39. Morgenstern, pp. 86, 90, 103, 106.
40. Watts, pp. 34–35, and n. 15 of this chapter, above. See K.A. Kitchen, *Ancient Orient and Old Testament*, pp. 102–6, for a persuasive counter-statement to the idea of a New Year's festival in ancient Israel at the time of the Feast of Tabernacles.

month as the Northern counterpart of the Feast of Tabernacles in Judah (1 Kings 12:32–33). There is simply no way to determine absolutely when and where vision 5 occurred. Because very few of the prophecies in the book concern Judah, it is probable that most of them were delivered in the sanctuaries of the Northern Kingdom, even though they may not have occurred there. Bethel is the only one we can be certain about. It is likely that all of them were announced there.

Purpose. As mentioned above, Morgenstern suggests that the first four visions provide an account of Amos's preparation for his ministry. There are other scholars who have suggested more specifically that these visions constitute his call.[41] Driver takes them merely as reinforcement of the lessons of the previous discourses,[42] and they are indeed that. Again we must recognize the speculative nature of the question. The only account of Amos's call that can be definitely identified is that of 7:14–15, which is a very general statement without the kind of detail that appears in the call of Jeremiah (chap. 1) and Ezekiel (chap. 1). Yet it should be noted that both of those prophets had visions in conjunction with their call. And although we ought not extrapolate from their experience backward to Amos, the idea that the first four visions may constitute the details of the prophet's call is worthy of our attention, especially because the only reference to the call is associated with the visionary records.

PURPOSE AND FUNCTION OF 7:10–17

Rather than consider this interchange between Amos and Amaziah as an intrusion, I have recognized it as an appendix to vision 3. The reference to the "house of Jeroboam" in 7:9 is no mere catch-word that joins the two passages. Rather it is quite likely that the threat against Jeroboam, delivered in the sanctuary at Bethel, provoked this strong reaction from the priest Amaziah. He heard in Amos's words no less than conspiracy against Jeroboam and his dynasty.

Peter R. Ackroyd's contention that its purpose was to pronounce doom against the dynasty of Jehu may be true enough, but his hypothetical assertion that 7:9–17 is not autobiographical, and that it is assocated with a grave tradition (like 2 Kings 13 and 23) of Amos in Bethel,[43] requires a hefty stretch of the imagination. Fosbroke also disassociates the passage from the prophet Amos and attributes it to a later writer who saw in Amos the greatness of a true prophet.[44] Yet the signature of Amos is obvious. The same irresistible compul-

---

41. E.g., J. P. Hyatt, "The Book of Amos," *Int* 3 (1949):344; Fosbroke, 765–66.
42. Driver, p. 135; Wolff, p. 200.
43. Peter R. Ackroyd, "A Judgment Narrative between Kings and Chronicles? An Approach to Amos 7:9–17," in *Canon and Authority: Essays in Old Testament Religion and Theology,* ed. George W. Coats and Burke O. Long (Philadelphia: Fortress, 1977), p. 85.
44. Fosbroke, p. 772.

sion that he expresses in 3:8 is present here. The character of those who forbade the prophets to prophesy, so pungently condemned in the oracle against Israel (2:12), is taken account of here also in the direct address to Amaziah— "you are saying, 'You shall not prophesy against Israel' " (v. 16). Moreover, the prediction of exile, so prominently declared elsewhere (5:27; 9:4), is part of this account (v. 17). There can be little doubt about the originality of this passage. It stands here as a report of the response to Amos's preaching in Bethel and a defense of his authority.

Amaziah's order that Amos return to Judah and carry on his prophetic work there ("Go, you seer, flee away to the land of Judah, and there eat bread and there do your prophesying!" v. 12) evoked from Amos a self-defense of his ministry, a statement that has been the point of much discussion: "I am not a prophet, nor am I the son of a prophet" (v. 14). Watts claims that the discussion of the time element (past or present) is a fruitless one. Rather, the syntactical problem is one of mood instead of tense. He calls it a kind of subjunctive of volition and renders the sentence: "No prophet did *I* choose to be! Nor did I seek to become one of the prophetic guild. For *I* (had chosen to be) a herdsman and a tender of sycamores, when Yahweh took me from following the flock."[45] Ackroyd prefers to interpret the negatives interrogatively: "Am I not a prophet?" That, of course, has the opposite effect normally assumed for the passage, giving Amos the status of prophet as well as assigning him to one of the prophetic guilds.[46] J. Albert Soggin's explanation, taking into account the past tense of the verbs in the passage, insists that the present could not be understood here (it is a verbless clause), only the past: "I was not a prophet, nor did I belong to an association of prophets." The implication would then be that Amos was not a prophet at first, but later he was.[47] Wolff takes the more traditional view, that Amos was denying any vocational connection with professional prophetism (i.e., he did not earn his living that way) either as a prophet or a prophet's disciple ("son of a prophet").[48] That interpretation does greater justice to the grammar of the sentence than the above attempts to make it say more than the obvious. In fact, Morgenstern's proposal, that Amos was disassociating himself from the older connotation of the professional prophets who were known to foment rebellion,[49] makes much sense in this context.

HYMNIC MATERIAL

Several scholars have identified the doxologies in 4:13; 5:8–9; and 9:5–6 as remnants of an older cultic hymn or hymns. These three passages laud Yahweh

---

45. Watts, p. 12 and n. 1.
46. Ackroyd, p. 83.
47. J. Alberto Soggin, *Introduction to the Old Testament*, pp. 241–42.
48. Wolff, pp. 313–14.
49. Morgenstern, p. 50 and n. 52.

as Creator and Sustainer of the earth, and they share a common refrain, "The Lord is His name" ("the Lord God of hosts" in 4:13). Watts argues that these fragments (he does not include 5:9) belong to an old hymn announcing Yahweh's coming and judgment, and that it was sung at the annual New Year's festival. In his view, the "Day of Yahweh" was the climax of the festival. The hymn originated sometime between Elijah and Amos.[50] Brevard S. Childs considers these fragments to be the effort of the redactor to reinforce the theological focus of the book.[51]

Although there is an obvious relationship among these three doxologies, it is not so obvious that they belong to an earlier hymn or that they represent a later theological emphasis. Harrison correctly observes that they are so well integrated into the text that they cannot be extricated and assigned to other sources.[52] The theological climate of the eighth century was sufficiently adequate for Amos to laud Yahweh as the Creator and Controller of the world. We must, therefore, adopt the position that Amos was the author of these doxologies, and that he himself used them to reinforce the theological focus of his message.

CONCLUDING ORACLES (9:11–15)

As part of the appendix to vision 5, two brief oracles are marked off here by an introductory formula ("In that day," v. 11; "Behold, days are coming," v. 13) and a concluding formula ("Declares the Lord who does this," lit., "utterance of the Lord" v. 12; "Says the Lord your God," v. 15). The first oracle predicts the rebuilding of the "fallen booth of David" and the conquest of Israel's arch-enemy, Edom. The "booth of David" has been understood as his dynasty, his empire (so the Targum), and his capital city, Jerusalem. If the reference is to the kingdom of David, as the Targum interprets, then there is no problem, for the kingdom of David had long disintegrated with the division of the united kingdom and the loss of other territories. That would then be another threat hurled against the house of Jeroboam. The Lord will again restore the united kingdom. But if the reference is to the future fall of Judah and the loss of the Davidic dynasty, which admittedly would satisfy the terms of this passage very well, there is still no reason to deny the prophecy to Amos. A few years later in this same historical time frame, Micah predicted the fall of Jerusalem (Mic. 3:12). The futuristic outlook, in fact, seems to be the most satisfactory.

The second oracle (9:13–15) in this concluding section speaks of future agricultural plenty and return from captivity. That, of course, amounts to a reversal of Amos's earlier prediction of exile. Although many scholars have

---

50. Watts, chap. 3.
51. Brevard S. Childs, *Introduction to the Old Testament as Scripture,* p. 405.
52. Harrison, p. 893.

ruled out any part for Amos in writing this oracle,[53] the critical question here is whether Amos had an eschatology that involved so abrupt a break with the conditions he saw developing in the immediate future. Could the prophet who said the Day of the Lord was darkness instead of light make such a clean break with his own message and declare a totally different future in the same theological framework? The only way to answer that question fully is to examine Amos in relation to other prophets of his own general time period; and when one approaches the scholarly literature, the vast array of presuppositions with which the literature is examined hopelessly confuses the undertaking. As we have indicated in the general introduction, however, the prophets of the eighth century did have a rather well-developed eschatology of the future. They were not merely prophets of doom. Amos, though a pioneer among the classical prophets, shared that view of eschatology. The glorious future predicted here is well within the expectations of the eighth-century constellation of prophets. The language of verse 13 is metaphorical, but the message is clear—the days of prosperity were coming. The association of that idea with verses 14–15 lead us to conclude that return from captivity and prosperity were to characterize the new era.

WRITING AND COMPILATION

We need to recognize that writing and compilation may be two different processes. It is possible, though in our opinion not probable, that Amos's part was limited to writing or dictating his prophecies, and admirers or disciples compiled the book. On the other hand, it is quite possible, perhaps likely, that Amos not only wrote the prophecies but also put the book in its present shape. As I have indicated in the general introduction, the prophets were concerned with the preservation of their message and the vindication of their prophetic office. With regard to Amos, some passages were written in the first-person singular style, for example his self-defense before Amaziah (7:10–17) and the five visions (7:1–3, 4–6, 7–9; 8:1–3; 9:1–4). Those give the most obvious expression of authorship by Amos himself. And as I have suggested above, there is sufficient grounds for believing that the oracles against the nations, including those against Tyre, Edom, and Judah, were written by the prophet Amos. In addition to those, Amos delivered many more oracles of both weal and woe, which he included to reinforce the message of the oracles and visions. We need not assume that they were delivered in the order in which they have been given in the book; but we can be certain that the present structure, which has theological implications, does not misrepresent the thrust and force of his prophetic ministry.

53. Wolff, p. 351; Kapelrud, pp. 57–58; Carl G. Howie, "Expressly for Our Time," Int 13 (1959):283; Hyatt, p. 340; Weiser, p. 244; Fosbroke, pp. 774–75, and others.

The earthquake appears to have marked the compilation of the book, although we should not assume that nothing was written before that time. As significant as the visions and national oracles were, Amos might have committed them to writing before that catastrophe, including the appendix to vision 3 in 8:4–14 in which the earthquake was predicted. When the calamity came, it provided the impetus to collect all the prophecies and give them a form to remind Israel that he had predicted what had actually happened and, further, to renew the prophecy of exile. Although we have no way of knowing, the earthquake, by its confirmatory force, may have opened the northern borders to Amos again. Perhaps on that occasion he both renewed the predictions of captivity and exile with the oracles of 9:7–10 and soothed the suffering of this people with his hopeful message of 9:11–15.

Weiser hypothesizes that there were two quite separate collections, the "visions," containing the visions proper in chapters 7–9, and the "words," containing the oracles of chapters 1–6. Watts has similarly proposed that the "words" of chapters 1–6 were spoken and copied down in the North and were probably taken to the South by refugees, where they were united with the other book of "visions" sometime between the fall of Samaria in 722 and the completion of the scroll of the twelve prophets.[54] The assumption is that Amos had little or nothing to do with the compilation of the book. In essence Fosbroke agrees with that late date of compilation, viewing the final stage to be represented by 4:13; 5:8–9; and 9:5–6, which extol Yahweh as Creator and Sustainer of nature.[55] Morgenstern's study led him to suggest that Amos wrote down the record of his message delivered at Bethel after the earthquake had occurred,[56] although he views much of the book as secondary.

Certainly we may assume that there was much interest in prophetic literature after the fall of Samaria, the event above all events that had confirmed the message of the eighth-century prophets. But it is not necessary to relegate the major work of compilation to that era, although much literary activity was probably associated with the reform of Hezekiah in Judah (2 Kings 18:4–6; 2 Chron. 31; Prov. 25:1). We can readily agree with Motyer that, although we cannot be certain that Amos compiled his own book, the opinion of scholarship a generation ago that he could not have done so has been discredited to a great extent by current research.[57]

54. Watts, p. 50 and n. 4.
55. Fosbroke, p. 775.
56. Morgenstern, p. 126.
57. Motyer, p. 19.

THE MESSAGE OF AMOS

GOD IS GREATER THAN RELIGION

The words of Amos reverberate from Bethel to Dan to Samaria to Gilgal, the places of religious and political authority, that there is an authority who supersedes the bloated self-confidence of the religious and political systems of Israel. He stands above them first in judgment and finally in grace. The power and prerogative of this God, Yahweh by name, are most clearly attributes that flow out of His nature as Creator and Sustainer of the world:

> He who made the Pleiades and Orion
> And changes deep darkness into morning,
> Who also darkens day into night,
> Who calls for the waters of the sea
> And pours them out on the surface of the earth,
> The Lord is His name.
> It is He who flashes forth with destruction upon
>   the strong,
> So that destruction comes upon the fortress.
>   (5:8–9)

The Lord is no fly-by-night, local deity whose dominion is circumscribed by geographical boundaries. By virtue of His creating power, He walks on the high places where the Israelites had built their pagan shrines and prayed to their nature god. It seems significant that, in view of the fertility emphasis of Baalism, Amos twice speaks of the Lord "who calls for the waters of the sea and pours them out on the surface of the earth" (5:8; 9:6). One might wonder if Amos did not snatch that right out of the Baal liturgy and annex it to his own description of Yahweh. He and Hosea after him knew full well that the rain, that most precious and vital commodity of nature, was Yahweh's prerogative, not Baal's. As Hosea's adulterous Israel came to consider in one of her better moments, perhaps Baal did not exercise the authority as Israel had supposed. At least it had been better for her with her old husband than in her new life (Hos. 2:7). But those prophets knew that Israel, so calloused by disobedience, had mistakenly attributed that authority over nature to another god. The Lord who created the world also sustained it.

Israel's true God had taken the initiative in the covenantal relationship that was fundamental to her welfare: "You only have I chosen among all the families of the earth" (3:2*a*). That special bond, far from ensuring privilege without responsibility, did not indemnify Israel against punishment. That was obviously a contradiction of the popular belief.[58] The fact that the Lord had

58. Barton, p. 49.

"known" (NASB "chosen") Israel is Amos's way of expressing the covenantal relationship. Hosea also uses that term along with the word *ḥesed*, lovingkindness, to describe the special affinity of Yahweh for Israel and vice versa. The latter term does not enter into Amos's vocabulary, even though he was aware of the concept. As expressions of the covenant, Yahweh had brought the Israelites out of Egypt (3:1; 2:10a; 9:7), led them in the wilderness forty years (2:10b), destroyed the awesome Amorites before them (2:9), and raised up prophets and Nazirites among them (2:11). In comparison to other nations, He had brought them into existence just as He had Israel:

> "Are you not as the sons of Ethiopia to Me,
> O sons of Israel?" declares the Lord.
> "Have I not brought up Israel from the land of
> Egypt,
> And the Philistines from Caphtor and the Arameans
> from Kir?"
>
> (9:7)

Yet He had endowed them with neither the privileges nor the responsibilities of His chosen nation, Israel. Because, therefore, privilege engendered responsibility, a principle that Israel had not comprehended, Yahweh would punish her for her default of the covenant responsibilities (3:2b; 9:8a).

In some respects Amos was a pioneer in prophetic thought. His theology laid a foundation for that of Isaiah a generation or so later. That is particularly true in his description of the Lord as Creator and Sustainer of the world, a concept Isaiah so beautifully developed. Further, his practical universalism, "Israel for the world's sake," rather than "the world for Israel's sake," as Harper expresses it,[59] prepared the way for Isaiah's advancement upon that theme.

RELIGION AND SOCIETY

There was no lack of religion in the Northern Kingdom. The patrons of the cult brought their offerings and tithes, and they enjoyed doing it; but contrary to their intended purpose, they amounted to more transgression:

> "Enter Bethel and transgress;
> In Gilgal multiply transgression!
> Bring your sacrifices every morning,
> Your tithes every three days.
> Offer a thank offering also from that which
> is leavened,
> And proclaim freewill offerings, make them known.
> For so you love to do, you sons of Israel,"
> Declares the Lord God.
>
> (4:4–5)

---

59. Harper, p. cxvii.

Their religion, though lavishly supplied with enough offerings and festivals to placate any self-gratifying god, could not pacify Yahweh, whose demands included justice and obedience:

> I hate, I reject your festivals,
> Nor do I delight in your solemn assemblies.
> Even though you offer up to Me
>   burnt offerings and your grain offerings,
> I will not accept them;
> And I will not even look at the peace offerings
>   of your fatlings.
> Take away from Me the noise of your songs;
> I will not even listen to the sound
>   of your harps.
>
> (5:21–23)

Religion that is confined to the sanctuary is worse than no religion at all, for it is false. Amos and the prophets generally issued their most stinging rebukes against those who practiced pseudo-piety. Hypocrisy is worse than atheism, for it camouflages the sickness that grace is meant to heal. It is a denial of both the reality of sin and the power of grace. And more hopeless still is hypocrisy that has advanced to the stage where it is not even recognized by its adherents. Amos's audience was at that stage:

> Seek good and not evil, that you may live;
> And thus may the Lord God of hosts be with you,
> Just as you have said!
>
> (5:14)

The enthusiasm that marked Israel's religion was branded by a spirit of self-gratification. Although performed with zeal and prodigality, the selfish motive was unmistakable:

> Hear this, you who trample the needy, to do away
> with the humble of the land, saying,
> "When will the new moon be over,
> So that we may buy grain,
> And the sabbath, that we may open the wheat market,
> To make the bushel smaller and the shekel bigger,
> And to cheat with dishonest scales,
> So as to buy the helpless for money
> And the needy for a pair of sandals,
> And that we may sell the refuse of the wheat?"
>
> (8:4–6)

We can be sure that Amos had not actually heard the people saying all those words, for they were too self-indicting, but he employs irony of attribution to describe their real motives. It is what he had heard in their actions.

For a people whose fear of famine and dread of infertility drove them to the Baal rituals, Amos was aware of a greater fear that should have motivated their actions. In fact, they had been contemptuously brazen in the face of that entity, the prophetic word, and had forbidden the prophets to prophesy (2:12). Their audacious cultic leader, Amaziah, had capsulized that spirit in no uncertain terms when Amos himself posed a threat to his liturgical realm (7:12–13). But even if the thing they feared did not happen, the thing they did not fear would—there would be a dearth of the prophetic word:

> "Behold, days are coming," declares the Lord God,
> "When I will send a famine on the land,
> Not a famine for bread or a thirst for water,
> But rather for hearing the words of the Lord.
> And people will stagger from sea to sea,
> And from the north even to the east;
> They will go to and fro to seek the word of the Lord.
> But they will not find it."
>
> (8:11–12)

The social texture of Israelite society in Amos's day was characterized by injustice in the court (5:10–12) and fraud in the marketplace (8:4–6). The poor had become the pawns of the rich, and poverty and injustice were virtually synonymous terms. Affluent living involved a winter and a summer house with ivory-inlaid furniture (3:15; 6:4), plenty of wine to drink (4:1), and the satisfaction of one's carnivorous appetites (6:4). Samaria and Jerusalem alike were seats of a lamentable false security (6:1).

Yet when the crust of that decaying society was removed, the creature inside was even worse still. Against the clamor of social festivities, commercial hawking, and liturgical chanting was the dreadful silence of society's patrons, who "have not grieved over the ruin of Joseph" (6:6). If there is a sin that bottoms out the empire of evil, that is it. Israel's social and political leaders had sunk to that level.

At some point in Amos's ministry, likely as early as his itinerant mission to Bethel, he offered a program to reverse the forces of decay that were wasting the society. It involved doing exactly what the Israelites thought they had been doing—seek Yahweh and live (5:4, 6, 14). But at that stage of the putrefaction he could only offer the hope of a fragile "perhaps": "Perhaps the Lord God of hosts may be gracious to the remnant of Joseph" (5:15).

The dreadful alternative to repentance was the curse of ancient Near Eastern culture—conquest and exile. Even though Amos never names the Assyrians, the time of his ministry demands that we identify the agent of destruction as the Neo-Assyrian Empire that Tiglath-pileser III built. One might topographically describe Samaria as located at the bottom of a shallow bowl whose sides are formed by the surrounding mountains. To itensify the humiliation and also provide the two witnesses needed for condemnation, the prophet summons Ashdod and Egypt to assemble on the mountains of Samaria and see the tumult and oppression in her midst (3:9).

Worship and the common life constitute the whole. Liturgy, however refined and well intended, is a broken reed without the validating effect of justice and morality in the sphere of everyday life. "Worship," says Carl G. Howie, "must be identification with the character and purpose of him whom we worship. God demands justice because he is just."[60] If God had to choose one over the other, Amos reminds us that He would unhesitatingly choose justice over liturgy, for the purpose of liturgy is to teach us who God is and what He requires. The essence of prophetic religion was ethical. The cult was auxiliary to that.

HOPE AND THE FUTURE

Moved by an irresistible force to proclaim doom in Israel, Amos introduced the term "the day of the Lord" (5:18–20), obviously a popular doctrine already, but with a repeal of its positive features. It would be "darkness instead of light" (5:20). Further descriptions of "that day" may be found in 2:16; 8:3, 9–10, 13; 9:11–12, and 13–15. The description found in 9:11–15 stands in contradistinction to the other references because "that day" ("days" in 9:13) is characterized as a day of restoration and renewal. The dynasty of David will be restored (v. 11), the kingdom of God will be widened (v. 12), the earth will become extremely fruitful (v. 13; cf. Gen. 3:17b–19), the people will be returned from captivity (v. 14), and they will be securely planted in the land of Israel again (v. 15). Many scholars will not acknowledge that that passage was written by Amos,[61] but that is to deny to him the prerogative of hope. Prophetic religion without hope, even as early as the time of Amos, was inconceivable. The eschatology of Amos's audience, so hopefully formulated, was founded on shifting turf. Although Amos deflated their false hope, we cannot conclude that he himself had no hope to offer them once divine judgment had been served upon their sins. It is impossible to judge just how distant he thought the day of restoration was. But we can be confident that he could not envision the day of doom apart from the day of renewal.

---

60. Carl G. Howie, "Expressly for Our Time," pp. 273–85, esp. pp. 278–81.
61. See pp. 75–76 above.

OUTLINE OF AMOS

I. Introduction (1:1–2)
   A. Superscription (1:1)
   B. Announcement of Judgment (1:2)
II. Oracles Against the Nations (1:3–2:16)
   A. Oracle Against Damascus (1:3–5)
   B. Oracle Against Gaza (1:6–8)
   C. Oracle Against Tyre (1:9–10)
   D. Oracle Against Edom (1:11–12)
   E. Oracle Against the Ammonites (1:13–15)
   F. Oracle Against Moab (2:1–3)
   G. Oracle Against Judah (2:4–5)
   H. Oracle Against Israel (2:6–16)
III. Additional Oracles (3:1–6:14)
   A. Hear This Word, People of Israel (3:1–15)
   B. Hear This Word, Cows of Bashan (4:1–13)
   C. Hear This Word, House of Israel (5:1–17)
   D. Woe to Impenitent Israel—Captivity beyond Damascus (5:18–27)
   E. Woe to Impenitent Israel—Destruction by Invasion from the North (6:1–14)
IV. The Visions and Appendixes (7:1–9:15)
   A. Vision 1—the Locust (7:1–3)
   B. Vision 2—the Devouring Fire (7:4–6)
   C. Vision 3 and Appendix A (7:7–17)
      1. Vision 3—the Lord's Plumb Line (7:7–9)
      2. Appendix A—Amos's Encounter with Amaziah (7:10–17)
   D. Vision 4 and Appendix B (8:1–14)
      1. Vision 4—the Basket of Summer Fruit (8:1–3)
      2. Four Oracles (8:4–14)
         a. Hear this, You Who Trample the Needy (8:4–8)
         b. Sundown at High Noon (8:9–10)
         c. The Unexpected Famine (8:11–12)
         d. The Devastating Drought (8:13–14)
   E. Vision 5 and Appendix C (9:1–15)
      1. Vision 5—the Lord by the Altar (9:1–4)
      2. Appendix C (9:5–15)
         a. The Lord, Creator and Sustainer of the Earth (9:5–6)
         b. The Lord, Israel, and the Nations (9:7–8)
         c. Judgment upon Skeptical Israel (9:8–10)
         d. Restoration of David's Dynasty and Kingdom (9:11–12)
         e. Renewal of the Earth, the People, and the Homeland (9:13–15)

4

HOSEA: A PROPHET'S DILEMMA

HOSEA EXEMPLIFIED THE DILEMMA of the ancient Israelite prophet as well, if not better, than any of the writing prophets. Possessed by an awareness of having been grasped by God, a knowledge that dominated the prophet's activity, the Hebrew prophet was also held by intense love for his people. Hosea's personal life symbolized that traumatic predicament. Much could be said about the strength of this man in the face of personal and national crisis, but he, as well as the prophets in general, was acutely aware that his strength to face up to the crisis had its divine source. In fact, the determined grip of Yahweh on His elected people provided the courage for the prophet Hosea to storm the walls of a decaying society, pronounce divine judgment, and sue for peace between God and Israel. It was not an easy task even for the strongest of men. If it was not easy for Yahweh, it certainly could not be easy for His prophet. The divine anguish expressed from a father's perspective (11:8) parallels the pleading of husband and children to their negligent wife and mother (2:2).

To be caught up in one's mission was normative for the prophets. Personal involvement and risks were all part of the execution of the call. No prophet took a greater risk than Hosea, and no prophet suffered more personal anguish than he. Yet risk and suffering were means by which his heart was borne more closely to God. But to be borne toward God was not to be carried away from the people in whose behalf he ministered. Rather, to be close to God was to be close to Israel, whom God had elected. Thus the dilemma of the prophet was Yahweh's dilemma:

> How can I give you up, O Ephraim?
> How can I surrender you, O Israel?
> How can I make you like Admah?
> How can I treat you like Zeboiim?
> My heart is turned over within Me,
> All my compassions are kindled.
>
> (11:8)

HOSEA THE MAN

Due to the biographical and autobiographical accounts in the book (chaps. 1 and 3) we know a good deal about this prophet. Although the book does not inform us of the place of Hosea's birth, the internal evidence suggests that he was a native of the Northern Kingdom, for he knew that region very well; and judging from his beautiful metaphors, it was a land that he loved very much. Adolphe Lods and Robert H. Pfeiffer[1] have suggested that he might have originated in the part of Benjamin that belonged to Israel, because he knew that land so well (4:15; 5:8; 6:7; 9:9; 10:9; 12:11). But that may require too much of those texts. His references to Judah are general, and never does he mention the name of any Judean city, not even Jerusalem. Israel is called "the land" (1:2) and her king "our king" (7:5), although Hosea is not proud of the Northern monarchy (13:10–11).

Nothing is known of Hosea's father, Beeri, unless he was the person by that name whom Tiglath-pileser deported (1 Chron. 5:6), as early Jewish tradition held. But that is not at all certain. Leviticus Rabba (VI.6; XV.2) preserves the tradition that Berri was a prophet and that his prophecy is preserved in Isaiah 8:19 and following.[2]

Even though Hosea was intimately familiar with the ways of the farmer (6:11; 8:7) as well as the baker (7:4–7), the book uses rich and diversified imagery. So on that basis we could easily assign to him several occupations. The truth is that we do not know what his occupation was, aside from being a prophet. We may, however, agree with R. K. Harrison[3] and others who propose that, based upon his knowledge of history and politics, he was not a peasant but likely a middle-class or upper-class citizen.

His marriage to Gomer, which will occupy our attention later, produced two sons and a daughter before the marriage fractured from Gomer's insistent promiscuity. His life and profession made such a negative impression on his contemporaries that they called him "a fool" and "demented" (9:7). But his courage and obedience never flagged, even when Yahweh instructed him to "go again" and retrieve the faithless wife who had heartlessly abandoned husband and child alike.

This prophet's public addresses were likely delivered in the cultic centers of Bethel and Gilgal, and perhaps also in the capital, Samaria. Based upon the speech forms of the legal dispute (2:4; 4:1, 4; 12:3) and the watchman (5:8; 8:1; 9:8), Hans Walter Wolff surmises that Hosea probably spoke in the city gates

---

1. Adolphe Lods, *The Prophets and the Rise of Judaism*, p. 87; Robert H. Pfeiffer, *Introduction to the Old Testament*, p. 566.
2. *Midrash Rabbah*, ed. H. Freedman and Maurice Simon, trans. J. Israelstam and Judah J. Slotki (London: Soncino, 1939), 4:86.
3. R. K. Harrison, *Introduction to the Old Testament*, p. 859. Also G. A. F. Knight, *Hosea*, p. 13.

of those urban centers. Of course, he may also have trespassed the courts of the cultic centers (2:4–17; 4:4–19; 9:1–9).[4]

DATING THE ACTIVITY OF HOSEA

The dating of Hosea's activity hinges upon two generally accepted facts and one contingency. The facts are that the superscription (1:1) distinctly places his prophecy within some part of the reign of Jeroboam II. Further, it is also generally agreed that his ministry likely ended before the fall of Samaria because that event is nowhere mentioned in the book. The contingency is whether or not the Syro-Ephraimite War is alluded to in the book. If not, Hosea's prophecy must have ended before or about 735 B.C.

Among those who hold that Hosea does not mention the Syro-Ephraimite War are G. A. Smith and F. C. Eiselen.[5] Smith, for example, notes that Gilead and Galilee, taken by Tiglath-pileser III in 734–733, are still referred to as part of the political entity of Israel (5:1; 6:8; 12:11). But that is a weak case, because conquest and Assyrian provincial status would not necessarily mean that they were not still thought of by the natives as belonging to Israel. Moreover, other times than those years prior to 735 could accommodate those references. Wolff, in fact, finds in 12:11 an allusion to Tiglath-pileser's conquest of Gilead as a punishment for her sins.[6] He would date 11:12—12:14 in the beginning of the reign of Shalmaneser V, because Ephraim again is suspended between Assyria and Egypt.[7] The imagery of Israel as a "silly dove" (7:11) flitting between Egypt and Assyria also fits into that period (727–726).

John Mauchline, while finding reference to the Syro-Ephraimite War in 5:8–10, 13, sees no evidence that Hosea continued after 734.[8] Yet, as Harrison suggests,[9] the relations of Israel to Egypt mentioned in 7:11; 9:6 and 12:2 would push the date down into the reign of Hoshea, the last king of Israel.

A host of scholars have identified references to the Syro-Ephraimite War, especially in 5:8–14, following A. Alt's study.[10] The reference to Ephraim's oppression in 5:10 leaves the impression that the devasting hand of the Assyrians had fallen upon them. That would qualify well for 733 B.C., when the Northern

4. Hans Walter Wolff, *Hosea*, p. xxii.
5. G. A. Smith, *The Book of the Twelve Prophets*, 1:225; F. C. Eiselen, *The Minor Prophets*, p. 16.
6. Wolff, p. 215.
7. Ibid., p. 209.
8. John Mauchline, *The Book of Hosea*, 5:563.
9. Harrison, p. 860.
10. A. Alt, "Hosea 5.8–6.6 Ein Frieg und sein Folgen in prophetischen Beleuchtung," pp. 163ff. Also Anderson and Freedman, Harrison, Mays, Selling and Fohrer, Eissfeldt, Wolff, and others.

tribes fell into Tiglath-pileser's hands. Actually it could even cover the tribute paid by Menahem to the Assyrians in 739–738 (2 Kings 15:19–20). But the "wound" of Ephraim (5:13) implies some heavy blow, answering perfectly to the conquest of Gilead and Galilee.

Thus Hosea's ministry likely spanned at least three decades, perhaps around 752 to 724 B.C., from the later years of Jeroboam II's reign to the last years of the Israelite monarchy.

Perhaps a word about Yehezkel Kaufmann's novel thesis[11] is in order, although it has not gained much support. Noting that the two explicit references to the Baal cult in chapters 4–14 (9:10; 13:1) refer to the past, he proposes that chapters 1–3, which clearly have the Baal cult in view, must have predated the reign of Jehu, who destroyed the cult (2 Kings 10:28). Unfortunately Kaufmann makes no allowance for its revival in the century that came between the rise of Jehu and the death of his descendant Jeroboam II. Further, the historical references to the Baal cult in chapters 4–14 illustrate Hosea's interest in explaining the roots of Israel's sins, just as he construes the nation's political conniving to go all the way back to the patriarch Jacob (12:1–4, 12–14).

THE LITERARY NATURE OF HOSEA

POETRY OR PROSE?

The form of the Masoretic text and its resultant form in our modern English versions would suggest that most of the book is written in poetry. However, the literary style is not uniform throughout. Chapters 1–3 are not easily scanned as poetry because they do not consistently exhibit the typical Hebrew parallelism. Yet their form is not prose either. Francis I. Anderson and David Noel Freedman[12] prefer to speak of a special literary style between prose and poetry, a style characteristic of the prophets. William Rainey Harper[13] explains the difference between psalm poetry and prophetic poetry by the fact that the former was written and the latter was spoken, the spoken form allowing much more freedom in style. Norman Snaith[14] answers the question differently, suggesting that chapters 1 and 3 (excepting 1:10–11) are prose, whereas 2:2–23 is written in oracular form and is poetry, following Mowinekel's Type A (Type A—oracular and poetic; Type B—biographical and prosaic; and Type C—autobiographical and prosaic[15]).

The work of Anderson and Freedman has further explored the nature of

11. Yehezkel Kaufmann, *The Religion of Israel*, pp. 368–69.
12. Francis I. Anderson and David Noel Freedman, *Hosea*, p. 132.
13. William Rainey Harper, *A Critical and Exegetical Commentary on Amos and Hosea*, p. clxiv.
14. Norman Snaith, *Mercy and Sacrifice: A Study of the Book of Hosea*, p. 28.
15. Sigmund Mowinckel, *Zur Komposition des Buches Jeremia* (Np.: Kristiania, 1914).

chapters 4–14, and the conclusion they draw is that those chapters are the most "poetic" of all prophetic writings. That conclusion is based upon the occurrence of certain prose elements, the Hebrew article (*h*), the sign of the definite object (*eth*), and the relative pronoun (*'asher*).[16] Because those particles have a lower frequency level in chapters 4–14, that would point toward the poetic nature of the segment.

THE LITERARY FORM AND PURPOSE OF CHAPTERS 1–3

The critical question at this point is the relationship between chapters 1 and 3 and the place of chapter 2 in that interrelationship. Stylistically chapter 1 is written in the third person, whereas chapter 3 is first person. Both accounts record Hosea's marriage, first (chap. 1) to Gomer and then (chap. 3) a subsequent marital experience with an unnamed woman. Perhaps then the best way to approach the literary nature of the chapters is to consider Hosea's marriage.

The Marriage(s) of Hosea. Some have considered the prophet's marriage a dream or vision (e.g., Maimonides[17]). Others, like Kimchi and Calvin,[18] insisted that it was a parable. A recent proposal by Kaufmann[19] is that it was a stage play. Obviously those positions are adverse to a literal interpretation, as Calvin muses: "How could he expect to be received on coming abroad before the public, after having brought on himself such a disgrace?"[20] Yet if the events here recorded did not actually take place, the impact of the story is greatly diminished. Prophetic symbolism even at that early time was practiced by Hosea's contemporary, Isaiah, who walked naked and barefoot for three years as a sign of the Assyrian defeat of Egypt and Cush (Isa. 20). Actually the Pentateuch forbids a priest to marry a harlot (Lev. 21:7), implying that it was permissible for a layman. However, if Gomer was a cult prostitute, we really have no legal judgment on such a case, because Leviticus 21:7 seems to refer to a non-cultic prostitute. We may be sure of one thing, however: Fidelity within marriage was strictly enjoined. The literal interpretation, although perhaps offensive to our moral decorum, does justice to the personal involvement of the prophet in his message. The message of the eighth-century prophets was sometimes graphic and animated, as illustrated not only by Isaiah but by Micah as well (Mic. 1:8).

Three distinctive interpretations of the order of the events of chapters 1–3 can be found in the literature. The accounts are (1) about different events and

16. Anderson and Freedman, p. 132.
17. Moses Maimonides, *The Guide of the Perplexed*, p. 406.
18. See David Kimchi's comments 2:4 in his commentary on Hosea (Hebrew); John Calvin, *Commentaries on the Twelve Minor Prophets*, 1:44–45.
19. Kaufmann, p. 371.
20. Calvin, 1:44.

different women; (2) about different events but the same woman; (3) parallel and variant records of the same event.

Different events and different women? The first position takes into account that chapter 1 names the woman whereas chapter 3 does not. Moreover, the details of the events are sufficient to differentiate them from one another. In chapter 1 three children are born to the marriage, whereas in 3:3 the woman must be sexually abstinent. In chapter 1 no price is paid, but in chapter 3 Hosea pays a considerable sum for her. It has been suggested that the unnamed woman of chapter 3 was a secondary wife,[21] that being permitted by the law (Deut. 21:15–17). But that possibility seems remote because it would destroy Hosea's message that the Lord loved Israel even though she had been unfaithful.

Although he does not call the woman of chapter 3 a secondary wife, that seems to be the gist of Pfeiffer's proposal that "again" in 3:1 modifies the verb of the introductory formula, thus giving the reading, "And the Lord said unto me *a second time.*" Further, he understands the meaning of 1:2 to be figurative of religious apostasy, thereby removing "the slanderous insinuations against Gomer's wifely virtue." The woman of chapter 3, submits Pfeiffer, was a different person, a common streetwalker, and the action did not involve Hosea's family life at all. By that action he merely symbolized the message that the Lord still loved the adulterous Israel and would take measures to bring her to her senses.[22]

Sellin and Fohrer[23] see Hosea's developing theology in the two stories. They conclude that Hosea married two women, the first marriage inaugurating his career and the second concluding it. The first signified the judgment of Yahweh, whereas the second denoted hope for Israel.

Different events but the same woman? This view has many proponents in current scholarship, and there are a variety of species within this category. H. H. Rowley, Harrison, Harper, and a host of other scholars take this view with variations.[24] H. Wheeler Robinson, opting for this position, remarks that its chief fault seems to be that "it has lost the charm of novelty."[25] The story runs approximately as follows. Hosea was commanded by Yahweh to marry a prostitute. In the course of the next five to ten years the couple had three children, to whom they gave portentous names. Perhaps after the children were born Gomer became enamoured of other lovers and left her family (2:5). Subsequently she fell into difficult circumstances and mused on her former life with her husband and children (2:6–7). Some of the links in the chain of events

21. Snaith, p. 31.
22. Pfeiffer, pp. 567–69.
23. Ernst Sellin and Georg Fohrer, *Introduction to the Old Testament*, p. 421.
24. H. H. Rowley, "The Marriage of Hosea," in *Men of God*, pp. 66–97; Harrison, pp. 864–65; Harper, p. 215.
25. H. Wheeler Robinson, *Two Hebrew Prophets*, p. 17.

have been lost, but Hosea was instructed by the Lord to go again and love the adulteress, whereupon he paid the price of a slave for her and subjected her to disciplinary measures for a time (chap. 3).

The major advantage of this view with its order of events is that it does justice to the message of Hosea. That is to say, God loved Israel even when she was idolatrous, and He entered into a covenant with her. When she subsequently returned to her idolatrous ways, He resolved to pay whatever price was necessary to show her that He still loved her. But the penalty for her own erring behavior was a period of isolation, which seems to allude to exile.

Robert Gordis has shown that the adverb "again" (*'odh*) in 3:1 can be construed with either the verb of the opening formula ("And the Lord again said to me") or the imperative of the oracle ("Go again"), because the Masoretes have supplied both words with a disjunctive accent, setting "again" off from the preceding and following words.[26] Therefore, we must decide the matter of the relationship of the two experiences on other grounds.

Harper, Harrison, Davison, Archer,[27] and others, although distinguishing the two events, have advanced the suggestion that "wife of harlotry" in 1:2 is used proleptically (i.e., in anticipation of the event), especially in view of the moral problem such a marriage would have posed for Hosea and in view of the use of the rare phrase "wife of harlotries" (plural form). But that still avoids the clear notion of the text that Gomer is called a "wife of harlotry"(1:2) and ignores the message behind the symbolism, "for the land commits flagrant harlotry, forsaking the Lord." The simple interpretation, therefore, is to be preferred because the situation necessitating this object lesson was one of flagrant harlotry (idolatry). For Hosea to have taken a wife from among the prostitutes perfectly symbolized the historical situation.

An interesting proposal by J. Lindblom places chapter 3 before chapter 1 in the order of events, yet maintains that they are distinct stages in the experience of Hosea. He married a woman known to be immorally inclined, disciplined her for a while by denying to her social and sexual intercourse, and later had the first child by her. Afterwards she was found to be an adulteress, prompting Hosea to give the next two children names of ill omen.[28] The description of Gomer as a wife of harlotry (1:2) is therefore after the fact. That view diverges from the proleptic views above in that Lindblom has rearranged the order of events, not merely reading Gomer's adulterous character back into the events of chapter 1. The same criticism, however, applies to Lindblom's position as to the one above.

---

26. Robert Gordis, "Hosea's Marriage and Message," p. 29.
27. Harper, p 207; Harrison, p. 865; A. B. Davidson, "Hosea," *A Dictionary of the Bible*, ed. James Hastings (Edinburgh: T. & T. Clark, 1899), 2:422a; Gleason L. Archer, Jr., *A Survey of Old Testament Introduction*, p. 323.
28. J. Lindblom, *Prophecy in Ancient Israel*, pp. 166–68.

Parallel Events? The view that chapters 1 and 3 are two versions of the same story has been propounded by many of Hosea's modern expositors.[29] One of the easiest ways to arrive at this hypothesis is to consider "again" (*'odh*) as an editorial insertion, as does Henry McKeating, who explains the differences as the result of different purposes. Perhaps, hypothesizes McKeating, the prophet told the story as it is preserved in chapter 3, and a disciple or collector of the oracles composed chapter 1.[30]

Gordis propounds the view that the two accounts represent two interpretations of the same event by Hosea at two different times in his career, the first (chap. 1) prior to 743 B.C. and the second (chap. 3) before the fall of Samaria about twenty years later. In the first account is couched the prophet's message of judgment upon idolatrous Israel, whereas the second extends hope to the nation tottering on the brink of disaster.[31] Yet, as Rowley observes, if chapter 3 is a parallel record, it is certainly curious that the author should pass over so many details recorded in chapter 1.[32] The price paid for the woman and her period of isolation in chapter 3 would be divergent details that are hard to explain. The consummation of the marriage evidently took place according to chapter 1 without a quarantine.

Actually Hosea's reunion with his wife in the autobiographical account of chapter 3 is anticipated in 2:6–7:

> Therefore, behold, I will hedge up her way with
> thorns,
> And I will build a wall against her so that she
> cannot find her paths. . . .
> And she will seek them, but will not find them.
> Then she will say, "I will go back to my first
> husband,
> For it was better for me then than now!"

Assuming that chapter 2 has an intermediate relationship to the chapters on either side, we may conclude that the reclamation of chapter 3, so materialistically conceived in Gomer's mind, was already contemplated during the prodigal wife's estrangement from her husband. Moreover, the message of Hosea is further clarified by that anticipation. Although Israel may return to Yahweh for materialistic benefit, Yahweh will take her back in love ("love a woman," 3:1). The selfish motives of Israel and the selfless love of Yahweh are put side by

---

29. Henry McKeating, *The Books of Amos, Hosea and Micah;* Lindblom, p. 168; Robert Gordis, HUCA 25 (1954):9–35; J. M. P. Smith, *The Prophets and Their Times,* p. 59; see Rowley, p. 71, n. 1, for a fuller list.
30. McKeating, pp. 76–77.
31. Gordis, pp. 30–32.
32. Rowley, p. 72.

side to elevate divine love and mercy. Even though Israel's return to Yahweh was marked by social and material exigency, Yahweh's return to Israel was motivated by love and grace.

Composition of Hosea 1–3. Opinion on the nature of the literary units has vascillated between long discourses and short sayings. Harper identified longer segments, twenty in all, but found within them many shorter insertions by later editors.[33] That has been followed by other scholars, most recently Anderson and Freedman,[34] who mark out longer discourses, viewing 1:2—2:25 as a literary whole, with 3:1–5 as an appendix. James Luther Mays also recognizes 1:2–9 and 3:1–5 as longer units, but believes that 2:2–15 is composed of shorter sayings with a cohering theme.[35]

The other side of the spectrum is represented by those who view chapters 1–3 to be composed of smaller units. Among those scholars are Sellin and Fohrer, and Wolff. Sellin and Fohrer consider 1:2–9 as an account that may go back to the prophet himself, corresponding to the first-person account of the marriage in chapter 3. To those two units have been added utterances of a threatening nature (2:2–13) and then sayings of a promising nature (2:14–23). Although those last two pericopes may appear long, actually these scholars see them constituted by smaller units.[36] Wolff proposes that accounts from the early period of Hosea's ministry (1:2–4, 6, 8f) were united with words from a later period of the prophet's preaching (2:4–17; 3:1–5) and that that was enlarged by sayings from 733 and later (1:5; 2:1–3, 18–25). The Judaic redactor subsequently inserted 1:1,7 and 3:5*b*.[37]

I shall have more to say later about the so-called Judean glosses, but for now I would point out that there is a definite literary pattern in chapters 1–3 that points toward literary unity. The two accounts of Hosea's marital experiences (A: 1:2–9 and A₁: 3:1–5) counterbalance each other. The reestablished covenant and reversal of judgment make up the content of units B (1:10–2:1) and B₁ (2:14–23), which follow and precede unit A and A₁. The renewed convenant in 1:10*a* incorporates terms of the Abrahamic covenant (cf. Gen. 22:17), whereas that in 2:14, 18–20 expresses renewal in the words of a return to the wilderness and the reawakening of love between Yahweh and Israel. In addition, the two units include a cancellation of Yahweh's judgment upon the erring nation: "You are not My people" / "sons of the living God" (1:10*b*), "Say to your brother, 'My people,' and to your sister, 'She has obtained pity' " (2:1, RSV). That is matched by the declaration in 2:23*b,c*: "And I will have pity on Not pitied, and I will say to Not my people, 'You are my people' " (RSV). A

---

33. Harper, pp. clix–clxii, esp. his table of analysis on p. clx.
34. Anderson and Freedman, p. 139.
35. James Luther Mays, *Hosea, A Commentary,* pp. 5–6.
36. Sellin and Fohrer, p. 423. See the literary types and their composition on p. 422.
37. Wolff, p. 12.

third set of comparative units (C: 2:2–4, C$_1$: 2:9–13) pronounces Yahweh's judgment upon Israel, using the imagery of harlotry in the first unit and the Baal fertility cult in the second, which amounts to an explication of the first unit. At the center of the whole literary composition is a summary of Yahweh's indictment and judgment of Israel's sin introduced by the Hebrew *kî*, "for" or "because" (D: 2:5–8).

The crux of the indictment is Israel's failure to know the Lord (2:8), so visibly expressed in her harlotry (idolatry). In terms of content and arrangement, the pattern gives us a palistrophe,[38] as the following diagram illustrates:

A (1:2–9)   Hosea's marriage and
            birth of children

    B   (1:10–2:1)   Renewal of covenant
                           Cancellation of judgment
                           (children's names changed)

        C   (2:2–4)   Yahweh's judgment on Israel
                           using the imagery of harlotry

            D   (2:5–8)   Indictment and Judgment
                           because Israel does not
                           know the Lord

        C$_1$ (2:9–13)   Yahweh's judgment on Israel,
                           using the terms of the Baal
                           fertility cult

    B$_1$ (2:14–23)   Renewal of covenant
                           Cancellation of judgment
                           (children's names changed)

A$_1$ (3:1–5)   Reunion of Hosea and his adulterous wife

This pattern does justice to the theology of the book as a whole because it identifies the fundamental sin of Israel to be the lack of knowledge of the Lord. As we shall discuss later, that is a foundational theme of the prophecy, the theme, in fact, with which the second part of the book opens (4:1).

THE LITERARY NATURE OF CHAPTERS 4–14

The older view that chapters 4–14 were an expansion of the prophecy of chapters 1–3, put forth by no less a biblical scholar than C. F. Keil, still has validity. The first part, explained Keil, is a condensed form of Hosea's labors

---

38. See Gordon J. Wenham, "The Coherence of the Flood Narrative," pp. 336–48.

and message, and the second part is the fuller form.[39] E. B. Pusey viewed chapters 4–14 to have the same relation to chapter 3 (an expansion and application) as chapter 2 to chapter 1. That is, just as chapter 2 expands upon the theme of Israel's idolatrous ways, in like manner chapters 4–14 are a fuller statement of God's mercy and love toward Israel, the theme of chapter 3.[40] Although that is an oversimplification, there is indeed ample witness in this major section to the mercy of Yahweh so tenderly recorded on Hosea's scroll of life in chapter 3.

The approach of modern criticism has ranged all the way from the attempts of form criticism to explicate the *Sitz-im-Leben* of Hosea's addresses to the outright rejection of the method. Walter Brueggemann concludes from his form critical study of the book that the forms have their immediate frame of reference for Hosea in the covenant tradition of Israel.[41] On the other hand, Anderson and Freedman have pronounced a judgment of futility upon the efforts of form criticism to identify and define the literary units and the life-setting behind each one: "Hardly any of the 'forms' in Hosea match the models in the inventory of modern form criticism. This raises a fundamental doubt about the premises of this approach."[42] It should be acknowledged that those two scholars, although pointing up the problems with form critical method in Hosea, do not methodologically overrule form criticism generally for Old Testament studies. As Brueggemann's own analysis shows (following Claus Westermann's study[43]), the prophetic speech forms normally regarded as basic do not have any perfect correspondences in the speeches of Hosea. That, it may be observed, is a problem with which the form critic must deal in applying his method to any genre or corpus of literature in the Old Testament.

Wolff's very interesting proposal deserves mention. He speaks of "kerygmatic" units, whose beginning may be identified in three ways: by the naming of the addressee, the distinct introduction of a new theme, and the absence of a conjunction (4:1, 4; 5:1, 8; 8:1; 9:1, 10; 10:1, 9; 11:1). The series of sayings within such a unit was spoken by Hosea on the same occasion. Between the rhetorical units that compose the kerygmatic unit "the audience may have voiced its objections, or the speaker may have turned from one group to address another." For example, he identifies 5:8—7:16 as a kerygmatic unit composed of sayings that belong to the time of 733 B.C., when Tiglath-pileser III invaded Israel and captured the upper Jordan Valley, Gilead, and the Jezreel Plain. In Wolff's opinion, most of Hosea's sayings recall the form of the legal dispute that has its *Sitz-im-Leben* in the legal assembly of elders at the city

39. C. F. Keil, *The Twelve Minor Prophets*, 1:23.
40. E. B. Pusey, *The Minor Prophets*, 1:13.
41. Walter Brueggeman, *Tradition for Crisis: A Study in Hosea*, p. 88.
42. Anderson and Freedman, p. 315.
43. Claus Westermann, *Basic Forms of Prophetic Speech*.

gate.[44] Brueggemann sees that as a covenant lawsuit with the prophet as the prosecuting attorney.[45]

In dialogue with Wolff, Sellin and Fohrer doubt the historical/form-critical approach and advocate a much less logical process by which collections of individual sayings from various periods and situations have been assembled on the basis of catchwords or subject matter.[46]

As tempting as is the effort of the form critic to describe the literary genesis of the literature, the conclusion of Anderson and Freedman is well taken. We must, they insist, deal with the literature as it has come to us, and the continuity of themes and literature texture make it impossible to analyze the material of chapters 4–14 into definite units. The whole complex appears to have been put together by one person. They divide the text into twenty sections varying in length between three and sixteen verses.[47]

In regard to the date of the final form of chapters 4–14, Sellin and Fohrer see evidence that an edition was made during the Deuteronomic period (seventh century), and that the final editing took place in the exilic or post-exilic period.[48] But, as Anderson and Freedman observe,[49] there is no compelling evidence in the complex that would mitigate against an eighth-century date of completion. Further, it is not very likely that the complex circulated independently of chapters 1–3, simply because the first complex of the prophecy provides the background and flesh-and-blood enactment of the alarming concerns and the tender love of the second complex. Although the latter might very well make sense without the former, the pain of Yahweh at the very thought of giving Israel up, for example (11:8–9), is much more meaningful in view of the personal tragedy of Hosea's marriage and the retrieval of his wayward wife. One complex complements the other.

Although chapters 4–14 likely represent a much longer period of Hosea's prophetic ministry than chapters 1–3, both probably came into being in the prophet's lifetime. It is, of course, possible that the book received its final form in the hands of a faithful disciple of Hosea. But if that was the case, we still are not likely dealing with the editorial editions attributed by some scholars to the compiler(s). In fact, because history had validated the prophet's message and vindicated his integrity, accuracy of accounting would be even more important. The failure of many scholars to allow that Hosea could have both written (or used an amanuensis) and compiled his own book is an unjustifiable delimitation

---

44. Wolff, pp. xxiii, xxx, 110-11. But see Anderson and Freedman's convincing reasons against this hypothesis, p. 127.
45. Brueggeman, p. 87.
46. Sellin and Fohrer, p. 422.
47. Anderson and Freedman, pp. 316–17.
48. Sellin and Fohrer, p. 424.
49. Anderson and Freedman, p. 317.

on the prophets. Indeed, they had a vested interest in the truthfulness of their message and the vindication of their integrity. Isaiah, Hosea's contemporary, was instructed to preserve his message among his disciples: "Bind up the testimony, seal the law among my disciples" (Isa. 8:16). At least we must keep open the option that the prophet conducted the process of writing and compiling his own book, perhaps with the aid of his disciples.

THE "JUDAH" REFERENCES AND HOPE IN HOSEA

There are fifteen references to Judah in the book. Because Hosea prophesied to the Northern Kingdom, the question of their purpose in the prophecy naturally arises. Scholarship in the past century has often assigned these references to a later editor in Judah, who sought to highlight the contrast between Israel's apostasy and Judah's faithfulness. Harper judges all the occurrences except 4:15 and 5:5 as secondary on the grounds that no sufficient reason can be found for Hosea to have referred to Judah, and because they occur in passages with late vocabulary, or they interrupt the rhythmic structure.[50] In varying degrees Pfeiffer, G. A. Smith, and Eissfeldt,[51] among others, view the "Judah" passages to suggest later editing. Sellin and Fohrer take the historical approach and point to 5:8–14, with the Syro-Ephraimite War as its background, and observe that Judah was originally mentioned there. Thus all the "Judah" passages, they suggest, could not be secondary.[52] Martin J. Buss has remarked that, because all the references to Judah in chapters 4–11 and 12–14 (except possibly one) are negative, that suggests a common literary history for the two complexes. He attributes them to a Northern contingent that fled south and sought to apply the critical thrust of the prophecy to Judah also. In contrast, the occurrences of "Judah" in chapters 1–3 are favorable, signifying a transmission through patriotically minded circles in the South, receiving its final form perhaps not earlier than the Babylonian Exile.[53]

On the opposite side of the discussion ledger are those who believe that these references are genuinely Hosea's and belong to the original form of the book. Harrison appropriately points out that the purpose of comparing Judah's fidelity with Israel's apostasy after 722 B.C. was virtually nullified by the demise of the state of Israel.[54] Of the three occurrences in chapters 1–3, two are favorable (1:7; 2:2) whereas one (1:1) may be considered neutral, unless Hosea's dating of his ministry largely by the kings of Judah is viewed as showing favor toward Judah, a position that is entirely possible. When we examine the twelve verses

---

50. Harper, p. clix.
51. Pfeiffer, pp. 566–67; G. A. Smith, 1:221; Otto Eissfeldt, *The Old Testament, an Introduction*, p. 387.
52. Sellin and Fohrer, p. 422.
53. Martin J. Buss, *The Prophetic Word of Hosea, A Morphological Study*, p. 33.
54. Harrison, p. 869.

in chapters 4–14, we see that ten are unfavorable (5:5, 10, 12, 14, 6:4, 11; 8:14; 10:11; 11:12; 12:2), as over against one favorable (4:15) and one neutral (5:13). With that kind of imbalance it can hardly be claimed that an editorial effort was aimed at achieving a favorable hearing for Judah.

The more likely rationale is that Hosea had a genuine interest in the history and destiny of Judah, and, like his contemporaries Amos and Isaiah, he alluded to the state of affairs in both kingdoms. Moreover, although Hosea spoke of "our king" (7:5) when referring to the Northern monarch, he may hint that he believed the monarchy in Israel was illegitimate:

> They set up kings, but not by Me;
> They have appointed princes, but I did not know it.
>   (8:4a)

His interest in Judah and the Southern monarchy is further reinforced in 3:5, where he declares that "the sons of Israel will return and seek the Lord their God and David their king." So it should not be surprising that Hosea should speak of Judah, hoping that she would not acquire the same guilt Israel had (4:15), yet recognizing that Judah was following in the erring pattern of Israel (5:5; 6:4; 11:12; 12:2), and judgment could not long be suspended for her either (5:10, 14; 8:14). There are simply no compelling reasons for objecting to the Hoseanic nature of the "Judah" references.

In company with the "Judah" references, the passages tendering hope have made up a much-contended group. They are 1:10–2:1; 2:14–23; 3:5; 11:8–11, and 14:4–7. Harper worked from the presupposition that Hosea was a prophet of irreversible disaster soon to come, and that hope was inconsistent with his theological point of view.[55] Snaith modifies that extreme position and assigns those passages that look forward to a re-united kingdom (1:10–2:1) and a restored Davidic dynasty (3:5) to a Southern origin. Yet those predictions of a new Israel (2:14–23; 14:4–7) and reversal of judgment signalled by the name changes (1:10–11; 2:1; 2:23) are authentic to the eighth-century Hosea.[56] Harrison seems even more inclined to accept the authenticity of them all.[57] As Mauchline has properly observed,[58] Hosea's personal experience with Gomer reflected a basic hope that should not surprise us when incorporated in his message generally. G. A. Smith recognizes the basic flaw in the thinking of those who reassign the hopeful passages and insists that it would be almost incredible that Hosea, with his impetuous heart of love for Israel, should not "burst out with such verses of promise and of prospect as the verses in

---

55. Harper, pp. clix-clx.
56. Snaith, pp. 50–51.
57. Harrison, p. 868.
58. Mauchline, 6:563.

question.''[59] An appropriate word of caution to all scholars would be to examine the presuppositions we bring to our prophetic studies so that we not impose the same premises on the prophets themselves.

THE MESSAGE OF HOSEA

Hosea's message is rooted in Israel's past, in which Yahweh had expressed His overflowing love for His people by calling them out of Egypt (11:1). With tender nostalgia He recalls His infant son's toddling days as He himself taught him how to walk, taking him up in His arms (11:3), and under a different metaphor, leading him with "bonds of love" (11:4). Judging from Hosea's imagery, we can be confident that he was a tender and gentle father whose love knew no bounds; he saw Yahweh as that kind of Father to Israel. Motivated by love, Yahweh had called Israel out of Egypt (11:1; 12:13), spoken tenderly to and cared for him in the wilderness just as He would do again (2:14; 13:5), and secured him in the land of Canaan. But Israel's idolatry had not germinated in Canaanite soil. Its roots went all the way back to the pre-Canaanite period when the people went after Baal-Peor at Shittim (9:10; cf. Num. 25). And if one was not satisfied with that explanation of origins, one could find reflections of the deceitful disposition of Hosea's Israel in the patriarch Jacob himself. He had not always behaved properly (12:2–3), and had fled to Aram where his life became dominated by the pursuit of a wife (12:12). In contrast to the patriarch's woman-dominated life, Yahweh had sought to guide Israel by a prophet (12:13). By implication the object of Yahweh's love could not set the agenda for Him. Hosea demonstrated that in his own marriage, which, when threatened by infidelity, he saved by the tender imposition of his love upon Gomer.

The primary imagery of the book is Hosea's marriage, which symbolized the marriage of Yahweh and Israel, Yahweh being the Husband and Israel the wife (2:16). Hosea, unlike Amos, polemicized against the idolatrous Baalism of the eighth century (8:4–6). Prostitution was the symbol of that idolatry. The aim that the Lord sought to achieve was the fidelity of Israel to Him alone. His emotional tie was one of love: "Go again, love a woman who is loved by her husband, yet an adultress, even as the Lord loves the sons of Israel, though they turn to other gods and love raisin cakes" (3:1). Israel from the inception of that relationship had been a special object of Yahweh's love (11:1). He saw the nation as "grapes in the wilderness," "the earliest fruit on the fig tree" (9:10), "a luxuriant vine" (10:1), and "a trained heifer that loves to thresh" (10:11). Yahweh's delight with His people in the early stages of love is evident. There was something truly revolutionizing in that idea of Yahweh's love for Israel, as H. Wheeler Robinson aptly remarks:

---

59. G. A. Smith, 1:234.

When Hosea argued from the moral relations between his adulterous wife and himself to those between Israel and Yahweh, the principle involved was more important than that which Newton discovered when he linked a falling apple to a moving star. It made a spiritual pathway along which thought could and did move with confidence.[60]

Israel's response to the love so freely given was ingratitude and more infidelity. As Ezekiel later described Judah (Ezek. 16), Israel went so far as to hire lovers, quite an inversion of the business of prostitution (Hos. 8:9). She refused to reciprocate Yahweh's love with devotion and gratitude. In fact, when any response to her Lord was at all visible, it was purely utilitarian in nature:

> And she will pursue her lovers, but she will not
>   overtake them;
> And she will seek them, but will not find them.
> Then she will say, "I will go back to my first
>   husband,
> For it was better for me then than now!"
>
> (2:7)

The initiative was Yahweh's in the beginning, and the renewal would be instituted by Him. It is simply not true, as Sellin and Fohrer have contended,[61] that Hosea was unfamiliar with covenantal theology. On the contrary, he faulted Israel for violating the covenantal laws (4:2; 8:1). It was the quality of those laws, not their quantity, that Israel had despised (8:12). The cancellation of the covenant had come, in fact, in terms of Yahweh's revelation of His name to Moses: "Call his name NOT-MY-PEOPLE, for you are not my people, and I am not I-AM to you" (1:9, author's trans.; cf. Ex. 3:14). Yahweh's initiative, however, in reversing that condition is seen immediately in 1:10 as He reverts to the language of His covenant with Abraham (Gen. 22:17) to articulate His new relationship with Israel. The theme of divine initiative is further developed in 2:14–23 and 14:47. Actually Israel did not have the internal motivation to respond to her Lord. Her half-baked politics, her incognizance of waning strength at the hands of aliens, and oncoming senility of which she was oblivious (7:8–9) were symptoms of the anesthetization by the cultic devotion to which she had committed herself. Yahweh would turn the Valley of Achor, where Achan had sinned and Israel had been humiliatingly defeated (Josh. 7:20–26), into a door of hope (Hos. 2:15). Even though Yahweh's own heart might break with the blow of the Assyrian destruction, it was the only way to

---

60. Wheeler Robinson, *The Religious Ideas of the Old Testament*, p. 40.
61. Sellin and Fohrer, p. 424.

bring Israel to her knees before her loving Lord. Anything less, as Theodore H. Robinson says, would have been a "cruel kindness."[62] The crucial message of Hosea was that Israel did not know the Lord. As I have suggested above, the crux of the indicting word is found in 2:5–8 and the redeeming word to Israel in 2:20: "I will betroth you to Me in faithfulness. Then *you will know the Lord* (italics added)." In verbal form the idea of the knowledge of the Lord occurs also in 5:4 and 6:3, the first predicting the Israelites' inability to turn to the Lord because their deeds had rendered them incapable of repentance, and the latter occurring in a prayer of repentance and return, which Yahweh was waiting to hear from Israel. Twice the verb "to know" is followed by the object describing Yahweh's actions (2:8, 11:3). The fundamental sin of Israel was that "there is no faithfulness or kindness or knowledge of God in the land" (4:1). The content of that phrase and the accompanying terms is explicated in 4:2: "There is swearing, deception, murder, stealing, and adultery. They employ violence, so that bloodshed follows bloodshed." That is, it has moral connotations, and 4:6 describes the deficiency of knowledge to be tantamount to forgetting the law of God.

John L. McKenzie identifies the knowledge of God (Elohim) as "the knowledge of traditional Hebrew morality, understanding knowledge in the dynamic Hebrew sense, therefore the practice of traditional Hebrew morality, moral integrity."[63] Although his attempt to distinguish between the meaning of the "knowledge of God" (Elohim) and the "knowledge of Yahweh" is interesting, it would appear to exact too much from the use of the divine names. Mays's more general understanding of the phrase "knowledge of God/Yahweh" as Hosea's formula for normative faith is much more likely,[64] because the prophet employs both names for God, even though he admittedly uses "Yahweh" more frequently. This general description of faith is the consummate demand of Yahweh upon Israel:

> "For I delight in loyalty rather than sacrifice,
> And in the knowledge of God rather than burnt
> offerings."
>
> (6:6)

The knowledge of God was also at the heart of Isaiah's message to Judah, as it was in Ezekiel's prophecy several generations later. It was, as we have observed, far more than a mere cerebral function, for it included man's will and emotions. Rather than a function of the mind, it was the reflex of the total person, the response of one to God and His revelation of himself in law,

---

62. Theodore H. Robinson, *Prophecy and the Prophets in Ancient Israel*, pp. 86–87.
63. John L. McKenzie, "Knowledge of God in Hosea," p. 27.
64. Mays, p. 63.

history, and prophetic word.[65] Even though we must be cautious in speaking of synonymous concepts in the Old Testament, we might suggest that the knowledge of God was to the prophets who use the phrase what the fear of the Lord was to the wisdom writers and the psalmists. It is the totality of man's relationship to God. Hosea understood that Israel was tragicallly mistaken in her assumption that she knew God: "They cry out to Me, 'My God we of Israel know Thee!' " (8:2). The deficiency itself was tragic, but believing that the deficiency did not exist was fatal.

OUTLINE OF HOSEA

Introduction (1:1)

 I. Hosea's Marital Experience (1:2–3:5)
    A. Marriage and Family, Symbols of Covenant
        and Judgment (1:2–9)
    B. Covenant Renewal (1:10–2:1)
    C. Israel's Idolatry and God's Judgment (2:2–4)
    D. Indictment and Judgment (2:5–8)
    E. Israel's Harlotry with Baalism (2:9–13)
    F. Covenant Renewal (2:14–23)
    G. Hosea's Marital Reconciliation, Symbol of
        Covenant Renewal (3:1–5)

 II. Hosea's Message (4:1—14:9)
    A. Yahweh's Dispute with Israel (4:1–5:14)
        1. General Accusation (4:1–3)
        2. Dispute with the Priesthood (4:4–10)
        3. Dispute with the Populace (4:11–19)
        4. Dispute with the Leaders (5:1–14)
    B. A Liturgy of Repentance and the Realities
        of Sin (5:15–6:10)
        1. A Liturgy of Repentance (5:15—6:3)
        2. A Morning Cloud and Early Dew (6:4–5)
        3. Steadfast Love and Knowledge of God/
            Israel's Harlotry (6:6–10)
    C. Images of Judgment (6:11–7:16)
        1. A Harvest for Judah (6:11)
        2. Thieves Within and Without (7:1–3)

---

65. H. B. Huffmon, "The Treaty Background of Hebrew Yada'," pp. 31–37, shows that the verb "to know" in the ancient Near Eastern treaties carries the idea of "acknowledge, recognize" regarding the authority of the suzerain.

  3. A Heated Oven (7:4–7)
  4. A Cake Not Turned (7:8–10)
  5. A Flitting Dove (7:11–12)
  6. A Treacherous Bow (7:13–16)
 D. Religious and Political Improprieties (8:1–14)
 E. Israel's Harlotry and the Prophet's Behavior (9:1–9)
 F. Images and Infringements of Yahweh's Covenant
  (9:10 —11:12)
  1. Grapes in the Wilderness (9:10–17)
  2. A Luxuriant Vine (10:1–10)
  3. A Trained Heifer (10:11–15)
  4. A Toddling Child (11:1–12)
 G. History and Harlotry (12:1—13:16)
  1. Jacob and His Ways (12:1–6)
  2. The Exodus and Wilderness Renewal (12:7–9)
  3. Moses the Prophet (12:10–14)
  4. The Exodus and Wilderness Rebellion (13:1–9)
  5. The Impotent Monarchy (13:10–11)
  6. Judgment on Samaria (13:12–16)
 H. Call to Repentance and Covenant Renewal (14:1–9)
  1. National Confession (14:1–3)
  2. Covenant Renewal (14:4–8)
  3. A Word to the Wise (14:9)

5

MICAH: JUDGMENT, HOPE, AND PROMISE

MICAH TOOK HIS PLACE in the prophetic constellation of the eighth-century prophets as significantly and prominently as any of its luminaries. Although he has not received as much academic attention as Amos, Hosea, and Isaiah, he is nevertheless fixed in his stellar orbit as firmly as they. And although his oracles do not run on at the length of theirs, his brevity is marked by deep insight into the social, religious, and political movements of the eighth century. His ability to grasp the essence of the Hebrew faith and to verbalize it in memorable form has gotten for him the reputation of providing the "golden rule" of the Old Testament (6:8). He was not more perceptive or silver-tongued than Isaiah, his contemporary, but his impact upon his and subsequent generations could still be measured in the memory of the Judean elders who heard a message of comparable passion from Jeremiah (Jer. 26). The power of his message and the appeal of his courage are both verified and buttressed by his personal absorption into the message he proclaimed. There was no duplicity about his oracular style, for he had his finger of indictment pointed directly at Samaria and Jerusalem (1:5) and the leaders, prophets, and priests who populated their lucrative offices. Micah pitted his message against a society whose overconfidence and self-indulgence had become the false gospel of the pseudo-prophets: " 'Do not preach'—thus they preach—'one should not preach of such things; disgrace will not overtake us' " (2:6, RSV). It is little wonder that he should feel as hopeless as those who find that the grapes have not only been gathered but gleaned (7:1). Yet a message of hope and promise punctuates the entire book.

MICAH THE MAN

Micah is preceded in his courage and social and professional alienation by a prophet of the same name, Micaiah son of Imlah (1 Kings 22). Despite, however, the similarities in name and disposition, as well as the identical formula of 1:2 and 1 Kings 22:28 ("Hear, O peoples, all of you"), there seems to be no connection between them.

Unlike Amos and Hosea, Micah has related no account of his call to be a prophet, only the experiences of carrying out his awesome task. Amos satisfies our curiosity by telling us what his occupation was. Hosea relates an intriguing story about his life that includes his prophetic call. But Micah neither feeds our curiosity nor anesthetizes it with an emotional drama. Coming from the small town of Moresheth in the Shephelah, it seems logical that he might have been a small farmer or craftsman,[1] but we have no sure way of knowing that. His hometown, designated Moresheth-Gath in 1:14 because of its location within the area of Gath, has been identified with present-day Tell el-Judeideh, about twenty-five miles southwest of Jerusalem, about twenty miles west of the Mediterranean coast, and approximately twelve miles northeast of the ancient city of Lachish. It is situated about one thousand feet above sea level, overlooking the coastal highway in the plain, over which countless armies and commercial caravans had traversed the distance between Egypt and Mesopotamia.[2] The "elders of the land" who rose to Jeremiah's defense a century later called him "Micaiah of Moresheth" (Jer. 26:18), simply using the longer form of his personal name than is found in 1:1.

Although Micah was from Moresheth-Gath, his major prophetic activity was probably not there, because that would have posed the problem of transmitting his message to the capital cities, Jerusalem and Samaria. It is very likely that he, like Isaiah his contemporary, prophesied in Jerusalem. Perhaps, as James Luther Mays suggests, the inference to be drawn from the name-type that included his place of origin (also "Amos of Tekoa" and "Nahum the Elkoshite") is that he acquired the name away from home.[3] Whereas Micah addressed the "house of Jacob" (2:7) and "heads of Jacob and rulers of the house of Israel" (3:1, 9), the evidence in 4:1–2 seems to confirm his use of "Jacob" as an epithet for Judah. There he refers to the Temple as "the house of the God of Jacob." Even though he prophesied the destruction of Samaria in 1:6–7, his concerns in the rest of the book do not focus on the Northern Kingdom but on Judah. Therefore, Jerusalem would be the logical place for him to carry on his prophetic career. In further support of that, Micah gave Jerusalem and the Temple a high profile in the book (1:2, 5; 3:10—4:4; 4:8, 10, 13; 7:8–11). Moreover, he was well acquainted with the activities of her leaders, prophets, and priests (3:1–4, 5–7, 9–11).

Hans W. Wolff proposes the interesting hypothesis that the elders' appeal to Micah in Jeremiah 26 suggests that Micah himself belonged to that group called "the elders of the land." That would have involved the prophet in visits to Jerusalem during the great festivals, perhaps at the direction of the king (1 Kings 8:1; 2 Kings 23:1). That, in Wolff's view, would explain many unusual

---

1. Bruce Vawter, *The Conscience of Israel: Pre-exilic Prophets and Prophecy*, p. 133.
2. B. A. Copass and E. L. Carlson, *A Study of the Prophet Micah*, p. 79.
3. James Luther Mays, *Micah, A Commentary*, p. 15.

features of the book, such as his virtual preoccupation with the inequities perpetrated by the "heads of Jacob and rulers of the house of Israel." It would also explain the use of "my people" (1:9; 2:4, 8, 9; 3:3, 5; 6:3, 5), which he interprets to be the country population that Micah represented. Further, according to Wolff's view, Micah adopted the kind of wisdom cultivated by the elders who judged the people at the gate.[4] Even though the hypothesis has certain features to commend it, Wolff's resulting criterion for judging the authenticity of disputed passages, that is, whether they can be explained as having originated with an elder in a Judean country town in the last third of the eighth century, subjects Micah to a critical hypothesis that is both tenuous and presumptive. Actually, our knowledge of speech and literary form in Judean country towns is minimal. We are assured that Micah had deep sympathy for the people in whose behalf he spoke, who were not the upper social echelons but the common people and perhaps, as Wolff suggests, the country people. Moreover, it would not be necessary for him to have been an "elder of the land" to visit Jerusalem or to deliver such indicting words against the leaders of Judah. If Micah did function in the office of "elder of the land," that would indeed have given him a platform for denouncing the leadership and their sins. Yet the hypothesis cannot be substantiated with certainty.

Judging from the addresses, Micah directed his message to *the leaders of Judah* (3:1, 9) who hate the good and love the evil (3:2) and "build Zion with bloodshed and Jerusalem with violent injustice" (3:10). They were responsible for the people's welfare. But he also aimed his indictment at *the people* themselves. In 6:1–5 the Lord lays out His controversy with His people and demands an answer:

> My people, what have I done to you,
> And how have I wearied you? Answer Me.
> (6:3)

In historical review the Lord reminded them of the counsel of Balak, king of Moab, and the answer of the prophet Balaam. The Lord's deeds in history were designed so that His people "might know the righteous acts of the Lord" (6:5).

Another component of the people's audience was the false prophets, "who lead my people astray" (3:5–7). Micah's courage and confidence may be seen in his condemnation of their misguided program of peace, motivated purely by their own gastric rumblings. The Lord would remove from them all semblances of the prophetic experience, but in contrast Micah himself was filled with the Spirit of the Lord (3:8).

---

4. Hans W. Wolff, *Micah the Prophet*, pp. 18–24.

Only once are "the peoples," that is, the Gentile nations, addressed (1:2), and there the purpose is to call them as a witness against Israel (cf. Amos 3:9). In the other instances when the peoples are mentioned, words of salvation and judgment are pronounced upon them (4:1, 3, 5, 13; 5:7, 8), except in 4:5, where the prophet compares the nations' walk with their particular gods and Israel's devotion to Yahweh.

We might conclude, therefore, that Micah aimed largely at the civil and religious leaders of Judah, but he was not blinded to the sins of the people whose cause he took up and defended.

DATE OF MICAH'S ACTIVITY

The scholarly views regarding the time when Micah was an active prophet fall roughly into four classes. First, there are those who confine his activity to the period before the fall of Samaria. Wolff belongs to this class, dating Micah's appearance in 734 at the very latest and suggesting a terminal date of 728, although he leaves open the possibility of a longer ministry.[5]

Second, some believe that Micah's ministry commenced before the fall of Samaria, because his reference to Samaria in 1:5–7 presupposes the existence of the Northern Kingdom, and it concluded sometime after that great crisis, perhaps before the time of the Assyrian invasion of 711 B.C. Ernst Sellin and Georg Fohrer take this view, advocating that Micah was not acquainted with the Assyrian campaigns of 711 and 701.[6] This and the following opinion are influenced by the note in Jeremiah 26:18 placing Micah in the reign of Hezekiah. Yet there is no reason to confine him exclusively to Hezekiah's reign, and an interpretation of Jeremiah's association to that effect requires too much of the reference to King Hezekiah.

Third, other scholars have opted for a time frame that has Sennacherib's invasion of 701 B.C. as the focus. Rolland E. Wolfe is among them, confining the prophet's ministry to the reign of Hezekiah. According to his view, the first phase fell within the years just prior to the Assyrian invasion under Sargon II in 711 B.C., a campaign Micah predicted would annihilate Jerusalem. When that did not happen, surmises Wolfe, the prophet was discredited in the eyes of the people and did not publicize his message again until the crisis of 701, when he was again discredited by Jerusalem's survival.[7] The appeal of that message of doom in the time of the Neo-Babylonian crisis of the early sixth century would then reappear when the survival of Jerusalem was threatened again. That had been the substance of Micah's pronouncement over the city (3:12). This position, however, seems to be much more a reflection of recent critical

---

5. Ibid., p 3.
6. Ernst Sellin and Georg Fohrer, *Introduction to the Old Testament*, pp. 443–44.
7. Rolland E. Wolfe, "The Book of Micah," p. 898.

methodology than the nature of ancient Hebrew prophecy. Both long- and short-range predictions characterized prophetic preaching and were not necessarily a result of the historical process of re-interpretation, as the traditionist school contends, even though some reinterpretation is not ruled out completely (as Daniel attests). At last, according to this line of reasoning, Micah was vindicated by the fall of Jerusalem to the Babylonians in 586. But it would seem strange indeed that a prophet who had been twice so rudely discredited by historical events should rise to renewed credibility. Isaiah's intervention at the time of Sargon's invasion of 711 was probably a factor that staved off an Assyrian destruction of Jerusalem at that time (Isa. 20). In the later crisis of 701 Isaiah and the writer of Kings inform us that divine intervention was the saving factor (Isa. 36–38; 2 Kings 19). It hardly sounds as though the turn of those events would have discredited this prophet. Actually, in the Jeremiah account of Micah's prophecy the elders of the land themselves offer the explanation for the delay of the destruction. It was found in the repentance of King Hezekiah (Jer. 26:19), an observation which is made also in Isaiah 37 and 2 Kings 19. The matter, therefore, was not one of discreditation/reinterpretation, but one of the basic nature of the prophetic word and Yahweh's relationship to it. His options were enlarged by repentance.

Fourth, still others have taken quite seriously the superscription that dates Micah's activity in the reigns of the Judean kings Jotham, Ahaz, and Hezekiah. That would provide a potential time span from 739–686, about fifty years in which he could have been active. Although we admit that a tenuous date must be assigned to many of the passages within the book, the inference that Samaria was still standing is certainly to be drawn from 1:6, which predicts Samaria's destruction. Even aside from any predictive powers, an astute prophet could have already drawn that conclusion as early as the Syro-Ephraimite coalition of 734–732, when the Assyrians were called to the aid of Judah against the allied powers of Syria and Israel. Given the prophetic inspiration to perceive and predict future events, Micah could have issued his word of doom for Samaria any time during the reigns of Jotham and Ahaz prior to the event. But given the public confidence in their own security, the likelihood that he found a more credulous audience grows as the form of the events takes shape in the international political arena. The affairs of 734–732 certainly furnish an appropriate atmosphere in which the message of Samaria's doom would fall on believing ears.

Because Micah, however, makes nothing of the fall of Samaria, we might suggest that a leave of absence from public view during the latter years of the reign of Ahaz should be considered. His re-entry was at a time when the shock of Samaria's fall had waned. Perhaps he was back in Moresheth during this time, but that is left to our imagination. The years prior to Sennacherib's invasion in 701 were possibly the time when Micah renewed his prophetic career. The temporary revival of the Chaldean ruler Merodach-baladan (703 B.C.) in Babylon was evidently a time when the hopes of Judah were fanned by current events (Isa. 39; 2 Kings 20). The oracle of 4:9–13 with its foreboding announcement that Judah would be exiled to Babylon would fit comfortably into that time reference. Or perhaps that oracle could have been issued even a decade earlier, when Merodach-baladan first asserted his independence against Assyria during Sargon's reign.

THE LITERARY NATURE AND PLAN OF THE BOOK

STYLE

The literary style of Micah has been characterized as "rough and rugged."[8] That, of course, is a judgment made in comparison to the styles of Amos, Hosea, and Isaiah. The specific observations include his abrupt transitions from threat to promise (2:1–11, 12, 13; 3:9–12; 4:1–5, etc.), from one subject to another (7:1–7 and 11–13), and sudden changes in grammatical person and gender (1:10; 2:12; 6:16; 7:15–19).[9] Yet judging from the use of paranomasia and alliteration in the Hebrew prophets, we are given the impression that a skillful use of those forms marked a good writer. In that case, Micah would be classified as adept in his literary style, for he used paranomasia cleverly (1:10–16) and used alliteration to a limited extent (1:16). Moreover, his imagery is impressively arresting and serves as a clear vehicle for his message (e.g., 1:3–4, 8; 3:2–3; 4:13; 7:1). So although his impetuous style would not be applauded by our literary standards, we should not depreciate the quality of his literary form by that kind of comparison. In fact, one can hardly evaluate his literary competence to be any less than Isaiah's, although in the case of Isaiah we have much more material upon which to make a judgment.

AUTHENTICITY

Chapters 1–3. Although the first two major sections of the book appear to be chapters 1–2 and 3–5, much of the scholarly literature follows the division into chapters 1–3 and 4–5, for reasons that will become obvious in our discussion. Perhaps our survey will be facilitated by temporarily following that division.

Generally speaking, chapters 1–3 have been accepted as authentic words of Micah. Before the rise of modern criticism, it was taken for granted that the whole book was written, or at least spoken, by him. John Calvin, for example, does not even discuss the matter of authorship. But whereas the precritical scholars assumed that the book attributed to Micah must have been written by

---

8. Keil, *The Twelve Minor Prophets,* 1:421.
9. Ibid.

him, modern critics have assumed much on the other side, sometimes swinging to the opposite end of the spectrum and assuming that nothing was written by the prophet until literary analysis could demonstrate otherwise. Bernard Stade in 1881 proposed that Micah's sayings were confined to chapters 1–3.[10] More recently Mays, for example, had found those borders acceptable to his analysis of the book.[11] Judging from the reference to the regathering of the exiles in 2:12–13, many scholars assign that passage to the exilic or post-exilic period.[12] Yet we are not convinced that the pre-exilic prophets did not predict the Exile *and* the regathering. Leslie C. Allen has pointed out that a similar prediction of return is found in Isaiah's prophecy that is linked with the invasion of Sennacherib (37:32).[13] Because Micah was probably an active prophet at that time, it should not be assumed that he did not have the same interest as Isaiah in the return from exile, although the crisis precipitated by Sennacherib's invasion did not conclude with exile. That was yet to come during the Neo-Babylonian period. If we understand the eighth-century prophets to have predicted both exile and return, there is no reason to deny any of the material of chapters 1–3 to Micah. We must, in fact, come to an understanding of prophetic eschatology, which painted a dark horizon of judgment and then fractured that darkness with bright hues of the breaking new day. That is the general diagram of their program of the future, not the exception.

Chapters 4–5. These chapters have not fared so well as 1–3 in the hands of critical scholars. The range of opinions extends the whole gamut, from no authentic Mican words to total authenticity. Examples of those who represent the nihilistic side are the century-old studies of Stade and the recent commentary of Mays.[14] The latter scholar conducts his analysis along the lines of the traditio-historical method, concluding that the salvation oracles of chapters 4–5 (except 5:10–13) were added to the judgment oracles of chapters 1–3 to counterbalance them and show that Yahweh's purposes included salvation as well as judgment. That was a stage in the re-use of Micah's sayings, a process that extended into the post-exilic era.[15] In his view the book is "the outcome of a history of prophetic proclamation and is itself in its final form

10. Bernard Stade, "Bemerkungen über das Buch Micah," pp. 161–72.
11. Mays, p. 13. Also W. O. E. Oesterley and Theodore H. Robinson, *An Introduction to the Books of the Old Testament*, p. 384; Wolfe, p. 899; Otto Eissfeldt, *The Old Testament, an Introduction*, p. 409; Arthur Weiser, *The Old Testament: Its Formation and Development*, p. 253; Leslie C. Allen, *The Books of Joel, Obadiah, Jonah, and Micah*, p. 241; G. A. Smith, *The Twelve Prophets*, 1:362.
12. E.g., Eissfeldt, Mays, Weiser, Sellin and Fohrer.
13. Allen, p. 242.
14. Stade, pp. 161–72. A summary of his views are given by J. M. P. Smith et al in *A Critical and Exegetical Commentary on Micah, Zephaniah, Nahum, Habakkuk, Obadiah and Joel*, p. 10. See also Mays, p. 13.
15. Mays, pp. 24–27.

prophecy.''[16] Although reasoning differently, Sellin and Fohrer conclude that virtually nothing from Micah is contained in chapters 4–5, which comprise a collection of sayings originating with unknown eschatological prophets of the post-exilic period.[17] Joining those representative voices is J. M. P. Smith, whose commentary, in collaboration with Ward and Bewer, aligns him with the position of Stade (except in the case of 4:14 and 5:9–12). These two chapters, in their view, have no more in common than a hopeful outlook for the future.[18]

Among those who identify some of the sayings in this collection as authentically Mican is Otto Eissfeldt, who contends that all but 4:1–5:8 (leaving only 5:9–14!) is genuine.[19] Allen is more conservative on the matter, designating only 4:1–4 and 4:6–8 to be unauthentic.[20]

Among the noncommitted are Driver, who weighs the evidence against and in favor of authenticity but does not come out strongly on either side,[21] and Weiser, who sees no compelling reason for or against the authenticity of these chapters.[22]

The position that all of chapters 4–5 originated with Micah is represented by G. A. Smith, R. K. Harrison, Edward J. Young, and B. A. Copass, and E. L. Carlson.[23] In general, that group of scholars sees no ideas in Micah 4–5 that are inconsistent with the eighth-century prophets. Of special interest is the eschatology of a glorious future for Israel, a doctrine whose development has frequently been assigned to the exilic and post-exilic periods. In chapters 4–5 Micah includes the ideas of Zion's elevation (4:1), the turning of the nations to the Lord (4:2), an ensuing age of peace eventuating in social stability (4:3–4), the repatriation of the exiles ("the lame" and "the outcasts") whom the Lord will make a strong nation (4:6–7), the birth of a true leader in Bethlehem Ephrathah (5:2–5), and the triumph of the remnant over their enemies (5:7–9). That eschatological program, although it is highly optimistic and quite advanced in its development, is a part of the eighth-century prophets in varying degrees. Isaiah certainly shared the hope of the elevation of the Temple (Isa. 2:2–4) in a passage that is almost a duplicate of Micah 4:1–3. He also predicted the birth of a ruler from the lineage of David (Isa. 11:1–10), a doctrine that Amos taught in the form of the restoration of the "booth of David" that had

16. Ibid., p. ix.
17. Sellin and Fohrer, pp. 445–46.
18. J. M. P. Smith et al, p. 12. Also Oesterley and Robinson, pp. 384–85, discount any genuine Mican passages and propose that the collection is not earlier than the fifth century B.C., with 5:5–6 perhaps being of Maccabaean origin.
19. Eissfeldt, pp. 410–12.
20. Allen, p. 251.
21. Driver, pp. 329–30.
22. Weiser, pp. 253–54.
23. G. A. Smith, *Minor Prophets*, 1:368–69; R. K. Harrison, *Intro.*, p. 924; Young, *Intro.*, pp. 258–60; Copass and Carlson passim.

fallen (Amos 9:11–12). Further, the doctrine of the remnant is shared by the eighth-century prophets Micah (2:12; 4:7; 5:6; 7:18), Amos (5:15), and Isaiah (e.g., 37:32), the last reference being associated with the invasion of Sennacherib. If we begin, as many scholars do, with the presupposition that such a well-developed eschatology could not have been a part of the theology of the pre-exilic prophets, then any or all of those passages can be precluded from consideration. The point should be clear, however, from these cursory remarks, that only a radical editing of the eighth-century prophetic material could accomplish that kind of superimposed doctrine of the future. Given the esteem and veneration, or at least the fear of the prophetic word that the prophets had come to enjoy over the long history of the prophetic movement, it is most unlikely that their words were subjected to such radical reshaping.

The special problem of 4:1–4. If there is any material in chapters 4–5 that does not originate with Micah himself, it is likely 4:1–4 (v. 4 is not in Isa.), which is included with minor variations in Isaiah 4:2–4. This passage speaks of the elevation of the Temple to a position of international prominence and the conversion of the nations to Yahweh, resulting in an age of world peace. The four solutions generally offered to resolve the problem of this duplicate text are: (1) Micah authored it; (2) Isaiah authored it; (3) it was interpolated into both prophets by a later editor; and (4) it is by neither prophet, and both borrowed it from a common source. This is a most unusual case in prophetic literature, for the prophets were not given to quoting one another. If the passage were inserted awkwardly in either context, that might give us a clue that it was original to the one where the connection was most logical. But actually it fits well enough in both contexts to caution against resolving the problem too easily by this criterion. Though Copass and Carlson proceed cautiously and steer clear of a dogmatic pronouncement, they do make the point that Micah begins with his message of the spiritual kingdom and then presents the steps by which it is developed. First, the faithful are delivered from the captivity of sin, symbolized by Babylon (4:9–10). Second, Israel is victorious over the powers of sin, represented by warring nations (4:11–5:1). Third, Israel accepts the person and power of her King (5:2–5*a*). And fourth, support for His rule comes from the surviving remnant and the renovation of worship (5:5*b*–15).[24] Admittedly that explanation may be an overspiritualization of the text, but they are correct to recognize the thread of the kingdom of God running through the context.

Some studies are inclined to attribute the oracle to Isaiah,[25] and the interconnections of the two prophets might seem to support that thesis.[26] But there is no foolproof way to demonstrate it.

24. Copass and Carlson, p. 118.
25. T. C. Vriezen, "Prophecy and Eschatology," pp. 199–229; Hans Wildberger, "Die Volkerwallfahrt zum Zion," pp. 62–81.
26. Keil, 1:420, gives these interconnections: Mic. 2:11/Isa. 28:7; Mic. 3:5–7/Isa. 29:9–12; Mic. 3:12/Isa. 32:13, 14: Mic. 4:1–5/Isa. 2:2–5; Mic. 5:2–4/Isa. 7:14; 9:5.

One of the most popular positions in recent years has been the attribution of both texts to a later editor. Mays propounds that view, pointing out that the destruction of Zion predicted in 3:12 and its elevation in 4:1 stand in stark contradiction. He advocates a post-exilic setting, perhaps after the completion of the Temple in 516/15 B.C., and, in his view, it was "an exuberant announcement of what YHWH's reign from 'his house' might mean for the entire world."[27]

J. M. P. Smith's analysis brings him to a similar conclusion, based in part upon his belief that the conversion of the nations appears nowhere else in Micah, but does occur in other prophetic passages, which he dates in the post-exilic era (e.g., Isa. 11:10; 56:6, 7; 60; 66:23, and Jonah). His proposal is the Greek period.[28] Coming to a similar conclusion is E. Cannawurf's more recent article in which he draws upon the Jerusalem/Zion parallel, which, submits Cannawurf, was a product of the Josianic reform by which Zion was given a central position, thus eventuating in the two names becoming interchangeable.[29] Yet all of those studies are based upon certain presuppositions that predetermine their conclusions.

Other important studies have concluded that the parallel texts are quoted from an original that was written by neither prophet. Allen's perspective study leads him to that conclusion, proposing that the original was closely related to the Songs of Zion found in the Psalms.[30] Arvid S. Kapelrud's article on the problem outlines the reasons for regarding the oracle as having a cultic origin, possibly being an oracle from the autumn and New Year festival. The ideas in the oracle, he correctly insists, were current in Micah's day. Yet he does not advocate Mican authorship, but rather regards the oracle in both prophets to be derived from a common source.[31]

There seems to be something in Kapelrud's article worthy of consideration. Whereas the biblical evidence for the so-called New Year festival is meager indeed, Micah 4:1–4 seems an appropriate response to the miraculous deliverance of Jerusalem from the aspiring world dictator Sennacherib. Perhaps the oracle of 3:9–12 describes the spirit of the country that Hezekiah inherited from his predecessor Ahaz. The leaders judged for bribes, the priests had mercenary motives, and the prophets thought only of a comfortable living. Yet univocally their actions and attitudes chanted, "Is not the Lord in our midst? Calamity will not come upon us" (3:11). It was that kind of self-confidence that Hezekiah's reform attempted to dismantle, a disposition implied by the religious neglect on the part of the priests and people when Hezekiah took the throne (2 Chron.

27. Mays, pp. 95–96.
28. J. M. P. Smith et al., p. 84. Smith surveys scholarly opinions up to his time on p. 84.
29. E. Cannawurf, "The Authenticity of Micah IV:1–4," pp. 26–33, esp. p. 32.
30. Allen, pp. 243–44, 323.
31. Arvid S. Kapelrud, "Eschatology in the Book of Micah," pp. 392–405, esp. pp. 395–96.

30:3). The account of his reign in 2 Kings 18:1–8 leaves the impression that he conducted his religious reforms early in his reign, and a decade or so later, in the fourteenth year, Sennacherib invaded Judah (2 Kings 18:13). Given the cyclical pattern of religious revival and apostasy in Israel and Judah, even that short interval of a decade or more was time enough for the Temple and cult, so recently resuscitated, to fall from its central position again. At least the military precautions and preparations taken by Hezekiah at the prospect of the siege (2 Chron. 32:2–6) may yield the inference that religious matters at the moment were not foremost in their minds, although the chronicler relates that Hezekiah eventually summoned Judah to man the spiritual ramparts as well (2 Chron. 32:7–8), and ultimately appealed to Isaiah for help (2 Chron. 32:20–23; 2 Kings 19:1–7; Isa. 37).

The point is that the miraculous deliverance of Jerusalem from Sennacherib might well have elicited from Israel the worshipful response recorded in Micah 4:1–5. The oracle of 3:12, assigned by Jeremiah to the reign of Hezekiah (Jer. 26:18), and perhaps spoken by Micah early in Hezekiah's reign to encourage reform, had set the stage for the awesome destruction of the Temple:

> Therefore, on account of you,
> Zion will be plowed as a field,
> Jerusalem will become a heap of ruins,
> And the mountain of the temple will become
> high places of a forest.

The reform itself staved off that awful contingency, and the miraculous deliverance from Sennacherib in 701 B.C. affirmed the centrality of the Temple and buoyed the confidence of those who relied on its system.

Eduard Nielsen has appropriately suggested that the theme of Zion's elevation may be as old as the Davidic dynasty itself.[32] Thus the cultic response of 4:1–5, borrowed by both Isaiah and Micah from the Temple liturgy or adopted from a third prophetic source, expressed the prophets' own confidence in the coming day when the religion of Israel would dominate the world with centrifugal force.

The liturgical response in Micah 4:5 and that in Isaiah 2:5, although different, seem to point to a worship setting for the passage. In any event, the theme of the oracle was in line with the eschatological program of the pre-exilic prophets. Despite their criticism of the cult, they had not abandoned it but instead hoped for its elevation to a central position in the religious system of Israel and the world. The theme of the centrality of the Jerusalem Temple deals a devasting blow to the hypothesis that Josiah's reign a century later was the

---

32. Nielsen, *Oral Tradition*, p. 91.

time when the so-called Deuteronomic school waged the successful campaign for the exclusive recognition of Jerusalem as the cultic center. With the incipient dictum of centrality of worship that called Israel to rally around the single Tabernacle in the wilderness, David's strategic location of the ark on Mount Zion was a natural outgrowth of a persuasion imbedded in Mosaic theology. We know for sure that the wilderness era had left its impression on Micah's mind (6:5), and it does not seem coincidental that Micah and Isaiah stressed that theme. They took it from the era whose formative influence was a premise of their sense of history.

The special problem of 4:10. A further problem with an eighth-century date for chapters 4–5 is the reference to Babylon in 4:10. The oracle of 4:6–13 seems to apply to the time when Jerusalem was under the Assyrian siege in 701 B.C. The reference to Babylon ought not be considered as a later gloss, as many scholars do. Harrison resolves the problem by considering "Babylon" a metonymy for Mesopotamia.[33] Yet the only problem with taking the term literally is the specificity involved. It is true that one might be surprised to hear Micah, so long before the rise of the Neo-Babylonian Empire, speak of Babylon as the place where Judah would survive and from which she would be delivered. That is, in the face of the Assyrian threat by Sennacherib, Micah talked about Judah's road to survival via Babylon.

In view of the rather recent visit of Merodach-baladan's embassy to Hezekiah (c. 703 B.C., 2 Kings 20/Isa. 38), I suggest that it is prophetic irony. Babylon as a Judean ally and a place of survival during the brief interlude of Chaldean rule might make only the slightest bit of sense, but in view of the weakness of Babylon compared to the great Assyrian kingdom, this reference was ironic indeed. Yet Micah's insight into Judah's future program of salvation was accurate even though much delayed. In fact, Micah was a master of irony. As he described the conflux of the nations to gloat over Judah's tragedy, he perceived the irony that was involved: they did not know that they were observing, not simply Judah's fall, but an episode in the drama of their own ultimate disaster (4:11–13). In the following passage (5:1–5*a*), against the background of Sennacherib's siege, a ruler who will provide the ultimate peace in this chaotic world of greed and power arises from the unpretentious little village of Bethlehem. Defying the military siege and the consequent political paralysis the Assyrians might effect in Jerusalem, the Lord sketches out His sovereignty in a little town six miles away, working behind the enemy lines to establish His rule. There is also a strong note of irony in the announcement that Jerusalem will be plowed like a field and become a heap of ruins (3:12), but the prophet further predicted that the mountain of the Lord's house would "be established as the chief of the mountains" and be "raised above the hills"

---

33. Harrison, p. 924.

(4:1). Prophetic irony is not prophetic contradiction. It is a literary method that characterizes prophetic preaching and thought.

Chapters 6–7. The spectrum of pronouncements made regarding the authenticity of these chapters is wide and discordant. The range of dates involved reaches all the way from the eighth century to the Maccabean era. Eissfeldt, expressing a sentiment that seems more and more to be found in current scholarly literature, sees features in 6:1—7:6 that do not fit Micah's time, allowing that 7:7–20 is probably, as Hermann Gunkel proposed, a post-exilic liturgy. Yet Eissfeldt is willing to admit that Mican authorship for this final segment should be considered.[34] Bruce Vawter is also accommodating but noncommittal, stating that chapters 6–7 could be from the eighth century.[35] Allen commits himself to the authenticity of all except 7:8–20, which he dates in the post-exilic era. That last passage, he submits, fixes the final editing of the book.[36] W. O. E. Oesterley and Theodore H. Robinson fix the date of chapters 6–7 not earlier than the last half of the fifth century, although they go so far as to admit that 6:6–8, 14–16 may be by Micah.[37] J. M. P. Smith assigns 7:7–20 to the age of the Maccabees,[38] a position virtually abandoned by more recent scholars.

The question we should put forth is: What in these chapters is inconsistent with the age of Micah and incongruent with his message in the first five chapters? This section of the book begins with a scene in the law court, as Yahweh confronts Judah about the strained relationship that had developed between them (6:1–5). Very much in the vein of Amos's oracle against Israel (Amos 2:6–16), the Lord reminds Judah of His historical acts in her behalf, from the Exodus to the first victorious encampment in the promised land at Gilgal (Josh. 4:19). In plain view of those events Micah then lays out the ethical basis for the relationship that had lapsed (6:6–8), followed by the Lord's oracle detailing the sins of Jerusalem and the punishment that would come as a consequence (6:9–16). The book is concluded with a lament by the prophet over his times, which are destitute of the unshakeable foundation stones of the community of faith: goodness, justice, and walking humbly with God (7:1–6). Micah had described his lamentive style in 1:8, instigated by the incurable wound of Judah. Thus the prophet began his collection of oracles with a personal note on the magnitude of his own sorrow and concluded with a similar notice. In the final lines of the book we hear the prophet speaking for Jerusalem with words of trust and penitence (7:7–13), to which is added a brief prayer of intercession (7:14) that the Lord would fulfill His promise to raise up a

34. Eissfeldt, pp. 411–12.
35. Vawter, p. 131.
36. Allen pp. 251–52.
37. Oesterley and Robinson, pp. 384–85.
38. J. M. P. Smith et al, p. 16.

Shepherd for Judah (5:4). Significantly, the voice of Yahweh is heard again
tendering a promise that He would renew the Exodus from Egypt (6:4) and
instill awe and fear of Israel in the nations as He did on the former occasion
(7:15–17). Most appropriately, the final words are a hymn of adoration,
perhaps spoken by Judah, extolling the loving and compassionate nature of the
Lord (7:18–20). These chapters definitely have an organic relationship to the
first five. The prophetic tone, at once indicting and assuring, permeates this
collection, as it does chapters 4–5. The inordinate ambitions of the people and
their leaders, distorting the value of life and property, come up for prophetic
denunciation here as in chapters 1–3 (6:11–12; 7:2–6; 2:8–11; 3:1–5, 9–11). E.
Hammerschaimb correctly observes that Micah's castigation of the leaders in
the community occupies a central place in his preaching.[39]

Underlying the entire book is an ethical system that has its roots in the
covenant faith, the essence of which is so unmistakably distilled in 6:8. It is
marked by justice and respect for one's neighbor and unalloyed devotion to
Yahweh. These characteristics are generally implied in Micah. But in 6:8 he
explicates what has been implied:

> He has told you, O man, what is good;
> And what does the Lord require of you
> But to do justice, to love kindness,
> And to walk humbly with your God?

In the same oracle Micah's attitude toward sacrifice as a non-essential
element of religion conforms to that of Isaiah his contemporary (Isa. 1:10–15).
And it may be observed that the pagan practice of child sacrifice mentioned in
6:7 was also known in Micah's day, a practice that King Ahaz observed (2
Kings 16:3).

Up to this point I have principally shown the consistency of ideas in chapters
6–7 with those in the rest of the book and with the attested ideas and customs
of Micah's time. That is obviously the kind of method that can be used to prove
different points of view. Sellin and Fohrer, for example, point to the individual-
istic emphasis in 6:1–8, characteristic of wisdom theology, and the description
of social justice given in 7:1–6, and they conclude that 6:1—7:7 should be
dated before Nehemiah in the fifth century.[40] Yet it should be clear that an
analysis of ideas does not rule this section out of the eighth century. It seems
likely that the prophetic books do not represent a history of ideas, contrary to
what form and tradition criticism has insisted in modern scholarship. Kapelrud
maintains that editors did not radically alter the thought of the books but may
have used ideas that they believed were clearly expressed in the prophet's

39. E. Hammershaimb, "Some Leading Ideas in the Book of Micah," in *Some Aspects of Old
    Testament Prophecy from Isaiah to Malachi*, p. 36.
40. Sellin and Fohrer, p. 446.

writings.[41] Although he may not help our case for Mican authenticity, he at least throws the method of dating by concepts into sharper relief. The burden of proof for shifting prophetic oracles away from a prophet and his era must lie with the biblical critic. Perhaps the integrity of the compilers has been grossly ignored.

Even in the case of 7:7–20, to which Gunkel applies his form-critical method, there are sound reasons for attributing the verses to Micah. The numerous similarities with the psalms recognized by Gunkel are undeniable. Investigating the literary forms and the occasions for their use, he concludes that it was composed of four units, 7:7–10, 11–13, 14–17, and 18–20, the first being a dirge of Zion to which God answers in the second, followed by a dirge of Israel concluded by a hymn of assurance. The entire poem is artistically woven into a liturgical piece that was used on a festival occasion in the Jerusalem Temple.[42] Although Gunkel did not connect the poem to 7:1–6, Bo Reicke has made a convincing argument for the organic unity of the whole chapter, the prophet employing the liturgical traditions of festivals such as the Day of Atonement and Tabernacles and speaking on behalf of the people.[43]

In conclusion, we cannot find sufficient grounds for doubting the authenticity of chapters 6–7. Although there are problems associated with Mican authorship, they do not lead us away from the eighth century B.C., and they do not convince us that any of these chapters is alien to Micah's thought.

PLAN OF THE BOOK

Most commentators have observed that a pattern of threat/promise characterizes the plan of this book. Yet the beginnings of the major divisions have been marked out by the imperative "Hear" (1:2, 3:1; 6:1), giving us the division of chapters 1–2 (I), 3–5 (II), and 6–7 (III). John T. Willis has pointed out that each division opens with an oracle of doom (1:2—2:11; 3; 6:1—7:6) and closes with an oracle of hope (2:12–13; 4–5; 7:7–20), and he has called attention to the symmetry of the book provided by the four balancing pericopes found in sections I and III: (a) a covenant lawsuit (1:2–7 and 6:1–8); (b) a lament (1:8–16 and 7:1–6); (c) an explanation for the impending catastrophe (2:1–11 and 6:9–16); and (d) an oracle of hope (2:12–13 and 7:7–20).[45] Allen has observed the same division into three major sections, with chapters 3–5 making up the middle section, and remarked that the whole book presents "a kaleido-

---

41. Kapelrud, pp. 395, 397.
42. Hermann Gunkel, "The Close of Micah: A Prophetical Liturgy," in *What Remains of the O.T. and Other Essays*, pp. 122–24, 142, 147.
43. Bo Reicke, "Liturgical Traditions in Mic. 7," pp. 349–67, esp. p. 366.
44. "Hear!" occurs also in 3:9; 6:2, 9 in secondary positions.
45. John T. Willis, "The Structure of Micah 3–5 and the Function of Micah 5:9–14 in the Book," pp. 191–214, esp. p. 197.

scopic picture of the judgment and salvation of God's city and God's people,'' with the focal point being 5:1–6 and its emphasis on the Davidic king.[46]

Two reasons surface for breaking the first collection of oracles after chapter 3 rather than at the end of chapter 2. First, many modern scholars believe Micah's authentic oracles are contained in chapters 1–3, even though some, as we have already seen, are willing to admit that there may be random oracles in the other two sections. Second, the prophecy against Mt. Zion in 3:9–12 is considered to be in contradiction with the restoration and elevation of Zion predicted in 4:1–5. Yet, as we have already observed, the prophetic program of eschatology involved not only doom but hope. Thus in light of Micah's concern for the Lord's continuing rule in Judah, it is not at all inconsistent for him to intermingle the destruction and the elevation of Zion. Doom in Micah's message, as well as the message of the prophets more generally, was a means toward Israel's reformation and ultimate salvation, not an end in itself. Therefore, the word of hope was a vital element in prophetic preaching.

Consequently I see no obstacle to sectioning the book by the clue "Hear." Moreover, Micah has left his prophetic signature on each of these collections. In section I (1–2) he related how lament over Israel's pitiable state had come to domineer his life-style (1:8), and in section II (3–5) he drew a sharp contrast between himself and the false prophets who sold their sermons of war and peace at public auction (3:8). Finally, he has autographed section III (6–7) by a lament over the moral desolation of his times, even though he may have spoken for Jerusalem (7:1). That is not to imply, however, that Micah personally collected and edited the book. Yet the intimate and personal tone that we hear in these notices points toward someone who knew Micah and perhaps even shared his sorrow as well as his expectant hope. An early seventh-century date for the book is quite probable.

THE MESSAGE OF MICAH

YAHWEH AND HIS PEOPLE

Micah's insight into the spiritual and social problems of the eighth century was as penetrating as Isaiah's. To throw those problems into sharper relief, Micah's view of God, known to the prophet by His covenant name Yahweh, left his audience no room to escape the consequences of their sins or to accuse Him of arbitrary behavior. He was a God who demanded moral obedience of his people rather than sacrificial appeasement (6:6–8). Of Judah's leaders He required that they know justice (3:1), but their response had been to pervert it (3:9).

---

46. Allen, p. 260.

It is worth noting that Micah does not summon members of the community to repentance or to change their ways, as do Amos, Hosea, and Isaiah. Rather his imperatives subpoena them to the Lord's court of law—"plead your case" (6:1)—where He is the key witness and judge (1:2–7). The urgent imperative "Hear!" inscribes the structure of the book (1:2; 3:1; 6:1) and punctuates it (3:9; 6:2; 6:9). That critical tone is heard against a backdrop of bloated self-confidence that permeates the rank and file as well as the leadership. The priests and prophets, whose fraudulent practices exposed the hollow devotion of their offices, leaned on the Lord and said, "Is not the Lord in our midst? Calamity will not come upon us" (3:11). Perhaps Micah had perceived in the religious and political leaders of Judah an adamant spirit that could only be changed by the dissolution of the structures in which they trusted and the institutions that provided the cover for their underhanded actions.

> For her wound is incurable,
> For it has come to Judah;
> It has reached the gate of my people,
> Even to Jerusalem.
>
> (1:9)

So Micah announced doom and wailed over the fact that he had to do so. For the political leaders there would be destruction of the system in which they trusted and exile to Babylon (4:10); visionless nights would come for the false prophets (3:5–7); and for the priests, the Temple mount would be reduced to a farmer's field (3:12). If Micah called those people to repentance, those oracles have not been preserved for us. Yet he preached a message of hope that a new day would break through the gloom of collapse.

Yahweh's soverign rule stretched across national lines and geographical boundaries to include the whole earth (4:1–4, 13; 7:16–17). Therefore, Israel's doom and redemption had implications for the nations. Even though Micah did not conceive of Israel's existence as a means to the goal of the nation's redemption, as did Isaiah, his theology at least took account of the nations' spiritual and national welfare. The elevation of Mt. Zion above the Ephraimite and Judean hills would signal to the nations that the time for their conversion had come, and imploringly they would turn to the Lord's Temple to learn His ways and walk in His paths. Micah depicted an age of international peace flowing out of that era of salvation, initiated by Yahweh's own arbitration of the disputes among the nations. To prove His power, He would turn a nation of handicaps into a commonwealth of strength over which His own coronation would begin a radically new day (4:1–8). The inevitability of that future was assured by the forgiving, loving, and compassionate nature of the Lord Himself. He was angry, but would not forever be so, for He delights in steadfast love, and would tread the iniquities of Judah under His feet and cast their sins into the depths of the sea. That was not a new face of Yahweh, for He had long ago sworn His steadfast love to Abraham (7:18-20).

HISTORY AND DESTINY

Micah's grasp of the importance of history can be seen in his references to past events and the response to which they called the Lord's people. In the legal dispute between the Lord and Judah in 6:1-5 the Lord reminded them, as Amos reminded Israel a generation earlier (Amos 2:10), that He had redeemed them from Egypt. Moreover, He recalled the opposition of Balak, king of Moab, and how Balaam the prophet answered him. In one phrase, "from Shittim to Gilgal" (6:5), the Lord summed up the victorious entrance into Canaan that included the defeat of Jericho. Shittim was the last encampment of the Israelites on the eastern side of the Jordan River, and Gilgal was the first major encampment on the western side (Num. 22:1; 25:1; Josh. 4:19-20). Intrinsic to all those historical events was the purpose "that you might know the righteous acts of the Lord" (v. 5). That was Judah's destiny, implied and explicated in her history. The overarching controls of her history, however, were to be found in the "truth" and "unchanging love" (*hesed*) that God swore to Abraham, a point that Hosea underscored when he recalled the Lord's promise to Abraham, which overarched even His covenant with the Mosaic community (Hos. 1:9-10).

History held the key to the future. In Yahweh's gracious dealings with Judah in bygone days the outlines of His program for her future could be detected. His demand of moral obedience indicted His people for their sins, and exile was inevitable; but His unchanging love painted the bright hues of a breaking new day on an otherwise dark horizon, and return from exile was as much a part of the program of the future as was doom. The new Exodus, so much like the first with its miraculous accompaniments, would inspire fear in the nations as the former had done (Josh. 2:9-11). They would come creeping out of their fortresses and cower before the Lord and His people (7:15-17). The warring spirit of the nations would be shattered into the implements of peace and security (4:3-4).

That new age, miraculously introduced into history, would be ruled by a new King whose unpretentious origins could not belie the magnitude of His mission. Jerusalem, that city of kings, must yield to Bethlehem, so little among Judah's clans, and the emerging King would reign over the age in which the Northern tribes returned to the national fold (5:2-5a). To lift this prophecy out of history and fail to see its fulfillment in the return from Babylonian Exile is to defy the historical element in the prophets. Yet, to obscure the messianic thrust of this and other texts like it in the prophets is tantamount to defying the divine plan for Israel and the world. The chief priests and scribes of the first Christian century perceived the latter as they responded to the wise men's inquiry (Matt. 2:5–6). If not yet in actuality, at least in symbolic form the nations in the person of the magi had come to the Lord to learn His ways and walk in His paths. The chronological depth of the prophetic vision of the future was perhaps only faintly understood by the prophets, but they knew that they were serving a generation yet unborn (1 Pet. 1:12).

MORALITY, IDOLATRY, AND THEOLOGY

The balance on the moral ledger of ancient Judah was regularly an indication of the deeper spiritual condition. Micah had focused his sights on the leadership level of his society. They who were responsible for justice (3:1) had an inverted sense of good and evil (3:2a). Instead of feeding the flock like respectable shepherds should, they had fed off the flock and molested the sheep who were at their mercy (3:2b–3). Their hatred of justice could be seen in the perverted way they did their job, building Zion with bloodshed and Jerusalem with violent injustice (3:10). The times, so destitute of justice, were like the vineyard that had been stripped of its fruit by harvesters and gleaners and left barren. Their olympic performance of injustice had turned man against man, and their ambidextrous ability to do evil had made the best of them like a briar and the most upright a thorn bush. Friend and foe had become indistinguishable, and the security of family and kinship had become a battleground of selfish interests. Civil leaders and priests alike were motivated by financial gain (3:11a).

Although the indicting oracle of 2:1–5 was not addressed to the leaders, it bears the marks of their craze for power and property. They spent their nights devising wicked schemes, which they eagerly executed when morning came, seizing the property of their helpless subjects and violating the ancient law that made one's house and field a sacred right. Isaiah observed the same illicit practice (5:8), thus confirming the moral corruption that typified the leadership of the eighth century.

If immoral behavior was the ledger balance, revealing the depravity of the times, the idolatry of pre-exilic Israel was no less than spiritual bankruptcy. Micah did not confront idolatry directly as did Hosea and Isaiah; his method was more oblique. Idolatry was the object of divine judgment as Yahweh swept away the vestiges of Judah's boldest impudence (1:7; 5:13–14; 6:16). Even Hosea's passionate message had not removed the pagan cultic practices in the Northern Kingdom, so Yahweh would smash her idols and return her "harlot's earnings" (1:7). Idolatry, that most blatant sin of rebellion against the sovereign Lord of the world, was slated for the burning wrath of Yahweh.

Even though Micah did not issue an imperative summons to repentance or apodictically enjoin Judah to abandon her idolatrous ways, he knew as clearly as any eighth-century prophet what the Lord required of His people. The comprehensive and potent expression of prophetic theology in 6:8 countermanded the foggy notions of social righteousness and perverted religious piety that the community intoned. Perhaps Micah accosted them at the Temple with their sacrifices with the subpoena of 6:1–5. And either sarcastically or sincerely they inquired what the Lord wanted of them:

> With what shall I come to the Lord
> And bow myself before the God on high?
> Shall I come to Him with burnt offerings,
> With yearling calves?
> Does the Lord take delight in thousands of rams,
> In ten thousand rivers of oil?
> Shall I present my first-born for my rebellious acts,
> The fruit of my body for the sin of my soul?
>
> (6:6–7)

Micah's answer summed up and affirmed the teaching of the three great prophets of his age: Amos's appeal for justice, Hosea's exposition of steadfast love (*ḥesed*), and Isaiah's call to a life of humble devotion to Yahweh:[47]

> He has told you, O man, what is good;
> And what does the Lord require of you
> But to do justice, to love kindness,
> And to walk humbly with your God?
>
> (6:8)

"Justice" (*mishpāt*) is a term that comprehends the covenant responsibilities, whereas "kindness" (*ḥesed*) is the duty of man to man, which grows out of Yahweh's gracious love expressed in His covenant relationship to mankind. "To walk humbly" with God is to maintain communion with Him.[48] God confronts man and leaves him inexcusable. In light of the clarity of the requirements that God had already shown the people of Israel, it is more understandable that Micah should not come in with a "do this-do that" message. They already knew His demands and were fully responsible for doing

---

47. G. W. Anderson, "A Study of Micah 6:1–8," pp. 191–97, makes a convincing argument for the unity of 6:1–8.

48. Ibid., pp. 194–96. J. Philip Hyatt examines the phrases "to love kindness" ('ahavat ḥesed) and "to walk humbly" (*hatasanēa' leket*) in the light of their occurence in the Qumran Manual of Discipline, conjecturing that Micah 6:6–8 originated in the fourth or third century B.C. in a group of pious Jews strongly influenced by the prophets and wisdom teachers, 232–39. Yet there is no reason to assume that the Qumram covenanters were not influenced directly by Micah and took up those phrases from his book.

them. It would certainly appear that this passage is the heart of Micah's message and probably the structural vertex of the entire book.

MICAH AND THE PROPHETS

No warped sense of professional loyalty marked the preaching of this prophet. He knew there were prophets whose credentials had been forged and who abetted the crime and decay. They were cohorts with the civil and priestly leaders whose commercial motive propelled them and who hypocritically leaned on the Lord and muttered their false notions of security and divine approval: "Is not the Lord in our midst? Calamity will not come upon us" (3:11). Micah indicted them for leading Yahweh's people astray and proclaiming oracles of peace when they were well paid, but predicting war when their income diminished (3:5–7). The courage of our prophet can be seen as he pitted himself against the falsity and egotism of the pseudo-prophets:

> On the other hand I am filled with power—
> With the Spirit of the Lord—
> And with justice and courage
> To make known to Jacob his rebellious act,
> Even to Israel his sin.
>
> (3:8)

A. S. Van der Woude has offered an interesting argument in favor of 2:6–11 as a disputation speech between Micah and the false prophets.[49] If that is so, then we may have a few more words from them than is the case in 3:5–8. One thing for certain, the false prophets, judging from the confrontations that occur between them and the canonical prophets, were evidently an influential group among the ancient Israelites. A further inference may be drawn, the idea that the prophetic word was a widely sought means of reassurance and revelation. Probably at critical times in Israelite history the false prophets carried on a flourishing business and contributed greatly to the false sense of confidence and security that Micah and other canonical prophets found so threatening to genuine security and peace.

---

49. A. S. Van der Woude, "Micah in Dispute with the Pseudo-prophets," pp. 244–60. He also proposes that 4:1–14 is such a disputation speech, but the argument there is less convincing.

OUTLINE OF MICAH

Introduction (1:1)

  I.   Exile and Restoration (1:2—2:13)

THREAT: A. The Case against Jerusalem and Samaria (1:2–7)
           B. Micah's Lament over Judah's Incurable Disease (1:8–9)
           C. The Itinerary of Judgment (1:10–16)
           D. The Crime and the Punishment (2:1–5)
           E. Dispute with False Prophets (2:6–11)
PROMISE: F. Return from Exile (2:12–13)

  II. The Fall and Rise of a Nation (3:1—5:15)

THREAT: A. Against the Princes (3:1–4)
           B. Against False Prophets (3:5–7)
           C. Micah the True Prophet (3:8)
           D. The Sins of Leadership and Jerusalem's Fall (3:9–12)
PROMISE: E. Elevation of the Lord's House (4:1–4)
           F. A Public Confession (4:5)
           G. The Lord's Reign (4:6–8)
THREAT: H. Exile to Babylon (4:9–10)
PROMISE: I. Israel's Victory over the Nations (4:11–13)
THREAT: J. Announcement of Assyrian Siege (5:1)
PROMISE: K. The Emerging King (5:2–6)
           L. A Powerful Remnant (5:7–9)
THREAT: M. Destruction of Idolatry (5:10–15)

  III. Final Indictment, Lament, and Promise (6:1—7:20)

PROMISE: A. The Case Against Judah (6:1–5)
           B. The People's Response (6:6–7)
           C. The Lord's Essential Demands (6:8)
THREAT: D. The Sins of Leadership and Their Consequences (6:9–16)
           E. A Lament over Judah's Transgressions (7:1–7)
PROMISE: F. Jerusalem's Lament and Hope (7:8–13)
           G. A Final Word from the Lord (7:14–17)
           H. A Final Confession of Judah (7:18–20)

6

ISAIAH: PROPHET PAR EXCELLENCE

ISAIAH WAS PROPHET PAR EXCELLENCE of the classical era of prophecy. Along with Amos, Hosea, and Micah, he was a bright star in the prophetic constellation of the eighth century B.C., soaring like an eagle in his literary and theological distinction. No prophet of his time more fully comprehended the gravity of the Assyrian threat and its implications for the immediate present and remote future.

His oracles comprehended the extremities of the prophetic message, which the rabbis called "words of comfort" and "words of reproof," with varying degrees of counsel in between. The wide variation of those oracles, to be discussed later, is a witness both to the genius of the man and the long and rich career he fulfilled. His prophetic field of vision was broad, widening out to the messianic age when Israel's hopes and destiny found fulfillment in Christ.

With his eyes fixed on the troubled societies of Israel and Judah and his heart fixed on the faithful covenant God, Isaiah exemplified the spiritual trauma such a dilemma created in the heart of a prophet. It was no less than Yahweh's own distressing dilemma lived out in His servants the prophets. Isaiah's "Lord, how long?" (6:11a) was the distress signal of a heart crushed by Israel's hardened nature (6:9–10) and compelled by an irresistible call to prophesy (6:6–8).

ISAIAH THE MAN

In view of the volume of material in the book of Isaiah, one would think that we should have a lot of information about the prophet himself. In a sense we do, especially when compared to some of the so-called minor prophets, like Micah and Zephaniah. But if we compare our information to what we know about Jeremiah and Ezekiel, we really do not have much biographical information about Isaiah. When we would almost get to know him, our attention is diverted to the Lord he served or the people to whom he spoke. From a theological point of view, that may be a positive feature, but from a biographical point of view, it leaves us rather impoverished.

Yet perhaps the most important thing about a prophet, or any individual, is what he thought and said as it issued forth in what he did. So we can be grateful that we are allowed into the depths of Isaiah's soul. Without doubt we are brought to the core of his being in the immortal record of his call in chapter 6. His self-image, cut from the same fabric as Israel's, was that of a man "of unclean lips." And having seen the vision of the Lord sitting on His throne in majestic glory, proclaimed by the seraphim as thrice holy, he keenly sensed the judgment of God on his personal condition; ("Woe is me, for I am ruined! . . . For my eyes have seen the King, the Lord of hosts" (6:5). At Isaiah's confession, which was at the same time a plea for pardon, the seraph's cleansing touch with a coal from the altar removed the prophet's sin and extended the range of his hearing past the seraphim's hymn to the threefold holiness of God (trisagion) to the voice of Yahweh himself: "Whom shall I send, and who will go for Us?" (6:8). Forgiven and summoned to a mission for the Lord, Isaiah responded with the unembellished, "Here am I. Send me!" Yet when the Lord had detailed the awesome assignment, the prophet's "Lord, how long?" exposed the deep trauma he felt over a mission with such dreadful prospects of failure (6:9–11a.).

Certain rabbinic commentators noted the tradition that Isaiah's father, Amoz, and King Amaziah of Judah (796–767 B.C.) were brothers, thereby making Isaiah of royal descent.[1] Perhaps this tradition owes its origin in part to the accessibility that our prophet had to the kings of Judah, but otherwise it is not well attested.

The death of Uzziah (740 B.C.), marking the end of an era of prosperity and relative peace in Judah, coincided with the momentous year of Isaiah's inaugural vision (6:1). The exact date of his call could have been either prior to or after the king's inauspicious passing, but it is clear that Isaiah saw his call providentially linked with that event and the ensuing era, which was imprinted with the Neo-Assyrian threat. It was more than a date.

Two of the four Judean kings in whose reigns Isaiah prophesied (1:1) had significant involvements with him. Ahaz (732–716 B.C.), having fallen ungrateful heir to the political implications of the Syro-Ephraimite alliance, was the object of Isaiah's challenge and rebuke (chap. 7). Against the background of invasion by the allied armies of Syria and Israel, Isaiah brought at least two oracles to Ahaz, first assuring him that the plans of the allies would not succeed (7:3–9), and then challenging him to ask a sign of the Lord that would portend the failure of this ill-conceived scheme (7:10–25). As the narrative reveals, Ahaz rejected the challenge, but the Lord gave him a sign nevertheless, and a far more wonderful one than he might have asked for—the sign of Immanuel.

The second king in whose affairs Isaiah became intricately involved was Hezekiah (716/15–686 B.C.), who was more religiously devout than Ahaz. In point of fact, the religious reform that he instigated (2 Kings 18:1–7a/ 2 Chron.

---

1. See the commentaries (Hebrew) of Rashi and David Kimchi on Isa. 1:1.

29–31) was probably inspired by the tragic events in the Northern Kingdom that culminated with the fall of Samaria in 722. Based upon the moral and spiritual indictments Isaiah delivered against Judah, Hezekiah's religious zeal and reformation staved off disaster on Judah for more than a century longer. When Sennacherib, vaunting himself to be Yahweh's agent of destruction (Isa. 36:10), dispatched his arrogant messenger to Jerusalem, Hezekiah sent an embassy of inquiry to the prophet Isaiah seeking a word from the Lord (701). The exchange of messages between king and prophet confirmed the sovereign power of the Lord, and Judah was miraculously delivered (chap. 37–38). The communication channel between Hezekiah and Isaiah was called into service on two other occasions that we know about, first when the king was facing a personal physical crisis, and then upon the subsequent diplomatic visit of Merodach-baladan's envoys from Babylon (chaps. 38–39, c. 704–703).

Having ready access to kings may imply that Isaiah was an official in the royal court. The proposal that he was a priest[2] has little hard evidence to back it up. An interesting suggestion is that he was a scribe, implied by 2 Chronicles 26:22, where the writing of Uzziah's court history is attributed to the prophet Isaiah, a practice the Chronicler knew about in the case of other prophets (Rehoboam—Shemaiah the prophet, 2 Chron. 12:16; Abijah—Iddo the prophet, 13:22; Jehoshaphat—Jehu, 20:34). As a scribe he would also be responsible for educating the children of the royal court, perhaps explaining what is meant by his "disciples" (8:16).[3] Further in that regard, W. W. Hallo's proposal on Isaiah 28:9–13, that the people accused the prophet of sounding like a tutor trying to teach children their alphabet, is tantalizing.[4]

Isaiah was married, but, unlike Hosea, we do not know his wife's name or anything about her personality. She is referred to as "the prophetess" in 8:3. Whether that implies that she too engaged in prophetic functions is not clear. More than likely, however, it was a term that simply referred to his wife rather than a profession.[5] To the marriage was born at least two sons, both of whom had symbolic names, following the practice that Hosea had popularized. Shear-jashub ("a remnant will return," 7:3) and Maher-shalal-hash-baz (lit., "the spoil speeds, the prey hastes," 8:1–4) symbolized respectively the hope that Isaiah held for Judah and the judgment he anticipated for Israel. In addition, some scholars have held that Immanuel was a third son, but that opinion is tenuous, and we cannot consider its merits or demerits here.

As with Hosea before him, Isaiah's family life was bound up with his prophetic ministry. There is no evidence, however, that he endured anything like the trauma that Hosea did. Yet when the names of one's children symbol-

---

2. I. Engnell, *The Call of Isaiah.*
3. Robert T. Anderson, "Was Isaiah a Scribe?" pp. 57–58.
4. W. W. Hallo, "Isaiah 28:9–13 and the Ugaritic Abecedaries," pp. 324–38.
5. But see Otto Kaiser, *Isaiah 1–12*, p. 111.

ize the destiny of nations, there is likely no total escape from whatever grief or joy they symbolize.

In respect to Isaiah's home, it was most likely Jerusalem, the city he knew so well. Its destiny was intertwined with his own, and the nation's faith and hope were peculiarly concentrated in that city.

The vast spiritual and mental resources represented by this prophet are unsurpassed by any other persons of prophetic vintage. The literary complexities of his book reflect that fact, and perhaps modern scholarship has given too little attention to his resourcefulness. Although all of the problems relating to composition and compilation cannot be resolved in that manner, some of them may at least receive illumination by a new appreciation for the man Isaiah and his personal, spiritual, and cultural assets.

DATE OF ISAIAH'S ACTIVITY

According to the superscition (1:1), Isaiah's ministry took place during the reigns of Uzziah, Jotham, Ahaz, and Hezekiah. If, as is generally thought, chapter 6 records his call, then he began prophesying in the last year of Uzziah's life (740 B.C.) and continued into Hezekiah's reign (which ended in 686). His ministry very likely extended beyond that date, because the last definite historical incident mentioned is the death of Sennacherib in 681 (37:38).

In addition to the year that Uzziah died, there are other date markers in the book. The "days of Ahaz" (7:1) refers generally to that king's reign and specifically to the early period when the Syrian/Israelite alliance (734–732) threatened his security. A second date in Ahaz's reign marks the year of his death (716 B.C., 14:28), dating the oracle against the Philistines, who might have been tempted to renew hostilities now that Ahaz was dead.

His successor, Hezekiah, had much interaction with Isaiah, some initiated by him and some by the prophet. In that regard, the first time marker was the offensive launched by Sargon's commander against the rebellious city of Ashdod (711 B.C., 20:1). Chronologically next in line was Hezekiah's illness. Although undated, it obviously preceded the visit of Babylon's diplomatic core, which can be dated from Babylonian records as 703 B.C. Thus Hezekiah's illness occurred in about 704, and Isaiah and the king's interaction regarding the latter's divulgence of classified information in the same year of the diplomatic visit. A very specific date is given to fix Sennacherib's invasion and siege of Jerusalem (the fourteenth year of Hezekiah, 701 B.C., 36:1).

Assuming that Isaiah authored the record of Sennacherib's defeat and assassination (37:36–38), we are brought down to the year 681, even though we cannot confidently assign any material other than the historical record to that last year. Thus the configuration of Isaiah's ministry would look like the following:

740 B.C.   His call
734–32   Encouraged Ahaz against the Syrian/Israelite crisis
716   Ahaz's death and Isaiah's warning to the Philistines
711   Sargon's expedition against Ashdod and Isaiah's oracle against
            Egypt and Ethiopia
704   Hezekiah's illness
703   Embassy of Merodach-baladan to Hezekiah
701   Sennacherib's siege of Jerusalem
681   Death of Sennacherib

These dates, however, are only significant dates, and perhaps indicate the most active periods of the prophet's ministry. Characteristically they were very critical times in Judah's history. Thus these time concentrations give us a skeleton plan for discussing Isaiah's prophetic activity.

Undoubtedly the prophet was active between crises, but the extent of the intermediate periods of ministry is difficult to ascertain. We ought not think of a prophet's ministry in terms of a modern clergyman who works all year long for a succession of years to complete his professional career. Rather the prophets, Isaiah not excluded, were pressed into service at critical junctures and in some instances followed other professions to sustain themselves and their families (for example, Amos). They sometimes had long careers, as did Isaiah, and sometimes short ones, as did Haggai (the dates in that book allow for three months) and Zechariah (about two years).

THE LITERARY NATURE AND AUTHENTICITY OF ISAIAH

In light of so much material in this book, spread out over a long period of time, we should not be surprised to find a rich diversity in style and subject matter. That will occupy our attention when we consider the authorship of chapters 40–66. For the time being we must make allowance for Isaiah's prophetic and literary genius, an assumption, to be sure, but just as valid as the assumption made by the critics who begin by disallowing that genius. If, of course, we can show just cause why either assumption is invalid, then the course of our discussion may take a different turn. It is my conviction, however, that such just cause has not yet been shown.

To illustrate the extremities of opinions, George Buchanan Gray has suggested that chapters 1–39 alone may contain the work of as many authors as the Book of the Twelve.[6] Those who fall within the general framework of that position are legion. One of the more promising studies that espouses the general view that the book is a composite of oracles by different authors in the

---

6. George Buchanan Gray, *A Critical and Exegetical Commentary on the Book of Isaiah I-XXVII*, p. xlix.

Isaiah tradition is that of William H. Brownlee. An obvious scribal break is indicated between chapters 33 and 34 of the Isaiah scroll from Qumran Cave 1, leading him to propose an ancient practice of writing the book on two scrolls. In his view chapters 34–35 formed an introduction to the second volume. Both volumes (I—chaps. 1–33; II—chaps. 34–66) developed at the same time, although volume one contained the bulk of the real Isaiah's work. As they developed, exilic and post-exilic traditions crept into volume one, and some pre-exilic oracles may have been included in volume two, all for the sake of literary balance. Brownlee goes so far as to suggest lines of development for a bifid structure for the book.[7]

More recently Avraham Gileadi has proposed the bifid structure and has worked out many of the details in his seminal study *The Apocalyptic Book of Isaiah.* As with Brownlee's study, he divides the book into two major parts, part I consisting of chapters 1–33 and Part II of chapters 34–66. Each of the halves breaks down into seven subunits with parallel subject matter. The general outline of the structure is as follows:

		Part I (chaps. 1–33)	Part II (chaps. 34–66)
a.	1–5	Ruin and Renascence	34–35
b.	6–8	Biographical Material	36–40
c.	9–12	Agents of Divine Deliverence and Judgment	41–46
d.	13–23	Oracles against Foreign Powers	47
e.	24–27	Suffering and Salvation	48–54
f.	28–31	Sermons on Loyalty and Disloyalty	55–59
g.	32–33	Dispossession of the Wicked; Inheritance by the Righteous[8]	60–66

My purpose is not to espouse Gileadi's hypothesis in its entirety, but to illustrate how a recent scholar has approached a topic considered by many other scholars to be a settled issue and has offered new insights and intriguing possibilities. It would be surprising indeed if under close scrutiny these categories did not present some problems, but Isaiah studies will probably always be characterized by the problematic, whatever theological camp the student is in. However, we should insist that any serious study of the composition of the prophetic books must approach the literature with assumptions that are built upon an analysis of ancient Near Eastern literature and literary method rather than modern literature, and Gileadi has made a genuine effort in that direction.

7. William H. Brownlee, *The Meaning of the Qumran Scrolls for the Bible,* pp. 247–59.
8. Avraham Gileadi, *The Apocalyptic Book of Isaiah, A New Translation with Interpretative Key,* pp. 171–83.

More general agreement among Isaiah scholars may be found on seven main divisions of the book:

1. Chaps. 1–12   4. Chaps. 28–33
2. Chaps. 13–23   5. Chaps. 34–35
3. Chaps. 24–27   6. Chaps. 36–39
                        7. Chaps. 40–66

In view of these customary divisions, I shall follow this outline in my discussion of the material.

ISAIAH 1–12

Our discussion of these sections in chronological order should not be taken to mean that the book took shape in that fashion. As it has come to us, the book is an anthology of Isaiah's oracles, collected by the prophet himself and perhaps some of his close disciples (cf. 8:16).[9] Any attempt to reconstruct the process by which the book took shape is speculative, and probably the process is forever irretrievable. Yet we need not remain mute, for certain things can be said with some degree of confidence.

These twelve chapters contain materials that stretch from Isaiah's call in 740 B.C. to approximately 732, and some scholars would say to Sennacherib's invasion in 701. The prophet's commission in chapter 6 may be viewed as the center of the collection. Whereas Hosea, Jeremiah, and Ezekiel begin with the call narrative, Isaiah (and Amos) opens with a description of the sins of Judah and Israel, and only after that condition has been vividly painted does the call narrative occur. The Book of Immanuel (chaps. 7–12), which follows, highlights the Lord's saving actions. On the one side of Isaiah's call (chaps. 1–5) the major emphasis falls upon the sinful condition of Judah and impending judgment, whereas the overarching stress on the other side of the call narrative is salvation.

First series of oracles, 1:2–31. Introducing the book is a compilation of oracles announcing Judah's transgression and lamenting the devastation of the land by war (1:2–23), concluding with an oracle of hope (1:24–31). Judah's loss of trust in Yahweh had reduced its people to animal status—no, even lower, for

> An ox knows its owner,
> And a donkey its master's manger,
> But Israel does not know,
> My people do not understand.
>
> (1:3)

9. The word *limmudîm* also occurs in 50:4 (twice) and 54:13, where it less certainly refers to Isaiah's disciples.

A land devastated by war, Judah was like a body covered with bruises, sores, and bleeding wounds, so that there was no spot for another blow or lash (1:5–9). The time of the first oracle is frequently identified with Sennacherib's invasion in 701 B.C. According to his account, he besieged and took forty-six fortified cities and many small towns, but Jerusalem was spared (2 Kings 18:13–19:36).[10] An earlier date may even be possible, during the Syrian/ Israelite siege of Jerusalem in 734 when those two northern neighbors tried to force Judah into an anti-Assyrian alliance. At that time the Edomites to the southeast and the Philistines to the southwest took advantage of the situation and confiscated Judean territory (2 Chron. 28:17–18).[11]

To reinforce the description of Judah's shameful apostasy, a second oracle associates the rulers and people with Sodom and Gomorrah (1:10–31), lamenting the nation's abusive religious system and calling for substantive repentance. Even though the nation as a whole was the object of Isaiah's indictment, Jerusalem was the national symbol and the prophet's special concern (vv. 8, 21–26, 27). In fact, he could hardly think of one without implicating the other (cf. 1:1; 2:1; 3:1, etc.). Whereas many scholars break those verses down into several oracles, the component parts fit together well if prophetic preaching is allowed to include both judgment and hope. The form of the oracle may be that of the messenger speech, the prophet delivering a word from Yahweh to Judah ("Hear the word of the Lord"). The concluding part of the oracle promises redemption to those who meet God's demands, reiterating judgment to the disobedient (1:27–31).

Second series of oracles/song of the vineyard/concluding woe's, 2:1—5:30. The second clearly marked group of oracles begins at 2:1 with the introductory statement, "The word which Isaiah the son of Amoz saw concerning Judah and Jerusalem," and it extends through 4:6. Because the "Song of the Vineyard" in 5:1–7 has a different literary form (parable) from the oracles that precede, we may justifiably distinguish it from the group that constitutes chapters 2–4. The conclusion to the "Song" is a well-balanced series of "woes" and "therefores," declaring Judah's sin and detailing the reasons for the Lord's judgment. The first series commences with two woes indicting those who abuse power and wealth and those who drink early and carouse late (5:8, 11). It ends with two "therefores" that attribute Judah's exile to a lack of knowledge of the Lord, as did 1:3, and promises an enlargement of Sheol to receive the numerous dead that the disaster would produce (5:13–14).

The second series doubles the number of woes to four (5:18, 20, 21, 22), condemning those who had become skeptical about God's work in the world

---

10. Cf Gray, p. 12; Kaiser, p. 9; James B. Pritchard, *Ancient Near Eastern Texts Relating to the Old Testament,* pp. 287–88.
11. C. von Orelli, *The Prophecies of Isaiah,* p. 14.

(vv. 18–19), who misjudged good for evil (v. 20), whose own wisdom had become the standard of prudence (v. 21), and who were heroes in drinking wine but cowards in dispensing justice (vv. 22–23). The conclusion begins at verse 24 ("therefore," *lākhēn*), threatening decomposure and disbursement. Verse 25 offers a broader explanation for Yahweh's anger against Judah, "On this account (*'al kēn*) the anger of the Lord has burned against His people." The collection concludes with a very graphic description of the Lord's sovereignty in the world as Isaiah depicts Him lifting up a signal to the nations and whistling for the advance of the Assyrians (vv. 26–30; cf. also 10:5).

Commentators have recognized the relationship of this last oracle (5:25–30) to 9:8–10:4, based upon the refrain, "For all this His anger is not spent,/But His hand is still stretched out" (v. 25; 9:12, 17, 21; 10:4).[12] If the oracles were preserved in short collections, such as the one we have been discussing, it could very well be that the collection found in 6:1—9:7 was inserted into the middle of another collection. The reason Isaiah or the editor would do that, however, is not obvious. The assumption made by many modern critics that the oracles have been put together in a somewhat bungling fashion is not acceptable. There is no reason Isaiah could not use the same phraseology on other occasions; and although the similarities are real, the oracles may not belong to the same speaking occasion. Therefore, they were not included in the same mini-collection. It is best to leave them where they are and try to deal with them in their ancient context rather than create a new context for them. In the case before us, 5:25–30 forms a logical conclusion to a section that has indicted Judah for social and religious sins and closed with a brief word about judgment (v. 24). The purpose of verses 25–30 is to define further the rationale of judgment as well as its agent. Further, the nations, especially Assyria, have not taken matters into their own hands—Yahweh still has everything under His control. He Himself was calling together the forces of destruction.

Isaiah's call, chapter 6. As already indicated, Isaiah's call and commission to prophesy constitutes a center for chapters 1–12. Here, after enough threatening oracles in chapters 1–5 to intimidate any people and their rulers, it was about time that Isaiah introduce his credentials. What right did he have to say such things? What word had he received that validated the hope as well as judgment that he liberally pronounced upon Israel and Judah? Chapter 6 is the answer, the validation of his right to speak. Here we must seek an editorial explanation. Certainly the prophet's call came before he had spoken the oracles recorded here, but as he put the oracles in a logical and coherent order, he chose to record his call only after he had laid out Israel's dilemma and culpability. Perhaps also it is more than coincidence that in the first five

---

12. Gray, pp. 95, 179–80, gives his reasons for believing that 5:26–29 originally formed the conclusion to 9:7—10:4; Kaiser, pp. 133–34, sees 5:25–30 as the conclusion of 9:8–21.

chapters the advancing foe of Judah and Israel is not mentioned by name. Not until 7:17 does the name Assyria occur, and that rather dramatically: "The Lord will bring on you, on your people, and on your father's house such days as have never come since the day that Ephraim separated from Judah, the king of Assyria." The point is that after Isaiah had presented his prophetic credentials he could then be more explicit and identify the foe that Yahweh was calling into service. Without that validation, the kind of words he had spoken were nothing short of treason.

In a visionary experience transcending time and history, Isaiah saw the Lord enthroned in majestic glory (6:1–13). Even His seraphic attendants veiled their eyes from His resplendent presence. So it was no surprise that the earthling should sense that he was doomed. The sins of the people, which he had described in chapters 1–5, had infected him too. He was one with them, hopelessly entombed in a doomed nation, until one of the Lord's seraphim turned his attention to him: "Behold, this has touched your lips; and your iniquity is taken away, and your sin is forgiven" (v. 7). The point of identity with his own people should have elicited a hearing from some of them, and the seraph's cleansing touch should have brought hope to them. Contaminated by earth and cleansed by heaven—that was Isaiah's testimony. And as his message unfolds, we become conscious that that also was his hope for Judah.

The clock of history had struck another solemn hour—Uzziah was dead. At least, it was the year of his death. With Assyria on the horizon and the political uncertainty at home added to the decline of social and religious standards, the tenuous future hung on the thread of God's mercy. That mercy summoned a listening prophet: "Whom shall I send, and who will go for Us?" With lips newly touched and cleansed, Isaiah made his unembellished, unqualified response, "Here am I. Send me!" (6:8).

Isaiah made his final response to that awesome experience only after Yahweh had detailed his assignment (vv. 9–11), which was more an analysis of the situation and the prospects than straightforward instructions. Faced with so little hope of success, he cried, "Lord, how long?" It is also the psalmist's cry of distress, "How distressingly long?"[13]

The Book of Immanuel, chapters 7–12. The Book of Immanuel, as it has been called, opens with a date and a crisis. The "days of Ahaz" is the date (c. 734 B.C.). The crisis is the threat of the Syrian/Israelite war that had weakened Judah by a siege of Jerusalem (1 Kings 16), with Edomite and Philistine campaigns against the Southern Kingdom furthering the disaster (2 Chron. 28). In an effort to enlarge the western front against Tiglath-pileser III, Syria and Israel entered into an anti-Assyrian treaty and tried to force Ahaz of Judah to join the alliance. With enemy forces surrounding his country on three sides

13. Pss. 6:3; 74:10; 80:4; 82:2; 90:13; 94:3.

(Edom on the southeast, Philistia on the southwest, and Syria and Israel on the north), Ahaz appealed to Tiglath-pileser for help. That overture brought Assyria westward on a second major campaign to deal with the problem.

Before Ahaz had taken that political gamble, however, Isaiah offered him a decidedly different alternative: "Ask a sign for yourself from the Lord your God; make it deep as Sheol or high as heaven" (7:11). J. Lindblom takes 6:1—9:6 to be the first collection made by an early collector of Isaianic revelations,[14] although he considers the call narrative to be only loosely connected to chapter 7. But we have indicated that the call narrative provides the prophet with the credentials necessary for proclaiming judgment and hope. That seems to have been the purpose of the call narrative in the prophetic collections. Only after Amos had been called to account for his words of judgment against the house of Jeroboam did he relate the experience of his call (Amos 7:10–17).

The sign, rejected by Ahaz but offered nevertheless by the Lord, consisted in this: ". . . a virgin will be with child and bear a son" (v. 14). The word "sign" (*'oth*) is used in two ways in the OT. First, it is a phenomenon that promotes belief in the immediate situation, like the signs Moses was given for the Egyptians (Ex. 4:8–9). Second, "it is designed to follow a series of events, to confirm them as acts of God and to fix a stated interpretation upon them."[15] The second usage is the appropriate one here. The birth of Isaiah's son Maher-shalal-hash-baz (8:1–4) could not have fulfilled the terms of the Immanuel prophecy. The prophet's wife hardly qualifies as the virgin of 7:14, and in this case Isaiah rather than the mother was to name the child.

Isaiah was fond of abstracting time measurements from the lives of individuals and laying them down on the grid of history to gauge coming events. Here in 8:4 he takes the time span required for Maher-shalal-hash-baz to learn to say "My father or my mother" (about a year) and uses it as a gauge of the interval before Damascus and Samaria will be devastated by the Assyrian king. A similar abstraction of time occurs in 16:14 and 21:16, where the years of a hireling are used to measure in the first instance the time span before judgment on Moab and in the second judgment on Kedar; "Within three years, as a hired man would count them, the glory of Moab will be degraded along with all his great population, and his remnant will be very small and impotent" (16:14). Therefore, Isaiah's time abstraction from Immanuel's life ("For before the boy will know enough to refuse evil and choose good," [7:16], perhaps four or five years) to measure the lapse of time before Assyria devastated the two kings in the north is not foreign to Isaiah's method.

---

14. J. Lindblom, *A Study on the Immanuel Section in Isaiah* (Isa. vii, 1-ix, 6), Scripta Minora (Lund: CWK Gleerup, 1958), p. 3.
15. J. A. Motyer, "Context and Content in the Interpretation of Isaiah 7:14," p. 120.

The sign can have a temporal value in the undated future. Further evidence that the prophecy was distant can be seen in the narrative of chapter 8, "Bind up the testimony, seal the law among my disciples. And I will wait for the Lord who is hiding His face from the house of Jacob; I will even look eagerly for Him" (vv. 16–17). Similar language in Daniel signaled the remote nature of his prophecy (Dan. 12:9, 12). J. A. Motyer has pointed out the Isaianic method of allowing room for false identifications before he finally and conclusively offered the true identity. For example, in chapters 41 and 42 one might identify the servant as Israel, then in 43–48 as Cyrus, then the remnant in 49–51, until 52–53, where the Servant becomes clearly a universal Savior.[16]

The purpose of the Maher-shalal-hash-baz oracle is to offer immediate evidence that the distant prediction will come to pass. It is another prophetic method. Jeremiah used it when he encountered the false prophet Hananiah (Jer. 28). He had predicted seventy years until the Exile ended, but he was contradicted by Hananiah, who said it would only last two years. The reliability of Jeremiah's prophecy was confirmed when he made the more immediate prediction that within the year Hananiah would die (28:16–17). The fulfillment of the immediate prediction confirmed Jeremiah's reliability as predictor of the remote future. Another example of the method is found in 1 Kings 13. The man of God from Judah predicted the birth of Josiah and his religious reform. To confirm the reliability of the remote prediction, he offered a sign that was fulfilled in the immediate future, ". . . the altar shall be split apart and the ashes which are on it shall be poured out." It happened just as the prophet forecasted (vv. 2–3, 5), thus lending reliability to his remote prediction. That seems to be the purpose of the prophecy of 8:1–4. It was the more immediate confirmation of Isaiah's predictive ability. With that confirmation to his credit, his credibility was heightened. Although Immanuel may be yet future, the prophet's predictive reliability was validated by the incident from the life of his own son.

Interpreted in that way, Matthew's understanding of the sign as the virgin birth of Jesus is not forced (Matt. 1:18–25). Due to the alleged ambiguity of the Hebrew word 'almāh (the usual Hebrew word for "virgin" is bethûlāh), translated by the Septuagint as parthenos ("virgin"), many modern scholars have discounted Matthew's understanding of the prophecy as mere messianic nonsense. Yet in the OT the word 'almāh is always used of an unmarried woman (some refute this by referring to Prov. 30:19, but there is no certainty that the woman referred to there was married), whereas the word bethûlāh definitely applies to both married and unmarried women.[17] That being the case, the word 'almāh is less ambiguous in referring to a virgin than the word bethûlāh.

The identity of the child has been a perplexing question for many. Other proposals have been made. One is based upon a collective reading of "virgin"

16. Ibid., p. 119.
17. Edward J. Young, The Book of Isaiah, 1:286–88.

(understood by the proponents of this position as "young woman") and suggests that the danger from the northern kings would disappear so soon that women who were pregnant at the time would name their sons Immanuel ("God with us") out of gratitude for the deliverance.[18] Rabbinic commentators have identified the woman as the prophet's wife, thus the child as Isaiah's son (so Rashi),[19] and the son of King Ahaz (so Kimchi).[20]

The child, first called Immanuel, is the possessor of the land of Judah (8:8), the protector against foreign plots (8:10), David's heir and successor (9:6-7), the mighty God (10:21), and the righteous ruler (11:1-10). In this section of the book the Syrian/Israelite alliance forms the background for 7:1-25; 8:1-15; and 9:1-21. Lindblom is a bit more restrictive, associating six pieces in the book with this time: 7:2-17; 8:1-4; 8:9-10; 8:11-15; 9:1-6; and 17:1-6.[21] It is Isaiah's practice to move back and forth between the historical era and the Messianic. The reason is simple—he saw Israel's hope for the present and future in Immanuel. That is clearly indicated in chapter 9. The introduction (9:1-2) rests in the years 733-732, when the Galilean tribes of Zebulun and Naphtali fell under Assyrian control. Interjected with the messianic hope of verses 2-7, those words are then followed by oracles that are again set in the historical context, if not that of 9:1-2, at least the Assyrian period. The Book of Immanuel closes with a long, memorable section on the righteous Ruler (11:1-5) and the age that He will inaugurate (11:6—12:6).

ISAIAH 13-23: ORACLES AGAINST THE NATIONS

The inclusion of oracles against the nations in prophetic collections is frequent. Our best examples, in addition to these chapters, are Amos 1-2, Jeremiah 46-51, and Ezekiel 25-32. We do not have much information from Isaiah on the manner in which their information was transferred to the nations concerned, if at all (but Jeremiah does provide some data). However, direct addresses are frequent, and in 18:2 Isaiah may be speaking directly to the Ethiopian envoys who visited Jerusalem.

18. E. g., Kaiser, *Isaiah 1-12*, p. 103.
19. See Herbert M. Wolf, "A Solution to the Immanuel Prophecy in Isaiah 7:14—8:22," pp. 449-56, for a well-researched study of the problem, concluding that Maher-shalal-hash-baz was the fulfillment of the Immanuel prophecy. Wolf, however, seeks to preserve both the integrity of Isaiah and Matthew. In a less convincing thesis, Norman K. Gottwald, "Immanuel as the Prophet's Son," pp. 36-47, speculates that the "young woman" (*hā'ālmah*) could have been Isaiah's wife or even another wife of the prophet (p. 42). He further associates his wife ("the prophetess," *hannebhî'â*) with the Temple service, suggesting that *ha'almāh* in 7:14 as in Ps. 68:25 (Heb., v. 26) is a female musician and that the term "the prophetess" (*hannebhi'a*) is a more restricted word for an ecstatic (p. 44). That, however, is a tenuous hypothesis, depending far too much upon the alleged cultic associations of the prophets.
20. Cf. Solomon B. Freehof, *Book of Isaiah*, p. 53.
21. Lindblom, *A Study on the Immanuel Section in Isaiah*, p. 28.

One fact is certain, however. Isaiah was not uninvolved in these oracles, and he did not view the nations with cold calculation. Weeping and terror seized him as he contemplated the judgments he pronounced (15:5; 16:9; 21:3–4; 22:4). Aage Bentzen's association of national oracles with the Egyptian execration texts is unconvincing,[22] for that implies more personal hostility than is evident in this collection.

The time span in which Isaiah delivered these oracles stretches from 734 to 701 B.C., at the least. They apply, however, to a much wider spectrum, extending into the Messianic era. Sometimes the prophet spoke in the past tense to describe future events (prophetic perfect), so certain was he that they would come to pass.

The arrangement of these oracles is difficult to explain, for they do not seem to follow any chronological or geographical order. The word *massā'*, generally rendered "oracle," occurs ten times and introduces most of the prophecies. The following list is an attempt to date the oracles, however risky that may be in some instances.

	Nation/Person	Date
13:1—14:23	Babylon	703 B.C.
[14:24–27]*	Assyria	702–701
14:28–32	Philistia	716–715
15:1—16:14	Moab	713–711
17:1–14	Syria and Israel	734
[18:1–7]	Ethiopia	714
19:1–25	Egypt	714
[20:1–6]	Ethiopia and Egypt	713–711
21:1–10	Babylon	703
21:11–12	Edom	703
21:13–17	Arabia	703
22:1–14	Jerusalem	713–711
[22:15–25]	Shebna	713–711
23:1–18	Tyre	701

*Brackets indicate those oracles not introduced by the word *massā'*.

13:1–14:23: Babylon. Babylon figures very prominently in this collection, here and probably as well in 21:1–10. Although for the most part this country in southern Mesopotamia was under Assyrian control during Isaiah's lifetime, the Chaldeans, led by Marduk-appal-iddin (Merodach-baladan), gained power in Babylonia during the years 721–710 and briefly in 703. During the last period of control the envoys visited Hezekiah (Isa. 39; 2 Kings 20:12–21). Although the Babylon of Isaiah's time could hardly qualify as "the beauty of

22. Aage Bentzen, "The Ritual Background of Amos i.2–ii.16," pp. 85–99.

kingdoms," Isaiah's keen political mind inspired by the Holy Spirit could perceive the viability of this sleeping giant. Ironically he predicts the destruction of Babylon by her ally, the Medes (13:17–22). Micah engaged in the same kind of irony when he intimated that Judah would go to Babylon and be rescued from there, even though Assyria, not Babylon, was the likely subject of captivity in the eighth century (Mic. 4:10). Yet the Medes and Persians under Cyrus the Great captured Babylon in 539 B.C. It is significant that Yahweh commanded the Babylonian army (13:3), just as He had ordered the Assyrians into action (7:18, 20; 10:5–6). The names had changed, but Israel's God had not.

Gray dates this oracle in the Exile because of the reference to the Medes, [23] but we are dealing here with the prophetic phenomenon of prediction.[24] In like manner 14:3–23 has been assigned to the post-exilic period,[25] but for no better reasons.

The king of Babylon in chapter 14 may be a personification of the monarchy. In arresting language the prophet depicts the tyrant king descending to Sheol just like all other tyrants (14:9–11), even the rulers of Jerusalem (5:14). A king whose egomania set him in ambitious defiance against God was brought to the lowest regions of Sheol (14:13–20), creating even astonishment among the residents of Sheol that the tyrant of earth should be so debased in the netherworld. Verse 12, unlike Luke 10:18, does not refer to the fall of Satan but to the downfall of the Babylonian king.

14:24–27: Assyria. Just as the Babylon of the future would fall, so the present Assyrian foe would also fall. The Assyrians were never very far from Isaiah's mind.

14:28–32: Philistia. Perhaps this oracle was delivered early in the reign of Sargon when the King of Hamath and the Philistine king Hanno, joined by Damascus and what was left of Samaria, raised opposition to Assyria.[26] The year 716/715, anticipating the rebellion of the Philistine city of Ashdod in 713, seems plausible, although there are differences of opinion on the year of Ahaz's death.

15:1—16:14: Moab. Using the prophetic perfect to describe Moab's downfall, Isaiah's heart was moved for them (15:5; 16:11). These chapters are difficult, and R. B. Y. Scott has remarked that they convey little to the modern reader, whereas Otto Procksch has called them "the problem child of exegesis."[27]

The question is whether this oracle is a lament, thus spoken after the event,

---

23. Gray, p. 237.
24. Cf. H. C. Leupold, *Exposition of Isaiah*, 1:238–39.
25. Otto Kaiser, *Isaiah 13–39, A Commentary*, p. 2.
26. Leupold, 1:269.
27. R. B. Y. Scott, "*The Book of Isaiah*, Chapters 1–39," p. 269; Procksch cited by Leupold, 1:273.

or a prediction. The predictive element can be identified in 15:9; 16:2, 12, thus indicating actual prediction. A reasonable date is 713–711, when Moab joined the coalition organized by Ashdod against Assyria.[28]

17:1–14: Syria and Israel. This oracle concerns both Syria and Israel, both victims of the Assyrian invasion of 734–732. A date of 735/734 seems to be demanded.

18:1–7: Ethiopia. Although called a land that lies "beyond the rivers of Cush," (v. 1), it is generally agreed that the country is Cush or Ethiopia itself. Located south of Egypt, her emissaries had come to Jerusalem to invite Judah to join an anti-Assyrian plot (c. 714 B.C.). The direct address, "Go, swift messengers" (v.2), leaves the impression that the oracle may have been spoken directly to the envoys upon their visit.

19:1–25: Egypt. This passage depicts another awesome visitation of the Lord to Egypt, this time riding upon a cloud and throwing the land into terror. The oracle breaks down into four parts, verses 1–4, 5–10, 11–15, and 16–25. The second part (vv. 5–10) describes the effect of Yahweh's visitation in terms of the Nile drying up, which would be a totally devastating thing for Egypt. Many scholars will not allow that verses 16–25 (esp. 18–25) are Isaianic, because of content and style; but as to content, C. von Orelli has pointed out that without them the oracle would be a torso.[29] A time around 714 B.C. before the establishment of the alien Ethiopian dynasty appears reasonable.[30]

The conclusion establishing the international trilogy of blessing in the world—Egypt, Assyria, and Israel—a mixed trio, to be sure, thrusts the passage into the Messianic era.

20:1–6: Ethiopia and Egypt. In 713 Ashdod rebelled against Assyria, inviting her neighbors to join in, and in 711 Sargon sent his commander-in-chief to put out the fire of insurrection. Isaiah opposed the alliance by a sign that seemed out of character with what we know of him. By posing as a prisoner of war on the way to captivity, going naked and barefoot (probably wearing only an undergarment), he thus symbolized the captivity of Egypt and Ethiopia at the hands of the Assyrians. Once Ashdod, standing as a sentinel on the highway to Egypt, was crushed, Egypt was next in line.

21:1–10: Babylon. This oracle, pronounced against the "wilderness of the sea," is probably directed against Babylon, whose fall is announced in verse 9.[31] Perhaps spoken at a time when Judah was looking toward Babylon for support (703 B.C.), the oracle concerns the fall of that city in 539. Note Isaiah's troubled heart (vv. 3–4) even though he speaks of a foreign nation.

28. Ibid., pp. 274–75; Gray, pp. 274–95, favors the lament.
29. von Orelli, p. 119.
30. Scott, p. 278, dates only the first and third sections to 714, whereas Gray, p 322, favors a post-exilic date.
31. See Young, *The Book of Isaiah*, 2:60; von Orelli, p. 123. Against identification with Babylon, see Gray, p. 348.

21:11–12: Edom. The name *Dumah* means "stillness," perhaps used in deference to the quiet stillness that follows destruction. There is a word play here, for *E-dom* and *Dum-ah* in Hebrew are essentially the same syllables interchanged. The message relates to the fall of Babylon in 539, and the watchman is probably the prophet (cf. Ezek. 33:2).

21:13–17: Arabia. The Dedanites were neighbors of the Edomites (cf. Ezek. 25:13; Jer. 49:8). The gist of this oracle seems to be a warning to the caravans to stay off the desert trails because they have been made unsafe by marauding enemies.[32]

22:1–25: Jerusalem and Shebna. These two oracles actually belong together, because the man Shebna held the important position of a scribe in Jerusalem (2 Kings 18:18 = Isa. 36:3). Called "the valley of vision," the levity that filled this city forms a contrast with Isaiah's troubled heart (compare v. 4 and vv. 12–13; cf. also 15:5; 16:9; 21:2–3).

The oracle against Shebna, the only invective Isaiah pronounced against an individual, predicts that he will be deposed and replaced by Eliakim. Otto Kaiser constructs a growth chart for this oracle, drawing a line from some unknown steward to an editorial identification with Shebna and a subsequent application to the Eliakim of 2 Kings:18,[33] but it is not convincing.

23:1–18: Tyre. This city of fame and infamy in the OT was known for her commercial activity. Situated on the Phoenician coast, she trafficked in wares of all kinds. Isaiah calls her a harlot (vv. 15–18), having illicit relations with all the nations of the world. Tiglath-pileser III subdued Tyre (by 738 B.C.)[34], and Sennacherib brought her under submission in the campaign of 701.[35] Nebuchadnezzar also took the mainland city, but the island city of Tyre was not captured until Alexander the Great (332). Von Orelli's helpful comment on this passage suggests a fulfillment in stages: "It is clear from what has been said, that here, as in chs. xiii, xiv, the prophetic gaze sees together in one picture what was realized in history *gradatim.*"[36]

ISAIAH 24–27: ESCHATOLOGICAL SUMMATION

These chapters have a very definite relationship to chapters 13–23. They form the capstone of the oracles against the nations. Isaiah's personal involvement in those prophecies (15:5; 16:11) receives further validation here as his heart is moved by Yahweh's world offensive (24:16), which not only included

---

32. Leupold, 1:341.
33. Kaiser, *Isaiah 13–39*, p. 4.
34. John Bright, *A History of Israel*, p. 253. Cf. Young, 2:143–45, where he gives a brief summary of Tyre's history.
35. Bright, p. 268.
36. von Orelli, p. 139.

the nations in judgment but also salvation (25:6–9).[37] The hermeneutical principle that prophecy equals the sum of its parts in one sense applies here. That is, the prophets sometimes broke down universal judgment and salvation into their component parts, reserving, of course, that ample measure of each for the eschatological age that loomed in the distant future.[38]

Nature of the literature. In proportion to its size, this section of Isaiah has posed as many problems for interpreters as chapters 40–66. One of the more interesting topics is the type of literature. Called by many the "Isaiah Apocalypse," these four chapters have been critical for understanding the development of apocalyptic literature. Until recent years, the prevailing opinion has been that apocalyptic sources were located in Persian literature and religion. Yet in recent research attention has shifted from Persian to Canaanite sources.[39] Opinions vary on the relative place of these chapters in that development, from proto- (William R. Millar), early (Paul D. Hanson), and late (Gray). Another alternative is to view them as eschatological rather than apocalyptic (Yehezkel Kaufmann). The broad difference between apocalyptic and eschatology is that apocalyptic has taken the visions of the age to come and systematized them (compare these chapters to Daniel).[40] Kaufmann has pointed out that the imagery of the so-called "Isaiah Apocalypse" is that of early Israelite prophecy, which later apocalyptists borrowed.[41]

Authorship and date. In the majority of modern studies the question of authorship has been connected to the gradual growth theory applied to much of the book of Isaiah. I have acknowledged that the book is an anthology—but an anthology of genuine Isaiah prophecies. The prevailing view in Isaiah scholarship today is that the book is a collection of oracles written by members of an Isaianic school that continued for perhaps a century or more after the prophet's death.[42] Others would extend the compilation and composition of these chapters into the late post-exilic period. Gray marvels that any part of the prophetic canon could be late enough to contain them. He prefers a date of about 400 B.C., plus or minus.[43] But in view of the indisputable relationship to chapters

---

37. Young, *The Book of Isaiah*, 2:146–47, points out the close relationship of these chapters to chaps. 13–23, comparing 24:13 with 17:5–6; 24:16 with 21:2; 27:9 with 17:8; and 25:3 with 1:8 and 23:18.
38. C. Hassell Bullock, "Entree to the Pentateuch Through the Prophets," pp. 60–77.
39. William R. Millar, *Isaiah 24–27 and the Origin of Apocalyptic*, p. 71. Yehezkel Kaufmann, *The Religion of Israel*, p. 384, also suggests Canaanite sources.
40. J. Lindblom, *Prophecy in Ancient Israel*, p. 422.
41. Kaufmann, p. 384.
42. Paul D. Hanson, *The Dawn of Apocalyptic*, pp. 313–14; Millar, p. 118; J. H. Eaton, "The Origin of the Book of Isaiah," p. 151.
43. Gray, p. 401. Kaiser, *Isaiah 13–39*, pp. 173, 179, looks to the late post-exilic era, perhaps as late as the Hellenistic period. Due to the reference to the resurrection (26:19) he gives 167–64 B.C. as a *terminus ad quem*. Hanson, pp. 313–14, tends toward 520 B.C., and Millar, p. 120, sometime in the last half of the sixth century.

13–23, and the unfolding possibilities that prophetic eschatology in its pre-apocalyptic form was a normal part of prophetic thought, I consider these chapters within the range of Isaiah's theology and eschatology of the future. In fact, given the earlier range of prophetic eschatology already outlined broadly by Amos (Amos 5:18–20; 9:11–15), Isaiah's advancement in that branch of theology is realistic.

Content. In 24:1–23 world destruction is the summation of the individual prophecies of judgment in chapters 13–23. This God, so terrible in judgment, is the God of Israel (24:15–16, 23).

A hymn celebrating the eschatological judgment and salvation composes 25:1–12. The "fortified city" of verse 2 ("strong city" in 26:1 and perhaps also the "city of chaos" in 24:10) may be a definite city, but no clear identification can be agreed upon. Proposals include Babylon, an unknown Moabite city, Jerusalem, and a general reference describing the devastation of divine judgment when cities will be made ruins. The last option seems to satisfy best the problems of the text. It is a general reference to the eschatological day of destruction.[44]

The hymn celebrates the day when the Lord will remove the horrible veil of death that affects the whole world (25:7–8). Moreover, God will remove Israel's reproach, and the Israelites will acknowledge Him as their God (vv. 8–9). As the Lord gives His people victory, Moab will again be no obstruction in Israel's path on the way to the new promised land (vv. 10–12).

In 26:1–21 another hymn of salvation celebrates the strong city prepared and secured for Israel (cf. 1:26). The new inhabitants should not be downcast because of the death wrought in that city in the past, for they will live, and their bodies arise (v. 19). Consequently, the Lord's people should wait until His wrath is passed. Perhaps Isaiah by those words comforts and encourages the present generation that labors under the fear and fact of Assyrian oppression and threat.

Chapter 27 is connected to the preceding one by its last verse (26:21). Here we have the description of the judgment that Yahweh will dispense upon Israel's enemies (v. 1), and the exile of Israel, which will be His chastisement (vv. 7–8). By that means He will remove Israel's guilt. Most appropriately, the prophecy ends with the prediction of return. Yahweh's chastisement by exile was a means to purging Israel. The return was the subsequent chapter in His plan for her.

ISAIAH 28–33: JERUSALEM, EGYPT, AND A PROPHET IN BETWEEN

Even those scholars who see little of Isaiah in chapters 24–27 will admit that there is much of him in this section of the book. The geographical foci of these

---

44. Young, *The Book of Isaiah,* 2:186–87.

prophecies are Jerusalem and Egypt. The latter, ruled by a vigorous king, Shabako (c. 710/9–696/5), seemed a likely source of help against the Assyrians to the east. The diplomatic relations that developed during that part of Hezekiah's reign (703–701) were probably inspired by the death of Sargon and the accession of his less capable son, Sennacherib, in 705. Hezekiah refused to give the new king the obedient homage he demanded (2 Kings 18:7), and the diplomatic channel between Jerusalem and Egypt was opened (30:1–7; 31:1–3). Isaiah was firmly opposed to that.

This broad outline divides the text into five major sections, each introduced by "woe" (Heb. *hoi*):

28:1—Woe to the drunkards of Ephraim
29:1—Woe to Ariel
30:1—Woe to those who seek a pact with Egypt
31:1—Woe to those who rely on Egypt
33:1—Woe to the destroyer not destroyed (Assyria)

These divisions are not exactly coextensive with the oracles themselves, for each contains suboracles, as the discussion will show.

Most fitting to begin this section is the comparison of Judah's sins to Samaria's (28:1–13). The change of subject is obvious in the Hebrew text (v. 7), which shifts from Israel to Judah by "and these also." Isaiah had risked his reputation to say these things, and it had brought him the mockery of his compatriots (vv. 9–10). To them he sounded like a tutor teaching children their alphabet.[45] The prophet's response in vv. 11–13 is essentially, "If you think such an elementary exercise makes no sense, the Lord is going to speak to you through a foreign language that you know absolutely nothing about." His message will be of judgment, even though He had said in the past, "Here is rest, give rest to the weary." Yet against the background of defiant unbelief (vv. 14–15) the Lord lays in Zion a foundation of genuine faith and confidence (vv. 16–17).

Addressing Jerusalem as "Ariel" in 29:1, Isaiah foresees the reduction of the city to ashes.[46] Yet her enemies need not think they are invincible, for they will disappear like a dream in the night (vv. 7–8).

Isaiah's urgency to prophesy was not limited to oral delivery. He was constrained, as in 8:16, to write down his words as a witness against his generation (30:8).

After his indictments of diplomacy with Egypt in chapters 30 and 31, the prophet turns from the society he loved but that caused him such pain of heart, and describes the reverse side of that social order, a king and princes who rule

45. Hallo, pp. 324–38.
46. "Ariel" appears to mean "altar hearth" in Ezek. 43:15, 16. The citizens of Jerusalem would become the victims on the altar.

in justice (32:1–8). That has been applied to Hezekiah, but that application is only appropriate in a limited sense. There is a ring of the messianic here, as in 11:1–5. The interruption of the theme in 32:9–14 to condemn the women who symbolize the life of ease and false confidence moves smoothly into a section (vv. 15–20) that picks up the theme of justice and righteousness sounded in the first part of the chapter. Amos had used the same language to indict the leaders of Samaria (Amos 6:1).

The conclusion to the section predicates Yahweh's exaltation against the unnamed enemy (most likely the Assyrians, 33:1–13), describes the righteous who can survive the day of judgment (vv. 14–16), and ends with a sketch of the new age in which Yahweh will be king (vv. 17–24).[47]

ISAIAH 34–35: ESCHATOLOGICAL SUMMATION

By this point we can see a pattern in the arrangement of the prophecies in the book. The first major section (chaps. 1–12) concluded with a description of the eschatological age (chap. 12), and the second similarly closed with a lengthy delineation of the future age (chaps. 24–27). Likewise chapters 34–35 are the capstone of chapters 28–33.

In chapter 34 Isaiah describes the judgment of the world (vv. 1–4), the destruction of Edom (vv. 5–15), and the affirmative Word of the Lord (vv. 16–17), whereas chapter 35 presents the transformation of the wilderness and the return of the redeemed to Zion, giving a description of the preparations as well as the effects of their return.

Generally these two chapters are considered a unit. C. C. Torrey viewed them as the beginning of "Second Isaiah," augmented (with the exception of chaps. 36–39) by chapters 40–46.[48] As we have noted above, the Dead Sea scroll has a break after chapter 33. Yet that may be merely a scribal convenience, because the Masoretes noted that this was the middle point of the book.

Authorship is much disputed. Edward J. Kissane comments that the reference to the Edomites is the principal reason for attributing chapter 34 to a post-exilic author (vv. 5–6). When Jerusalem fell in 586, the nonfraternal behavior of the Edomites toward Judah was condemned (Ps. 137:7; Lam. 4:21–22; Ezek. 25:12–14; 35:5, 10), and hostility developed toward them during the Exile and post-Exile. Kissane would emend the text to read *Adam* ("man") rather than Edom (the consonants are the same) and preserve the composition for Isaiah.[49] Yet there is no textual support for the emendation. Edward J. Young has contended that "Edom" belongs in the text: In the larger

---

47. Franz Delitzsch, *Biblical Commentary on the Prophecies of Isaiah*, 2:66, 68; Young, 2:428; Kaiser, *Isaiah 13–39*, p. 353.
48. C. C. Torrey, *The Second Isaiah, A New Interpretation*, p. 53.
49. Edward J. Kissane, *The Book of Isaiah*, 1:381.

plan of the book, Edom is introduced as the representative of the world against God; Isaiah affirms in relation to chapters 28–35 that God's wrath will punish the evil world, just as the presence of Moab in chapter 25 asserted the world of chapters 13–23 would feel God's wrath.[50] Moreover, a strong case has been made for Zephaniah's use of chapter 34 as well as Jeremiah's.[51] The eschatological program formulated by the earlier prophets became the basis of eschatology for the later prophets. Isaiah was a pioneer in describing the future age.

That chapters 34 and 35 are a piece with chapters 28–33 is supported by the parallel themes of the oppressor's overthrow and the restoration of Zion, as well as minor details that overarch the two sections.[52]

ISAIAH 36–39: THE HISTORICAL APPENDIX

Three events are recorded that focus upon the relations between King Hezekiah and Isaiah: (1) Sennacherib's unsuccessful attempt to take Jerusalem (chaps. 36–37); (2) Hezekiah's sickness and recovery (chap. 38); and (3) the Babylonian envoys from Merodach-Baladan and the prediction of Babylonian Exile (chap. 39). 2 Kings 18:13–20:19 is a parallel account. Chronologically these events are recorded in reverse order, for Sennacherib's invasion occurred in 701[53] and Hezekiah's illness about 704, with the Babylonian diplomatic core arriving in 703 when Merodach-Baladan was king of Babylon again for nine months.[54]

Literary nature and content. The three events are related in prose, as we would expect historical material to be. Isaiah has included other prose accounts (e.g., chaps. 6–8, 20). Otto Eissfeldt's assessment of this material as three legends[55] is typical of current scholarship. At least, 37:36–38 and chap. 38 are widely suspected. It is true that the Assyrian records say nothing about the miraculous deliverance of Jerusalem, nor should we expect them to. Moreover, the story of Isaiah's healing Hezekiah does seem out of character with the prophet. We need not rule it non-historical because no other passages in the book corroborate that kind of activity for the prophet. We are dealing with material as genuine to Isaiah as that in chapter 20, where he also engages in noncharacteristic behavior.

50. Edward J. Young, "Isaiah 34 and Its Position in the Prophecy," pp. 93–114.
51. Delitzsch, 2:67, compares Zeph. 1:7, 8, and 2:14 with Isa. 34:6, 11. Young, "Isaiah 34," pp. 105–6, finds eight passages in Jeremiah dependent upon Isa. 34: Jer. 46:10/Isa. 34:3–8; Jer. 25:31/Isa. 34:2 and 66:16; Jer. 25:33/Isa. 34:2 and 66:16; Jer. 25:34/Isa. 34:2; Jer. 50:27/Isa. 34:7; Jer. 51:40/Isa. 34:6; Jer. 50:39/Isa. 34:14; Jer. 50:60ff./Isa. 34:16.
52. See Kissane's list of parallels, 2:381–82.
53. See John Bright, *History of Israel*, p. 270, reiterated in *Peake's Commentary on the Bible*, "Isaiah I," p. 514, for the opinion that Sennacherib invaded Judah twice, this particular invasion occurring in 688. For the one-invasion theory, see H. H. Rowley, "Hezekiah's Reform and Rebellion," pp. 395–431.
54. See J. A. Brinkman, "Merodach-Baladan II."
55. Otto Eissfeldt, *The Old Testament: An Introduction*, p. 328.

Relationship to 2 Kings 18:13–20:19. The general opinion of current scholarship is that 2 Kings has priority of authorship. It is believed that Isaiah would not have been alive when Sennacherib was assassinated in 681 (37:37–38). Yet the tradition in the Ascension of Isaiah (Pseudepigrapha) that the prophet outlived Hezekiah at least leaves open the possibility. Some appeal to 2 Chronicles 32:32 and say that the prophet wrote an historical monograph about the reign of Hezekiah like the one the Chronicler said he wrote on the reign of Uzziah (2 Chron. 26:22).[56] The compiler of Isaiah then used that for chapters 36–39. John H. Walton has pointed out the consistency of the reversed chronology in Isaiah, where chronology is not always a concern, but its inconsistency in Kings where a chronological pattern is normally followed.[57] Thus Walton concludes that Kings took the material from Isaiah, and the inverted order was a prophetic design to prefix to chapters 40–66 the Babylonian portion of the material, which closes with the prediction of Exile to Babylon (39:5–8). Thus the prophet appropriately bridged the Assyrian and Babylonian periods that occupied his concern.[58]

ISAIAH 40–66 (ISA. II)

The heart of Isaiah the prophet is best revealed as he opens these chapters with comfort. Compared to the earlier task, so laden with contradiction and failure, his painful response, "Lord, how long?" (6:11) modulates to tenderness and hope. One gets the impression that Isaiah as a prophet and a literary artist flourished when hope became the essence of his message. We have earlier called attention to Isaiah's literary genius, and perhaps we need to consider as well the depth of his heart in trying to understand the differences in style, tone, and thought that are exhibited in Isaiah II (a term I shall use for convenience in referring to chaps. 40–66). Yet our prophet, whether pronouncing weal or woe, was ready to proclaim the message. His trusting "Here am I. Send me!" (6:8) is here matched by "What shall I call out?" (40:6).

Section 1, chapters 40–48. Isaiah II falls into three sections of nine chapters each. The first (chaps. 40–48) announces release from captivity and the preparations made to effect it, along with the name of Yahweh's agent of redemption (Cyrus). Engaging in a polemic with idol worshipers, the prophet establishes the indisputable sovereignty of Israel's God, who could predict the future and bring it to pass.

Section 2, chapters 49–57. In this second section Cyrus and his conquest of

---

56. Although we may surmise that the Chronicler had in mind chapters 36–39, there is nothing in the book that could qualify as a monograph on Uzziah's reign. Most likely he knew of these two separate works.

57. But see Kissane, 1:395, who takes the opposite view on the Kings literary method, but is less convincing.

58. John H. Walton, "Positive Redaction Criticism and the Date of Isaiah."

Babylon fades as the Servant of the Lord occupies center stage. Already introduced in 42:1–4, He is now seen to be the real Savior of Israel. Moreover, the abuse that the nation had heaped upon Yahweh through her history is heaped upon the Servant, but He meekly bears Israel's sins.

Section 3, chapters 58–66. Isaiah in the third section is absorbed by the thought of Zion restored. He is concerned for the proper removal of evil among the people in order to prepare for the glorious restoration that will extend beyond Israel to the nations.

The geometric lines. Very early in this last half of the book the Exile comes clearly in view. Yet the description in the opening chapters of Isaiah II of the tragedy that Judah has suffered is clarified only in light of the closing chapter of Isaiah I, until we have the unmistakable identity of the place of the Exile as Babylon in 43:14. Whereas in chapter 39 the emphasis falls upon captivity, here it is upon the return rather than expatriation. Hezekiah, shortsighted and insensitive to the future, had rejoiced that exile would not occur in his day (39:8), so it remained for the prophet to take up the cause of the unborn generation.

Yet the agent of deliverance remains a bit ambiguous. The Lord stirred up "one from the east" (41:2) with prospects of terrible and rapid conquest. Although the agent went unnamed, the Prime Mover cannot be mistaken— Yahweh was the power who moved the conqueror: "I, the Lord, am the first, and with the last. I am He" (41:4). Nor should Israel tremble like the nations at the conqueror's appearance, for Yahweh will help him and uphold him by His victorious right hand (41:10, 13–14). The "one from the north" (41:25) was likely the same conqueror of kingdoms as the one from the east, but his identity was still unclear. Even his mission was indistinct, although his motive of conquest was unmistakable. The identity of the deliverer is finally revealed in 44:28 and 45:1 as Cyrus.[59] Styled as a second Moses, he is called the Lord's "shepherd" (44:28) whose task is to set the captives free (45:13). The Lord will go before him as He went before Moses (45:1–2; Ex. 23:23; 32:34), and will give him the treasures of Babylon just as He gave Israel the treasures of Egypt (45:3; Ex. 3:22; 11:2; 12:35–36).[60]

Is he the one Isaiah wanted to declare as Israel's Redeemer? Isaiah leads his audience along as if Cyrus may be that Moses-like prophet for whom Israel had long been looking (Deut. 18:15–22). He is called the Lord's "anointed," a title used for kings and priests in Israel and given to the Messiah who would combine both offices, reigning as "a priest on His throne" (Zech. 6:13). But as important to the divine plan as Cyrus was, he was hardly more than a precursor of Israel's true Redeemer whose portrait (52:13–53:12) is a striking contrast to Cyrus. Introduced by a poem celebrating Cyrus's accomplishments and the redemption of and return to Zion (52:7–12), the portrait of the Suffering Servant is thrown into sharp relief. The Lord goes before Israel as He has promised Cyrus He would go before him (52:12). With that introduction, the Suffering Servant is presented as the real Hero of redemption, bearing Israel's sin (53:6) and even making Himself an offering for sin (53:10).

Cyrus played another intriguing role in the prophecies. The sovereign Lord of Israel, proclaimed supreme throughout the book, laid the plans for and executed the second exodus not merely through a Moses-like agent. In fact, He allowed all the odds to stack up against Him, using not an Israelite believer, but a pagan king to accomplish His work. If there had ever been any question about Yahweh's sovereignty, there should be none left when He performed His newest miracle, employing a pagan for redemption rather than for the usual sordid task of punishment, which at other times was assigned to the pagan Assyrians and Babylonians.

Isaiah's theological geometry draws two lines from the Exile to the great Redeemer. The first we have already delineated as Cyrus. The second is the Servant, entrusted with light, covenant, and a prophetic word for the world (42:6, 9). He constitutes the countertheme that runs alongside the unfolding identity of the political liberator. In a sense, Cyrus, pagan king and conqueror, liberator and rebuilder of Jerusalem, represents the royal face on the coin, whereas the Servant symbolizes the humbler offices in Israel. In 42:1–4 he executes the office of judge and establishes justice, in 49:1–6 he assumes the prophetic office and returns Israel to the Lord, and in 50:4–11 he is the faithful teacher who sustains the weary. Finally, in 52:13–53:12 he becomes the priest who intercedes for Israel and offers Himself as a sacrifice for them. Again Isaiah runs the risk of misidentification until the Servant is finally identified as the Redeemer of Israel in the last Servant Song. The two geometric lines meet in the Suffering Servant. The one is a Gentile who will call on the Lord's name (41:25), and the other is an Israelite who suffers for Israel without a word (53:7). Thus the universalism of Isaiah is in part justified along these two lines until they meet in the Savior of the World (52:15; 53:8).

Once Isaiah has dealt fully with the return from Babylonian captivity on one level, effected by Yahweh's shepherd, Cyrus, and the higher salvation of Israel on another level, proceeding from the Suffering Servant, the prophecy intertwines concerns of the political and spiritual kingdoms in chapters 56–66. The closing section (66:5–24) corresponds to those eschatological capstones that concluded other sections of the book (chaps. 12, 24–27, 34–35).

Authorship. For about two centuries OT critics have questioned the Isaianic authenticity of chapters 40–66. Appeal has been made to 2 Chronicles 36:22–23, which attributes the prophecy of Cyrus to Jeremiah rather than Isaiah. Bernard

Duhm in 1892 brought Isaiah studies to a plateau with his commentary that designated chapters 40–55 as Deutero-Isaiah ("Second" Isaiah), written about 540 B.C., and chapters 56–66 as Trito-Isaiah ("Third" Isaiah), composed just prior to Nehemiah's time. That position in some modified form has virtually dominated Isaiah studies since the end of the nineteenth century.[61] Torrey in his 1928 study and translation proposed the unity of chapters 40–66 and added chapters 34–35 to them, resorting to emendation to explain the mention of Cyrus in 44:28 and 45:1 as well as the references to Babylon. He believed the prophecy addresses Israel as God's chosen people to save the world, and he assigned it to a late fifth-century author in Palestine.[62]

The trend in recent scholarship has been to follow the suggestion of Mowinckel that the book should be regarded as the work of Isaiah's disciples.[63] R. E. Clements even attempts to shift the discussion from a unity based on authorship to a unity based upon theme. Taking the Babylon prophecies as a "commentary on Judah's fortunes" in relation to Babylon over a period of two centuries, that model becomes a microcosm of the entire book.[64] Two forms of that hypothesis are identifiable today. The one, which Clements represents, views the book as a composite of oracles, poems, and so forth, composed by Isaiah and a school of disciples that followed his teachings. The other views the book as a collection of Isaianic materials that was preserved and edited by Isaiah's disciples.[65] We must recognize, however, the hypothetical nature of that argument. There is little evidence outside of Isaiah 8:16 for prophetic schools that popularized the teachings of their masters, with one exception of the non-writing prophets and court prophets.

In defense of the unity of chapters 40–66, S. R. Driver's work is probably representative, citing evidence in two broad categories: language and style, and theology and thought.[66] In more recent studies arguments based on vocabulary and style are often viewed with less confidence. For example, commenting on chapters 40–55, John L. McKenzie states, "The vocabulary alone is not decisive. Nor is the style alone any more decisive. What is decisive—for chapters xl–lxvi as a whole . . . is that the work moves in a different world of discourse from that of First Isaiah."[67]

In one sense, McKenzie is right; but the crucial question is why that is so. Does the writer speak from the Neo-Assyrian or the Neo-Babylonian context?

---

61. For a history of criticism see R. K. Harrison, *Introduction to the Old Testament*, pp. 765–74; Young, *Studies in Isaiah*, pp. 9–101.
62. Torrey, pp. 40–54.
63. Sigmund Mowinckel, *Jesaja-disiplene. Profeten fra Jesaja til Jeremia.*
64. R. E. Clements, "The Unity of the Book of Isaiah," pp. 117–29, esp. p. 120.
65. See W. S. LaSor, D. A. Hubbard, and F. W. Bush, *Old Testament Survey*, pp. 371–78. These authors waffle between these two positions.
66. S. R. Driver, *Isaiah: His Life and Times*, pp. 192–212.
67. John L. McKenzie, *Second Isaiah*, p. xvi.

Most will agree that he does speak about the Babylonian Exile and return. Yet to claim a completely different world of discourse is hardly accurate. In fact, the religious conditions described in Isaiah II are precisely those of the historical Isaiah's time. The low profile of the righteous (57:1; 59:2–8), profanation of the Sabbath (58:13; compare Amos 8:5), pagan cultic rites (57:4–10; 66:17),[68] and the practice of idolatry (40:18–20; 41:21–24; 44:9–17; 45:16, 20; 46:5–7; 57:13) characterized the eighth and early seventh centuries. In the case of the last item, the Exile seemed to have cured Israel of idolatry. It would then be surprising to find that it was such a troublesome problem in the Exile and the post-exilic period. Further, Isaiah's concern for the disadvantaged (41:17; 57:1–10; 58:7; 59:2–8, 14; 61:1–3), the call to repentance (44:22; 45:22; 55:6–7; 56:1), and the operation of the Jerusalem Temple and sacrificial system (43:23–24, 28; 55:6–7; 58:2; 66:3) point to an eighth- or early seventh-century date. The Neo-Assyrian world is certainly in evidence in these twenty-seven chapters.

That, of course, is not to deny that there is ample evidence of the Neo-Babylonian age also (between 605 and 539 B.C.). The Exile itself is the best evidence (43:14; 44:28; 46:1; 47:1, 6; 48:14. 20–22; 52:2–5). The mention of Cyrus's name further projects the reader into the end of the Neo-Babylonian era. The material, therefore, may go either way. The case is not as clean as it is made out to be.

Conservative defenses of Isaianic authorship have been ample and erudite,[69] in no way deserving James Muilenburg's comment that such attempts have "led to the most tortuous kind of reasoning and are at variance with the whole nature of Hebrew prophecy where the oracles, however predictive in character, are always related to the concerns and issues of the time in which the prophet is living."[70] In fact, few conservatives would disagree with the nature of prophecy as he has defined it. However, the assumption that prediction was not endemic to the nature of Hebrew prophecy is absolutely wrong. Prediction was a major characteristic of prophecy, from the earliest times of the classical prophets (Amos 3:7) to the New Testament era. If the predictive element is removed from Isaiah II, especially chapters 40–48 where lies the crux of the problem for critics, the prophecy collapses. The polemic against idolatry that Isaiah carries through those nine chapters capitalizes on Yahweh's ability to predict the future as over against the idols that cannot even speak, much less

---

68. Child sacrifice was practiced by Manasseh (2 Kings 21:6). See Kissane, 2:xlvi–lv, for an excellent discussion of the social and religious conditions in the eighth century as reflected in Isaiah 40–66.
69. Joseph Addison Alexander, *Earlier Prophecies of Isaiah,* and *Later Prophecies of Isaiah;* Kissane; O. T. Allis, *The Unity of Isaiah;* Young, *Studies in Isaiah;* Rachel Margalioth, *The Indivisible Isaiah: Evidence for the Single Authorship of the Prophetic Book;* Harrison, pp. 764–800; Gleason L. Archer, Jr., *A Survey of Old Testament Introduction.*
70. James Muilenburg, "Isaiah 40–66," p. 383.

predict the future. In 41:21–24 Isaiah challenges the idols to declare the things that are coming hereafter if they are really gods (v. 23). In contrast, Yahweh has announced them from the beginning (41:25–29; also 46:10–11). The former things have come to pass, so now He is announcing new things (42:9; 48:6–8). The same challenge is flung at the idols in 44:6–8 to declare "the events that are going to take place" (v. 7). The polemical narrative against idolatry follows that challenge (44:9–20). The Lord's predictive ability again becomes the critical difference between Him and the idols in 45:20–21:

> Who has announced this from of old?
> Who has long since declared it?
> Is it not I, the Lord?
>
> (v. 21*b*)

Indeed, Yahweh had used prediction for apologetic purposes. He had announced things in advance, lest idolators should say their idols did them (48:3–5). The most critical test of Yahweh's predictive ability, however, and thus His self-validation, was calling Cyrus by name (44:28).

> And I will give you the treasures of darkness,
> And hidden wealth of secret places,
> In order that you may know that it is I,
> The Lord, the God of Israel, who calls you by your name.
>
> (45:3)

Calling Cyrus by name was part of the Lord's strategy aimed at convincing him that He was the only God. Whether Josephus correctly reported that Cyrus built the Temple because Isaiah had mentioned his name 210 years before his birth may be a valid question, but Josephus had certainly read the text correctly.[71] The theology of Isaiah II particularly stands or falls on the predictive element. Remove it, and the framework is gone—and so is the sovereignty of Israel's God over mute idols.

The identity of the Servant. Following Duhm's epoch-making study in which he delineated four pieces that he called "Servant Songs," these passages have come to be generally recognized as distinct songs or poems describing a special servant of Yahweh. There is some disagreement over the extent of the songs and whether or not they are intruders in their present contexts or native to their literary habitats. Usually the following delineations are given: (1) 42:1–4; (2) 49:1–6; (3) 50:4–9; (4) 52:13–53:12. Duhm believed they were written by an author different from the author of Isaiah II during the post-exilic period. The servant was an historical person, anonymous in the songs, who became a martyr for his faith.

71. *Antiquities* 11.1a–b.

Five major theories can be identified in the quest for the identity of the servant: (1) an anonymous individual of Isaiah's time; (2) the prophet himself; (3) the collective theory; (4) the mythological; (5) the Messianic.

(1) The anonymous individual theory, first introduced in the modern era by Duhm, with other versions offered by R. Kittel and W. Rudolph,[72] has not found many supporters. Obviously, because the identity of the servant must remain anonymous, that limits the credibility of any hypotheses that might be proposed.

(2) The interpretation that the servant was the prophet himself was known as early as the first century A.D. (Acts 8:34). Most recently it is presented by R. N. Whybray, who proposes that in the first three songs the servant is the prophet, whereas in the last he is Israel.[73] That interpretation will be found in varied forms. The twelfth-century Jewish commentator David Kimchi viewed the servant in songs 2 and 3 as the prophet, but in song 1 as the Messiah, and in the last as Israel.[74]

(3) The collective theory has been rather popular among interpreters. H. Wheeler Robinson, working with the corporate personality idea, which he recognizes to be endemic to biblical thought, proposes a fluidity between the individual and corporate interpretations. Thus the servant could be both the prophet as representative of the nation and the nation in its prophetic role.[75] H. H. Rowley essentially agrees with him but extends its application.[76] Other proposals include the righteous remnant[77] and Israel personified.[78]

(4) The mythological interpretation, set forth by Christopher R. North in his very helpful study of the Servant Songs, draws upon ancient Canaanite mythology and concludes that we have a portrait of the servant that exemplifies truth but is not likely to be true itself. It is a portrait within which a real person could fit, and within which Jesus did find His own mission.[79] His view is not far from the "ideal personality" interpretation.

---

72. See Christopher R. North, *The Suffering Servant in Deutero-Isaiah: An Historical and Critical Study*, p. 3.
73. R. N. Whybray, *Isaiah 40–66*, pp. 135, 150–51, 169.
74. See Kimchi's commentary on Isaiah (Hebrew); also Sheldon H. Blank, *Prophetic Faith in Isaiah*, p. 78.
75. H. Wheeler Robinson, "The Hebrew Conception of Corporate Personality," pp. 49–62.
76. H. H. Rowley, "The Servant Mission," 259–72. Also Driver, pp. 175–78.
77. E.g., H. G. Mitchell, "The Servant of Yahweh in Isa. 40–55," pp. 113–28.
78. Blank, p. 101, proposes that the servant in Song 4 is Israel personified in the manner of Jeremiah. Although a bit different, W. O. E. Oesterley's "ideal personality" may best fit into this category (*Studies in Isaiah XL–LXVI*, pp. 85–104). Perhaps also Lindblom's allegorical interpretation, which is a modification of Israel personified, at least on his view of Song 4. His emphasis, however, is not on "who" but "what." He sees the servant of the last song as signifying Israel in exile. (*The Servant Songs in Deutero-Isaiah, A New Attempt to Solve an Old Problem*, p. 48).
79. North, p. 218.

(5) The Messianic view has had many exponents. The evangelist Philip applied Isaiah 53 to Jesus: "and beginning from this Scripture he preached Jesus to him" (Acts 8:35). Whereas some interpreters have been willing to allow the Messianic as a secondary interpretation (e.g., North), others have insisted that the primary meaning of the servant was the Messiah, and that song 4 was the climax of the portrait. Franz Delitzsch articulates the pyramid model, which allows for some fluidity between Israel and the Messiah but reaches its apex in the Messiah. The idea of "the servant of Jehovah" assumes, to speak figuratively, the form of a pyramid. The base is Israel as a whole; the central section is Israel, not merely Israel according to the flesh, but according to the spirit also; and the apex is the person of the Mediator of salvation springing out of Israel.[80] O.T. Allis in his excellent study on Isaiah has endorsed a similar position,[81] which J. A. Alexander had put forth a century earlier in his commentary.[82]

The explicit nature of the Cyrus prophecies falls into direct contrast to the inexplicit nature of the Servant passages. As indicated above, they form two geometric lines in Isaiah's future expectancy, converging in the Suffering Servant of song 4. Both lie in the distant future, one more distant than the other. And as Isaiah was projected by the Holy Spirit into the exilic age to comfort the exiles and assure them that Cyrus would set them free, he simultaneously gave them hope on a different plane, that of forgiveness of sins purchased by the death of One who would suffer in their behalf, quite a contrast to the political redemption that Cyrus gained by military conquest. The Israelites could easily conceive of military conquest, even though freedom given by a king who did not know Yahweh might stretch the imagination. But that an innocent Israelite (not an animal sacrifice!) should atone for their sins by suffering and death (53:8) and rise to life again (53:10b, 11) was as inconceivable as a virgin having a child. As indicated in our discussion of the Immanuel prophecy, the more immediate fulfillment of the Maher-shalal-hash-baz prophecy (8:1–3) boosted confidence in the reliability of the remote prophecy of Immanuel. Seeing Isaiah's prediction of Cyrus fulfilled before their eyes, the exiles might have believed anything the prophet foretold, regardless of how spectacular or inconsonant with reality. The Cyrus prophecy, so explicit, as over against the inexplicit Servant prophecies, likely served the same function for the exilic community that the prophecy of Isaiah's son served for the people of Ahaz's day. Perhaps that would help to explain the strong Messianic hope that we find in the post-exilic prophecy of Zechariah. Not only did Cyrus restore the exiles to their home, but he indirectly renewed messianic hope in Israel.

80. Delitzsch, 2:174.
81. Allis, pp. 81–101.
82. Alexander, *The Later Prophecies of Isaiah*, p. 50.

Isaiah's Theology

The rich diversity of Isaiah's theology is impossible to summarize in a few pages. Yet, at the risk of oversimplification, some benefit may be found in looking for the prominent outline of his thought.

Two Encompassing Ideas

In good editorial style, Isaiah has given us the encompassing ideas in the beginning of the book. Their condensed form is found in the two phrases "My people" and the "the Holy One of Israel" (1:3-4). The first term is the stamp of the Lord's claim upon Israel, implying Israel's covenant relation to Him,[83] whereas the second term emphasizes Yahweh's distinctiveness and sets Him apart from Israel.[84] In fact, Isaiah stressed the sin and rebellion of the nation, placing it in the context of the holiness of Yahweh. "My people" means that Israel could never be "free" to go her own way. There was no world big enough in which she could lose herself to the watchful care of her God, whether by her own rebellious behavior or the militancy of a pagan nation. The covenant, a concept basic to prophetic theology, had the divine pronoun "My" as its vanguard. In that pronoun was contained election and providence.

The phrase "the Holy One of Israel" marks the high and sublime God who stood above the nation and required justice and righteousness of His people. He is the God whom the seraphim declared holy (6:3), the sight of whom brought Isaiah an excruciating consciousness of his and his people's sinfulness. That experience, which formed the center of the first literary section, like the Damascus road where a later hero of faith was condemned and forgiven, left its mark upon Isaiah's theology. Living under the pronominal claim of this God was no easy task. Its demands were ethical and could not be thrown off even by the scrupulous exercise of religious ritual (1:10-17). The ethical center of Isaiah's theology, that place where the holy God and a sinful people came to terms, was expressed in the memorable words, "Here is rest, give rest to the weary"; and the prophet's painful realism would not let him forget that "they would not listen" (28:12). His political philosophy was closely tied to his theology. It required returning to Yahweh and trusting in Him rather than foreign alliances (30:15). It is significant that in the first half of the book the Holy One of Israel is set over against Israel's spiritual rebellion and sinful condition (except 10:20;

---

83. The term "my people" (*'amî*) is applied twenty-two times to Israel and once to Egypt: 1:3; 3:12, 15; 5:13; 10:2, 24; 19:25 (Egypt), 22:4; 26:20; 32:13, 18; 40:1; 43:20; 47:6; 51:4, 16; 52:4, 5, 6; 53:8; 57:14; 63:8; 65:22.
84. "The Holy One of Israel" occurs nineteen times as an epithet for Yahweh: 1:4; 5:19, 24; 10:20; 12:6; 17:7; 30:11, 12, 15; 31:1; 37:23; 41:14; 43:3, 14; 45:11; 47:4; 48:17; 54:5; 60:14. Several variants also occur: "the Holy One of Jacob" (29:23), "his Holy One" (10:17; 49:7), "Holy One" (40:25; 57:15), "the Holy God" (5:16), and "the Lord your Holy One" (43:15).

12:6; 17:7; 29:23), but in the last half that name is expressly identified with Israel's "Redeemer" or His saving acts.

THE MEANS OF RECONCILIATION

When the holy God and a sinful nation stand apart, what is the means of reconciliation? In Isaiah we see three personal lines of redemption, all appointed by the Lord: the prophet, Cyrus, and the Messiah. Even though he identified with Israel's sinful condition, Isaiah became an example of obedience in contrast to Israel's disobedience (compare 6:8 with 1:19; 28:12; 30:15). On his kind the people leveled their insults, aimed ultimately against the Holy One of Israel,

> For this is a rebellious people, false sons,
> Sons who refuse to listen
> To the instruction of the Lord;
> Who say to the seers, "You must not see visions";
> And to the prophets, "You must
>   not prophesy to us what is right,
> Speak to us pleasant words,
> Prophesy illusions.
> Get out of the way, turn aside from the path,
> Let us hear no more about the Holy One of Israel."
> (30:9–11)

Isaiah's heart was quickly moved for Israel. He prayed for her (2:6–9, 22; 33:2–4), and we have already observed that he was also moved to compassion over the ill destiny of the nations (15:5; 16:9–11; 21:3–4). So when his message turns largely to comfort in the last twenty-seven chapters, we see this prophet at his best. In hope and promise of redemption his literary method and style were shaped to form.

Cyrus, as observed earlier, was Israel's political deliverer, and his success in returning the exiles home was the result of Yahweh's sovereign action in the world.

The Messiah in this prophecy is the centerpiece of redemption. At times we can see only the era in which He brings about God's will, whereas in other instances we get a revealing glimpse of His Person. The age of peace and justice, introduced as early as 2:2–4, is an earmark of Isaiah's future age. Described in various places in the book, that day will be known by the supremacy and purification of Zion, along with renewal of the covenant with its ancient symbols of the Lord's presence, "a cloud by day . . . and the brightness of a flaming fire by night" (4:2–6). Not until 7:14 does the person of the Messiah come into our view, but His identity remains even then inconclusive, except for the fact that He symbolizes God's presence with Israel. If Immanuel was not, as we have suggested, a contemporary of Isaiah, then He was not just typical. His birth must be identified in the future age.

Whereas the sign of Immanuel was given as assurance of Yahweh's presence in a time of war, the figure in chapter 9, a prince of David's lineage, has come as the establisher of peace. The Davidic descent is again evident in chapter 11, where the Messiah is seen to be capable of discerning the inner character of individuals. At last the perfect judge has arrived on the scene to establish equitably the kingdom of justice and righteousness that has earlier caught our attention in the Messianic portraiture. The kingdom of peace will be so effective that the enmity between wild and domestic beasts, and between man and beast, will be removed.

The thread weaves its way to the portrait of the Servant in 42:1–4. The Lord's Spirit that endowed the descendant of David (11:2) also empowers the Servant, whose mission, like that described in chapter 11, is the establishment of justice. Moreover, the nations that had resorted to the "root of Jesse" (11:10) now wait eagerly for the Servant's law (42:4) and receive the light radiated by redeemed Israel (49:6). The Lord had formed Him in the womb (cf. 7:14) to bring Israel back to Him and to transmit His salvation to the earth's extremities.

That mission, which the prophet had announced but not accomplished, and whose way for future development Cyrus had paved, was uniquely effected by the obedient suffering of the Servant (50:5–6). But not until the fourth Servant song do we know that His suffering was not due to His own sin but to that of Israel (53:5–6, 9). Finally, tying all the threads together, the future era that Isaiah had predicted and the Servant who had suffered to establish it are united (61:1–11). The Servant (although not mentioned by the name, He has all the marks of the Servant) comes announcing the good news that the day of liberation has arrived. Cyrus only foreshadowed the liberty that the real Servant proclaimed and actualized. The real triumph was not to Assyria or Babylon or Cyrus, but to the Lord's Servant.

OUTLINE OF ISAIAH

I. Oracles of Judgment and Hope (1:1–12:6)
   A. Judah Condemned (1:1–5:30)
      1. Oracles Concerning Coming Devastation (1:1–23)
      2. Oracle of Hope (1:24–31)
      3. Oracles Concerning Judah and Jerusalem (2:1–4:6)
         a. The Future Kingdom of Judah (2:1–4)
         b. Judah's Corruption and Judgment (2:5–4:1)
         c. Judah's Future Glory (4:2–6)

    4. Song of the Vineyard (5:1–7)
    5. Oracles of Woe Against the Wicked (5:8–30)
  B. Isaiah's Call and Commission (6:1–13)
  C. The Book of Immanuel (7:1–12:6)
    1. The Sign of Immanuel and Its Implications (7:1–25)
    2. The Assyrian Invader (8:1–9:7)
    3. Prophecy Against Israel (9:8–10:4)
    4. The Power of Assyria and the Power of Yahweh (10:5–34)
    5. The Righteous Ruler (11:1–5)
    6. The Kingdom of the Righteous Ruler (11:6–12:6)
II. Oracles Against the Nations (13:1–23:18)
  A. Against Babylon (13:1–14:23)
  B. Against Assyria (14:24–27)
  C. Against Philistia (14:28–32)
  D. Against Moab (15:1–16:14)
  E. Against Syria and Israel (17:1–14)
  F. Against Ethiopia (18:1–7)
  G. Against Egypt (19:1–25)
  H. Against Ethiopia and Egypt (20:1–6)
  I. Against Babylon (21:1–10)
  J. Against Edom (21:11–12)
  K. Against Arabia (21:13–17)
  L. Against Jerusalem (22:1–14)
  M. Against Shebna (22:15–25)
  N. Against Tyre (23:1–18)
III. Eschatological Summation (24:1–27:13)
  A. Eschatological Judgments (24:1–23)
  B. Eschatological Triumphs (25:1–12)
  C. The Eschatological City (26:1–21)
  D. The Eschatological Israel (27:1–13)
IV. Jerusalem, Egypt, and a Prophet in Between (28:1–33:24)
  A. Woe to the Drunkards of Ephraim (28:1–29)
  B. Woe to Ariel (29:1–24)
  C. Woe to Those Who Seek a Pact with Egypt (30:1–33)
  D. Woe to Those Who Rely on Egypt (31:1–32:20)
  E. Woe to the Destroyer Not Destroyed (33:1–24)
V. Eschatological Summation (34:1–35:10)
  A. Summation of Judgment (34:1–17)
  B. Summation of Blessings (35:1–10)
VI. Historical Bridge (36:1–39:8)
  A. Hezekiah and Sennacherib (36:1–37:38)
  B. Hezekiah's Illness and Recovery (38:1–22)
  C. Hezekiah's Misplaced Joy over Postponed Judgment (39:1–8)

VII. Oracles of Consolation (40:1–66:24)
- A. Release from Captivity (40:1–48:22)
  1. Promise of Restoration (40:1–31)
  2. The Liberator (41:1–29)
  3. God's Righteous Servant (42:1–25)
  4. Israel as God's Servant (43:1–44:23)
  5. Cyrus as God's Servant (44:24–45:25)
  6. Judgment on Babylon (46:1–47:15)
  7. The Deliverance of Judah (48:1–22)
- B. The Servant of the Lord (49:1–57:21)
  1. The Servant's Commission (49:1–26)
  2. The Servant's Faithfulness (50:1–11)
  3. Restoration of Zion (51:1–52:12)
  4. The Servant's Suffering and Triumph (52:13–53:12)
  5. Restoration Assured (54:1–55:13)
  6. Blessings to All Who Are Righteous (56:1–8)
  7. Rebuke of the Unrighteous (56:9–57:21)
- C. Zion Restored (58:1–66:24)
  1. Worship Without Righteousness (58:1–14)
  2. Judah's Sin (59:1–21)
  3. The Glory of Restored Jerusalem (60:1–22)
  4. The Servant's Ministry to Israel (61:1–11)
  5. The Restoration of Zion (62:1–12)
  6. The Judgment on God's Enemies (63:1–6)
  7. The Confidence of God's People (63:7–64:12)
  8. The Repentance of Sin (65:1–25)
  9. Condemnation of the Hypocrites (66:1–4)
  10. Rejoicing in Salvation (66:5–24)

THE PROPHETS OF THE NEO-BABYLONIAN PERIOD

ZEPHANIAH
HABAKKUK
JEREMIAH
NAHUM
EZEKIEL
OBADIAH
LAMENTATIONS

THE NEO-BABYLONIAN PERIOD AND THE PROPHETS[1]

ANY HOPE FOR Judah's well-being and security that was created by Hezekiah's religious piety and anti-Assyrian policy was dashed by Manasseh's about-face on both counts. When this rebel son of Hezekiah ended his reign (686–642 B.C.), the fortunes of the Assyrian Empire were also changing. The Chaldeans had been a formidable force in Babylonian culture for two centuries. During the last quarter of the eighth century they gained political dominance in Babylon for a decade in the person of Merodach-baladan II (721–710) and later for nine months in 703. In that year he dispatched an embassy to Jerusalem to congratulate Hezekiah upon his return to health, and very likely to test the waters for a possible anti-Assyrian alliance (Isa. 39/2 Kings 20:12–19). Merodach-baladan's resurgence, however, did not last long enough to make a difference in the political balance. But this assertion of Chaldean influence was a harbinger of the Chaldean dynasty that came into being three-quarters of a century later. When the Assyrian-appointed governor of Babylon, Kandalanu, died in 626, a Chaldean usurper, Nabopolassar, seized the throne. Although Assyria continued to be a fairly effective power for two decades longer, eventually the Chaldeans and the Medes brought the weakening government to its knees with the fall of Asshur in 614 and the toppling of Nineveh in 612. Nahum celebrated the latter event in his unforgettable poetic imagery.

With Assyria dead or dying, control of Palestine hung in the balances with hopeful Egypt to the southwest and aspiring Babylonia to the east. In 609 Pharaoh Necho launched a campaign to the northeast, perhaps to offer consolation and military assistance to the few Assyrians still holding out at Harran. When Josiah tried to head off this campaign at Megiddo, he lost his life, and with it went the hope of Judah's independence. Necho proceeded to remove Josiah's successor, Jehoahaz, from the throne and elevate his own choice, Jehoiakim (609–598).

While Jeremiah became a prophet in the year 628/27, Jehoiakim's reign raised this prophet's profile to a new level of visibility. Jeremiah was no friend

---

1. See pp. 192–95 for further discussion of the Neo-Babylonian period.

of Jehoiakim, and it was a mutual adversarial relationship, for Jehoiakim was certainly no friend of Jeremiah's.

As the Neo-Babylonian consolidation took shape, Habakkuk read the headlines and addressed the theological issue of God's justice that would select a pagan nation like Babylonia to mete out punishment to God's people, rebellious and sinful though they be.

As Babylonia's star was rising, Pharaoh Necho's plummeted toward the decisive Battle of Carchemish on the Euphrates River in 605 B.C. There Nebuchadnezzar dealt the Egyptians a reeling blow. Within months his father, Nabopolassar, was dead, and he was king. The fortunes of Judah continued their downward slide under the Chaldean domination of this aggressive king (605–562 B.C.). At some point in his father's last days, Nebuchadnezzar's army raided Jerusalem and took Daniel and his three loyal friends into captivity, along with other members of the royal court of Judah. Daniel's long life in Babylon extended into the early years of the Persian period, and his visions of the rise and fall of kingdoms were not without foundation in his personal experience.

The prophets line up along the sides of Nebuchadnezzar's reign. When he besieged Jerusalem in 597, Jeremiah's voice was still strong, and the prophet's ministry continued well beyond the fall of Jerusalem to the Babylonians in 586. The fateful Babylonian siege of Jerusalem in 598/97 ended in exiling the Judean king, Jehoiachin. Among the 3,023 Jews exiled at that time (Jer. 52:28) was a young man whose destiny, by genealogy aimed toward the priesthood, was diverted to prophetic pursuits on Babylonian soil. Ezekiel began his prophetic career in 593 and was active at least until 571. Joining Jeremiah and Ezekiel was Obadiah whose sensitivities could not let the Edomite plunder of Jerusalem in the wake of her fall pass without prophetic comment. As in the Neo-Assyrian period, so in the Neo-Babylonian, the prophets were present to offer warning, rebuke, and hope.

7

ZEPHANIAH: PROFILE OF A PEOPLE

THE LONG REIGN of Hezekiah's wicked son Manasseh (687/86–642/41 B.C.) reversed whatever good Hezekiah was able to accomplish. Manasseh's pro-Assyrian politics may have been a survival game, but in the mind of the prophets one did not play that game. There was only one way to survival, and that was to entrust the life and destiny of the nation to God. In our historical sources for Manasseh's period (2 Kings 21:1–18; 2 Chron. 33:1–20) we have information, however slight it is, that the prophetic voice was not silent (2 Kings 21:10–15; 2 Chron. 33:10), even though extensive preaching like that of the eighth-century prophets had subsided. Of interest is the fact that few or no prophetic oracles survived the reign of Manasseh in the collections that achieved canonical status. Perhaps that in itself is a silent witness to the religious suppression that characterized his reign.

The Chronicler gives the peculiar account of Manasseh's exile to Babylon and his subsequent restoration (2 Chron. 33:10–13), a bit of history whose authenticity some scholars write off as theological embellishment.[1] That train of events became the impetus for the converted king to institute a religious reform in a land that had, by his own corrupt management, become for the time being incorrigible. The Chronicler plaintively observes, "Nevertheless the people still sacrificed at the high places, although only to the Lord their God" (33:17). That confusion of pagan and Yahweh worship is reflected in Zephanaiah 1:4–5 (italics added):

> And I will cut off the remnant of Baal
> from this place,
> And the names of the idolatrous priests
> along with the priests.
> And those who bow down on the
> housetops to the host of heaven,
> And those who bow down and swear
> to the Lord and yet swear by Milcom.[2]

---

1. This temporary exile of Manasseh could have occurred during the rebellion of Babylonia under Asshurbanapal's brother, Shamash-shum-ukin, between 652 and 648. Cf. John Bright, *Jeremiah*, p. xxxv.
2. The Hebrew text has "their king" (*malkām*), but the Versions (LXX, Vulgate, Syriac) read *Milkom* (the same consonants), the name of the Ammonite god. This textual variant is preferable to the Masoretic reading because of the context, which deals with pagan worship.

The author of Kings informs us that Manasseh erected altars for Baal and worshiped "the host of heaven" (2 Kings 21:3, 5). By the time Amon (642/41–640/39) succeeded his father to the throne, Judah was entrenched in idolatry and pagan religious ritual. Take the spirit of a people whose affinities had been with idolatry for time immemorial, add that to the policies of a king who indulged pagan religious tastes, and the result is almost intractable.

PROFILE OF THE PROPHET

The information in Zephaniah's personal profile is minimal. His name means "The Lord has hidden." His genealogy of four generations (1:1) seems to signal something of importance, for he is the only prophet to trace his lineage back that far. The rabbinic commentators Ibn Ezra and David Kimchi believed that *Hizkiyyah* ("Hezekiah") in the list was King Hezekiah. Some Christian scholars have followed that opinion. C. F. Keil, for example, avoids the problem that he is not directly called "king" by taking "king of Judah" at the end of the verse, obviously applied to Josiah, to apply also to Hezekiah.[3] Gleason L. Archer insists that the four generations do not fit comfortably in the time frame,[4] whereas S. M. Lehrman defends the royal descent by appealing to early marriage, which was common in the ancient Near East.[5] Others argue that the prophet's familiarity with the royal court (1:8–9) favors his royal ancestry, but that is not decisive. However appealing the identification of *Hizkiyyah* with King Hezekiah, it cannot be substantiated. Yet being the last named in the list, we surmise that he was a very important man.

The book gives no explicit information about the place of the prophet's residence. However, judging from his familiarity with Jerusalem (1:10–11), he most probably delivered the prophecies in the capital city, even though we cannot be sure he hailed from there.

PROFILE OF A PEOPLE

Whereas the prophet's profile is indistinct, his profile of the people of Judah is marked by perceptive familiarity. Zephaniah's reading of the popular religious attitude includes an awareness of those people whose hearts were stagnant, and who thought that Yahweh was stagnant too, uninvolved in Judah. They concluded, "The Lord will not do good or evil!" (1:12). In an oracle against Jerusalem he remarks that divine judgment, rather than bringing the Judeans back to the Lord, merely made them more eager to do their evil deeds (3:6–7). Over against the too few poor of the land who sought the Lord (2:3) were set the "proud, exulting ones" who carried their haughty spirit even to

---

3. C. F. Keil, *The Twelve Minor Prophets*, 2:117.
4. Gleason L. Archer, Jr., *A Survey of Old Testament Introduction*, p. 354, n. 1.
5. S. M. Lehrman, "Zephaniah," p. 231.

the Temple (3:11). They used their servants to take ill-gotten gain by violence and fraud (1:9). Theirs was a shameless nation (2:1; 3:5).

In addition to their deplorable spirit, the popular religion was, as we have already mentioned, a mixture of Yahwistic and pagan elements. The worship of Baal and planetary deities was widespread (1:4–5, 9). To add insult to injury, the functionaries on whom ancient Judean society depended for orderly operation merely fortified an already corrupt system. The officials were roaring lions, the judges evening wolves, the prophets wanton, faithless men, and the priests violators of the Torah (3:3–4). With this character sketch of a people and her leaders, we do not wonder that Zephaniah announced the nearness of the Day of the Lord (1:7, 14).

HISTORICAL OR MORAL OCCASION FOR THE PROPHECY?

Manasseh's pro-assyrian administration had likely been instrumental in saving the country from Assyrian devastation, but it seems to have created many enemies who believed Judah should not just acquiesce to the Assyrians. When his son Amon acceded to the throne, members of his court, perhaps opposed to the pro-Assyrian stance which he also represented, assassinated him, and the "people of the land"[6] elevated his eight-year-old son, Josiah (640/39–608), to the throne (2 Kings 21:19–26). The risk involved in breaking away from Assyria was a serious one, even with internal problems that had harrassed that empire. After Assurbanipal in 648 retook Babylon, which his brother Shamash-shum-ukin had led away from him, he continued his policy of conquest, destroying Elam (c. 640) and reasserting his supremacy in Palestine.[7] It is impossible, with so little information, to determine whether the "people of the land" and the assassins in the royal court were on the same side, pro-Assyrian or anti-Assyrian. However, it was a troubled time in Judah.

THE UNNAMED ENEMY

Zephaniah never mentions by name the foe that would be the agent to punish God's people. One hypothesis favored by some scholars[8] is that when the Scythians invaded Palestine on their way to Egypt, they waged war against

6. The phrase "people of the land" may have been a technical term for the landed gentry, or it may designate the grass-roots population as over against the court officials and royalty. See John Bright, *A History of Israel*, pp. 294–95.
7. Ibid., pp. 292–93.
8. J. M. P. Smith, *A Critical and Exegetical Commentary on Micah, Zephaniah, Nahum, Habakkuk, Obadiah and Joel*, p. 207, proposes that 1:18 ("Neither their silver nor their gold will be able to deliver them") is an echo of the Egyptian bribery to avert the Scythian plunder. See also his *The Prophets and Their Times*, pp. 131–48. G. A. Smith favors the Scythian hypothesis *(The Book of the Twelve Prophets*, pp. 15–17); also Otto Eissfeldt, *The Old Testament: An Introduction*, p. 424.

Jerusalem.[9] There is, however, no evidence to support that view. Other proposals are that the enemy was the Assyrians[10] or the Chaldeans.[11] In view of the outlay of history in the following years, the Chaldeans are the logical identification, because they, along with the Medes, desolated Nineveh in 612 B.C., and in 586 the Chaldeans dealt Jerusalem the reeling blow that ended the Southern Kingdom.

PRE- OR POST-JOSIANIC REFORM?

The majority opinion[12] is that Zephaniah prophesied before Josiah's reform of 621 B.C. (2 Kings 22:1—23:30/2 Chron. 34–35). The grave religious perversion that the reform was designed to reverse was the order of the day (1:4–6; 3:1–2, 4, 7). Keil holds the minority position that the prophecy came after 621. He appeals, as do others, to the "remnant of Baal" in 1:4, inferring that Josiah's reform had begun to stamp out Baalism but had not yet totally succeeded, thus the "remnant."[13] E. B. Pusey makes a helpful comment on that point: "The emphasis seems to be rather on the completeness of the destruction, as we should say, that He would efface every remnant of Baal, than to refer to any effort which had been made by human authority to destroy it."[14]

The evidence for Zephaniah's ministry points to a date before the Josianic reform, perhaps even early in Josiah's reign. The date generally given to harmonize with the Scythian hypothesis is 630–625. Yet it is possible that the preaching of Zephaniah pricked Josiah's conscience and helped to initiate the reform. The Chronicler relates that he began to seek the Lord in the eighth year of his reign, instituted the reform in the twelfth year, and in the eighteenth year the Book of the Law was discovered (c. 632, 628, 622 respectively; 2 Chron. 34:3, 8). If Zephaniah's ministry sparked this king's religious interests, then the period of his activity likely falls between 640 and 632 B.C., at least prior to the beginning of the reform in 628. The latest possible date would of necessity be the fall of Nineveh in 612, because from Zephaniah's perspective that event

---

9. The Scythians came from the area of the Caucasus Mountains, and according to Herodotus (1:103–6) they ruled Asia for twenty-eight years, dominating Media for a time. On their expedition to plunder Egypt when they were bought off by Psammetichus I (c. 630–625 B.C.), some of them plundered the temple of Aphrodite in Ashkelon, but Herodotus does not mention any other Palestinian cities plundered by them. On the contrary, Zephaniah says Jerusalem will be plundered by the unnamed foe (1:13), the fortified cities devastated (1:15–16), and Nineveh destroyed (2:13). None of those things are recorded by Herodotus. See Keil, 2:124.
10. R. K. Harrison, *Introduction to the Old Testament*, p. 941.
11. B. K. Waltke, "Book of Zephaniah," 5:1051–55.
12. E.g., Eissfeldt, p. 424; Ernst Sellin and Georg Fohrer, *Introduction to the Old Testament*, p. 456; Waltke; E. B. Pusey, *The Minor Prophets with a Commentary*, p. 438; G. A. Smith, pp. 41–45; N. K. Gottwald, *All the Kingdoms of the Earth*, p. 219; Harrison, p. 940; John D. W. Watts, *The Books of Joel, Obadiah, Jonah, Nahum, Habakkuk and Zephaniah*, p. 155.
13. Keil, 2:119–20.
14. Pusey, p. 437.

was still in the future (2:13). However, the evidence does not support so late a date as that.

Because the Scythian hypothesis hardly stands on firm historical grounds, the logical occasion for the prophecy, supported by internal evidence, was moral decline. The aftereffect of Manasseh's religious policies could be seen all over the land. Zephaniah may have had much to do with the changes that occurred in Josiah's thinking and quite likely should receive a great deal of credit for the bold and courageous reform that grew out of them.

A date for Zephaniah after the reform has not found many exponents. In view of the literary dependence upon Isaiah, Jeremiah, and especially Ezekiel, Louise Pettibone Smith and Ernest R. Lacheman argue that the book was a pseudepigraph and should be read against the background of 200 B.C.[15] A less radical proposal is made by J. Philip Hyatt, who believes the problem of Nineveh's destruction and other perplexities are removed if the book is dated in the reign of Jehoiakim (608–597 B.C.).[16] Neither of those proposals is convincing.

THE NATURE OF THE LITERATURE

The book is composed of two major sections. The first (1:2–3:8), largely made up of oracles against Judah and foreign nations, is held together by the opening prophecy of universal judgment (1:2–3) and a concluding word of world punishment (3:8). That section (1:2–3:8) is constituted an inclusion by the two prophecies of universal judgment that brace either side of it, and it is intermediately punctuated by the conversion of the Gentiles (2:11). Zephaniah's Day of the Lord is the sum of the judgments against Judah and the various nations:

> Against Judah—1:4–2:3
> Against the Philistines—2:4–7
> Against Moab and Ammon—2:8–11
> Against Ethiopia—2:12
> Against Assyria—2:13–15
> Against Jerusalem and Judah—3:1–7.

Balancing the first part, which broadly describes the judgmental aspect of the Day of the Lord, is the second major section, a collection of promises regarding the salvation of the world and Judah (3:9–20). It begins with the idea that all of the nations shall call on the Lord's name in the eschatological day (3:9). The promises that follow in verses 10–20 deal with Judah's salvation and the resulting esteem that that would earn him among the nations. Thus the book is well balanced between judgment and promise.

---

15. Louise Pettibone Smith and Ernest R. Lacheman, "The Authorship of the Book of Zephaniah," pp. 137–42.
16. J. Philip Hyatt, "The Date and Background of Zephaniah," pp. 25–29.

Critical scholarship has questioned the authenticity of 2:4–15 because the material is a bit difficult to fit into the historical period prior to 621 B.C.[17] Here, however, we should ask whether we ought to look for the appropriate historical conditions or whether the oracles arise out of a broad eschatological plan and interest which Zephaniah represented. My contention is that he has described the Day of the Lord in general terms and broken that judgment down into its constituent parts.[18] The prophecy is of a rather general nature, as Keil has pointed out:

> It is in this comprehensive character of his prophecy that we find the reason why Zephaniah neither names, nor minutely describes, the executors of the judgment upon Judah, . . . He does not predict either this or that particular judgment, but extends and completes in comprehensive generality the judgment, by which God maintains His kingdom on the earth.[19]

Pusey takes cognizance of the same characteristic by his remark that Zephaniah's prophecy was "more than those of most other prophets, apart from time, to the end of time. He prophesies of *what* shall be, not *when* it shall be, nor *by whom*."[20] Even at this stage of modern prophetic studies, much remains to be understood about the prophets' eschatology. The predictive nature of 2:4–15 poses a problem for some critical scholars. The fall of Nineveh, for example, is clearly forecast (2:13). Yet Zephaniah's political insight imbued with the Spirit of Yahweh brought the vision of Nineveh's end into his eschatological program. Any nation opposed to Israel's God was slated for judgment, especially a nation that had so blatantly defied Yahweh's people and His sovereign rule of the world.

A second passage that is often attributed to post-exilic authorship is 3:18–20 (or vv. 14–20), which uses the language of return from exile.[21] The terms of 3:19 ("the lame" and "the outcast") appear also in Micah 4:6–7, where they describe the returning exiles, even though that passage is also under post-exilic suspicion. What we are dealing with here is a whole set of presuppositions espoused by critical scholarship, which not only disavows a strongly predictive element in the prophets, but also confidently sorts the material on the basis of vocabulary that is thought to be confined to specific periods. Indeed that is the case with these terms. It cannot be proved that this language belonged to the post-exilic era. On the contrary, it was part of the prophetic language of future expectation. Zephaniah had a rich prophetic tradition behind him, and he drew liberally from it.[22]

---

17. Sellin and Fohrer find only nine genuine sayings: 1:4–5, 7–9, 12–13, 14–16; 2:1–3, 4, 13–14; 3:6–8, 11–13 (pp. 456–57), whereas Eissfeldt considers most of the book genuine (p. 424).
18. C. Hassell Bullock, "Entree to the Prophets Through the Pentateuch," pp. 60–77.
19. Keil, 2:123.
20. Pusey, p. 441.
21. See Brevard S. Childs, *Introduction to the Old Testament as Scripture*, p. 461.
22. See Pusey, pp. 441–43, for an excellent and germinal discussion of Zephaniah's use of his prophetic predecessors' language.

In its present form the book could very well have come into being during the reformatory years of Josiah's reign. Zephaniah's ministry did not likely continue as late as the fall of Nineveh, for there is no evidence that he took notice of the event. However, the compilation of his prophecies could have emanated from the spiritual impact Nineveh's fall had on Judah. The book was perhaps edited by the prophet himself or one of his devotees. Yet it is not absolutely necessary to assume such a lapse of time between delivery and writing. The language of waiting, which Isaiah and Habakkuk also used in anticipation of fulfillment, occurs in 3:8 (compare Isa. 8:17; Hab. 2:3):

> "Therefore, wait for Me," declares the Lord,
> "For the day when I rise up to the prey.
> Indeed, My decision is to gather nations,
> To assemble kingdoms,
> To pour out on them My indignation,
> All My burning anger;
> For all the earth will be devoured
> By the fire of My zeal.

The fulfillment of events that the prophets had predicted vindicated them in the eyes of their compatriots. Thus waiting was part of the program of prophetic vindication. In Isaiah 8:16–17 the writing down of Isaiah's words and the waiting (for fulfillment) are tied together. In that light it is conceivable that Zephaniah recorded and arranged his own messages.

PURPOSE AND MESSAGE

PURPOSE

We have concluded that the condition that occasioned the prophecies in this book was the moral decay that grew out of the soil of Manasseh's reign. He had reversed the effects of his father's religious reform of the previous century. During his reign the prophetic voice, though not entirely mute, was muffled by the oppressive policies of that wicked king. Toward the end of Asshurbanipal's reign and early in Josiah's rule, again the prophets began to address the spiritual and political affairs of the time. Zephaniah was in the vanguard of that renewal. He stepped forth to announce the nearness of the Day of the Lord and to confer hope on the remnant that still kept Yahweh's commandments (2:3).

MESSAGE

Zephaniah did not explicitly champion the cause of the poor as Amos, Isaiah, and Micah had done. Yet he was keenly aware of injustice (3:3–4), and he was just as acutely conscious of Yahweh's daily dispensation of justice among His people (3:5). It was out of that sense of justice that Zephaniah perceived the sharp lines of the Day of the Lord.

The Day of the Lord. Amos, who had announced the Day of the Lord and described it as "darkness and not light" (Amos 5:18; compare Zeph. 1:15), had removed the silver lining from around that anticipated day thought by the Israelites to be a day of triumph for them and of woe for their enemies. In a related vein, Zephaniah called Judah to silence before the Lord God in deference to the nearness of that awful day (1:7). His glossary of terms for it includes "the day of the Lord's sacrifice" (1:8*a*), "that day" (1:9, 10; 3:11, 16), "that time" (1:12; 3:19), "the great day of the Lord" (1:14), "the day of the Lord's wrath" (1:18), and simply "day of wrath" in 1:15; 2:2 and 3 use a synonym for "wrath" [*af*], "day of trouble and distress," "day of destruction and desolation," "day of darkness and gloom," "day of clouds and thick darkness," and "day of trumpet and battle cry" (1:15–16*a*).

Whether Zephaniah was personally aware of how long it would be until his prophecies of judgment came to pass is impossible to determine. However, the prophets telescoped future events so that in their description of them they appeared close to one another. But when we see them on a time line, we recognize the time lapse that separated them. It was obvious to our prophet that the Day of the Lord was near. In fact, in 1:14 he twice puts the word "near" (*qārôv*) in the front part of the line to emphasize its impending nature. He differs from Amos in that he views the Day of the Lord in broader scope. It included judgment on Judah and the nations. No doubt he saw the gathering events of the time as the initial phase of the terrible day.

Zephaniah's contemporaries, Jeremiah and Habakkuk, both named the agency of destruction that God would use to punish Judah. However, as we have already noted, Zephaniah leaves the foe unnamed. Yet there is no question about the power that moves that foe—it is Yahweh Himself (1:2–4, 8–9, 12, 17; 2:5, 11, 13; 3:6, 8). And just as surely as He was the primary agency of destruction, He was also the One who restored Judah and saved the nations (3:9, 12, 18–20).

Of great importance also is the idea that the Day of the Lord will visit not only judgment on Judah and the nations but also salvation. The conversion of the Gentiles is predicted both in 2:11 and 3:9, whereas Judah's salvation shall come through the remnant (2:7), and the Lord will restore her fortunes (2:7; 3:20). The latter references are probably to the return from exile, but that too became a foundation stone in the prophetic eschatology with implications that reached beyond that point of history into the gospel era.

The inconsistency of grace. There was a gross inconsistency between Yahweh's calling Judah "my people" and their endorsement of pagan idolatry. We have already made this observation in Isaiah, and it bears repeating here: Although Judean society was replete with idolatrous religion and plagued by injustice, the

Lord still claimed them as His people. And it is not insignificant that those terms of ownership and endearment in Zephaniah occur in contexts of judgment. Yahweh's decision of judgment called forth His covenantal commitment of grace. In the oracle against Moab He used both the words *'am* ("people") and *goi* ("nation," 2:8–9), the first normally applied to Judah or Israel, and the second the regular term for a Gentile nation (also occurs in 2:1). Further, the phrases "God of Israel" (2:9) and "the people of the Lord of hosts" (2:10) reinforce the covenantal relationship that undergirded the theology of Zephaniah. From the human point of view, grace is inconsistent with the sin it covers. No merits draw it forth from God's heart—that was certainly clear in Zephaniah's Judah. But from the divine point of view as revealed in OT prophecy, Yahweh's sentence of condemnation often bore also His offer of mercy.

The tenuous thread. Zephaniah calls upon the minority people, whom he names the "humble of the earth" (2:3), to seek the Lord, to seek righteousness and humility:

> Perhaps you will be hidden
> In the day of the Lord's anger.

Repentance was the only way to avert disaster, and it was only the hinge of a door that might or might not swing open. Amos had recognized the tenuous nature of divine mercy (Amos 5:15), tenuous in the sense that there was no guarantee that repentance and mercy were like hand in glove or that one followed the other with mechanical precision. Yet that intangible "perhaps" of God's mercy was far more preferable than the tangible effects of injustice and idolatry, which the society eagerly sought.

OUTLINE OF ZEPHANIAH

I. Universal Judgment (1:1–3:8)
    A. Superscription (1:1)
    B. Universal Judgment (1:2–3)
    C. Oracles Against the Nations (1:4–3:7)
        1. Against Judah (1:4–2:3)
        2. Against Philistia (2:4–7)
        3. Against Moab and Ammon (2:8–11)
        4. Against Ethiopia (2:12)
        5. Against Assyria (2:13–15)
        6. Against Jerusalem and Judah (3:1–7)
    D. Universal Judgment (3:8)
II. Promises of Salvation (3:9–20)
    A. Salvation of the Nations (3:9)
    B. Salvation of Judah (3:10–20)

8

HABAKKUK: PROPHET OF TRANSITION

FROM THE VERY BEGINNING of the classical era of the prophets to the year 626, or possibly as late as 612 B.C., the Assyrian Empire had posed either a viable or a real threat to the tiny kingdoms of Israel and Judah. Perhaps the only writing prophet in that century and a half who did not live in a time of authentic Assyrian menace was Jonah. We have already observed that he prophesied in a period of Assyrian weakness.[1] With Tiglath-pileser's rise to power around 745 a new era dawned in Near Eastern politics and diplomacy. His reign alone, with its greedy seizure of land and power, touched the ministries of four great pre-exilic prophets, Amos, Hosea, Isaiah, and Micah. The prophets of the Assyrian era who followed in their train lived in the frightful shadow of Tiglath-pileser's dynasty and empire. When Josiah's reign began in 641/40 there was probably not a living person who had had any experience of life without Assyria. She was a tyrant of veritable strength and dominion. Her sway over Mesopotamian countries and their western neighbors had held firmly until the middle of the seventh century, when internal problems began to intimate terminal trouble.

Habakkuk was the prophet who concentrated his attention upon the transition from Assyrian to Babylonian domination of Judah. Whether or not he actually referred to Assyria is a question we shall deal with in the discussion below, but there is no question about his anticipation of the rise of the Neo-Babylonian Empire. Led by the Chaldeans, an ethnic group in Babylonia whose advanced culture had long silhouetted an aspiring people, that emerging empire began to take shape with the rise of the Chaldean Nabopolassar to the Babylonian throne in 626 B.C. In that year he defeated the Assyrians at the city of Babylon, thus giving notice of a new day in Near Eastern politics.

Both Isaiah and Micah had foreseen the transition from Assyrian to Babylonian domination (Isa. 39:5–7; Mic. 4:10), but neither had raised the acute theological question of why God should deal with His chosen people through instruments so soiled and devoid of true faith as Assyria and Babylonia. It was a new dimension of prophetic thought. The prophets had spoken to Israel about

1. See pp. 51–52.

Yahweh's demands, but Habakkuk spoke to Yahweh about Judah's dilemma. George Adam Smith has observed, and with some qualification we can agree, that in Habakkuk we find the beginning of speculation in Israel.[2] The qualification is that prophetic speculation seems to have its incipience in Habakkuk, but speculation as an endeavor of wisdom thought was older than that.[3] We should further observe that speculation never became an earmark of the prophets. In the post-exilic era it was assumed to a lesser degree by apocalyptic and to a larger degree by wisdom literature.

Therefore, Habakkuk was a transition prophet in that he focused on the changing political fortunes of his world, the shift from the Neo-Assyrian to the Neo-Babylonian period. Further, he signalled a transition movement in Israelite thought. He was contemplative and spoke to God about Judah's concerns rather than to Judah about God's. He asked "Why?"—a question that prophets rarely posed to Yahweh. In that respect he signaled the transition to another thought movement, from prophetic thought to wisdom speculation.

That in no way means that the prophetic movement was in decline and its purpose would soon terminate. The movement was to continue for another two centuries at least. Yet the burden of theological speculation that the great tragedy which befell Judah in 586 placed upon prophetic thinking eventually proved, by the very nature of prophecy itself, to be too heavy for prophetic thought to bear. Such thought was not designed to speculate—it was designed to announce Yahweh's Word. It was not introspective by its nature, even though it called Israel to introspection. The "Why?" of Habakkuk was a resident alien in prophetic literature. Its presence could be justified and defended, but it could have no permanent home there. The function of the prophet was not speculation—it was proclamation. Perhaps it is not overstating the case to say that Habakkuk, who admissibly conducted a successful inquiry of God, offered the first hint that the future held a task that prophecy could not fulfill.

HABAKKUK THE MAN

Unfortunately we do not know any more about Habakkuk than we do about Zephaniah, Nahum, and Obadiah, all prophets of the last days of Judah. The nearest thing to personal information about him is that he is called "prophet" in 1:1 and 3:1. We do not even have the advantage of a superscription dating him by the kings in whose reigns he may have prophesied. Some traditions about this prophet have been preserved in Jewish literature, but none of them is

2. George Adam Smith, *The Book of the Twelve Prophets*, 2:131.
3. That, of course, depends upon the date of Job and Ecclesiastes. Many scholars today are willing to allow a pre-exilic date for Job, but the general opinion is that Ecclesiastes belongs in the post-exilic period. See the author's discussion of these issues in *An Introduction to the Old Testament Poetic Books*, pp. 66–68, 199–200.

very reliable. In *Bel and the Dragon*, one of the apocryphal additions to the book of Daniel, the prophet Habakkuk is pictured taking food to reapers in the field when an angel whisks him away to Babylon, where he offers the food to Daniel in the lions' den. Then the prophet is transported back to Judea (vv. 33–39). Another tradition places him in the reign of Manasseh, along with Joel and Nahum, stating that because Manasseh was not a worthy king those prophets did not mention his name.[4]

In modern scholarship Habakkuk has often been associated with the Temple. That notion is based largely on the literary nature of chapter 3, which is called a psalm, and which provides liturgical notes (3:1, 3, 9*a*, 13). That is not impossible, but the book as a whole does not seem to have had a liturgical usage.

LITERARY FORM AND ANALYSIS OF THE BOOK

BASIC PROBLEMS

The identity of the oppressor in 1:2–4. One of the basic questions that must be answered in order to understand Habakkuk's prophecy is the source of the oppression perpetrated on the Judeans in 1:2–4. This oppressor would presumably be synonymous with the "wicked" of verse 4. Basically two answers have been given to this question. First, it is speculated that they were unjust Judeans perpetrating evil upon their brothers and sisters.[5] According to this view, the problem that troubled Habakkuk was social disorder within Judah, and the purpose of the Lord's raising up the Chaldeans in 1:5–11 was to punish the evildoers in Judah. It would also follow that the Chaldeans would likely be the oppressor described in 1:12–17. In favor of this position is the general view of the prophets since Amos that God would use foreign invaders to punish Israel and Judah for their immorality and idolatry. Furthermore, the terms used to describe the oppression in 1:2–4[6] are words that normally represent domestic evils.

Second, it is thought that the oppressor was a foreign enemy. Perhaps the most common identification in this category is the Chaldeans.[7] The problem with this interpretation, however, is that the Chaldeans are specifically mentioned in 1:6 as the nation that the Lord would raise up, presumably to punish

---

4. The tradition is found in *Seder Olam* and is also mentioned by David Kimchi in his commentary (Hebrew) on Hab. 1:1.

5. Representatives are William Hayes Ward, *A Critical and Exegetical Commentary on Habakkuk*, p. 4; Ernst Sellin and Georg Fohrer, *Introduction to the Old Testament*, p. 455; John D. W. Watts, *The Books of Joel, Obadiah, Jonah, Nahum, Habakkuk and Zephaniah*, pp. 124–25; Ralph L. Smith, *Micah–Malachi*, p. 99.

6. *Shōd*, "destruction"; *ḥāmās*, "violence"; *rîv*, "strife"; *mādôn*, "contention"—v. 3.

7. E.g., J. Lindblom, *Prophecy in Ancient Israel*, p. 254.

the oppressor of 1:2–4. That, of course, would give the impression that the Chaldeans brought about their own punishment. This problem was obviated by Karl Budde, who proposed that the oppressor of Judah in 1:2–4 and 1:12—2:4 was Assyria, and in his opinion the issue of the Chaldeans in 1:5–11 was out of place in the book. According to Budde the prophet intended to say that the Chaldeans would rise up to punish the Assyrians. Therefore, Budde moved 1:5–11 after 2:4 to give the proper historical sequence in the book.[8] G. A. Smith followed the contours of the hypothesis but proposed that the oppressor of 1:12–17 was more likely Egypt during the years 608–605 B.C.[9]

The content of the "vision" (2:2–3). There are three distinct possibilities here. First, Yahweh's command to write the vision may be a reference backward to the revelation that He was raising up the Chaldeans to punish the oppressors (1:6). In that case, 1:5–11 would be the basic content of the vision the prophet recorded.

The second possible interpretation is that the vision consisted of the following revelation found in 2:3–5, assuring the readers that vengeance would come, even if slowly, and exhorting them to be patient. Moreover, the only way to live is by faith in God's promises to punish the wicked and save the righteous. The way of brute power manifested by the Babylonians is the opposite of the way of faith, which will sustain the righteous. In this case the vision, consisting in a message of reassurance and encouragement to live by faith in Yahweh, is in deference to the picture of the self-confident, idolatrous Chaldeans described in 1:5–17. Thus, if the vision consists of 2:3–5, it is still only understood in reference to the message of 1:5–11. Therefore, when Habakkuk recorded it, he may have recorded the "vision" of reassurance along with the prediction that the Chaldeans would be the executors of justice. This position seems the most natural.

A third proposal is that the vision consisted of the revelation of Yahweh's appearance in chapter 3. This view is held by Ernst Sellin and Georg Fohrer and is supported by Artur Weiser, who advocates that 3:2–16 was the content of the vision.[10] There is some logic to this proposition, especially because the words of instruction in 2:2–3 imply a time of vindication, and the Lord's appearance in chapter 3 has as its purpose the judgment of the wicked and the salvation of His people (3:12–16). Yet, if Habakkuk was the editor of the book, which is quite conceivable, why should he place the contents of the vision so far away from the command to write it down? Moreover, the psalmic form of

8. Karl Budde, "Die Bücher Habakuk und Zephanja," pp. 383–93.
9. G. A. Smith, 2:123–24; also more recently J. H. Eaton, *Obadiah, Nahum, Habakkuk and Zephaniah: Introduction and Commentary*, p. 82.
10. Sellin and Fohrer, p. 454; Artur Weiser, *The Old Testament: Its Formation and Development*, p. 261.

chapter 3 with its liturgical notes is not the normal character of a prophetic vision.

As indicated above, the content of the vision was likely the reassurance given in the instructions of 2:2–5. But that message is hardly complete unless it is viewed in light of the oracle concerning the rise of the Chaldeans in 1:5–11. The purpose of chapter 3 appears to be confirmation of Yahweh's faithfulness to revenge His enemies and save His people, couched in the imagery and language of the Exodus from Egypt and the revelation at Sinai. The point is that should there be any reluctance to believe the Lord would vindicate and save, let the readers recall the great vindication and salvation of history. Therefore, Habakkuk's vision contained the word of reassurance that faith, not arrogance, would sustain the prophet and his people (2:2–5) but it also included the vision of the coming Chaldeans (1:5–11). Chapter 3 was recorded as a capstone confirmation of the certainty that Yahweh would, as promised in 2:2–5, bring vindication to the oppressor (Chaldea) and salvation to the oppressed (Judea) as He had done under Moses. The rehearsal of those events was sufficient to elicit a renewed resolution to wait for the day of Yahweh's reprisal (3:16). Judging from the use of the verb "saw" in 1:1 (*ḥāzāh*), from which the word "vision" (*ḥizayôn*) is derived, the entire book assumes a visionary character, although the "vision" per se is constituted only by 1:5–11 and 2:2–5.

The psalm (ch. 3). In light of the emphasis in modern scholarship on the cult of Jerusalem and the prophets' associations with it, a number of scholars have proposed that chapter 3 was composed for use in the Temple liturgy. G. A. Smith, for example, believed that it had a liturgical origin after the Exile and was later adapted in Psalm 77:17–20.[11] William F. Albright advocated that the author of the psalm and chapters 1–2 was probably one and the same person who lived and wrote in an archaizing style during the last years of the first Temple.[12] The occasion for the recital of the psalm has been identified by a number of scholars as an autumn festival, in which Yahweh's covenant with Israel and the world was renewed.[13] The hypothesis that such an annual festival of covenant renewal existed in ancient Israel is a questionable one. There is insufficient evidence in the Pentateuch to support it, and the hypothesis is largely built upon the analogy of the Babylonian autumn festival. Nevertheless, the psalm of Habakkuk, although perhaps acquiring a liturgical usage at some point, was probably written for the purpose of affirming the promise of 2:3–5 that Yahweh would act in His own time, just as He had acted in Israel's glorious past. In fact, 2:20 closes the first major section, expecting Yahweh's awesome appearance in chapter 3,

11. G. A. Smith, 2:126–27.
12. William F. Albright, "The Psalm of Habakkuk," pp. 1–18.
13. E.g., Sigmund Mowinckel, "Zum Psalm des Habakuk," pp. 1–23; Watts, p. 144.

> But the Lord is in His holy temple.
> Let all the earth be silent before Him.

Therefore, as R. K. Harrison observes, it is difficult to see how chapters 1 and 2 could have been used liturgically.[14] Brevard S. Childs also disagrees with the liturgical hypothesis, calling attention to the autobiographical nature of the book, which militates against it.[15]

The fact that chapter 3 is not included in the Habakkuk Scroll from Qumran proves nothing. In light of the hermeneutical interests of that community, chapter 3 likely did not serve their purposes very well.

LITERARY FORM AND ANALYSIS

Four kinds of material have been identified in the book: complaint, prophetic oracle, prophetic woes, and a psalm.[16] Actually, however, the complaint is a prayer, and so is the psalm of chapter 3. Therefore, there are three types of material: prayer, prophetic oracle, and prophetic woes. The material alternates between prophetic prayer and divine answer, interrupted by the prophet's words of confidence (2:1; 3:16–19), condemnation (2:6–19), and admonition (2:20). The contours of Habakkuk's style divide the book into two main parts (see outline at the end of the chapter).

Part I (chaps. 1–2). The book of Habakkuk is a very personal book. The prophet logs his theological inquiry, opening Prayer One (1:2–4) with a question that sets the tone for the prophecy:

> How long, O Lord, will I call for help,
> And Thou wilt not hear?
> I cry out to Thee, "Violence!"
> Yet Thou dost not save.
>
> (1:2)

The problem that he set forth is basically a domestic one. His prayer had been provoked by the wrongs he had observed in Judean society: violence, iniquity, wickedness, destruction, strife, contention, abuse of the law, and perverted justice—the list is long and malicious.

Answer One (1:5–11) contains a solution to the problem of Judah's iniquities that is not any different from that detailed by Jeremiah: Yahweh is raising up the Chaldeans to punish the nation (Jer. 6:7, 22–26, etc.). He had not blindly chosen them as His agent of judgment, for He was aware of their sins: They seized habitations that were not theirs (1:6), recognized no standard of justice

---

14. R. K. Harrison, *Introduction to the Old Testament*, p. 936.
15. Brevard S. Childs, *Introduction to the Old Testament as Scripture*, p. 452.
16. Charles L. Taylor, Jr., "The Book of Habakkuk," 6:973.

but their own (1:7), perpetrated violence (1:9), and took captives (1:9, 15*b*). They are guilty men who had made their own brute force into their god (1:11).

Prayer Two (1:12–17) focuses on the nature of God. He is eternal (1:12*a*), sovereign (1:12*b*), and too pure to look on evil (1:13), yet He was silent when the wicked (Chaldeans) swallowed up the man more righteous than he (1:13). Here Habakkuk raises the question of theodicy. How could a holy God use a wicked agent to punish His people, evil though they be? He closes the prayer as he had opened it, with a question (as in 1:2),

> Will they therefore empty their net
> And continually slay nations without sparing?
> (1:17)

Habakkuk's confidence and faith, perhaps implied in 2:4, is clearly affirmed in 2:1 and 3:16. He will wait and trust.

Answer Two (2:2–5) is of far greater import than its length would imply. The Lord commanded Habakkuk to preserve the vision because the time had not yet come for its fulfillment ("the vision is yet for the appointed time," 2:3*a*). The answer to the question posed in 1:13 is specifically given in 2:4–5. The Chaldeans were puffed up with pride and morally decadent ("not right"), but a righteous one (Habakkuk or any Judean who hoped in God) shall live by his faith. The Septuagint rendering of verse 4, "If he shrink back, my soul does not find pleasure in him; for the righteous shall live by my faith," seems to be based upon a scribal error, having read the Hebrew word "puffed up" (*upplāh*, NASB "proud one") as "shrink back" (Heb. *ullpāh*—note the interchange of letters)[17]. The description of the Chaldeans in 2:5 is not as abrupt as it first appears if we recall that the Lord had described them in verse 4 also.

The second word of the prophet that does not belong to his prayers introduces a series of five woes (2:6–19) pronounced against the Chaldeans. The preceding material prepared the readers for that condemnation by detailing the sins of the Chaldeans (1:5–11, 13*a*–16). Admittedly, the Chaldeans are not mentioned in the woes,[18] but they are evidently the object. Although questions have been raised about the genuineness of this material,[19] they are integrally related to the earlier material in chapters 1 and 2, where the same sins are attributed to the Chaldeans as here. The first woe (2:6*b*–8) promises that the roles will be reversed on the Chaldeans, and they will become the prey of the

---

17. C. F. Keil, *The Twelve Minor Prophets*, 2:72–73.
18. Taylor, 6:976, advances the thesis that 2:5–20 was written after the exile of 597, and the prophet delivered the woes against the Chaldeans but could not use their name because they were in power in the land.
19. Ward, p. 6, assigned numbers two through five to the Maccabean period.

nations (2:7). Already the Lord had pronounced judgment on them in 1:6. The second woe (2:9–11) condemns the oppressor for unjustly having gained their status in the world, and it is aligned with the indictments found in 1:15, 17 and 2:5b. The third woe (2:12–14) asserts that, although the Lord permits them to amass their ill-gotten wealth, their work will count for nothing. Indeed, in gaining their possessions unjustly, they had usurped God's glory. So He will destroy their ill-gotten fame and fill the whole earth with the knowledge of His own glory (2:14). The Chaldeans had already been indicted for usurping God's earth in 2:5. The fourth woe (2:15–17) denounced them for forcing the cup of wrath on the nations. The Lord too has a cup, and He will make the Chaldeans drink it, and they will become inibriated on His wrath rather than drunken on their false glory. The violence they had perpetrated in the earth is a theme sounded earlier in 1:9. The fifth woe (2:18–19) is inverted, the subject being introduced (v. 18) before the woe is pronounced (v. 19). It is a resounding condemnation of idolatry, not unlike those that Isaiah so eloquently pronounced. Earlier in 1:16 Yahweh had taken cognizance of the idolatrous ways of the Chaldeans.

Part II (chap. 3). The closing verse of chapter 2 (v. 20) leads quite naturally into the prayer of chapter 3, for all the earth is admonished to keep silence in deference to the awful judgment and great salvation that Yahweh will bring.

Prayer Three (3:2) is connected to chapters 1 and 2 in two ways: (1) it is reassurance that the God who promised weal and woe would deliver the Judeans as He had so frightfully and gloriously done in the Exodus; (2) it is a prayer that Yahweh might "in wrath remember mercy." The prayer proper consists of only one verse, whereas verses 3–15 take the form of an answer to the prayer. The larger content falls into these sections:

3:2   Habakkuk recalls Yahweh's ancient saving work and prays for its renewal.

3:3–12   Description of the theophany in imagery suggesting the Exodus from Egypt and the revelation at Sinai.

3:13–15 The purpose of the theophany, described as the salvation of Yahweh's people and punishment of the wicked.

3:16–19 The prophet's response of faith and confidence to the theophany.

The theme of Yahweh's anger runs through this prayer as it does in the prophecies of the Neo-Babylonian era.[20]

DATE OF THE PROPHET

Because Habakkuk gave us no explicit information about the time of his ministry, we must depend upon implicit data to place him in the history of

---

20. Four Hebrew words are used to designate Yahweh's wrath, *ḥārāh*, *'af, 'evrāh* [3:8], and *za'am* [3:12—also *'af* is repeated here]).

Israel. The issue of date hinges largely upon the identification of the oppressor in 1:2–4 and 1:12–17.

One of the most radical proposals was put forth by Bernard Duhm, who amended the term *Kasdim* (Chaldeans) to *Kittim* (Greeks) and dated the book about 332 B.C.[21] C. C. Torrey followed that line of reasoning and advocated that the book was a meditation on the conquests of Alexander the Great. He dated it between 334 and 331.[22]

We have already taken note of the Jewish tradition that Habakkuk prophesied in the reign of Manasseh. If the social chaos described in 1:2–4 was domestic, then the reign of Manasseh or Amon, plagued by social ills, would be a possibility. That time period has had its defenders among modern scholars, represented by no less of a scholar than C. F. Keil. Because Habakkuk presents the work of God as an incredible one ("You would not believe it if you were told," 1:5), that rules out the possibility of his prophecy in the first years of Jehoiakim's reign or the closing years of Josiah's, when the Chaldean rise was apparent. Moreover, in the reign of Manasseh it is said that the Lord caused His prophets to announce the coming of such a calamity, "that whoever hears of it, both his ears shall tingle" (2 Kings 21:12), namely, the destruction of Jerusalem and rejection of Judah. Keil believes one of those prophets was Habakkuk.[23]

There are also proponents of a Josianic date, particularly those who believe that the sins enumerated in 1:2–4 were those of the oppressor rather than the Judeans. The assumption is that the Josianic reform had all but eradicated that kind of transgression.[24] A date after 622/21 is favored. A further assumption by proponents of Josiah's reign is that the oppressor was the Assyrians, and the Chaldeans were slated to bring judgment upon them.[25]

However, the majority opinion in modern scholarship is a date in the latter part of Jehoiakim's reign, between 605 and 598 B.C.[26] The assumption behind this date is that the Chaldeans became the primary power in the Near East when they defeated the Egyptians at Carchemish in 605. At that point Chaldea became a credible force and a threat to Judah as well. This view, however, weakens the predictive element.

A date in the declining years of the Neo-Assyrian period but before the rise of the Chaldeans seems preferable for two reasons. First, the Lord told the

21. Bernhard Duhm, *Das Buch Habakkuk.*
22. C. C. Torrey, *The Second Isaiah: A New Interpretation,* p. 96.
23. Watts, pp. 122–23; Yehezkel Kaufmann, *The Religion of Israel,* p. 399; Harrison, p. 935; Albright, p. 2; Gleason L. Archer, Jr., *A Survey of Old Testament Introduction,* p. 356.
24. S. M. Lehrman, "Habakkuk," p. 211; J. H. Eaton, *Obadiah, Nahum, Habakkuk and Zephaniah: Introduction and Commentary,* p. 84.
25. Sellin and Fohrer, p. 455; Eissfeldt, p. 422.
26. Keil, 2: 51–52.

prophet and his compatriots that He was doing a work in "your days" (1:5), the implication being that it would occur in their lifetime. Second, credibility was lacking when the prophecy was delivered ("You would not believe if you were told," 1:6). Therefore, a date during the first decade of Josiah's reign would satisfy those qualifications. The adults to whom the prophet spoke lived to see the Chaldeans rise to power in 605 and perhaps even the exile of 597.[27] Moreover, the early part of Josiah's reign, between 641/40 and 628/27, was a time when the Judean sins enumerated in 1:2–4 were in evidence.

THE MESSAGE OF HABAKKUK

THE JUSTICE OF GOD

Habakkuk was bold enough to broach the subject of divine justice. Whether or not he was acquainted with Job, he nevertheless took the issue that Job had raised and probed on a personal level and dealt with it on an international plane. There is a distinct difference, however. Job defended his innocence and moral integrity, whereas Habakkuk admitted the sins of Judah. Yet the prophet still could not comprehend what justification Yahweh had for using such a haughty, God-defying agent to punish His people. It was the question of God's justice. Kaufmann has observed that Habakkuk was the only prophet to treat the problem of the success of the wicked in the historical-national realm.[28]

The answer that Yahweh provided was a confirmation of what the prophet already believed. He well knew that God was of purer eyes than to look on evil (1:13), but the circumstances contravened that conviction, although they could not suppress it. Yahweh's reassurance was that the "righteous will live by his faith" (2:4). International circumstances, though they may appear to contradict His sovereignty and sense of justice, are only temporary. His justice in universal affairs can be relied upon. Faith and fact are not always compatible in the world of sense and sight, but that is not the whole world. There is a world of justice that only God fully comprehends. His people must accept by faith what they cannot confirm in fact.

THE POLEMIC AGAINST IDOLATRY

With the prophet Habakkuk the prophetic polemic against idolatry entered a new phase. Now it was directed to pagan ears: "Woe to him who says to a piece of wood, 'Awake!' To a dumb stone, 'Arise!' " (2:19). Kaufmann's keen observation has drawn attention to this new shape of the argument against idols.[29] The nation that had piled success upon success, catching men and

---

27. E. B. Pusey, *The Minor Prophets with a Commentary*, p. 399.
28. Kaufmann, pp. 399–400.
29. Ibid.

women like fish in its net, had shown its dullness of spiritual insight by offering sacrifice to that net (1:16). The absurd limits of idolatry were evident among the Chaldeans. The primitive stage, represented by idols of wood and stone guilded with gold and silver was perhaps, relatively speaking, the most "innocent" phase. If the worshiper could understand that the idol cannot breathe, cannot speak, cannot comprehend, perhaps he could be turned toward the truth. But a nation that had made power and success its god (1:11) had advanced to the ultimate stage of idolatry. To turn human attributes and achievements into idols that are worshiped is the greatest defiance of the true and truly sovereign God.

OUTLINE OF HABAKKUK

I. PART I (chaps. 1–2)
    A. Superscription to Part I (1:1)
    B. Prayer One (1:2–4)
    C. Answer One (1:5–11)
    D. Prayer Two (1:12–17)
    E. Prophet's Word of Confidence (2:1)
    F. Answer Two (2:2–5)
    G. Prophet's Word of Condemnation (2:6–19)
        1. First Woe (2:6*b*–8)
        2. Second Woe (2:9–11)
        3. Third Woe (2:12–14)
        4. Fourth Woe (2:15–19)
        5. Fifth Woe (2:18–19)
    H. Prophet's Word of Admonition (2:20)
II. PART II (chap. 3)
    A. Superscription to Part II (3:1)
    B. Prayer Three (3:2)
    C. Answer Three (3:3–15)
    D. Prophet's Word of Confidence (3:16–19)

9

JEREMIAH: PROPHET TO THE NATIONS

THE SCOPE OF JEREMIAH'S MINISTRY extended beyond his native Judah to the nations. In that respect he truly represented a prophetic plateau, for Jonah, Amos, Isaiah, Zephaniah, and Habukkuk had turned their attention to the nations in varying degrees, and Nahum, Habakkuk, Obadiah, and Ezekiel would yet set their sights beyond Israel's national boundaries. Yet Jeremiah stands out among the prophets in that Yahweh specifically appointed him a "prophet to the nations" (1:5, 10). Although he obviously was preoccupied with Judah, whose changing political fortunes shifted through Assyrian, Egyptian, and Babylonian cycles before his forty-year ministry terminated, the oracles against the nations at the end of the book (chaps. 46–51) in part justify that job description. Moreover, there is additional evidence that Jeremiah actually communicated with the kings of other countries in his role as prophet to the nations. In chapter 25 Yahweh commanded him as early as Jehoiakim's fourth regnal year (605 B.C.) to take the cup of divine wrath and cause all nations to drink it. Among those countries were the familiar names of Jerusalem, Egypt, Uz, Philistia, Edom, Moab, Ammon, Tyre, Sidon, Elam, and Media, and others both named and unnamed (25:15–31). Even though we do not know how precisely he carried out that mandate, during Zedekiah's reign (597–586) Yahweh instructed him with more explicit detail.

> Make for yourself bonds and yokes and put them on your neck, and send word to the king of Edom, to the king of Moab, to the king of the sons of Ammon, to the king of Tyre, and to the king of Sidon by the messengers who come to Jerusalem to Zedekiah king of Judah. And command them to go to their masters, saying, "Thus says the Lord of hosts, the God of Israel, thus you shall say to your masters . . ."
>
> (27:2b–4)

That is one of the clearest indications in Scripture that the prophets on occasion communicated directly with foreign rulers. Evidently Jeremiah made yokes for each of the kings and sent them by the hands of their ambassadors who had come to consult with Zedekiah over the Babylonian crisis, for the Hebrew text reads "send them," that is, the bonds and yokes (rather than NASB, RSV, etc. "send word," which, of course, is implied). On another occasion in the fourth year of Zedekiah's reign (594 B.C.) he sent a special message to the Babylonian king by the hand of Seraiah, who accompanied Zedekiah to Babylonia on a mission (51:59–64a). Just how much more communication of that nature he had with foreign kings cannot be determined, but those texts are an indication that it may have been considerable and that he took seriously Yahweh's appointment of him as "prophet to the nations."

Perhaps, moreover, the explanation of his call to be a prophet to the nations is not complete until we have understood the theological tenets that Jeremiah espoused and preached. Convinced of Yahweh's universal sovereignty, he saw no national limits to his own ministry.[1] Certainly in his lifetime he saw nations rise and fall, and he was absolutely sure that the Lord was the power behind those events. His urgent appeal to the kings of Edom, Moab, Ammon, Tyre, Sidon, and Judah to submit to Nebuchadnezzar (chap. 27), calling him Yahweh's "servant" (27:6; also 25:9; 43:10), reveals a dimension of that theological tenet. Sometimes the Lord chose instruments outside of Israel and put His welfare in their charge. In Jeremiah's conviction of Yahweh's universal rule and control he did not go beyond Isaiah, but in the practical aspects of his ministry he advanced to the stage of actually transmitting his message to foreign monarchs in the name of Yahweh. He not only spoke *about* the foreign nations but spoke *to* them.

JEREMIAH: THE MAN AND HIS MINISTRY

THE MAN

We know more about this prophet than any other in the OT, even though the biblical sources outside the book of Jeremiah are sparse. The historical account of Jeremiah's period in 2 Kings 21–25 does not even mention Jeremiah. The Chronicler, however, took cognizance of his strategic role in the declining days of the Judean state (2 Chron. 36:12, 21, 22; Ezra 1:1), and Daniel made one reference to Jeremiah's prophecy of the seventy-year Exile (Dan. 9:2). The book of Jeremiah remains the basic document for our knowledge of his life.

His family. Hailing from the little town of Anathoth (1:1) about three miles northeast of Jerusalem,[2] Jeremiah's priestly family may have descended from the family of Abiathar, David's high priest, who was deposed by Solomon and banished to Anathoth (1 Kings 2:26–27). In that case the priest and judge Eli (cf. 1 Sam. 2:27–36) would be his ancestor. Of course, it is also possible that more than one priestly family lived in Anathoth, and Jeremiah did not belong

1. J. A. Thompson, *The Book of Jeremiah*, p. 146.
2. Anathoth is identified with the site known as Ras el-Kharrubeh near the modern village of Anata, which preserves the ancient name.

specifically to Abiathar's clan. The only thing we know for certain about his genealogy, aside from the fact of priestly lineage, is his father's name, Hilkiah (1:1). Although it is tempting to identify Jeremiah's father with the priest by the same name who discovered the law scroll in the Temple in 622 (2 Kings 22:8), there is no basis in Jeremiah or Kings for connecting the two. As early as Jerome the identification was made, but we should not press it.

He was not married, and in 16:1–4 he explains why:

> The word of the Lord also came to me saying, "You shall not take a wife for yourself nor have sons or daughters in this place." For thus says the Lord concerning the sons and daughters born in this place, and concerning their mothers who bear them, and their fathers who beget them in this land: "They will die of deadly diseases, they will not be lamented or buried."

His personality. Introspective and possessed of a conviction that God's will was irresistible, both for him as prophet (20:9) and for the nations (27:8), Jeremiah discharged his ministry with a peculiar yet creative fusion of courage and reluctance. No doubt a personality that might have under other conditions been receding, when imbued with the strong sense of call and the promise of God's undergirding presence he could indeed become "as a fortified city, and as a pillar of iron and as walls of bronze" (1:18). Yet the intractable will of his native Judah, forged upon the anvil of idolatry and covenant violation, could and would assault that fortress of a prophet and leave him a broken spirit, if but only temporarily daunted. Like Amos of an earlier generation (Amos 5:15), and like Ezekiel his younger contemporary in exile (Ezek. 12:3), Jeremiah's success was suspended on the tenuous thread of "perhaps" (21:2; 26:3; 36:3, 7).

The pattern of Jeremiah's personality was sketched in moments of solitude, alone with himself and with God. In point of fact, it was forged in eternity.

> "Before I formed you in the womb I knew you,
> And before you were born I consecrated you."
> (1:5)

He withdrew from social functions because he knew that God was about to put an end to joy and mirth (16:5–9), and his own morose personality became a symbol of that calamity. His grief and reproach were so great that he, like Job, lamented the day of his birth (20:14–18). Like Isaiah's Servant, he was a man of sorrows and acquainted with grief.

HIS CALL AND MINISTRY: A SUMMONS FROM THE TIMES

Even the ministry of Isaiah, which was punctuated by five Assyrian invasions into Israelite and Judean territory, was not marked by the level of anxiety, terror, and tragedy that stalked Jeremiah's long ministry of at least forty years. Whereas Isaiah had seen the destruction of Samaria and the exile of her citizens to the distant East, Jeremiah lived to see the awful destruction of Jerusalem, that city that had stood almost inviolable through the days of his predecessors in prophecy. The Assyria of Isaiah's time was in the throes of death when Jeremiah's call came to him. The long reign of Asshurbanapal (668–631 B.C.), the last great king of the Neo-Assyrian Empire, had ended, and the harbingers of a new era appeared on the international horizon. In Babylonia the Chaldeans, whose cultural influence had already made deep impressions in that land, were prepared to fill the vacuum that was developing in empirical politics. Hardly a century earlier they had made their political prowess felt when Merodach-baladan, of Chaldean extraction, had seized the Babylonian throne, and the decline of Assyrian power in the last half of the seventh century cleared the way for a comeback. It occurred when Nabopolassar took Babylon in 626. At that time Jeremiah was a novice at his profession, having received his call in the thirteenth year of Josiah (627/26 B.C.; 1:2; 25:3).

In Judah Josiah had had a religious conversion in the eighth year of his reign and in the twelfth year, the year prior to Jeremiah's call, had inaugurated religious reform (2 Chron. 34:3). The ground for our prophet's ministry had been prepared, even if only the thin layer of topsoil had been turned.

A summons from eternity. Not only was he summoned by the exigencies of the times, but his summons emerged out of eternity. The Lord knew him before He ever formed him in his mother's womb, and He had consecrated Jeremiah a prophet to the nations outside of the time frame in which he must carry out that role. His objections to Yahweh's call grew out of the feeling of inadequacy, and perhaps over against the awesomeness of the task as he had assessed it,

> Then I said, "Alas, Lord God!
> Behold, I do not know how to speak,
> Because I am a youth."
>   (1:6)

But a prophet whom eternity had summoned could not be overwhelmed by the exigencies of the time,

> But the Lord said to me,
> "Do not say, 'I am a youth,'
> Because everywhere I send you, you shall go,
> And all that I command you, you shall speak.
> Do not be afraid of them,
> For I am with you to deliver you," declares the Lord.
>   (1:7–8)

It was another version of Isaiah's admission,

> "Woe is me, for I am ruined!
> Because I am a man of unclean lips,
> And I live among a people of unclean lips."
> (Isa. 6:5*a*)

And the Lord's gracious touch of Jeremiah's mouth was as dramatic as the seraph's cleansing touch of Isaiah's lips. The word that Yahweh put in his mouth (1:9) burned its way into his heart and made itself an indispensible and irresistible part of the prophet's existence (20:9).

Methods of communication. Here we want to consider briefly the methods of communication that this prophet used to carry out his call. They do not differ substantially from those methods already long established by the prophets. The primary mode was *speaking*. The form critics insist that the prophets used certain literary forms from the social structures of their times, such as the messenger speech from international diplomacy, the lament from the religious liturgy, and the lawsuit from the legal assembly. Given the normal interchange among cultural forms and social functions in any society, and given the need of literature to assume structures that communicate concrete ideas as well as certain emotions and images, that assumption is logical. A question arises, however, over whether the social and cultural forms were stamped upon the oral message before or after its delivery. Perhaps both options are possible. The prophets were among the most adept literary figures of their times, and an address in the form of a messenger speech or some other literary form reflecting social structures and patterns is quite conceivable, even without prior writing. On the other hand, it is also possible that sometimes those forms were refined or the literature rephrased accordingly after the oral delivery. So we may surmise, for example, that the "confessions"[3] could have first been spoken in essentially their present form, especially by one who was steeped in psalmic poetry. Yet there is no reason they should not be edited by Jeremiah or the prose sections by his amanuensis, Baruch, when they were committed to writing. The point is that even though the message may have been first given orally and then written down, which was by no means the general rule, the message could have been cast in the literary form in its oral stage.

The second mode of communication that Jeremiah used was *writing*. Instructions came from Yahweh in the fourth year of Jehoiakim (605), "Take a scroll and write on it all the words which I have spoken to you concerning Israel, and concerning Judah, and concerning the nations, from the day I first spoke to you, from the days of Josiah, even to this day" (36:2). When Jehoiakim had

---

3. See pp. 197–98 below.

shredded that scroll and burned it in the fire, the Lord instructed the prophet to take another scroll and write on it the words of the first one (36:27–28). At Jeremiah's dictation Baruch completed the second scroll containing the content of the first plus many similar words (36:32). The fact that Jeremiah seems to have been barred from the Temple at the time, thus explaining his use of Baruch as his messenger, ought not suggest that writing the message down was an extraordinary means of communicating it. In fact, the first scroll was a compilation of prophecies over a period of approximately twenty-three years (from the thirteenth year of Josiah—627 B.C.—to the fifth year of Jehoiakim—604). Having scribal assistance, he likely had committed many, if not most, of his oracles to writing during those years.[4] On still another occasion after the exile of Jehoiachin in 597, Jeremiah wrote a letter to the exiles in Babylonia, encouraging them to settle down and live a normal life, because the captivity would last seventy years (chap. 29). His correspondence to Babylonia included words to the Babylonian king informing him of the fate his country would suffer in the future (51:59–64a). In a more comforting vein, he consoled Judah and promised restoration in a series of undated prophecies that he committed to writing (30:2).

The third method of communicating his message was by means of the *acted sign*. Prophetic symbolism, as it is called, had been known since the days of Hosea and Isaiah, but Jeremiah gave it popularity, and Ezekiel mastered the art as no other prophet had. Among Jeremiah's signs were the linen waistcloth (chap. 13), the potter's house (chap. 18), the broken jar (chap. 19), the bonds and yokes he wore (chaps. 27–28), and the purchase of his kinsman's field in Anathoth (chap. 32). Some of these were performed or observed in private and some publicly, always accompanied by interpretation.

Places of communication. Jeremiah's earliest ministry may have taken place in his hometown of Anathoth (11:21), but most of his activity occurred in Jerusalem, even though 11:6 suggests that he prophesied in other cities of Judah as well. The specific locations where he proclaimed his messages depended upon two factors: gathering a crowd and his personal circumstances. Even though all of Jeremiah's prophecies were not intended for public consumption, he wanted those that were to be heard by as many as would listen. For example, the Temple was a place where crowds gathered. So he preached there (7:2; 26:2), and when he himself was debarred from the Lord's house, he sent Baruch to read the scroll on a festival day when large crowds converged (36:5; cf. also 7:2; 26:2; 28:1). Another place where he could easily find an audience was the city gate where people gathered socially (11:6; 17:19). On another occasion he found his audience in the king's house (22:1; 37:17). Yet

---

4. The king's house had a chamber for his scribe, Elishama (36:12). The recording of important events and documents was the norm, not the exception. See also Jeremiah's land purchase and the written transaction (32:6–15).

when the circumstances of his life did not allow him to go where he would, he issued his message from whatever place he was confined to, even from prison (32:2). When he held a private audience with the Rechabites, he used a chamber of the Temple (35:2, 4).

Sociological dimensions of Jeremiah's ministry: his enemies. The candor with which this prophet spoke about Judah's sins, added to the unpopular message of submission to the Babylonians that he later proclaimed, made many enemies for Jeremiah. Among his strongest opponents were the prophets who were optimistic about the future but had no cause to be. They were joined by the priests who were evidently influenced greatly by the prophets (27:16–18). The influence of the prophets on the priests is confirmed in 28:1–4, where Hananiah performs his act in the presence of the priests in the Temple, obviously to sway them to his position. That class of prophets seems to have been closely attached to the Temple, an idea that is confirmed by the letter of the exile Shemaiah to the priest Zephaniah in Jerusalem inquiring why he had not reprimanded Jeremiah for his promise of a long exile (29:24–28). The implication of that passage is that the priests had the upper hand over the prophets and could censure them. Interestingly, in the majority of cases when Jeremiah mentions the prophets, he also mentions the priests in the same context.[5] The point of contention between Jeremiah and the false prophets is clear. The latter practitioners dispensed a message of peace when there was no peace (6:13–15; 8:11; 14:13–16; 23:17). They were guilty of bringing false hope to a people that was doomed by its idolatry. Together the priests and prophets indicted him for predicting the destruction of the Temple, and his life was spared only by the intervention of the elders of the land (26:7–19, 24).

Jeremiah's ministry began amidst opposition. The men of his own native town of Anathoth sought to kill him (11:21–23; 12:6). Once he had transferred his credentials to Jerusalem, he fared no better (18:18, 22–23). Jehoiakim despised him and burned his scroll, giving orders for his and Baruch's arrest, "but the Lord hid them" (36:20–26). He was opposed by Passhur the priest, who had him beaten and thrown in prison because he had prophesied the destruction of Jerusalem (20:2), and Zedekiah took measures to quiet his debilitating preaching that called for surrender to Babylonians during the siege of Jerusalem in 588/87. He arrested him and kept him in the court of the guard of the king's palace (32:2–5). Yet conflict seemed to call forth the strength of Jeremiah's personality. Publicly he never backed down in the face of challenge or danger, even though in solitude his courage and resoluteness receded into introspection.[6]

---

5. See 2:8; 5:31; 6:13–15; 8:1–2; 13:13; 18:18; 23:33–40; 26:7–24; 27:14–22; 32:32.
6. A. B. Davidson, "Jeremiah the Prophet," 2:569.

His friends. It is not surprising that Jeremiah also elicited a deep sense of devotion from certain individuals. Perhaps his most loyal friend was his scribe, Baruch (36; 43:6; 45). Others were Baruch's brother, Seraiah (51:59; 32:12), the royal eunuch Ebed-melech (38:7–13), Ahikam, who saved his life on one memorable occasion (26:24), and Ahikam's son, Gedaliah (39:14; 40:5). King Zedekiah consulted Jeremiah on critical occasions (37:3, 16–21), and when approached by Ebed-melech, he sent him to mitigate the prophet's suffering (38:7–13). Even the Chaldeans treated him kindly and allowed him to choose whether he would go to Babylonia with the exiles or remain in Judah (40:1–6). He chose the latter.

HISTORICAL BACKGROUND

Reading Jeremiah without a knowledge of the history of his time is like reading the New Testament without an awareness of the Jewish and Roman events and influences in the first century A.D. To a large extent his life and ministry were shaped by the historical events of the day. That may be said of any of the classical prophets. Jeremiah was certainly no exception.

REIGN OF JOSIAH (640–609 B.C.)

The declining power of the Assyrian Empire lowered a cloud of uncertainty over the ancient Near East while it also created new aspirations. The death of Assurbanipal (668–631 B.C.), the last great king of the empire, left a void that could not be immediately filled. The aspiring Chaldean, Nabopolassar in Babylonia, defeated the Assyrians at the city of Babylon in 626 and became king of Babylon. With external events having given Judah virtual freedom from foreign domination, internal events began to create hope for a better future. Josiah's youthful accession to the throne (at eight years of age) introduced a pliable personality to the political stage, and by the eighth year of his reign (632/31) he had begun to show a definite religious inclination for Yahweh, which led to the initiation of religious reform in his twelfth regnal year (628/27). Only one year later (627/26) Jeremiah received his call to be a prophet. Those early years of religious reform were marked by renewed hope for Judah, and the discovery of the scroll of the law in 622/21 reinforced and abetted the renewal (2 Chron. 34–35/2 Kings 22–23).

Jeremiah's attitude toward the reform has been the subject of much debate. The general opinion is that he first supported the reform and later became disappointed with it. The view that after 622/21, when the law scroll was found, Jeremiah fell into silence for several years is merely hypothetical. Although it is difficult to date his prophecies issued during Josiah's reign, it is unlikely that he was silent for any long period of time. Further, judging from his personal opposition to idolatry, we would conclude that he very much supported Josiah's efforts to destroy the pagan cult and restore the sanctuary in Jerusalem. Begun in 628/27, the reform at first was directed against the public cult, whose evidences could be seen on every green hill.[7] Josiah extended the religious purge even to Israel, killing the priests of the cult (2 Chron. 34:3–8) and giving special attention to purging Bethel, the ancient site of Jeroboam's golden calf (2 Kings 23:15). Centralizing worship in Jerusalem, he did not defrock the priests in the rural sanctuaries of Judah, but they joined their brothers in Jerusalem, although they were not permitted to serve at the altar (2 Kings 23:9). Jeremiah's sympathies with the reform may be seen in 11:1–12. Further, the men of the reform and their sons came to Jeremiah's defense and saved his life (26:24; 36). Moreover, he had great admiration for Josiah (22:15–16), and the Chronicler credits him with the composition of a lament for Josiah (2 Chron. 35:25). Given the renewed emphasis upon the cult, it may be that the reform resulted in a tenacious hold of the priesthood and cult on the life of the people.[8] That induced him to speak rather strongly against the abuse of the sacrificial system (6:20; 7:21–26; 11:15).

The fatal blows to the expiring Neo-Assyrian Empire were dealt by the Medes and Babylonians, first to the city of Asshur in 614, and two years later to Nineveh in 612. When the Assyrian king Asshur-uballit repaired to Haran to preserve a remnant of his empire, the allies of the forming Babylonian axis took Haran. Meantime the Egyptians, seeing some political advantage to keeping a vestige of the Assyrian Empire viable, launched a rescue expedition to the Euphrates. When Josiah attempted to cut off Pharaoh Neco II (609–593) at Megiddo, the Judean monarch was killed (609), thus concluding a very hopeful era in Judean history.

JEHOAHAZ TO JEHOIACHIN (609–597 B.C.)

The people's choice for Josiah's successor was his son, Jehoahaz. Having reigned only three months, he was summoned by Neco II to Riblah and was deposed and subsequently exiled to Egypt. Thereupon Pharaoh Neco, feeling his Megiddo victory, elevated his brother, Eliakim (throne name "Jehoiakim"), to the throne and exacted heavy tribute (2 Kings 23:28–35). Early in that king's reign Jeremiah, standing in the court of the Temple in Jerusalem, delivered the shocking prophecy that promised the destruction of the sanctuary if Judah did not repent. It is not surprising that he became a victim of the ire of the

---

7. Yehezkel Kaufmann holds that the type of idolatry in Jeremiah's time was the cult of Ishtar, identified with the "queen of heaven" (7:17–18; 44). In his opinion, the popular cult that the kings promoted until the reform of Josiah was not reinstituted after the death of that king. The fate of Judah was determined by the sins of Manasseh (2 Kings 21:10–12; 23:26–27; 24:3–4, 20). The death of Josiah, therefore, did not terminate that aspect of his reform (*The Religion of Israel*, pp. 405–9).

8. John Bright, *Jeremiah*, p. xcv.

disgruntled priests and prophets who functioned in the Temple. Arraigned before the court, Jeremiah's life was at stake as he was tried for treason. Certain elders, however, intervened and cited the prophetic precedent of Micah, who had also predicted the destruction of the Temple. Ahikam, one of the elders, played a strong hand in bringing about Jeremiah's acquittal (chap. 26; 2 Kings 22:12, 14).

Jehoiakim's eleven-year reign saw the filling of the power vacuum that the demise of Assyria had created. Even though the Egyptians enjoyed a brief interregnum in which they flexed their military muscles in Syria-Palestine (609–605), the international showdown came in 605 when Neco met Nebuchadnezzar at Carchemish on the Euphrates and received a humiliating defeat at the hands of the soon-to-be Babylonian king. Assuming the throne in Babylon upon the death of his father, Nabopolassar, in that same year, Nebuchadnezzar had already tilted the balance of power in Babylon's direction. Jehoiakim became a Babylonian vassal (2 Kings 24:1). In that momentous year (605) Jeremiah received Yahweh's command to write his prophecies on a scroll (chap. 36). They were nothing like Jehoiakim wanted to hear, so he destroyed them, only to necessitate a second and more prolific effort to collect Jeremiah's prophecies of the previous quarter of a century.

A subsequent confrontation between Nebuchadnezzar and Pharaoh Neco in 601 B.C. was less decisive than the Battle of Carchemish. Perhaps the outcome was an encouragement to Jehoiakim to rebel against Babylon. At first Nebuchadnezzar did not himself launch a campaign against Judah, although the Syrian, Moabite, and Ammonite marauders into Judean territory may have been incited by the Chaldeans (2 Kings 24:2). In any event, the Babylonians besieged Jerusalem in 598, and before the outcome of the three-month siege could be determined, Jehoiakim died. As might have been expected, Nebuchadnezzar's army established Babylonian control over Judah. The new king, Jehoiachin, son of Jehoiakim, reigned for the duration of the siege but was then exiled to Babylonia along with the royal family and other influential members of the society (2 Kings 24:8–17).

ZEDEKIAH TO GEDALIAH (597–586/5)

To head up the new government Nebuchadnezzar appointed another son of Josiah, Mattaniah (throne name "Zedekiah"), to the throne. A. B. Davidson describes him as "a prince of good intentions, but weak and irresolute."[9] His years were not marked by slavish loyalty to Babylonia, as one might expect, for in 594/93 ambassadors from Edom, Moab, Ammon, Tyre, and Sidon met in Jerusalem to discuss the prospects of rebellion against Babylon (27:3). The

9. A. B. Davidson, p. 571.

occasion was appropriate for Jeremiah to dispatch his message to the sponsoring kings, advising submission to Nebuchadnezzar.

After nine years of Babylonian tutelage Zedekiah rebelled against Nebuchadnezzar. During the two years that the siege was underway, Jeremiah spent part of that time under house arrest in Zedekiah's palace. The reason was simple—he had advised surrender to the Babylonians, a program that Zedekiah thought would break down the national morale and weaken the war effort. It was Zedekiah's way of keeping him quiet and circumventing his influence on the people (chaps. 37, 38). The events of chapters 21, 32–34, and 37–38 took place during the siege. The Babylonians finally breached the wall on the ninth day of Ab, 586 B.C., and had the city in their control within a month (2 Kings 25:1–12).

Nebuchadnezzar appointed Gedaliah, the son of Ahikam, governor (2 Kings 25:22–26/Jer. 40:7–41:18). Evidently he was not of royal lineage, although his grandfather, Shaphan, had been secretary and financial officer to King Josiah. It was he who had carried the Scroll of the Law to the king (2 Kings 22:3–13), and his son, Ahikam, was part of the commission that took the scroll to the prophetess Huldah for verification of its authenticity (2 Kings 22:12–14). Gedaliah set up the seat of his government in Mizpah. Jerusalem was probably so devastated as to be inappropriate for the daily operations of the new administration (Lam. 2:13; 4:1). We might infer from the account of Nebuchadnezzar's kind treatment of Jeremiah after the conquest (Jer. 39:11–14) that he knew about his reputation. It is possible that he had heard about his advocacy of submission to Babylon, thus disposing him favorably toward the prophet.[10] Whatever the reason, Jeremiah was put into the friendly charge of Gedaliah, the son of the same man (Ahikam) who had saved his life early in the reign of Jehoiakim (26:24).

Taking political asylum from the ravages of the Babylonian conquest was a man of the royal family, Ishmael (41:1). When he, encouraged by the Ammonites, carried out a plot to murder Gedaliah, Johanan, a supporter of the governor, attempted to avenge his death but failed. That led eventually to Johanan's decision to flee to Egypt lest he and his compatriots be deemed anti-Babylonian (chaps. 41–42).

The final stage of Judean statehood is bound inextricably to the ministry of the prophet Jeremiah. He would have remained in the land after Jerusalem fell, but Johanan refused Jeremiah's word from the Lord that they should not flee to Egypt, and he took Jeremiah and Baruch along with them in defiance of that word (chap. 42).

---

10. It is doubtful that the message that Jeremiah dispatched to Babylonia by the hand of Seraiah about 594 B.C. had reached Nebuchadnezzar (51:59–64a), for Seraiah was to read it and cast it into the Euphrates. The impression is that it was read as an apostrophe rather than to particular individuals.

THE LITERARY NATURE AND AUTHENTICITY OF JEREMIAH

STRUCTURE OF THE BOOK

We have already observed that the prophetic books are collections of prophetic oracles and compositions. The book of Jeremiah is one of the best witnesses to that fact. Neither of the standard criteria for arranging the prophetic books, chronology and subject matter, works very well in an analysis of this book. The best that can be hoped is to discover segments of the book that have come together according to identifiable criteria and make use of those "centers" to understand the book as a whole. The identification of three separate "books" is a rather standard procedure.[11]

"Book" One: The Basic Collection (1:1–25:13). The first "book" is marked off at the beginning by Jeremiah's call in the thirteenth year of Josiah (627) and at the end by a concluding reference to "this book," a prophecy dated in the fourth year of Jehoiakim (605)—"And I will bring upon that land all My words which I have pronounced against it, all that is written in this book, which Jeremiah has prophesied against all the nations" (25:13).

The basic content of these chapters is judgment on Judah and Jerusalem. That judgment is described in several ways, most of which use the "north" as the direction from which it will come. First announced in Jeremiah's vision of the boiling pot facing away from the north (1:13), it is called "the evil" that comes or looks from the north (1:14; 4:6; 6:1), "families" from the north (1:15; 25:9), a nation from afar (5:15), a people from the north land (6:22–23), iron and bronze from the north (15:12), and serpents and adders that cannot be charmed (8:17). The name of the foe is left anonymous[12] until it is explicitly identified as Babylon in 20:4. In the final oracle at the end of the book of Jeremiah, the phrase will be turned against Babylon rather than Judah, and Jeremiah will describe in similar terms the agent that will reek vengeance on Babylonia: a nation out of the north (50:3), a horde of great nations from the north land (50:9), a people from the north (50:41), and destroyers from the north (51:48).

Judah's sins are also detailed in these chapters, most graphically depicted in the idolatry that was practiced in Jeremiah's day.[13] It was of the most horrible kind, blatant and open, and included child sacrifice after the Canaanite fashion

---

11. Bright, *Jeremiah*, pp. lvii–lix; Thompson, pp. 27–32.
12. Some scholars have believed that the "foe from the north" was the Scythians. See, e.g., H. H. Rowley, "The Early Prophecies of Jeremiah in Their Setting," 198–234 esp. pp. 199–200 n. 8, 213, 217. When the Scythian hordes did not invade Palestine as he predicted, Jeremiah went into a period of silence. However, the Scythian hypothesis is not widely accepted today. See the discussion on Zephaniah, pp. 168.
13. 2:20; 3:1–5; 7:9, 17–18, 30–31; 8:19; 9:14; 10:2–10, 14; 11:12–13, 17; 17:3; 18:15; 19:4–5. Outside of the first twenty-five chapters the theme of idolatry is not as prominent.

(7:30–31; 19:4–5). The gods of Judah were as numerous as their cities, and the altars as many as the streets of Jerusalem (11:12–13). Yet Jeremiah had no desire merely to transfer the religious devotion from the Baal sanctuaries to the Jerusalem Temple. In fact, the Temple too had become a fetish to the people. They were overconfident about it, thinking that their personal ethics had nothing to do with the security the Temple provided (7:3–10). Idolatry is a concern outside these chapters, but not very frequently (32:29, 34–35, 44:9–10, 16–19). The same violation of covenant fidelity is expressed in the phrases (both negative and positive) "to know the Lord/Law," "to forget the Lord," "to forsake the Lord/Law," and "to reject the Lord/Law."[14] The point of our discussion is that in this first "book" the judgment and the sin that called it forth are explicated.

Within chapters 1–25 are smaller collections that can be identified by the titles. The first is 14:1–15:4, titled "That which came as the word of the Lord to Jeremiah in regard to the drought" (Heb. "droughts"). The date is not clear, but the occasion is vivid enough. Judah languished as a result of drought. The false prophets were on the scene with their unfounded hopes: "You will not see the sword nor will you have famine, but I will give you lasting peace in this place" (14:13).

A second shorter collection is titled "To the household of the king of Judah" (21:11–23:8). It begins with words about the monarchy's responsibility and the consequences for not fulfilling it (21:12–22:9), followed by messages about Jehoahaz (22:10–12), Jehoiakim (22:13–23), Jehoiachin (22:24–30), and concluding with a word of judgment against the "shepherds" (kings) who had not attended to the Lord's flock—so the Lord will attend to them in judgment (23:1–8).

The third collection is the condemnation of the false prophets, called simply "As for [concerning] the prophets" (23:9–40). It stands after the condemnation of the kings, perhaps because the prophets, along with the priests, made up the second major class of flawed leadership. The three groups whom Jeremiah held most responsible for Judah's tragic situation were the kings, priests, and prophets.

Although the "confessions" are not grouped together in one collection, they do constitute a homogeneous classification by virtue of their emotional tone and subject matter. Furthermore, all of them are found within this first "book." The list is fairly standard, although some variations among lists will occur: 11:18–23; 12:1–6; 15:10–21; 17:14–18; 18:18–23; 20:7–18.[15] The deeply emo-

---

14. 4:22; 5:4–5; 8:7; 9:3, 6, 24; 14:18/13:25; 18:15/5:7, 19; 9:13; 16:11; 19:4/6:19; 8:9; 15:6.
15. This is Otto Eissfeldt's list, *The Old Testament: An Introduction*, p. 357. See also Bright's list, p. lxvi; James Philip Hyatt, "The Book of Jeremiah," 5:782; Sheldon H. Blank, *Jeremiah: Man and Prophet*, pp. 106–112. Blank's helpful discussion of Jeremiah's prayers (pp. 105–28) deals also with their form.

tional passage found in 8:18–9:3 contains a mixture of divine and prophetic lament. Basically these confessions or p. ayers conform to the emotional disposition of Jeremiah as we know it outside the confessions. On that basis they quite definitely derive from Jeremiah himself.

When we speak of authenticity we have in mind the origin of the materials in 1:1—25:13. Did they originate with Jeremiah? If that question is answered affirmatively, that still does not rule out the hand of Jeremiah's scribe, Baruch, who may have contributed in an editorial way as the prophet dictated the messages to him. But it may also be noted that Baruch is nowhere mentioned in these chapters (not until chap. 32), although he was involved with Jeremiah as early as 605 B.C. (36:1). It is not to be doubted that this section came into being over a considerably long period of time. Certainly chapter 1 belongs to 627 B.C. in the reign of Josiah, and 3:6–10 also comes from that time.[16] Judging from the fact that King Jehoiakim cut up the first scroll three or four columns at a time and threw the pieces into the fire (36:23), we might surmise that the scroll that Baruch wrote at Jeremiah's dictation in 605 was of considerable length. It contained prophecies from a period of twenty-three years. Just how much of the material comes from Josiah's reign is difficult to determine. The criterion must generally be the appropriateness of a passage (both in content and tone) for Josiah's time. For example, the passages that deal with the false peace pronounced by the prophets may belong to Josiah's time, when there was national peace, but Jeremiah recognized that it was an insecure one (6:13–15; 8:10–11; 14:13–16; 23:17). The reform of Josiah, in addition to its positive effects, perhaps lulled the priests and prophets, who came into a new position of prominence, into believing that a new day had truly dawned. But Jeremiah was perceptive enough to recognize that they had prematurely announced the day of peace.

It is obvious, however, that chronology was not the primary basis for the collection, because chapter 21 is dated in the reign of Zedekiah during the siege of Jerusalem, and 10:17–18 and 25, though undated, must come from the time of the siege and the fall also. Even the Exile finds description in 13:15–19 ("All Judah has been carried into exile, wholly carried into exile" [v. 19]). Moreover, 8:14–15 reveals a time when national optimism, likely that of Josiah's reign of peace and reform, had turned to horror in a subsequent period ("We waited for peace, but no good came; for a time of healing, but behold, terror!" [v. 15]).

We may confidently say that the materials of these first twenty-five chapters were written or dictated by Jeremiah. Most likely also this "book" circulated in self-contained form or at least was written on a separate scroll for a time.

16. R. K. Harrison, *Introduction to the Old Testament*, p. 816, assigns tentatively all of chaps. 1–10 and 18–20 to Josiah's reign.

The fact that the Septuagint inserted the oracles against the nations (chaps. 46–51) after 25:13[17] suggests that the Greek translator found that to be an appropriate place to insert the oracles, which were also probably a separate collection. Yet we should admit that that proposition is not absolutely certain, although the reference to the book in 25:13 does give that inference.

"Book" Two: The Book of Consolation (30–31). The second "book" is constituted by chapters 30–31. Composed mainly in poetry, these chapters are commonly called the "Book of Consolation." The Lord instructed Jeremiah, "Write all the words which I have spoken to you in a book" (30:2), and 30:3 defines the content of the prophecies as concerning restoration. The reference to rebuilding the city (31:38) seems to fix the date at the end of the Judean kingdom after Jerusalem had fallen.

Jeremiah's eschatology elsewhere, especially in the first book (12:14–17; 16:14–15), is in agreement with the plan of the future set forth in the Book of Consolation. The new covenant (31:31–34), predicted the prophet, will become the landmark covenant of history rather than that of Moses, and Yahweh will write the words on tablets of flesh rather than tablets of stone. That passage draws the same kind of comparison that Jeremiah drew in 23:1–8. When the Lord returned Judah to his homeland, He would make that return rather than the Exodus the landmark of history.

"Book" Three: The Oracles against the Nations (46–51). The third "book" is the collection of national oracles in chapters 46–51. It is introduced by the formula, "That which came as the word of the Lord to Jeremiah the prophet concerning the nations" (46:1). Included are prophecies against Egypt (46:2–28), Philistia (47:1–7), Moab (48:1–47), Ammon (49:1–6), Edom (49:7–22), Damascus (49:23–27), Kedar and the kingdoms of Hazor (49:28–33), Elam (49:34–39), and Babylon (50:1–51:58). This collection appropriately concludes the book and balances the opening prophecies of chapter 1, in which the Lord appointed Jeremiah a "prophet to the nations" (1:5).

The oracle against Egypt (46:2–28) is dated in the fourth year of Jehoiakim (605). Verses 2–12 deal largely with Pharaoh Neco's defeat by Nebuchadnezzar at Carchemish in that same year, whereas verses 13–24 probably deal with the Chaldean capture of Ashkelon in 604 B.C. The oracle concludes with an appendix assuring Israel that the Lord will save him and make an end of the nations (vv. 27–28).

The oracle against Philistia (47:1–7) probably dates around 601 B.C. when Neco and Nebuchadnezzar fought to a stalemate on the Egyptian border.[18] The reference to the ruin of Ashkelon perhaps relates to Nebuchadnezzar's sack of the city in 604.

17. See the discussion on Septuagint below.
18. D. J. Wiseman, *Chronicles of Chaldaean Kings (626–556 B.C.) in the British Museum,* pp. 29–31.

The oracles against Moab and Ammon (48:1–47 and 49:1–6) may have their setting in the events recorded in 2 Kings 24:1–4. Bands of Chaldeans were joined by marauders from Syria, Moab, and Ammon in raids upon Judah. An interesting feature of these oracles, shared also by the oracle against Elam (49:39), is Yahweh's promise to restore the fortunes of these nations.

Edom is slated for defeat and humiliation (49:7–22). Perhaps this prophecy centers upon the events surrounding Nebuchadnezzar's attack on the Edomites in 594, when she joined Ammon and Moab in an anti-Babylonian rebellion.

Three more oracles, against Damascus (49:23–27), Kedar and the kingdoms of Hazor (49:28–33), and Elam (49:34–39), round out the list before the major oracle of the series against Babylon. The prophecy against Damascus, in which Hamath and Arpad are also mentioned, is difficult to pinpoint in history. The oracle against Kedar, an Arab tribe located in the Syrian desert, and the "kingdoms of Hazor"[19] may be assigned to the year 599/98, when Nebuchadnezzar conducted a campaign against the Arabs.[20] The oracle against Elam is provided with a date early in Zedekiah's reign. However, the events that Jeremiah refers to are much more difficult to date. A broken place in the Babylonian Chronicle may refer to an attack by Nebuchadnezzar on Elam in 596/95, but that is not certain.[21]

The longest oracle of them all is that against Babylon. It was definitely written from the perspective of the destruction of Jerusalem, for messengers flee from Babylon to declare to Zion that the Lord has taken vengeance for His Temple (50:28), and the prophecy takes cognizance of the desecration of the sanctuary (51:51). Yet the destruction of Babylon is still future (51:58). When the fall of the city is spoken of as accomplished (51:8), it is the prophetic perfect that is used.

The oracle is probably a compilation of shorter poems about the fate of Judah's archenemy. At points it is interspersed with words of reassurance and comfort for Judah: the return to Zion (50:4–7), pardon of the remnant of Israel (50:17–20), the messenger's word that the Lord has avenged Zion (50:28), the promise that Judah's Redeemer will give rest to the earth but none to Babylon (50:33–34), and the beautiful image of the lion coming up out of the jungle of the Jordan and the Lord frightening him away from the sheepfold (50:44–46). The primary guilt of Babylon consisted in the atrocities she had committed against the Lord and Zion (51:5, 24).

There is an interesting note in 51:59–64 that Jeremiah wrote all these things against Babylon and sent Seraiah, who went with Zedekiah to Babylon in 594, to read them by the Euphrates. If that applies to the entire oracle, then he

---

19. See Thompson, pp. 726–27, for the opinion that the phrase "the kingdoms of Hazor" should be understood as "village chieftains."
20. Wiseman, pp. 31–32.
21. Ibid., p. 36.

composed it before that date. We can be confident that part of it does predate that event, but other parts may have been added after the fall of Jerusalem. This section of the book of Jeremiah ends with the note, "Thus far are the words of Jeremiah." That implies that the editor of the book added chapter 52.

Two biographical interludes. Between the three "books" are two prose narratives that relate incidents in the life and ministry of Jeremiah. The principle of arrangement used in these collections seems to be no more than the fact that Jeremiah is their leading character.

The first biographical interlude (chaps. 26–29) incorporates events from the beginning of Jehoiakim's reign (chap. 26, c. 609/8) as well as the beginning of Zedekiah's rule (chaps. 27–29, c. 597/96). Jeremiah's trial before the elders occurred in the early part of Jehoiakim's reign (chap. 26), and the conflict with Hananiah the prophet in the early reign of Zedekiah (chaps. 27–28). The letter of Jeremiah to the exiles, also from Zedekiah's reign, was written soon after the exile of 597. The chronological scheme of this section is the following:

Biographical Interlude I (chaps. 26–29)

Jehoiakim	Zedekiah
26 (c. 609/08)	27–28 (c. 597/96)
	29 (same time)

The second *biographical interlude* (chaps. 32–45) is connected to the Book of Consolation (chaps. 30–31) in that 32–33 record Jeremiah's purchase of a field in Anathoth when that town was already under Babylonian control in 588/87 (chap. 32), and they include promises of restoration of the kingdom and the Davidic monarchy (chap. 33). Hope is the connection to the Book of Consolation. In fact, whereas chapters 32–34 record events during the Babylonian siege of Jerusalem (588–586), chapters 35–36 jump back to the reign of Jehoiakim. The commendation of the Rechabites for faithfulness to their father's precepts likely occurred in the final days of Jehoiakim (598) when the Babylonians had besieged Jerusalem, and the Rechabites, normally a nomadic people, had taken refuge inside the city walls (chap. 35). Yet chapter 36 is earlier still, the dictation of the first scroll (36:1–8) in the year 605 B.C. and the second scroll in 604 (36:9–32). Then the narrative makes another jump forward to Zedekiah's reign in chapters 37–39 to present events that occurred during the siege of Jerusalem. First is the approach of Pharaoh Hophra (Apries) of Egypt to relieve the besieged city, and then Jeremiah's arrest when he was seen leaving the city, supposed by his accusers to be deserting to the Chaldeans (chap. 37). The account of Zedekiah's consultation with Jeremiah in chapter 38 belongs to the same period, and chapter 39 is a summary of the siege and fall of Jerusalem in 588–586. The narrative moves chronologically to the days after the capture of Jerusalem during the governorship and assassination of Gedaliah and the flight to Egypt of those who attempted to avenge his death (chapters 40–44). The historical narrative of 40:7–41:18 parallels and greatly supplements the brief account of the events in 2 Kings 25:23–26. So we have the following parallels within Jeremiah and between these historical sections and the book of Kings:

Jer. 52:1–30 parallels and greatly supplements
2 Kings 24:18–25:21.

Jer. 52:31–34 parallels
2 Kings 25:27–30.

Jer. 40:7–41:18 parallels and greatly supplements
2 Kings 25:23–26.

Jer. 39:1–10 parallels
Jer. 52:4–16 parallels
2 Kings 25:1–12.

Concluding this section is the account of Baruch's self-pity (chap. 45), which belongs not to the last days of Judah but to the fourth year of Jehoiakim, when he had written the original scroll for Jeremiah (chap. 36). Perhaps the Lord's promise of Baruch's life as booty (45:5) is in deference to the threats of annihilation of those who fled to Egypt (chap. 44).

In summary, this section of narrative has the following chronological scheme:

Biographical Interlude II (chaps. 32–45)

Jehoiakim	Zedekiah	Gedaliah
36:1–8 (605)		
45 (605)		
36:9–32 (604)		
35 (598)		
	32–34 (588/87)	
	37–39 (588–586)	
		40–44 (586–582)

Historical appendix (52). The final installment of the book is a historical narrative briefly summarizing the reign of Zedekiah and relating the stages of the Babylonian siege of Jerusalem, the number of the captives taken to Babylon in the three exiles, and the release of King Jehoiachin from prison. The narrative of 52:1–30 parallels and generously supplements that of 2 Kings 24:18–25:21, whereas 52:31–34 is more or less a parallel account of 2 Kings

25:27–30. Because the scope of this appendix extends to the death of Nebuchadnezzar in 562, Jeremiah could hardly have written this narrative. In fact the editor has given us the cue in 51:64 that Jeremiah's words were ended ("Thus far are the words of Jeremiah").

COMPILATION AND AUTHENTICITY

The prophecies of Jeremiah span a period of about forty years, from 627/26 to 586. The reconstruction of the process by which they were written and brought together in this collection must remain hypothetical. Yet R. K. Harrison is likely right when he states that the process of transmitting the oracles from Jeremiah's lips to their ultimate form "was considerably less complex than has been assumed by the majority of liberal writers on the subject."[22] On the other side of the spectrum, Davidson claims one can scarcely talk about Jeremiah's literary style because "strictly speaking, we have no literature from him."[23] My assumption is that the material comes from Jeremiah, most likely through the hand of his scribe Baruch, unless it can be proved otherwise. As a review of modern scholarship on the subject reveals, that process of proof is often subjective and prejudiced against the prophet. Of course, the charge can be made in the other direction, and sometimes justifiably so. Yet the assumptions upon which many critical scholars approach the prophets are based upon those materials that they will allow to these biblical spokesmen. For example, some interpreters will not allow universalism in the pre-exilic prophets because they assume that idea was a post-exilic belief. Even literary style is an elusive criterion for determining authenticity and must be used cautiously, although it certainly is not an invalid one.

Although the book of Jeremiah is not plagued by the number and scope of controversial issues that have shrouded the book of Isaiah for the past century, it nevertheless has been the subject of much discussion. It is widely agreed that some form of the book came into being during Jeremiah's lifetime, and as early as 605–604 (chap. 36).

The First and Second Scrolls. In my discussion above I tried to delineate major sections within the book from the vantage point of the book as we have it today. However certain is the compilation of a scroll containing Jeremiah's prophecies of the first twenty-three years, the content of that scroll is only vaguely defined for us in the book. Three things are clear from the account: (1) it was intended to elicit repentance (36:3); (2) its contents should have caused fear and made the king and his servants mourn (36:24); and (3) it predicted that the King of Babylon would come and destroy man and beast (36:29). Thus we may draw one inference and one certain conclusion. We infer that Jeremiah

---

22. Harrison, p. 815.
23. A. B. Davidson, p. 575.

included prophecies that called Judah to repentance, and with certainty we can conclude that he predicted destruction at the hands of the Babylonians. Otto Eissfeldt has satisfactorily shown that chapters 1–25 do contain such materials, although he limits them to sayings predominantly of a threatening kind. In his view chapter 25 is the conclusion to the original scroll. The second scroll then added the first-person narratives (chaps. 24, 27, 28, 32, 35).[24] J. A. Thompson has reviewed major proposals and concludes with John Bright and others that trying to determine its content is so speculative as to be futile.[25] Yet it is quite probable that the contents of the first scroll are imbedded in chapters 1–25. All the ingredients, however vague their description in chapter 36, are there. As I have shown above, Judah's sins are most clearly laid out in that section of the book. Further, the theme of the foe from the north and finally the clear prediction that Babylon is the enemy to be feared (20:4) are contained there. Somewhere in those chapters lies the substance of the first scroll; speculation beyond that is not helpful.

All we know about the second scroll is that it contained the words of the first and "many similar words" (36:32). It is not satisfactory to limit one type of material to the original scroll (e.g., Eissfeldt's sayings) and conjecture that the second scroll contained an additional type (e.g., Eissfeldt, first-person reports;[26] and Pfeiffer, "confessions"[27]) because Jeremiah's literary forms were probably spread out over his ministry. It is not likely that he wrote the "confessions" in one short period of time, because they were his prayers that represented a long and disheartening career. If the three descriptive points mentioned above can give any guidance, the second scroll contained more of the same: more prophecies that explicated Judah's idolatry and sinful history and perhaps even additional prophecies about the Babylonian threat. Of course, the possibility of other contents should not be excluded, but neither should it be limited to one literary category.

Categorization of the literature. Since Sigmund Mowinckel's work on Jeremiah, his divisions of the literature of the book into three categories has become a standard way to view the material,[28] even if the composition of the three types and their relationship to Jeremiah are not widely agreed upon. Mowinckel called the prophetic oracles written in poetic form *Type A.* He believed these to be genuine oracles of the prophet Jeremiah recorded without introductory material or concluding formulas. Much of this kind of material is to be found in chapters 1–25. It includes the "confessions" of Jeremiah. Other examples are 2:2*b*–3, 5–37; 4:1–2, 3*b*–4, 5*b*–8. This type represents the poetic form in which

---

24. Eissfeldt, pp. 350–54.
25. Thompson, pp. 56–59; Bright, p. lxi.
26. Eissfeldt, p. 353.
27. Robert H. Pfeiffer, *Introduction to the Old Testament*, p. 501.
28. Sigmund Mowinckel, *Zur Komposition des Buches Jeremia* (Kristiana, 1914).

Jeremiah spoke his oracles. For the most part, there is wide agreement that Type A originated with Jeremiah.

The literature that Mowinckel called *Type B* material was the historical narratives about Jeremiah. Most of chapters 26–29 and 34–44 fall into this category. Jeremiah is referred to in the third person. The Jeremianic nature of this material is not as generally held, as with Type A. Mowinckel thought it came from an Egyptian background during the century after Jeremiah's death (c. 580–480 B.C.). Other scholars have held that it originated during the prophet's lifetime. The natural inclination is to attribute this work or its editorial style to the scribe Baruch. The narratives sound as though they were recorded by someone contemporary with Jeremiah and perhaps even an eyewitness. Eissfeldt agrees that Baruch contributed significantly to this material.[29] Thompson insists that the best candidate for the "biographer," as he is called, is Baruch.[30] H. L. May has not been willing to accept Baruch's part in these biographical sections and insists that Baruch was merely Jeremiah's amanuensis, not his biographer, and the author of Type B materials could not be earlier than the first half of the fifth century, because he wrote in the style of the Deuteronomic redactor.[31]

Because we have no writings that we know for certain came from Baruch's hand, it is impossible to say what his part in the composition of this type of material was. It is more likely that he wrote materials in collaboration with Jeremiah. His involvement with the prophet began at least as early as 605 (chap. 36) and continued to the end of Jeremiah's public ministry in Judah. The two men went to Egypt together at the insistence of Johanan and his party. Because Baruch's profession was that of a scribe and his employment with Jeremiah utilized his professional skills, anything less than a significant role in the editorial stage of the book would be inconceivable. He was known to be a man of great influence (43:3).

Mowinckel called the third class of material *Type C*. In this category he included the speeches written in a repetitive prose style and marked by Deuteronomic language. They are scattered throughout the book, examples being chapter 27; 29:16–20; 32:17–44; 34:12–22; 35:12–17. This material, urged Mowinckel, was not from Jeremiah but belonged to the efforts of later editors. There has been much discussion about this category. Bright has clearly shown that, although there are correspondences in style between Jeremiah and Deuteronomy, there are also significant differences. He concludes that it is a style in its own right and that it belongs to the prose of the seventh to sixth

29. Eissfeldt, p. 355.
30. Thompson, p. 43.
31. H. G. May, "Towards an Objective Approach to the Book of Jeremiah: The Biographer," pp. 139–55 (esp. pp. 140, 146, 152).

centuries.[32] No wide agreement on Type C material is in view, but many scholars are more willing to admit today that the material is much more Jeremianic than had been assumed earlier. Perhaps enough credence has not been given to the variety and development within Jeremiah's writings. Many scholars insist on development of his thought over the forty years of his ministry but allow for little or no development in literary style and forms.

The Septuagint version of Jeremiah. The Greek translation of the Hebrew text of Jeremiah is estimated to be about one-eighth shorter than the Masoretic version. The omissions are largely single verses and parts of verses, but some longer passages are missing, such as 17:1–5a; 29:16–20; 33:14–26; 39:4–13; 51:44b–49a; 52:27b–30. Those omissions may be due to scribal errors like homoioteleuton or simple oversight.[33] Yet some may indicate that the translator was working with a different version of the Hebrew text than has come to us, whereas still others reveal an ineptness on the part of the Greek translator.[34]

One of the most obvious differences between the Greek and Hebrew versions is the position and order of the oracles against the nations (chaps. 46–51). In the LXX they occur after 25:13a, with verse 14 omitted, whereas the Hebrew text (and English translations) places them at the end of the book. The sequence of the nations is quite different, with only Edom occupying the same position in both lists. It is most probable that the book had reached its present form three centuries before the Septuagint translation (c. 250–150 B.C.), although there may have been other rescensions of the book in existence. If the LXX translator used another edition of Jeremiah, it was not superior to the Hebrew. Although the LXX readings may occasionally be preferred over the Hebrew, the opposite is more often the case. It has further been observed that the order of the Hebrew oracles is closer to that of the order of the nations given in 25:17–26 than to the Greek (both begin with Egypt and end with Babylon); and even though that may be true, it is hardly close enough to make a case for the Hebrew order and position on that basis. The list in chapter 25 was evidently not intended to be a parallel to the list in chapters 46–51, for it adds some names and omits Damascus and Kedar. Perhaps the Greek translator was attempting to arrange the book more logically.[35] The Lord's promise to punish Babylon after the seventy-year Exile had elapsed (25:12–13a) perhaps seemed to him a good place to insert the oracles, following them with the oracle about Yahweh's cup of wrath that Jeremiah should cause the nations to drink (25:17–26).

32. John Bright, "The Date of the Prose Sermons of Jeremiah," pp. 15–35; also *Jeremiah*, pp. lxx–lxxii. Thompson expresses plausibly the view that Jeremiah was the inheritor of a literary prose style that was impressed upon the Deuteronomistic history (Joshua–II Kings) as it was on Jeremiah's prose discourses (*Jeremiah*, p. 43). W. L. Holladay, "A Fresh Look at 'Source B' and 'Source C' in Jeremiah," pp. 394–412, reviews the work of H. Weippert, *Die Prosareden des Jeremiabuches*, who concludes that the ties to Deuteronomic-Deuteronomistic speech are weak (p. 408).
33. Eissfeldt, p. 349, attributes the omission of 39:4–13 to homoioteleuton.
34. See A. B. Davidson's list of faults with the Greek version, p. 574.
35. Edward J. Young, *An Introduction to the Old Testament*, p. 232.

We can speculate about the reasons for putting those prophecies at the end of the Hebrew version. It may have been intended to balance out Jeremiah's call to the nations in the beginning of the book or perhaps to put the oracle against Egypt close to the flight of the Judeans to that country. An even better reason may be inferred from the final position of the oracle against Babylon and the prose account that concludes it. Babylon had been the agent of Yahweh's judgment on Judah, but He had promised to turn on Babylon when the seventy years were passed. The book ends with that expectation. In that case the present form of the book would certainly precede the fall of Babylon in 539 B.C. In fact, the entire book was probably finished around 560, because the closing narrative records Nebuchadnezzar's death and Jehoiachin's release from prison, another note of expectancy and hope. The LXX version of those oracles was too far removed from the events of the sixth century to be concerned with such matters. Most probably the Hebrew order is the original one.

The following table will help to make the comparisons between the oracles in the two versions:

GREEK		HEBREW
25:15–20	Elam	49:34–39
26	Egypt	46:2–38
27–28	Babylon	50:1–51:58
29:1–7	Philistia	47:1–7
30:1–16	Edom	49:7–22
30:17–22	Ammon	49:1–6
30:23–28	Kedar	49:28–33
30:29–33	Damascus	49:23–27
31	Moab	48:1–47
32	The nations	25:15–38

THE MESSAGE OF JEREMIAH

The Lord promised to make Jeremiah like a "pillar of iron and as walls of bronze" against Judah (1:18; 15:20), a people whose will, as it turned out to be, was also made of bronze and iron (6:28). It was the will of God over against the will of Judah. The hope behind Jeremiah's ministry was that he would make the difference. As already observed, in public Jeremiah never flinched. He was invincible. Whether it was the king seeking a word from the Lord or a false prophet who publicly contradicted his message, this prophet of iron and bronze braced himself against the leaning wall of Judah's idolatrous and immoral conduct. Yet in private he agonized over his dreadful task. When those two images are seen together in the book, Yahweh's power to call and equip His prophet is all the more evident. And all the more obvious is the fact that His prophets were but men.

THE PURPOSE OF THE BOOK

The book of Jeremiah seems to involve two aims in its purpose. First, Jeremiah announced the sin of Judah, which consisted basically in forsaking the Lord and devising a religious system that epitomized disobedience to the Lord:

> Then I said,
> "How I would set you among My sons,
> And give you a pleasant land,
> The most beautiful inheritance of the nations!"
> And I said, "You shall call Me, My Father,
> And not turn away from following Me."
> Surely, as a woman treacherously departs from her lover,
> So you have dealt treacherously with Me,
> O house of Israel," declares the LORD.
>
> (3:19–20)

What Yahweh really wanted was not more and better ritual but obedience (7:21–26; 9:13; 11:7–8). It all boiled down to the fundamental requirement that Hosea and Isaiah made of Israel—to know the Lord and live out that knowledge in obedience to the ethical demands of the covenant: "But let him who boasts boast of this, that he understands and knows Me, that I am the Lord who exercises lovingkindness, justice, and righteousness on earth; for I delight in these things," declares the Lord" (9:24).

The second aim was to announce judgment if repentance was not forthcoming. The form of that judgment was the "evil from the north," which Jeremiah eventually came to understand as being Babylonia. Yet Yahweh was ready to relent in His punishment of Judah if the people would only allow Him to remake them as the potter reshapes the spoiled vessel at his wheel (18:1–11). The announcement of judgment included Jeremiah's role as prophet to the nations (1:5), and there was also an element of reassurance involved in some instances (48:47; 49:6, 39).

JUDAH AND GOD: AN UNNATURAL RELATIONSHIP

In graphic imagery that the Judeans could understand, Jeremiah laid out the dilemma:

> For My people have committed two evils:
> They have forsaken Me,
> The fountain of living waters,
> To hew for themselves cisterns,
> Broken cisterns,
> That can hold no water.
>
> (2:13)

In a land where water was at a premium, the spiritual condition of Judah was that of one who had turned away from a flowing stream of water only to hew out cisterns with holes in them, two illogical actions. Forsaking the water she desperately needed to prepare a useless cistern for water she had already forsaken—what an absurdity! Yet that describes the dilemma the nation had fallen into.

If one inquired among the nations of the world, Judah's apostasy could not be duplicated:

> Has a nation changed gods,
> When they were not gods?
> But My people have changed their glory
> For that which does not profit.
>
> (2:11)

> Therefore thus says the Lord,
> "Ask now among the nations,
> Who ever heard the like of this?
> The virgin of Israel
> Has done a most appalling thing.
>
> For My people have forgotten Me,
> They burn incense to worthless gods
> And they have stumbled from their ways,
> From the ancient paths,
> To walk in bypaths,
> Not on a highway."
>
> (18:13, 15)

In more sentimental terms, Judah had done what a bride could not do,

> Can a virgin forget her ornaments,
> Or a bride her attire?
> Yet My people have forgotten Me
> Days without number.
>
> (2:32)

Judah had made unnatural conduct the norm. Yet she had inherited a tradition of apostasy from her fathers who found no injustice in Yahweh but forsook Him nevertheless (2:5; 9:14; 44:9–10, 16–19).

The most blatant form of apostasy in ancient Judah was idolatry in its worst form. Jeremiah, like Hosea, used the term *harlot* to describe Judah's pagan worship (e.g., 2:20), for the people had stooped even to child sacrifice (7:30–31; 19:5; 32:35). The Yahwism of Jeremiah's day was a blend of Mosaic and

Baalistic elements, sometimes committed openly in the Temple (7:30–31; 32:35). Like Isaiah, Jeremiah gibes the makers of idols and their products,

> They decorate it with silver and with gold;
> They fasten it with nails and with hammers
> So that it will not totter.
> Like a scarecrow in a cucumber field are they,
> And they cannot speak;
> They must be carried,
> Because they cannot walk!
> Do not fear them,
> For they can do no harm,
> Nor can they do any good.
>
> (10:4–5)

In contrast, Judah's God was maker of the heavens and earth (10:12; 32:17; 33:2; 51:15). He had called the people of Israel His children, but they had not called Him their Father (3:19). Rather, the people had turned to the symbols of Baalism and called a tree their father, and to a stone they said, "You gave me birth" (2:27). Yet the blend of the two religions was so crafty that sometimes they could not recognize that they had opted for Baalism (2:23).[36]

THE COVENANT OLD AND NEW

Using the imagery of Israel as God's bride, Jeremiah depicts Yahweh's special covenant relationship to the nation (2:2–3). It was rooted in the historical Exodus from Egypt,[37] and its principal character was to be found in obedience (7:23; 11:4). The Judeans were quite religious, for they never stopped sacrificing and fulfilling the ritual requirements, but they had been able to disassociate religion from morality, the benefits of the covenant from its responsibilities. They committed their moral violations, breaking the Ten Commandments, and came to the Temple and felt secure (7:1–11). The ceremonial law was to them a manipulative tool, and they had learned to use it well, or so they thought. Perhaps that was the design of their actions in 34:8–22 when, in the midst of the Babylonian siege, they released their Hebrew slaves in compliance with the Mosaic covenant (Ex. 21:2). The insincerity of that act was transparent when they took them back, believing the crisis had passed. Ritual without morality could not satisfy the demands of a just God who required righteousness and holiness of His people (6:20; 11:15).

The history of Yahweh's covenant dealings with Israel was paralleled by the prophetic movement, yet the words of the prophets were served upon a

36. 2:6; 7:22, 25; 11:4, 7; 16:14; 23:7; 31:32; 32:21; 34:13.
37. 2:6; 7:22, 25; 11:4, 7; 16:14; 23:7; 31:32; 32:21; 34:13.

disobedient people (7:25–26). Jeremiah saw himself in that long chain of witnesses whom Israel had rejected and abused. His professional loyalty was pledged to the God who called him, however, and not to that company that went under the name of "prophets." He really felt quite alone, and as Abraham pleaded that Sodom be spared if only five righteous persons could be found there, Jeremiah looked for only one such person in Jerusalem so that Yahweh might pardon the city (5:1).

What a tragic history Israel had lived. The conclusion to her story was woven out of the threads she had spun. Nevertheless the Lord would not accept the conclusion that was woven in the darkest hues of destruction and exile. Rather, He would inaugurate a new day when Jerusalem would not be known as the resting place of the ark but the Throne of God (3:16–17). The Exodus from Egypt would cease to be the landmark of history, replaced by the return from exile as the new landmark,

> "Therefore behold, days are coming," declares the Lord, "when it will no longer be said, 'As the Lord lives, who brought up the sons of Israel out of the land of Egypt,' but, 'As the Lord lives, who brought up the sons of Israel from the land of the north and from all the countries where He had banished them.' For I will restore them to their own land which I gave to their fathers." (16:14–15; cf. 23:7–8)

The covenant that had been so peripheral for Israel would become a vital organ of existence. Written formerly on tablets of stone, the new age would be characterized by a covenant written on the heart of Israel (31:31–34). Nothing short of that could erase the sin that was written with an iron stylus upon Israel's heart (17:1–4). The sin and apostasy that had blackened her past would be outdistanced by God's grace, which would distinguish her future.

THE FUTURE OF JUDAH

The centerpiece of Jeremiah's future age was the return from exile. We have already noted that once that event occurred it would take a more prominent place in history than the Exodus. Purified by the Exile, Yahweh's people would return after seventy years (25:12; 29:10). Yet Jeremiah saw farther into the future than the Exile. His foresight included a renewed Jerusalem that would reflect God's holiness (31:23–25) and bear a new name, "The Lord is our righteousness" (33:16). The Messianic age comes into view in our prophet's eschatology distinguished by a restored Davidic Ruler, the Righteous Branch, who will dispense equity and justice (23:5; 33:14–16). Both Judah and Israel will come to Zion (50:4–5), and the Gentiles will benefit from the blessings of that new day (3:17). The new covenant will be written on the hearts of men and women, and the law of God will be thus internalized (31:31–34).

OUTLINE OF JEREMIAH

I. "Book" One: The Basic Collection (1:1–25:13)
   A. Superscription (1:1–3)
   B. The Call of Jeremiah (1:4–10)
   C. Two Visions (1:11–19)
   D. Judah's Apostasy (2:1–3:5)
   E. Judah's Punishment (3:6–6:30)
      1. Israel and Judah Compared (3:6–11)
      2. A Call to Repentance (3:12–4:4)
      3. The Coming Judgment (4:5–6:30)
         a. Evil from the North (4:5–31)
         b. Reasons for Judgment (5:1–31)
         c. Judgment Predicted (6:1–30)
   F. Judah's False Religion (7:1–10:25)
      1. Indictment of False Religion (7:1–8:3)
         a. The Temple Sermon (7:1–15)
         b. Descriptions of Judah's False Religion (7:16–8:3)
      2. Punishment of False Religion (8:4–10:25)
         a. God's Retribution (8:4–9:26)
         b. Foolishness of Idolatry (10:1–16)
         c. Jeremiah's Lament and Intercession (10:17–25)
   G. Judah's Broken Covenant (11:1–13:27)
      1. The Covenant Broken (11:1–7)
      2. The Plot Against Jeremiah (11:18–12:6)
      3. Consequences of the Broken Covenant (12:7–17)
      4. Warnings of Judgment (13:1–27)
   H. Drought in Judah (14:1–15:4)
      1. The Message of the Drought (14:1–6)
      2. Lament and Intercession (14:7–15:4)
      3. Lament over Jerusalem (15:5–9)
   I. The Travail of the Prophet (15:10–17:27)
      1. The Prophet's Dilemma (15:10–21)
      2. The Prophet's Restrictions (16:1–9)
      3. Explanation of Judgment (16:10–17:27)
   J. The Potter's House and Other Prophecies (18:1–20:18)
      1. The Potter and the Vessel (18:1–23)
      2. The Broken Vessel (19:1–15)
      3. Jeremiah Persecuted (20:1–6)
      4. Jeremiah's Complaint (20:7–18)
   K. Prophecies to the Kings of Judah (21:1–23:8)
      1. Zedekiah's Question and Jeremiah's Answer (21:1–10)

  2. The Responsibility of the Monarchy (21:11–22:9)
  3. A Message Concerning Jehoahaz (22:10–12)
  4. A Message Concerning Jehoiakim (22:13–23)
  5. A Message Concerning Jehoiachin (22:24–30)
  6. Judgment against Judah's Shepherds (23:1–8)
 L. Concerning the Prophets (23:9–40)
 M. Summary Prophecies of Captivity (24:1–25:38)
  1. Vision of Two Baskets of Figs (24:1–10)
  2. The Duration of Captivity (25:1–14)
  3. Judgment on the Nations (25:15–38)
II. Biographical Interlude I (26:1–29:32)
 A. The Temple Sermon and Jeremiah's Trial (26:1–24)
 B. Jeremiah Versus the False Prophets (27:1–29:32)
  1. Jeremiah's Yoke (27:1–22)
  2. Contrasting Prophecies Between Jeremiah and Hananiah (28:1–17)
  3. Jeremiah's Letter to the Captives (29:1–32)
III. "Book" Two: The Book of Consolation (30:1–31:40)
 A. Promise of Restoration (30:1–31:30)
 B. The New Covenant (31:31–34)
 C. Yahweh and Israel in the New Jerusalem (31:35–40)
IV. Biographical Interlude II (32:1–45:5)
 A. Jeremiah's Symbolic Land Purchase (32:1–33:26)
  1. The Purchase at Anathoth (32:1–15)
  2. Jeremiah's Prayer (32:16–25)
  3. Yahweh's Reply to Jeremiah (32:26–44)
  4. Promise of Restoration of the Kingdom and Monarchy (33:1–26)
 B. Events in the Reigns of Jehoiakim and Zedekiah (34:1–39:18)
  1. Message in Zedekiah's Reign (34:1–22)
  2. Events in Jehoiakim's Reign (35:1–36:32)
   a. Praise of the Rechabites (35:1–19)
   b. Jehoiakim's Antagonism (36:1–32)
  3. Events in Zedekiah's Reign (37:1–38:28)
   a. Jeremiah's Counsel to Zedekiah (37:1–10)
   b. Jeremiah Imprisoned as a Traitor (37:11–16)
   c. Removal to the Court of the Guard (37:17–21)
   d. Jeremiah in the Dungeon Again (38:1–6)
   e. Jeremiah Aided by Friends (38:7–13)
   f. Jeremiah's Further Counsel to Zedekiah (38:14–28)
  4. The Fall of Jerusalem (39:1–18)
 C. Events After the Fall of Jerusalem (40:1–45:5)
  1. Jeremiah in the Land (40:1–43:7)
   a. The Governorship and Assassination of Gedaliah (40:1–41:3)

2. Jeremiah in Egypt (43:8–45:5)
   a. Invasion of Egypt Prophesied (43:8–43:13)
   b. Jeremiah's Final Oracle of Condemnation (44:1–30)
   c. Baruch's Despair (45:1–5)
V. "Book" Three: the Oracles Against the Nations (46:1–51:64)
   A. Oracles Against Egypt (46:1–28)
      1. Against Pharaoh at Carchemish (46:1–12)
      2. Prophecy of Nebuchadnezzar's Campaign Against Egypt (46:13–24)
      3. Israel's Final Superiority (46:25–28)
   B. Oracle Against the Philistines (47:1–7)
   C. Oracle Against Moab (48:1–47)
   D. Oracle Against the Ammonites (49:1–6)
   E. Oracle Against Edom (49:7–22)
   F. Oracle Against Damascus (49:23–27)
   G. Oracle Against Kedar and the Kingdoms of Hazor (49:28–33)
   H. Oracle Against Elam (49:34–39)
   I. Oracle Against Babylon (50:1–51:64)
VI. Historical Appendix (52:1–34)

10

NAHUM: THE REALITY OF JUDGMENT

FEW VOICES among the pre-exilic prophets have resounded with such immediacy of divine vindication as Nahum. The preaching of judgment by the prophets had primarily taken the form of judgment against Israel and Judah. Yet the other side of that message of Yahweh's vengeance against sin and idolatry was their message, strongly worded and emotionally charged, against the nations. We have those collections in Amos, Isaiah, Zephaniah, Jeremiah, and Ezekiel. However, in only two cases, Nahum and Obadiah, is a prophet preoccupied with his message against a foreign nation. Jonah might also be included in that category, but that book does not belong generically to the oracles against the nations as do Nahum and Obadiah. Nahum even distinguishes himself from Obadiah in the sense that he zooms in on the event of vindication and gives his audience an audio-visual experience by means of his powerful poetic style. If there was any doubt that the Lord would take vengeance upon Nineveh, the evil capital of Assyria, Nahum with his graphic word pictures of her fall would remove it out of mind. The sight of warriors dressed in red, flashing steel, madly racing chariots, frantic Assyrian soldiers hurrying to the wall, galloping horses, piles of corpses, combined with the sounds of women moaning like doves, leaves the audience with the feeling of having tuned in on the devastation. The scenes with all their visual horror, painted with the colorful hues of Nahum's vocabulary, give an immediacy to divine judgment that mere threats and promises cannot give. The threat of judgment is present in the book (1:8, 14; 3:5–6), but the reality of judgment is the thing that Nahum seeks to bring to his audience.

It has been recognized that the prophets often envisioned future events with such confidence of their reality that they spoke of them as having already occurred. In grammatical terms that phenomenon has been called the "prophetic perfect."[1] For example, Isaiah used that grammatical construction to predict the new day for Israel after the Assyrian conquest of the Galilean region:

---

1. The term perfect in Hebrew grammar signifies "completed" action and is not synonymous with the same term in English grammar.

> The people who walked in darkness have seen a great light;
> those who dwelt in a land of deep darkness,
> on them has light shined.
>
>   (Isa. 9:2, RSV)

The light is a future event described in Messianic terminology in the succeeding verses, but Isaiah was so certain of it that he spoke about it as completed action.

Nahum is that kind of prophecy. Although the fall of Nineveh was in the future (1:13–14), our prophet was so certain it would happen that he described it, not as already having occurred, but as transpiring before the eyes of his audience (2:3–7; 3:1–7). If we could speak of a "prophetic present," then that is what we have in Nahum. He paints a word portrait of the vindication that the Lord would take on the Assyrian capital.

NAHUM THE MAN

Our knowledge of the prophet is so minimal that we can hardly justify this category. With John Merlin Powis Smith we recognize that he is "little more to us than a voice."[2] The only personal information the book provides is that he was an "Elkoshite" (1:1). Unfortunately the location of the town of Elkosh is uncertain. Three places have been suggested. The first is modern Al-Kish, a town about twenty-four miles north of the ancient site of Nineveh. However, there is no substantive evidence that Nahum ever lived there, and the tradition itself is late. The second location is found in Jerome's commentary on Nahum. He identified it with Helkesei, or Elkese, in Galilee (perhaps modern El-Kauzeh).[3] In Jerome's time it still existed. Valid questions, however, have been raised about Nahum's association with Galilee.[4] The third proposal is the southern part of Judah. A Syriac version of the prophets, ascribed to Epiphanius, locates Elkosh "beyond Bet Gabre, of the tribe of Simeon."[5] The value of that tradition may be questionable, but it does point in the right direction, that is, to a southern provenance, for Nahum obviously spoke to Judah (1:15 [Heb. version 2:1]).

---

2. John Merlin Powis Smith, Wiliam Hayes Ward, and Julius A. Bewer, *A Critical and Exegetical Commentary on Micah, Zephaniah, Nahum, Habakkuk, Obadiah and Joel*, p. 269.
3. C. F. Keil, *The Twelve Minor Prophets*, 2:3, advances the idea that Nahum was born in Galilee during the Assyrian invasions, and he later emigrated to Judah, where he lived and prophesied. Although that harmonizes the Northern and Southern traditions, it is nevertheless speculative.
4. George Adam Smith, *The Book of the Twelve Prophets*, 2:79.
5. Ibid., pp. 79–80.

HISTORICAL BACKGROUND AND DATE OF THE PROPHECY

HISTORICAL BACKGROUND

The decline of the Assyrian Empire had been in process for some time when Nineveh, the capital, gave way to an enemy attack in the year 612 B.C.[6] The Medes and Babylonians in alliance against the imperial city marched up the Tigris in the summer of 612 and within three months took Nineveh, looting the temple and turning the city into a pile of debris. No details of the assault are given in the Babylonian Chronicle, which leads D. J. Wiseman to remark that that silence may support the classical theory[7] that the final breach of the walls resulted from a high flood of the Tigris River. In the autumn Asshur-uballit, the reigning Assyrian monarch, rallied his supporters to the provincial capital of Harran and reaffirmed his sovereignty over the empire.[8]

The internal evidence of the book of Nahum points to some Assyrian invasion of Judah in the past that had caused great suffering for the nation (1:9, 12, 15). That may be a specific invasion or a reference to an aggregate of the Assyrian invasions, for the Assyrians had harassed them since the days of Ahaz. The latter seems to be the better option. It was the aggregate sins of Assyria against Judah and the nations that justified God's wrath (1:12; 3:4).

Regardless of when scholars would date the ministry of Nahum and the composition of the book, it is almost a universal opinion that the prophecy is concerned with the fall of Nineveh in 612 B.C. The name of the city only occurs three times in the book. Outside of the superscription (1:1) it does not occur in the prophecy itself until 2:8, and then the last time in 3:7, but the pronouns in 1:8, 9, 11, 13–14, and 2:1 refer to Nineveh.

DATE OF THE PROPHECY

The *terminus a quo* and *terminus ad quem* of Nahum's activity can be easily established. His reference to the capture of Thebes (No-Amon) in 3:8–9, which fell to Assurbanipal in 663 B.C., fixes the *terminus a quo,* and the fall of Nineveh in 612 establishes the *terminus ad quem.* A few scholars have thought the book was written after the event, but their view has not been generally accepted. The majority opinion is that Nahum prophesied a few years before the fall of Nineveh, perhaps as late as 614. That position seems tenable, especially in view of the fact that it was the period in which the Medes and Babylonians were gaining momentum, and Assyrian power and glory were in decline. The period between the rise of Nabopolassar, as a result of his defeat

---

6. See discussion of "Historical Background" for Jerermiah, pp. 192–95.
7. Zenophon *Anabasis* 3.4, 7–12; Diodorus 2:27.1; Nahum 1:8.
8. D. J. Wiseman, *Chronicles of Chaldean Kings (626–556 B.C.) in the British Museum,* pp. 16–18.

of the Assyrians at Babylon (626 B.C.), and the fall of Asshur is a likely time for the prophecy. We should not assume, however, that Nahum merely read the political events of his times and forecast what seemed obvious to him. He saw the fall of Nineveh through the inspiration of the Holy Spirit, whether he was close to or distant from the event. Certainly he was a keen observer of political events, as were most of the prophets, and that has a place in any theory of how the prophets predicted the future, but it was secondary, whereas the Word of Yahweh was primary.

Proposals for an early date have also been made. C. F. Keil was of the opinion that the defeat of Sennacherib at Jerusalem in 701 probably furnished the occasion for the prophecy.[9] Walter A. Maier has formulated a case for a date between the fall of Thebes to Assurbanipal and the year of its recapture by Psamtik I, because the prophet seemed not to know about the restoration of the city to the Egyptians. He dates Nahum between 668/67 and 654.[10]

LITERARY FORM AND ANALYSIS

The book is an extended poem that predicts the fall of Nineveh and the collapse of the Assyrian Empire.

STYLE

As a poet Nahum comes very close to Isaiah.[11] He is bold and picturesque in his imagery, crisp and dignified in his expressions.[12] He uses no superfluous wordage, and perhaps because of his word conservation he makes sudden transitions from one idea to another, producing marked contrasts. For example, in 1:2 Nahum uses the word "avenge" three times, but in 1:3 he introduces the patience of the Lord. In 1:14 he pronounces doom upon Nineveh, and in 1:15 he sees the good news of her fall flashed from mountain top to mountain top.

LITERARY FORM

Hypothesis of an acrostic in chapter 1. The literary form of chapter 1 has been identified as an incomplete alphabet acrostic. It begins, it is supposed, in verse 2a and is sustained with much irregularity through verse 10, with the *ayin* and *tsade* lines (i.e., beginning with the 16th and 18th letters of the Hebrew alphabet) perhaps preserved in verses 13 and 14. Ever since Hermann Gunkel attempted to reconstruct the acrostic of the poem,[13] many efforts have been expended in that direction. J. M. P. Smith in his 1911 commentary commented

9. Keil, 2:5–6.
10. Walter A. Maier, *The Book of Nahum: A Commentary*, pp. 31, 34–37.
11. S. R. Driver, *An Introduction to the Literature of the Old Testament*, p. 336.
12. S. M. Lehrman, "Nahum," p. 192.
13. Hermann Gunkel, "Nahum 1," pp. 223–44.

that the acrostic structure was "too clearly apparent to be a subject of reasonable doubt." He mentioned that the only doubters of his day were A. B. Davidson and George Adam Smith.[14] The original opening, in his view, had been lost and replaced by the acrostic poem.[15]

When an examination of chapter 1 is made, however, the acrostic hypothesis is rather unconvincing. The following analysis follows the Masoretic divisions of the lines and indicates how disruptive is any attempt to follow the order of the letters of the Hebrew alphabet:

2a	——	*aleph*	(1st letter of Heb. alphabet)
2b	——	*nun*	(14th)
3a	——	*yod*	(10th)
3b	——	*beth*	(2d)
4a	——	*gimel*	(3d)
4b	——	*aleph*	(1st)
5a	——	*he*	(5th)
5b	——	*vav*	(6th)
6a	——	*lamed*	(12th)
6b	——	*heth*	(8th)
7a	——	*teth*	(9th)
7b	——	*yod*	(10th)
8a	——	*beth*	(2nd)
8b	——	*kaph*	(11th)
9a	——	*mem*	(13th)
9b	——	*lamed*	(12th)
10a	——	*kaph*	(11th)
10b	——	*kaph*	(11th)
11a	——	*mem*	(13th)
11b	——	*yod*	(10th)
12a	——	*kaph*	(11th)
12b	——	*lamed*	(12th)
13a	——	*ayin*	(16th)
14a	——	*tsade*	(18th)
14b	——	*lamed*	(12th)
14c	——	*mem*	(13th)
14d	——	*aleph*	(1st)

(The conjunction [*vav*] has been ignored except in verse 5b where it would naturally follow *he*.)

14. J. M. P. Smith, et al, p. 296.
15. Ibid., p. 269. A more recent defense of the acrostic poem hypothesis is S. J. De Vries, "The Acrostic of Nahum in the Jerusalem Liturgy," who believes that the idea is assured and that the acrostic produced only half the alphabet, ending with the letter *kaph*. He breaks vv. 2–8 down into alternating triads and couplets (vv. 2a, 2b, 3a—triad/vv. 3b, 4a—couplet/vv. 4b, 5a, 5b—triad/vv. 6a, 6b—couplet/vv. 7a, 7b, 8a—triad).

As is obvious from the above list, unless the acrostic has been tortured almost beyond recognition (as some suggest!), there is too much confusion in the order of the letters for the acrostic hypothesis to be convincing. Oswald T. Allis has suggested that, instead of an acrostic, we should think in terms of topical emphasis. Other literary devices that figure prominently in the book are repetition, alliteration, assonance, and paronomasia.[16]

The assumption that the acrostic has been lost has led to the further speculation that little of chapter 1 can be identified with Nahum. J. M. P. Smith says the first genuine Nahum material appears in 1:11, 14 and 2:1, 3; the rest of the book is genuine except 3:18–19.[17] Otto Eissfeldt seriously questions 1:2–9 but does not reach a hard conclusion on the matter.[18] For the most part, with the exception of chapter 1, the critics have given the material good marks for genuineness. Further, if chapter 1 is not treated as a badly mauled acrostic poem, there is no good reason to exclude it from Nahum's genuine works. It certainly is in harmony with the tone of the book, and it beautifully prepares the stage for the major theme of the book.

The liturgical hypothesis. Paul Haupt first proposed that Nahum was not a prophecy but a liturgy.[19] The liturgical hypothesis was adopted by Paul Humbert, who conjectured that it was a New Year's liturgy for the year 612 B.C.[20] Ernst Sellin and Georg Fohrer have followed that line of thinking, isolating three prophetic liturgies: (1) 1:12–13, 15; 2:2; (2) 1:10–11, 14; 2:1, 3:13; (3) 3:1–7.[21]

An alternating pattern between addresses to Nineveh and Judah is identifiable in chapter 2, but the kind of responses one would expect in a liturgy are hard to find in the book. Further, the superscription calls it an "oracle" and a "vision," terms that hardly qualify for a liturgical composition. There are two faulty underlying assumptions of this hypothesis. The first is that the prophets contain a considerable amount of cultic material. Indeed they were not diametrically opposed to the cult, but the cultic associations of the prophets have been overemphasized. If any of the writing prophets can legitimately be called "cult" prophets, it is doubtful that they composed any liturgies to be used in the services of the Temple. At least we do not have any clear examples of that in the prophetic books. The second questionable assumption is that the book

16. Oswald T. Allis, "Nahum, Nineveh, Elkosh," pp. 67–80.
17. J. M. P. Smith, et al, p. 269.
18. Otto Eissfeldt, *The Old Testament: An Introduction,* p. 416.
19. He ventured to suggest that the book was composed of four poems, the first two composed in the Maccabean age and the last two by a poet who had seen the fall of Nineveh. He conjectured that the book was a liturgical composition for the celebration of the Jews' victory over Nicanor on the 13th of Adar, 161 B.C. (Paul Haupt, "The Book of Nahum").
20. Paul Humbert, "Essai d'analyse de Nahoum 1,2–2,3," pp. 266–80.
21. Ernst Sellin and Georg Fohrer, *Introduction to the Old Testament,* pp. 449–51.

celebrates the fall of Nineveh after the fact. Yet there are clear indications that the event was yet future (1:14; 3:5, 7).[22]

The cultic-mythological hypothesis. Alfred Haldar developed the thesis that Nahum originated in the nationalistic cultic circles as propaganda against the declining Assyrian Empire. He saw numerous allusions to the mythological motifs in the Mesopotamian and Ugaritic religious systems. In agreement with A. Johnson and G. Widengren, he believed that he detected the cult of the dying and resurrected god as a major element of pre-exilic religion in Judah.[23] This hypothesis, still accepted by a number of leading scholars, is based largely upon the presupposition that Israel celebrated an annual festival in which Yahweh was re-enthroned, much like the *akitu* festival of Babylonia in which the death of the god was mourned and his resurrection from Sheol celebrated. However, aside from similar phraseology, which may be more poetic than mythical, there is very little substance in the OT for such a hypothesis. And certainly the anti-idolatry theme of the prophets would countermand such an emphasis. Haldar's hypothesis represents another instance of what has been called "parallelomania."

Analysis. The prophecy of Nahum opens with a description of God's character (1:2–3*a*) and a rehearsal of His sovereign power over nature (1:3*b*–5). The rhetorical question that follows in 1:6 anticipates the success of Yahweh's judgment upon Nineveh:

> Who can stand before His indignation?
> Who can endure the burning of His anger?
> His wrath is poured out like fire,
> And the rocks are broken up by Him.

Then 1:7–8 draws a contrast between the Lord as a stronghold for those who take refuge in Him and the Lord as the avenger of those who oppose Him. Thus the stage is set for a series of alternating addresses to Nineveh and Judah interspersed with graphic descriptions of the fall of the imperial city. The following pattern pertains:

GOD'S CHARACTER AS AVENGER AND SAVIOR (1:2–8)

As Avenger	1:2–3*a*
As Sovereign in Nature	1:3*b*–5
[Rhetorical Question]	1:6
In Relation to the Faithful	1:7
In Relation to His Enemies	1:8

22. See Walter A. Maier's helpful critique of this hypothesis in his commentary, pp. 42–46.
23. Alfred Haldar, *Studies in the Book of Nahum*, pp. 149–50, 153–54, and so on. The difference between Haldar's thesis and the liturgical theory (with which he disagrees) is that he advocates the origin of the book for political propaganda against Assyria rather than for use in a liturgical setting. See esp. pp. 150–51.

GOD'S CHARACTER MANIFESTED IN VENGEANCE ON
NINEVEH AND MERCY ON JUDAH (1:9–2:2)

Address to Nineveh	1:9–11
Address to Judah	1:12–13
Address to Nineveh	1:14
Address to Judah	1:15
Address to Nineveh	2:1
Comfort for Judah	2:2

GOD'S CHARACTER MANIFESTED IN THE FALL OF NINEVEH (2:3–3:19)

Description of Siege of Nineveh	2:3–9
Taunt against Nineveh	2:10–12
Address to Nineveh	2:13
Woe to Nineveh	3:1
Description of Siege of Nineveh	3:2–4
Address to Nineveh	3:5–6
Lament over Nineveh	3:7
Address to Nineveh	3:8–13
Address to Nineveh (prepare for the siege!)	3:14–17
Address to King of Assyria	3:18–19

It is not surprising that the words addressed to Judah are in the nature of comfort. That harmonizes with the description of Yahweh's vengeance and mercy related in 1:2–8 (particularly vv. 7–8). There is an alternating pattern between vengeance and comfort that extends from 1:9–2:2, and from that point the prophecy is exclusively preoccupied with the siege and fall of Nineveh. In that section of the prophecy the two literary centers are the graphic scenes depicting the city under siege (2:3–9; 3:2–4). Nahum's message is illustrated most vividly at those two points where the "visionary" nature of the prophecy becomes real. Furthermore, Nahum provides the reason for the destruction of Nineveh—her perfidy among the nations (3:4).

The literary form is not the regular oracular style of the prophets, even though the usual oracular formulas are used.[24] Nor is it dialogue, because Judah and Nineveh do not speak. Only Yahweh and the prophet are heard speaking in the book.

The literary style of 1:2–8 is that of a poetic oracle lauding Yahweh's nature as Judge and Savior, very much in psalmic style. Beyond that, however, the remainder of the book exhibits distinct similarities to the oracles against the nations. It is doubtful that Nahum communicated his prophecy to Nineveh, but

---

24. These formulas occur: "Thus says the Lord" (1:12), "The Lord has issued a command concerning you" (1:14), " 'Behold, I am against you,' declares the Lord of hosts" (2:13; 3:5).

he certainly delivered it to Judah. That seems to have been the case with most of the oracles against the foreign nations. They were spoken to Israel or Judah rather than to the foreign powers themselves, although Jeremiah provided exceptions.[25] The oracle of Jeremiah against Egypt is particularly helpful for purposes of comparison. It contains the same kind of instructions for preparing for battle, along with a description of combat, as we have in Nahum (Jer. 46:2–5; Nah. 2:1*b*, 3–7, 9; 3:2–3, 14). Further, Jeremiah's oracle against Egypt contains words of comfort for Israel (46:27–28), which is also a large element in Nahum's prophecy, as pointed out above. In fact, beginning with 1:9 the book falls into the category of the national oracles. It is designed to reassure Judah that the Lord was faithful to His own nature as Judge and Redeemer. As is the case with most of the oracles against the nations, Nahum is triumph, not warning.

RELATIONSHIP TO NATIONAL PROPHETS

Having indicated Nahum's relationship to the prophets who oracularized against foreign nations, the question naturally arises whether he was closer to such prophets as Amos, Isaiah, Jeremiah, and Ezekiel, who also issued oracles against the nations, or to the "national" prophets whom Jeremiah condemned as responsible for Judah's false security. The presence of this book in the canon of Holy Scripture is enough to settle the question in the minds of many who are committed to the inerrant work of the Holy Spirit in canonical formation. Whatever presuppositions about the nature of inspiration one brings to the study of the prophets, exploring the issue may turn out to be instructive. Nevertheless it has been raised by leading scholars, and a response seems appropriate.

J. M. P. Smith classed Nahum as "a representative of the old, narrow and shallow prophetism" that deposited its point of view through such men as Hananiah (Jer. 28) and the four hundred prophets who counterbalanced Micaiah ben Imlah's foreboding reputation (1 Kings 22).[26] An examination of the words of condemnation against the false prophets reveals a nationalism that was rather blind to Israel's sins and an optimism that could not be justified if the welfare of the nation was dependent upon adherence to ethical standards. In fact, the latter condition seems to have been the point of contention between the false prophets and their canonical counterparts. The latter insisted that Yahweh operated in history on the basis of moral absolutes that were an expression of His own moral nature. Israel's destiny was tied to a moral response to Yahweh's demands. On the other hand, the false prophets insisted that Yahweh paid no

25. See pp. 185–86.
26. J. M. P. Smith, et al., pp. 281–82. See also Artur Weiser, *The Old Testament: Its Formation and Development*, p. 258.

regard to ethical matters. They were much closer to the standards of the Mesopotamian prophets, who had the national welfare in front of their portfolio and cared little for the ethical concerns that distinguished the Hebrew prophets. That allegation, however, can certainly not be made against Nahum. He distanced himself from the national prophets in the opening poem, describing Yahweh as a moral deity, punishing evil and securing those who take refuge in Him. Even though Nahum does not, like most of the Hebrew prophets, indict Judah for his sins, the ethical undergirding of his theology is apparent. We can only guess why he did not do so. Some have thought that the reform of Josiah had effected such a moral change that there was no compelling need to indict the people. That, judging from Jeremiah, is hardly convincing. The relative success of the reform may have created new optimism, but it certainly did not clear away all of the evils of the nation. The most probable reason that Nahum did not indict the nation for its sins is to be found in the single purpose of his prophecy. Habakkuk also restricted his focus to a single issue and did not indict Judah for his sins. In like manner Nahum presented the fall of Nineveh as historical evidence that Yahweh would "by no means leave the guilty unpunished" (1:3). Nahum, therefore, belongs in the mainstream of prophetic thought and definitely parts company with the national prophets who preached security apart from ethical obedience.

MESSAGE AND THEOLOGICAL PROBLEM

The message of Nahum is two-pronged. Capsulated in 1:7–8, it proclaims the Lord as sovereign in judgment and salvation:

> The Lord is good,
> A stronghold in the day of trouble,
> And He knows those who take refuge in Him.
> But with an overflowing flood
> He will make a complete end of its site,
> And will pursue His enemies into darkness.

As already demonstrated in the analysis above, Yahweh's sovereign command of the world and its inhabitants (including even the Assyrians) is an expression of His essential being. When He, the God of vengeance, appears, who can stand before Him? Who can endure His fiery anger? (1:5). He is not a nature God who only prescribes and orders the operation of the physical world, but He is a universal God who relates judicially to those who oppose Him and mercifully to those who seek refuge in Him. To call Nahum a theologian would be an overstatement, but he understood the theological issue that preoccupied his message. Lest Yahweh should be accused of acting arbitrarily, the prophet lays down the ground principles on which God operates. Vengeance had been a long time in coming—"He is slow to anger"—but He could bring it to pass, for He is "great in power" (1:3). His wrath was a "well-considered wrath."[27]

For some interpreters Nahum poses a theological problem because he is so preoccupied with the wrath of Yahweh. However, the prophet himself was not vindictive. He certainly did not, for example, exhibit the tone of the imprecatory psalms (Pss. 35, 69, 109),[28] but rather he knew that vindication was in the Lord's hands. And Nahum was confident that the Lord could handle the Assyrian problem. Only those who cannot accept the wrath of God as a valid expression of Yahweh's nature will stumble on the theological ideas of Nahum. But then that same problem will exclude much more of Scripture. The interpreter's responsibility is to accept the God of Nahum as He is, not as he wishes Him to be.

The book of Nahum brings to mind the prophecy of Jonah. They have much in common. Both were concerned with the city of Nineveh. Both believed very strongly in the sovereignty of God over nature and nations. Jonah knew Yahweh as a "gracious and compassionate God, slow to anger and abundant in lovingkindness" (Jon. 4:2). Nahum knew Him as that kind of God. But "slow to anger" implies that the process, undiverted by repentance, would advance to incandescence. Jonah's message elicited repentance. He had not designed it that way, but God had. Nahum's message brought no repentance, nor did God intend it to. Nineveh's time had run out. Her fortifications would fall like ripened figs when the tree is shaken (3:12).

OUTLINE OF NAHUM

I. God's Character as Avenger and Savior (1:2–8)
  A. As Avenger (1:2–3*a*)
  B. As Sovereign in Nature (1:3*b*–5)
  C. Rhetorical Question (1:6)
  D. In Relation to the Faithful (1:7)
  E. In Relation to His Enemies (1:8)
II. God's Character Manifested in Vengeance on Nineveh and Mercy on Judah (1:9–2:2)
  A. Address to Nineveh (1:9–11)
  B. Address to Judah (1:12–13)
  C. Address to Nineveh (1:14)
  D. Address to Judah (1:15)
  E. Address to Nineveh (2:1)
  F. Comfort for Judah (2:2)

---

27. Theodore Laetsch, *The Minor Prophets*, p. 297.
28. See my discussion of these psalms in *An Introduction to the Old Testament Poetic Books*, pp. 144–46.

III. God's Character Manifested in the Fall of Nineveh (2:3–3:19)
- A. Description of Siege of Nineveh (2:3–9)
- B. Taunt Against Nineveh (2:10–12)
- C. Address to Nineveh (2:13)
- D. Woe to Nineveh (3:1)
- E. Description of Siege of Nineveh (3:2–4)
- F. Address to Nineveh (3:5–6)
- G. Lament over Nineveh (3:7)
- H. Address to Nineveh (3:8–13)
- I. Address to Nineveh (prepare for the siege!) (3:14–17)
- J. Address to King of Assyria (3:18–19)

11

EZEKIEL: THE MERGING OF TWO SPHERES

THE DEGREE TO WHICH the prophetic and priestly roles in ancient Israel were mutually cooperative or exclusively resistant is still an open question in OT studies. Most likely there was something of both in the history of prophecy. Some of the classical prophets had strong words to say against the sacrificial practices of their times, but the system had the authority of Moses and the prophets' God behind it, so it is not likely that they altogether rejected the cultic institution. On the other hand, much has been written about the cultic associations of the prophets Habakkuk, Nahum, Obadiah, and Joel. Whereas much of the theory that surrounds the study of those prophets is hypothetical, it does raise the issue, an important one indeed, regarding the relationship between prophecy and cult. We cannot further address the matter here, but the point should be made that with the prophet Ezekiel we clearly have a merging of the two thought strands, or classical roles, in Israelite history.

There is no certain way of knowing whether Ezekiel ever functioned as a priest in the Jerusalem Temple. It is my opinion that he did not, but that nevertheless his knowledge of the Temple and sacrificial system was acquired with a view toward the priestly profession. Perhaps only his exile to Babylonia prevented him from entering the priesthood. However that may be, it is obvious that he saw himself in the priestly ranks, for he calls himself a priest in 1:3, and his description of the new Temple and cultic functions in chapters 40–48 remove all doubt about his priestly orientation. In fact, he cast his vision of the future in the form of the new Temple and resumption of worship there.

In Ezekiel prophet and priest converge; it can hardly be said that one role serves the other. Despite the strong cultic elements in the book, he is foremost a prophet. Yet the two offices contribute their essential strengths through him to bring the coming kingdom of God into sharp focus. Each had that as their distinct religious function in Israelite life, so in combination they could theoretically usher in the kingdom with much greater power. The unutterable tragedy in 586 B.C. proved the accuracy of prophetic vision and delineated the necessity of the Temple system, especially the dejection of life without it. It is no accident that when the restoration began to take real shape in the days of Zerubbabel, it did so under the cooperative tutelage of prophets *and* priests. It would be presumptuous to suggest that Ezekiel had anything to do with that facet of restoration, but it is fair to say that he saw the potential of both offices, empowered by the Lord's Spirit, to produce the kingdom toward which both had aimed.

EZEKIEL THE MAN

In the opening verses of the book, Ezekiel identifies his location as the "land of the Chaldeans by the river Chebar" (1:3) and counts himself "among the exiles" (1:1). The exile of Jehoiachin in 597 B.C. is his point of reference, as he makes clear in 1:2. However, he does not explicitly state that he had been expatriated with Jehoiachin, but he implies as much in 40:1 when he dates his vision in the twenty-fifth year "of our exile." So there is no doubt that he was among the company of people whom the Babylonians exiled in 597.

He further informs us that he was a priest (1:3), a fact that is reinforced by his use of priestly language and his interest in the Temple. If the enigmatic "thirtieth year" (1:1) was the thirtieth year of his life, then he probably never actively served as a priest in the Temple, because there is reason to believe that the priests assumed their office at the age of thirty years (Num. 4:3), perhaps beginning their preliminary training at age twenty (1 Chron. 23:24). It may be that prior to exile Ezekiel had been involved in preparatory instruction for the priesthood. Certainly that would explain his knowledge of the law and the Temple even if in fact he had not functioned in the priestly office.

We also know that he was married, and that his wife, also with him in exile, died suddenly in approximately 587 B.C. while Jerusalem was under siege (24:16–27). But unlike Hosea and Isaiah, we have no knowledge of any children they may have had.

Just what respect he may have commanded among his compatriots who remained in Palestine cannot be determined with absolute confidence, but we may assume that the refugee who came from Palestine to announce the fall of Jerusalem came to Ezekiel because of the reputation the prophet had in Judah (33:21).

In the Jewish community of Babylonia his reputation was well known and respected, for the elders of the exilic community came to inquire of him on several occasions (8:1; 14:1; 20:1).[1]

THE LITERARY NATURE AND AUTHENTICITY OF EZEKIEL

In the modern era Ezekiel has undergone the same kind of critical scrutiny that the other major prophets have been subjected to. Gustav Hoelscher, for exam-

---

1. In 14:1 and 20:1 they are called the "elders of Israel," but Ezekiel prefers the name Israel for the Southern Kingdom, so we should understand the elders of Judah and Israel to be synonymous.

ple, believing that Ezekiel was a poet who wrote in *qinah* meter, found no more than 170 verses out of the 1273 in the book to be genuine.[2] The book fared little better at the hands of William A. Irwin, whose so-called "inductive study" of Ezekiel produced the conclusion that only 251 verses were genuine in whole or in part.[3] On the other hand, Moshe Greenberg's recent work has signalled a move in the other direction in Ezekiel studies, not to suggest that the radical positions of Hoelscher and Irwin ever represented a scholarly consensus. He believes the evidence is weighted in favor of the sixth-century prophet, who certainly shaped the book, if not provided the very words that have come to us.[4] A review of the literature on Ezekiel can be found in other sources,[5] so we want to approach our task by considering the critical problems that continue to preoccupy the scholarly literature.

GEOGRAPHICAL LOCATION

A question revolves around Ezekiel's location during his prophetic ministry. Most would agree that he originally lived in Palestine before his exile in 597, but not all agree that he prophesied exclusively in Babylonia. The crux of the issue comes mainly into focus in chapters 8–11. Based upon the vivid descriptions of events occurring in Palestine, the reader is left with the impression that the prophet was actually viewing the events as they occurred. Basically three explanations have been given for that phenomenon.

The three-residence theory. Alfred Bertholet proposed that he received his call while in Jerusalem in 593 B.C. (2:3–3:9), following which he prophesied to Jerusalem and Judah for the next six years until, during the siege, he moved to a village somewhere in Judah (12:3), where he received the news of the fall (33:21). Subsequently he left for Babylonia, where he received a second call to prophesy in the thirteenth year (emending "thirtieth" of 1:1 to "thirteenth") of Jehoiachin's exile (1:4–2:2, c. 585).[6] Other versions of the three-residence theory have been proposed. Robert H. Pfeiffer, following the general outline of other works, advances the view that Ezekiel received his call in 593 to go to Palestine (3:4), finally arriving there a year and two months later in 592 (8:1–4). He continued to prophesy in the city until sometime between January of 588 (24:1) and January of 585, when he returned to Babylonia in time to receive the bad news that Jerusalem had fallen (33:21).[7] All of the forms of this theory, however, require such radical interpretations of the text that we cannot accept them.

2. Gustav Hoelscher, *Hesekiel, der Dichter und das Buch.*
3. William A. Irwin, *The Problem of Ezekiel: An Inductive Study,* pp. 283–84.
4. Moshe Greenberg, *Ezekiel 1:20: A New Translation with Introduction and Commentary,* p. 27.
5. See H. H. Rowley, "The Book of Ezekiel in Modern Study," pp. 146–90; Carl Gordon Howie, *The Date and Composition of Ezekiel,* pp. 5–46.
6. Alfred Bertholet and Kurt Galling, *Hesekiel;* see Howie, p. 11.
7. Robert H. Pfeiffer, *Introduction to the Old Testament,* pp. 536–41.

The two-residence theory. As early as the Targum and Mechilta, the belief circulated in Jewish circles that Ezekiel began his prophetic career in the land of Israel and received some of his oracles there. (The Mechilta is a midrashic commentary on the book of Exodus, written in the second century A.D.) The problem that faced the rabbis was how a prophet could receive prophetic oracles in a foreign land. The idea of this theory is that the initial stages of the prophet's career began in Palestine before his exile to Babylonia, where he completed his career.[8] W. O. E. Oesterley and Theodore H. Robinson espouse this view in their introduction.[9] Yet little can be said in its support if the integrity of the text as it has come to us is maintained.

The one-residence theory. The overwhelming evidence of the book favors Babylonia as Ezekiel's single residence while engaged in his prophetic ministry. Exiled in 597 B.C. he received his prophetic commission in 592 and spent his entire career prophesying from his Babylonian residence. Much scholarly opinion presently favors the single residence of Babylonia. The problem of his knowledge of Judean events displayed in chapters 8–11 is easily solved when we take seriously Ezekiel's statement that "the Spirit lifted me up between earth and heaven and brought me in the visions of God to Jerusalem" (8:3). The visionary nature of the prophet's experience is hard to deny.[10] Furthermore, the problem that he mainly addressed the citizens of Judah rather than the exiles in chapters 1–24 is not difficult to solve. The communication channels between the exiles and the citizens still in Judah were kept open. Jeremiah corresponded with the exiles in Babylonia (Jer. 29), and there were probably messengers who delivered oral news from time to time. Certainly that

---

8. James Smith in *The Book of the Prophet Ezekiel, A New Interpretation* advanced a two-residence view that dated Ezekiel's ministry between 722 and 669 B.C. and placed him first in Northern Israel and later in Assyria among the Northern exiles. For a summary of his position, see pp. 90–100. Obviously this position requires a radical reinterpretation of the book and rejects the obvious historical setting. It is to the credit of modern Ezekiel scholarship that this view has not found many proponents.

9. W. O. E. Oesterley and Theodore H. Robinson, *An Introduction to the Books of the Old Testament*, pp. 324–25, 328–29. They essentially agree with the position of Volkmar Herntrich, *Ezechielprobleme*, that in the book two worlds are evident, that of Palestine and that of Babylonia. Herntrich believed the oracles of chaps. 1–24 were addressed to a Judean audience, and later an exilic editor gave the book its Babylonian facade. See Howie's summary of Herntrich's view, pp. 10–11.

10. David Noel Freedman propounds the theory, also put forth by others, that the vision consisted of things Ezekiel had seen and heard while he was a resident of Jerusalem before his exile ("The Book of Ezekiel," pp. 448–71, esp. p. 459). We can agree that the Spirit used images and experiences that Ezekiel had acquired prior to exile, but the contents of the visions themselves—the death of Pelatiah, for example (11:13)—need not have been something he had seen prior to 597. It may very well be that Pelatiah's death occurred as a result of Ezekiel's prophecy, but the prophecy did not have to be spoken directly to him for it to affect him. The oracles against the nations are perhaps the best evidence of the power of prophecy to affect persons and nations too distant to hear the oracles when spoken. In any event, Pelatiah's death became to Ezekiel a symbol of the destruction of Israel and the Temple.

was the case when Jerusalem fell (33:21). Moreover, Ezekiel's message to the Judeans did not necessarily have to be addressed directly to them to be effective, although we assume that would be the exception rather than the norm.

In conclusion, the evidence of the book is weighted heavily in favor of the one-residence theory, that is, Babylonia.[11]

THE PROPHETIC WORD IN EZEKIEL

Ezekiel employed four different modes to convey his message: oracles delivered orally, visions, symbolic actions, and prophetic discourse.

Oral communication. Ezekiel addressed the exiles orally and personally (e.g., 11:25; 14:4; 20:3). As with the prophets in general, that was his primary mode of communication. Generally they were prefaced with the prophet's word of reception ("Then the word of the Lord came to me saying") or Yahweh's directive (the imperative "say," "speak," "prophesy," etc.). In several instances he used the spoken oracle to address entities that were out of hearing range. On those occasions he *set his face* toward that entity and delivered the message.[12] The gesture is not unknown in preclassical prophecy (Num. 24:1; 2 Kings 8:11), and in the so-called Holiness Code, reflected clearly in Ezekiel, the Lord sets His face against offenders of the law (Lev. 17:10; 20:5). The expression connotes judgment in Ezekiel and the Holiness Code, although sometimes Yahweh sets His face toward His people in favor (Num. 6:25–26). Like the symbolic actions, Ezekiel was physically and emotionally involved in his oral messages.[13]

Visions. Ezekiel's visionary experiences, however, surpassed anything else in the pre-exilic prophets. The opening chariot vision (chap. 1), the visionary journey to Jerusalem (chaps. 8–11), which includes a second chariot vision poised over Jerusalem (chap. 10), the valley of dry bones (chap. 37), and the New Temple (chaps. 40–48) make up a significant part of the whole book, not only in terms of mass but of structural importance. The commissioning vision of chapter 1, received in his Babylonian home, is repeated when he is transported to Jerusalem and sees visions of events there (chap. 10). Moreover, once our prophet turned his attention to comfort and restoration, the confirming vision of the valley of dry bones and the miraculous resurrection placed a stamp of validity upon that section of the prophecy. The closing segment, like the opening, is visionary, thus binding the entire prophecy together between them.

---

11. There are scholars who have argued a one-residence view for Palestine. See Howie's review of those positions, pp. 6–9.
12. The instances are: the sketch of Jerusalem (4:4, 7), the mountains of Israel (6:2), the daughters of Israel (13:17), the Negeb of Israel (20:46), Jerusalem (21:2), the Ammonites (25:2), Sidon (28:21), Pharaoh (29:2), Mount Seir (35:2), and Gog (38:2).
13. Keith W. Carley, *Ezekiel Among the Prophets: A Study of Ezekiel's Place in Prophetic Tradition,* pp. 40–42.

Visions, therefore, authenticated the two major phases of Ezekiel's ministry, his prophecies of judgment and his prophecies of restoration.

Symbolic action. Ezekiel's symbolic actions were numerous,[14] surpassing even Jeremiah. Among the classical prophets, Hosea and Isaiah had earlier engaged in this type of prophetic expression, and Jeremiah capitalized on it, but Ezekiel virtually made it into a prophetic art. In these actions message and messenger were combined into one inseparable mode of communication. Consistently some words of interpretation accompanied them, and most often the dramatic signs focused on the destruction of Jerusalem and the resulting conditions of siege and exile. Walther Zimmerli and others have drawn attention to the interesting idea that Ezekiel took several metaphors found in other prophets and enacted them literally, for example, Jeremiah's metaphor of eating the Lord's words (Jer. 15:16) and Ezekiel's consumption of the scroll (3:1–3), Isaiah's metaphor of shaving Israel with a razor (Isa. 7:20) and our prophet's literal shaving of his head and beard (5:1–4).[15]

Prophetic discourse. This is one of the minor elements of the book in terms of the mass of material, but it is no less a significant part of the ministry of Ezekiel and the plan of the book. Taking the form of both prose and poetic narrative, it falls basically into the categories of historical-theological discourse (chaps. 16, 20, 23) and allegory (15, 16, 17, 19, 23, 27, 37). The literary modes, it should be observed, are not all exclusive types, for the historical-theological narrative of chapter 23 takes the form of an allegory, as does chapter 16. Further, the modes are often couched in oracular form, being messages that Ezekiel delivered to Israel and other persons or entities. These discourses may be distinguished from the oracles themselves by the fact that they are generally of considerable length, are usually drawn from history, and aim to teach a theological lesson.

EZEKIEL'S DUMBNESS

Apparently very soon after Ezekiel's call in 592 the Lord informed him that he would be dumb and unable to reprove the people (3:22). Seven years later,

---

14. The symbolic actions are: eating the scroll (2:8–3:3), modeling the siege of Jerusalem on a clay tile (4:1–3), lying on his left side 390 days and on his right forty days (4:4–8), rationing his food and cooking it on cow's dung (4:9–17), shaving his head and beard and disposing of the hair in three parts (5:1–17), clapping his hands and stamping his feet (6:11–14), digging through the wall and exiting with an exile's baggage (12:3–7), eating his meals nervously (12:17–20), sighing with a breaking heart (21:6–7), smiting his thigh (21:12), clapping his hands and striking the sword three times (21:14–17), setting up road signs to point the way for Nebuchadnezzar to Jerusalem (21:19–23), his unnatural behavior at the death of his wife (24:15–24), setting his face toward the objects of his oracles (see note 12 above), and putting two sticks together (37:15–23).

15. Walther Zimmerli, *Ezekiel 1*, pp. 19–20; also Walther Zimmerli, "The Message of the Prophet Ezekiel," pp. 131–57, esp. pp. 136–38; Walther Zimmerli, "The Special Form- and Traditio-Historical Character of Ezekiel's Prophecy," pp. 515–27, esp. pp. 520–21.

while Jerusalem was under siege, God promised that a fugitive would come and report the news of Jerusalem's fall, and on that day Ezekiel's mouth would be opened so that he could speak (24:26–27). By the time the fugitive arrived with the news, the Lord had already opened the prophet's mouth so that his speech was no longer restrained. Yet a seven-year silence is certainly inconsistent with the clear impression in chapters 4–32 that he continued his ministry of proclamation during those years (e.g., 11:25).

So in what sense was Ezekiel dumb? Five lines of argument have been followed to solve the problem. First, it has been suggested that his silence should be understood as total prophetic inactivity between 592 and 586. Moses Buttenwieser took this position and viewed the predictions of chapters 1–32 as after the fact.[16] That, however, requires a radical (and unjustified) reinterpretation of the book.

Second, it is suggested that 3:22–27 is out of place and probably belongs in chapter 24 or 33. This would have the effect of shortening the time of the prophet's silence to a brief period, perhaps just prior to the fall of Jerusalem. Walther Eichrodt follows this line of thought, suggesting a symbolic period of dumbness imposed upon Ezekiel shortly before the fall of Jerusalem; his disciples regarded it as a recurrent sign to the unbelieving people and placed it, like the call to be a watchman, at the beginning of the book.[17] John W. Wevers and Zimmerli also seek an editorial solution to the problem by considering the references to his muteness a product of later redactors.[18] But that position also requires the superimposition of an editorial interpretation that cannot be easily explained in light of the orderly structure of the book.

Third, the dumbness is explained as intermittent during those seven years and not permanently removed until the fall of the city.[19] Although this may be plausible in that Ezekiel only spoke the words that Yahweh instructed him to say, it is more speculative than textually verifiable.

Fourth, it is speculated that the experience was visionary, as were also others of the peculiar activities described in 3:22–5:17.[20] This explanation, however, has no textual support. Normally Ezekiel informs us when his experiences took the form of visions.

Fifth, some believe that the silence was some form of inhibited speech that lasted until the Babylonian conquest of Jerusalem. This line of argument has the advantage that it eliminates the need to resort to textual reductionism or a

16. Moses Buttenwieser, "The Date and Character of Ezekiel's Prophecies," pp. 1–18, esp. pp. 2–7.
17. Walther Eichrodt, *Ezekiel: A Commentary*, p. 76.
18. John W. Wevers, *Ezekiel*, pp. 58–59, 194, 253; Zimmerli, *Ezekiel 1*, pp. 161, 508–9.
19. John Skinner, *The Book of Ezekiel*, pp. 53–54; Charles Lee Feinberg, *The Prophecy of Ezekiel*, pp. 30–31.
20. This seems to be the preference of Howie, p. 81, following Herbert W. Hines, "The Prophet as Mystic," pp. 37–71.

redactional explanation. In recent scholarship, Robert R. Wilson has pointed the way to a viable solution. Interpreting the word *môchîah* in 3:26 as a legal term meaning "arbitrator" rather than "reprover," he proposed that Ezekiel was forbidden to be a mediator or arbitrator between Yahweh and Israel.[21] Greenberg, although not following Wilson's definition of *môchîah*, agrees that it was related to his preaching. He interprets it in the context of the command to be shut indoors with the ban on reproving: "As they rejected the prophet, so God withdraws from their midst the healing presence of the prophet."[22] The solution is to be found in the text of 3:22–27, something John Calvin recognized long ago. He connected the command not to reprove with the prophet's dumbness.[23] However, unless we are willing to assign 14:6 and 18:30–32 to a later period of his ministry, then we must admit that the kind of reproving that called Israel to repentance is found among the earlier oracles. But viewed in the context of the prophet's isolation from the public, as the command "shut yourself up in your house" (3:24) implies, then his dumbness consisted in the inhibition against public reproof of Israel that summoned her to repentance.[24] In a sense, it was the cancellation of his public role as watchman (3:17–21) until he was reinstated to that office just prior to his release from silence (33:1–10).

THE "THIRTIETH" YEAR

Although this is a minor problem, it deserves brief comment. In 1:2 Ezekiel specifies that the calendar on which his dates are based is the exile of King Jehoiachin to Babylonia in 597 B.C. He never again refers explicitly to that system of dating except in the reference to "our exile" in 40:1, but all of the other dates doubtlessly use 597 as the reference point. So the most obvious explanation of the "thirtieth" year of 1:1 is the thirtieth year of Jehoiachin's exile, which would be 568/67. A number of scholars have taken that to be the year in which Ezekiel published his prophecies.[25]

The clue to the enigma is the synchronism given in 1:1–2: the "thirtieth" year is the same as the "fifth" year of Jehoiachin's exile, that is, 592 B.C.

---

21. Robert R. Wilson, "An Interpretation of Ezekiel's Dumbness," pp. 91–104.
22. Greenberg, *Ezekiel 1–20*, p. 120; "On Ezekiel's Dumbness," pp. 101–5. In the latter article Greenberg draws attention to Josephus's record (*War* 6.5.3) of a man named Jesus, son of Ananias, who went about the streets and alleys of Jerusalem for seven and a half years crying, "Woe to Jerusalem!" He neither spoke to citizens personally nor answered those who questioned him. He merely cried out against the city. He isolated himself from the society in a similar way as did Ezekiel. Yet Ezekiel depended upon the elders' coming to him. He evidently did not go outside of his house to speak to them.
23. John Calvin, *Commentaries on the First Twenty Chapters of the Book of the Prophet Ezekiel*, p. 167.
24. So A. B. Davidson, *The Book of the Prophet Ezekiel*, p. 26.
25. E.g., Howie, pp. 41, 92, following William F. Albright, "The Seal of Eliakim and the Latest Preexilic History of Judah, with Some Observations on Ezekiel," pp. 77–106.

Contrary to the obvious, the thirtieth year belongs to another calendar, and "fifth day" is the synchronizing factor:

1:1	year 30	month 4	day 5
1:2	year 5	———	day 5

The Targum interpreted the date as the thirtieth year after Josiah's reform,[26] perhaps suggested by Huldah's prediction of evil upon Jerusalem when she commented upon the discovery of the law scroll in the Temple (2 Kings 22:8–20). Really, however, there is no more support for this theory than for David Kimchi's view that it was the thirtieth year of the current Jubilee,[27] because neither Jubilee reckoning nor the Josianic reform seemed to have much significance in Ezekiel's day.

A plausible view, though conjectural like all the rest, is that it was the thirtieth year of Ezekiel's life, the year in which he would have, under different circumstances, entered fully into his priestly profession (Num. 4:3, 30, 35, 39, 43, 47). R. K. Harrison, cautiously accepting that position, comments that it would not disturb the chronology of the book and would likely accord with what we would expect Ezekiel's age to be at that time.[28] Although I am inclined in that direction, one final alternative, obvious enough but not always easily admissible, is to declare it an enigma and acknowledge that we do not know its significance beyond the fact that it was coincident with the fifth year of Jehoiachin's exile.[29]

EZEKIEL AND APOCALYPSE

Sometimes called the "father of apocalyptic," Ezekiel has a place of distinction in the development of the literary genre known as apocalypse. Several elements of apocalypse appear incipiently in the book: journeys under the propulsion of the Spirit or the hand of Yahweh[30] (8:3; 11:1; 37:1; 40:1–2), visions accompanied by an interpreter or guide (chaps. 40–48), and review of history under the guise of symbolism with accompanying interpretation, followed by prediction (17:3–10/12–21/22–24).[31]

When the apocalyptic texts are compared to Ezekiel, however, it becomes

26. See Targum on 1:1.
27. 1:1 in Rabbi David Kimchi's commentary on Ezekiel (Hebrew).
28. R. K. Harrison, *Introduction to the Old Testament*, p. 838.
29. This is Greenberg's conclusion, *Ezekiel 1–20*, pp. 39–40.
30. The "hand of Yahweh" is similarly applied to Elijah's race from Carmel to Jezreel (1 Kings 18:46) and Elisha's prophesying upon the request of a minstrel (2 Kings 3:15). See Carley, pp. 13–23.
31. Note the similar pattern (history under the form of symbolism, interpretation, prediction) in 1 Enoch 85–90; 2 Esdras 3–14; 2 Baruch 53:1–12/56:1–74:4; Dan. 7, 8.

apparent that the pattern of history telling, which became elaborate and highly symbolic in apocalyptic literature, is in its elementary stages, as is also the use of interpretation as a prophetic tool.[32] Nevertheless, in spite of all of these characteristics, Yehezkel Kaufmann is correct to maintain that Ezekiel lacks the most essential element of apocalypse, the revelation of heavenly secrets. He, like his prophetic predecessors, reveals the will of God for Israel and mankind, not the secrets of the universe.[33] But even if he cannot accurately be considered the father of apocalypse, he is certainly one of the major tributaries.

LITERARY STYLE

The "I" style of the book is the most extended first-person material in the prophets. In fact, the entire book (except 1:3) is a combination of the "I" style and the direct words of Yahweh to Ezekiel. Usually the Lord addresses the prophet as "son of man," a phrase that has no special messianic overtones but carries the simple meaning of "human being."[34] Ezekiel is the narrator of his own experiences and visions, reporting the words that Yahweh speaks to him. Even the numerous popular sayings reported in the book are, with one exception (20:49), couched in the words of Yahweh.[35] Compared to other pre-exilic prophets, we are more conscious of the role of Ezekiel in the transmission of Yahweh's oracles to Israel. The oracles normally include the directive element instructing the prophet to "say," "speak," "prophesy," "propound a riddle," to name a few, and generally the word of accomplishment (e.g., 11:25, "Then I told the exiles all the things that the Lord had shown me") is missing.

Yet that should not lead to the erroneous conclusion that the prophet is more prominent than Yahweh. To the contrary, he is absorbed in his task. Yahweh's Word and the prophet's performance are brought together into a harmonious whole, especially in the symbolic actions. Even though Ezekiel employs the first person to relate his experiences, the words of the book are largely Yahweh's words, and the actions are directed by Him.

The question of Ezekiel's state of mind during his reception of revelation has been much discussed. The term *ecstasy* has been applied to the kind of experiences described in this book. J. Lindblom's definition of ecstasy is an abnormal state of consciousness in which one is so intensely absorbed by one

---

32. The use of interpretation appears in a very simple and brief form in Isa. 5:1–7. It becomes a very effective and much more elaborate instrument in later apocalyptic works (e.g., 1 Enoch 52:3–4, etc.; 2 Esdras 2:44–45; 2 Baruch 53:1–12/55:3–74:4, and frequently in Daniel).
33. Yehezkel Kaufmann, *The Religion of Israel*, pp. 437–38. See also Buttenwieser, pp. 1–18, esp. p. 7.
34. See C. Hassell Bullock, "Ezekiel, Bridge Between the Testaments," pp. 23–31, esp. pp. 27–29.
35. The sayings are located in the following places (the diagonal indicates a different saying): 8:12/ 9:9/ 11:3/ 11:15/ 12:22/ 12:27/ 13:6, 7; 22:28/ 13:10/ 18:2/ 18:25, 29; 33:17, 20/ 20:32/ 20:49/ 33:10/ 33:24/ 33:30/ 37:11.

single idea or one single feeling, or by a group of ideas or feelings, that the normal stream of physical life is more or less arrested.[36] Ezekiel seems to fit in that category. He was physically and emotionally involved in all of his visions, even though the physical activity may have been more a state of mind than body. Moreover, he seems to have been incognizant of events around him during those deep visionary states. Yet we should not confuse that state of consciousness with the kind of ecstatic behavior that characterized some of the non-writing prophets (1 Sam. 19:24). The distinguishing factor is the apparent dismantling of the mental processes in the latter case and their engagement in Ezekiel's visions.

STRUCTURE

Chronological indications. The fourteen dates[37] may be viewed as one but not the single key to the structure. Those dates given in the first twenty-four chapters predate the fall and stretch from Ezekiel's call in 592 to the beginning of the Babylonian siege in 588.[38] All of the other dates fall within the siege or after it. The following table indicates their occurrences:

Year	Month	Day	System	Event/Message	
1:1–2	30/5	4	5	Jehoiachin's exile	Chariot vision
3:16	[5]	[4]	[12]	[ ]*	Call to be a watchman "at the end of seven days"
8:1	6	6	5	[ ]	Vision of Temple
20:1	7	5	10	[ ]	Historical-Theological Discourse
24:1	9	10	10	[ ]	Day of Siege
26:1	11		1	[ ]	Against Tyre
29:1	10	10	12	[ ]	Against Pharaoh
29:17	27	1	1	[ ]	Against Egypt
30:20	11	1	7	[ ]	Against Pharaoh
31:1	11	3	1	[ ]	Against Pharaoh
32:1	12	12	1	[ ]	Lament over Pharaoh
32:17	12		15	[ ]	Lament over Egypt
33:21	12	10	5	[ ]	"The city has fallen"
40:1	25	"first of year"	10	"of our exile"/14th after fall of Jerusalem	Vision of New Temple

[ ]-information is implied

36. J. Lindblom, *Prophecy in Ancient Israel*, p. 4.
37. Sixteen if the "thirtieth year" of 1:1 and "fourteenth year" of 40:1 are counted separately.
38. For a discussion of the events and the dates of this period, see A. Malamat, "The Last Kings of Judah and the Fall of Jerusalem: An Historical—Chronological Study," pp. 137–56. On p. 156 he gives a chronological table of the siege of Jerusalem.

Despite the generous help Ezekiel provides through his dates, a structure can hardly follow the lines they draw. As is obvious from the table, the dates in the last half of the book are not consistently chronological.

Theological structure. A theological criterion is much more workable for determining the structure of the book. Running through several of the prophets during this unsettling era is the theme that the Day of the Lord is impending. Zephaniah and Jeremiah stressed its imminence. When Jerusalem fell, the authors of Lamentations and Obadiah declared that the Day had come for Judah, and they anticipated the Day of the Lord for the nations. Ezekiel was preoccupied with the same judgment that had long been predicted for Israel. When it occurred, he turned to announce the counterpart of that day on the nations:

> Wail, "Alas for the day!"
> For the day is near,
> Even the day of the Lord is near;
> It will be a day of clouds,
> A time of doom for the nations.
> (30:23)

The Day of the Lord in the late pre-exilic prophets is not a single day but a complex of events. A pattern emerges that puts Israel's disaster of 586 in front, followed by similar disaster on his enemies. Then, either simultaneous to international judgment or following it, Israel's restoration occurs.

Eschatological movement. That eschatological pattern is detectable in Ezekiel. Eichrodt calls it "the prophet's mighty forward march from judgment to salvation."[39] The book falls into an eschatological outline. The first major section (chaps. 1–24) contains prophetic oracles and actions that focus on the national Day of the Lord for Israel—Israel's doomsday.

Then the prophet in the second major section (chaps. 25–32) turns to the nations to consider the fate that will come to them on the Day of the Lord (30:3). In several instances the national oracles specify the sin or injustice that the particular nation has perpetrated against Israel, thereby sealing its doom (25:3, 8, 12, 15; 26:2).[40]

The third major section (chaps. 33–48) turns upon Israel's restoration and subdivides into two parts: (1) events and oracles regarding restoration (chaps. 33–39) and (2) restoration idealized in the restored Temple and worship (chaps. 40–48). Restoration was a major feature of prophetic eschatology. It was the light at the end of the tunnel.

---

39. Eichrodt, p. 22.
40. Only Egypt and Sidon are not directly charged with an offense against Israel, but such a crime is implied against Sidon in 28:24. Both Egypt and Tyre are accused of having a haughty spirit and behaving like they were gods (28:2, 6; 29:9; 31:10).

AUTHORSHIP

A word about Ezekiel's part in the composition of the book is in order. The dating system that almost consistently uses Jehoiachin's exile as its reference point, the homogeneity of thought, the well-balanced prophetic/priestly approach to Israel's present dilemma and future hope, and the consistency of language patterns all point to a single author. Moreover, it is likely that the editorial process was also supervised by Ezekiel sometime in the decade of the 560s. At any rate, the book in its present form must have been completed before the death of Nebuchadnezzar, for there is nothing of the flurry of excitement and hope that might have been created by the release of Jehoiachin from prison after the Babylonian monarch's death. The Talmud states that the men of the Great Synagogue wrote Ezekiel, the Twelve Prophets, Daniel, and the Scroll of Esther.[41] The meaning of that statement, however, has nothing to do with composition but with authoritative revision and reissuing by the Jewish authorities.[42] During the Tannaitic period the school of Shammai rejected the book because of discrepancies between Ezekiel's cultic prescriptions and the Pentateuch.[43] The commentary on the book that Chananiah ben Hezekiah, head of the school of Shammai, wrote to explain the differences is a strong indication that efforts had not been made to remove those discrepancies.[44]

ANALYSIS OF THE BOOK

EVENTS AND ORACLES CONCERNING THE NATIONAL DAY OF THE LORD: ISRAEL'S DOOM (CHAPS. 1–24)

These chapters, filled with unspeakable judgments against Yahweh's people, predict, justify, and announce the end of the kingdom of Judah. Prefacing those judgments, however, are the words of Ezekiel's call, as is the case with Hosea and Jeremiah. This first half of Ezekiel divides into four subsections: (1) Events and Oracles Relating to Ezekiel's Call and Ministry (chaps. 1–5); (2) Predictions of the End: The Day of the Lord (chaps. 6–7); (3) Visions of Temple Abominations and Departure of the Glory of the Lord (chaps. 8–11); and (4) Realities of Judgment Against Jerusalem (chaps. 12–24).

Events and oracles relating to Ezekiel's call and ministry (chaps. 1–5). The center of this first subsection is obviously the chariot vision of chapter 1. Occurring in the year 592 B.C. in the fourth month, the same month in which the Babylonians seven years later breached the walls of Jerusalem (2 Kings 25:2–4), Ezekiel saw the glory of the Lord poised above the chariot throne.

41. Babylonian Talmud, *Baba Bathra* 15a.
42. S. Fisch, *Ezekiel*, p. xiv.
43. See Bullock, pp. 27–29.
44. See the discussion of the Day of the Lord, pp. 172, 241, 254, 271–72.

That was the prophet-priest's version of Isaiah's "I saw the Lord" (Isa. 6). Here the throne is mobile, moving with lightning speed across the sky, supported and mobilized by four sets of gyroscopic wheels and flanked on all four sides by the cherubim with four faces.

Ezekiel's reaction to that sight was predictable. He fell upon his face and thereupon heard a voice speaking (1:28). The content of Yahweh's speeches and the prophet's response follow in 2:1–3:15. Here the significance of the chariot vision is clarified in Ezekiel's call. The central focus of 2:1–3:15 is composed of the prophet's consumption of the scroll, that is, the assimilation of the message of "lamentations, mourning and woe" written uncustomarily on both sides (2:10). The major thrust of Ezekiel's message becomes lucid in this section. He was to be a prophet of judgment, and he should have no false illusions about the difficulty of the task (2:3–5; 3:5–7). Although he could hope for little more, he would leave with them the knowledge, minimal to be sure, that a prophet had been among them (2:5; also 33:33).

The title "son of man," by which Yahweh addresses Ezekiel, simply means "human being." In this book it has no Messianic overtones. Those were to come later, and the phrase was to receive its clearest Messianic dimension in the use Jesus made of it. But here the term "son of man," that is, human being, stands in stark contrast to the "glory of the Lord."

The appearance of the "glory of the Lord" in Babylonia gave signal expression to the fact that the Lord was not confined to the Temple in Jerusalem. The chariot throne was the vehicle of His glory. When the Spirit transported Ezekiel to Jerusalem, "the glory of the God of Israel was there," like the vision he had seen in the plain (8:4). There is some confusion over the identity of the cherubim in 9:3, whether they were those in the Holy of Holies (so the Targum) or those Ezekiel had seen in the Babylonian plain. In actuality it is probably of little consequence, because the symbolism is the all-important element. Yet it would appear that the cherub of 9:3 was not located in the Temple proper. The "glory of the Lord," in disdain for the abominations that were taking place in the Temple (8:5–17), had already departed from the Holy of Holies, for in 8:6 the Lord accuses the abominators of driving Him from His sanctuary. When the purging of the Temple began in chapter 9, the glory of the Lord had come to rest upon the Temple threshold (9:3)[45] and at some unspecified time returned to the cherubim, subsequently coming to rest a second time upon the threshold (10:3–4). Then it resumed its place on the chariot throne as it moved with the living creatures to the East Gate of the city (10:18–19), finally coming to rest upon the Mount of Olives on the city's east side (11:23).

---

45. The threshold is not mentioned in 1 Kings 6, but it was probably the space at the east entrance of the Temple proper (not the entrance to the court). See G. A. Cooke, *The Book of Ezekiel*, 1:106.

Only in Ezekiel's vision of the New Temple did it return to its place in the sanctuary (43:1-5).

The prophetic symbolism in which Ezekiel engages in chapters 1-5 (aside from eating the scroll) is directed toward the sin of Israel and the impending siege and conquest of Jerusalem. There is good reason to assume that these prophecies were spoken to the exiles (3:11, 15).

Predictions of the end: the Day of the Lord (chaps. 6-7). The theme of Yahweh's wrath, which was a major component of the prophetic message of doom, is seen to be a principal theme in Ezekiel as well. Already introduced in 5:13, chapters 6 and 7 raise the din of God's outpoured wrath to deafening decibels. And to no surprise, the fearful product of divine wrath is the end of Israel. Announced with a frightful repetitiveness, the prophet leaves no room for doubt—the end had come (7:2, 3, 6, 24). In Ezekiel's mind and vocabulary, as with most of the prophets of Judah's declining days, that was the "Day" of the Lord, "The time has come, the day has arrived" (7:12). The announcement, inherent with terror, is superimposed with two statements to make the fate unspeakably intolerable. First, the Lord's eye would not spare the people or have pity on them (7:4, 9). Second, the Lord would turn His face from them, allowing their enemies to profane His Temple (7:22).

In this subsection the recognition formula ("You/They shall know that I am the Lord," and its variants) emphasizes Yahweh's justification for executing His wrath upon Israel. His actions in history were designed to reveal His sovereignty both in judgment and redemption. There was nothing arbitrary about them.[46]

Visions of Temple abominations and the departure of the glory of the Lord (chaps. 8-11). Dated in 591 (8:1), one year and one month after Ezekiel's chariot vision, the prophet was transported by the Spirit to Jerusalem, where he saw the horrible abominations that were committed in the Temple. The visionary nature of this experience is clearly stated, bracketed by the assertion that the Spirit transported Ezekiel in visions to Jerusalem (8:3) and then returned him in like manner to the exiles (11:24). So Ezekiel remained bodily in Babylonia.

A number of commentators consider the references that duplicate the chariot-throne vision of chapter 1 (8:2; 9:3; 10; 11:22-23) to be editorial accretions. However, it should be observed that each time the explicit identification with the vision of chapter 1 is made, the statement is in the characteristic first-person

---

46. The recognition formula is applied both to Israel and the nations. To Israel: 6:7, 10, 13, 14; 7:4, 9, 27; 11:12; 12:15, 16, 20; 13:9, 14, 21, 23; 14:8; 15:7; 16:62; 20:20, 26, 38, 42, 44; 22:16; 23:49; 24:24, 27; 28:22, 24, 26; 29:21; 33:29; 34:27; 36:11, 38; 37:6, 13. Variants: 5:13; 14:23; 20:12; 34:24; 39:22, 28. To the Nations: 25:5, 7, 11, 14, 17; 26:6; 28:22, 23; 29:9, 16; 30:8, 19, 25, 26; 32:15; 35:4, 9; 38:23; 39:6. Variants: 17:24; 21:5; 29:6; 35:12, 15; 36:23, 36; 37:28; 38:16; 39:7, 23.

style of Ezekiel ("which I saw," 8:4; 10:15, 20, 22). Further, even though the word "cherubim" is not introduced until 9:3, the identification of the four cherubim with the four "living beings" of chapter 1 (10:15, 20) need not be redactional, for the unfolding consciousness of the meaning of his vision in the plain is part of the texture of his experiences in Jerusalem. That we are dealing with textual corruptions that have resulted from scribal copying and notations is also highly probable. Yet the longer unit is well structured. It moves from the Temple abominations (8:3–18) to the purge of the sanctuary and city by the six executioners (chap. 9) and continues the same theme under the form of burning coals scattered over the city by the priestly figure of chapter 9 (chap. 10). The difficulty of 11:1–13 is its placement after the judgment has been dispensed. The clue to understanding that, however, is in the nonsequential nature of events. The sudden death of Pelatiah, evidently a consequence of Ezekiel's prophecy, is a parenthesis in the vision, and the time element is ambiguous. It serves the purpose of explaining the actual means by which the Lord would execute judgment upon the sanctuary and city, symbolized by the executioners and burning coals. Judgment would come by foreign conquest (11:8–11). The unit closes with a word of hope for the exiles, whose fate had been interpreted by those left in Judah as Yahweh's dispossession of them (11:15). When Ezekiel emerged from his vision, he told it to the exiles (11:25), probably the elders who were gathered in his house when the vision occurred (8:1).

Realities of judgment against Jerusalem (chaps. 12–24). The bond that holds the last two subsections together is the theme of exile, dramatically performed by our prophet in chapter 12. The impending doom of Israel is announced, the time when prophetic word and divine action would converge at a single point in time (12:25). The time lapse between prediction and fulfillment was growing thin. The literary pins that hold this long section together are the publications of Ezekiel as a "sign" to Israel in the beginning (12:6, 11) and at the end of the unit (24:24, 27). The material offers further explication of Yahweh's plans for Israel, in both judgment and redemption, and puts them in the light of the justifying factors, Israel's incorrigible sins that justify Yahweh's judgment and Yahweh's grace that is the sole justification of redemption.

Three discourses on Israel's history form the pillars of this extended section. First, the tender parable of the abandoned baby girl confirms the incorrigibility of Israel (chap. 16) and broadly outlines Yahweh's plan of judgment (16:35–52) and redemption (16:53–63). The second discourse on history affirms God's unrelenting grace from the Exodus to the conquest (chap. 20). Israel's history stretched across the episodes of time because Yahweh would not sacrifice His good reputation before the nations by annihilating His people. He would lead them ultimately to participation in the farthest reaches of His grace, a second wilderness and occupation of the land (20:33–44). The sins of Israel, black harbingers of the end, marked the road to destruction (chap. 22) just as Ezekiel posted the roadsign to direct the king of Babylon to Jerusalem (21:18–25). The third discourse on history, constituting an allegory on the two indecent sisters, confirms the incorrigibility of Israel's sins, which requisition that awful day of judgment (chap. 23).

Other materials are interspersed in this section. The condemnation of the prophets (chap. 13), the allegory of the eagles (chap. 17), and the lament over the plight of Judah's last kings (chap. 19) reinforce the rationale for Yahweh's announced judgment.

The thread of divine grace is woven into the fabric of this unit. Judgment could not be averted, and even the righteous Noah, Daniel, and Job could save only their own lives by their righteousness (14:12–20). In fact, that was Yahweh's way of preserving a remnant. The individual could personally turn and be spared (chap. 18), but corporate mercy was out of the question.

The sudden death of Ezekiel's wife and the Lord's command to show no outward signs of mourning form an appropriate conclusion to this section (24:15–27). The final subsection is dated in 588, the day on which Nebuchadnezzar laid siege against Jerusalem (24:1–2). Though not stated, we may assume that his wife's death occurred soon after that time.

EVENTS AND ORACLES CONCERNING THE INTERNATIONAL DAY OF THE LORD: THE NATIONS' DOOM (CHAPS. 25–32)

The eschatological arrangement of Ezekiel begins to take form in the second major section of the book. Ezekiel shared the generally held notions on Israel's future, judgment on the nations being one of the major features of prophetic theology that underscored the inevitability of divine wrath on the unrepentant. In 30:3 Ezekiel announces the Day of the Lord for the nations. One of the purposes of this collection is evidently the announcement that the Day of the Lord is also impending for the nations, just as he had announced Israel's doomsday in the first section.

The oracles against the nations constitute a distinct collection, as they do in Amos, Isaiah, Zephaniah, and Jeremiah, but whether they ever circulated independently as a collection cannot be determined with certainty. All of the national oracles were not, however, included, for oracles against Ammon (21:28–32) and Edom (chap. 35) appear elsewhere in the book and follow the standard form of the oracles in this collection. In two instances explicit words of comfort for Israel are injected, though Israel is not directly addressed (28:24–26; 29:21).[47] That, however, may be indicative of one of the purposes of the oracles against the nations. They were intended not only to indict Israel's

47. Jer. 46:27–28 interrupts a long oracle against Egypt and is addressed directly to Israel. Indirect words of comfort for Israel are also found in Jeremiah's oracles (50:19–20, 33–34; 51:5a).

enemies but to comfort Israel. The words of restoration directed to Egypt in 29:13–16, although somewhat surprising, are also not without precedent (Jer. 48:47; 49:6, 39).

In seven instances the oracles are dated, placing them within the tenth to twelfth years of Jehoiachin's exile (588/87–586 B.C.), excepting 29:17–21, which is dated in the twenty-seventh year (571/70). Thus the bulk of the oracles comes from the period when Jerusalem was under Babylonian siege. They are arranged as follows:

	Nation/City/Ruler	Date	Offended Israel
25:1–7	Ammonites	yes (25:3, 6)	
25:8–11	Moab		yes (25:8)
25:12–14	Edom		yes (25:12)
25:15–17	Philistines		implied (25:15)
26:1–28:19	Tyre		yes (26:2)
26:1–21	Tyre	11/ /1	
27:1–36	Tyre		
28:1–10	Tyre		
28:11–19	King of Tyre		
28:20–26	Sidon		implied (28:24)
29:1–32:16	Egypt/Pharaoh		
29:1–16	Pharaoh	10/10/12	
29:17–21	Egypt	27/1/1	
30:1–19	Egypt		
30:20–26	Pharaoh	11/1/7	
31:1–18	Pharaoh	11/3/1	
32:1–16	Pharaoh	12/12/1	
32:17–32	Egypt	12/ /15	

As the table indicates, six of the seven nations are indicted for some offensive behavior against Israel. The absence of such an indictment against Egypt may reflect the effort of Pharaoh Hophra to relieve the siege in early 587 (Jer. 37:5–7). Because the dates are not strictly chronological, the oracles have obviously been grouped according to the location.

In literary form the major oracles follow a fairly standard pattern, but there are significant internal variations. Basically the literary form is the following: (1) a word of reception, "And the word of the Lord came to me saying" (25:1; 26:1; 27:1; 28:1, 11, 20; 29:1, 17; 30:1, 20; 31:1; 32:1, 17); (2) a word of address to the prophet as "son of man," usually accompanied by speaking or acting instructions ("prophesy against them and say," "raise a lamentation against . . . and say," "say," "set your face against . . . and say," "wail"); (3) a word of validation, "thus says the Lord God"; (4) a word of indictment, introduced by "because" (Heb. prep. *ya'an*); (5) a word of confirmation, usually taking the form of the recognition formula "and they shall know that I am the Lord" or the phrase "declares the Lord God."

Oracles against Israel's Palestinian neighbors (chap. 25). The first group of oracles is directed against Ammon (25:1–7), Moab (25:8–11), Edom (25:12–14), and Philistia (25:15–17). There are actually five oracles, the oracle against Ammon being broken down into two (25:1–5, 6–7). Being shorter and less complex than the other oracles, the literary pattern is more standardized. The word of reception (1) is much longer than any of the others, whereas the word of address is missing from all except the first, where it is probably intended to stand at the head of the group. The word of validation (3) is standardized in all five (except the addition of "for" or "because" in 25:8), as is also the form of the word of indictment (consistently introduced by "because"). An additional feature is the standard word of judgment introduced by "therefore" (25:4, 7, 9, 13, 16), which does not always appear in the oracles outside this group in this form. The word of confirmation (4) also follows a standard form ("you will know that I am the Lord"), with the exception of 25:14*b.*

All four neighbors are condemned, presumably for their scornful treatment of Judah at the time the Babylonians defeated them. That is most clear in the first Ammon oracle (25:3). Therefore, these oracles appear to have been written soon after the fall of Jerusalem.

Oracles against Tyre (26:1–28:19). Perhaps the Sidon oracle ought to be included in this group, as it is in Isaiah 23. It is broken down into four smaller units (see table above). The chief city of Phoenicia, Tyre was known by her commercial and religious reputations. Two cities carried the name, one on the mainland and another, called insular Tyre, located in the sea. The latter, suggested by 26:5, 14, seems to be the subject of the oracles. After Nebuchadnezzar conquered Jerusalem, he turned northward and conducted a thirteen-year siege against Tyre[48] with limited success (cf. 29:17–21). Not until a hundred and forty years later did it fall to Alexander the Great (332 B.C.). Because 26:14 predicts utter destruction and says the city will never be built again, the question of fulfillment has been vigorously debated. Some scholars have noted the change from the singular (26:7–11) to the plural (26:12) and suggest that the prophecy extends to the invaders of the successive centuries.[49] However, such number change is not unusual for Ezekiel. Another approach is to appeal to the conditionality of prophecy (Jer. 18:7–10), assuming some unknown change of condition caused Yahweh to change His mind.[50] Still others have insisted that the categories of right and wrong are inappropriate for prophetic prediction. The thing that really matters is what the community of faith did with those prophecies and how they, fulfilled or unfulfilled, affected

48. Josephus *Ant.* 14.2.
49. E.g., Feinberg, pp. 148–49.
50. E.g., H. L. Ellison, *Ezekiel: The Man and His Message,* p. 103.

the community's thought and history.[51] The problem is real, and none of the approaches enumerated may be a satisfactory solution. Ezekiel in another passage (chap. 20) affirms that sometimes the rationale for God's actions recedes into His own mysterious nature and hinges upon His own best interests, which human beings cannot always comprehend.

Oracles against Egypt (29:1–32:32). The third and longest series is broken down into seven smaller oracles (see table above). The pharaoh of this series is Hophra (588–569 B.C.), grandson of the famed Pharaoh Neco (609–594), who had slain Josiah at Megiddo and had been defeated by Nebuchadnezzar at Carchemish in 605. All of the oracles except 30:1–19 are dated, mainly falling in the years 587–585 (29:17–18 is dated in 571/70). The question of fulfillment arises again in relation to 29:11–16. Our knowledge of Egyptian history does not provide confirmation of a forty-year exile and return. But perhaps John B. Taylor is right to propose that the language is not literal but metaphorical, predicating the humiliation that awaited Egypt.[52] The Babylonian records do speak of Nebuchadnezzar's invasion of Egypt in 568/67 to deal with the revolting Amasis, a general whom he had set on the throne of Egypt in 572 B.C. after defeating Apries (Hophra).[53] However, the success of that invasion is not fully known.

EVENTS AND ORACLES CONCERNING THE NATIONAL DAY OF THE LORD: ISRAEL'S RESTORATION (CHAPS. 33–48)

Comfort for Israel (chaps. 33–48). The fall of Jerusalem was a turning point in the ministry of Ezekiel. Basically the first two major sections were reproof and judgment, but in this section Ezekiel turns largely to comfort. The eschatological scheme that has been followed in the arrangement of the book becomes even more visible here. The first phase of Israel's Day of the Lord, partitioned into judgment and restoration, is tersely announced by the fugitive: "The city has been taken" (33:21). Ezekiel identified the fall of Jerusalem, the day when the sheep were scattered, as the Day of the Lord by his use of the phrase "day of clouds and thick darkness" (34:12 [RSV]), a phrase that Zephaniah had used to speak of that Day (Zeph. 1:15). Joel later employed the same phrase to describe a renewed phase of that Day (Joel 2:2).

The message of restoration dominates the section. Even the words of judgment against Mt. Seir and Gog and Magog fall as much in the category of

---

51. Robert P. Carroll, *When Prophecy Failed: Cognitive Dissonance in the Prophetic Traditions of the Old Testament*, pp. 57–58; also with a stronger emphasis upon faith rather than dissonance, David Thompson, "A Problem of Unfulfilled Prophecy in Ezekiel: The Destruction of Tyre (Ezekiel 26:1–14 and 29:18–20)," pp. 93–106.
52. John B. Taylor, *Ezekiel, An Introduction and Commentary*, p. 200.
53. D. J. Wiseman, *Chronicles of Chaldaean Kings (626–556 B.C. in the British Museum,)* pp. 30, 94–95.

Israel's comfort as judgment against her enemies. After the indictment of Edom for immoral conduct in the wake of the Jerusalem disaster (chap. 35), the theme turns clearly to restoration (chaps. 36–37). History was about to be repeated. Just as Yahweh had acted for the sake of His own Name in past historical eras, the restoration would be another such episode. In chapter 20 Ezekiel had depicted Israel's survival in history as a consequence of Yahweh's grace, His acting for the sake of His own Name, that it might not be profaned among the nations. Yet having spared Israel as an act of grace, Israel ultimately succeeded in doing what Yahweh's grace had precluded in earlier eras—she had profaned the divine Name among the nations, for she had requisitioned the exile by her shameful sins. So Yahweh, whose grace can never be outdone by man's sin, would do what Israel could not accomplish: He would give the people a new heart and a new spirit (36:26–32). It is that theme that is illustrated in chapter 37, associating the new spirit with return from captivity (v. 14). The valley of dry bones and their resuscitation primarily constitute a message of return from captivity and restoration to the land, although overtones of physical resurrection may be read from the text. Yet the earmark of the return to the land would be the reestablishment of Yahweh's sanctuary, the ultimate witness to His presence in Israel (37:26–28). That theme is drawn out in chapters 40–48 with the description of the New Temple.

That still leaves the function of chapters 38–39 to be accounted for. The invasion of the land of Israel by Gog, the foe from the north (38:15; 39:2), seems to be an extension of the eschatological plan beyond the simple judgment/ salvation scheme that we have normally seen in the prophets. That is, Ezekiel, perhaps toward the end of his ministry and well into the Babylonian Exile, has already begun to reexamine and reapply the outline of the Day of the Lord, especially as it concerns the restoration and the conclusive judgment on the nations. The invasion of Gog was to take place when Israel was again secure upon her land, that is, after the return from captivity (38:8, 11, 14). So Ezekiel has taken another step in the development of prophetic eschatology by defining more precisely the time factor between Israel's restoration to the land and judgment upon her arch enemy. The purpose of associating return to the land with judgment upon Gog is to show conclusively to the nations why the Exile occurred (39:23–24, 28–29). It is evident that Israel had begun to despair over the delay of the Day of the Lord for the nations (38:8; 39:8). Furthermore, the return was still in the future (39:25). Therefore, just as chapter 33 (especially vv. 10–20) was an antidote for those who despaired because of the Exile, so chapters 38–39 function as encouragement to those who despaired because the Day of the Lord for the nations had not yet received its final installment of divine wrath. Here Ezekiel has gone a step well beyond the concept of the Day of the Lord in the oracles against the nations by correlating it with the return. That reexamination of eschatological expectations set a precedent, consciously or unconsciously, for the reexamination that Daniel a generation later would conduct (Dan. 9).

The third section may be broken down into these units: (A) Renewed Call and Summons to Repentance (chap. 33); (B) The Divine Shepherd (chap. 34); (C) Condemnation of Edom (chap. 35); (D) Israel's Restoration (chaps. 36–37); (E) Yahweh's Decisive Judgment Against the Ultimate Foe (chaps. 38–39); and (F) The New Temple (chaps. 40–48).

The New Temple (chaps. 40–48). To conclude our analysis we should make some observations on Ezekiel's fascinating description of the New Temple. That has been anticipated in 37:26–28. In chapters 40–48 the prophet-priest ties the threads of the book together. The Temple, so central and vital to Israel's interests, is the symbol of the new nation. With obvious appreciation for the Temple, its functions, and functionaries, Ezekiel provides detailed descriptions of the Temple complex (40:5–42:20), the returning glory of the Lord (43:1–12), the altar (43:13–27), the Temple functionaries (44:1–45:8), offerings and cultic regulations (45:9–46:24), the new life that flowed from the sanctuary (47:1–12), new tribal divisions gathered around the centralized Temple, (47:13–23), and the boundaries of the land (48:1–29). The return of the glory of the Lord to the Temple is of signal importance, contributing to Jerusalem a new name, "The Lord is there" (48:35).

The contents were given in a vision that came to him in the twenty-fifth year of Jehoiachin's exile (572 B.C.). His escort and interpreter was a man whose appearance was like bronze. That may not be the same escort who led him through his visions of Jerusalem (8:2). The figure shares the description of the Lord enthroned on the chariot (1:27), whereas the guide in the final section is described more briefly and less regally. Likely the escort is an angel and not the Lord Himself.

If the Temple had not been the central feature of the classical prophets' religious focus, it certainly was for Ezekiel. He saw it as the main authenticating institution in the life of Israel. The future, whatever shape it took, was inconceivable without it. Yet the obvious question that arises is whether our prophet really believed that particular structure would be built. There is really no question that he believed the Temple would be restored, but did Ezekiel intend to supply a blueprint for the New Temple and its services? Four views have taken shape in response to this question.

The first is the literal view. As the term implies, this position anticipates the literal construction of the Temple as Ezekiel describes it. The wording in 43:10–12 seems to encourage the literal expectation. Further, because the post-exilic prophets Haggai and Zechariah encouraged the reconstruction of the Jerusalem sanctuary, it would certainly appear that the restoration of the Temple was an important feature of hope during the exilic period. However, when the Temple was actually restored, it did not follow Ezekiel's plans. So the proponents of this view must face up to the problem of nonfulfillment.

The second view is the symbolic one, holding that Ezekiel has symbolically described the Christian age in terms of the Temple. So those who hold this position do not anticipate a literal fulfillment. Rather they see its fulfillment in the age of the Christian gospel. Jesus' use of Temple symbolism for His resurrection (John 2:18–22) and John's interpretation of the Lord God as the Temple of the New Jerusalem (Rev. 21:22) lend support to this view.

The third view is the dispensational one, which assumes that all prophecies about Israel must be literally fulfilled. So those who hold this position yet anticipate the reconstruction of the Temple, perhaps in the millennial age. The strength of this view is that Scripture is taken very seriously. Its weakness is that it fails to identify the symbolic and spiritual dimensions of future predictions about Israel.

The fourth view is to interpret these chapters as apocalypse. We have observed above how the book of Ezekiel is related to apocalyptic literature. According to this position chapters 40–48 predict in highly symbolic terms the Messianic Age.[54] It is closely akin to the symbolic view but differs in that it does not insist upon covenantal theology, on which the symbolic view is based. The proponents of this position insist that the prophecy must remain anchored in history and not lifted above it. Further, some future realities transcend the ability of human language to describe them, so the familiar and fundamental realities of Israel's life became the basis for representing the indescribable.

It seems that, because the prophecy demands the historical fulfillment, and because the literature is so characteristically apocalyptic, we must insist that the prophecy is fulfilled in part by the historical reconstruction of the Temple in 520–16. Yet to restrict the meaning of these chapters to the historical is to ignore the supernatural elements, such as the river that flows from the Temple and transforms the Dead Sea (47:1–12) and the abiding presence of the Lord (48:35). So although the restoration led by Zerubbabel, Haggai, and Zechariah fulfilled the prophecy in one respect (the Temple was rebuilt), in another respect they did no more to exhaust its full meaning than did the historical return from exile to deplete Isaiah's program of restoration (e.g., Isa. 35, 40, 43). The prophecy calls for both the historical and the eschatological, for as A. B. Davidson says, there is "so much of earth, so much of heaven" in it.[55]

---

54. Taylor, pp. 251–53.
55. Davidson, p. 288.

THE MESSAGE OF EZEKIEL

MAN'S POLARITY AND GOD'S RESOLUTION

The polarity that human disobedience had created in Israel was a major subject of prophetic preaching. It had put Israel in opposition to God. The prophets' ethical imperative that called men and women to reform their ways often left the Israelites unmoved and even more often unchanged. The fall of Jerusalem, to which Ezekiel was an auditor, and the Exile, of which he was a victim, were the incontestable evidences of Israel's moral inflexibility. Ezekiel, as clearly as any of the prophets, set up the opposite poles and then showed how Yahweh resolved the polarization. On the one hand God declares that He will turn His face from Israel (e.g., 7:22), and on the other that He will not hide His face from them any more (39:29). At one pole Israel drives Yahweh from His sanctuary (8:6), and at the other Yahweh gives instructions for a new Temple where He will take up His everlasting residence (37:26–28; 40–48). The glory of the Lord leaves the Temple (11:23), and it returns (43:1–5). He gives up the land to destruction so that even Noah, Daniel, and Job could not save it (14:12–20), and He reclaims and repartitions the land for His people (47:13–48:35). On the one side Israel breaks the Mosaic covenant (16:59), and on the other the Lord establishes an everlasting covenant. The shepherds neglect His flock (34:10), and He Himself becomes the good Shepherd (34:11). Israel's idolatrous abominations are pitted against Yahweh's holiness. Repentance has a low profile in the book, giving place to Yahweh's initiative to bring about the drastic changes that could save and restore Israel. The use of the emphatic first person to reinforce the subject of the verb (God) illustrates this shift of emphasis from human repentance to divine action:

> "I myself will remember my covenant with you in the
>   days of your youth" (16:60).
> "I myself will establish my covenant with you" (16:62).
> "I myself will take a sprig from the high cedar" (17:22).
> "Behold, I myself will search out my sheep" (34:11).
> "I myself will shepherd my sheep" (34:15).
> "I myself will judge between the fat sheep and the
>   lean sheep" (34:20, author's translation).

Poised precipitously on the ledge of disaster, Israel had heard the prophets but had not understood. Yet, inevitably the ultimate disaster had come. Ezekiel had said little about averting it. The unenviable responsibility that had fallen to him was that of interpreting the calamity. And now in the face of appalling destruction and despair, hope could be found only in the Person and actions of Yahweh Himself. It was an old prophetic theme to which Israel had virtually become deaf, and in Ezekiel the people's deafness had been paired with prophetic muteness. Yet when they could hear and the prophet could speak, the word of salvation was as graciously astonishing as the word of judgment had been terrifyingly devastating.

THE GOAL OF PROPHETIC PREACHING

The recognition formula ("You/They shall know that I am the Lord" and its variants) picks up a prominent theme in the earlier prophets.[56] To bring Israel to the knowledge of the Lord was the aim of classical prophecy. We have seen that very clearly in our study of Hosea.[57] Further, Jeremiah, Ezekiel's contemporary, had couched the new covenant in terms of the knowledge of the Lord (Jer. 31:31–34). Yet Ezekiel's stress on that object far outruns any OT prophet and anticipates the emphasis that Jesus in the gospel of John places on His mission to establish the knowledge of God.[58] The degrees of that knowledge range from mere recognition of Yahweh as sovereign God of the world to knowledge of Him as Savior of Israel. It encompasses a range that extends from mental perception to dynamic interaction with Yahweh's moral demands and acts in history. Even His judgment on the nations eventuates in the knowledge of the Lord, although it is likely sovereign knowledge rather than saving knowledge. However, at last the whole world will know Him as Yahweh, will know that He is Israel's God and that there is no match for Him among the gods of the nations. Ezekiel was not so much concerned with the salvation of the nations. His focus was divine justice meted out to them. Therefore, it is not clear whether his application of the formula to the nations carried any salvific connotation.

That concept, directed at Israel and the nations, serves another purpose. It is the great vindication of Yahweh's character. Ezekiel's apologetic for the nature of God can be traced throughout the book. Chapter 20 is a classic expression of that apologetic applied to the national history. It was Yahweh's own name and character that He was concerned with, not Israel's. When His covenant people and the nations around them came to acknowledge who He was, then He would be truly vindicated. To say, however, that He was intent upon protecting His own reputation is not in the least to suggest that He had no concern with Israel's. Rather it is to suggest that the Lord was most true to His people when He was most true to Himself. When He was true to Himself, He could not be false to Israel.

---

56. See Carley's study on the relationship of Ezekiel to the preclassical prophets, pp. 13–47, esp. pp. 37–40 for the recognition formula.
57. See pp. 92–93.
58. See Bullock, pp. 25–27.

OUTLINE OF EZEKIEL

I. Events and Oracles Concerning the National Day of the Lord: Israel's Doom (chaps. 1–24)
   A. Events and Oracles Relating to Ezekiel's Call and Ministry (chaps. 1–5)
      1. Superscription (1:1–3)
      2. The Vision of the Lord's Chariot-throne (1:4–28)
      3. Ezekiel's Commission (2:1–3:15)
      4. The Watchman (3:16–21)
      5. Ezekiel's Dumbness (3:22–27)
      6. Four Symbolic Actions (4:1–5:17)
   B. Predictions of the End—the Day of the Lord (chaps. 6–7)
      1. Prophecy Against the Mountains of Israel (6:1–14)
      2. The End (7:1–27)
   C. Visions of Temple Abominations and the Departure of the Glory of the Lord (chaps. 8–11)
      1. Visions of Jerusalem and the Glory of God (8:1–6)
      2. Elders Practicing Idolatry (8:7–13)
      3. The Tammuz Cult (8:14–15)
      4. Worship of the Sun (8:16–18)
      5. Executioners in Jerusalem (9:1–11)
      6. The Chariot-throne and Punishment of Jerusalem (10:1–8)
      7. The Chariot and the Cherubim Described (10:9–17)
      8. The Departure of the Glory of the Lord from the Temple (10:18–22)
      9. The Death of Pelatiah (11:1–13)
      10. A New Heart for the Exiles (11:14–25)
   D. The Realities of Judgment Against Jerusalem (chaps. 12–24)
      1. Two Symbolic Acts (12:1–20)
      2. Popular Sayings Counteracted (12:21–28)
   E. Against Prophets and Prophetesses (13:1–23)
   F. Polemic Against Idolatry (14:1–11)
   G. The Ineffectiveness of Righteousness to Deliver Jerusalem (14:12–23)
   H. Allegory of the Vine (15:1–8)
   I. Allegory of the Unfaithful Wife (16:1–63)
   J. Allegory of the Two Eagles (17:1–24)
   K. The Doctrine of Individual Responsibility (18:1–20)
   L. Justification of Judgment (18:21–32)
   M. Lament for the Kings and Nation (19:1–14)
   N. Discourse on History (20:1–44)
   O. Judgment on Judah (20:45–21:32)

P. Three Oracles on the Evil of Jerusalem (22:1–31)
Q. Oholah and Oholibah (23:1–49)
R. The Rusty Cauldron (24:1–14)
S. The Death of Ezekiel's Wife (24:15–27)
II. Events and Oracles Concerning the International Day of the Lord: The Doom of the Nations (chaps. 25–32)
A. Against Neighboring Nations (25:1–17)
1. Against Ammon (25:1–7)
2. Against Moab (25:8–11)
3. Against Edom (25:12–14)
4. Against the Philistines (25:15–17)
B. Against Tyre and Sidon (26:1–28:19)
1. Against Tyre (26:1–28:19)
2. Against Sidon (28:11–19)
C. Against Egypt (29:1–32:32)
III. Events and Oracles Concerning the National Day of the Lord: Israel's Restoration (chaps. 33–48)
A. Renewed Call and Summons to Repentance (33:1–33)
B. The Divine Shepherd (34:1–31)
C. Condemnation of Edom (35:1–15)
D. Israel's Restoration (36:1–38)
E. The Lord's Decisive Judgment Against the Ultimate Foe (38:1–39:29)
F. The New Temple (40:1–48:35)
1. Introduction to the Vision (40:1–4)
2. Description of the Courts (40:5–47)
3. Description of the Temple and Its Auxiliary Buildings (40:48–41:26)
4. The Priests' Chambers (42:1–14)
5. The External Measurements of the Temple Area (42:15–20)
6. The Return of the Glory of the Lord to the Temple (43:1–12)
7. The Altar (43:13–27)
8. The Ministers and Their Duties (44:1–45:8)
9. The Offering and Other Regulations (45:9–46:24)
10. The River Flowing from the Temple (47:1–12)
11. The Tribal Boundaries (47:13–23)
12. The Tribal Allotments of the Land (48:1–29)
13. The Gates of Jerusalem and Its Measurements (48:30–35)

12

OBADIAH: EDOM'S DAY OF THE LORD

THE DAY OF THE LORD was an ominous concept in prophetic thought. Yet judging from Amos (5:18–20) the idea did not likely receive its initial impulse from the prophets but from the popular religion of Israel. In the success-oriented society of Jeroboam II, that two-sided concept of bane and blessing had developed into an optimism that blinded Israel to the ethical demands of religion. Amos's corrective became more than that. It became a prophetic way of describing the future crisis that would materialize if Israel and Judah persisted on their collision course with the ethical requirements that Yahweh had laid down for them. They did persist, and the fall of Israel in 722 B.C. proved that Yahweh's covenant with His people was not inviolable from His side of the arrangement. The unjustified optimism of Judah's citizens, possessors of the Torah and occupants of Yahweh's favored city, was not sufficiently shattered by the fate of Israel, and the prophets continued to announce judgment and plead for repentance. As the history of Judah came to a close, Zephaniah and Jeremiah renewed the threat of the Day of the Lord. When the Day actually came in 586 B.C., the author of Lamentations acknowledged it and prayed that God might actualize the other aspect of that fateful Day upon Judah's enemies (Lam. 1:21).[1] Obadiah looked from the vantage point of the disaster that had befallen Jerusalem, reviewed its tragedy, and announced that the Day of the Lord was near for the nations, and for Edom in particular (Obad. 15).

OBADIAH THE MAN

Personal information about this prophet is totally lacking. The name ("servant of Yahweh") is borne by several individuals in the OT. The Babylonian Talmud identified him as King Ahab's steward,[2] a devout worshiper of Yahweh (1 Kings 18), but that tradition does not seem to rest on anything more substantive than the common name and his religious devotion. Further, the

---

1. See pp. 271–72.
2. Babylonian Talmud, *San.* 39b.

book itself is so brief that indirect information gleaned from the prophet's words is not helpful.

The country of Edom, lying on the southeastern edge of the Dead Sea, was bordered on the north by the Brook Zered, which distinguished between two kinds of land, the plateau of Moab to the north and the highlands of Edom to the south.[3] In pre-exilic times the Arabah seems to have been the southern border.[4] Through that elongated strip of land ran the King's Highway between Ezion-geber and Damascus in ancient times, and by that route countless caravans of traders had carted their wares. The Edomites, controlling the highway for about seventy miles of its north-south route, profited from the tolls they collected along the land ports built mainly for that purpose (Isa. 21:13–14; Job 6:19; Ezek. 27:15).

A nation known from early times for its wisdom, Edom was the home of Job's friend Eliphaz, who came from Teman, a city in the southern sector of the little kingdom. Job also likely hailed from some place in Edom, for Lamentations 4:21 puts Edom and Uz in parallel lines, suggesting that Uz was located within the bounds of Edom. Obadiah was aware of that wisdom tradition and quips that his "understanding" (a frequent synonym for wisdom) would not be able to figure out what the Lord was doing (v. 7). To deplete further the wisdom of the nation, the Lord would destroy the sages that were resident in Edom (v. 8).

The ancestral kinship of Israel and Edom went all the way back to the conflict between Isaac's sons Esau and Jacob, the eponymous patriarchs of Edom and Israel respectively (Gen. 25:19–34; 27:1–28:9; 32–33). Although the Edomites obstructed the migrating Israelites as they sought to traverse the King's Highway during the wilderness wanderings (Num. 20:14–21), the two neighbors seem to have lived peacefully until the reign of Saul (1 Sam. 14:47).[5] David's reign was especially marked by conflict with the Edomites, and he defeated them in the Valley of Salt (2 Sam. 8:13–14). Later Joab conducted a six-month campaign in Edom aimed toward genocide of Edomite males (1 Kings 11:14–25). After Solomon's reign a deputy governor ruled Edom during the time of Jehoshaphat (873–848 B.C.; 1 Kings 22:47), evidently under the tutelage of Judah, for when Jehoshaphat's son, Joram (853–841 B.C.), became king, the Edomites successfully revolted against Judah and set up their own king (2 Kings 8:20–22). The later Judean successes against Edom, one about fifty years later

---

3. Denis Baly, *The Geography of the Bible*, pp. 239–41.
4. Nelson Glueck, "The Boundaries of Edom," pp. 141–57.
5. John D. W. Watts, *Obadiah: A Critical Exegetical Commentary*, p. 15, and Watts's helpful discussion of Edomite history on pp. 11–19.

under Amaziah (2 Kings 14:7) and another by his son Uzziah (2 Kings 14:22), seem to have been quite temporary, because the writer of Kings implies that the Edomite revolt against Joram had held until his day (2 Kings 8:22). The fall of Edom is shrouded in uncertainty. Evidently in 586 the country was still independent and relatively free from the Babylonian devastation that brought Judah down, because Jeremiah mentions that some of the Jews had fled to Edom for safety (Jer. 40:11). Some have speculated that by the time of Nehemiah (mid-fifth century) Edom had fallen. However that may be, by the year 312 their homeland was dominated by the Nabataeans.[6] Nelson Glueck describes the transition to Nabataean culture and control as both a displacement and an absorption of Edomite elements.[7] The name was preserved in the later designation of the region as Idumaea.

Obadiah wrote his prophecy as a reaction to the Edomites' scavenger approach to the devastation of Jerusalem. As I shall explain below in the discussion of Obadiah's date, my assumption is that the tragedy was the fall of Jerusalem to the Chaldeans in 586 B.C. From the historical survey of relations between the two countries, shaded by the historical memory of Jacob's treatment of Esau, it should not be surprising that the Edomites would swoop down upon wounded Jerusalem and take advantage of her disaster. Nor is it surprising to hear this oracle devoted exclusively to condemnation of Edom's perfidious behavior.

LITERARY FORM, ANALYSIS, AND COMPOSITION

LITERARY FORM: NATIONAL ORACLE AGAINST EDOM

The literary genre of the book of Obadiah, like Nahum, is the national oracle.[8] Four other oracles against Edom occur in the prophets: Amos 1:11–12, Isa. 21:11–12, Jer. 49:7–22, and Ezek. 25:12–14. There are no elements common to them all, but the vengeful conduct of Edom against Israel occurs in Amos, Ezekiel and Obadiah (v. 12), and the sense of security Edom had developed in his craggy home is condemned in Amos, Jeremiah (49:16, 22), and Obadiah 3, 4. Although we cannot discuss the purpose(s) of those oracles here,[9] suffice it to say that the salvation of the nations was not a basic theme in them. In three instances, however, Jeremiah promised restoration to the nations whom he addressed (Moab— Jer. 48:47, Ammon—49:6, and Elam—49:39[10]),

---

6. Diodorus *Bibliotheka*, 2.48 and 19.94–100.
7. Nelson Glueck, *The Other Side of the Jordan*, pp. 166–67.
8. Amos 1:3–2:16; Isa. 13–23; Zeph. 2:4–15; Jer. 46–51; Ezek. 25–32.
9. See pp. 29–30, 185–86, 215, 223–24.
10. The fact that in the LXX the promise of restoration appears only in the oracle against Elam probably points to the peculiarities of the Greek translation of Jeremiah and not to any theological distinctives of that version.

and of interest also is the fact that the Lord promised in Jeremiah's Edom oracle that He would keep alive the orphans and widows (Jer. 49:11). The reason for that may be connected to the likely explanation of why the prophets did not call the nations to repentance as they did Israel. Not being partners in the covenant, there was no basis upon which the nations could respond to Yahweh except a broadly shared general ethic. Yet that ethical sense alone should have directed them to the better Torah that Yahweh had imparted to Israel.

The book of Obadiah, therefore, is basically a condemnation of Edom, in character generally with the national oracles. No words of comfort or hope appear, at least not for Edom. Yet the effect of the oracle for Judah is greatly comforting, both directly and indirectly. Directly, Obadiah extends a promise of repatriation to the exiles (vv. 19–21), but indirectly, the pledge that Edom will be destroyed (vv. 4, 6, 15, 18) is to Judah a comforting message of divine justice.

ANALYSIS

Dramatically the book opens with the announcement that the Lord has issued tidings and has sent a messenger among the nations calling them to rise up in battle against Edom (v. 1*d*). The rest of the book (vv. 2–21) contains Yahweh's message, directed not to the nations but to Edom. The prophecy can be subdivided into the following sections:

Superscription	1*a*
The Messenger's tidings	1*b-d*
Indictment of Edom for his pride and threat of Edom's fall ("I will bring you down")	2–4
Announcement of Edom's Day of the Lord	5–9
Description of Judah's Day of the Lord/ Explanation of Edom's judgment	10–14
Announcement of Edom's Day of the Lord	15*a*
Description of Edom's Day of the Lord	15*b*–18
Promise of Judah's Repatriation	19–21

The book employs comparison and surprise. The comparison consists in the explication of the two phases of the Day of the Lord, consisting of the Day of the Lord for Judah and the Day for the nations (in this case, Edom). In this book the second phase (for Edom) is introduced first (verse 8), followed by an explanation of why that judgment had become necessary. It was necessitated by Edom's plunder of Jerusalem in her time of helplessness. After the term "day" is introduced in verse 8, the prophet in hammer-like style drives home the idea that Judah's "day" had already occurred, and Edom had no compassion on him. The recurring use of the term throughout verses 11–14 is reminiscent of a similar style in Zephaniah 1:14–16, announcing the Day of the Lord. Whereas in Zephaniah it was future, here in verses 11–14 it is past. Once Obadiah has dealt with the terrible realism of Judah's Day of the Lord, he returns to explicate the Day of the Lord for Edom (vv. 15–18), a thought already introduced in verse 8. The fact that Obadiah introduced the description as the Day of the Lord for all the nations should not confuse the picture, for the other aspect of that Day was judgment upon the nations. Edom's participation in that day of judgment was the central message of Obadiah.

The surprise occurs in the form of Edom's question, "Who will bring me down to earth?" (v. 3) and Yahweh's answer, "I will bring you down" (v. 4). When Edom was deceived by its own precipitous heights into believing that it was invincible, the Lord declared His intention to bring down the haughty nation.

COMPOSITION

Though brief in scope, the book has had its ample share of critical theories. T. H. Robinson proposed that it was a collection of poetic fragments against Edom from various periods (verses 1–5, 6–7, 8–11, 12–14, 15–16, 17–18, 19–21).[11] Those who have viewed the prophecy more wholistically fall into three groups. First, some attribute only vv. 1–14 and 15b to Obadiah. Julius A. Bewer, following Wellhausen, takes this position, reasoning that those verses deal with concrete historical situations, whereas the other verses deal with eschatology.[12] The second position, represented by Artur Weiser and Otto Eissfeldt, divides verses 1–18 into two oracles going back to Obadiah, verses 1–14 and 15b, and 15a and 16–18, denying only verses 19–21 to the prophet. In fairness, however, it should be said that neither of those scholars categorically denies verses 19–21 to Obadiah.[13]

The third position, represented by John A. Thompson, attributes the whole book to Obadiah.[14] The unity of the book, contrary to the older view that history and eschatology were not written by a single prophet, is indicated by the unified theme, the Day of the Lord for Edom, and the natural outgrowth of that theme that tenders the future restoration of Judah. In prophetic eschatology the salvation of God's people follows a purge of their sins and is associated with the punishment of Israel's enemies. So the book of Obadiah is a fine model of

---

11. T. H. Robinson, "The Structure of the Book of Obadiah," pp. 402–8.
12. Julius A. Bewer, *A Critical and Exegetical Commentary on Obadiah and Joel*, p. 4.
13. Artur Weiser, *The Old Testament: Its Formation and Development*, pp. 248–49; Otto Eissfeldt, *The Old Testament: An Introduction*, pp. 402–3.
14. John A. Thompson, "The Book of Obadiah," 6:859.

that eschatological scheme. The punitive aspect of the Day of the Lord had already passed for Judah, and now the Jews awaited the restoration that would come when Yahweh brought vengeance upon their enemies. In the prophet's mind those last two ideas were inseparable.

RELATIONSHIP TO OTHER PROPHETS

Obadiah has definite verbal affinities with Jeremiah's oracle against Edom. The phraseology of Obadiah 1–5 is frequently verbatim with Jeremiah 49:14–16, and 9, with sometimes slight changes.[15] That has of course raised the question of priority. In the scholarly literature one generally finds three positions assumed to solve this kind of problem. First, it is speculated that Obadiah was original, and Jeremiah borrowed from him. Since the study of P. C. Caspari in 1842, that opinion has been widely held.[16] Second, some believe that both Jeremiah and Obadiah drew upon a common source. The reason behind this position is that the order of the two texts is different, so Obadiah adhered more closely to the original source, and Jeremiah used it with more freedom.[17] The third position is that Jeremiah was original, and Obadiah drew from him.[18] If the occasion for Obadiah's prophecy was the fall of Jerusalem in 586 B.C. and its subsequent plunder by the Edomites, then it was possible for him to have drawn upon Jeremiah's oracle.

The question of priority, however, is never an easy one to resolve. E. B. Pusey argued in his erudite manner that Jeremiah drew from Obadiah just as he also drew upon Isaiah.[19] Yet there are other cases of borrowing in the prophets,[20] which may suggest that Jeremiah was not alone in the practice. So it is hardly sufficient to argue that thesis. Perhaps the different arrangement of the material by the two prophets suggests a common source that each one treated differently. At any rate, none of the positions can be definitively demonstrated.

---

15. Obad. 1/Jer. 49:14; 2/49:15; 3*a*/49:16*a*; 4/49:16*b*; 5/49:9; 6/cf. 49:10*a*; 8/cf. 49:7; 16/cf. 49:12.
16. P. C. Caspari, *Der Prophet Obadja*; espoused by E. B. Pusey, *The Minor Prophets with a Commentary*, p. 228 and notes, t, u, x, y; followed by Gleason L. Archer, Jr., *A Survey of Old Testament Introduction*, p, 301; and others.
17. E.g., Robert H. Pfeiffer, *Introduction to the Old Testament*, p. 585; Thompson, 6:858; Watts, *Obadiah*, p. 23; Leslie C. Allen, *The Books of Joel, Obadiah, Jonah and Micah*, pp. 132–33.
18. E.g., Julius A. Bewer, *A Critical and Exegetical Commentary on Obadiah and Joel*, p. 3; S. Goldman, "Obadiah, Introduction and Commentary," *The Twelve Prophets, p. 127.*
19. Jer. 48:29; 30/Isa. 16:6; 48:31/Isa. 15:5; 16:7, 11; 48:32/Isa. 16:8, 9, 10; 48:34/Isa. 15:4–6; 48:36/Isa. 16:11; Isa. 15:7, 48:37/Isa. 15:2, 3; 48:43, 44/Isa. 24:17, 18; 50:16/Isa. 13:14; 50:39/Isa. 13:21, 20; 50:40/Isa. 13:9; 49:27/Amos 1:4; 49:3/Amos 1:15. See Pusey, p. 228, notes t, u, x, y.
20. Thompson, 6:858, draws attention to the similarities (mostly phrases) between Obadiah and Joel, proposing that Joel borrowed from Obadiah.

DATE AND PURPOSE

DATE

Smith has remarked that Obadiah "has been tossed out of one century into another by successive critics, till there exists in their estimates of its date a difference of nearly six hundred years" (899 to soon after 312 B.C.).[21] The main two criteria for dating the book are the devastation of Jerusalem in verses 10–14 and Obadiah's relationship to Jeremiah 49. Either of those can be answered more than one way, so neither of them is the kind of criteria that will produce dogmatic results.

Regarding the date of the devastation of Jerusalem described in verses 10–14, some commentators have proposed that it took place in the reign of Jehoram (853–841). That proposal is based upon the Edomite revolt during that time, mentioned in 2 Kings 8:20 and 2 Chronicles 21:8–17. Yet there is no reference in either of those texts to the kind of total conquest that is described in verse 11 (". . . foreigners entered his gate and cast lots for Jerusalem"). The fall of Jerusalem to the Babylonians in 586 B.C. is the only event that qualifies for that kind of conquest. Further, as we have noted above, Obadiah was aware that the Day of the Lord had come for Jerusalem, thus suggesting the finality that the phrase implied. Looking from the vantage point of Judah's day of judgment, he predicts the coming of the Day of the Lord for the nations and Edom in particular. Those who opt for a pre-exilic date must explain verses 10–14 satisfactorily. Outside of the events of 586 B.C. it is extremely difficult to do that.

The second criterion, the relationship of Obadiah to Jeremiah, is, as we have already indicated, one that gives an uncertain sound. The critical question is the identification of the events in verses 10–14. Externally Joel utilizes several distinctive phrases that are found in Obadiah,[22] thus perhaps giving a terminus ad quem.[23] Although the description of the events of 586 in verses 10–14 does not leave the impression of an eye-witness account as in Lamentations, the emotions relating to Edom's unbrotherly behavior are very strong and may belong within a generation of the fall of Jerusalem. The early years after 586 B.C., perhaps within the decade, seem the most favorable time for Obadiah's prophecy.

---

21. George Adam Smith, *The Book of the Twelve Prophets*, 2:164.
22. Thompson, 6:858, lists several phrases from Obad. 10, 11, 15, 17, 18, noting that the clause "as the LORD has said" in 2:32 seems to refer directly back to Joel.
23. Bewer, pp. 6–7, dates the book between 586 and Joel's prophecy; John D. W. Watts, *The Books of Joel, Obadiah, Jonah, Nahum, Habakkuk and Zephaniah*, p. 51, places it at the end of the sixth or early fifth century B.C.

PURPOSE

The purpose of Obadiah is bound up more generally with the purpose of the national oracles. More than likely we should speak in terms of *purposes*, a topic we have only mentioned above. It is not clear whether the messenger in verse 1 was literally sent among the nations, but there is a precedent for such a thing in Jeremiah 27:1-11. However, in view of the loss of national status and diplomatic channels, it is not likely that Judah could send ambassadors to the nations. If that avenue of communication is eliminated, then the book was probably spoken as comfort to those citizens who felt the brunt of Edomite plunder after the fall of Jerusalem.

John D. W. Watts has speculated that the book of Obadiah was a collection of oracles arranged in the form of a prophetic liturgy for a larger Day of the Lord ritual, perhaps at the "New Year's festival."[24] The conjectural nature of Watts's theory, however, must be emphasized. As we have pointed out in our discussion of Nahum, very little evidence can be found in the Pentateuch for such a festival.

THE MESSAGE OF OBADIAH

BETWEEN BROTHERS

Some of the most bitter conflicts in history have occurred between brothers. The biblical account of Esau and Jacob is an indicting model of that fact, reminding us that even the most ancient of enmities deposit their bitter seeds in the soil of history and bring forth their spiteful offspring. The enmity that existed between Israel and Edom, however, cannot be so easily explained, for the ongoing generations bore responsibility also. They could break the chain, which they sometimes seem to have done (cf. Jer. 40:11), or they could forge new links, which they most often did. It is a mark of immaturity and irresponsibility for the children always to blame the fathers for their problems. That lesson is only implicit in Obadiah. Yet the ancestral relationship between Judah and Edom could not be forgotten, and Obadiah indicted Edom for gloating over the day of his brother's misfortune (v. 12). If only they could have lived peacefully as allies, history might have taken a different course for both nations. At any rate, talking about the "if" of history cannot change the facts of it, but it can alert us to the treacheries that lie in our own paths.

THE JUSTICE OF GOD

The most prominent theological motif of the book is the justice of God. It belongs naturally to the themes of this particular age. As we have observed in

24. John D.W. Watts, *Obadiah, A Critical Exegetical Commentary* (Grand Rapids: Eerdmans, 1969), pp. 24-26.

other prophets of this era, the wrath of God, dispensed out of an unalterable commitment to divine justice, had brought retribution to Judah for his sins. Yahweh had used the Chaldeans to effect that justice. Yet the spiteful behavior of Edom was not part of that network of justice. The Lord had not directed the Edomites to pillage Jerusalem. It was their own doing. Even if He had, He would still have exacted punishment for their sins, as He required of Assyria and Babylonia. The principle operative in Obadiah's announcement of the Day of the Lord for Edom was that of retributive justice: "As you have done, it will be done to you. Your dealings will return on your own head" (verse 15). Apart from repentance and divine grace, that was the principle to which all offenders must surrender. Esau, Edom's patriarch, had been deceived by his brother, and now he had been deceived again by his arrogance and false sense of security (verse 3). The justice of God took the form of the Day of the Lord for Edom and the nations (vv. 15–16). But when justice is dispensed, it should not evoke enmity and greed from the bystanders, but compassion. That was Edom's sin: He had not shown compassion in the day of his brother's distress. God's moral government of the world is a confidence that permeates the book of Obadiah as it did Habakkuk, Nahum, and Lamentations of this same era.

OUTLINE OF OBADIAH

Superscription (1*a*)
The Messenger's Tidings (1*b-d*)
Indictment of Edom (2–4)
Announcement of Edom's Day of the Lord (5–9)
Description of Judah's Day of the Lord and Explanation of Edom's
   Judgment (10–14)
Announcement of Edom's Day of the Lord (15*a*)
Description of Edom's Day of the Lord (15*b*–18)
Promise of Judah's Repatriation (19–21)

13

LAMENTATIONS: REFLECTIONS OF THE SOUL

RARELY DOES THE OT afford the reader the luxury of reveling in theological contemplation so fully and clearly as in the Book of Lamentations. Job is certainly one of those books, but the theological reflection there centers upon the suffering of the individual and widens out to apply the implications of Job's suffering more generally to the human race.[1] In contrast, Lamentations is a treatment of national suffering. It is one of the most important theological treatises in the OT. Norman K. Gottwald has called attention to its importance for understanding OT religion and has remarked how most of the books written on the history and religion surrounding the Exile totally bypass or only casually mention this book.[2]

TITLE AND PLACE IN CANON

The title "Lamentations" comes into our English translations through the Septuagint and Latin versions, in which the book is called *Threnoi* and *Threni* ("Lamentations") respectively. In ancient Jewish literature the book was also called by that title (*Qinoth*).[3] However, the title in the Hebrew Bible follows the common practice of naming the book by the first word(s), and there it is called *Êkhāh* ("How").

In the Septuagint and Vulgate the book of Lamentations follows the book of Jeremiah because of its traditional association with Jeremiah. That explains its position among the prophetic books in our English translations. Yet in the Hebrew Bible it is included in the third division, which is known as the "Writings," or by its Greek name, Hagiographa. In the list of biblical books in the Talmud (*Baba Bathra 15a*) Lamentations is placed near the end of the Writings. Moreover, it is not grouped with the Five Megillot, which are five short books that have come to be used for liturgical purposes in the synagogue. In the Hebrew Bible those five books are grouped together. They are the Song

---

1. See C. Hassell Bullock's discussion of Job, *An Introduction to the Old Testament Poetic Books*, pp. 63–112.
2. Norman K. Gottwald, *Studies in the Book of Lamentations*, p. 20.
3. Babylonian Talmud, *Baba Bathra 14b*.

of Songs, Ruth, Lamentations, Ecclesiastes, and Esther. In the liturgy of the synagogue the Song of Songs came to be read on the Festival of Passover, Ruth on Shavuoth (Pentecost), Lamentations on the Ninth of Ab (commemorating the destruction of both Temples), Ecclesiastes on the Feast of Tabernacles, and Esther on Purim. As early as the first century A.D. Josephus knew the practice of placing Lamentations with Jeremiah (*Contra Apionem* 1.8).

The position of Lamentations among the prophets is a natural one. The book truly stands in the prophetic tradition, for it treats the fall of Jerusalem in 586 in the light of the message of the prophets.[4] Delbert R. Hillers has remarked that the book is the "Amen" of the prophetic pronouncement of judgment for Israel's sins.[5] The Exile, which the prophets predicted, had occurred, and it had brought all the horror and devastation they had promised, and more. Now Jerusalem sat in shock contemplating the disaster and its cause. The book of Lamentations is not prophecy in the strictest sense of the word, but it is a vindication of the prophets and their view of Israel's covenantal relationship to Yahweh along with their assessment of the consequences for violating it.

LITERARY STRUCTURE AND ANALYSIS

STRUCTURE

Lamentations is composed of five poems coterminus with the five chapters. The first four poems are alphabetic acrostics. Each poem begins with the first letter of the Hebrew alphabet, and each new stanza (each new line in chap. 3) introduces the next letter of the alphabet until all twenty-two letters have been used. The last poem is not an acrostic, although it conforms to the twenty-two stanza pattern. Poem I has three lines in each stanza, and only the first word of the first line conforms to the alphabet. That pattern is followed also in Poem II, whereas Poem IV exhibits the same acrostic form, but each stanza having only two lines instead of three. Poem III in comparison has a three-line stanza like Poems I and II, but each letter of the alphabet begins the three lines of the stanza assigned to it rather than only the first line. Another minor difference occurs in Poems II, III, and IV as compared to Poem I. The letters *ayin* and *pe* are interchanged, as they are also in the acrostic poem found in Proverbs 31. Some have reasoned that that peculiarity may allude to a more standard sequence of letters, but that does not seem to be the case, because the Ugaritic abecedaries (alphabets) a millennium before Lamentations follow the same sequence as the Hebrew alphabet.

Some scholars have depreciated the artistic quality of the acrostic poem because it is so rigid and limits the author in his range of ideas. Other examples

---

4. Gottwald, pp. 113–15.
5. Delbert R. Hillers, *Lamentations*, p. xvi.

of the form are Psalms 9–10, 25, 34, 37, 111, 112, 119, 145, and Proverbs 31:10–31. The popularity of the form may have been due to its mnemonic value. Yet in the case of Lamentations it may have another function as suggested by several scholars and accepted by Gottwald in his stimulating study of the book: "to encourage completeness in the expression of grief, the confession of sin and the instilling of hope."[6] The idea was that once the entire range of the alphabet had been exhausted to vent the deep grief of Jerusalem and Judah, about all that could be said had been said.

The following comparative table may help to assimilate some of these observations on the literary form of the book:

Poem I	*Poem II*	*Poem III*	*Poem IV*	*Poem V*
22 vv.	22 vv.	66 vv.	22 vv.	22 vv.
Begins with 1st letter of alphabet and ends with last.	Same as I, except *ayin* and *pe* (vv. 16 and 17) are interchanged.	Same as II.	Same as II and III.	Not an acrostic but conforms in number to alphabet.
Each stanza has three lines and 1st word of 1st line conforms to alphabet.	Same as I.	Each stanza has three lines and 1st word of each line conforms to alphabet.	Each stanza has two lines and 1st word of 1st line conforms to alphabet.	

The metrical pattern of these poems has been much discussed. Karl Budde identified a metrical pattern that he called the *Qinah* ("lament") meter because he viewed it as the standard meter for mourning or lamentation. The meter had a falling pattern, with three stresses in the first half of the line and two in the second (3 + 2).[7] That theory, along with the older metrical theories of Hebrew poetry, has been criticized in recent years. It has been observed that the Qinah pattern is not limited to the lamentation or funeral song (cf., e.g., Isa. 1:10–12; Song of Songs 1:9–11). Further, many of the lines in Lamentations exhibit a balanced pattern (3 + 3) rather than the falling type.[8]

Form critics have attempted to offer insights on the literary type of each poem. Hermann Gunkel proposed that Poems I, II, and IV were examples of the national funeral song, Poem III mainly an individual lament, and Poem V a communal lament.[9] Otto Eissfeldt is in agreement with that position.[10] Gottwald

---

6. Gottwald, pp. 28, 32.
7. Karl Budde, "Poetry (Hebrew)," *A Dictionary of the Bible*, ed. James Hastings, 5 vols. (Edinburgh: T & T Clark, 1902), 4:2–13. For a brief discussion of Hebrew poetry and other suggested readings, see Bullock, pp. 41–48.
8. See Hillers, pp. xxx–xxxvii, for a helpful discussion of meter, syntax, and strophe.
9. Hermann Gunkel, "Klagelieder Jeremiae," 3, cols. 1049–52.
10. Otto Eissfeldt, *The Old Testament: An Introduction*, p. 501.

also seeks help in the form critical method and advances the suggestion that national lament is the primary type, although he acknowledges that the author fused types.[11] Hillers, on the other hand, offers the opinion that form criticism has given us very little help in understanding these poems. Perhaps his word of caution is in order, and the greatest insight we can receive from form criticism is that the poems are written in the style and tone of lament.

Robert Gordis's proposal that chapter 3 is best understood under the rubric of fluid personality, vacillating between individual and communal lament,[12] seems an appropriate way to view that central poem. In addition to recognizing that the book is a lament, we may also observe that it is a literary personification. Poems I, II, IV, and V are basically a lament from the mouth of Jerusalem personified, interspersed with commentary by the author. For example, in 1:12–16 we hear the city of Jerusalem speaking:

> Is it nothing to all you who pass this way?
> Look and see if there is any pain like my pain
> Which was severely dealt out to me,
> Which the Lord inflicted on the day of His fierce anger.
>
> The Lord has rejected all my strong men
> In my midst;
> He has called an appointed time against me
> To crush my young men;
> The Lord has trodden as in a wine press
> The virgin daughter of Judah.
>
> (1:12, 15)

The author's commentary follows in verse 17 with reference to Zion in the third person, and the lament of the personified city is resumed in verse 18.

Poem III may be viewed as a lament spoken by the nation personified. It has been observed that Jerusalem is a feminine figure in the poems, so "I am the man" is out of character. However, if Judah is speaking in chapter 3, then that explains the opening words, "I am the man who has seen affliction because of the rod of His wrath" (3:1). Because the wrath of Yahweh is such a strong theme in most of the poems and Jerusalem contemplates the fact and purpose of divine wrath, it is only natural for the nation to speak at some point in the book and come to terms with the terrible reality of the fall and Exile. Of course, that could also apply to the author. However, having once engaged in personification, we might expect our author to adhere to the same art form throughout. Admittedly the question is a difficult one and can with justification go either way, author/personified city or personified city/personified nation.

11. Gottwald, p. 34.
12. Robert Gordis, *The Song of Songs and Lamentations*, p. 174.

ANALYSIS

The destruction of Jerusalem and Judah and exile to Babylonia constitute the indisputable subject matter of this book. The ultimate disaster befell Jerusalem and the nation in 586 B.C. Although the number of exiles deported to Babylonia at that time was smaller than that in 597, the horrible events of 586 ended the history of Judah as a nation and dethroned the Davidic dynasty that had ruled for four centuries. And worse still, among the physical rubble of destruction the spiritual relationship to Yahweh lay in shambles.

Poem I is a lament over Jerusalem's pitiable condition after the Babylonian destruction. The theme of the chapter is the lonely and comfortless plight of the city.

> How lonely sits the city
> That was full of people!
> She has become like a widow
> Who was once great among the nations!
> She who was a princess among the provinces
> Has become a forced laborer!
> She weeps bitterly in the night,
> And her tears are on her cheeks;
> She has none to comfort her
> Among all her lovers.
> All her friends have dealt treacherously with her;
> They have become her enemies.
>
> (1:1–2)

Here the theme of the chapter is introduced. The absence of comforters is repeated in verses 9, 16, 17, and 21. Of further significance is the admission in verse 18 that the Lord was right in what He had done because Jerusalem had rebelled against His Word. The poem is not lacking in the self-disclosure that the nation's sins had brought about the disaster (1:5, 14, 20, 22). This graphic picture of desolation, a city forlorn and musing over her humiliation, sets the stage for the entire book.

Poem II deals with Yahweh's anger. The poet or the nation weeps and calls Jerusalem to weep also (2:11–19). The author uses three different Hebrew nouns for Yahweh's wrath and two verbal expressions.[13] He views the recent catastrophe as the "day of the Lord's anger," (2:1, 22) a phrase that Zephaniah had used to describe the coming Day of the Lord (Zeph. 2:2–3). Jeremiah had also frequently used the language of divine wrath to predict the approaching destruction of Judah. Further, the historical appendix to Jeremiah offers the

---

13. The nouns are: *af*—2:1, 3, 6, 21, 22; *'evrah*—2:2; *hamah*—2:4. The verbs *b'r* (to burn) and *'kl* (to consume) occur in 2:3.

same explanation for the fall of Jerusalem and the Exile to Babylonia (Jer. 52:3). That vocabulary of Yahweh's wrath is rather prominent in the three middle poems (II, III, IV) of the book.[14] As we have already seen, the theme of chapter 1 focuses on self-confession, and chapter 5 again mourns the pitiable plight of Jerusalem and raises the question why the Lord should forsake her for so long. Thus the three middle chapters reflect upon the wrath of God, bringing it into a new light in chapter 3, where the poet affirms its redemptive purpose of returning Judah to the Lord (3:40).

Poem III is connected to chapter 2 by the idea of divine wrath, introduced in 3:1 and concluded in the final verse (v. 66). The man who laments may be the nation, or, if we follow Gordis's proposal of fluid personality,[15] the poet may be speaking. The author believed that Judah's tragedy was the Day of the Lord. Although he does not use the phrase, he uses the language of Amos ("darkness and not light," 3:2/Amos 5:18) to describe it. He even draws upon Amos's imagery of the bear and lion as the fierce executors of that Day (3:10/Amos 5:19). After introducing the idea that the nation suffers because of the rod of the Lord's anger, the poet engages in a Joban complaint (vv. 3–20), followed by affirmation of trust in the Lord (vv. 21–36). Then the last part of the chapter proceeds through an admission that the catastrophe was the Lord's doing (vv. 37–39), a call to repentance (vv. 40–42), another complaint (vv. 43–54), and concludes with a consideration of what the Lord would now do about His enemies (vv. 55–66). This chapter is the core of the book. C. W. Eduard Naegelsbach speaks of 3:19–40 as the peak of the mountain jutting out of the darkness into the sunlight; from there the poet begins his descent into the gloom again.[16] The poet's explanation for the nation's suffering is of consequence to an understanding of the book. The Lord had executed the awful events because of Judah's sins (v. 42), but He had a redemptive purpose, to return the nation to the Lord (v. 40). The greatness of ancient Israel in part consisted in the fact that the Israelites could and did face up to their sin and its consequences. The book of Lamentations is one of the profound expressions of that greatness.

Poem IV describes the appalling ruin of Jerusalem and the famine and suffering that followed. The city was reduced to rubble (4:1), and famine and death stalked every street. Even the princes were not exempt from the ravages of famine. Their countenances were black like soot, and their skin shriveled on their bones (4:8). Women boiled their children to appease their gnawing appetite (4:10). It is an ugly picture. The poem is so descriptive that it is hard to believe that the poet did not himself personally witness the terrible things he describes. Perhaps the conditions were made even more intolerable by the

---

14. See 3:1, 43, 66; 4:11, 21, and one verbal form in 5:22. Also the "day of His [the Lord's] fierce anger" occurs in 1:12.
15. Gordis, p. 174.
16. C. W. Eduard Naegelsbach, *The Lamentations of Jeremiah*, p. 4.

Edomite scavenger operation after the fall (see Obadiah). The blame of these events was again positioned, not on the people generally, but on the prophets and priests. Rather than enjoying their former honored stations in society, they wandered around in the city so defiled with blood that none could touch their garments (4:13–16). That laying of blame on the prophets and priests is reminiscent of Jeremiah.[17] The poem ends with the announcement that the punishment for the iniquity of the daughter of Zion is finished (4:22).

Poem V is a prayer in which the poet continues to lament the pitiable state of Jerusalem and poses the question of why the Lord had forsaken them for so long (5:20). The idea of bearing the iniquities of the fathers, which is found in 5:7, has been used to disqualify Jeremiah as the author, because he, like Ezekiel, strongly urged personal responsibility for one's sins rather than suffering for the sins of the fathers (Jer. 31:29–30; compare Ex. 20:5–6). However, these words are not those of the poet himself, but they belong to the personified nation or city. Evidently blaming the fathers for one's woes was a popular escapism of the time, for both Jeremiah and Ezekiel quoted the proverb that justified the idea, "The fathers have eaten sour grapes, and the children's teeth are set on edge" (Jer. 31:29; Ezek. 18:2). So these words merely reflect the popular rationalization of the day. The poem ends with a verse whose translation is disputed (v. 22). Perhaps in keeping with the tone of rejection in the book, the King James translation of the initial Hebrew words (*kî 'im*) as an adversative is the best rendering: "But thou hast utterly rejected us; thou art very wroth against us."[18]

AUTHORSHIP AND DATE

The Hebrew version of Lamentations does not attribute the book to Jeremiah. The Greek and Latin versions do, however, perhaps based upon the Jewish tradition that Jeremiah authored the book. The Septuagint begins with this introductory statement, not found in the Hebrew: "And it came to pass, after Israel was taken captive, and Jerusalem made desolate, that Jeremias sat weeping, and lamented with this lamentation over Jerusalem, and said." Some scholars believe that the Jewish tradition of Jeremianic authorship was based upon Jeremiah 9:1 (Hebrew version, 8:23),

> O that my head were waters,
> And my eyes a fountain of tears,
> That I might weep day and night
> For the slain of the daughter of my people!

17. See p. 197.
18. See Hillers, pp. 100–101, for the translational options and this preference.

Gordis represents the broad consensus of modern scholarship that the book was composed between 586 and 530 B.C. (after the fall and before the return under Zerubbabel). He views chapters 2 and 4 to be composed by an eyewitness of the fall of Jerusalem and dates them around 570–60. Chapter 1 speaks of the Temple as something further removed in time than the events of chapters 2 and 4 seem to be, so Gordis proposes a date of around 530 for that poem. Yet the identification of the poet with his suffering people, which is evidenced in 3:39–48, would put the composition of chapter 3 closer to the events lamented in the book, around 550–40 in his opinion. That leaves chapter 5, which, in Gordis's assessment, reflects a long period of desolation and should be dated about 530 B.C.[19] That view also represents the position of many scholars that the five poems are not a unity. Yet that is certainly not a universal rule. Gottwald, for example, although not accepting Jeremiah's authorship, advances the opinion that the first four poems do form a literary unit written by one poet. Yet he is not dogmatic about chapter 5. He dates all of the poems, however, between 586 and 538 B.C.[20] Hillers is inclined toward literary unity of the entire book.[21]

Much has been said about the similarities and differences between Jeremiah and Lamentations.[22] They both lived to see the destruction of Jerusalem, had the same conviction that Judah's sins had caused it, shifted the blame more directly to the shoulders of the prophets and priests, and spoke about the city in the same terminology. The differences are generally exaggerated. To illustrate, Jeremiah's reference to the Temple as a "den of robbers" (Jer. 7:11) ought not exclude any affections he may and probably did have for it (e.g., Lam. 2:1, 6; 4:2). Nor should his preference for personal responsibility obscure his perception of the "sour grapes" theology that enjoyed popularity in his day. Further, Jeremiah, although imprisoned by Zedekiah, does not seem to have been his enemy. In fact, Zedekiah had on occasion consulted and helped him.[23] So if "the breath of our nostrils, the Lord's anointed" in 4:20 is applied to Zedekiah, it hardly contradicts what we know about his relationship to that king. The similarities seem to outweigh by far the differences, contrary to the frequently expressed opinion in favor of the opposite view.

An interesting comparison of the similarities and differences in vocabulary between the two books is given by Naegelsbach in his commentary. His observations lead him to conclude that Lamentations was not written by Jeremiah, but certainly by an eyewitness of the fall.[24] W. H. Hornblower, the subsequent

---

19. Gordis, pp. 126–27.
20. Gottwald, p. 21.
21. Hillers, p. xxii.
22. Gordis, pp. 124–26; S. R. Driver, *An Introduction to the Literature of the Old Testament*, pp. 462–64.
23. See p. 192.
24. Naegelsbach, pp. 10–15.

editor and enlarger of Naegelsbach's commentary, followed up on that study with a defense of Jeremianic authorship. His predecessor had capitalized on expressions that were frequent in Lamentations but not used often or at all in Jeremiah. The intriguing approach of Hornblower was to conduct a comparison between the vocabulary of Shakespeare's poems and his plays. Within only a few verses selected from the Shakesperian poems he found several words that did not occur at all in his many plays.[25] His point was to show the tenuous nature of dependance upon vocabularic studies for disproving the matter of authorship.

We must agree with R. K. Harrison's conclusion that Jeremiah could have written the book, but we may at the same time respect its anonymity and refuse to dogmatize on the matter. Harrison's terminus ad quem for its composition is 550 B.C.[26] However, there is really nothing in the book that would demand a date any later than the end of the decade in which Jerusalem fell. The hope that becomes evident in chapter 3 was already present in germinal form in the preaching of the prophets. Now that their prediction of judgment had materialized, that was a strong reason for trusting their message of hope. The truly repentant did not have to wait for events to create that hope that had its origin in a relationship to the Lord.

THEOLOGY AND MESSAGE

EXILE AND THE DAY OF THE LORD

There are strong indications that the poet of Lamentations believed that the Day of the Lord had come. As already observed above, in chapter 1 our poet takes up the issue of divine wrath and gives that problem central attention in chapter 2, sustaining its overtones through chapters 3 and 4. Lamentations employs one of the phrases, "the day of wrath," that Zephaniah had used to describe the awful day of judgment that was coming upon Judah (Zeph. 2:2–3). The disaster that befell Jerusalem and the Exile to Babylonia were the effects of Yahweh's anger (1:12; 2:1, 21, 22). In the language of Amos it was "darkness and not light." The bear and lion from which Amos's compatriots had escaped only to be bitten by a serpent had ultimately attacked in all their savagery (3:10).

Our author was also aware that the Day of the Lord was to be a two-edged sword. Not only was Judah to receive his just punishment, but so were the Lord's enemies. So Jerusalem exclaims,

---

25. Ibid., pp. 19–35. Hornblower's explanation of the differences of vocabulary, illustrated from Shakespeare's poems and plays, as applied to Jeremiah and Lamentations is given on pp. 29–35.
26. R. K. Harrison, *Introduction to the Old Testament*, p. 198.

> They have heard that I groan;
> There is no one to comfort me;
> All my enemies have heard of my calamity;
> They are glad that Thou hast done it.
> O that Thou wouldst bring *the day*
>   *which Thou hast proclaimed,*
> That they may become like me.
>
> (1:21)

He is confident that the Day had come for Judah and that it was awaiting his enemies, so he prays for its arrival.

TEMPLE, PRIESTS, PROPHETS, AND FESTIVALS: RELIGION IN RUIN

The pathos that surrounds the demolished Temple is intense in the book. The joy that accompanied the festal assemblies has been asphyxiated by death and destruction. The Lord abandoned His own sanctuary and delivered it into enemy hands (2:6). The din of mad conquerors and greedy pillagers created a clamor in the Temple that was in some respects not unlike the noise that filled the Temple on festival days (2:7). The unemployed priests perished in the city while looking for food (1:19). The day of the appointed festivals arrived, and no one came (1:4). The priests moaned. The religious institution was ruined, and just as well, for it had posed no obstruction in the path of the judgment. If anything, its functionaries, along with the false prophets, had abetted the process that prepared the way for destruction (4:13–16). Advancing from visions that were false and deceptive (2:14), the prophets had made progress— they saw no visions at all (2:9). The shame that attached to prophet and priest after the fall was well deserved and best received in the foreign lands where they had been scattered (4:16).

This book, so full of regret and penance, opens up Judah's soul to God and man. The honest confession of sin, the conviction that Yahweh was Judge and Redeemer, and the hope of renewed mercy every morning were foundation stones on which the new Israel could and did arise. The soul of this people had sunk low and all but breathed its last. But on the ruins of the past the Lord began to build the future. Israel's soul revived because he despaired of his sins and he hoped in the Lord. The Book of Lamentations exposes that soul, shamed by sin and ennobled by grace, to all mankind.

OUTLINE OF LAMENTATIONS

I. The Pitiable State of Jerusalem (1:1–22)
    A. Lament for Jerusalem (1:1–11)
    B. Lament by Jerusalem (1:12–22)

II. Yahweh's Anger (2:1–22)
   A. Yahweh's Judgment (2:1–10)
   B. The Author's Anguish (2:11–22)
III. Judah's Lament (3:1–66)
   A. The Suffering Nation (3:1–2)
   B. Judah's Complaint (3:3–20)
   C. Trusting in Yahweh (3:21–36)
   D. Yahweh's Judgment (3:37–39)
   E. Call to Repentance (3:40–42)
   F. Further Complaint (3:43–54)
   G. Yahweh's Enemies (3:55–66)
IV. Jerusalem's Ruin (4:1–22)
   A. Famine and Suffering (4:1–12)
   B. Sins of the Prophets and Priests (4:13–20)
   C. The Punishment Concluded (4:21–22)
V. Final Lament (5:1–22)
   A. Description of Ruin (5:1–18)
   B. Prayer for Restoration (5:19–22)

THE PROPHETS OF THE PERSIAN PERIOD

PERIOD

DANIEL
HAGGAI
ZECHARIAH
JOEL
MALACHI

With the dwindling fortunes of the Neo-Babylonian Empire after Nebuchadnezzar's passing (562 B.C.), the alignment of nations began to assume another shape. The greatest challenge to Babylonian sovereignty was Media, ruled by King Astyages (585–550). As divine sovereignity would have it, however, one of that monarch's vassals was Cyrus the Persian, king of Anshan in southern Iran. Hoping against hope to contravene the Median power, the Babylonian king, Nabonidus (556–539), endorsed Cyrus and his exploits against Media, and by 550 Cyrus had unseated Astyages and gained control of the Median empire. In 547/46 he extended his rule to Lydia in Asia Minor when he captured the Lydian capital, Sardis. Egypt, with whom Nabonidus had subsequently sided when he saw the aggressive disposition of Cyrus, was unable to put together a defensive alliance that could hold the Persians in check. Therefore, Babylon was surrounded by the spreading tentacles of Cyrus's growing empire, and in 539 the city fell to the Persian king's general, Ugbaru. Thus the Neo-Babylonian Empire expired, and the control of Palestine was transferred to Cyrus.

His famous decree of 538, which gave the Jews permission to return to Judah and rebuild their Temple (Ezra 1, 2), was like waking from a bad dream. Daniel stood in conquered Babylon and viewed the changing international horizons and spoke of the future of God's people.

The Persians appointed Sheshbazzar governor of Judah, and amidst bursting enthusiasm the foundation of the Temple was laid (Ezra 5:16). But with heightening difficulties that included drought and political tensions between the returnees and the indigenous population of Judah, enthusiasm waned and hope smoldered. Cyrus's death in 530 practically terminated the restoration movement. His son and successor, Cambyses (530–522), seemed to have no interest in supporting that particular edict of his father. However, after Darius I took the throne (522) and stabilized his realm, the prophets Haggai and Zechariah, buttressed by the support of the Judean governor, Zerubbabel, and the high priest, Jeshua, renewed interest in the reconstruction of the Temple. Within weeks architecture was again on the minds of the Judeans, and the Temple was reconstructed within a four-year period (520–516) and rededicated (Ezra 6:13–18).[1]

Though there is a scholarly difference of opinion on the matter, Joel might have prophesied within a generation of the completion of the Temple.

A later wave of Babylonian exiles returned to Judah in the middle of the fifth century. Ezra returned in 458 during the reign of Artaxerxes I (465–424 B.C.) and instituted religious and social reforms, while Nehemiah became governor in 445 and effected social reform as well as significant building accomplishments in Jerusalem. The prophecy of Malachi seems to fit into that period just prior to Ezra and Nehemiah because no evidence of their reforms is to be found in his oracles.

---

1. See pp. 302–3 for further discussion of the early years of the restoration.

14

DANIEL: WITNESS IN BABYLONIA

THE BEAUTY AND POWER of the book of Daniel have often been obscured in the modern era by the complex of problems that has surrounded the study of the prophecy. Frequently the problems have preempted the positive dimensions of research, leaving the book devoid of historical value. We can allow that the spiritual merits of the book can, to some extent, be ascertained by those who deny its historical basis, but a book that reputes to be of a historical nature and seeks to teach spiritual realities based in its historical premises cannot be put on an equal footing with the book that lays no such claim to history. History and spiritual reality are like body and soul, to use a metaphor inappropriate to the Old Testament, but one that we understand. On the one hand, it is no great concession to hypercritical scholarship to acknowledge the nature of the historical problems related to Daniel and his book. Nor is it, on the other hand, any infringement of scholarly integrity to seek to establish the historical nature of the material. Therefore, our task is a dual one.

DANIEL THE MAN

The prophets had no propensity for mentioning their professional predecessors or contemporaries. When they did, it was the exception rather than the rule. The elders in Jeremiah mentioned Micah (Jer. 26:18), and Daniel mentioned Jeremiah (Dan. 9:2); both of those references were in regard to critical predictions and their subsequent fulfillment. However, Ezekiel, Daniel's contemporary in Babylonia, made reference to Daniel in three instances (Ezek. 14:14, 20; 28:3), not for his prophetic ability but for his righteousness and wisdom. In the first two instances Ezekiel mentioned him in company with Noah and Job, who, by their own righteousness, could not reclaim the land of Judah from its advanced moral declension. They could save only their own lives. In the third reference Daniel is held up to the Prince of Tyre as a paragon of wisdom.

That brief character sketch of the prophet harmonizes with his character description in the book of Daniel. Recognized for his wisdom (1:4; 2:48; 5:11), he was also perceived as a man of impeccable character. The rulers of Darius's realm shrank from attacking his character and chose rather to undermine the law of his God (6:5, also v. 22). Ezekiel's exile to Babylonia in 597 B.C. occurred almost a decade after Daniel's banishment to that land in 605 B.C., allowing ample time for Daniel to have established his reputation there. Ezekiel's acquaintance with Daniel's renown is not surprising in view of his own residence in Babylonia. Nor should the knowledge of that reputation in Judah be any less surprising in light of the correspondence that took place between the expatriates and the Palestinian community.

Further, the proposal that Ezekiel had in mind the "Danil" of Ugaritic mythology is inconsonant with that prophet's theology. No OT prophet was more vocal in his opposition to idolatry and pagan religion than Ezekiel was, having predicted and been witness to its inevitable consequences. To hold forth a figure from such a tradition as an exemplar of righteousness and wisdom would belie his own deep convictions about pagan idolatry. Harold H. P. Dressler observes that in the Ugaritic Aqhat Text neither the word "wise" (*ḥkm*) nor "righteousness" (*tsdq*) is applied to the Danil of that document.[1]

Although not a priest, Daniel represented the loyalty of the laity to the Mosaic law. Well acquainted with the dietary laws (1:8–16), he was a transition figure between pre-exilic religion and Judaism. Daniel's advice to King Nebuchadnezzar, to "break away now from your sins by doing righteousness, and from your iniquities by showing mercy to the poor, in case there may be a prolonging of your prosperity" (4:27), was not a new thought (cf. Prov. 14:21), but it did silhouette the prophetic emphasis upon the care of the indigent, which came to be a major tenet of Judaism. Further, the centrality of the Torah in Judaism may be seen in incipient form in this book. Perhaps Daniel represented a strand of orthodoxy whose roots were anchored in the Reform of Josiah with its renewed accentuation on Torah. Moreover, the custom of praying three times a day, corresponding to practice in later traditional Judaism,[2] is already attested in Daniel's religious code.

Nothing definite is known about this prophet's family or his Palestinian roots. That he was young is implied (1:4), and that he was from the nobility is suggested by the text (1:3).

He was deported to Babylonia in the year 605 B.C., when Nebuchadnezzar

---

1. Harold H. P. Dressler, "The Identification of the Ugaritic 'Dnil' with the Daniel of Ezekiel," pp. 152–161, esp. p. 154. A rejoinder to Dressler's article was written by John Day, "The Daniel of Ugarit and Ezekiel and the Hero of the Book of Daniel," but his counter arguments are inadequate to turn the evidence back around in favor of the Ugaritic Daniel. In fact, he does not really respond properly to the charge that Daniel, as a representative of the Baal cult, stood opposed to all that Ezekiel preached regarding idolatry. He believes the Ugaritic portrait of Daniel has fed into the stream of tradition, producing the portrait of the biblical Daniel in the second century, even though he does not argue that Ezekiel knew our present Aqhat Text.

2. See *Berakhot* 4.1. Also Ps. 55:17.

evidently made a raid upon Judah.[3] He lived to be an old man, as his activity in the reigns of Belshazzar of Babylon and Cyrus the Great attests. The latest date in the book is the third year of Cyrus as king of Babylon (536 B.C.).

MAJOR PROBLEMS IN THE BOOK

The major obstacles that lie in the interpreter's path to confident historical credibility fall into two classes, the historical and linguistic. Daniel's historical details have often, as already noted, presented difficulties which some scholars have pronounced insurmountable for historical inquiry. Therefore, the book does not, in the opinion of numerous researchers, qualify for the category of history. From a linguistic standpoint, the issue revolves around the date and purpose of the long Aramaic section of the book (2:46–7:28) and the presence of Persian and Greek words in the text. Thus, at the risk of beginning on a negative note, we should consider the problems that are associated with these two categories.

DANIEL 1:1: THE "THIRD YEAR OF JEHOIAKIM" AND DANIEL'S EXILE

Having taken the throne in the year 608, Jehoiakim's third year would be 605 B.C., according to the *accession-year system* of reckoning, which was used in Babylonia and thus was used by Daniel. By that system the year in which the king ascended the throne was considered his "accession year," and the first year of his reign began on new year's day of the following year (his first full year). However, Jeremiah's dates, it would appear, followed the *nonaccession-year system*, which began counting the king's first year from the date he assumed the throne.[4] That means that the nonaccession-year dates will normally be one year higher than the same date in the accession-year system. Jeremiah correlates the "fourth year of Jehoiakim" with the "first year of Nebuchadnezzar" (Jer. 25:1), which was 605 B.C. according to Jeremiah's nonaccession-year system and 604 B.C. according to the Babylonian accession-year method.[5] The following comparison of the two systems indicates that the "third year of Jehoiakim" was the year 605 B.C. according to Daniel's accession-year system:

Daniel's Babylonian System	Jeremiah's Palestinian System
Year of Jehoiakim's Accession (608)	First Year of Jehoiakim (608)
First year of Jehoiakim (607)	Second Year of Jehoiakim (607)
Second year of Jehoiakim (606)	Third Year of Jehoiakim (606)
Third Year of Jehoiakim (605)	Fourth Year of Jehoiakim (605)

3. See below on Dan. 1:1.
4. Edwin R. Thiele, *The Mysterious Numbers of the Hebrew Kings*, pp. 14–15, 19–20.
5. Ibid., pp. 159–60. This view was set forth by Robert Dick Wilson, *Studies in the Book of Daniel: A Discussion of the Historical Questions*, pp. 43–59; favored also by Edward J. Young, *The Prophecy of Daniel: A Commentary*, p. 269, and others.

D. J. Wiseman has pointed out that in apparent contradiction to Daniel 1:1 the Babylonian Chronicle gives no explicit evidence of any action by Nebuchadnezzar in Judah in 606 or 605 B.C. or any siege of Jerusalem, for that matter, before 597 B.C.[6] Nevertheless, the Chronicle does state that Nebuchadnezzar led his father's army up the Euphrates to Carchemish where he met the Egyptians in battle and summarily defeated them. Subsequently his troops marched through Syria and reached Egypt early in the month of Ab (Aug. 605), suggesting that the Battle of Carchemish likely took place in May–June of that year. Further, the Chronicle records, "At that time Nebuchadrezzar conquered the whole area of Hatti" (Syria and Palestine).[7] Thus the Babylonian foray into the Judean hill country, resulting in the captivity of Daniel and other members of the nobility, most likely occurred while the Babylonian army was en route to Egypt or very soon after the Egyptian operation in early August of 605 B.C. Josephus, citing the Babylonian historian Berosus, verifies that chronology, stating that Jewish captives were taken by Nebuchadnezzar shortly before his father Nabopolassar died, which would be the third year of Jehoiakim, according to Daniel's accession-year system.[8] Moreover, the Babylonian Chronicle attests that Nabopolassar died on the eighth of Ab (15th/16th Aug., 605). Upon hearing the news, Nebuchadnezzar and a small party returned immediately to the capital where he became king on the day he arrived (first of Elul, i.e., 6th/7th Sept., 605).[9] Admittedly we must argue from the silence of the primary historical documents for such an invasion, but the witness of the book of Daniel ought not be dismissed out of hand. Whereas some scholars would acknowledge neither Josephus nor Daniel as a credible source of information, Robert Dick Wilson's remark on the subject seems appropos: "Daniel, at whatever time it was written, would probably know more than we do to-day; for *we know nothing*. No evidence proves nothing."[10]

Neither of the references in 2 Kings 24:1 and 2 Chronicles 36:6–7 to a siege of Jerusalem during the reign of Jehoiakim mentions the date, but the usual interpretation is that they refer to the siege of 597. Two details in Chronicles provide correlative and noncorrelative information with Daniel—that Nebuchadnezzar took away some of the Temple vessels and that he bound Jehoiakim in bronze chains "to bring him to Babylon" (2 Chron. 36:6). The correlative statement regarding the Temple vessels has inclined some major commentators to observe that these texts conform to the description of the siege in Daniel

6. D. J. Wiseman, "Some Historical Problem in the Book of Daniel," in D. J. Wiseman, ed., *Notes on Some Problems in the Book of Daniel*, p. 16.
7. D. J. Wiseman, *Chronicles of Chaldean Kings (626–556 B.C.) in the British Museum*, pp. 24–25.
8. Josephus *Contra Apionem*, 1.19.137.
9. Wiseman, *Chronicles of Chaldean Kings*, p. 27.
10. Wilson, p. 81.

1:1.[11] But such an action was typical of foreign invaders. On the other hand, the noncorrelative statement, that Nebuchadnezzar bound Jehoiakim in bronze chains "to bring him to Babylon," leaves us wondering if the incident was not part of the siege of 597. That the Chronicler believed it was is indicated by the form of the narrative in which the detail is contained. The finality of the incidents as recorded in 2 Chronicles 36:5–8 is rather obvious, indicating that the Chronicler was relating the last days of Jehoiakim's reign, not intermediate incidents. Note the introductory and concluding formulas between which the details are given ("Jehoiakim was twenty-five years old when he became king, and he reigned eleven years in Jerusalem . . . Now the rest of the acts of Jehoiakim and the abominations which he did"). If the last days of Jehoiakim's reign are related there, as seems to be indicated by the form of the narrative, then he did not live to be exiled to Babylon. The Chronicler does not say that the deed was actually carried out, only that it was intended.

The lapse of Jehoiakim's three years of vassalage to Nebuchadnezzar (2 Kings 24:1) could easily fit into the years between 605 and the campaign of the Babylonian army in Hatti (Syria-Palestine) in 601 B.C., when the military presence assisted the district governors to collect and forward the annual tribute to Babylon.[12] That requires us, of course, to make the assumption that Judah, like so many other Babylonian vassals, paid the tribute most grudgingly and sometimes had to be forced to do it. That accords perfectly with Josephus's statement that Nebuchadnezzar, after he had reigned four years and Jehoiakim had ruled eight, came against Judah and required tribute of Jehoiakim.[13] Nebuchadnezzar personally joined his army in Syria and marched to Egypt, where he engaged Pharaoh Neco II in battle, both suffering heavy losses.[14]

BELSHAZZAR AND NABONIDUS

In chapters 5, 7, and 8 Belshazzar is called the king of Babylonia, and according to 5:30–31 he was king when Cyrus conquered the city of Babylon. It is known, however, that Nabonidus, his father, was the legitimate monarch, reigning from 556 to 539 B.C. Yet Raymond Philip Dougherty has shown from the Babylonian cuneiform records that Nabonidus spent the seventh, ninth, tenth, and eleventh years of his reign in Tema as a devotee to his god, Sin. He ruled the western part of his empire from Tema, while Belshazzar was co-regent in Babylonia.[15] To be sure, we cannot determine the extent of Belshazzar's

---

11. E.g., Young, p. 270; C. F. Keil, *Biblical Commentary on the Book of Daniel*, pp. 58–59.
12. See Wiseman's discussion of this campaign in *Chronicles of Chaldean Kings*, pp. 29–30.
13. Josephus *Antiq.* 10. 6. 87. 6
14. Wiseman, *Chronicles of Chaldean Kings*, p. 29.
15. Raymond Philip Dougherty, *Nabonidus and Belshazzar: A Study of the Closing Events of the Neo-Babylonian Empire*, p. 105. Dougherty discusses historical, commercial, and administrative documents to show Belshazzar's association with his father, Nabonidus, in the administrative affairs of the Neo-Babylonian Empire (pp. 105–37).

powers as co-regent, but they must have been considerable, for he performed royal functions that would not have been expected of a mere administrator. Although he is never called "king" in the cuneiform documents, he virtually functioned in that capacity and is so called by Daniel. But it should be noted that our prophet was quite aware of his position as second ruler, for in 5:16 and 29 Belshazzar offers Daniel the *third* position in the kingdom.

DARIUS THE MEDE

As John C. Whitcomb, Jr. has observed, Daniel gives more information about Darius the Mede than he does about Belshazzar or even Nebuchadnezzar.[16] In addition to being called a Mede, we learn that he was sixty-two years old when he received the kingdom (5:31), that he was called "king" (chap. 6), and that he was the son of Ahasuerus (9:1). Unknown by that name in the cuneiform sources, Darius has been a puzzle to scholars. The major theories that have been proposed to solve the riddle are the following:

A Fictitious Person. H. H. Rowley made a study of the problem and concluded that Darius the Mede was a "fictitious creation." The author of Daniel, he said, confused certain traditions about Darius I-Hystaspes (521–486 B.C.) and Cyrus the Great (539–530 B.C.).[17] The problem is partly found in the fact that Daniel places Darius's reign before Cyrus.[18] If then the author had Darius I in mind, he inverted the reigns of the two kings. But as Whitcomb has commented, a Jewish author of the second century (Rowley's assumed date of composition) had the succession of kings readily available in Ezra 4:5–7: Cyrus, Darius, Xerxes (Ahasuerus), and Artaxerxes.[19] So there was no reason for him to make such a blunder. Further, Wilson has maintained that the statements in 5:31 that "Darius the Mede *received* the kingdom" and in 9:1 that "Darius . . . *was made king*" are indicative of the fact that he was made king by his overlord, Cyrus.[20]

Cyrus the Persian. This theory, proposed by Wiseman, holds that Cyrus was himself Darius the Mede. Wiseman bases the identification upon 6:28, where he interprets the Hebrew conjunction *vav* ("and") as appositional, thus "Dan-

16. John C. Whitcomb, Jr., *Darius the Mede; A Study in Historical Identification*, p. 8.
17. H. H. Rowley, *Darius the Mede and the Four World Empires in the Book of Daniel*, pp. 54–60.
18. Cyrus II became king of Babylon in the year 539 B.C. when it fell to his Persian army, although he had become vassal king of Anshan in the east around 559 B.C., soon uniting all the Persian tribes under his rule, and ultimately incorporating Media in his empire ca. 550—A. T. Olmstead, *History of the Persian Empire*, pp. 34–4, 37.
19. Whitcomb, p. 59. Wilson, p. 145, has shown that a second-century writer would have had several works dealing with the history of the Persian Empire at his disposal, among them Herodotus, Ctesias, Berosus, and Menander. Josephus, writing in the first century A.D., said he consulted forty different historians in preparing his treatise *Contra Apionem*.
20. Wilson, pp. 143–44.

iel prospered in the reign of Darius, that is, the reign of Cyrus the Persian.'' Wiseman also identifies the appositional use of that conjunction in 1 Chronicles 5:26. Further, the Babylonians could have called Cyrus a Mede because he incorporated the Medes into his empire around 550 B.C.[21] However, against the book of Daniel, which calls Darius the son of Ahasuerus (9:1), the historical sources reveal that Cyrus was the son of Cambyses.[22]

Gubaru. The identification of Darius with Gubaru, governor of Babylon, is judiciously set forth by Whitcomb. He shows that in the Nabonidus Chronicle two persons were mentioned who played a significant role in the conquest and governance of Babylon, Ugbaru and Gubaru. The first was associated with the conquest of Babylon on October 12, 539 B.C., dying three weeks later. Subsequently Gubaru was appointed by Cyrus as governor of Babylon and the region beyond the river, a position he held for at least fourteen years.[23] Obviously this necessitates identifying Darius the Mede with a person of a different name in the cuneiform documents based upon his function as governor of the city. Nowhere is the equation of Darius and Gubaru explicitly presented. However, the function of the two is certainly, according to Whitcomb, parallel.

Even though our current information is inadequate to solve the riddle beyond doubt, we should not relinquish hope of more information still to be unearthed at some archaeological site or awaiting the philologist's scrutiny in some silent museum archive. In the meantime Whitcomb's work deserves serious attention. The assured minimum at this point, however, is, as Joyce G. Baldwin has observed, that "there is too much evidence of him as a person in history" to reject the historicity of Darius.[24] As has been observed, the same uncertainty and speculation surrounded the search for the identification of Belshazzar before the discovery of the cuneiform documents that settled the matter that Belshazzar was Nabonidus's son.[25]

THE ARAMAIC OF DANIEL

The central section of the book is written in Aramaic (2:4*b*–7:28), the language of diplomacy in the eighth century B.C. (2 Kings 18:26) and the language of the Medo-Persian Empire. Two issues arise out of this fact: Why is Aramaic introduced in the middle section of the book, and what bearing does that have on dating the composition of Daniel?

21. Wiseman, "Some Historical Problems in the Book of Daniel," pp. 9–18. Joyce G. Baldwin, *Daniel: An Introduction and Commentary,* pp. 26–28, sympathetically discusses Wiseman's theory but stops short of embracing it.
22. Olmstead, p. 34. See Whitcomb's critique, pp. 46–49.
23. Whitcomb, pp. 22, 23.
24. Baldwin, *Daniel,* p. 28.
25. Edwin M. Yamauchi, "The Archaeological Background of Daniel," pp. 3–16, esp. pp. 13–14.

Purpose of the Aramaic section. To write a book in Hebrew and Aramaic, even though the latter is a dialect of the former, is a strange phenomenon to the modern reader.[26] Yet in a world where a knowledge of other languages was a necessity, especially for commercial and diplomatic purposes, bilingualism was not uncommon. But still that does not answer the question of why Daniel would compose his book in two different languages. Two explanations have been generally offered.

The first explanation accounts for the phenomenon in the hypothesis that the entire book was originally written in Aramaic and that later 1:1–2:4a and chapters 8–12 were translated into Hebrew. R. H. Charles proposed this thesis, explaining that three translators later rendered the Hebrew portions into that language with the motive of getting the book into the canon. He believed the date of the translation was the Maccabean period, around 164–145 B.C.[27] H. C. Leupold has satisfactorily argued against this thesis on linguistic grounds.[28] It may further be observed that if, as Charles argued, the Hebrew portions were done to bring about canonization of the book, then why did the translators not go all the way and translate the entire book so as to assure greater certainty of canonical acceptance?

The second explanation, and perhaps the most satisfactory one proposed as yet, is that the Aramaic portion in 2:4b—7:28 was the part of the book most germane to non-Jews. Thus it was written in the language of the empire for their consumption.[29] The last five chapters (8–12) applied the eschatological /theological insights of chapters 2–7 to the people of God and were therefore in Hebrew, as was also the introduction to the book (1:1–2:4a).

The bearing of Aramaic on the date of the book. Scholarly debate in recent years has largely revolved around the issue of date rather than purpose as regards the Aramaic section of Daniel. Since the publication of Rowley's study of biblical Aramaic in 1929, many scholars have been inclined to accept uncritically his conclusion that the Aramaic of Daniel stood "somewhere between the Aramaic of the papyri and that of the Nabataean and Palmyrene inscriptions," i.e., the second century B.C.[30] Yet, as other documents have come to light, including the Dead Sea Scrolls, a re-examination of the data has begun to take effect. K. A. Kitchen has observed that nine-tenths of the vocabulary of the book is attested in fifth-century texts or earlier. Although the

---

26. Other portions of the OT written in Aramaic are Ezra 4:8–6:18; 7:1–26; and Jer. 10:11.
27. R. H. Charles, *A Critical and Exegetical Commentary on the Book of Daniel*, pp. xviii, xxx–xxxix, xlvi–l. The general form of this hypothesis has been espoused and defended by Frank Zimmermann, "The Aramaic Origin of Daniel 8–12," pp. 258–72, "Some Verses in Daniel in the Light of a Translation Hypothesis," pp. 349–54; and H. Louis Ginsberg, *Studies in Daniel*, pp. 41–61.
28. H. C. Leupold, *Exposition of Daniel*, pp. 37–39.
29. Accepted, e.g., by Baldwin, *Daniel*, pp. 29–30, and Leupold, p. 29.
30. H. H. Rowley, *The Aramaic of the Old Testament* (1929).

unattested one-tenth could be from a later period, it is equally possible that it could be from an earlier period.[31] One of the most interesting phenomena in the Aramaic of Daniel, however, is the word order, which usually follows the pattern of subject-object-verb. That stands in sharp contrast to certain Dead Sea documents in Aramaic, the *Genesis Apocryphon* and the *Targum of Job*, both close to the time of the supposedly second-century composition of Daniel. As Kitchen has observed, the word order of Daniel agrees with the Asshur ostracon of the seventh century B.C. and with the freedom of word order that characterized the fifth-century Aramaic papyri from Egypt.[32] Although Peter W. Coxan has no interest in disproving a second-century date for Daniel, he has re-examined the seven points that Rowley noted as differences between biblical Aramaic and the papyri and has concluded that four of the points have no parallel in Qumran. He deems it unwise to conclude that the syntax of Daniel was either early or late, but he is intrigued by the "eastern" word order we have just mentioned.[33]

Admittedly the data do not permit a dogmatic decision. However, the confidence with which the second-century date for Daniel, based upon the Aramaic, was once held has been eroded.

LOANWORDS

The often quoted dictum of S. R. Driver delineates the problem here:

> The verdict of the language of Daniel is thus clear. The *Persian* words presuppose a period after the Persian empire had been well established: the Greek words *demand*, the Hebrew *supports*, and the Aramaic *permits*, a date *after the conquest of Palestine by Alexander the Great* (B.C. 332).[34]

There are in the book of Daniel seventeen words from the Persian language, three Greek, and possibly one Egyptian. If, however, Daniel moved in the circles of the New Persian government, he would have picked up some of the vocabulary. Leupold has commented that twelve of the seventeen Persian words belong to governmental terminology, names of officials, technical terms, and so on. Because Daniel was writing for the new generation that had come under Persian rule, the use of the current Persian terms communicated better than would have the former Babylonian terms.[35]

31. K. A. Kitchen, "The Aramaic of Daniel," pp. 32–33.
32. Ibid., p. 76. The North-West Semitic word order of the *Genesis Apocryphon* has been elucidated by Gleason L. Archer, Jr., "The Aramaic of the Genesis Apocryphon Compared with the Aramaic of Daniel," pp. 160–69.
33. Peter W. Coxon, "The Syntax of the Aramaic of Daniel: A Dialectal Study," pp. 107–22, esp. p. 122.
34. S. R. Driver, *An Introduction to the Literature of the Old Testament*, p. 508.
35. Leupold, pp. 23–24.

The three Greek words occur in 3:5 and are Greek names of musical instruments. Yet that is not a great block of evidence for a late date, especially when it is recognized that the exchange of musicians and musical instruments was a very common thing in the royal courts of the ancient world.[36] Gleason L. Archer, Jr., has observed that even though these words do not occur in Greek literature until the time of Plato (*ca*. 370 B.C.), that is still an insufficient basis for determining the date of Daniel, for extant Greek literature is estimated to be no more than one-tenth of the Greek literature that once existed.[37]

The possible Egyptian loanword *hartummîm* ("magicians"), found in 1:20; 2:2, 10, 27; 4:4, 6, also occurs in Genesis 41:8, 24. If it is a loanword, then there was no reason it should not appear in Daniel, because Egyptians were in Babylonia during the sixth and fifth centuries B.C.[38]

In conclusion, the cultural and personal interchange in the ancient world easily explains the use of foreign words in Daniel.

THE DATE AND UNITY OF THE BOOK

DATE

Ever since the third-century philosopher Porphyry wrote his disclaimer to the historicity of the book of Daniel, alleging that Daniel was a second-century B.C. composition that recorded history in the form of prediction (*vaticinium post eventum*), the book of Daniel has been shrouded by doubts concerning its historicity and authenticity.[39] The reasons for assigning the book to the second century can be summarized in three categories: history, language, and place in the canon. Many scholars, as already noted, contend that the author's supposedly vague acquaintance with the historical details of the Neo-Babylonian and early Medo-Persian periods is a clue to the late date of composition. Further, it is supposed that the detail surrounding the exploits of Antiochus IV Ephiphanes in chapter 11 is so specific that it must be history rather than prediction. In our consideration of the historical problems above we have indicated that the author was far better acquainted with the historical data of the Neo-Babylonian and Medo-Persian periods than he has been credited. Baldwin has examined five Assyrian/Babylonian "prophecy" texts and concluded that Daniel shows definite affinities with that type of Babylonian literature. As she observes, it would be strange for a second-century Jew in Palestine to exhibit such a knowledge of Babylonian cuneiform literature.[40] In view of that evidence, it is my conclusion

---

36. Edwin M. Yamauchi, "The Archaeological Background of Daniel," p. 12; *Greece and Babylon* (Grand Rapids: Baker, 1967), pp. 19–24.
37. Gleason L. Archer, Jr., *A Survey of Old Testament Introduction*, pp. 386–87.
38. Yamauchi, "The Archaeological Background of Daniel," p. 10.
39. Gleason L. Archer, Jr., trans. *Jerome's Commentary on Daniel*.
40. Baldwin, "Some Literary Affinities of the Book of Daniel," pp. 77–99, esp. pp. 97–98.

that none of the historical problems constitute a formidable obstacle to the sixth-century date.

The explicit information about Antiochus Ephiphanes poses a slightly different problem, however, hinging upon the nature of prophecy itself. On the one hand, we must admit that normally OT prediction was given in general terms. Yet there are exceptions, as we have noted in Isaiah's prediction of Cyrus. In fact, the predictive nature of that section of Isaiah (esp. chaps. 40–48) is the one thing that separates Israel's God from the pagan gods. Only the God who could predict the future was the truly sovereign God of the world.[41] Leupold, citing E. W. Hengstenberg, draws attention to the specificity of Jeremiah's prediction of the conquest of Babylon, especially the mode and agent (Medes and their allies) of conquest (Jer. 50, 51; esp. 50:38; 51:32, 36; 51:39, 57), as well as the prophecy of Zechariah 9:1–8, which remarkably foretells the victories of Alexander the Great.[42]

Another way of solving the problem is that represented by C. F. Keil, who understands the prophecy to be a general description of what will happen to the people of God in the end times (10:14), rather than a regular prophetic prediction of historical events and persons.[43] Still another approach is to view chapter 11 as a predictive prophecy either up to verse 36[44] or to verse 40,[45] and from there on as general prophetic description. The traditional position is to interpret those last verses as applying to the Antichrist. The question is a difficult one. Although the simplest method would be to follow either the predictive or general prophecy interpretation, it must be recognized that after having set forth the historical pattern for the persecution of God's people, a shift to the general sense may best satisfy the nature of the passage and at the same time not represent a violation of the nature of Hebrew prophecy in general.

Arguments for a second-century date, once thought to be supported by the strongest evidence, have in recent years begun to give way to new discoveries of Aramaic documents that put the Aramaic of Daniel within the possible if not probable range of Imperial Aramaic (7th-3rd centuries B.C.), thus allowing for a sixth-century date of composition.

Another reason for the second-century date is the fact that Daniel is not included among the Prophets in the Hebrew canon of Scripture. Rather it is

---

41. See pp. 151–52; also Baldwin has a helpful discussion of chapter 11 from a predictive point of view, *Daniel*, pp. 182–203.
42. Leupold, pp. 471–72. See also this book, pp. 317.
43. Keil, p. 428.
44. Leupold, pp. 510–24; Young, pp. 246–53.
45. E. W. Heaton, *Daniel*, p. 240.

contained in the Writings, or Hagiographa,[46] generally deemed to be the latest literary corpus of the OT to achieve canonical status. In view of the evidence from the Dead Sea collection, however, the canonical status of the Writings may have been achieved earlier than is often thought, certainly prior to the Septuagint translation.[47] Date of composition, although important, was hardly the reason that Daniel was not included in the collection of the Prophets, which was likely canonized by the end of the fifth century B.C. It is far more likely that some literary criteria were involved, perhaps the apocalyptic sections that predominated in the book. Daniel was a new stage in apocalyptic, anticipated to be sure by Ezekiel, but well advanced beyond the genre as it was incipiently represented by Isaiah 24–27 and Ezekiel 38–39. We may conjecture that the developing genre did not immediately find a place among the prophetic books. It came to acceptance more slowly than the standard genre of prophetic material; therefore, it stood outside the regular collection of prophets. The fact that history vindicated Daniel's prophecies, as it did those of Zechariah 9–14,[48] lent support to the legitimacy of the book. Thus the lapse of time required for historical authentication would be one of the reasons Daniel was not included among the Prophets in the Hebrew canon.[49]

Twice Daniel is commanded to keep his words a secret (8:26; 12:4) and to seal the book until the time of the end (12:4). Isaiah also sealed his words for a later time (Isa. 8:16). We may assume that those prophets took their instructions literally, for they were sensitive to the issue of fulfillment, and without it their prophetic ministries could not be fully vindicated. So it is quite possible that the book of Daniel was hidden for a while and only brought to public attention at an appropriate time, possibly as early as the time of Alexander the Great when the lines of fulfillment had begun to become distinct. Although Daniel's prophecy of "another kingdom inferior to you" (2:39) was made in

---

46. The Hebrew OT has a threefold division:
   I.   Torah (Pentateuch)
   II. Prophets
        A. Former Prophets (Josh., Judg., Sam., Kings)
        B. Latter Prophets (Isa., Jer., Ezek., Twelve Minor Prophets)
   III. Writings (Hagiographa)
47. The Writings were probably canonized by the end of the fourth century B.C., i.e., in the early Hellenistic period.
48. Zechariah, which in contrast did achieve canonical status among the Prophets (despite the apocalyptic nature of the book), was assisted by his historical role in the restoration of the Temple, as well as his association with the Davidic descendant, Zerubbabel. Moreover, he prophesied in Palestine, whereas Daniel lived his entire prophetic career, so far as we know, in Babylonia and Persia.
49. The fact that the prophets predicted historical events that were subsequently fulfilled was evidently an important element that contributed to the canonization of certain prophetic books. The fall of Samaria in 722 vindicated Amos and Hosea, just as the fall of Jerusalem in 586 vindicated Jeremiah and Ezekiel, as did also the return from Babylonian captivity. Although this was not the sole criterion determining canonicity, it was an important one.

the second year of Nebuchadnezzar (603), time would be required, even upon the commencement of that kingdom in 539 B.C., for that assessment to be made. The other future prophecies fall much later in the Neo-Babylonian period.

Dates in Daniel According to the Monarchs

Jehoiakim	Nebuchadnezzar	Belshazzar	Darius	Cyrus
3d yr.	2d yr.—2:1	1st yr.	1st yr.	1st yr.
—1:1	603 B.C.	—7:1	—9:1	—1:21
605 B.C.		552/51 B.C.	—11:1	538 B.C.
			538 B.C.	
	[3d yr.]	3d yr.		3d yr.
	12 months after	—8:1		—10:1
	dream of chap. 2	550/49 B.C.		also
	—4:29			same yr.
	604 B.C.			24th day
				1st month
				—10:4
				536 B.C.

As the above table indicates, the last year that Daniel mentions is the "third year of Cyrus" as king of Babylon, that is, 536 B.C. The book could have been complete by the end of that decade. Judging from the eastern type of Aramaic and the use of the Babylonian calendar system, the book was most likely written in Babylonia.

UNITY

The unity of Daniel has been both attested and contested. Even major defenders of a second-century date, like Robert H. Pfeiffer[50] and H.H. Rowley,[51] have found no reasons to reduce the book to disparate fragments. The reasons generally given are that the same system of thought and the same world view are present in both parts.

Chapters 1–6 are especially characterized by backward reflections. In 2:48–49 Nebuchadnezzar gives Daniel high honors and sets the three Hebrews over the affairs of the provinces of Babylon. The position of the three Hebrews is recalled by certain Chaldeans in 3:12. Daniel's interpretive gift, first seen in 2:25–45, is recalled by Nebuchadnezzar in 4:18. The same reflective style is seen in the Belshazzar narratives of chapters 5–6, Belshazzar recalling the raid his father had made on the Temple in Jerusalem (5:2–4, 13, 23/1:1–2, 3–7),

---

50. Robert H. Pfeiffer, *Introduction to the Old Testament*, p. 761. Pfeiffer also gives a list of those scholars who have opted against literary unity (pp. 760–61).
51. H. H. Rowley, "The Unity of the Book of Daniel," 249–80; *Darius the Mede*, pp. 176–78.

and the queen reminding the king of Daniel's interpretive powers in the days of Nebuchadnezzar (5:10–12/chap. 2). Further, Daniel recollects the madness of Nebuchadnezzar before Belshazzar (5:18–21/4:28–33).

Chapters 5–6 form a transition from the story narrative to the apocalyptic section. The focus shifts from the court setting of Belshazzar to the court of Darius the Mede (5:30–31), and the same piety and wisdom that Daniel had manifested in the Babylonian court are remanifested under the Medo-Persian authority, concluding with a brief description of his status in the regime: "So this Daniel enjoyed success in the reign of Darius and in the reign of Cyrus the Persian" (6:28). The fact that two of the visions are dated in the reign of Belshazzar (7:1; 8:1) and are contained in the last part of the book rather than the first only means that they conform more closely to the type of literature in the last six chapters than that of chapters 1–6. Even in the last half the visions are not in chronological order (see above table). The role of Belshazzar in both parts of the book may also be viewed as support for its unity.

GENRE, STRUCTURE, AND ANALYSIS

GENRE

The book of Daniel as a whole cannot be assigned to any one genre of ancient literature. Chapters 1–6 contain stories about the experiences of Daniel and his fellow Jewish captives in the Babylonian court, whereas chapters 7–12 are apocalyptic in form. Chapter 2, sharing both story narrative and apocalyptic, may be viewed as a model of the entire book. There the dream of Nebuchadnezzar and Daniel's interpretation are set in the story of the failure of the Babylonian magicians to interpret the dream and Daniel's heroic intervention that spared all of the wise men. Thus it is against the backdrop of the Babylonian court stories that the visions of the world empires come to Daniel. And what better background could there be! For Babylon was the center of the ancient Near Eastern world during most of Daniel's lifetime. Moreover, in the court setting of the stories, God establishes His sovereign rule over the decisions and actions of a world monarch, and likewise in chapters 7–12 He establishes His sovereignty over world empires.

It is hardly debatable that Daniel 2 and 7–12 belong to the genre of apocalypse. The OT beginnings of that type of literature can be seen in Isaiah 24–27, Ezekiel 38–39, 40–48, and Zechariah 9–14. It is a genre that is difficult, if not impossible, to define. Certain characteristics, however, recur in the literature, though not distributed uniformly in every apocalypse. Some of them are: the presence of heavenly messengers or interpreters; cosmic disturbances designed to bring about the kingdom of God; a definite pattern in history that is aimed toward the consummation of God's reign over the world;

transmission of heavenly secrets about the future to human beings; use of highly symbolic language; and visions and dreams as media of communication. In late Jewish apocalyptic, pseudonymity was also associated with the genre, but that was not the case in the early stages of development. That Daniel qualifies for several of those characteristics is evident even to the casual reader. Dreams and visions constitute the media of communication (chaps. 2, 7–12), interpreters assist Daniel in his understanding of the message (8:13–14, 16–17, 19–26; 9:22–27; 11:2–12:4), secrets about the future are revealed (2:29; 8:17, 19, 26; 11:35; 12:9), a four-phase plan of history is put forth (chaps. 2, 7),[52] and symbolism plays a prominent role in the dreams and visions.

Apocalyptic arose directly out of the prophetic experience.[53] Although the ethical demands of the prophets faded into the background, they were not totally forgotten (4:27, 37; 9:4–19). Moreover, the apocalyptists became more intent upon the end times, compared with the prophets' concentration upon repentance to divert the disaster anticipated on the Day of the Lord. Although the phrase "Day of the Lord" does not appear in Daniel, he was preoccupied with the last days, which was an associate concept of the Day of the Lord. We have already pointed to evidence in Ezekiel (38:8; 39:8) that God's people had begun to despair over the delay of the Day of the Lord for the nations. Furthermore, Ezekiel's correlation of that Day of wrath with the return of Israel to the land has its counterpart in Daniel's musing over Jeremiah's seventy years and its meaning for Israel and the world. Evidently the return had not commenced at the time of Daniel's searching inquiry, but the vision turned Jeremiah's seventy years into a whole age of restoration, stretching out into the Messianic age. Thus, although not using the phrase, Daniel nevertheless understood the concept and employed it with the wider meaning of the kingdom of God in the world.

STRUCTURE

There are two major divisions in the book. The first is the collection of stories (chaps. 1–6), with an apocalyptic insertion in chapter 2. The framework of the stories about Daniel and his three Hebrew friends, Hananiah, Mishael, and Azariah, is third-person narrative, with Daniel, the friends, Babylonian

---

52. See Baldwin, *Daniel*, pp. 55–56, for her discussion of the four-phase plan of history.
53. Gerhard von Rad, *Old Testament Theology*, 2:306–07, 311, hypothesizes that apocalyptic originated in wisdom thought. But, although intriguing, it is not convincing. In the first place, wisdom had little concern with history. Second, the revelational character of apocalypse is not normative for wisdom, a genre that is much more contemplative than is prophecy. In apocalyptic, as in prophecy, divine communication is quite direct albeit frequently through intermediaries. Revelation is indirect in wisdom (with the exception of Job 28:28 and the God Speeches in chaps. 38–41). Nor can it be said without qualification, as von Rad maintains, that the idea that loyalty to Yahweh leads to suffering is to be identified with wisdom as opposed to prophecy (cf. Isa. 53).

monarchs, and Darius the Mede speaking in appropriate places.[54] It is of interest that Cyrus, the great Persian conqueror, never speaks in the book, even though he is mentioned by name on three occasions (1:21; 6:28; 10:1). That may reflect the historical fact that he delegated his authority to a governor, Darius the Mede (Gubaru).

The visions of Daniel are collected in the second part, chapters 7–12. In the first division our prophet was the interpreter of the dreams/visions of the rulers, whereas in this division he is the receptor of visions and is aided by angelic interpreters.[55]

The two divisions break down further into the ten individual stories and visions of the book:

1:1–21	6:1–28
2:1–49	7:1–28
3:1–30	8:1–27
4:1–37	9:1–27
5:1–31	10:1–12:13

Alexander A. DiLella's pronouncement upon these units, that any one of them could have stood by itself and have been "as intelligible, or unintelligible, as it now stands in the Book of Daniel,"[56] is not a fair assessment of the interrelationships of these units. As we have indicated above, there are definite cross-references among the stories, and the visions have the common goal of delineating the world kingdoms and the establishment of God's rule in the world.

The structure may be viewed as a construct of God's sovereignty over world history and kingdoms. Nebuchadnezzar is brought to that acknowledgment in three different settings: Daniel's interpretation of his dream (2:46–47), the friends' survival in the fiery furnace (3:28–29), and his own madness (4:34–35, 37). In contrast, Belshazzar's use of the sacred vessels Nebuchadnezzar had confiscated from the Temple was an act of defiance against God's sovereignty. And the clear confession of God's rule was not forthcoming from that monarch. It is, therefore, not coincidental that during his reign the kingdom fell to the Persians (5:30–31). On the other side of that narrative is the account of Daniel's deliverance from the lions' den and Darius's confession of the sovereignty of God (6:21–22), followed by the climactic visions of Daniel that

---

54. Daniel speaks in 1:12–13; 2:15, 20–23, 24, 27–45; 4:19c–27; 5:17b–28; 6:21–22. The three friends speak in 3:16–18. These speeches of the Hebrew actors in the stories are balanced by the words of the Babylonian monarchs, Nebuchadnezzar and Belshazzar and Darius the Mede.
55. 8:13b, 14, 16b, 17b, 19–26; 9:22–27; 11:2–12:4.
56. Louis F. Hartman and Alexander A. DiLella, *The Book of Daniel*, p. 9.

establish divine sovereignty over world kingdoms. That is to say, confessions of God's sovereignty in the world flank the gross defiance of His regal power by the ill-fated Belshazzar.

ANALYSIS OF THE DREAMS AND VISIONS (CHAPS. 2, 7–12)

Nebuchadnezzar's dream (chap. 2). The date of this dream was Nebuchadnezzar's second year (603 B.C.). Aside from the date of Daniel's exile (1:1), it is the earliest date in the book. Whereas the king's personal acquaintance with Daniel in chapter 1 (esp. v. 19) appears inconsonant with his ostensible ignorance of him in chapter 2, the access that the youthful prophet had to Nebuchadnezzar seems to confirm the acquaintance (2:16), even though the king probably had no knowledge of Daniel's interpretive powers, to which he had had no occasion for introduction. The statement that "Daniel even understood all kinds of visions and dreams" (1:17) is a proleptic observation and need not imply that Nebuchadnezzar was aware of that ability.

The king may have forgotten the dream, but more likely he believed that if the Chaldeans could relate its contents to him, then he could be confident of the validity of their interpretation, as 2:9 implies.

The colossal statue, composed from the head down of gold, silver, bronze, and iron, stands insecurely on the brittle feet of iron and clay. It is a symbol of history between the Exile and the Messianic age. About the identity of the head of gold there is no disagreement, for Daniel identified it with Nebuchadnezzar and the Neo-Babylonian kingdom (vv. 37–38). Moreover, the devaluating metals represent the Medo-Persian, Greek, and Roman Empires,[57] with the stone "cut out without hands" (v. 34) being the Messiah. The extended description of the fourth kingdom (vv. 40–43) gives way to the everlasting kingdom of God (vv. 44–45), set in order by the Messiah's work. The opinion that the second kingdom was a legendary Median empire and the third and fourth were Persian and Greek empires fits nicely with the second-century dating of Daniel but has little to support it.

Vision of the four beasts (chap. 7). The date is the first year of Belshazzar (*ca.* 552/51 B.C.), some fifty years after the dream of Nebuchadnezzar, but the subject matter parallels that of chapter 2. The difficulties of identifying these kingdoms are formidable, and dogmatic positions that draw battle lines among interpreters are hardly in order. Yet I shall seek to represent an interpretation that commands the loyalty of many in the evangelical wing of the Christian church. But admittedly, even there no unanimity exists.

According to our interpretation the four kingdoms again span the time from the Neo-Babylonian empire to God's everlasting kingdom (7:18). The four

---

57. We cannot discuss the problem of the identity of the second and fourth empires here, but see Young's helpful discussion, pp. 275–94.

beasts arise out of the sea, the first a lion with eagle's wings, the second a bear with the evidence of his three victims still in his mouth,[58] the third a leopard with four wings and four heads, and the fourth an unidentified species of beast with ten horns, iron teeth, and bronze claws. Like chapter 2, the vision is preoccupied with the fourth kingdom (7:7–11, 19–27), for that is the phase of history that opens out into the kingdom of God. The ten horns are the spiritual successors of the Roman Empire, and the little horn may represent the Antichrist. The appearance of the Son of Man coming with clouds (7:13–14), evidently a messianic figure, is reminiscent of the revelation of God on Sanai when His glory appeared in a cloud (Ex. 16:10; 19:9). Confessedly the Christian is inclined to look at this vision through the spectacles of NT eschatology, and through those spectacles the little horn well answers to the period of the Antichrist before the return of Christ (2 Thess. 2:3–4).

Vision of the ram and goat (chap. 8). Dated in the third year of Belshazzar (*ca.* 550/49 B.C.), a momentous year in which Cyrus the Great established the joint state of the Medes and the Persians, this vision identifies the ram with two horns as the "kings of Media and Persia" (v. 20) and the goat as the kingdom of Greece (v. 21). Only once before (2:37–38) has an explicit interpretation of the kingdoms (Babylon) been given. The ram pushing westward, northward, and southward is an appropriate figure for the rapid conquests of Cyrus and Darius, as also the rapid advance of the he-goat fittingly represents the rise and conquest of Alexander the Great. The breaking of the large horn symbolizes the death of Alexander, and the four horns in its place represent the four divisions of his kingdom: (1) Macedonia under Cassander, (2) Egypt under Ptolemy, (3) Thrace and Asia Minor under Lysimachus, and (4) Syria under Seleucus. The little horn, it is generally agreed, was Antiochus Epiphanes. Leupold comments that the purpose of this expansion upon the second and third kingdoms of chapter 7 was to teach readers what should precede the days of the Messiah.[59]

The seventy years (chap. 9). Daniel's solicitude over Jeremiah's prediction of seventy years for the Exile is hardly a match for the apprehension the interpretors of the passage have felt through the centuries.[60] The date was a memorable year, for the first year of Darius (the Mede) was approximately 538 B.C., the year after Cyrus conquered Babylon. Reckoning from the year of Daniel's exile (605 B.C.), the seventy years of Jeremiah's prophecy (Jer. 25:11–12; 29:10) were virtually expired. Daniel's prayer was directed toward

---

58. The three ribs probably represent the countries of Babylon, Lydia, and Egypt, which the Medo-Persians conquered.
59. Leupold, p. 331.
60. See, for example, Jerome's review of the interpretations of the church Fathers, *Jerome's Commentary on Daniel*, pp. 90–110. For modern interpretations see the summaries of Young, pp. 192–95; Leupold, pp. 404—5; Baldwin, *Daniel*, pp. 172–78.

the concern that the period of humiliation come to an end (esp. vv. 16–19). The answer brought by Gabriel was in effect a message that, even though the end of Jeremiah's seventy years might conclude at that point, "seventy sevens" were decreed for God's people and would commence in that period. Verse 24 is the critical verse for interpeting the chapter. First we have to decide whether or not these statements are messianic. In view of the extended scope of chapters 2 and 7, which stretched into the everlasting kingdom of God, we might also expect the scope of this chapter to be as comprehensive. Edward J. Young's division of these six provisions into two groups of three each, the first negative and the second positive, is justifiable and divides the prophecy into two clear purposes.[61] The first group established the completion of God's work of judgment on Israel and the world, whereas the second appointed His future redemption.

The difficulties of verse 25 are tremendous, but the mention of the "sixty-two weeks" as a distinct period in verse 26 would support the view that in verse 25 the "seven weeks and sixty-two weeks" are not one single time period but two. Moreover, if "sixty-nine weeks" were intended, the normal way to express that would be "nine and sixty weeks." Thus the scope of history involved would divide into three distinct periods: (1) seven weeks (sevens) from the decree to restore Jerusalem until the building of the city,[62] (2) followed by sixty-two weeks between the building of the city and the coming of the Anointed One, (3) concluded by the seventieth week, in which the Messiah will be cut off and the Temple destroyed. The marker that signals the conclusion of the seven and sixty-two weeks is the appearance of the Anointed One, a topic that is continued in verse 26, whereas the concluding comment of verse 25, "it will be built again, with plaza and moat, even in times of distress," seems to refer to the carrying out of the decree to build Jerusalem. We cannot discuss here the interpretive options for this prophecy, but the Decree of Cyrus in 538 B.C. (Ezra 1:1–4) that permitted the Jews to return to Palestine qualifies well for the terminus a quo of (1), whereas the terminus ad quem would be the period of rebuilding under Ezra and Nehemiah. Admittedly more than forty-nine years elapsed between those events, but the numbers may be merely symbolic rather than literal. The terminus ad quem of the sixty-two weeks would be the appearance of the Messiah, and in that seventieth week He is cut off, and the Temple and city are destroyed. The death of Christ, therefore, and the destruction of the Temple in A.D. 70 characterize the third and final period. Although we assume that the final week has an end, there is no marker in the text that signals its termination. Rather it is left open-ended. Only sixty-nine and a half weeks are fulfilled, implying that the end has not yet arrived. Perhaps the most tenable interpretation of verse 27 is to understand the first clause, as does Young, as

61. Young, pp. 197–201.
62. See the pattern of seven sevens for calculating the Jubilee Year in Lev. 25:8–24.

"he will cause a covenant to prevail" and view it as the redeeming work of Christ for the world.[63] The second major event of the seventieth week as described in that verse would perhaps be the destruction of the Temple by Titus in A.D. 70. On the other hand, some interpreters would refer the entire verse to the Antichrist.

The final vision (chaps. 10–12). This prophecy is hardly less difficult than the rest of the visions. Dated in the third year of Cyrus (536 B.C.), it presents the briefest history of the Persian kings (11:2) and concentrates largely on the Greek Empire and the successors of Alexander the Great (11:3–20), with special attention to Antiochus Ephiphanes (11:21–45).[64] The explicit nature of this prophecy, detailing historical personalities and events, is unmatched by any other OT predictions, thus causing many interpreters to view it as written under the guise of prediction after the events had occurred. However, we should not limit the power of the sovereign God to reveal the future. So for those who believe He has and exercises that power, there is no real difficulty here. Yet that is not to deny that all of the problems of the prophecy are smoothed out by the simple belief that God can detail future events. Although we cannot discuss the details here, we should observe that the scope of this section extends from the Persian period to the resurrection in the last day.

THEOLOGICAL REFLECTIONS ON DANIEL

The prophets had declared and the Lord had demonstrated His sovereignty in the fall of Jerusalem. Ezekiel, Jeremiah, Obadiah, and the book of Lamentations predicted and anticipated the day when the nations would acknowledge that Yahweh was the sovereign Lord of the world. The book of Daniel, written as the Exile was fading into the historical past, was the greatest prophetic declaration of the sovereignty of God. It was no longer a theoretical matter, but rather it had been manifested in the great events of history. First, the Lord brought Judah to his knees at the hands of the Babylonians, chosen and used as His instrument of judgment. Second, the Babylonians had been wrestled to the ground by the sovereign work of God in history, and the new age, predicted by Jeremiah, was dawning. The witness to God's sovereignty during the closing years of the Exile was especially pertinent, for the tragic events of the sixth century had been sufficient evidence to the contrary. That is, one could read them, as Isaiah recognized, as evidence of the weakness of Israel's God. His Temple had been reduced to debris, and His people had gone into exile. It was enough to turn orthodoxy to agnosticism, piety to skepticism, and faith to irresolution. Daniel, giving witness to the sovereign rule of Israel's God even

---

63. I have found Young's interpretation, pp. 201–21, to have the fewest difficulties associated with it.
64. Jerome saw the Antichrist from 11:21 on (Archer, *Jerome's Commentary on Daniel,* p. 129). Young, pp. 246–47, interpreted 11:36 to begin speaking about the Antichrist.

through the glorious reign of Nebuchadnezzar, struck the note that caused the strains of prophetic theology to reverberate anew with faith and hope.

Confessed by Nebuchadnezzar (4:34–35, 37) and reaffirmed by Darius (6:25–28), the visions, as already noted, served the function of confirming that vital doctrine of prophetic theology. Belshazzar, the king who did not acknowledge the regal power of Daniel's God, was the king in whose reign judgment befell Babylon. The book of Daniel is a bridge that, like no other prophetic book, connects the two realms of Israel's history, the realm of tragic failure and the realm of incredible restoration. The chasm that the Exile had created in history, a trough of humiliation and despair, is spanned by Daniel's bridge built of the basic stuff of prophetic belief and proclamation. God was sovereign, and in the historical events of this prophet's long life He had demonstrated it with His determined and resolute acts.

OUTLINE OF DANIEL

I. Stories about Daniel (1:1–6:28)
   A. Daniel's Commitment (1:1–21)
      1. Daniel's Captivity (1:1–7)
      2. Daniel's Purity (1:8–16)
      3. Daniel's Wisdom (1:17–21)
   B. Nebuchadnezzar's Dream of the Statue (2:1–49)
      1. Failure of the Wise Men (2:1–11)
      2. The King's Anger and Daniel's Intervention (2:12–16)
      3. The Dream Revealed to Daniel (2:17–23)
      4. Daniel's Interpretation (2:24–45)
      5. The King's Honor of Daniel (2:46–49)
   C. The Golden Image (3:1–30)
      1. The Royal Command (3:1–7)
      2. Accusation of the Jews (3:8–12)
      3. Jews on Trial (3:13–18)
      4. The Fiery Furnace (3:19–25)
      5. Nebuchadnezzar's Recognition of God (3:26–30)
   D. Nebuchadnezzar's Dream of the Tree (4:1–37)
      1. The Proclamation (4:1–3)
      2. Summoning the Wise Men (4:4–9)
      3. The Dream (4:10–18)
      4. Daniel's Interpretation (4:19–27)
      5. The Fulfillment of the Dream (4:28–33)
      6. Nebuchadnezzar's Restoration (4:34–37)
   E. Belshazzar's Feast (5:1–31)
      1. The Feast (5:1–4)
      2. The Mysterious Handwriting (5:5–12)

        3. Daniel's Interpretation (5:13–28)
        4. Daniel Rewarded (5:29)
        5. Belshazzar's Death (5:30)
    F. The Lion's Den (6:1–28)
        1. Daniel's Position in Babylon (6:1–9)
        2. Accusation and Punishment of Daniel (6:10–19)
        3. Daniel's Deliverance (6:20–24)
        4. Darius's Decree (6:25–28)
II. The Visions of Daniel (7:1–12:13)
    A. Vision of the Four Beasts (7:1–28)
        1. The Vision (7:1–14)
        2. The Interpretation (7:15–28)
    B. Vision of the Ram and Goat (8:1–27)
        1. The Vision (8:1–8)
        2. The Interpretation (8:9–26)
        3. Daniel's Sickness (8:27)
    C. The Seventy Years (9:1–27)
        1. Jeremiah's Seventy Years (9:1–3)
        2. Daniel's Prayer (9:4–19)
        3. Gabriel's Interpretation (9:20–27)
    D. The Final Vision (10:1–12:13)
        1. Introduction (10:1–3)
        2. The Vision (10:4–8)
        3. Daniel's Reception of the Revelation (10:9–11:1)
        4. The Kings of Persia (11:2)
        5. The Greek Period (11:3–20)
        6. Antiochus Epiphanes and the Final Conflict (11:21–45)
        7. The Last Things (12:1–13)

15

HAGGAI: THE TEMPLE AND
THE FUTURE

MORE FAVORABLE WINDS began blowing on the prophetic movement in the early post-exilic era. They had been created in the exchange between national suffering and self-examination. Political events served as the weather vane for Israel's hope, and Cyrus's decree of 538 brought a mighty gale of optimism. Haggai both encouraged and benefited from that optimism. He encouraged it when he found that the Palestinian community had dropped into a lull after the initial and unsuccessful effort to rebuild the Temple. His benefits became apparent when his first oracle received an obedient response from the governor of the land, the high priest, and the remnant of the people (1:14).

Outside of Ezekiel, there was no prophet more zealous for the Temple than Haggai. Even more than the monarchy, it was the symbol of the community restored to God's favor. The main focus of Haggai's message concentrated on that time.

HAGGAI THE MAN

In the prophetic reception formulas (except 2:20) Haggai is called "the prophet" (1:1; 2:1, 10; also Ezra 6:14), and in 1:13 he is called "the messenger of the LORD." Both of those titles suggest the stature he enjoyed in the community. Mentioned in Ezra 5:1 and 6:14 with Zechariah, the two prophets presumably acted as a team to encourage the reconstruction of the Temple and resumption of worship.

He is not listed among the returnees in Ezra 2, so speculation that he grew up in Palestine receives some encouragement from that silence. It is possible that both he and Zechariah grew up in Palestine and witnessed the waning enthusiasm for Temple restoration.[1] However, there is a Jewish tradition that he, having lived most of his life in Babylonia, was an old man who remembered the first Temple (2:3). A Christian tradition, perhaps fostered by the attribution of Psalms 138 and 146–149 to Haggai and Zechariah in the Septuagint, held that he was a priest. Yet he himself consulted the priests on levitical uncleanness (2:11) and did not seem to identify with that class of individuals.[2]

1. R. K. Harrison, p. 945.
2. Eli Cashdan, p. 252.

Although his passion for the Temple and its worship was unmistakable, that does not necessarily mean that he was a priest. The opinion that he was a cult prophet[3] has no better substantiation. What is important, however, is that in the early post-exilic era Haggai and Zechariah do not have the same adversarial relationship to the priesthood and the cult that generally characterized the pre-exilic prophets. Assuming that the prophets before the Exile opposed not the Temple and priesthood, as such, but the corruption of the priesthood and their misguidance of Temple worship,[4] then Haggai is a good representative of the prophetic disposition toward the Temple when the abuses they censured were absent.

HISTORICAL BACKGROUND

The historical sources that provide information on the first years of the post-exilic period are Ezra 1:1–4:5 and the Cyrus Cylinder. After Cyrus had captured Babylon in 539 B.C. he issued a proclamation that all the Jews could return to their homeland (Ezra 1:2–4). The first wave of returnees left their land of captivity carrying with them the sacred vessels that Nebuchadnezzar had taken from the Temple and were led by the Judean prince and governor, Sheshbazzar (Ezra 1:5–11). The people who returned numbered 42,360, accompanied by 7,337 servants (Ezra 2:64). An influx of so many people at once was a mixed blessing. It brought new enthusiasm for the restoration, which resulted in laying the foundations of the Temple (Ezra 5:16). Yet so many new settlers, coupled with drought and crop failure, made life extremely difficult. Furthermore, the presence of the homecomers created tension between the returnees and the native population (Ezra 4:4–5). The strain came to a climax when the second attempt at Temple reconstruction, led by Zerubbabel the governor, Joshua the high priest, and Haggai and Zechariah the prophets, was launched. In that case the adversaries of Judah and Benjamin, perhaps the Samaritans, were descendants of the people Esarhaddon who had settled on the land in 676 B.C. (Ezra 4:2).

We do not know when Haggai and Zechariah, along with Zerubbabel and Joshua, returned to the land. Likely they were part of a second wave of returnees that came late in the reign of Cambyses or early in that of Darius I. They were certainly in the land during the second year of Darius (520).

Further opposition came from Tattenai, governor of the province "beyond the River," who appealed to Darius I for a ruling on the legality of the project. When Darius's archivists found the record of Cyrus's decree and promise of financial assistance to rebuild the Temple, that settled the matter, and the work

3. Otto Eissfeldt, *The Old Testament: An Introduction*, p. 426.
4. See pp. 197, 270, 342.

on the Temple was continued with the blessing of the Persian monarch (Ezra 5:1–6:22).

Cyrus died in battle in 530 B.C. while fighting barbarian tribes to the northeast of Persia. His son, Cambyses, succeeded him. Paranoid that someone might assassinate him, he himself assassinated his own brother, Bardiya, who was quite popular with the people.[5] The great achievement of his reign was adding Egypt to his empire in 525. Then in July of 522, on his way back from Ethiopia, he received the news that a usurper, pretending to be his dead brother, Bardiya, had seized the throne in the eastern part of the empire. Thereupon Cambyses committed suicide. A member of his entourage, Darius, son of the governor of Susa, laid claim to the throne. Having the confidence of the army, he proceeded to deal with the uprising and executed the usurper.[6]

The result of that train of events was not stability, however, but revolts all over the Persian Empire. Yet by the end of 520 Darius had secured his throne and had quieted the numerous insurgents.

The work on the Temple was resumed on the twenty-fourth day of the sixth month in the second year of Darius (Sept.–Oct. 520; Hag. 1:15) and completed on the third day of Adar in Darius's sixth year (Feb.–March 516; Ezra 6:15). When the Passover was celebrated in the following month, The Temple was standing as a symbol of God's gracious favor (Ezra 6:19–22).

STYLE, STRUCTURE, AND DATE

STYLE

The book is composed of four short messages written in the third person narrative style. Paul F. Bloomhardt proposed that the genuine words of Haggai exhibited a distinct poetic meter, whereas the narrative passages (1:1, 12, 14; 1:15 and 2:20; 2:1, 2, 10, 11) were added by a later editor, perhaps the Chronicler, in about 350 B.C. He attempted to restore the original poetry.[7] Peter R. Ackroyd, espousing a similar opinion, calls it "poetic prose."[8] Although Haggai's style frequently follows the patterns of Hebrew parallelism,[9] we need not, however, look for a poetic form behind the prose. It was likely the original style of writing rather than prose that was based upon a poetic original.

---

5. Joyce G. Baldwin, *Haggai, Zechariah, Malachi: An Introduction and Commentary*, pp. 15–16; John Bright, *A History of Israel*, p. 346.

6. Ibid., p. 351.

7. Paul F. Bloomhardt, "The Poems of Haggai," pp. 153–95.

8. Peter R. Ackroyd, "Studies in the Book of Haggai" (JJS 2), pp. 163–76, esp. p. 165; "Studies in the Book of Haggai" (JJS 3), pp. 1–13. In this view he follows Hinckley G. Mitchell, John Merlin Powis Smith, and Julius A. Bewer, *A Critical and Exegetical Commentary on Haggai, Zechariah, Malachi and Jonah*, pp. 37–39.

9. For example, 1:6: "You have sown much, but harvest little; you eat, but there is not enough to be satisifed; you drink, but there is not enough to become drunk; you put on clothing, but no one is warm enough; and he who earns, earns wages to put into a purse with holes."

For such a small book, taking second place in length only to Obadiah among OT books, Haggai provides generous datings for his oracles. All six dates given belong to 520 B.C., the second year of Darius (although in 2:1, 18, and 20 that is assumed), ranging over a period of less than four months (1:1, 15; 2:1, 10, 18, 20). The day is consistently given, but the month is assumed in 2:20 (9th month), and the year only occurs in half the cases. The order (year, month, day) varies. Based upon the prophetic precedent already set by Jeremiah, Ezekiel, and Daniel, it should not be surprising to find dates attached to Haggai's prophecies. And having that tradition behind him, it is hardly justifiable to assume with Ackroyd that the dates are secondary.[10]

The use of rhetorical questions is a favorite way the prophet broaches the issue with which the Lord has impressed him (1:4, 9; 2:3, 12–13, 16, 19).

Haggai's addressees are Zerubbabel, Joshua, and the people. In 1:1 and 2:2 all three are addressed, whereas in 2:20 only Zerubbabel.

STRUCTURE

Each of the four messages begins with a date and the messenger formula ("the word of the LORD came by the prophet Haggai . . ." and its variant forms). The following configuration of the messages applies:

Message I   Date + messenger formula (1:1)
             Messenger formula + oracle (1:2–11)
             Narrative material (1:12)
             Messenger formula + oracle (1:13)
             Narrative material + date (1:14–15)
Message II   Date + messenger formula (2:1)
             Oracle (2:2–9)
Message III Date + messenger formula (2:10)
             Messenger formula + oracle (2:11–19)
                 First question to priests and answer (2:12)
                 Second question to priests and answer (2:13)
                 Oracle of application (2:14–19)
Message IV   Messenger formula + date (2:20)
             Oracle (2:21–23)

Considered on the basis of their subject matter, the four messages form a chiasmic scheme. Messages I and III deal with the devastating agricultural failure, the first being an explanation of the poor harvest and the third a declaration that the work on the Temple had reversed the effects of the drought. Messages II and IV involved the promise of a seismic shaking of the heavens

10. Ackroyd, p. 173.

and earth. The first shaking results in filling the New Temple with the Lord's glory (2:7); the consequence of the second was making Zerubbabel the Lord's signet ring (2:23). Thus we have the following pattern:

Message I (1:1–15)	Message II (2:1–9)
Message III (2:10–19)	Message IV (2:20–23)

The variant forms of the messenger formula in this book are not unusual in the OT prophets, but such a variety (at least nine forms) in so short a book is interesting.[11] It is a mistake, however, to assume that such diversity alludes to different levels of editing. For a writer so conscious of the poetic possibilities of prose, Haggai varied his phraseology to that end. It was good prophetic style, illustrated very effectively in Ezekiel.[12]

DATE

The date of Haggai's prophetic activity is not in doubt. Almost universally the year 520 B.C. is accepted. However, the date of compilation is another matter. The optimism that develops as a result of Temple rebuilding and priestly renewal is characteristic of the years in which the reconstruction was taking place. The breakdown of hope and the lagging enthusiasm that Ezra found in Jerusalem are not represented in Haggai. Therefore, the tone of Haggai is that of the hopeful age in which Temple, priesthood, and monarchy are all new signs of a bright future. The closing prophecy, which envisions the revival of the Davidic dynasty, certainly implies the early years of Zerubbabel's governorship. It would thus seem fair to date the compilation of the book within the years 520–16 while the Temple was under construction, or soon thereafter in celebration of its completion, an accomplishment that could be largely attributed to Haggai's encouragement.

ANALYSIS

MESSAGE I: A POPULAR SAYING AND HAGGAI'S RESPONSE (1:1–15)

This first message was prompted by a current popular saying, that the time to rebuild the house of the Lord had not arrived (v. 2). The community's

---

11. 1. "The word of the Lord was by (*beyad*) Haggai the prophet, saying" (1:1, 4; 2:1). 2. "The word of the Lord was to (*'el*) Haggai the prophet, saying" (2:10, 20). 3. "Thus says the Lord of Hosts, saying" (1:3). 4. "Thus says the Lord of Hosts" (1:5, 7; 2:6, 11). 5. "Says the Lord" (1:8). 6. "Says the Lord of Hosts" (2:7–8). 7. "Utterance (*neum*) of the Lord of Hosts" (1:9; 2:4, 8–9). 8. "Utterance (*neum*) of the Lord" (1:13; 2:4 [twice], 14, 17). 9. "Haggai, the messenger of the Lord, spoke by the deputation of the Lord to the people, saying" (1:13).
12. See Ezekiel's oracles against the nations (chaps. 25–32) for an example of the diversity of messenger formulas.

expectation of prosperity and plenty, warranted by the restoration preaching of the pre-exilic prophets, had been disappointed (v. 9), but they could still not perceive the reason. Haggai stepped between the people and the Lord to clarify the reason for their crop failures: they had attended to their own houses and neglected God's (vv. 4–6). In fact, the Mosaic law had laid down the principle of the interrelationship between moral obedience to God's law and agricultural prosperity (Lev. 26:14–20). The solution, once the problem was clearly comprehended, was simple and straightforward: "Rebuild the temple" (v. 8).

The positive response made by Zerubbabel, Joshua, and the remnant of the people (1:12–15) only twenty-three days after Haggai's appeal was a refreshing reaction to prophetic preaching. The pre-exilic prophets had waited in vain for that kind of obedience, and, in its absence, the tragic Exile had occurred. But history was no more out of God's control now as when He appointed the Babylonians to destroy the Temple, for the Lord assured them, "I called for a drought on the land" (v. 11). He was still ordering the events of history. The reassurance of Yahweh's presence with the community, "I am with you" (v. 13), certified His abode among them even though the Temple did not exist. His presence was not tied to the Temple. Rather the Temple was merely the formal place where the Lord was glorified (v. 8).

MESSAGE II: THE GLORY OF THE NEW TEMPLE AND THE GLORY OF THE OLD (2:1–9)

The date (seventh month, twenty-first day) places this message almost one month after the resumption of work on the Temple. The diligence of that effort had already begun to reveal the character of the new edifice, and it was obvious that the new Temple would not match that of Solomon in beauty. Ezra recalled the mixture of joy and weeping when the foundations of the new Temple were laid, the sounds of weeping coming from those who had seen Solomon's beautiful Temple (Ezra 3:12–13).

This day was the seventh day of the feast of Tabernacles (Lev. 23:34–36), a festival of great rejoicing for the Lord's guidance through the wilderness and His blessings in the annual harvest. However, as Haggai has already recognized in his first message, the harvest had been sparse and gave little reason for rejoicing. Moreover, both Isaiah and Ezekiel had predicted that the latter Temple would surpass the former in beauty and glory. So we can understand why Haggai spoke to all three constituents of the community and offered a word of encouragement from the Lord: "But now take courage . . . and work; for I am with you" (2:4). Yahweh was still with His people as He had been when He brought them out of Egypt. Further, He would once more reveal Himself to Israel as He had done in Sinai and fill this house with His glory. The inferiority of the new Temple would be rectified when the nations, alarmed and drawn by the new revelation, would come bringing their wealth to the

Temple. It was only a matter of time until the glory of the new Temple surpassed the former as the prophets had predicted.

MESSAGE III: PRIESTLY LESSONS FROM THE LAW (2:10–19)

This message, like Message I (1:6, 10–11), deals with the subject of the poor harvest (2:15–19). It is unnecessary to relocate verses 15–19 to follow 1:15a, with Otto Eissfeldt and others.[13] Although it is true that the subject matter is the same, the point in the first message was that the poor harvest was a result of apathy toward and neglect of the Temple rebuilding, whereas here Yahweh recognizes the response of the leaders and people to His prophet and declares that from this day (twenty-fourth day of the ninth month) He will bless them. As we have pointed out above, the book is very well balanced between the emphasis upon the poor harvest in Messages I and III and the emphasis in Messages II and IV upon the shaking of the heavens and the earth. The words were spoken exactly three months after the resumption of work on the Temple (cf. 1:15). Thus the twenty-fourth day of the ninth month became a landmark day: "From this day on I will bless you" (2:19).

The significance of the questions posed to the priests and their answers is twofold. Haggai used the questions to drive home a moral lesson, and the answers showed that the priests had retained their legal knowledge and were prepared to resume service in the newly built Temple. The first question regarded "holy meat" (v. 12), which is the flesh of sacrificial animals (Jer. 11:15). According to Leviticus 6:27 the lappet of the priest's robe was made holy by the holy flesh, but that could not be transferred any farther (Hag. 2:12). The second question regarded the spread of legal defilement that was caused by touching a corpse. That was one of the strongest kinds of defilement and could only be removed after sprinkling the defiled person during a seven-day period with water prepared from the ashes of the red heifer (Num. 19). Holiness could not be transferred beyond the lappet of the priest's robe, whereas the defilement of a people was dangerously contagious. The new Temple could not transform the community into a holy people, but their moral defilement could infect the whole land.

MESSAGE IV: HOPE FOR REVIVAL OF THE DAVIDIC DYNASTY (2:20–23)

This brief oracle is of great importance, for it complements the renewal of Temple worship with renewal of the Davidic dynasty. The shaking of the heavens and earth connects the two promises, thus giving us the two pivotal ideas of the book. The one doing the shaking, which was of earthquake proportions, was Yahweh. The restoration was in His hands and under His

---

13. Eissfeldt, p. 427.

control. He would make Zerubbabel, a descendant of David, His signet ring, that is, the symbol of Davidic sovereignty. With the Temple and Davidic monarchy in place again, the restoration could not fail to succeed.

THE MEANING OF THE BOOK

HAGGAI AND THE TEMPLE

The exilic period with its loss of monarchy, Temple, and priesthood was a time of deep soul-searching. It was also a time of adjustment to a totally different way of life. The loss of the Temple, which had given the Judeans a sense of security, false though it was, necessitated critical adjustments in their thinking and practice. They discovered that faith could survive and even thrive without the Temple. Perhaps that partly accounts for the neglect of Temple rebuilding as they endeavored to reinstate themselves in the land in those early years of the post-exilic age. Yet by its absence the Temple also found a fonder place in the hearts of the exiles, who saw its true significance in religious and social life. The Davidic house and the priesthood, urged on by the prophets Haggai and Zechariah, became part of the Temple consensus and moved forward toward restoring the central institution of ancient Israel.

The Temple's centrality in the post-exilic age was greatly attributable to the prophet Ezekiel (chaps. 40–48), who described the Messianic era in terms of the reconstructed Temple and renewed worship. According to Ackroyd, Ezekiel's scheme required the rebuilding of the Temple after the international upheaval described in chapters 38–39.[14] The same word used in Haggai 2:6 and 21 (*r'sh*) also occurs in Ezekiel 38:19 to describe the earthquake that would shake Israel and send the nations into trepidation as the new age dawned. Whether Haggai's interpretation of the political upheaval in the Persian Empire during 522–21 B.C.[15] was influenced by Ezekiel is an open question. It could be posited, and maybe even defended, that he had no concern with it at all. However, the pivotal place of the Temple in the new order as evidenced in Haggai should most naturally be traced to Ezekiel's theology. Although Yahweh was not confined to the Temple (the Exile proved that), His covenant relationship by design involved the Temple as a vital part of covenant reality. If a misplaced zeal for the temple, issuing in copious sacrifices and additional gods and rituals, was deemed by the pre-exilic prophets to be loathsome to God, indifference to the Temple was just as abhorrent. God had connected His favor to the Temple and its worship, and apathy toward cessation of sanctuary and sacrifice was no small thing in His eyes.

14. Ackroyd, p. 4.
15. D. Winton Thomas, "The Book of Haggai," p. 1039.

HAGGAI AND THE ETHICAL PREACHING OF THE PROPHETS

It has been contended that Haggai had little in common with the great Hebrew prophets of the pre-exilic age, because his intense concern was the Temple and purity of the cult rather than the moral wickedness of his people.[16] Obviously he did not issue the call to repentance found in the preaching of his predecessors, but the apathy toward the Temple and sacrifice was definitely a moral issue. Twice he commanded the community to "consider your ways!" (1:5,7; lit., "Set your heart on your ways!"). It was a call to consider the moral implications of their behavior. That, of course, was not the same as calling Israel to repent of the gross sins that distinguished their conduct prior to the Exile. However, Haggai's moral interest is clear. Moreover, when he questioned the priests about contact with a corpse, he applied the lesson of infectious uncleanness to the people (2:14). Everything that this unclean people touches would become unclean. The moral implications of Haggai's message were quite strong. In that sense he represents the legacy of his prophetic forerunners.

OUTLINE OF HAGGAI

I.   Message I: A Popular Saying and Haggai's Response (1:1–15)
   A.   Introduction (1:1)
   B.   The Popular Saying (1:2)
   C.   Haggai's Reprimand (1:3–6)
   D.   Haggai's Solution (1:7, 8)
   E.   The Drought (1:9–11)
   F.   The Positive Response (1:12–15)
II. Message II: The Glory of the New Temple and the Glory of the Old (2:1–9)
   A.   Introduction (2:1–2)
   B.   The Glory of the New Temple and Age (2:3–9)
III. Message III: Priestly Lessons from the Law (2:10–19)
   A.   Introduction (2:10)
   B.   Two Lessons on Holiness and Ritual Purity (2:11–14)
   C.   Promise of Renewed Blessing (2:15–19)
IV. Message IV: Hope for Revival of the Davidic Dynasty (2:20–23)
   A.   Introduction (2:20)
   B.   The Lord's Shaking of Heaven and Earth (2:21–22)
   C.   Zerubbabel the Lord's Signet Ring (2:23)

16. Robert H. Pfeiffer, *Introduction to the Old Testament*, p. 603.

16

ZECHARIAH: PROPHET OF THE NEW KINGDOM

IN VIEW OF THE REVERSAL of Judah's misfortunes in the two decades that followed the decree of Cyrus, it is all too easy to fail to appreciate the critical nature of that era. The momentum set in motion by the Persian decree could not be expected to maintain itself without other encouragements from the traditional structures of the Judean community, both exilic and non-exilic. Haggai brought first witness to the declining enthusiasm for Temple restoration, and Zechariah advanced upon the hopeful disposition that his colleague Haggai had enunciated. Without the assistance of those two prophets, one can only wonder how long it might have taken to restore the Temple and insure its centrality in the new community. Obviously Persian benevolence was insufficient by itself, and even that too failed with the passing of Cyrus.

What Ezekiel was to the late pre-exilic and exilic eras, Zechariah was to the post-exilic age. Not only did he outline the program of restoration, the heart of which was the Temple and priesthood, but he, like Ezekiel, filled in much detail about the eschatological age that lay ahead. That is particularly true of the last six chapters of his book. With a new urgency to establish a durable kingdom, he proclaimed the Lord as king over Judah and promised that He would become king over all the nations.

ZECHARIAH THE MAN

Zechariah was a priest who succeeded his father as head of his particular priestly family (Neh. 12:16). Very likely he functioned in the priestly office while he was active as a prophet. It is of significance that the post-exilic prophets were closely associated with the Temple, for the Temple became the rallying point of that community. The monarchy remained only a figment of historical memory and a future hope that did not materialize in Zechariah's lifetime. When the entire community needed a cohesive center around which to shape its new life, the one that fell within the permissive boundaries of Persian political policy was the religious institution. The liberality of Cyrus the Great and Darius I in religious matters gave the prophets a sphere in which their program of restoration could succeed, attached to an institution that could legitimately endure under foreign domination. The sovereign nature of the kingship ruled out that option. Zechariah's priestly descent and Haggai's cultic orientation in no small way assured the triumph of their efforts.

Mentioned in company with Haggai in Ezra 5:1 and 6:14, Zechariah was perhaps the younger contemporary of Haggai. His assumption of the head of his priestly clan (Neh. 12:16) seems to support the idea that he was a young man when he began his prophetic career in 520. In 1:1 the names of both his father (Berechiah) and grandfather (Iddo) are given, but in the Ezra references he is known as "son of Iddo." It is not unusual in the OT for one to be called "son" of his grandfather. Speculation may suggest that Berechiah died at an early age and Zechariah was reared by his grandfather. Or it may simply imply that Iddo was better known or more prominent than Berechiah, thus the use of the grandfather's name.

Of the many occurrences of the name Zechariah in the OT, this one is the best known. He must be distinguished from the Zechariah, also of priestly lineage, whom King Joash killed (2 Chron. 24:20–22) and to whom Jesus referred in Luke 11:51.

HISTORICAL BACKGROUND

Zechariah's ministry as prophet began in the same year that Haggai prophesied (520 B.C.). The three dates given in the book spread over two years and one month (2d yr. of Darius/8th mth. to the 4th yr./9th mth.), but it is likely that the last six chapters were even much later than the completion of the Temple in 516 B.C. Yet for the most part, the reconstruction of the historical background of Zechariah is the same as that for Haggai.[1]

THE LITERARY NATURE AND AUTHENTICITY OF ZECHARIAH

LITERARY GENRE

An identification of the genre of Zechariah will largely be determined by one's definition of apocalyptic literature. In addition to the more general characteristics, such as visions, the presence of heavenly interpreters, and the use of highly symbolic language, Robert North has urged that a clear framework of ages characterizes apocalyptic literature, for example, Daniel's division of history into four phases. Whereas Daniel and the Revelation of John clearly exemplify that characteristic, North does not believe it is true of Ezekiel and Zechariah.[2] Yet the basic two-eon theory of the prophets still forms the basis of their eschatology, even though the apocalyptists may delineate more

1. See pp. 302–3.
2. Robert North, "Prophecy to Apocalyptic via Zechariah," p. 53.

refined divisions of history. The present evil age will give way to the age of the Kingdom of God.

Yehezkel Kaufmann sees the distinctive criterion of apocalyptic to be the revelation of heavenly secrets not accessible to man by ordinary means.[3] Yet there is something of the extraordinary in all of prophetic literature. Kaufmann's distinction, reaching beyond the phenomenon of predictive prophecy, lays the emphasis upon the more uncommon disclosure of divine plans for history, such as is found in Daniel 7–12. Yet in doing that, he has really identified a common strain that unites prophecy and apocalyptic—they both disclose divine plans that are not ordinarily available to man, one simply using a higher frequency of symbolism and apocalyptic media than the other.

George Eldon Ladd's term "prophetic-apocalyptic"[4] is an appropriate one for Zechariah. He shares at least two basic perspectives with the classical prophets that illustrate his continuity with them. The coming of the kingdom of God, which is a mutually shared concept of prophecy and apocalyptic, figures prominently in Zechariah. That notion of the approaching rule of God in history is seen in the basic prophetic form of the Day of the Lord, which appears as early as Amos. And not only the form, but also the divine interruption of history to bring it about, can be detected in Amos's dramatic reversal of the popular view of that Day:

> Will not the day of the LORD be darkness instead of light,
> Even gloom with no brightness in it?
>
> (Amos 5:20)

Already the incipient idea of the divine interruption of history had been set in motion by Amos. In a word, the Kingdom of God is a prophetic thesis that can be traced from the classical prophets to the OT apocalyptic writings.

A second perspective, the ethical basis for prophetic preaching, is also continued in Zechariah. In point of fact, the entire prophecy is set within that context by Zechariah's appeal to the words of the former (pre-exilic) prophets. The Exile had come as a consequence of the anger of the Lord because the fathers of Israel had spurned the prophetic message (1:2, 12). Moreover, the words and statutes the prophets had commanded the people overtook them in the disaster of the Exile. Divine judgment for failing to keep Yahweh's laws caught up with them (1:6; 7:12).

The genre of Zechariah shares features with both classical prophecy and apocalyptic literature. It occupies a median position.

---

3. Yehezkel Kaufmann, *The Religion of Israel*, p. 348.
4. George Eldon Ladd, "Why Not Prophetic-Apocalyptic?" pp. 192–200.

STRUCTURE

The book divides into two major parts. Part I (chaps. 1–8) consists of an introduction (1:1–6), the night visions, which comprise the central section of Part I (1:7–6:15), and the oracles related to fasting (7:1–8:23). Part II (chaps. 9–14) is subdivided by the heading *Massa'* ("oracle" or "burden," 9:1—"the burden of the word of the Lord is against the land of Hadrach" and 12:1—"the burden of the word of the Lord concerning Israel") into two sections, chapters 9–11 and 12–14. Some scholars refer to Part I as Proto-Zechariah and Part II as Deutero-Zechariah. A minority even uses the term Trito-Zechariah for chapters 12–14.

Joyce G. Baldwin, following the work of P. Lamarche, who proposed that a chiastic structure could be detected in Part II, has identified a similar chiasmus in the arrangement of Part I. According to her analysis the outline takes the following form:

PART I

I. Introduction: The Covenant Still Stands (1:1–6)
II. Eight Visions and Accompanying Oracles (1:7–6:15)
   a. Vision 1. A patrol of the whole earth reports (1:7–17)
   b. Vision 2. The nations meet retribution (1:18–21)
   b^1. Vision 3. Jerusalem has a divine protector (2:1–13; Heb. vers. 2:1–4)
   c. Vision 4. The high priest reinstated (3:1–10)
   c^1. Vision 5. Divine resources for high priest and prince (4:1–14)
   b^2. Vision 6. Evil meets retribution (5:1–4)
   b^3. Vision 7. Jerusalem is purified (5:5–11)
   a^1. Vision 8. God's patrols compass the earth (6:1–15)
III. Messages Prompted by the Question on Fasting (7:1– 8:19)
   a. The question (7:1–3)
   b. The first sermon (7:4–14)
   c. Relevant sayings (8:1–8)
   b^1. The second sermon (8:9–17)
   a^1. The answer (8:18–19)
IV. Conclusion: Universal Longing for God (8:20–23)

PART II

I. Triumphant Intervention of the Lord: His Shepherd Rejected (9:1–11:17)
   a. The Lord triumphs from the north (9:1–8)
   b. Arrival of the king (9:9, 10)
   c. Jubilation and prosperity (9:11–10:1)

    d. Rebuke for sham leaders (10;2–3*a*)
      c^1. Jubilation and restoration (10:3*b*–11:3)
        b^1. The fate of the good shepherd (11:4–17)
II. Final Intervention of the Lord and Suffering Involved (12:10–13:1)
    c^2. Jubilation in Jerusalem (12:1–9)
      b^2. Mourning for the pierced one (12:10–13:1)
        d^1. Rejection of sham leaders (13:2–6)
      b^3. The shepherd slaughtered, the people scattered (13:7–9)
    c^3. Cataclysm in Jerusalem (14:1–15)
a^1. The Lord worshiped as King over all (14:16–21)[5]

This structure demonstrates the literary similarity between the two parts, even though the analysis may press the chiastic scheme too far. The interconnection of the sections within each part is easier to establish for Part I than Part II, but this analysis helps to show that there is an internal order in Part II as well.

AUTHENTICITY

By this term we have in mind the genuineness of the book as a product of Zechariah's prophetic ministry. Admittedly this is an extremely complex question, and the authorship of Zechariah has been almost as heatedly debated as that of Isaiah. Authenticity is not the same question as unity, however, for unity could be given to a book through an editorial process. Further, an editor might arrange authentic material, but he could not create oracles that would be authentic to the prophet. Unity of thought (but not of structure) follows as a corollary of authenticity, but the reverse is not true.

    The issue of authenticity centers mainly upon Part II. Generally Part I is largely attributed to Zechariah. Ernst Sellin and Georg Fohrer, whose view is rather typical of modern scholarship, isolate two types of material in Part I, sayings and reports. Two kinds of reports are given, the night visions (1:7–6:8) and the reports that deal with concrete events (6:9–15; 7:1–3; 8:18–19). Other sayings that may or may not be genuine occur in 1:1–6, 16, 17; 2:8–9, 10, 11–12, whereas the sayings in 7:1–8:19 are not genuine.[6] Otto Eissfeldt agrees that non-genuine sayings may have slipped into that category, but he admits that there is no real ground for suspecting any one of them.[7]

    Arguments against authenticity and unity have ordinarily involved (1) the difference in atmosphere between Parts I and II; (2) the absence of any

  5. Joyce G. Baldwin. *Haggai, Zechariah, Malachi*, pp. 85–86.
  6. Ernst Sellin and Georg Fohrer, *Introduction to the Old Testament*, pp. 461–63. George Adam Smith, *The Book of the Twelve Prophets*, 2:257, accepts the entirety of chapters 1–8, with the exception of a few interpolations, as genuine.
  7. Otto Eissfeldt, *The Old Testament: An Introduction*, p. 433.

reference in Part II to the recent reconstruction of the Temple; (3) the reference in 9:13 to Greece as the dominant power rather than Persia; and (4) the apocalyptic scenes in chapter 14, which are taken to be characteristic of late apocalypse.

The case for authenticity of the whole book has been argued by such scholars as E. B. Pusey, Edward J. Young, Eli Cashdan, and H. C. Leupold.[8] R. K. Harrison and Joyce Baldwin have presented strong favorable arguments for unity but stopped short of adopting a clear position on authorship.[9] An argument for unity has also been advanced by Rex A. Mason, who finds five emphases in the book that give coherence to Parts I and II: (1) prominence of the Zion tradition; (2) divine cleansing of the community; (3) universalism; (4) appeal to the earlier prophets; and (5) the provision of leadership as a sign of the new age. He views the line of continuity to be the result of an ongoing Zecharian tradition (perhaps disciples), much like that postulated for "Second Isaiah."[10]

Brevard S. Childs, based upon his canonical analysis of the book, has made a convincing case for unity of chapters 9–14 and a definite canonical relationship between Parts I and II. His approach is to attribute their compatibility to the common use of Isaiah, Jeremiah, and Ezekiel at the redactional level. His impressive list of congruous elements includes (1) a new Jerusalem protected by Yahweh (2:5/9:8; 14:11); (2) return of Edenic fertility to the land (8:12/14:8); (3) use of the covenant formula as promise (Yahweh and Israel's mutual recognition, 8:8/13:9); (4) the canvassing curse in 5:3 and the time when it is removed in 14:11; (5) divine judgment on the nations (1:18–21/14:16–17), their conversion (8:22–23/14:16), and worship of Yahweh (8:20–21/14:16); (6) regathering of the exiles (8:7–8/10:9–11); (7) the outpouring of the Spirit to inaugurate the new age (4:6/12:10); (8) purging the land of those who swear falsely in the Lord's name (5:4/13:3); and (9) the messianic figure of one who triumphs, not by power, but in humility (4:6/9:9–10).[11]

Whereas Child's presuppositions and methodology compel him to posit his theory of unity at a redactional level, the disparities between the two parts may rather be explained as the changing perspective of Zechariah through several years of theological and eschatological thought. For example, in the later years of the prophet's ministry Yahweh's protecting presence predominated his thought, because experience had shown that the restoration of the Temple was

8. E. B. Pusey, *The Minor Prophets*, pp. 503–11; Edward J. Young, *An Introduction to the Old Testament*, pp. 271–73; Eli Cashdan, "Zechariah," pp. 269–70; H. C. Leupold, *Exposition of Zechariah*, pp. 6–13.

9. R. K. Harrison, *Introduction to the Old Testament*, pp. 950–56; "Book of Zechariah," 5:1044. Baldwin, pp. 66–70.

10. Rex A. Mason, "The Relation of Zech. 9–14 to Proto-Zechariah," pp. 227–39.

11. Brevard S. Childs, *Introduction to the Old Testament as Scripture*, pp. 482–83.

less important than Yahweh's spiritual presence. The Temple was the symbol of His presence. That theme had already been stated clearly in the message of Haggai (Hag. 2:1–9), and the passing of time had verified it in Zechariah's thinking. In addition, if any hopes of national revival had clung to the Davidic line, by the early fifth century both time and historical experience had strongly insinuated that restoration in the fullest sense could only come by divine intervention. And Yahweh's unpretentious entry into history would take the tyrant nations by surprise. If they had calculated that the strongest defense was a military one, they had miscalculated, for God had in mind a king "humble, and mounted on a donkey" (9:9). The "redaction," to use the critical term, had occurred in the mind of the prophet as God had clarified to him His plan for the future.

The question of the authenticity of Zechariah 9–14 is one of the most formidable issues of prophetic studies. Although our discussion has largely concentrated upon unity, when that is established as a plausible hypothesis and is joined to the view that Part I is authentic to Zechariah, then the authenticity of Part II becomes an hypothesis to be reckoned with seriously. The heavier burden of proof rests upon those who would impugn the authenticity of those chapters. If we assume, as Nehemiah 12:16 implies, that the prophet was young when he wrote chapters 1–8, he was likely still alive when the fortunes of the Persian Empire began to shift in favor of the Greeks at the Battle of Marathon in 490 B.C. and at Salamis in 480. With the international signs of an impending changing of the guard, Zechariah comforted Judah and Israel. As can be seen in the history of the prophetic movement, those historical moments when empires fell called for prophetic insight and divine reassurance.

DATE

There is hardly any question about the date of chapters 1–8, with the exception of some scholars who date the so-called interpolations in later periods. Three specific dates nail down Part I in time:

    1:1   8th month/2d yr. of Darius
    1:7   11th month/2d yr. of Darius/24th day
    7:1   9th month/4th yr. of Darius/4th day

Thus, judging from these dates, the prophecies of Part I extend at least over the space of twenty-five months during the years 520–518 B.C.

The dating of Part II, however, is not so easy. In the nineteenth century European scholarship assigned chapters 9–14 to the pre-exilic period. When Pusey wrote his erudite commentary on the minor prophets, he remarked that with one notable exception, the scholars who severed these chapters from

Zechariah were unanimous in placing them before the captivity.[12] Chapters 9–11 were usually assigned to the eighth century, based upon references to both Israel and Judah (9:10, 13; 10:6), mention of Assyria and Egypt, and the historical description of Syria-Palestine in chapter 9. Yet those chapters speak of the Exile as past (9:11; 10:3–5). Scholarly opinion took a turn in the late nineteenth century and began assigning so-called Deutero-Zechariah to the Greek period.[13] It was believed that 9:1–8 reflected the rapid advance of Alexander the Great, and the third-century rule by the Ptolemies could be detected in 9:11; 10:10–11; 14:18–19. Moreover, efforts to make a historical identification of the three shepherds in 11:4–17 have influenced some to look to the Maccabean period.[14]

Historical allusions are hard to find in chapters 12–14. Rather, the eschatological nature of those oracles is evident in their subject matter. They regard the deliverance of Jerusalem, the salvation of God's people, and judgment on the nations, couched in language reminiscent of the Day of the Lord ("in that day"). Dating those chapters by their subject matter to a later period is at best tenuous, for all of the topics could well have been discussed by Zechariah. They are all part of the prophetic heritage passed on by the pre-exilic prophets. As already stated above, it is conceivable that Zechariah could have spoken those oracles in the early decades of the fifth century B.C.

ANALYSIS

PART I (CHAPS. 1–8)

Introduction (1:1–6). Dated in the eighth month of the second year of Darius (about Oct. 520), only weeks before Haggai's last dated message, Zechariah joined his voice to the numerous prophetic voices that had called Israel to repentance. There is no clearer admission of the truth of the prophetic message than verse 6, "But did not My words and My statutes, which I commanded My servants the prophets, overtake your fathers?" A similar note of Israel's repentance can be found in Daniel's prayer (Dan. 9:4–19), and analogous confessions of the justice of Yahweh's action are found in Lamentations 2:17 and Ezra 9:6–15. But the main thrust of this introduction is to call Zechariah's own generation to repentance (1:3–4), citing the consequences of their fathers who refused to obey the prophets' words (1:5–6).

---

12. Pusey, p. 506.
13. Childs traces this to the publication of B. Stade's articles, "Deuterozacharja." E. W. Hengstenberg had already shown that chaps. 9–14 were greatly dependent upon Jeremiah and Ezekiel and other prophets. So Stade's shift was a concession to that demonstrated evidence. Still today, following Stade, Eissfeldt, p. 438, takes the *house of Joseph* and *Ephraim* in 10:3–12 to be archaiac language and *Assyria* and *Egypt* as code references to Seleucid Syria and Ptolemaic Egypt.
14. See Harrison, p. 953.

The night visions (1:7–6:15). Occurring all in one night (Feb. 15, 520 B.C.), the visions contain three types of material: (1) a description of what Zechariah saw, often introduced by standard formulae, "I saw at night, and behold," (1:8), "Then (again) I lifted my eyes and looked, and behold," (1:18; 2:1; 5:1; 6:1), "Then the LORD (he) showed me," (1:20; 3:1), "And behold" (5:7); (2) Zechariah's responses, which include (a) interrogation of the angelic interpreter about the meaning of the visionary images, phrased as a question (1:9, 19a, 21a; 2:2a; 4:4, 11, 12; 5:6a, 10; 6:4), (b) the prophet's response to the angelic interpreter's questions (4:2b–3, 5b, 13b; 5:2b), and (c) brief instructions and oracles (2:9, 11c–12, 13; 3:5a; 4:9b); and (3) responses of the vision personnel, (a) first the angelic interpreter who answers Zechariah's questions and explains the visionary actions and objects (1:9b, 10b, 19b, 21b; 2:2b, 3–4; 3:6–10; 4:6–7, 14; 5:3–4, 6b, 8a, 11; 6:5–6, 8), instructs the prophet and vision personnel (1:14–17; 3:4; 5:5; 6:7b), intercedes for Israel (1:12), and interrogates Zechariah (4:2a, 5a, 13a; 5:2a); (b) the horsemen (1:11b), (c) another angel (2:4), and (d) Yahweh (1:13; 2:5–8, 10–11b; 3:2; 4:8–9a; 6:9–15). The descriptions of the visionary content are introduced very early in each vision, though the unfolding drama is stretched out in Visions 4 and 8. Whereas Zechariah interrogates the angel in Visions 1, 2, 3, 7, and 8, the angel interrogates Zechariah in Visions 5 and 6, with the interrogation style absent from Vision 4. It should be further noted that because the angel is communicating the Lord's words to Zechariah and other vision personnel (3:6–10; 4:6–7), the angel's words and the Lord's are virtually indistinguishable (for example, 3:2, 4; 4:5a, 6–9a; 6:8–15). We may deduce, therefore, that when Zechariah says "the word of the LORD came to me" (4:8; 6:9), he received it from the angelic interpreter. In the same regard, the "gracious" and "comforting" words that Yehweh spoke to the angel in 1:13 were probably the message that follows in verses 14–17.

In regard to structure, there is great fluidity within the visions. We may infer from that that the prophet wrote them down very soon after he received them and left them virtually in the form in which he had received them. Subsequent editing would probably have produced a more standard form.

A number of scholars have sought to discover a plan in the visions. Klaus Koch has observed that geographically the events begin in the west and move over the center of the earth to the east. He suggests that that progression in space may correspond to a temporal sequence of evening, midnight, and morning, producing a symmetry in which the middle vision (by his count, Vision 5 of the lampstand) is the zenith. Koch removes Vision 4 as an interpolation, pairs the two outer visions (1 and 8), which are set beyond the human sphere, relates Visions 2 and 3 (elimination of external political hindrances) to visions 6 and 7 (elimination of internal spiritual hindrance—sin), and sees a climax in Vision 5.[15] Baldwin sees a chiastic structure in the visions (a b b c c b b a), with the climax in the fourth and fifth visions.[16] The advantage her pattern has over Koch's is that it does not require the dubious elimination of Vision 4 from the scheme. Both see progression in the visions. From Vision 1, with its concern for the restoration of Jerusalem and Judah, the visions advance to the announcement of the messianic person, the Branch, who will build the Temple of the Lord and bear both royal and priestly honor.

The visions may be summarized as follows. In Vision 1 (1:7–17) the four horsemen are sent out to see if the earth had been shaken according to the promise of Haggai 2:7–8, 22–23 in order to avenge Jerusalem and Judah,[17] but they find it quite peaceful. The angel's concern then turns to the vindication of Jerusalem, followed by the promise that the Temple will be built and the city restored.

Vision 2 (1:18–21) describes the four horns and four smiths. The horns, symbols of strength, represent the nations that have scattered God's people. Quite appropriately they are matched by the same number of smiths, who will deal God's judgment to the nations at peace.

In Vision 3 (2:1–13) "a man with a measuring line," an angelic architect, draws the master plan for the reconstruction of Jerusalem, thus implementing Yahweh's plans to restore the city, which will symbolize His omnipotent protection, for He will be both a wall around it and the glory within it.

Vision 4 (3:1–10) describes the reinstatement of the high priest. With the assurance that Yahweh will again return with His glory to Jerusalem, the setting of the visions shifts to the Temple, where Joshua's ritually unclean garments are removed, and he is clothed in vestments appropriate to his station. The Lord has chosen Jerusalem, and, against any contradiction, this vision reiterates His determination to restore it as the center of worship.

Vision 5 (4:1–14) is of a golden lampstand and two olive trees. Having distinguished Joshua in his place as high priest, this vision places Zerubbabel, the governor, alongside him but fails to elevate him to the Davidic throne. Nevertheless, his role in the reconstruction of the Temple is clarified, and before him the mountain of opposition would become a plain.

Vision 6 (5:1–4) depicts the flying scroll. Once the role of Joshua and Zerubbabel in restoration has been made clear, this vision brings the purging of the land into focus.

Vision 7 (5:5–11), the woman in the ephah basket, shows that the persistent removal of evil from the land is culminated by transfer of wickedness, symbolized by the woman in the basket, to Babylon, the epitomy of idolatrous practice.

---

15. Klaus Koch, *The Prophets*, 2:166–71.
16. Baldwin, p. 80.
17. C. F. Keil, *The Twelve Minor Prophets*, 2:234.

Vision 8 (6:1–15) depicts the four chariots. Similar imagery marks the relationship of this vision to Vision 1. There the patrol found the nations unvindicated, whereas here the Lord's Spirit has been vented against Israel's enemies. The gold crown set on Joshua's head represents the combining of the royal and priestly offices in the messianic person called the Branch.

Question about fasting and related messages (7:1–8:23). Dated in the fourth year of Darius, fourth day, ninth month (Dec. 7, 518 B.C.), this section relates to the question of fasting in the fifth month (when Jerusalem was burned) and seventh month (when Gedaliah was assassinated), as had been the custom for seventy years (7:1–7). Zechariah's immediate response was to remind them that disobedience had characterized the pre-exilic population and had occasioned the Exile (7:8–14). A second word from Yahweh promises that He will return to Zion and dwell in her midst again (8:1–17). He would be as intent upon restoration as He had been on judgment. The program of the new society is prescribed: " 'These are the things which you should do: speak the truth to one another; judge with truth and judgment for peace in your gates. Also let none of you devise evil in your heart against another, and do not love perjury; for all these are what I hate,' declares the Lord" (8:16–17).

In the context of Yahweh's reversal of His disposition toward Judah (wrath to compassion), He reverses the fasts of the fourth (when the Babylonians breached the walls of Jerusalem), fifth, seventh, and tenth (when the Babylonians began the siege of Jerusalem) months and makes them festivals of joy and gladness (8:18–19). The turnabout set the tone for the new age. In 7:2 the representatives of Bethel come "to seek the favor of the Lord," and at the end of this section the nations are seen coming "to seek the LORD of hosts in Jerusalem and to entreat the favor of the LORD" (8:22).

PART II (CHAPS. 9–14)

The first oracle (9:1–11:17). The interpretation of chapters 9–14 is a difficult task. The general theme, however, is the kingdom of God, for which we have been prepared in chapters 1–8. The first oracle (chaps. 9–11) deals with God's judgment on Israel's enemies (9:1–8). The very different kind of king, whose image is projected in 9:9–17, "humble and mounted on a donkey," is seen against the backdrop of the military figure who moves by swift conquest through Syria and Philistia on his way to Egypt. It is reminiscent of the Lord's resolve to restore His people by His Spirit rather than military power (4:6). The redemption theme is continued in 10:1–12, where Egypt and Assyria are symbolic of Israel's captivity. The wonders that will accompany the restoration are described in terms of a new Exodus.

In contrast to that bright and glorious day, the rejection of the shepherd, so unappreciated, illustrates the bizarre fact that when the perfect leader should arise in history, rather than being hailed and honored, he would be rejected

(11:1–17). The shepherd's flock is Israel, and he is a native Israelite. Perhaps the prophet himself acted out the parable.

The second oracle (12:1–14:21). The eschatological day that has been anticipated in chapters 1–8 and especially in 9–11 comes into sharp focus here. The frequent occurrence of "in that day" drives home the point that the prophet envisions the day when God's Kingdom will truly be consummated. The Israelites will come to recognize their sin and repent (12:10–14). The final state of the kingdom will be the condition of holiness that preponderated in the Temple (14:20), and the nations of the world will come to Jerusalem to worship the King, the Lord of Hosts, and celebrate the Feast of Tabernacles, the most joyful festival of the year (14:16).

THE MESSAGE OF ZECHARIAH

INTERPRETING THE FORMER PROPHETS

Zechariah's use of the term "former prophets" is a reference to the pre-exilic prophets, who, in his mind, had been Yahweh's powerful spokesmen for righteousness. The Exile had occurred precisely because the "fathers" had spurned the message of the prophets (7:11–14). The dynamic force of the prophetic word can be seen in Zechariah's rhetorical question, "But did not My words and My statutes, which I commanded My servants the prophets, overtake your fathers?" (1:6).

Zechariah affirms the prophetic theme that Israel's religiosity had been designed for his own benefit rather than God's (7:7). In agreement with prophetic theology, rather than well-ordered ritual he urges the practice of justice and compassion and the care of widow, orphan, and alien (7:9–10).

With Jeremiah (23:6; 50:20) and Ezekiel (37:16–19), Zechariah sees the reunion of Israel and Judah and a future in which their oneness is indissoluble (1:19; 8:13; 10:6). At the dedication of the Temple that unity was reaffirmed with the sacrifice of a sin offering (twelve he-goats, according to the twelve tribes) for all of Israel (Ezra 6:17), and at the celebration of Passover that year the repatriated exiles joined the Israelites who had separated themselves from idolatry to worship the Lord (Ezra 6:21). Zechariah believed, as Jeremiah and Ezekiel had predicted, that the age of reunion had dawned.

Whereas Zechariah made numerous direct and indirect appeals to the pre-exilic prophets,[18] his greatest patron was Ezekiel. Like Ezekiel, he was both priest and prophet, and he shared not only Ezekiel's official titles but his theological/ eschatological plan. Cameron Mackay's remark that Zechariah was

---

18. See the list of connections in Pusey, pp. 504–05; and Hinckley G. Mitchell, John Merlin Powis Smith, and Julius A. Bewer, *A Critical and Exegetical Commentary on Haggai, Zechariah, Malachi and Jonah,* pp. 101–2.

the earliest "commentary" on Ezekiel 40–48 captures the point well.[19] The centrality of the Temple, as sketched out in Ezekiel's prospectus of the future (chapters 40–48), and the de-emphasized role of the Davidic dynasty in the coming age[20] are underscored in Zechariah.[21] Reanimating an ancient concept, the Temple becomes the symbol of the new age of Yahweh's kingship (Ex. 15:18), and that new kingdom is to be constituted as a kingdom of priests (Ex. 19:6).

THE KINGDOM OF GOD

The phrase does not occur in Zechariah, but the book is replete with the description of the coming kingdom of God. Admittedly there is much in chapters 9–14 that is difficult, if not impossible, to explain. However, certain ideas are rather clear. Yahweh will cut off the implements of war and establish His kingdom of peace through the humble king who makes His royal entry riding on a donkey (9:9–10). Indeed, Yahweh Himself will take the task of conquest in His own hands and set the captives free (9:11–15).

The royal person who will dominate the new age will be more than a king—he will be the shepherd of the Lord's flock (11:4–7), who will be ungratefully detested by the sheep. When he should ask for his wages, they will certify their ungrateful spirit by paying him the price of a slave (11:12/Ex. 21:32). The king and the shepherd of Zechariah are evidently one and the same person, for in 11:6 the two words occur in parallel language. The royal status of the shepherd is further substantiated by the description of him as "My Associate" (13:7).[22] The image of the shepherd-king has already been set forth by Ezekiel (34:23–31; 37:24), and Zechariah mixes the hues of that imagery with those of the Suffering Servant to paint the portrait of the Messiah on his apocalyptic canvass. The gospel writers knew those precious phrases from Zechariah, and in them they heard the traumatic events of the passion of Christ expressed.[23]

The kingdom that Zechariah announces is one in which Israel and Yahweh will come to perfect harmony, as the covenant stipulated (13:9/Ex. 19:5). In other vivid imagery, the holiness that distinguished the Temple precincts and the sacred vessels would be expanded into the common sphere of life. So

19. Cameron Mackay, "Zechariah in Relation to Ezekiel 40–48," p. 197.
20. W. J. Dumbrell, "Kingship and Temple in the Post-Exilic Period," pp. 34, 36, observes that the Davidic representative is called a "prince" (*nāsî*) rather than "king," and he is barred from entering the new Temple (Ezek. 45:4–7).
21. Cameron Mackay's article cited above is a stimulating and elucidating study of this topic, and I gratefully acknowledge my debt to him.
22. F. F. Bruce, *The New Testament Development of Old Testament Themes,* p. 102.
23. Mark 14:27/Zech. 13:7; Matt. 21:4/Zech. 9:9; Matt. 26:15/Zech. 11:12; Matt. 27:9–10/Zech. 11:12–13; John 19:37/Zech. 12:10. See Bruce, pp. 100–114, for a detailed discussion of these texts.

thoroughly disseminated would be Temple holiness that any cooking vessel in Judah could be used for sacrificial purposes (14:20–21). Thus the logic of the centrality and prominence of the Temple, a critical issue in Zechariah, comes into focus. In the coming age the entire land would be purified and consecrated to the Lord in the same degree as vessels in the Lord's House. The Temple, therefore, became in Zechariah's view not only the center of life in the new age but the standard by which the land would be purified.

OUTLINE OF ZECHARIAH

I. Part I: The Night Visions and Questions about Fasting (chaps. 1–8)
    A. Introduction (1:1–6)
    B. The Night Visions (1:7–6:15)
        1. Vision 1: The Four Horsemen (1:7–17)
        2. Vision 2: The Four Horns and Four Smiths (1:18–21)
        3. Vision 3: A Man with a Measuring Line (2:1–13)
        4. Vision 4: Reinstatement of the High Priest (3:1–10)
        5. Vision 5: A Golden Lampstand and Two Olive Trees (4:1–14)
        6. Vision 6: The Flying Scroll (5:1–4)
        7. Vision 7: The Woman in the Ephah Basket (5:5–11)
        8. Vision 8: The Four Chariots (6:1–15)
    C. Questions About Fasting and Related Messages (7:1–8:23)
        1. The Question (7:1–3)
        2. The Answer (7:4–8:23)
            a. God's Requirements (7:4–14)
            b. Decalogue of Promises (8:1–23)
II. Part II: The Kingdom of God (chaps. 9–14)
    A. Oracle One: Judgment of Israel's Enemies (9:1–11:17)
    B. Oracle Two: The Coming of the Kingdom (12:1–14:21)

17

JOEL: THE DAY OF DECISION

THE FRESH WINDS of the Spirit blow through the oracles of Joel, renewing hope that too soon dwindled in ancient Judah. The time for decision had come. Joel calls Israel to it by his numerous imperatives. Perhaps only the Gentile nations were to be gathered in the Valley of Jehoshaphat for the divine verdict (3:1–3), but if Israel was not there to hear his own sentence, it was only because he had responded to the call of the prophets to repent (2:12–13). The thin thread of "perhaps" on which his future hung (2:14) turned out to be the thread of divine grace, the strength of which was dependent, not on the texture of the thread, but on the faithfulness of the Weaver. The Lord's covenantal grace, periodically obstructed by a national agenda for immorality, encountered no wall it could not scale and no foe it could not subdue. Joel's prophecy of the outpouring of the Spirit, when men and women in universal order would join the ranks of the prophets, is a colossal testimony to that truth. Even the ravaging locust plague, harbinger of the Day of the Lord, like the Exile that left Judah reeling in wrathful intoxication, only closed one disappointing chapter and opened up a more hopeful one.

JOEL THE MAN

Aside from the name of his father, Pethuel, we know nothing personal about Joel. Any information must be inferred from the book itself.

He was obviously from Judah, a fact that can be deduced from his numerous references to Zion (2:1, 15, 23; 3:17) and to Judah and Jerusalem (2:32; 3:1, 6, 8, 17–20). His intimate knowledge of and a healthy respect for the priests might also indicate that he lived somewhere in the environs of Jerusalem, or at least in Judah. However, he evidently was not a priest, for he sets himself apart from them (1:13; 2:17). We may also suggest that he was not one of the elders of Israel, inasmuch as he addresses them as a group (1:2) and calls for their assemblage to avert the terrible Day of the Lord (2:16).

Whether he was a Temple prophet, as A. S. Kapelrud has proposed,[1] is

---

1. A. S. Kapelrud, *Joel Studies*, pp. 176–80.

difficult to say. He recognized the priests as leaders of the community and their role in Israel's destiny as strategic (2:17). Yet he had no biased loyalty to the priesthood that caused him to hide moral misconduct under a camouflage of correct Temple ritual. Although Joel's passion was not the sins of the people, it is safe to assume that the Temple ritual was functioning normally, and the devastation of crops by the locusts that resulted in the discontinuance of the cereal and drink offering was deplorable in his eyes (1:9, 13). Indeed, the resumption of those offerings was numbered among the blessings of the new day he hoped for (2:14). Judging the disposition of the Temple prophets by the political coalition the priests and prophets had formed during Jeremiah's time (Jer. 29:24–32), then Joel was not a Temple prophet. If more honest, less politicized Temple prophets existed in OT times, then we may entertain the notion that Joel belonged among them. However, the respect and sympathy that he bore toward the Temple and priesthood are more likely the healthy side of the prophets' view of the cult, a side we rarely see in the pre-exilic prophets, but which becomes evident among the post-exilic prophets, especially in Haggai and Zechariah.[2]

LITERARY NATURE AND AUTHENTICITY

STYLE

Written in Hebrew poetry, the language of the book manifests a poet's eyes and a scribe's skilled pen. His imagery is artful, the product of a mind that thinks in similes and poetic images. The emotional trauma and the horrible devastation of a land stripped bare by a plague of locusts did not blind his artistic mind to the details of the devastation and the devastators. His poetic eye moved from the rather humorous, howling drunkards, now deprived of their intoxicating spirits (1:7, 13), to the much more serious cessation of the drink and cereal offerings in the Temple (1:9). His glance fell upon the anguished faces of those who saw the locust invasion (2:6) and the aimless roaming of cattle that had been robbed of their meagre grain by the pillaging pestilence (1:18). The defoliated fig trees, with their whitened branches, attracted his observant view (1:7),[3] and the storehouses and granaries posed with their stark emptiness all around the land (1:17).

Joel's metaphors and similes are carefully and richly endowed by his descriptive ability. The locusts are an invading nation, "mighty and without number."

---

2. See p. 302.
3. John D. Whiting, "Jerusalem's Locust Plague," 511–50, esp. p. 529, describes the locust plague of 1915 in Palestine and observes that the locusts gnawed off the small limbs of the fig trees, resembling "white candles on a dried up Christmas tree." George Adam Smith also details descriptively a swarm of locusts he personally saw in the Middle East, *The Book of the Twelve Prophets*, 398–99.

They have the "teeth of a lion" and "the fangs of a lioness" (1:6). He develops the war imagery in chapter 2, describing the locusts as horses, their movement as the running of cavalry (2:4), the sound like the rumbling of chariots and the crackling of fire devouring the stubble (2:5). They are like warriors, and like soldiers they scale the wall (2:7–9). The coming judgment is the harvest and the wine press, while literally multitudes of people are crowded into the Valley of Jehoshaphat on that dark day, void of sun, moon, and stars, for the awful verdict (3:14–15).

The impact of Joel's literary style is further seen in the numerous imperatives with which his book is punctuated. Some forty-five occurrences of the imperative mood[4] declare the urgency of his message. Perhaps that feature also implies that the time differential between the speaking of the oracles and their written form was insignificant, because the urgency remains clearly woven into the fabric of the oracles.

STRUCTURE

Two popular divisions of the book are found in the literature, each dividing the book into two major parts. The one, based mainly upon content, insists that Part I deals with the present reality of a locust plague (1:1—2:27), and Part II presents the future realities of the eschatological age (2:28—3:21).[5] The other division, based upon literary form, views Part I to be a lament (1:2—2:17) and Part II Yahweh's response to the lamentation (2:18—3:21).[6] The latter partition seems more satisfactory, for as Hans W. Wolff observes, 2:19b–20 already tells about the reversal of the disaster.[7] Thus 2:18 becomes the hinge; "Then the LORD will be zealous for His land, and will have pity on His people."

As has been pointed out frequently by scholars, there is an easily discernible symmetry in the book. After the introduction calling the elders and people to the incomparable occasion of the prophecy (1:2–3), Part I divides into two sections. The first (1:4–20) describes the locust plague with its horrible effects on man and beast and on the social and religious functions of Judah. That is balanced by the announcement of the approaching Day of the Lord, described with imagery that advances upon the plague of chapter 1, and a call to repentance (2:1–17). Part II subdivides into two sections also, the first (2:18–32)

4. 1:13 alone, for example, contains five. That does not include a generous number of jussives (normally expressed with "let . . ."), which also carry imperative force.
5. Representatives are John A. Thompson, "The Book of Joel," 6:729, and John Merlin Powis Smith, William Hayes Ward, and Julius A. Bewer, *A Critical and Exegetical Commentary on Micah, Zephaniah, Nahum, Habukkuk, Obadiah and Joel*, pp. 49–56.
6. Representatives are C. F. Keil, *The Twelve Minor Prophets*, 1:171; S. R. Driver, *The Books of Joel and Amos*, pp. 110–11; Hans W. Wolff, *Joel and Amos*, pp. 7–8; and Leslie C. Allen, *The Books of Joel, Obadiah, Jonah and Micah*, pp. 39–42.
7. Wolff, p. 7.

presenting Yahweh's response to Judah's repentance (cf. 2:12–14) and especially to the priestly intercession of 2:17. The eschatological age comes clearly in view there. The second section (3:1–21) then draws a contrast between repentant Judah's blessings and the fate of the unrepentant nations.

The verse divisions of the OT text originate in ancient Jewish tradition as it was written into the text by the Masoretes of Tiberias in the Middle Ages. However, the chapter divisions were given to the Vulgate text by Stephen Langton (ca. A. D. 1205). He subdivided the text of Joel into three chapters, a division that was introduced into the Septuagint and most other translations in the fourteenth century. That division was imposed even on the Hebrew Bible for a brief time, but in the second Rabbinic Bible of Jacob ben Hayyim (1524–1525) the text was redivided into four chapters, subdividing chapter 2 into two chapters (2:1–32 became 2:1–27 and 3:1–5). Thus the English versions and the Hebrew compare as follows:

English	*Hebrew*
1:1–20	1:1–20
2:1–27	2:1–27
2:28–32	3:1–5
3:1–21	4:1–21

UNITY/AUTHENTICITY

The unity of the book is supported by the majority of modern scholars. The symmetrical arrangement, featuring a concern for the present and eschatological hope for the future, a combination that characterizes the prophetic books generally, vouches for the unity of the book. That balance may also be seen in the anticipation of the Day of the Lord in Part I and its description in Part II. Even though the imagery of the locusts does not appear after 2:27 of Part II, the reality of the Day of the Lord, of which Joel proclaimed the locusts a harbinger, becomes the prominent feature. Further, a common religious point of view permeates both parts, one calling for repentance and the other describing the Lord's blessing upon repentant Judah.

Generally speaking, the authenticity of very little of the book has been questioned. Among modern commentators, Julius Bewer declared all references to the Day of the Lord in chapters 1 and 2 as interpolations and attributed only 2:28–31a and 3:2a, 9–14a of chapters 3 and 4 (Heb.) to Joel.[8] However, few exponents for such extensive editing can be found in recent years. Wolff, while making a strong case for unity, questions the authenticity of only 3:4–8, on the basis of sentence structure and viewpoint.[9] Yet, although the judgment upon

8. Smith, Ward, and Bewer, pp. 50–56.
9. Wolff, p. 8.

the nations is delayed until 3:9, verses 4–8 are an expansion of the ideas of 3:1–3, the scattering of God's people by the Gentile nations.[10]

The nature of Part I (1:2–2:17), with its addresses to the elders, citizens of the land, and priests, furnishes evidence that Joel orally delivered that message in Judah soon after the locust plague, perhaps even before it had entirely ended. The urgency of his message, as noted above, leaves the impression that the crisis was still very real. Part II (2:18–3:21), with the exception of 2:18–27, may have been written a bit later in more reflective moments. At least the urgency of Part I has disappeared, but the lesson that the crisis had taught Judah, that the Lord would judge the unrepentant nations who had dispersed His people and bless repentant Judah, is drawn out. Whether or not a time lapse existed between the two parts is impossible to determine. However, we can be fairly confident that the same prophet wrote them both.

DATE

The dating of Joel has had as much latitude as Obadiah, ranging from the ninth to the fourth centuries B.C. Fortunately there are no cardinal points of orthodoxy at stake in the matter. With no indication of date in the superscription and no clear corroborative evidence in other prophetic and historical books (as with Jonah), the matter must rest in the uncertain hands of internal evidence.

PRE-EXILIC

Early pre-exilic. The case for an early date was ably made by K. A. Credner in 1831.[11] Among his arguments were (1) the absence of allusions to Syria, Assyria, and the Babylonians on the one hand, and the references to Egypt and Edom on the other; (2) the absence of references to the king, whereas the elders and priests are the prominent leaders; (3) the affinities of the book with Amos (Amos 9:13/Joel 3:18; Amos 9:13/Joel 3:16), assuming that Amos borrowed from Joel; and (4) the second-place position of the book in the Minor Prophets. Credner reasoned that the early years of the reign of Joash, when Jehoiada the priest was the regent (2 Kings 11:21–12:3), was a time when priestly leadership would be recognized. The international scene also was believed to fit the clues given in Joel, because Egypt was a strong power. Further, under Joash's grandfather, Jehoram, the Edomites and Philistines made successful incursions into Judah (2 Kings 8:20–22/2 Chron. 21:16–17). Thus the date would be early in the reign of Joash (835–796 B.C.)[12] before the Assyrian period, perhaps making Joel the earliest of the writing prophets.

---

10. Allen, pp. 111, 114.
11. K. A. Credner, *Der Prophet Joel.* See S. R. Driver, pp. 13–14, for a summary of Credner's arguments and A. F. Kirkpatrick's helpful review of the arguments in his defense of an early date, *The Doctrine of the Prophets,* pp. 57–73.
12. Thiele's chronology.

Late pre-exilic. A date in the generation before the Exile (late Assyrian) has found proponents in Kapelrud and Klaus Koch.[13] Both recognize the affinities that Joel has with Zephaniah. Koch observes that the impending Day of the Lord is the most critical point in determining the late Assyrian vintage of the book. Moreover, it would explain Joel's strong affinities with Isaiah.

POST-EXILIC

A date after the Exile has found the most supporters in modern scholarship. Among the major reasons for post-exilic dating are (1) the reference to exile in 3:2–3; (2) the absence of the sins that preoccupied the pre-exilic prophets' preaching; (3) the absence of any mention of a king would fit equally well the post-exilic period; (4) the hostility the Edomites showed toward Judah when Jerusalem fell in 586 (Obad. 10–16; Ezek. 25:12–14; 35; Lam. 4:21–22); and (5) the normal operation of the Temple services with no apparent competition from pagan cults, which might qualify better for a post-exilic date than the time of Joash, who did not remove the high places (2 Kings 12:3).

Early post-exilic. The strong role of the priests in the community and the evidence of normal Temple functions suggest a time of priestly rule similar to the period of Haggai and Zechariah. S. R. Driver is inclined toward a date shortly after those two prophets, and G. W. Ahlstrom and Leslie C. Allen express the same preference.[14] Admittedly the certainty we wish for cannot be achieved, but the period between Haggai and Zechariah and Malachi has much in its favor. The picture of a stable cultic community emerges from Joel. Moreover, the burning concerns of the prophets for moral reformation are not deliniated clearly in Joel, an observation that can also be made of Haggai and Zechariah. By the time of Malachi, however, prior to the reforms of Ezra and Nehemiah, the moral fabric of the community had deteriorated.

Late post-exilic. It must be admitted that the same arguments can be used to favor a date after Ezra and Nehemiah. George Adam Smith proposed that time.[15] The mention of the wall in 2:7 has been seen as a reference to Nehemiah's wall. However, portions of the wall evidently were not destroyed, so that is not a reliable clue.

Based upon essentially the same arguments as outlined above, and adding to them the fact that the Greeks were not yet a world power (3:6), the time of Ezra-Nehemiah (*ca.* 444 B.C.) has been used as the early date and the year of the destruction of Sidon by Artaxerxes III (345 B.C.) the latest date, because for

---

13. A. S. Kapelrud, *Joel Studies*, (1948).
14. Driver, p. 25; G. W. Ahlstrom, *Joel and the Temple Cult of Jerusalem*, p. 129; Allen, p. 24.
15. Smith, 2:379.

Joel Sidon's judgment still lay in the future (3:4).[16] A host of scholars has found this the most satisfactory period.[17]

METHODS OF INTERPRETING JOEL

The critical interpretive question involves the reality of the locusts described by Joel. Were they real and historical? Part I of the book (1:1–2:17) is the crux of the hermeneutical quandry. The question has been answered with three interpretive applications: the historical-literal, the allegorical, and the apocalyptic.

The historical-literal method insists that Joel described a locust plague that occurred during his lifetime. The fact that he called upon the elders and citizens to search their historical memory to see if such a thing as that had ever happened, and his directive to tell the future generations about it (1:2–3), substantiate the historical reality of the locust plague. The highly metaphorical language is attributable to Joel's excellent poetic ability, and it should be observed that interspersed in his poetic description of the disaster are clues to its literal nature, for example, the cessation of the cereal and drink offerings and the failure of the crops. Illuminating support for the literal interpretation has been provided by John Whiting, who described the locust plague of 1915 in Palestine. He even observed that the invaders came from the northeast, rather than the south, which amounts to a verification that "the northerner" in 2:20 is not an allegorical term.[18]

The second method, the allegorical, holds that the description of the locusts exceeds the bounds of reality and can best be explained as an allegory of an invading army. Proponents of this view have pointed to "the northern army" (2:20) as an allegorical term. Further, the petition of the priests, "Do not make Thine inheritance a reproach, a byword among the nations" (2:17), implies a fear of foreign invasion and conquest. Some have even viewed the four stages of the locust (1:4; 2:25) to represent the four great powers at whose hands Israel successively suffered: the Assyro-Babylonian, the Medo-Persian, the Greek, and the Roman. Yet the clues of allegorical language that we normally expect are missing in the text. A. F. Kirkpatrick astutely remarks that the conclusive

---

16. Thompson, 6:732. Marco Treves, "The Date of Joel," pp. 149–56, opts for 312 B.C., when Ptolemy Soter conquered Jerusalem. But he finds specificity in the text of Joel that is elusive to other scholarly scrutiny.
17. Thompson, around 400 B.C.; Robert H. Pfeiffer, *Introduction to the Old Testament*, p. 576, around 350; R. K. Harrison, *Introduction to the Old Testament*, p. 879, somewhat in advance of 400 B.C.; Otto Eissfeldt, *The Old Testament, An Introduction*, in the fourth or early third century B.C.; Wolff, p. 5, first half of fourth century; F. R. Stephenson, "The Date of the Book of Joel," pp. 224–49, views 2:31 historically and searches for dates of a total solar eclipse. Astronomical calculations show that such a phenomenon occurred in 357 and 336 B.C. He proposes one of those years for Joel's ministry.
18. Whiting, p. 511.

argument against the allegorical interpretation is that the locust plague is itself compared to an army (2:2–11).[19]

The third method, the apocalyptic, views the locust plague of chapters 1 and 2 as eschatological or apocalyptic description of future woes, addressed not to Joel's contemporaries but to those whose eyes would behold that awful day. The locusts become not a natural pestilence but extraterrestrial invaders who usher in the Day of the Lord. Not widely held, this view can be disqualified with the same arguments used against the allegorical view.

ANALYSIS

PART I: LAMENTATION OVER THE LOCUST PLAGUE (1:1–2:17)

Introduction (1:2–3) and description of the plague (1:4–20). In the brief introduction Joel asks the elders and citizens if such a devastating locust plague has ever occurred. The instructive impact of recent events comes into view as the prophet commands them to communicate the message to future generations.

Credner proposed that the four stages of the locust's development are given by Joel's four terms in 1:4. The same words occur in 2:25 but in a different order. Ovid R. Sellers has made a case for the order of 2:25. The *arbeh*, he proposes, is the old locust that lays the eggs, the *yeleq* the wingless stage when the locust cannot walk or fly (wings still enfolded in sacs) but can jump, the *hasil* the pupa or nymph stage, when it can walk and jump but still not fly, and the *gazam* the stage when it has just become an adult and is ready to fly.[20]

The address to the priests to don sackcloth for lamentation and call a fast (1:13–14) is followed by the lament itself, which bewails the terrible devastation the locusts have produced (1:15–20). It begins on the awesome note that the Day of the Lord is imminent. Perhaps verse 19 is the prophet's own prayer amidst the lamentation of the community.

Announcement of the Day of the Lord (2:1–17). The symmetry of Part I may be seen in the fact that the locust catastrophe is again described, this time in terms of an invading army (vv. 4–11), followed by another fervent summons to repentance (2:12–14). The priests play a significant role in this section (2:17) as they also did in chapter 1.

The announcement of the Day of the Lord is made like the terror-inspiring call to war, with the soul-piercing notes of the ram's horn. A second time he declares that it is near (v. 1; cp. 1:15), and in language reminiscent of Amos (5:18–20), he paints the dark hues of that terrible day. The unequalled proportion of doom that the Day portends again deepens its impression upon the minds of his contemporaries (2:2b; cp. 1:2–3). The locusts found Judah looking

---

19. Kirkpatrick, p. 54.
20. Ovid R. Sellers, "Stages of Locust in Joel," pp. 82–84.

like the Garden of Eden and left it looking like a wilderness. If there are any questions about who is commanding this army of destroyers, Joel lays them to rest, for they are the Lord's army, which executes His Word (2:11).

PART II: THE LORD'S RESPONSE TO THE REPENTANCE AND THE FUTURE AGE (2:18–3:21)

The intercession of the priests in 2:17 is met with Yahweh's pity in 2:18. Thus the latter verse becomes the hinge between the two parts.

The Lord's response to repentance (2:18–32). The response follows two lines, the first a reversal of the devastation that the locusts had caused (2:19–26), which results in Judah's recognition that the Lord is uniquely their God (2:27). The second line is the new age when Yahweh will pour out His Spirit upon all flesh, irrespective of sex, age, or social rank (2:28–32). The new age will be characterized by a generalization of the phenomenon of prophecy, here described in terms of its major manifestations in oracles, dreams, and visions.

Contrast between repentant Judah's blessings and judgment of the unrepentant nations (3:1–21). The restoration of Judah's fortunes and the judgment of the nations in the Valley of Jehoshaphat seem to be occurring simultaneously. The judgment of the nations, in accord with the general prophetic view, is meted out because of the nations' ill treatment of Yahweh's people (3:1–8, 19). Although they did not have the Torah to instruct them, the presence of Israel, Yahweh's witness in the world, was sufficient reason to call the nations to account on moral grounds. The age of peace, artfully described by Isaiah (Isa. 2:4), would be no age of peace for the nations. Reversing Isaiah's metaphor, Joel summons the nations to "beat your plowshares into swords, and your pruning hooks into spears" (3:10). The war effort, requiring the conscription of even the infirm of the society, would be futile. To illustrate the futility, Joel declares that Egypt and Edom, Judah's arch enemies from time immemorial, would be desolated for the violence they had done to Judah (3:19). Interspersed in this eschatological message of judgment are words of reassurance for Judah (3:16–18, 20–21), like glowing candles in the black night of doom.

THE MESSAGE OF JOEL

THE DAY OF THE LORD

More than the locust invasion, the Day of the Lord is the true message to Joel. By his time the tradition had developed into a complex form. Basically two-sided, a time of judgment and subsequent blessing for Israel and judgment for the nations, since the fall of Jerusalem the thought of the nation's portion of the Day of the Lord had been a troublesome pondering for the prophets. When would it occur? How long must they wait? The destruction of Jerusalem was the capstone on the pagan edifice of atrocities the nations had erected against Israel for centuries. Joel could not forget that any more than his professional associates who had preceded him, among them Jeremiah, Obadiah, Ezekiel, Daniel, and Zechariah.

Yet Joel saw another potential dimension in the tradition, that Israel's Day of the Lord could strike again if he did not repent and humble himself before his God. A nation, as it were, so miraculously raised from the grave, had been reminded by the frightful pestilence that her welfare was forever tied to her relationship to Yahweh. A violation of it could result in renewal of judgment. Yet Joel is a further reminder of the power of repentance. His call to repentance was, as the text implies, as effective as Haggai's. A community whose heart was impervious to the preaching of the pre-exilic prophets had become thankfully responsive. So the explication of the Day of the Lord was applied to the nations, for Israel's repentance had evoked divine pity, as it always could and always would.

THE DAY OF UNIVERSAL PROPHECY

The preaching of the Day of the Lord had most often not fallen on listening ears. Amos had inverted the popular notion and had mercifully deprived Israel of an unjustifiable optimism. The prophetic phenomenon had become a blessing and a curse. The prophets were not given to arrogance, but they believed their word from the Lord was irresistible for both prophet and people. The lawgiver himself had once wished that all God's people were prophets (Num. 11:29). Joel finally envisions that society, open to the voice of God in oracle, dream, and vision, with every social rank of society responsive to His revelation (2:28–29). It is another form of the recognition formula, another way of declaring that finally the covenant people would recognize their God, acknowledge Him alone as Sovereign Lord, and submit to His commands (cf. 2:27; 3:17).

With inexpressible elation the apostle Peter announced that the coming of the Holy Spirit on the day of Pentecost had fulfilled Joel's prophecy. The age had dawned when all men and women would join the prophetic ranks, when all would hear the voice of God and render obeisance to His Name. Joel's day of universal prophecy was nothing short of Jeremiah's day when the Law of God would be written in human hearts, and no person would say, "Know the Lord," for the universalization of that knowledge would eliminate the need for its interpersonal communication (Jer. 31:31–34). It would exude from every transformed heart and fill the world with the knowledge of the Lord as the waters cover the sea.

OUTLINE OF JOEL

Superscription (1:1)
I. Part I: A Lament (1:2–2:17)
    A. Introduction (1:2–3)
    B. Lament (1:4–2:17)
        1. The Locust Plague (1:4–20)
        2. Announcement of the Day of the Lord and Call to Repentance (2:1–17)
II. The Lord's Response to the Lament and the Future Age (2:18–3:21)
    A. The Lord's Response to Judah's Repentance (2:18–32)
    B. Contrast Between the Repentant Judah's Blessings and the Judgment of the Unrepentant Nations (3:1–21)

18

MALACHI: PROPHET OF COVENANT LOVE

THE INITIAL WAVES of repatriates and the first surges of enthusiasm for a restored Temple and community had died away. Even the cultic passions of the priests, the central actors on the post-exilic stage, had turned into philandering. That a restoration so miraculous, so unheard of in history, could lose its wonder and be deprived of the loyalty of the community in two generations becomes more plausible when we recall the decline of enthusiasm that had occured only a generation or two previous. In less than two decades, between Cyrus's decree and the second year of Darius I, restoration enthusiasm had turned into survival strategy. The zealous voices of Haggai and Zechariah then blew the smoldering hopes into flame again. The Temple was rebuilt, and sacrifices resumed. But when the uncertain decades of the fifth century had begun to pile up and the fortunes of the Persian Empire had begun to totter, the inner life of Israel too showed signs of wear and moral decadence. The priesthood, vitally attached to the Temple, could not easily throw off its vested interest in Temple and sacrifice, from which its livelihood was derived. And from time to time an objective appraisal from within the profession became impossible. It needed the independent assessment of the prophets, as it had needed it for the many centuries of its existence.

Malachi, whose candor on cultic abuse was as ardent as Isaiah's, appeared at a time of social decadence and spiritual decline. Like Hosea, he had an emphatic message of God's love for Israel, re-enacted in the miraculous events of the past century. His theology, based largely upon that of Deuteronomy,[1] centered upon the unconditional nature of Yahweh's love. But "unconditional" did not mean that it made no demands. Laxity in adherence to cultic prescription and moral mandate bespoke Israel's abuse of Yahweh's covenant love.

MALACHI THE MAN

The question asked by modern scholars is whether the word "Malachi" is intended as a personal name or as the Hebrew possessive noun "my messenger." A popular view today is that the book is anonymous, and the term "my

---

1. See W. J. Dumbrell, "Malachi and the Ezra-Nehemiah Reforms," pp. 42–52.

messenger'' was taken from 3:1 and prefixed to the book. The word is the noun commonly used of an angel or messenger. Those who hold that position often consider the last three sections of the Minor Prophets to be anonymous, because all three are headed by the word *massa'*, ''Oracle,'' or ''burden'' (Zech. 9:1; 12:1; Mal. 1:1).

The Targum took it to be a title of Ezra the Scribe, a viewpoint that Jerome, the Babylonian Talmud (*Megilla* 15a), and Rashi also adopted. Beyond those fragments of tradition, however, we have no evidence of that identity.

There are other examples of names that occur with the ending *i* (''my''), Ethni (1 Chron. 6:41—''my gift'') and Beeri (Gen. 26:34; Hos. 1:1—''my well''). So either interpretation of the name is possible. In fact, it is more logical to read 3:1 in light of 1:1. That is, the reference to the eschatological prophet (''my messenger'') called forth associations with Malachi. He was a prophet who claimed the end; and the messenger that would arise to announce that the day has arrived would be of a similar disposition. But to assume that an editor identified the messenger of 3:1 as the prophet is to overlook the fact that the eschatological prophet is still anticipated at the end of the book.[2]

As to the person of Malachi, we know only what we deduce from the book itself. He obviously prophesied in Jerusalem near the Temple and priesthood. Quite likely he was born and lived his life in Judah.

His zeal for proper cultic observance was inseparable from his demand for moral integrity in personal affairs. Both were proper expressions of loyalty to the covenant. That was the real passion of Malachi's heart.

LITERARY NATURE AND AUTHENTICITY

The book is generally considered to be prose, even though it bears marks of poetic insight and imagination (e.g., 3:1–4). John Merlin Powis Smith's appraisal is representative: ''Neither in spirit, thought, nor form, has it the characteristics of poetry.''[3]

STRUCTURE

Form critical analysis has alerted us to the disputation form used by Malachi. The pattern is to raise a point that is made by certain people and then contradict it. It follows a point-counterpoint pattern. This form occurs in Jeremiah 2:23–25, 35–37; 8:8–9, and Ezekiel 12:21–28 and is evident also in Isaiah 40:27–28.[4] In Malachi the substance of the controversy is introduced by a statement or imperative, followed by a question articulating the people's quandry or counter-

---

2. Brevard S. Childs, *Introduction to the Old Testament as Scripture*, pp. 493–94.
3. John Merlin Powis Smith, *A Critical and Exegetical Commentary on the Book of Malachi*, pp. 4–5.
4. See Claus Westermann, *Basic Forms of Prophetic Speech*, p. 201.

point (1:2–5; 2:17; 3:7, 13). In two instances, however, the substance of the matter is transcribed by a question (1:6; 2:10). It may be of theological importance that the counterpoint most often occurs in the form of a question. In the examples cited from Jeremiah, the point takes the form of a popular statement, and the counterpoint is the prophet's rejoinder. The fact that the rejoinder takes the question form in Malachi may imply that the priestly and public opinions were not so fixed as those that Jeremiah and Ezekiel dealt with. Furthermore, there is an interaction with the prophet that does not characterize the form in Jeremiah and Ezekiel. That is, the prophet's word evoked a popular objection, which then was matched by Malachi's rejoinder. In fact, in 1:6–2:9 the questioning is doubly sustained ("How have we despised Thy name? . . . How have we defiled Thee?"). On the other hand, the examples we have cited above begin with the popular statement or belief and are matched by the prophet's rejoinder, and that is where the dialogue ends.

Six disputations, with Malachi and the Lord taking one side and the priests or people the other, compose the book:

1. Disputation about love (1:2–5)
2. Disputation about honor (1:6–2:9)
3. Disputation about faithlessness (2:10–16)
4. Disputation about divine justice (2:17–3:5)
5. Disputation about repentance (3:6–12)
6. Disputation about serving God (3:13–4:3)

An appendix (4:4–6) concludes the book, recalling Moses, the giver of the Law, and Elijah, the exemplar of prophecy.

AUTHENTICITY

A surprising concensus of scholarly opinion on Malachi exists. The authenticity of two passages has been questioned: 2:11–12 and 4:4–6 (Heb. version 3:22–24). The issue of marriage to foreign women in 2:11–12 has been considered to be out of context in a section that deals with divorce. Yet there is no compelling reason why Malachi should not deal with that problem in such a context.[5]

The widest agreement has been to consider the two appendices (4:4, 5–6) as an interpolation. It is true that the names Moses and Elijah are rather abrupt, because no mention has been made of them previously. However, the ideas of the Law and the eschatological prophet who will prepare the way for the terrible Day of the Lord are certainly not alien to the book. Malachi was

---

5. Robert C. Dentan, "The Book of Malachi," 6:1117, explains it as the author's attempt to deal with a complex social situation.

concerned about the stipulations of the Law, both cultic and moral, and predicted the coming of the eschatological prophet.

The work of linguistic analysis, still in its infancy, has led Yehuda T. Radday and Moshe A. Pollatschek to the conclusion that chapters 1–2 show evidence of unified authorship, but chapter 3 (Eng. version 3–4) stands apart from them. The anonymous fragments of chapter 3 were added at the end of the collection of the Book of the Twelve so they would not be lost.[6] But linguistic analysis does not have the capability, by these authors' own admission, to draw absolute conclusions. It can only indicate probability.[7] Yet caution must be exercised, despite the disclaimers, that the method not be given the regal status that literary analysis (especially of vocabulary and style) was accorded by a past generation and still to some extent enjoys.[8]

DATE

Basically three positions can be identified with regard to the date of Malachi's ministry. The first views him as contemporaneous with Nehemiah, based upon similar social and religious abuses and emphases.[9] That would put Malachi somewhere around 444 B.C.., because that was the year Nehemiah became governor of Judah.

The second position dates his ministry just prior to the governorship of Nehemiah, perhaps during the early years of Ezra's work (ca. 450 B.C.). Due to the similarity of the conditions that prevailed in his time and those described in Nehemiah 13:10–29, Malachi probably predated Nehemiah, because Malachi gives no evidence of any reforming force at work in the community.[10]

The third position dates the book just prior to Ezra. The rationale is that there is no mention of the legislation that Ezra and Nehemiah introduced (Ezra 10:3; Neh. 13:13, 23–27). Joyce G. Baldwin proposes that Malachi's preaching had already quickened the public conscience, and that would explain the surprising reaction to Ezra's day of repentance and fasting before he had actually begun to speak to the public (Ezra 9:1–10:5).[11]

There are no time indicators in the book, with the exception of the desolation

---

6. Yehuda T. Radday and Moshe A. Pollatschek, "Vocabulary Richness in Post-Exilic Prophetic Books," pp. 333–46.
7. Ibid., p. 334.
8. See E. B. Pusey's citation of the work of Stanley Leathes, who made comparative studies of certain works of Milton and Tennyson, finding wide divergences of vocabulary usage within the works of both authors, *The Minor Prophets* p. 505, n. "q."
9. Mal. 3:5; Neh. 5:1–13. Also tithing is stressed (Mal. 3:7–10; Neh. 10:37–39), and divorce and mixed marriages discussed (Mal. 2:10–16; Neh. 10:30; 13:23–29). C. F. Keil is a representative of this position, *The Twelve Minor Prophets*, 2:427.
10. A few exponents of this position are Dentan, p. 1118, R. K. Harrison, *Introduction to the Old Testament*, p. 961, and J. M. P. Smith, pp. 7–8.
11. Joyce G. Baldwin, *Haggai, Zechariah, Malachi*, p. 213.

of Edom (1:3–4), which could be dated during a broad range of years. We are really thrown back upon internal evidence, which includes a governor ruling in Judah (1:8), the general spiritual decline of laity and priesthood (1:6–2:9), carelessness in the payment of tithes and in cultic matters (3:8), and deteriorating respect for marriage and rising divorce rate added to the problem of foreign marriages (2:11–16). Thus we may think in terms of a decade or two before Ezra's coming to Palestine in 457 B.C.[12]

The fourth-century date championed by C. C. Torrey has not found many proponents.[13]

ANALYSIS

SUPERSCRIPTION AND FIRST DISPUTATION: GOD LOVES ISRAEL (1:1, 2–5)

The Deuteronomic theme of God's unconditional love (Deut. 7) is put into contrast with His rejection of Esau. To speak in terms of opposites is a typical Old Testament thought pattern. The verb "hate" must be understood in the light of God's election of Israel. It does not imply personal animosity toward Edom, but means that God did not choose Esau. In His inexplicable grace He chose Jacob.

The reference to the devastation of Edom in verses 3–4 is quite general. It is possible that it alludes to the Nabatean invasion of Edom (1 Macc. 5:25), which may have occurred in the late sixth or early fifth century B.C. By 312 B.C. the Nabateans were in control of Petra, driving the Edomites into the Negeb. According to Malachi, the Edomites were never to return and permanently restore their ancient homeland.

SECOND DISPUTATION: A SON HONORS HIS FATHER (1:6–2:9)

This section, occurring after the disputation about divine love, carries a step further the concept of covenant loyalty. Because Yahweh has chosen Israel out of His wonderful grace, the father/son master/servant relationship that the covenant implies should be taken very seriously. Especially should the priests, with whom this section is primarily concerned (1:14 may address the laity), be exemplary of covenant loyalty, because they were the functionaries responsible for the ongoing expression of loyalty through the Temple and its services. Yet they had permitted in sacrifice what the Law had forbidden (Deut. 14:21).

---

12. Andrew E. Hill, based upon his linguistic analysis of the book, proposes a date between Haggai and Zechariah and the beginning of Ezra's activity—"Dating the Book of Malachi: A Linguistic Reexamination," pp. 77–89.
13. C. C. Torrey, "The Prophecy of 'Malachi,' " pp. 1–15. He argued that the apocalyptic passages that sharply separate the righteous from the wicked, coupled with the similarities of the book with the late psalms and wisdom literature, called for a date in the first half of the fourth century.

A critical verse for exegesis is 1:11, one of the most difficult OT verses for interpreters. More liberal scholars have tended to see a profound note of universalism in this verse. Torrey's explication is typical, "that *all sincere worship of God* under whatever name, in whatever way, and by whomsoever offered, is accepted by Yahweh as offered to Him."[14] But if that is what the verse means, it stands by itself in the OT, for the universalism of the prophets is one that envisions the turning of the nations to Yahweh, acknowledging His name, and worshiping at His Temple. Moreover, Malachi could hardly have inveighed against foreign marriages if he had been so tolerant of foreign worship. Nor would we expect him to introduce Elijah, the fundamentalist of Yahweh worship, if his religious lenience was so broad as that interpretation suggests.

James Swetnam deals with the term "pure offering" (*minḥah tehorah*; NASB, "a grain offering that is pure"), proposing that it relates to the synagogue services and their relation to sacrifices in the Temple. Assuming that the synagogue was operative at that time, and that it was at first a substitute for Temple sacrifice, Malachi contrasts the misconduct of the Temple priests to the worthy performance of the cult as represented in the synagogue.[15]

Baldwin offers an eschatological interpretation. Noting that the use of the phrase "from the rising of the sun, even to its setting"[16] occurs in contexts that look toward the future revelation of the Lord to the world, she proposes that the implied verb "to be" should be interpreted as future, which Hebrew grammar permits. The use of the participles with a future sense is also a common phenomenon in Hebrew. Thus the proposal is to view 1:11 as a prediction of the future day when the nations would worship Yahweh and acknowledge the greatness of His Name[17] (NASB so renders it, " 'For from the rising of the sun, even to its setting, My name will be great among the nations, and in every place incense is going to be offered to My name, and a grain offering that is pure; for My name will be great among the nations,' says the LORD of hosts"). That interpretation respects the integrity of the verse as well as the theological integrity of the book and OT theology.

THIRD DISPUTATION: WE HAVE ONE FATHER (2:10–16)

This section builds upon the second, which appealed to the fifth commandment (Ex. 20:12). Here appeal is made to the seventh commandment, which mandates against unfaithfulness in marriage (Ex. 20:14). Actually, a combination of the first and seventh commandments is involved here. Intermarriage

14. Ibid., p. 8.
15. James Swetnam, "Malachi 1:11: An Interpretation," pp. 200–9.
16. Pss. 50:1; 113:3; Isa. 45:6; 59:9.
17. Joyce G. Baldwin, "Malachi 1:11 and the Worship of the Nations in the Old Testament," 117–24.

with foreigners was detrimental to the purity of the faith. But that was not the only problem in Malachi's community. Marriages were terminated for frivolous reasons, ignoring the covenantal nature of the relationship. Faithfulness in marriage finds its prototype in God's faithfulness to men and women. All of our relationships, and the regulation of them, can be traced back to the fatherhood of God.

FOURTH DISPUTATION: WHERE IS THE GOD OF JUSTICE? (2:17–3:5)

Justice is a central feature of God's operation of His world. So the repatriates had a reason to expect its manifestation in history. Yet the years had passed, and they still had not witnessed God's intervention into history to punish the nations and bring about the glorious day that was still anticipated. The delay had created cynicism. But to question God's justice was to question His existence. The repatriates approved of evil and doubted that God was involved in the world, a double offense.

The delay was not permanent. When the eschatological messenger had prepared the way, quite unexpectedly the Lord would appear in His Temple for judgment (3:1). That theme of beginning judgment at the house of God has been sounded before in the prophets. Amos and Ezekiel had seen the beginnings of that dreadful day in that awesome place (Amos 9:1; Ezek. 9:6). The cultic abuses described in 1:6–2:9 would be removed (3:4).

FIFTH DISPUTATION: THE UNCHANGING GOD STILL CALLS FOR REPENTANCE (3:6–12)

Got puts His unchanging nature up against Israel's undiminished aptitude for sinning. The Hebrew of 3:6 literally reads, "For I the Lord have not changed, and you, sons of Jacob, have not ceased [to do evil]." Repentance must be accompanied by tangible actions. The whole nation had defrauded Him by withholding His tithes. Their problem was lack of trust. The Lord, provided they brought the full tithes to the Temple, would open heaven's windows and pour out His generous blessings.

SIXTH DISPUTATION: YOUR WORDS HAVE BEEN STRONG AGAINST THE LORD (3:13–4:3 [HEB. VERSION 3:13–21])

The skepticism of the times, earlier seen in 2:17, comes into focus again. They have questioned the benefits of the covenant relationship (3:13) and have even called the arrogant blessed (3:15). Malachi puts them on notice, however, that the God-fearers have not or will not be forgotten by the Lord (3:16–17). The day will come when He will reinstate sound moral judgment (3:18). Nor has the Lord forgotten the wicked. Judgment is stored up for them on the day when the Lord acts (4:1–3).

What could be the model for the relationship between the Law and prophecy is given here. That the Temple and prophecy were not antithetical, either by basic design or historical reality, is coming more and more to be recognized. In the post-exilic prophets we see that model more clearly than in the pre-exilic prophets. Now at the end of Malachi the model of Moses and Elijah, the two men who, perhaps more than any others, determined the direction of Israel's history, appear. The great forces for good that characterized OT history have been brought together at the end of the prophets.[18] They both served the same function, to prepare Israel for the great Day of the Lord. Of particular interest is the use of Horeb as the name for the mount of revelation. Both Moses and Elijah received a revelation there (1 Kings 19:8–18). The book of Malachi ends as it began, by appealing to the Lord's covenant with Israel.

THE MESSAGE OF MALACHI

THE LORD LOVES JACOB

This theme, which initiates the book (1:2–5), is generally recognized to be Deuteronomic (Deut. 7), as are a number of the theological emphases of Malachi.[19] Having stated God's love for Israel and having entertained the inquiry for further explication, Malachi does not review Israel's history and point out historical evidences of His grace, as a prophet might have done.[20] Rather he centralizes attention upon God's choice of Jacob and His rejection of Esau. Assuming that the Nabatean conquest of Edom still stuck in the memory of the Judeans, that illustration was contemporary and relevant. Further, this language of love tapped a deep reservoir of emotions that might be unresponsive to legal terminology. Primary in the special relationship between Yahweh and Israel was His unconditional love. Perhaps it could be best seen in His choice of Jacob over Esau.

THE DAY OF THE LORD AND ITS PROPHET

The prophets generally have in one way or another pointed toward the Day of the Lord. It was a message that was close to their hearts and an integral part of their theology. The fact that the last of the prophets in the Book of the Twelve closes with a virtual announcement that the plan is in place and the preparer has already been chosen is of much significance. We are left waiting

---

18. George Adam Smith treats the entire book under the rubric "Prophecy Within the Law," *The Book of the Twelve Prophets*, 2:348–72.
19. Dumbrell offers some helpful observations on the relationship of the book to Deuteronomy.
20. G. A. Smith, 2:349.

for the coming of Elijah, the very mention of whose name implies much about the Day. Absolute in his demands for the worship of Yahweh, Elijah's imposing presence in the vestibule of the future age intimated a day of pure and absolute worship of Israel's God.

OUTLINE OF MALACHI

Superscription (1:1)
I.   Six Disputations (1:2–4:3)
    A.   First Disputation: About Love (1:2–5)
    B.   Second Disputation: About Honor (1:6–2:9)
    C.   Third Disputation: About Faithlessness (2:10–16)
    D.   Fourth Disputation: About Divine Justice (2:17–3:5)
    E.   Fifth Disputation: About Repentance (3:6–12)
    F.   Sixth Disputation: About Serving God (3:13–4:3)
II. Appendix: Moses the Lawgiver and Elijah the Exemplar of Prophecy (4:4–6)

ABBREVIATIONS IN BIBLIOGRAPHY

ALUOS *Annual of Leeds University Oriental Society*
BA   *Biblical Archaeology*
BASOR *Bulletin of the American Schools of Oriental Research*
Bib   *Biblica*
BJRL   *Bulletin of the John Rylands Univ. Library of Manchester*
BTB   *Biblical Theology Bulletin*
CBQ   *Catholic Biblical Quarterly*
CurTM *Currents in Theology and Mission*
EQ   *The Evangelical Quarterly*
ET   *Evangelische Theologie*
ExpTim *The Expository Times*
HTR   *Harvard Theological Review*
HUCA   *Hebrew Union College Annual*
IEJ   *Israel Exploration Journal*
Int   *Interpretation*
JAOS   *Journal of the American Oriental Society*
JBL   *Journal of Biblical Literature*
JETS   *Journal of the Evangelical Theological Society*
JJS   *Journal of Jewish Studies*
JNES   *Journal of Near Eastern Studies*
JQR   *The Jewish Quarterly Review*
JSOT   *Journal for the Study of the Old Testament*
JSS   *Journal of Semitic Studies*
JTS   *Journal of Theological Studies*
OTS   *Oudtestamentische Studien*
PEQ   *Palestine Exploration Quarterly*
RB   *Revue biblique*
RE   *Review and Expositor*
RevQ   *Revue de Qumran*
SJT   *Scottish Journal of Theology*
TynB   *Tyndale Bulletin*

TBT	*The Bible Today*
Them	*Themelios*
TZ	*Theologische Zeitschrift*
VT	*Vetus Testamentum*
ZAW	*Zeitschrift fur die alttestamentliche Wissenschaft*

BIBLIOGRAPHY

GENERAL OT INTRODUCTIONS AND BACKGROUNDS

Ackroyd, P. R. *Exile and Restoration. A Study of Hebrew Thought of the Sixth Century* B.C. Old Testament Library. Philadelphia: Westminster, 1968.

Albright, William F. "Archaeological Background of the Eighth-Century Prophets." JBR 8 (1940):131–36.

———. *Archaeology and the Religion of Palestine*. Baltimore: Johns Hopkins U., 1942.

———. *From the Stone Age to Christianity*. 2d ed. Garden City, N.Y. Doubleday, 1957.

———. "The Ancient Near East and the Religion of Israel." JBL 59 (1940): 85–112.

Alt, Albrecht. *Essays on Old Testament History and Religion*. Translated by R. A. Wilson. Garden City, N.Y. Doubleday, 1967.

Anderson, G. W. *The History and Religion of Israel*. London: Oxford, 1966.

Archer, Gleason L., Jr. *A Survey of Old Testament Introduction*. Rev. ed. Chicago: Moody, 1974.

Baly, Denis. *God and History in the Old Testament*. New York: Harper & Row, 1976.

———. *The Geography of the Bible*. New York: Harper and Brothers, 1957.

Bright, John. *A History of Israel*. 3d ed. Philadelphia: Westminster, 1981.

Childs, Brevard S. *Introduction to the Old Testament as Scripture*. Philadelphia: Fortress, 1979.

Dougherty, R. P. *Nabonidus and Belshazzar*. Yale Oriental Series No. 15. New Haven, Conn.: Yale U., 1929.

Driver, S. R. *An Introduction to the Literature of the Old Testament*. Meridian Books. Cleveland: World, 1963.

Eissfeldt, Otto. *The Old Testament: An Introduction*. Translated by Peter R. Ackroyd. New York: Harper & Row, 1965.

Gottwald, Norman K. *A Light to the Nations: An Introduction to the Old Testament*. New York: Harper & Row, 1959.

Harrison, R. K. *Introduction to the Old Testament*. Grand Rapids: Eerdmans, 1969.

Kitchen, K. A. *Ancient Orient and Old Testament*. Chicago: InterVarsity, 1966.

Kraus, Hans Joachim. *Worship in Israel: A Cultic History of the Old Testament*. Richmond: John Knox, 1966.

LaSor, W. S.; D. A. Hubbard; and F. W. Bush. *Old Testament Survey*. Grand Rapids: Eerdmans, 1982.

Maimonides, Moses. *The Guide of the Perplexed*. Translated by Shlomo Pines. Chicago: U. of Chicago, 1963.

Malamat, A. "The Last Kings of Judah and the Fall of Jerusalem: An Historical-Chronological Study." IEJ 18 (1968).

Meek, T. J. *Hebrew Origins*. New York: Harper and Brothers, 1936.

Midrash Rabbah. Edited by H. Freedman and Maurice Simon. Translated by J. Israelstam and Judah J. Slotki. London: Soncino, 1939.

Moran, William L. "New Evidence from Mari on the History of Prophecy." Bib 50 (1969):15–56.

Nielsen, Eduard. *Oral Tradition*. Chicago: Allenson, 1954.

Oesterley, W. O. E., and Theodore H. Robinson. *An Introduction to the Books of the Old Testament*. New York: Macmillan, 1937.

Pritchard, James B. *Ancient Near Eastern Texts Relating to the Old Testament*. Princeton, N.J.: Princeton, 1954.

Robinson, H. Wheeler. *The Religious Ideas of the Old Testament*. 2d rev. ed. by L. H. Brockington. London: Duckworth, 1956.

Rowley, H. H. "The Nature of Prophecy in the Light of Recent Study." HTR 37 (1945):1–38.

Sellin, Ernst, and Georg Forher. *Introduction to the Old Testament*. Translated by David E. Green. Nashville: Abingdon, 1968.

Snaith, Norman H. "The First and Second Books of Kings." In *The Interpreter's Bible*. New York: Abingdon, 1954.

Soggin, J. Alberto. *Introduction to the Old Testament*. Translated by John Bowden, Philadelphia: Westminster, 1976.

Thiele, Edwin R. *A Chronology of the Hebrew Kings*. Grand Rapids: Zondervan, 1977.

de Vaux, Roland. *Ancient Israel: Its Life and Institutions*. Translated by John McHugh. London: Darton, Longman & Todd, 1961.

Weister, Artur *The Old Testament: Its Formation and Development*. Translated by Dorothea M. Barton. New York: Association, 1961.

Westermann, Claus. *Basic Forms of Prophetic Speech*. Translated by Hugh Clayton White. Philadelphia: Westminster, 1967.

Wevers, John W. *Ezekiel*. Century Bible (new series). London: Thomas Nelson, 1969.

Wood, Leon. *A Survey of Israel's History*. Grand Rapids: Zondervan, 1970.
Young, Edward J. *An Introduction to the Old Testament*. Grand Rapids: Eerdmans, 1949.

GENERAL WORKS ON THE PROPHETS AND RELATED SUBJECTS

Ahlstrom, G. W. "Oral and Written Transmission, Some Considerations." HTR 59 (1966):69–81.

Alden, Robert L. "Ecstasy and the Prophets." JETS 9 (1966):149–56.

————. "Study of the Prophets Since World War II," pp. 131–45. In *New Perspectives on the Old Testament*. Edited by J. Barton Payne. Waco, Tex.: Word, 1970.

Allen, E. L. *Prophet and Nation: A Reconciliation of Divided Loyalties*. London: Nisbet, 1947.

Allen, G. F. "The Prophetic Interpretation of History." ET 51 (1940):454–57.

Anderson, B. W., and Walter Harrelson, eds. *Israel's Prophetic Heritage*. New York: Harper, 1962.

Berger, Peter L. "Charisma and Religious Innovation: The Social Location of Israelite Prophecy." *American Sociological Review* 28 (1963):940–50.

Blenkinsopp, J. *The Men Who Spoke Out: The Old Testament Prophets*. London: Darton, Longman & Todd, 1969.

Buber, Martin. *The Prophetic Faith*. Translated by C. Witton Davies. New York: Macmillan, 1949.

Bullock, C. Hassell. *An Introduction to the Old Testament Poetic Books*. Chicago: Moody, 1979.

Carroll, Robert P. *When Prophecy Failed: Cognitive Dissonance in the Prophetic Traditions of the Old Testament*. New York: Seabury, 1979.

Craghan, John F. "Mari and Its Prophets: The Contributions of Mari to the Understanding of Biblical Prophecy." BTB 5 (1975):32–55.

Davidson, A. B. *Old Testament Prophecy*. Edinburgh: T. & T. Clark, 1904.

————. "Prophecy and Prophets." In *Dictionary of the Bible*, 4:106*b*–27*b*, edited by James Hastings. New York: Scribner's, 1911.

De Vries, S. J. *Prophet Against Prophet: The Role of the Micaiah Narrative (1 Kings 22) in the Development of Early Prophetic Tradition*. Grand Rapids: Eerdmans, 1978.

Edersheim, Alfred. *Prophecy and History in Relation to the Messiah*. London: Longmans, Green, 1885.

Edgehill, E. A. *An Enquiry into the Evidential Value of Prophecy*. New York: Macmillan, 1912.

Eichrodt, Walther. *Theology of the Old Testament*. Philadelphia: Westminster, 1967.

Freeman, Hobart E. *An Introduction to the Old Testament Prophets*. Chicago: Moody, 1968.

Gerstenberger, Erhard. "The Woe-Oracles of the Prophets." JBL 81 (1962): 249–63.

Graham, William C. *The Prophets and Israel's Culture.* Chicago: U. of Chicago, 1934.

Guillaume, Alfred. *Prophecy and Divination.* London: Hodder and Stoughton, 1938.

Hanson, Paul D. *The Dawn of Apocalyptic.* Rev. ed. Philadelphia: Fortress, 1979.

Haran, M. "From Early to Classical Prophecy: Continuity and Change." VT 27 (1977):385–97.

Hayes, John. "Prophetism at Mari and Old Testament Parallels." ATR 49 (1967):397–409.

Hengstenberg, E. W. *Christology of the Old Testament and A Commentary on the Messianic Predictions.* Edinburgh: T. & T. Clark, 1863.

Heschel, Abraham J. *The Prophets.* 2 vols. New York: Harper & Row, 1962.

Hoffmann, Y. *The Prophecies Against Foreign Nations in the Bible* (Hebrew). Tel-Aviv: Chaim Rosenberg School for Jewish Studies, 1977.

Holladay, John S., Jr. "Assyrian Statecraft and the Prophets of Israel." JTR 63 (1956):277–84.

Huffmon, Herbert B. "The Origins of Prophecy." In *Magnalia Dei: The Mighty Acts of God,* pp. 171–86, edited by Frank Moore Cross, Werner E. Lemke, and Patrick D. Miller, Jr. Garden City N. Y.: Doubleday, 1976.

Hughes, P. E. *Interpreting Prophecy: An Essay in Biblical Perspectives.* Grand Rapids: Eerdmans, 1976.

Hyatt, J. Philip. "The Prophetic Criticism of Israelite Worship." In *Interpreting the Prophetic Tradition,* pp. 203–24, edited by Harry M. Orlinsky. New York: KTAV, 1969.

———. *Prophetic Religion.* New York: Abingdon, 1947.

Kaufmann, Yehezkel. *The Religion of Israel.* Translated by Moshe Greenberg. Chicago: U. of Chicago, 1960.

Kirkpatrick, A. F. *The Doctrine of the Prophets.* 3d ed. London: Macmillan, 1917.

Knight, Harold. *The Hebrew Prophetic Consciousness.* London: Lutterworth, 1947.

Koch, Klaus. *The Prophets.* 2 vols. Translated by Margaret Kohl. Philadelphia: Fortress, 1983.

Leslie, Elmer A. *The Prophets Tell Their Own Story.* New York: Abingdon, 1939.

Lindblom, J. *Prophecy in Ancient Israel.* Philadelphia: Fortress, 1965.

Lods, Adolphe. *The Prophets and the Rise of Judaism.* Westport, Conn.: Greenwood, 1937.

Lowth, Robert. *Lectures on the Sacred Poetry of the Hebrews.* Translated by G. Gregory. 2 vols. 1787; reprint. New York: Garland, 1971.

McKane, W. *Prophets and Wise Men.* Studies in Biblical Theology. London: SCM, 1965.

Malamat, Abraham. "Prophecy in the Mari Documents" (Hebrew). EI 4 (1956):74–84.

———. "Prophetic Revelations in New Documents from Mari and the Bible." Supp. VT 15 (Leiden: E. J. Brill, 1966):207–27.

Milton, J. P. *Prophecy Interpreted: Essays in Old Testament Interpretation.* Minneapolis: Augsburg, 1960.

Mowinckel, Sigmund. *Prophecy and Tradition.* Oslo: Jacob Dybwad, 1946.

Oesterly, W. O. E., and Theodore H. Robinson. *An Introduction to the Books of the Old Testament.* New York: Macmillan, 1937.

Overholt, Thomas W. "Jeremiah 27–29: The Question of False Prophecy." JAAR 35 (1967):241–49.

Parzen, Herbert. "The Prophets and the Omri Dynasty." HTR 33 (1940): 69–96.

Paterson, John. *The Goodly Fellowship of the Prophets.* New York: Scribner's, 1948.

Payne, J. Barton. *The Theology of the Older Testament.* Grand Rapids: Zondervan, 1962.

Ringren, Helmer. *Israelite Religion.* Translated by David E. Green. Philadelphia: Fortress, 1966.

Robertson, Edward. "The Role of the Early Hebrew Prophet," BJRL 49 (1959–60):412–31.

Robinson, Theodore H. *Prophecy and the Prophets in Ancient Israel.* London: Duckworth, 1923.

Rowley, H. H. *Studies in Old Testament Prophecy.* Edinburgh: T. & T. Clark, 1950.

Scott, R. B. Y. *The Relevance of the Prophets.* Rev. ed. New York: Macmillan, 1968.

Smith, George Adam. *The Book of the Twelve Prophets.* Two vols. New York: A. C. Armstrong and Son, 1903.

Smith, J. M. P. *The Prophets and Their Times.* Chicago: U. of Chicago, 1941.

Smith, W. Robertson. *The Prophets of Israel.* London: A. and C. Black, 1897.

Tucker, G. "Prophetic Speech." Int 32 (11979):31–45.

Vawter, Bruce. *The Conscience of Israel: Pre-exilic Prophets and Prophecy.* New York: Sheed & Ward, 1961.

von Rad, G. *The Message of the Prophets.* Translated by D. M. G. Stalker, 1968.

———. *Old Testament Theology.* Translated by D. M. G. Stalker, 2 vols. New York: Harper & Row, 1962.

Vriezen, T. C. *An Outline of Old Testament Theology.* Oxford: Basil Blackwell, 1958.

———. "Prophecy and Eschatology." Supp. VT 1 (1953): 199–229.

Widengren, Geo. *Literary and Psychological Aspects of the Hebrew Prophets*. Uppsala: A.-B. Lundequistska Bokhandeln, 1948.

Wildberger, Hans. "Die Vokerwallfahrt zum Zion." VT 7 (1957):62–81.

Williams, James G. "The Social Location of Israelite Prophecy." JAAR 37 (1969):153–65.

Wiseman, D. J. *Chronicles of Chaldaean Kings (626–556 B.C.) in the British Museum*. London: The Trustees of the British Museum, 1956.

Young, Edward J. *My Servants the Prophets*. Grand Rapids: Eerdmans, 1952.

MINOR PROPHETS

Calkins, Raymond. *The Modern Message of the Minor Prophets*. New York: Harper, 1947.

Calvin, John. *Commentaries on the Twelve Minor Prophets*. Translated by John Owen. Reprint. Grand Rapids: Eerdmans, 1950.

Cashdan, Eli. *The Twelve Minor Prophets*. London: Soncino, 1940.

Eiselen, F. C. *The Minor Prophets*. New York: Eaton & Mains, 1907.

Keil, C. F. *The Twelve Minor Prophets*. Trans. by James Martin. Reprint. Grand Rapids: Eerdmans, 1949.

Laetsch, Theodore. *The Minor Prophets*. St. Louis: Concordia, 1956.

Pusey, E. B. *The Minor Prophets*. 2 vols. New York: Funk & Wagnalls, 1885.

Robinson, G. L. *The Twelve Minor Prophets*. New York: George H. Doran, 1926.

Smith, George Adam. *The Book of the Twelve Prophets*. 2 vols. New York: A. C. Armstrong, 1903.

Weiser, Artur. *Das Buch der Zwolf Kleinen Propheten*. Goettingen: Vandenhoeck & Ruprecht, 1974.

JONAH

Aalders, G. Ch. *The Problem of the Book of Jonah*. London: Tyndale, 1948.

Allen, Leslie. *Joel, Obadiah, Jonah and Micah*. New International Commentary on the Old Testament. Grand Rapids: Eerdmans, 1976.

Anderson, Bernard W. *The Eighth Century Prophets: Amos, Hosea, Isaiah, Micah*. Proclamation Commentaries. Philadelphia: Fortress, 1978.

Bentzen, Aage. "The Ritual Background of Amos 1:2–2:16." *Oudtestamentische Studien* 8 (1950):85–99.

Bewer, Julius; J. M. Powis; and H. G. Smith. *A Critical and Exegetical Commentary on Haggai, Zechariah, Malachi, and Jonah*. International Critical Commentary. New York: Scribner's 1912.

Blank, Sheldon H. " 'Doest Thou Well to Be Angry?' A Study in Self Pity." HUCA 26 (1955):29–42.

————. *Understanding the Prophets*. New York: Union of American Hebrew Congregations, 1969.

Burrows, Millar. "The Literary Category of the Book of Jonah." In *Translating and Understanding the Old Testament: Essays in Honor of Herbert Gordon May*, pp. 80–107, edited by Harry Thomas Frank and William L. Reed. Nashville: Abingdon, 1970.

Childs, Brevard S. "The Canonical Shape of the Book of Jonah." In *Biblical and Near Eastern Studies: Essays in Honor of William Sanford LaSor*, pp. 122–28, edited by Gary A. Tuttle. Grand Rapids: Eerdmans, 1978.

————. "Jonah: A Study in Old Testament Hermeneutics." SJT 11 (1958): 53–61.

Clements, R. E. "The Purpose of the Book of Jonah." Supp. VT 28 (1975):16–28.

Cohen, Simon. "The Political Background of the Words of Amos." HUCA 36 (1965):153–60.

Fretheim, T. E. *The Message of Jonah: A Theological Commentary*. Minneapolis: Augsburg, 1977.

————. "Jonah and Theodicy." ZAW 90 (1976):227–37.

Graham, W. C. "Jonah." In *The Abingdon Bible Commentary*, pp. 787–90, edited by F. C. Eiselen, et al. Garden City, N.Y.: Doubleday, 1929 and 1957.

Holladay, J. "Assyrian Statecraft and the Prophets of Israel." HTR 63 (1970):29–51.

Johnson, A. R. "Jonah 2:3–10: A Study in Cultic Phantasy." In *Studies in Old Testament Prophecy: Presented to T. H. Robinson*, pp. 82–102, edited by H. H. Rowley. Reprint. Edinburgh: T. & T. Clark, 1957.

Keil, C. F. *The Twelve Minor Prophets*. Biblical Commentary on the Old Testament. Translated by James Martin. Reprint. Grand Rapids: Eerdmans, n.d.

Kidner, F. D. "The Distribution of Divine Names in Jonah." TynB 21 (1970):126–28.

Knight, George A. *Ruth and Jonah: Introduction and Commentary*. London: SCM, 1950.

Landes, George M. "The Kerygma of the Book of Jonah: The Contextual Interpretation of the Jonah Psalm." Int 21 (1967):3–31.

Macloskie, G. "How to Test the Story of Jonah." Bib Sac 72 (1915):334–38.

Merrill, Eugene H. "The Sign of Jonah." JETS 23 (1980):23–30.

Miles, John A. "Laughing at the Bible: Jonah as Parody." JQR 65 (1975):168–81.

Mitchell, Hinckley G.; John Merlin Powis Smith; and Julius A. Bewer. *A Critical and Exegetical Commentary on Haggai, Zechariah, Malachi and Jonah*. New York: Scribner's, 1912.

Nowell, Irene. "The Book of Jonah: Repentance of Conversion." TBT 21 (1983):363–68.

Peiper, Claude J. "Jonah and Jesus: The Prophet as Sign." TBT 21 (1983): 377–83.

Perowne, T. T. *Obadiah and Jonah.* The Cambridge Bible for Schools and Colleges. Edited by J. J. S. Perowne and A. F. Kirkpatrick. Cambridge: At the Univ. Press, 1905.

Pusey, E. B. *The Minor Prophets with a Commentary.* Oxford: J. H. & J. Parker, 1860.

Rayner, F. A. "The Story of Jonah: An Easter Study." EQ 22 (1950): 123–25.

Scott, R. B. Y. "The Sign of Jonah, An Interpretation." Int 19 (1965):16–25.

Soleh, A. "The Story of Jonah's Reflective Adventures." *Beth Mikra* 24 (1979):406–20 (Hebrew).

Smart, James. "Jonah." In *The Interpreter's Bible.* Edited by George Buttrick et al. Nashville: Abingdon, 1956.

Trumball, H. Clay. "Jonah in Nineveh." JBL 11 (1892);53–60.

Walsh, Jerome T. "Jonah 2:3–10: A Rhetorical Critical Study." Bib 63 (1982):219–29.

Walton, John. *Jonah, Bible Study Commentary.* Grand Rapids: Zondervan, 1982.

Wilson, Ambrose John. "The Sign of the Prophet Jonah and Its Modern Confirmations." PTR 25 (1927):630–42.

Wiseman, Donald J. "Jonah's Nineveh." TynB 30 (1979):29–51.

Wolff, H. W. "Jonah: The Reluctant Messenger." CurTM 3 (1976):8–19.

AMOS

Ackroyd, Peter R. "A Judgment Narrative Between Kings and Chronicles? An Approach to Amos 7:9–17." In *Canon and Authority: Essays in Old Testament Religion and Theology*, pp. 71–87, edited by George W. Coats and Burke O. Long. Philadelphia: Fortress, 1977.

Barton, John. *Amos's Oracles Against the Nations: A Study of Amos 1:3–2:5.* Cambridge: Cambridge U., 1980.

Bentzen, Aage. "The Ritual Background of Amos 1:2–2:16." *Oudtestamentische Studien* 8 (1950):85–99.

Bright, John. "Faith and Destiny. The Meaning of History in *Deutero-Isaiah.*" Int 5 (1951):3–26.

Brueggemann, Walter. "Amos 4:4–13 and Israel's Covenant Worship." VT 15 (1965):1–15.

———. *Tradition for Crisis: A Study in Hosea.* Richmond: John Knox, 1968.

Christensen, Duane. "The Prosodic Structures of Amos 1–2." HTR 67 (1974): 427–36.

Clements, R. E. *Prophecy and Tradition.* Atlanta: John Knox, 1975.

Coote, Robert B. *Amos Among the Prophets: Composition and Theology.* Philadelphia: Fortress, 1981.

Crenshaw, J. L. "Amos and the Theophanic Tradition." ZAW 80 (1968): 203–15.

———. "The Influence of the Wise upon Amos: The 'Doxologies of Amos' and Job 5:9–16; 9:5–10." ZAW 79 (1967):42–52.

Cripps, Richard S. *A Critical and Exegetical Commentary on the Book of Amos.* 2d ed. London: SPCK, 1955.

DeWaard, J. "The Chiastic Structure of Amos 5:1–17." VT 27 (1977): 170–77.

Driver, S. R. *Isaiah: His Life and Times.* New York: Anson D. F. Randolph, n.d.

———. *Joel and Amos.* The Cambridge Bible for Schools and Colleges. Cambridge: At the Univ. Press, 1901.

Farr, G. "The Language of Amos, Popular or Cultic." VT 16 (1966): 312–24.

Fensham, F. C. "Common Trends in Curses of the Near Eastern and Kudurru-Inscriptions Compared with Maledictions of Amos and Isaiah." ZAW 75 (1963):155–75.

Fosbroke, Hughell E. W. "The Book of Amos," In *The Interpreter's Bible.* Vol. 6. Edited by George A. Buttrick. New York: Abingdon, 1956.

Gaster, Theodore H. "An Ancient Hymn in the Prophecies of Amos." JMEOS 19 (1935):23–26.

Gordis, Robert. "The Composition and Structure of Amos." HTR 33 (1940): 239–51.

Gottlieb, Hans. "Amos and Jerusalem." VT 17 (1967):430–63.

Gottwald, Norman K. *All the Kingdoms of the Earth.* New York: Harper & Row, 1964.

Hammershaimb, E. *The Book of Amos.* Oxford: Basil Blackwell, 1970.

Harper, William Rainey. *A Critical and Exegetical Commentary on Amos and Hosea.* New York: Scribner's, 1905.

Hayes, John H. "The Usage of Oracles Against Foreign Nations in Ancient Israel." JBL 87 (1968):81–92.

Howie, Carl G. "Expressly for Our Time: The Theology of Amos." Int 13 (1959):273–85.

Hyatt, J. P. "The Book of Amos." Int 3 (1949):338–47.

———. "The Translation and Meaning of Amos 5:23, 24." ZAW 68 (1956): 17–24.

Irwin, W. A. "The Thinking of Amos." AJSL 49 (1932):102–14.

Kapelrud, Arvid S. *Central Ideas in Amos.* Oslo: Oslo U. 1961.

———. "God as Destroyer in the Preaching of Amos and in the Ancient Near East." JBL 71 (1952):33–38.

———. "New Ideas in Amos." Supp. VT 15, pp. 193–206. Leiden: E. J. Brill, 1966.

Knierim, Rolf P. " 'I Will Not Cause It to Return' in Amos One and Two." In *Canon and Authority, Essays in Old Testament Religion and Theology*, pp. 163–75, edited by George W. Coats and Burke O. Long. Philadelphia: Fortress, 1977.

McCullough, W. S. "Israel's Eschatology from Amos to Daniel." In *Studies of the Ancient Palestinian World*, pp. 86–101, edited by J. M. Weavers and D. B. Redford. U. of Toronto, 1972.

McKeating, H. *The Books of Amos, Hosea and Micah*. The Cambridge Bible Commentary on the New English Bible. Edited by P. R. Ackroyd, et al. Cambridge: Cambridge U., 1971.

Malamat, Abraham. "Amos 1:5 in the Light of the Til Barsip Inscriptions." BASOR 129 (1953):25–26.

Marsh, John. *Amos and Micah*. Torch Bible Commentaries. London: SCM, 1959.

————. *Amos, A Commentary*. The Old Testament Library. London: SCM, 1969.

Mays, James L. "Words About the Words of Amos: Recent Study of the Book of Amos." Int 13 (1959):259–72.

Moldenke, Harold N., and Alma L. Moldenke. *Plants of the Bible*. Waltham, Mass.: Chronica Botanica Co., 1952.

Morgenstern, Julian. *Amos Studies*. 2 vols. Cincinnati: Hebrew Union College, 1941.

Motyer J. A. *The Day of the Lion*. Downers Grove, Ill.: InterVarsity, 1974.

Paul, Shalom M. "Amos 3:15—Winter and Summer Mansion." VT 28 (1978): 358–60.

Ridge, F. M. *The Prophet Amos*. London: Epworth, 1951.

Robinson, H. Wheeler. "Amos." In *The Abingdon Bible Commentary*, pp. 775–83, edited by F. C. Eiselen, et al. Garden City, N.Y.: Doubleday, 1929 and 1957.

Schoville, Keith N. "A Note on the Oracles of Amos Against Gaza, Tyre, and Edom." In *Studies on Prophecy*, pp. 55–63. Supp. VT 26. Leiden: E. J. Brill, 1974.

Smith, J. M. P. *Amos, Hosea and Micah*. New York: Macmillan, 1914.

Snaith, Norman. *Amos, Hosea and Micah*. The Epworth Preacher's Commentary. London: Epworth, 1957.

Story, Cullen I. K. "Amos 3:15—Prophet of Praise." VT 30 (1980):67–80.

Terrien, Samuel. "Amos and Wisdom." In *Israel's Prophetic Heritage*, pp. 108–15, edited by G. W. Anderson and Walter Harrelson. New York: Harper and Bros., 1962.

Toy, Crawford. "The Judgment of Foreign Peoples in Amos i. 3– ii.3." JBL 25 (1906):25–28.

Tucker, Gene M. "Prophetic Authenticity: A Form Critical Study of Amos 7:10–17." Int 27 (1973):423–34.

Van der Wal, Adri. "The Structure of Amos." JSOT 26 (1983):107–13.

Vawter, Bruce. *Amos, Hosea, Micah, with an Introduction to Classical Prophecy.* Wilmington, Del.: Glazier, 1981.

Watts, John D. W. "The Origin of the Book of Amos." ET 66 (1954–55): 109–12.

————. *Vision and Prophecy in Amos.* Leiden: E. J. Brill, 1958.

Williams, A. J. "A Further Suggestion About Amos 4:1–3." VT 29 (1979): 206–11.

Wolfe, Rolland E. *Meet Amos and Hosea.* New York: Harper and Bros., 1945.

Wolff, H. W. *Amos the Prophet: The Man and His Background.* Philadelphia: Fortress, 1974.

————. *Joel and Amos.* Translated by Waldemar Janzen, et al. Philadelphia: Fortress, 1977.

Wright, T. J. "Amos and the 'Sycamore Fig.' " VT 26 (1976):362–68.

Zalcman, Lawrence. "Astronomical Illusions in Amos." JBL 100 (1981):53–58.

Zevit, Ziony. "Expressing Denial in Biblical Hebrew and Mishnaic Hebrew, and in Amos." VT 29 (1979):505–9.

HOSEA

Achtemeier, Elizabeth. "The Theological Message of Hosea: Its Preaching Values." RE 72 (1975):473–85.

Ackroyd, P. R. "Hosea and Jacob." VT 13 (1963):245–59.

Alt, A. "Hosea 5.8–6.6 Ein Frieg und sein Folgen in prophetischen Beleuchtung." In *Kleine Schriften II.* Munich: C. H. Beck, 1953.

Anderson, Francis I., and David Noel Freedman. *Hosea.* The Anchor Bible. Garden City, N.Y.: Doubleday, 1980.

Anderson, B. W. "The Book of Hosea." Int 8 (1954):290–303.

Anderson, G. W. "Hosea and Yahweh: God's Love Story (Hosea 1–3)." RE 72 (1975):425–36.

Barre, M. L. "New Light on the Interpretation of Hosea 6:2." VT 28 (1978):129–41.

Bentzen, Aage. "The Weeping of Jacob, Hosea 12:5a." VT 1 (1951): 58–59.

Bewer, Julius A. "Some Ancient Variants in Hosea with Scribe's or Corrector's Mark." JBL 30 (1911):61–65.

————. "The Story of Hosea's Marriage." AJSL 22 (1905–06):120–30.

Browne, S. L. *The Book of Hosea.* Westminster Commentaries. London: Methuen, 1932.

Brueggeman, Walter. *Tradition for Crisis: A Study in Hosea.* Richmond: John Knox, 1968.

Buss, Martin J. *The Prophetic Word of Hosea, A Morphological* Study. Berlin: Verlag Alfred Topelmann, 1969.

Cheyne, T. K. *The Book of Hosea.* The Cambridge Bible for Schools and Colleges. Cambridge: At the Univ. Press, 1913.

Cobb, William H. "On the Text of Hosea 4–14." JBL 36 (1917):63–74.

Coote, R. B. "Hosea 12." VT 21 (1971):389–402.

Craghan, J. F. "The Book of Hosea: A Survey of Recent Literature on the First of the Minor Prophets." BTB 1 (1971):81–100; 145–70.

———. "An Interpretation of Hosea." BTB 5 (1975):201–7.

Davidson, A. B. "Hosea." In *A Dictionary of the Bible.* 2:422*a.* Edited by James Hastings. Edinburgh: T. & T. Clark, 1899.

DeRoche, M. "The Reversal of Creation in Hosea." VT 31 (1981):400–9.

Eichrodt, W. "The Holy One in Your Midst: The Theology of Hosea." Translated by Lloyd Gaston. Int 15 (1961):259–73.

Emmerson, Grace. "The Structure and Meaning of Hosea 8:1–3." VT 25 (1975):700–10.

Gertner, M. "An Attempt at an Interpretation of Hosea 12." VT 10 (1960): 272–84.

Good, E. M. "Hosea 5:8–6:6: An Alternative to Alt." JBL 85 (1966): 273–86.

Gordis, Robert. "Hosea's Marriage and Message." HUCA 255 (1954):9–35.

———. "The Text and Meaning of Hosea 14:3." VT 5 (1955):88–90.

Gordon, C. H. "Hosea 2:4–5 in the Light of New Semitic Inscriptions." ZAW 54 (1936):277–80.

Harper, William Rainey. *A Critical and Exegetical Commentary on Amos and Hosea.* New York: Scribner's, 1905.

Haupt, Paul. "Hosea's Erring Spouse." JBL 34 (1915):41–53.

Holladay, William L. "Chiasmus, the Key to Hosea 12:3–6." VT 16 (1966): 53–64.

Johansen, John H. "The Prophet Hosea: His Marriage and Message." JETS 14 (1971):179–84.

Kelley, P. H. "The Holy One in the Midst of Israel: Redeeming Love (Hosea 11–14)." RE 72 (1975):465–72.

Kimchi, David. *Hosea* (Hebrew). In *Mikraoth Gedoloth.* New York: Pardes, 1951.

Kittel, Rudolf. "Classic Prophets, Amos and Hosea." Translated by Charlotte A. Knoch and C. D. Wright. In *Great Men and Movements in Israel,* pp. 229–49. New York: KTAV, 1968.

Knight, G. A. F. *Hosea, Introduction and Commentary.* London: SCM, 1960.

McKeating, Henry. *The Books of Amos, Hosea and Micah.* The Cambridge Bible Commentary. Cambridge: At the Univ. Press, 1971.

McKenzie, J. L. "The Knowledge of God in Hosea." JBL 74 (1955): 22–27.

Mauchline, John. "The Book of Hosea." In *The Interpreter's Bible*. Vol. 4. New York: Abingdon, 1956.

May, H. G. "An Interpretation of the Names of Hosea's Children." JBL 55 (1936):285–91.

———. "The Fertility Cult in Hosea." AJSL 48 (1932):73–98.

Mays, J. L. *Hosea, A Commentary*. London: SCM, 1969.

North, F. S. "Hosea's Introduction to His Book." VT 8 (1958):429–32.

———. "Solution of Hosea's Marital Problems by Critical Analysis." JNES 16 (1957):128–30.

Nyberg, H. S. *Studien zum Hosea Buch*. Uppsala: Lundequistska, 1935.

Owens, J. J. "Exegetical Study of Hosea." RE 54 (1957):522–43.

Paton, L. B. "Notes on Hosea's Marriage." JBL 15 (1896):9–17.

Paul, S. M. "The Image of the Oven and the Cake in Hosea 7:4–10." VT 18 (1968):114–20.

Ritschl, Dietrich. "God's Conversion: An Exposition of Hosea 11." Int 15 (1961):286–303.

Robinson, H. Wheeler. *The Cross of Hosea*. Philadelphia: Westminster, 1949.

———. "Hosea." In *The Abingdon Bible Commentary*, pp. 759–67. Edited by F. C. Eiselen et al. Garden City, N.Y.: Doubleday, 1929 and 1957.

———. *Two Hebrew Prophets*. London: Lutterworth, 1948.

deRoche, Michael. "The Reversal of Creation in Hosea." VT 31 (1981): 400–9.

Rowley, H. H. "The Marriage of Hosea." In *Men of God*, pp. 66–97. London: Thomas Nelson, 1963.

Rust, E. C. "The Theology of Hosea." RE 54 (1957):510–21.

Smith, J. M. P. *Amos, Hosea and Micah*. New York: Macmillan, 1914.

Snaith, Norman. *Amos, Hosea and Micah*. The Epworth Preacher's Commentary. London: Epworth, 1957.

———. *Mercy and Sacrifice: A Study of the Book of Hosea*. London: SCM, 1953.

Spiegel, Shalom. "A Prophetic Attestation of the Decalogue: Hosea 6:5 (with Some Observations on Psalms 15 and 24)." HTR 27 (1934):105–44.

Stinespring, W. F. "A Problem of Theological Ethics in Hosea." In *Essays in Old Testament Ethics*, pp. 131–44. Edited by J. Crenshaw and J. T. Willis. New York: KTAV, 1974.

Swaim, Gerald G. "Hosea the Statesman." In *Biblical and Near Eastern Studies: Essays in Honor of William Sanford LaSor*, pp. 177–83. Edited by Gary A. Tuttle. Grand Rapids: Eerdmans, 1978.

Tate, Marvin. "The Whirlwind of National Disaster: A Disorganized Society (Hosea 7–10)." RE 72 (1975):449–63.

Tushingham, A. D. "A Reconsideration of Hosea, Chapters 1–3." JNES 12 (1953):150–59.

Ward, J. M. *Hosea. A Theological Commentary*. New York: Harper & Row, 1966.

―――. "The Message of the Prophet Hosea." Int 23 (1969):387–407.

Waterman, L. "Hosea, Chapters 1–3 in Retrospect and Prospect." JNES 14 (1955):100–9.

―――. "The Marriage of Hosea." JBL 37 (1918):193–208.

Wenham, Gordon J. "The Coherence of the Flood Narrative." VT 28 (1978):336–48.

Williams, Donald L. "Annotated Bibliography on Hosea." RE 72 (1975): 495–501.

Wolfe, Rolland E. *Meet Amos and Hosea*. New York: Harper Bros., 1945.

Wolff, H. W. "Guilt and Salvation: A Study of the Prophecy of Hosea." Trans. by Lloyd Gaston. Int 15 (1960):274–85.

―――. *Hosea*. Hermeneia. Translated by G. Stansell. Philadelphia: Fortress, 1974.

MICAH

Allen, Leslie C. *The Books of Joel, Obadiah, Jonah, and Micah*. Grand Rapids: Eerdmans, 1976.

Anderson, B. W. *The Eighth Century Prophets: Amos, Hosea, Isaiah, Micah*. Proclamation Commentaries. Philadelphia: Fortress, 1978.

Anderson, G. W. "A Study of Micah 6:1–8." SJT 4 (1951):191–97.

Bewer, J., J. M. P. Smith, and W. H. Ward. *A Critical and Exegetical Commentary on Micah, Zephaniah, Nahum, Habbakuk, Obadiah, and Joel*. New York: Scribner's, 1911.

Burkitt, F. C. "Micah 6 and 7, A Northern Prophecy." JBL 45 (1926):159–61.

Calvin, John. "Calvin's Saturday Morning Sermon on Micah 6:6–8." Translated by A. David Lewis. SJT 23 (1970):166–82.

Cannawurf, E. "The Authenticity of Micah IV:1–4." VT 13 (1963): 26–33.

Cheyne, T. K. *Micah*. Cambridge Bible for Schools and Colleges. Cambridge: At the Univ. Press, 1901.

Copass, B. A., and E. L. Carlson. *A Study of the Prophet Micah*. Grand Rapids: Baker, 1950.

Crook, M. B. "Did Amos and Micah Know Isa. 9:2–7 & 11:1–9?" JBL 73 (1954):144–51.

―――. "The Promise in Micah 5." JBL 70 (1951):313–20.

Gunkel, Hermann. "The Close of Micah: A Prophetical Liturgy." In *What Remains of the Old Testament and Other Essays*, pp. 115–49. Translated by A. K. Dallas. New York: Macmillan, 1928.

Hammershaimb, E. "Some Leading Ideas in the Book of Micah." In *Some Aspects of Old Testament Prophecy from Isaiah to Malachi*, pp. 122–24. Denmark: Rosenkilde og Bagger, 1966.

Haupt, Paul. "The Book of Micah." AJSL 27 (1910):1–63.

Hillers, Delbert R. *Micah*. Hermeneia. Philadelphia: Fortress, 1984.

Hyatt, J. P. "The Book of Amos." Int 3 (1949):338–48.

————. "On the Meaning and Origin of Miach 6:8." ATR (1952):232–39.

Jeppesen, Knud. "New Aspects of Micah Research." JSOT 8 (1978):3–32.

Kapelrud, Arvid S. "Eschatology in The Book of Micah." VT 11 (1961):392–405.

McFadyn, John E. "Micah." In *The Abingdon Bible Commentary*, pp. 791–97. Edited by F. C. Eiselen et al. Garden City, N.Y.: Doubleday, 1929, 1957.

McKeating, Henry. *The Books of Amos, Hosea and Micah*. The Cambridge Bible Commentary on the New English Bible. Cambridge: Cambridge U., 1971.

Margolis, Max. *Micah*. Philadelphia: JPS, 1908.

Marsh, John. *Amos and Micah*. Torch Bible Commentaries. London: SCM, 1959.

Mays, James Luther. *Micah, A Commentary*. The Old Testament Library. Philadelphia: Westminster, 1976.

Reicke, Bo. "Liturgical Traditions in Mic. 7." HTR 60 (1967):349–67.

Smith, J. M. P. *Amos, Hosea and Micah*. New York: Macmillan, 1914.

———— et al. *A Critical and Exegetical Commentary on Micah, Zephaniah, Nahum, Habakkuk, Obadiah and Joel*. New York: Scribner's, 1911.

Snaith, Norman. *Amos, Hosea and Micah*. New York: The Epworth Preacher's Commentary. London: Epworth, 1957.

Stade, B. "Bemerkungen uber das Buch Micha." ZAW 1 (1881):161–72.

Taft, J. *The Prophecy of Micah*. New York: Scribner's, 1907.

Torrance, T. "The Prophet Micah and His Famous Saying." EQ 24 (1952):206–14.

Van der Woude, A. S. "Micah in Dispute with the Pseudo-prophets." VT 19 (1969):244–60.

Vawter, Bruce. *Amos, Hosea, Micah, with an Introduction to Classical Prophecy*. Wilmington, Del.: Glazier, 1981.

Willis, John T. "Authenticity and Meaning of Micah 5:9–14." ZAW 81 (1969):353–68.

————. "Micah 4:14–5:5, A Unit." VT 18 (1968):529–47.

————. "Micah 5:1." JQR 58 (1967–68):317–22.

————. "The Structure of Micah 3–5 and the Function of Micah 5:9–14 in the Book." ZAW 81 (1969):191–214.

Wolfe, Rolland E. "The Book of Micah." In *The Interpreters's Bible*. Vol. 6. New York: Abingdon, 1956.

Wolff, Hans W. *Micah the Prophet*. Translated by Ralph D. Gehrke. Philadelphia: Fortress, 1981.

ISAIAH

Ackroyd, P. R. "Isaiah 1–12: Presentation of a Prophet." Supp. VT 29 (1977):16–48.

Alexander, Joseph Addison. *Earlier Prophecies of Isaiah*. New York: Wiley and Putnam, 1846.

———. *Later Prophecies of Isaiah*. New York: Wiley and Putnam, 1847.

Allis, O. T. *The Unity of Isaiah*. Philadelphia: Presbyterian and Reformed, 1950.

Anderson, B. W. "Exodus and Covenant in Second Isaiah and Prophetic Tradition." In *Magnalia Dei: The Mighty Acts of God*, pp. 339–60. Garden City, N.Y.: Doubleday, 1976.

Anderson, Robert T. "Was Isaiah a Scribe?" JBL 79 (1960):57–58.

Bewer, Julius. *The Book of Isaiah*. New York: Harper and Bros., 1950.

Blank, Sheldon H. *Prophetic Faith in Isaiah*. London: Adam and Charles Black, 1958.

———. "Traces of Prophetic Agony in Isaiah." HUCA 27 (1956):86–90.

Bright, John. "Faith and Destiny. The Meaning of History in Deutero-Isaiah." Int 5 (1951):3–26.

Brinkman, J. A. "Merodach-Baladan II." In *Studies Presented to A. Leo Oppenheim*. Chicago: U. of Chicago, 1964.

Brodie, Louis. "The Children and the Prince: The Structure, Nature and Date of Isaiah 6–12." BTB 9 (1979):27–31.

Brownlee, William H. *The Meaning of the Qumran Scrolls for the Bible*. New York: Oxford U., 1964.

Bullock, C. Hassell. "Entree to the Pentateuch Through the Prophets: A Hermeneutics of History." In *Interpreting the Word of God*, pp. 60–77. Edited by Samuel J. Schultz and Morris A. Inch. Chicago: Moody, 1976.

Buttenwieser, M. "Where Did Deutero-Isaiah Live?" JBL 38 (1919):94–112.

Callaway, J. A. "Isaiah in Modern Scholarship." RE 65 (1968):397–407.

Cheyne, T. K. *The Prophecies of Isaiah*. New York: Whittaker, 1884.

Childs, Brevard S. *Isaiah and the Assyrian Crisis*. Studies in Biblical Theology, sec. series, no. 3. Naperville, Ill.: Allenson, 1967.

Clements, R. E. "The Prophecies of Isaiah and the Fall of Jerusalem in 587 B.C." VT 30 (1980):421–36.

———. "The Unity of the Book of Isaiah." Int 36 (1982):117–29.

Coggins, R. J. "The Problem of Isaiah 24–27." ExpTim 90 (1979):328–33.

Cross, F. M. "The Council of Yahweh in Second Isaiah." JNES 12 (1953):274–77.

Davidson, R. "Universalism in Second Isaiah." SJT 16 (1963):166–85.

Delitzsch, Franz. *Biblical Commentary on the Prophecies of Isaiah*. 2 vols. Translated by James Martin. Reprint. Grand Rapids: Eerdmans, 1949.

Driver, S. R. *Isaiah: His Life and Times*. New York: Anson D. F. Randolph, n.d.

Eaton, J. H. "The Origin of the Book of Isaiah," VT 9 (1959):138–57.

Engnell, I. *The Call of Isaiah*. Uppsala: Lundequistska, 1949.

Fohrer, G. "The Origin, Composition and Tradition of Isaiah 1–39." ALUOS 3 (1961):3–38.

Freehof, Solomon B. *Book of Isaiah*. New York: Union of American Hebrew Congregations, 1972.

Gehman, Henry S. "The Ruler of the Universe: The Theology of First Isaiah." Int 11 (1957):269–81.

Gileadi, Avraham. *The Apocalyptic Book of Isaiah, A New Translation with Interpretative Key*. Provo, Utah: Hebraeus Press, 1982.

Goldingay, John. "The Arrangement of Isaiah xli–xlv." VT 29 (1979): 289–99.

Gottwald, Norman K. "Immanuel as the Prophet's Son." VT 8 (1958):36–47.

Gray, George Buchanan. *A Critical and Exegetical Commentary on the Book of Isaiah I-XXVII*. Edinburgh: T. & T. Clark, 1912.

Hallo, W. W. "Isaiah 28:9–13 and the Ugaritic Abecedaries." JBL 77 (1958): 324–38.

Jackson, Robert Sumner. "The Prophetic Vision: The Nature of the Utterance in Isaiah 40–55." Int 16 (1962):65–75.

Jensen, Joseph. "The Age of Immanuel." CBQ 41 (1979):220–39.

Kaiser, Otto. *Isaiah 1–12, a Commentary*. Philadelphia: Westminster, 1972.

―――. *Isaiah 13–39, A Commentary*. Translated by R. A. Wilson, Philadelphia: Westminster, 1974.

Kaufmann, Yehezkel. *The Babylonian Captivity and Deutero-Isaiah*. Translated by E. W. Efroymson. New York: Union of American Hebrew Congregations, 1970.

Kissane, Edward J. *The Book of Isaiah*. 2 vols. Dublin: Browne and Nolan, 1941.

Leupold, H. C. *Exposition of Isaiah*. 2 vols. Grand Rapids: Baker, 1968.

Lindblom, J. *The Servant Songs in Deutero-Isaiah, A New Attempt to Solve an Old Problem*. Lund: C. W. K. Gleerup, 1951.

Lindblom, J. *A Study on the Immanuel Section in Isaiah (Isa. vii, 1–ix, 6)*. Scripta Minora: Lund: CWK Gleerup, 1958.

McCullough, W. S. "A Re-Examination of Isaiah 56–66." JBL 67 (1948): 27–36.

McKenzie, John L. Isaiah. The Anchor Bible. Garden City, N.Y.: Doubleday, 1968.

Margalioth, Rachel. *The Indivisible Isaiah: Evidence for the Single Authorship of the Prophetic Book*. New York: Sura Institute for Research, 1964.

Marshall, R. J. "The Structure of Isaiah 1–12." BR 7 (1962):19–32.

Milgrom, J. "Did Isaiah Prophesy During the Reign of Uzziah?" VT 14 (1964):164–82.

Millar, William R. *Isaiah 24–27 and the Origin of Apocalyptic.* Missoula, Mont.: Scholars Press, 1976.

Mitchell, H. G. "The Servant of Yahweh in Isa. 40–55." JBL 38 (1919):113–28.

Motyer, J. A. "Context and Content in the Interpretation of Isaiah 7:14." TynB 21 (1970):118–25.

Mowinckel, Sigmund. *Jesaja-disiplene. Profeten fra Jesaja til Jeremia.* Oslo: Forlagt Av. H. Aschhoug, 1925.

Muilenburg, James. "Isaiah 40–66." In *The Interpreter's Bible.* Vol. 5. New York: Abingdon, 1956.

North, Christopher R. *Isaiah 40–55.* London: SCM, 1952.

———. *The Suffering Servant in Deutero-Isaiah: An Historical and Critical Study.* London: Oxford, 1948.

Oesterley, W. O. E. *Studies in Isaiah XL-LXVI.* London: Robert Scott, 1916.

Orlinsky, H. M., and Snaith, N. H. *Studies on the Second Part of the Book of Isaiah.* Supp. VT 14. Reprint. Leiden: E. J. Brill, 1977.

Payne, J. Barton. "The Effect of Sennacherib's Anticipated Destruction in Isaianic Prophecy." WTJ 34 (1971):22–38.

———. "The Unity of Isaiah: Evidence from Chapters 36–39." JETS 10 (1963):50–56.

———. "Eighth Century Israelitish Background of Isaiah 40–66." WTJ 29 (1966–67):179–90; 30 (1967–68):50–58, 185–203.

Rembaum, Joel E. "The Development of a Jewish Exegetical Tradition Regarding Isaiah 53." HTR 75 (1982):289–311.

Rignell, L. G. "Isaiah 52:13–53:12." VT 3 (1953):87–92.

Roberts, J. J. M. "Isaiah in Old Testament Theology." Int 36 (1982):130–43.

Robinson, H. Wheeler. "The Hebrew Conception of Corporate Personality." In *Werden und Wesen des Alten Testaments,* pp. 49–62. Berlin: A. Topelmann, 1936.

Rowley, H. H. "Hezekiah's Reform and Rebellion." BJRL 44 (1961–62): 395–431.

———. "The Servant Mission: The Servant Songs and Evangelism." Int 8 (1954):259–72.

———. "The Servant of the Lord in the Light of Three Decades of Criticism." In *The Servant of the Lord and Other Essays on the Old Testament.* London: Lutterworth, 1952.

Schultz, Samuel. "Interpreting the Prophets." In *The Literature and Meaning of Scripture,* pp. 103–21. Edited by Morris A. Inch and C. Hassell Bullock. Grand Rapids: Baker, 1981.

Scott, R. B. Y. "The Book of Isaiah, Chapters 1–39." In *The Interpreter's Bible.* Vol. 5. New York: Abingdon. 1956.

————. "Isaiah 1–39." Int 7 (1953):453–65.

Smart, James D. History and Theology in Second Isaiah. Philadelphia: West-minster, 1965.

Smith, George Adam. The Book of Isaiah. 2 vols. The Expositor's Bible. Rev. ed. London: Hodder and Stoughton, 1927.

Snaith, Norman H. "The Servant of the Lord in Deutero-Isaiah." In Studies in Old Testament Prophecy, pp. 187–200, ed. H. H. Rowley. Edinburgh: T. & T. Clark, n. d.

Torrey, C. C. The Second Isaiah: A New Interpretation. New York: Scribner's, 1928.

Vasholz, Robert. "Isaiah Versus 'The Gods.' A Case for Unity." WTJ 42 (1980–81):389–94.

von Orelli, C. The Prophecies of Isaiah. Translated by J. S. Banks. Edinburgh: T. & T. Clark, 1895.

Walton, John H. "Positive Redaction Criticism and the Date of Isaiah." Unpublished paper read at Evangelical Theological Society, April 1984.

Westermann, Claus. Isaiah 40–66, A Commentary. Translated by D. M. G. Stalker. Old Testament Library. London: SCM, 1969.

Whedbee, J. Williams. Isaiah and Wisdom. Nashville: Abingdon, 1971.

Whybray, R. N. Isaiah 40–66. New Century Bible. London: Marshall, Morgan & Scott, 1975.

————. Thanksgiving for a Liberated Prophet. An Interpretation of Isaiah Chapter 53. JSOT Supp. 4 Sheffield: Dept. of Biblical Studies, 1978.

Whitcomb, John C., Jr. "Cyrus in the Prophecies of Isaiah." In The Law and The Prophets: Studies Prepared in Honor of Oswald T. Allis, pp. 388–401, ed. John Skilton. Philadelphia: Presbyterian and Reformed, 1974.

Wolf, Herbert M. "A Solution to the Immanuel Prophecy in Isaiah 7:14–8:22." JBL 91 (1972):449–56.

Young, Edward J. The Book of Isaiah. 3 vols. Grand Rapids: Eerdmans, 1965.

————. "Isaiah 34 and Its Position in the Prophecy." WTJ 27 (1955):93–114.

————. Isaiah 53. Grand Rapids: Eerdmans, 1952.

————. Studies in Isaiah. London: Tyndale, 1954.

————. "The Study of Isaiah Since the Time of Joseph Addison Alexander." WTJ 9 (1946):1–30; 10 (1947–48):23–56; 139–67.

ZEPHANIAH

Bewer, J. A. A Critical and Exegetical Commentary on Micah, Zephaniah, Nahum, Habakkuk, Obadiah and Joel. New York: Scribner's, 1911.

Davidson, A. B. The Books of Nahum, Habakkuk and Zephaniah. Cambridge Bible for Schools and Colleges. Cambridge: Cambridge U., n.d.

Eaton, J. H. Obadiah, Nahum, Habakkuk and Zephaniah. London: SCM, 1962.

Ferguson, Henry. "The Historical Testimony of the Prophet Zephaniah." JBL 102 (1983):42–59.

Gray, John. "A Metaphor for Building in Zephaniah 2:1." VT 3 (1953):404–7.

Hyatt, J. P. "The Date and Background of Zephaniah." JNES 7 (1948):25–29.

Kselman, John. "A Note on Jeremiah 49:20 and Zephaniah 2:6–7." CBQ 32 (1970):579–81.

Lehrman, S. M. "Zephaniah." In *The Twelve Prophets*. Edited by A. Cohen. Bournemouth: Soncino, 1948.

Smith, Louis Pettibone, and Ernest R. Lacheman. "The Authorship of the Book of Zephaniah." JNES 9 (1950):137–42.

Stonehouse, G. G. V. *The Books of the Prophets Zephaniah and Nahum*. Westminster Commentary. London: Methuen, 1926.

Waltke, B. K. "Book of Zephaniah." In *Zondervan Pictorial Encyclopedia of the Bible*, 5:1051–55. Edited by Merrill C. Tenney. Grand Rapids: Zondervan, 1975.

Williams, Donald L. "The Date of Zephaniah." JBL 82 (1963):77–88.

Habakkuk

Albright, William F. "The Psalm of Habakkuk." In *Studies in Old Testament Prophecy*. Edited by H. H. Rowley. Edinburgh: T. & T. Clark, 1950.

Birnbaum, S. A. "The Date of the Habakkuk Cave Scroll." JBL 68 (1949):161–68.

Brownlee, William H. "The Placarded Revelation of Habakkuk." JBL 82 (1963):319–25.

Budd, Karl. "Die Bücher Habakkuk und Zephanja." *Theologische Studien und Kritiken* 66 (1893):383–93.

Day, J. "Echoes of Baal's Seven Thunders and Lightnings in Psalm 29 and Habakkuk 3:9 and the Identity of the Seraphim in Isaiah 6." VT 29 (1979): 143–51.

Driver, G. R. "On Habakkuk 3:7." JBL 62 (1943):121.

Duhm, Bernard. *Das Buch Habakkuk*. Tübingen, J. C. B. Mohr, 1906.

Eaton, J. H. "The Origin and Meaning of Habakkuk 3." ZAW 76 (1964): 144–71.

Gaster, Theodore H. "On Habakkuk 3:4." JBL 62 (1943):345–46.

Lehrman, S. M. "Habakkuk." In *The Twelve Prophets*. Edited by A. Cohen. Bournemouth: Soncino, 1948.

Moriarity, F. J. "The Habakkuk Scroll and a Controversy." ThS 13 (1952): 228–33.

Mowinckel, Sigmund. "Zum Psalm des Habakkuk." TZ 9 (1953):1–23.

O'Connell, Kevin G. "Habakkuk—Spokesman to God." CurTM 6 (1979): 227–31.

Rast, Walter E. "Justification by Faith." CurTM 10 (1983):169–75.

Roth, Cecil. "The Era of the Habakkuk Commentary." VT 11 (1961):451–55.
Smith, John Merlin Powis; William Hayes Ward; and Julius A. Bewer. *A Critical and Exegetical Commentary on Micah, Zephaniah, Nahum, Habakkuk, Obadiah and Joel.* ICC. New York: Scribner's, 1911.
Stenzel, M. "Habakkuk 2:15–16." VT 3 (1953):97–99.
Talmon, S. "Notes on the Habakkuk Scroll." VT 1 (1951):33–37.
Taylor, Charles L., Jr. "The Book of Habakkuk." In *The Interpreter's Bible.* Edited by George A. Buttrick. New York: Abingdon, 1956.
Ward, William Hayes. *A Critical and Exegetical Commentary on Habakkuk.* ICC. New York: Scribners, 1911.

JEREMIAH

Anderson, Bernhard W. " 'The Lord Has Created Something New': A Stylistic Study of Jer. 31:15–22." CBQ 40 (1978):463–78.
Blank, Sheldon H. *Jeremiah: Man and Prophet.* Cincinnati: Hebrew Union College, 1961.
Bright, John. "The Book of Jeremiah." Int 9 (1955):259–78.
———. "The Date of the Prose Sermons of Jeremiah." JBL 70 (1951):15–35.
———. "An Exercise in Hermeneutics: Jeremiah 31:31–34." Int 20 (1966): 188–210.
———. *Jeremiah.* The Anchor Bible. Garden City, N.Y.: Doubleday, 1965.
———. "A Prophet's Lament and Its Answer: Jeremiah 15:10–21." Int 28 (1974):59–74.
Calkins, R. *Jeremiah the Prophet.* New York: Macmillan, 1930.
Calvin, John. *Commentary on the Book of the Prophet Jeremiah and the Lamentations.* Translated by John Owen. Reprint. Grand Rapids: Eerdmans, 1950.
Cheyne, T. K. *Jeremiah, His Life and Times.* New York: Revell, 1888.
Cunliffe-Jones, Hubert. *The Book of Jeremiah: Introduction and Commentary.* Torch Bible Commentaries. London: SCM 1961.
Davidson, A. B. "Jeremiah the Prophet." In *A Dictionary of the Bible,* 2:569–78. Edinburgh: T. & T. Clark, 1899.
Davidson, R. "Orthodoxy and the Prophetic Word: A Study in the Relationship Between Jeremiah and Deuteronomy." VT 14 (1964): 407–16.
Dijkstra, Meindert. "Prophecy by Letter (Jeremiah xxix.24–32)." VT 33 (1983):319–22.
Driver, S. R. *The Book of the Prophet Jeremiah.* London: Hodder and Stoughton, 1906.
Duhm, Bernard. *Das Buch Jeremia.* Handkommentar zum Alten Testament. Tübingen: J. C. B. Mohr, 1901.

Eissfeldt, Otto. "The Prophet Jeremiah and the Book of Deuteronomy." In *Studies in Old Testament Prophecy*, pp. 157–74. Edited by H. H. Rowley. New York: Scribner's, 1950.

Fox, Michael V. "Jeremiah 2:2 and the 'Desert Ideal.' " CBQ 35 (1973):441–50.

Friedman, Harry. *Jeremiah*. Soncino Books of the Bible. London: Soncino, 1949.

Freehof, S. B. *The Book of Jeremiah. A Commentary*. New York: Union of American Hebrew Congregations, 1977.

Hobbs, T. R. "Some Remarks on the Structure and Composition of the Book of Jeremiah." CBQ 34 (1972):257–75.

———. "Torah in the Book of Jeremiah." JBL 60 (1941):381–96.

Holladay, W. L. *The Architecture of Jeremiah 1–20*. Lewisburg, Pa.: Bucknell U., 1976.

———. "A Fresh Look at 'Source B' and 'Source C' in Jeremiah." VT 25 (1975):394–412.

———. "The Identification of the Two Scrolls of Jeremiah." VT 30 (1980):452–67.

———. "Jeremiah's Lawsuit with God: A Study in Suffering and Meaning." Int 17 (1963):280–87.

———. *Jeremiah: Spokesman Out of Time*. Philadelphia: United Church Press, 1974.

———. "Style, Irony and Authenticity in Jeremiah." JBL 81 (1962):44–54.

Horwitz, William J. "Audience Reaction to Jeremiah." CBQ 32 (1970): 555–64.

Hyatt, J. Philip. "The Beginning of Jeremiah's Prophecy." ZAW 78 (1966): 204–14.

———. "The Book of Jeremiah." In *The Interpreter's Bible*. Edited by G. A. Buttrick. 12 vols. New York: Abingdon, 1956.

———. "Jeremiah and Deuteronomy." JNES 1 (1942):156–73.

———. "The Peril from the North in Jeremiah." JBL 59 (1940): 499–513.

———. "Torah in the Book of Jeremiah." JBL 60 (1941):381–96.

Keil, C. F. *Biblical Commentary on the Book of Daniel*. Translated by M. G. Easton. Reprint. Grand Rapids: Eerdmans, 1971.

Kelso, A. P. "The Religious Consciousness of Jeremiah." AJSL 41 (1925): 233–42.

Kuist, Howard Tillman. "The Book of Jeremiah." Int 4 (1950):322–41.

Laetsch, Theodore. *Jeremiah*. St. Louis: Concordia, 1952.

Leslie, Elmer A. *Jeremiah Chronologically Arranged, Translated and Interpreted*. Nashville: Abingdon, 1954.

Lofthouse, W. F. *Jeremiah and the New Covenant*. London: SCM, 1925.

Ludwig, Theodore M. "The Shape of Hope: Jeremiah's Book of Consolation." CurTM 38 (1967):526–41.

Malamat, Abraham. "Jeremiah and the Last Two Kings of Judah." PEQ 83 (1951):81–87.

May, H. G. "The Chronology of Jeremiah's Oracles." JNES 4 (1945): 217–27.

———. "Towards an Objective Approach to the Book of Jeremiah: The Biographer." JBL 61 (1942):139–55.

Meek, Theophile. "The Poetry of Jeremiah." JQR 14 (1923–34):281–91.

Mitchell, H. G. "The Theology of Jeremiah." JBL 20 (1900):56–76.

Mowinckel, Sigmund. *Zur Komposition des Buches Jeremia*. Kristiania, 1914.

Nicholson, E. W. *The Book of The Prophet Jeremiah, Chs. 1–25*. Cambridge: University Press, 1973.

———. *The Book of the Prophet Jeremiah, Chs. 26–52*. Cambridge: University Press, 1975.

Nicholson, E. W. *Preaching to the Exiles*. Oxford: Basil Blackwell, 1970.

von Orelli, C. "Jeremiah." In *The International Standard Bible Encyclopedia*. 3:158–91. Chicago: Howard Severance Co., 1930.

Overholt, Thomas W. "Jeremiah 2 and the Problem of 'Audience Reaction.' " CBQ 41 (1979):517–32.

———. "Jeremiah 27–29: The Question of False Prophecy." JAAR 35 (1967):241–49.

———. "King Nebuchadnezzar in the Jeremiah Tradition." CBQ 30 (1968):39–48.

———. *The Threat of Falsehood: A Study in the Theology of the Book of Jeremiah*. Studies in Biblical Theology, second series. London: SCM, 1970.

Potter, H. D. "The New Covenant in Jeremiah xxxi.31–34." VT 33 (1983): 347–57.

Rowley, H. H. "The Early Prophecies of Jeremiah in Their Setting." BJRL 45 (1962–63):198–234.

Skinner, John. *Prophecy and Religion: Studies in the Life of Jeremiah*. New York: Cambridge, U., 1922.

Smith, G. A. *Jeremiah*. 4th ed. rev. and enlarged. New York: Harper and Bros., 1929.

Swetnam, James. "Why Was Jeremiah's New Covenant New?" Supp. VT 26 (1974):111–15.

Taylor, John B. *Ezekiel, An Introduction and Commentary*. Tyndale Old Testament Commentaries. London: Tyndale, 1969.

Thompson, J. A. *The Book of Jeremiah*. NICOT. Grand Rapids: Eerdmans, 1980.

Torrey, C. C. "The Background of Jeremiah 1–10." JBL 56 (1937): 193–216.

Vischer, Wilhelm. "The Vocation of the Prophet to the Nations: An Exegesis of Jeremiah 1:4–10." Translated by Suzanne de Dietrich. Int 9 (1955):310–17.

Wallis, Wilbur B. "Irony in Jeremiah's Prophecy of a New Covenant." JETS 12 (1969):107–10.

Watts, John D. W. *The Books of Joel, Obadiah, Jonah, Nahum, Habakkuk and Zephaniah.* The Cambridge Bible Commentary on the New English Bible. Cambridge: Cambridge U., 1975.

Welch, Adam C. *Jeremiah: His Time and His Work.* Oxford: Basil Blackwell, 1951.

Whitley, C. F. "Carchemish and Jeremiah." ZAW 80 (1968):38–50.

Woudstra, M. H. "A Prophet to the Nations: Reflections on Jeremiah's Call to the Prophetic Office." *Vox Reformata* 18 (1972):1–13.

NAHUM

Allis, Oswald T. "Nahum, Nineveh, Elkosh." EQ 27 (1955):67–80.

Arnold, William R. "The Composition of Nahum." ZAW 21 (1901):225–65.

Cathcart, Kevin J. "Treaty Curses and the Book of Nahum." CBQ 35 (1973): 179–87.

Christensen, Duane L. "The Acrostic of Nahum Reconsidered." ZAW 87 (1975):17–30.

Dahood, M. "Casual Beth and the Root NKR in Nahum 3, 4." Bib 52 (1971): 395–96.

Davidson, A. B. *The Books of Nahum, Habakkuk and Zephaniah.* The Cambridge Bible for Schools and Colleges. Cambridge: Cambridge U., 1920.

DeVries, S. J. "The Acrostic of Nahum in the Jerusalem Liturgy." VT 16 (1966):476–81.

Eaton, J. H. *Obadiah, Nahum, Habakkuk and Zephaniah.* Torch Book Commentary. London: SCM, 1962.

Gaster, Theodore H. "Two Notes on Nahum." JBL 63 (1944):51–52.

Graham, W. C. "The Interpretation of Nahum 1:9–2:3." AJSL 44 (1927–28): 37–48.

Gunkel, Hermann. "Nahum 1." ZAW 13 (1893):223–44.

Haldar, Alfred. *Studies in the Book of Nahum.* Uppsala: Lundequistska Bokhandeln, 1947.

Haupt, Paul. "The Book of Nahum." JBL 26 (1907):1–53.

Humbert, Paul. "Essai d'analyse de Nahoum 1,2–2,3." ZAW 44 (1926): 266–80.

Lehrman, S. M. "Nahum." In *The Twelve Prophets.* Edited by A. Cohen. Bournemouth: Soncino, 1948.

Levenson, J. D. "Textual and Semantic Notes on Nahum 1:7–8." VT 25 (1975):792–95.

Mihelic, Joseph L. "The Concept of God in the Book in Nahum." Int 2 (1948):199–207.

Smith, John Merlin Powis; William Hayes Ward; and Julius A. Bewer. *A Critical and Exegetical Commentary on Micah, Zephaniah, Nahum, Habakkuk, Obadiah and Joel.* ICC. New York: Scribner's, 1911.

van der Woude, A. S. "The Book of Nahum: A Letter Written in Exile." OS 20 (1977):108–26.

EZEKIEL

Ackroyd, Peter R. "An Interpretation of the Babylonian Exile: A Study of II Kings 10, Isaiah 38–39." SJT 27 (1974):329–52.

Albright, William F. "The Seal of Eliakim and the Latest Preexilic History of Judah, with Some Observations on Ezekiel." JBL 51 (1932):77–106.

Alexander, Ralph H. "A Fresh Look at Ezekiel 38 and 39." JETS 17 (1974):157–69.

Berry, G. R. "The Composition of the Book of Ezekiel." JBL 58 (1939): 163–75.

———. "The Title of Ezekiel." JBL 51 (1932):54–57.

Bertholet, Alfred, and Kurt Galling. *Hesekiel*. Tübingen: Mohr, 1936.

Bewer, J. *The Book of Ezekiel*. 2 vols. Harper Annotated Bible. New York: Harper and Row, 1952.

Blackwood, Andrew W., Jr. *Ezekiel: Prophecy of Hope*. Grand Rapids: Baker, 1965.

Broom, Edwin C., Jr. "Ezekiel's Abnormal Personality." JBL 65 (1946):277–92.

Bullock, C. Hassell. "Ezekiel, Bridge Between the Testaments." JETS 25 (1982):23–31.

Buttenwieser, Moses. "The Character and Date of Ezekiel's Prophecies." HUCA 7 (1930):1–18.

Calvin, John. *Commentaries on the First Twenty Chapters of the Book of the Prophet Ezekiel*. 2 vols. Translated by Thomas Myers. Edinburgh: Calvin Translation Society, 1849.

Carley, Keith W. *Ezekiel Among the Prophets: A Study of Ezekiel's Place in Prophetic Tradition*. Studies in Biblical Theology No. 31 (2d series). Naperville, Ill.: Allenson, 1974.

Cooke, G. A. *The Book of Ezekiel*. 2 vols. ICC. New York: Scribner's, 1937.

Davidson, A. B. *The Book of the Prophet Ezekiel*. Cambridge: Cambridge, U., 1892.

Kijk, H. J. Van. *Ezekiel's Prophecy on Tyre*. Rome: Pontifical Biblical Institute, 1968.

Eichrodt, W. *Ezekiel, A Commentary*. Translated by Gosslett Quin. The Old Testament Library. Philadelphia: Westminster, 1970.

Ellison, H. L. *Ezekiel: The Man and His Message:* London: Paternoster, 1956.

Feinberg, Charles Lee. *The Prophecy of Ezekiel*. Chicago: Moody, 1969.

Fisch, S. *Ezekiel*. Soncino Books of the Bible. Edited by A. Cohen. Bournemouth: Soncino, 1950.

Fishbane, Michael. "Sin and Judgment in the Prophecies of Ezekiel." Int 38 (1984):131–50.

Fox, Michael V. "The Rhetoric of Ezekiel's Vision of the Valley of the Bones." HUCA 51 (1980):1–15.

Freedman, David Noel. "The Book of Ezekiel." Int 8 (1954):446–71.

Geyer, John B. "Ezekiel 18 and a Hittite Treaty of Mursilis II." JSOT 12 (1979):31–46.

Greenberg, Moshe. *Ezekiel 1–20, A New Translation with Introduction and Commentary.* The Anchor Bible. Garden City, N.Y. Doubleday, 1983.

———. Ezekiel 17 and the Policy of Psammaticus II." JBL 76 (1957):304–9.

———. "Ezekiel 17: A Holistic Interpretation." JAOS 103 (1983):149–54.

———. "On Ezekiel's Dumbness." JBL 77 (1958):101–5.

Haran, Menahem. "The Law Code of Ezekiel 40–48 and Its Relation to the Priestly Code." HUCA 50 (1979):45–71.

Herntrich, Wolkmar. *Ezechielprobleme.* Giessen: A. Toepelmann, 1932.

Hoelscher, Gustav. *Hesekiel, der Dichter und das Buch.* Giessen: Alfred Toepelmann, 1924.

Howie, Carl Gordon. *The Date and Composition of Ezekiel.* JBL Series. Vol. 4. Philadelphia: Society of Biblical Literature, 1950.

Irwin, William A. *The Problem of Ezekiel, An Inductive Study.* Chicago: U. of Chicago, 1943.

———. "Ezekiel Research Since 1943." VT 3 (1953):54–66.

Keil, Carl F. *Biblical Commentary on the Prophecies of Ezekiel.* Translated by J. Martin. Reprint. Grand Rapids: Eerdmans, n.d.

Levenson, John D. *Theology of the Program of Restoration of Ezekiel 40–48.* Harvard Semitic Monograph Series. Edited by Frank Moore Cross, Jr. Missoula, Mont.: Scholars Press, 1976.

Lindars, B. "Ezekiel and Individual Responsibility." VT 15 (1965):452–67.

Lofthouse, William F. "The Book of the Prophet Ezekiel." In *Century Bible.* Edinburgh: T. C. and E. C. Jack, n.d.

Mackay, Cameron. "The Integrity of Ezekiel 40–48." EQ 32 (1960): 15–24.

———. "Why Study Ezekiel 40–48." EQ 37 (1965):155–67.

———. "Zechariah in Relation to Ezekiel 40–48." EQ 40 (1968): 193–96.

May, H. G. "The Departure of the Glory of Yahweh." JBL 56 (1937):309–21.

———. "Ezekiel: Introduction and Exegesis." In *The Interpreter's Bible,* pp. 41–338. Edited by George Buttrick, et al. Nashville: Abingdon, 1956.

———. "The King in the Garden of Eden: A Study of Ezekiel." In *Israel's Prophetic Heritage,* pp. 166–76. Edited by G. W. Anderson and Walter Harrelson. New York: Harper and Bros., 1962.

Mays, James L. *Ezekiel and Second Isaiah.* Proclamation Commentaries. Philadelphia: Fortress, 1978.

O'Connor, Michael P. "The Weight of God's Name: Ezekiel in Context and Canon." TBT 18 (1980):28–34.

Orlinksy, H. M. "Where Did Ezekiel Receive the Call to Prophesy?" BASOR 122 (1951):34–36.

Peifer, Claude J. "Ezekiel and the New Jerusalem." TBT 18 (1980):22–27.

Redpath, H. A. *The Book of the Prophet Ezekiel.* London: Methuen, 1907.

Rowley, H. H. "The Book of Ezekiel in Modern Study." BJRL 36 (1953–54): 146–90.

Sherlock, Charles. "Ezekiel's Dumbness." ExpTim 94 (1983):296–98.

Skinner, John. *The Book of Ezekiel.* The Expositor's Bible. London: Hodder and Stoughton, 1909.

Smith, James. *The Book of the Prophet Ezekiel, A New Interpretation.* London: SPCK, 1931.

Spiegel, Shalom. "Ezekiel or Pseudo-Ezekiel?" HTR 24 (1931):245–321.

———. "Toward Certainty in Ezekiel." JBL 54 (1935):145–71.

Stalker, D. M. G. *Ezekiel.* The Torch Bible Commentaries. London: SCM, 1968.

Taylor, J. B. *Ezekiel. An Introduction and Commentary.* Tyndale Old Testament Commentaries. London: Tyndale, 1969.

Thompson, David. "A Problem of Unfulfilled Prophecy in Ezekiel: The Destruction of Tyre (Ezekiel 26:1–14 and 29:18–20)." *Wesleyan Theological Journal* 16 (1981):93–106.

Torrey, C. C. *Pseudo-Ezekiel and the Original Prophecy.* New Haven, Conn.: Yale U., 1930.

———. "Certainly Pseudo-Ezekiel." JBL 53 (1934):291–320.

Tsevat, M. "The New-Assyrian and Neo-Babylonian Vassal Oaths and the Prophet Ezekiel." JBL 78 (1959):199–204.

Wevers, John W. *Ezekiel.* The Century Bible, new series. London: Thomas Nelson, 1969.

Whitley, C. F. "The 'Thirtieth' Year in Ezekiel 1:1." VT 9 (1959):326–30.

Wilson, Robert R. "An Interpretation of Ezekiel's Dumbness." VT 22 (1972):91–104.

———. "Prophecy in Crisis: The Call of Ezekiel." Int 38 (1984):117–30.

Zimmerli, Walther. *Ezekiel 1.* Hermeneia. Translated by Ronald E. Clements. Philadelphia: Fortress, 1979.

———. *Ezekiel 2.* Hermeneia. Translated by James D. Martin. Philadelphia: Fortress, 1983.

———. "The Message of the Prophet Ezekiel." Translated by Mrs. Lewis Wilkins and James P. Martin. Int 23 (1969):131–57.

———. "The Special Form- and Traditio-Historical Character of Ezekiel's Prophecy." VT 15 (1965):515–27.

———. "The Word of God in the Book of Ezekiel." *Journal for Theology and the Church* 4. Translated by Joseph C. Weber. Tübingen: J. C. B. Mohr, 1967.

OBADIAH

Allen, Leslie C. *The Books of Joel, Obadiah, Jonah and Micah.* NICOT. Grand Rapids: Eerdmans, 1976.

Beecher, Willis, J. "The Historical Situation in Joel and Obadiah." JBL 8 (1888):14–40.

Bewer, Julius A. *A Critical and Exegetical Commentary on Obadiah and Joel.* ICC. New York: Scribner's, 1911.

Caspari, C. P. *Der Prophet Obadja ausgelegt.* Leipzig: R. Beyer, 1842.

Davies, G. I. "A New Solution to a Crux in Obadiah?" VT 27 (1977):484–87.

Eaton, J. H. *Obadiah, Nahum, Habakkuk and Zephaniah.* Torch Book Commentary. London: SCM, 1962.

Glueck, Nelson. "The Boundaries of Edom." HUCA 11 (1936):141–57.

———. *The Other Side of the Jordan.* Cambridge, Mass.: American Schools of Oriental Research, 1970.

Goldman, S. "Obadiah, Introduction and Commentary." In *The Twelve Prophets.* Edited by A. Cohen. Bournemouth: Soncino, 1948.

Gray, John. "The Diaspora of Israel and Judah in Obadiah vs. 20." ZAW 65 (1953):53–59.

Lillie, James, R. "Obadiah—a Celebration of God's Kingdom." CurTM 6 (1979):18–22.

Perowne, T. T. *Obadiah and Jonah.* The Cambridge Bible for Schools and Colleges. Cambridge: Cambridge U., 1883.

Robinson, T. H. "The Structure of the Book of Obadiah." JTS 17 (1916):402–8.

Smith, John M. P. "The Structure of Obadiah." AJSL 22 (1906): 131–38.

Smith, John M. P.; William Hayes Ward; and Julius A. Bewer, *A Critical and Exegetical Commentary on Micah, Zephaniah, Nahum, Habakkuk, Obadiah and Joel.* ICC. New York: Charles Scribner's Sons, 1911.

Thompson, John A. "The Book of Obadiah." In *The Interpreter's Bible.* Vol. 6. New York: Abingdon, 1956.

Watts, John D. W. *The Books of Joel, Obadiah, Jonah, Nahum, Habakkuk and Zephaniah.* The Cambridge Bible Commentary on the New English Bible. Edited by P. R. Ackroyd et al. Cambridge: Cambridge U., 1975.

———. *Obadiah, A Critical Exegetical Commentary.* Grand Rapids: Eerdmans, 1969.

LAMENTATIONS

Budde, Karl. "Das hebraeische Klagelied." ZAW 2 (1882):1–52.

———. "Poetry (Hebrew)." In *A Dictionary of the Bible.* Edited by James Hastings.

Calvin, John. *Commentary on the Book of the Prophet Jeremiah and the Lamentations.* Reprint. Grand Rapids: Eerdmans, 1950.

Dahood, M. "New Readings in Lamentations." Bib 59 (1978):174–97.

Gordis, Robert. *The Song of Songs and Lamentations*. Rev. and enlarged ed. New York: KTAV, 1947.

Gottwald, Norman K. *Studies in the Book of Lamentations*. Studies in Biblical Theology No. 14. Chicago: Allenson, 1954.

Gunkel, Hermann. "Klagelieder Jeremiae." In *Die Religion in Geschichte und Gegenwart*. 2d ed. 3:1049–52. Tübingen, 1929.

Habel, Norman C. *Jeremiah. Lamentations*. Concordia Commentary. St. Louis: Concordia, 1968.

Hillers, Delbert R. *Lamentations*. The Anchor Bible. Garden City, N.Y.: Doubleday, 1972.

Kuist, Howard Tillman. *Jeremiah and Lamentations*. The Layman's Bible Commentary. Richmond: John Knox, 1960.

Naegelsbach, C. W. Eduard. *The Lamentations of Jeremiah*. Translated and enlarged by W. H. Hornblower. New York: Scribner's, 1892.

Peake, A. S. *Jeremiah and Lamentations*. The New Century Bible. Edinburgh: T. C. and E. C. Jack, 1910–1912.

Shea, W. H. "The *qinah* Structure of the Book of Lamentations." Bib 60 (1979):103–7.

Streane, A. W. *The Book of the Prophet Jeremiah Together with the Lamentations*. Cambridge: Cambridge U., 1899.

DANIEL

Archer, Gleason L., Jr. "The Aramaic of the Genesis Apocryphon Compared with the Aramaic of Daniel." In *New Perspectives on the Old Testament*, pp. 160–69. Edited by J. Barton Payne. Waco, Tex.: Word, 1970.

———. "The Hebrew of Daniel Compared with the Qumran Sectarian Documents." In *The Law and the Prophets: Old Testament Studies Prepared in Honor of Oswald T. Allis*, pp. 470–80. Edited by John Skilton. Philadelphia: Presbyterian and Reformed, 1974.

———, trans. *Jerome's Commentary on Daniel*. Grand Rapids: Baker, 1958.

Baldwin, Joyce G. *Daniel: An Introduction and Commentary*. Downers Grove, Ill.: InterVarsity, 1978.

———. "Some Literary Affinities of the Book of Daniel." TynB 30 (1979): 77–99.

Bulman, James M. "The Identification of Darius the Mede." WTJ 35 (1972–73): 247–67.

Calvin, John. *Commentary on the Book of Daniel*. Translated by Thomas Meyer. Reprint. Grand Rapids: Eerdmans, 1948.

Charles, R. H. *A Critical and Exegetical Commentary on the Book of Daniel*. ICC. Oxford: Clarendon, 1929.

Collins, J. J. *The Apocalyptic Vision of the Book of Daniel*. Harvard Semitic Monographs No. 16. Missoula, Mont.: Scholars Press, 1977.

Coxon, Peter W. "The Syntax of the Aramaic of Daniel: A Dialectal Study." HUCA 48 (1977):107–22.

Day, John. "The Daniel of Ugarit and Ezekiel and the Hero of the Book of Daniel." VT 30 (1980):174–84.

DiLella, Alexander A. "The One in Human Likeness and the Holy Ones of the Most High in Daniel 7." CBQ 39 (1977):1–19.

Dougherty, Raymond Philip. *Nabonidus and Belshazzar: A Study of the Closing Events of the Neo-Babylonian Empire*. New Haven, Conn.: Yale U. 1929.

Dressler, Harold H. P. "The Identification of the Ugaritic 'Dnil' with the Daniel of Ezekiel." VT 19 (1979):152–61.

Driver, S. R. *Daniel*. The Cambridge Bible for Schools and Colleges, Cambridge: Cambridge U., 1901.

Ginsberg, H. Louis. *Studies in Daniel*. New York: The Jewish Theological Seminary of America, 1948.

Gurney, R. J. M. "The Seventy Weeks of Daniel 9:24–27." EQ 53 (1981):29–36.

Hartman, Louis F., and Alexander A. DiLella. *The Book of Daniel*. The Anchor Bible. Garden City, N.Y.: Doubleday, 1978.

Hasel, Gerhard, F. "The Four World Empires of Daniel 2 Against Its Near Eastern Environment." JSOT 12 (1979):17–30.

Heaton, E. W. *Daniel*. Torch Bible Commentaries. London: SCM, 1956.

Hillers, Delbert. R. "History and Poetry in Lamentations." CurTM 10 (1983):155–61.

Jones, B. C. "The Prayer in Daniel 9." VT 18 (1968):488–93.

Keil. C. F. *Biblical Commentary on the Book of Daniel*. Translated by M. G. Easton. Reprint. Grand Rapids: Eerdmans, 1971.

Kline, Meredith G. "The Covenant of the Seventieth Week." In *The Law and the Prophets: Old Testament Studies Prepared in Honor of Oswald T. Allis*, pp. 452–69. Edited by John Skilton. Philadelphia: Presbyterian and Reformed, 1974.

Knowles, Louis E. "The Interpretation of the 70 Weeks of Daniel in the Early Fathers." WTJ 7 (1944):136–60.

Lacocque, A. *The Book of Daniel*. Translated by David Pellauer. London: SPCK, 1979.

Leupold, H. C. *Exposition of Daniel*. Columbus: Wartburg, 1949.

McCullough, W. S. "Israel's Eschatology from Amos To Daniel." In *Studies on the Ancient Palestinian World*, pp. 86–101. Edited by J. M. Weavers and D. B. Redford. Toronto: U. of Toronto, 1972.

Montgomery, J. A. *A Critical and Exegetical Commentary on the Book of Daniel*. ICC. New York: Scribner's, 1927.

Newman, Robert C. "Daniel's 70 Weeks and the Old Testament Sabbath Year Cycle." JETS 16 (1973):229–34.

Olmstead, A. T. *History of the Persian Empire*. Chicago: U. of Chicago, 1948.

Payne, David. "The Place of Daniel in Old Testament Eschatology." Them 4 (1967):33–40.

Payne, J. Barton. "The Goal of Daniel's Seventy Weeks." JETS 21 (1978): 97–115.

Porteous, Norman. *Daniel, A Commentary*. The Old Testament Library. Philadelphia: Westminster, 1965.

Rowley, H. H. *The Aramaic of the Old Testament*. London: Oxford U., 1929.

———. "The Composition of the Book of Daniel." VT 5 (1955): 272–76.

———. *Darius the Mede and the Four World Empires in the Book of Daniel*. Cardiff, Wales: U. of Wales, 1959.

———. "The Meaning of Daniel for Today: A Study of Leading Themes." Int 15 (1961):387–97.

———. "The Unity of the Book of Daniel." In *The Servant of the Lord and Other Essays*, pp. 249–80. Oxford: Oxford U., 1965.

Thiele, Edwin R. *The Mysterious Numbers of the Hebrew Kings*. Chicago: U. of Chicago, 1951.

Towner, W. Sibley. *Daniel*. Interpretation. Atlanta: John Knox, 1984.

———. "The Poetic Passages of Daniel 1–6." CBQ 31 (1969): 317–26.

Vasholz, Robert I. "Qumran and the Dating of Daniel." JETS 21 (1978):315–21.

Waltke, Bruce K. "The Date of the Book of Daniel." Bib Sac 133 (1976): 319–29.

Whitcomb, John C., Jr. *Darius the Mede: A Study in Historical Identification*. Grand Rapids: Eerdmans, 1959.

Wilson, Robert Dick. *Studies in the Book of Daniel: A Discussion of the Historical Questions*. New York: Putnam's, 1917.

Wiseman, D. J. *Chronicles of Chaldean Kings (626–556 B.C.) in the British Museum*. London: The Trustees of the British Museum, 1956.

———, ed. *Notes on Some Problems in the Book of Daniel*. London: Tyndale, 1965.

Wood, Leon. *A Commentary on Daniel*. Grand Rapids: Zondervan, 1973.

Yamauchi, Edwin M. "The Archaeological Background of Daniel." Bib Sac 137 (1980):3–16.

———. "Daniel and Contacts Between the Aegean and the Near East Before Alexander." EQ 53 (1981):37–47.

———. "Hermeneutical Issues in the Book of Daniel." JETS 23 (1980):13–21.

Young, Edward J. *The Prophecy of Daniel, A Commentary*. Grand Rapids: Eerdmans, 1949.

Zimmerman, Frank. "The Aramaic Origin of Daniel 8–12." JBL 57 (1938): 258–72.

————. "Some Verses in Daniel in the Light of a Translation Hypothesis." JBL 58 (1939):349–54.

HAGGAI

Ackroyd, Peter R. "The Book of Haggai and Zechariah 1–8." JJS 3 (1952): 151–56.

————. "Some Interpretive Glosses in the Book of Haggai." JJS 7 (1956):163–67.

————. "Studies in the Book of Haggai." JJS 2 (1951): 163–76.

————. "Studies in the Book of Haggai." JJS 3 (1952):1–13.

————. "Two Old Testament Historical Problems of the Early Persian Period: the First Years of Darius I and the Chronology of Haggai, Zechariah 1–8." JNES 17 (1958):13–27.

Baldwin, Joyce G. *Haggai, Zechariah, Malachi, An Introduction and Commentary.* Tyndale Old Testament Commentaries. Downers Grove, Ill.: Inter-Varsity, 1972.

Bloomhardt, Paul F. "The Poems of Haggai." HUCA 5 (1928):153–95.

Koch, Klaus. "Haggai Unreines Volk." ZAW 79 (1967):52–66.

Mason, R. A. "The Purpose of the 'Editorial Framework' of the Book of Haggai." VT 27 (1977):413–21.

Mitchell, Hinckley G.; John Merlin Powis Smith; and Julius A. Bewer. *A Critical and Exegetical Commentary on Haggai, Zechariah, Malachi and Jonah.* ICC. New York: Scribner's, 1912.

Petersen, David L. *Haggai and Zechariah 1–8, A Commentary.* Philadelphia: Westminster, 1984.

Thomas, D. Winton. "The Book of Haggai." In *The Interpreter's Bible.* Vol. 6. New York: Abingdon, 1956.

Whedbee, J. William. "A Question-Answer Schema in Haggai 1: The Form and Function of Haggai 1:9–11." In *Biblical and Near Eastern Studies: Essays in Honor of William Sanford LaSor*, pp. 184–94. Edited by Gary A. Tuttle. Grand Rapids: Eerdmans, 1978.

Wolf, Herbert. " 'The Desire of All Nations' in Haggai 2:7: Messianic or Not?" JETS 19 (1976):97–102.

ZECHARIAH

Baldwin, Joyce C. *Haggai, Zechariah, Malachi.* Tyndale Old Testament Commentaries. Downers Grove, Ill.: InterVarsity, 1972.

Cashdan, Eli. "Zechariah." In *The Twelve Minor Prophets.* Edited by A. Cohen. Bournemouth: Soncino, 1948.

Dumbrell, W. J. "Kingship and Temple in the Post-Exilic Period." RTR 37 (1978):33–42.

Halpern, Baruch. "The Ritual Background of Zechariah's Temple Song." CBQ 40 (1978):167–90.

Harrison, R.K. "Book of Zechariah." In *The Zondervan Pictorial Encyclopedia of the Bible*, pp. 950–56. Edited by Merrill C. Tenney. Grand Rapids: Zondervan, 1975.

Jansma, T. *Inquiry into the Hebrew Text and the Ancient Versions of Zechariah 9–14*. Leiden: E. J. Brill, 1949.

Jones, D. R. "A Fresh Interpretation of Zechariah 9–11." VT 12 (1962):241–59.

Kraeling, E. G. H. "The Historical Situation in Zech. 9:1–10." AJSL 41 (1924):24–33.

Ladd, George Eldon. "Why Not Prophetic-Apocalyptic?" JBL 76 (1957): 192–200.

Leupold, H. C. *Exposition of Zechariah*. Columbus, O.: Wartburg, 1956.

Mackay, Cameron. "Zechariah in Relation to Ezekiel 40–48." EQ 40 (1968):196–210.

Mason, Rex A. "The Relation of Zech. 9–14 to Proto-Zechariah." ZAW 88 (1976):227–39.

Mastin, B. "A Note on Zecharah 6:13." VT 26 (1976):113–16.

May, H. G. "A Key to the Interpretation of Zechariah's Visions." JBL 57 (1938):173–84.

Mitchell, Hinckley G.; John Merlin Powis Smith; and Julius A. Bewer. *A Critical and Exegetical Commentary on Haggai, Zechariah, Malachi and Jonah*. ICC. New York: Scribner's, 1912.

Monro, W. D. "Why Dissect Zechariah?" EQ 10 (1938):45–55.

North, Francis Sparling. "Critical Analysis of the Book of Haggai." ZAW 68 (1956):25–46.

Petersen, David L. *Haggai and Zechariah 1–8, A Commentary*. Philadelphia: Westminster, 1984.

Radday, Yehuda and Dieter Wickmann. "The Unity of Zechariah Examined in the Light of Statistical Linguistics." ZAW 87 (1975):30–55.

Ringgren, Helmer. "Behold Your King Comes." VT 24 (1974):207–11.

Robinson, Donald Fay. "A Suggested Analysis of Zechariah 1–8." ATR 33 (1951):65–70.

Siebeneck, Robert T. "The Messianism of Aggeus and Proto-Zechariah." CBQ 19 (1957):312–28.

Stade, B. "Deuterozacharja." ZAW 1 (1881):1–96; 2 (1882):151–72, 272–309.

Treves, M. "Conjectures Concerning the Date and Authorship of Zechariah 9–14." VT 13 (1963):196–207.

JOEL

Ahlstrom, G. W. *Joel and the Temple Cult of Jerusalem*. Supp. VT 21. Leiden: E. J. Brill, 1971.

Allen, Leslie C. *The Books of Joel, Obadiah, Jonah and Micah*. NICOT. Grand Rapids: Eerdmans, 1976.

Beecher, Willis J. "The Historical Situation in Joel and Obadiah." JBL (1888):14–40.

Credner, K. A. *Der Prophet Joel*. Halle: Buchhandlung des Waisenhauses, 1931.

Driver, S. R. *The Books of Joel and Amos*. Cambridge Bible for Schools and Colleges. Cambridge: Cambridge, U., 1901.

Gray, G. B. "The Parallel Passage in Joel and Their Bearing on the Question of Date." Expos 458 (1893):208–25.

Hosch, Harold. "The Concept of Prophetic Time in the Book of Joel." JETS 15 (1972):31–38.

Jones, D. R. *Isaiah 56–66 and Joel*. Torch Bible Commentaries. London: SCM, 1964.

Kapelrud, A. S. *Joel Studies*. Uppsala: Almquist and Wiksells, 1948.

Mitchell, Hinckley G.; John Merlin Powis Smith; and Julius A. Bewer. *A Critical and Exegetical Commentary on Haggai, Zechariah, Malachi and Jonah*. ICC. New York: Scribner's, 1912.

Myers, J. M. "Some Considerations Bearing on the Date of Joel." ZAW 24 (1962):177–95.

Ogden, Graham S. "Joel 4 and Prophetic Responses to National Laments." JSOT 26 (1983):97–106.

Roth, C. "The Teacher of Righteousness and the Prophecy of Joel." VT 13 (1963):91–95.

Sellers, Ovid R. "Stages of Locust in Joel." AJSL 52 (1935):81–85.

Stephenson, F. R. "The Date of the Book of Joel." VT 19 (1969): 224–49.

Thompson, John A. "The Book of Joel." In *The Interpreter's Bible*. Vol. 6. New York: Abingdon, 1956.

——. "Joel." JNES 6 (1956):727–60.

——. "Joel's Locusts in the Light of Near Eastern Parallels." JNES 14 (1955):52–55.

Treves, Marco. "The Date of Joel." VT 7 (1957):149–56.

Whiting, John D. "Jerusalem's Locust Plague." NatGeo 27 (1915):511–50.

Wolff, Hans W. *Joel and Amos*. Translated by Waldemar Janzen et al. Philadelphia: Fortress, 1977.

MALACHI

Baldwin, Joyce G. *Haggai, Zechariah, Malachi*. Tyndale Old Testament Commentaries. Downers Grove, Ill.: InterVarsity, 1972.

——. "Malachi 1:11 and the Worship of the Nations in the Old Testament." TynB 23 (1972):117–24.

Dentan, Robert C. "The Book of Malachi." In *The Interpreter's Bible*. Vol. 6. New York: Abingdon, 1956.

Dumbrell, W. J. "Malachi and the Ezra-Nehemiah Reforms." RTR 35 (1976):42–52.

Fisher, James A. "Notes on the Literary Form and Message of Malachi." CBQ 34 (1972):315–20.

Hill, Andrew E. "Dating the Book of Malachi: A Linguistic Reexamination." In *The Word of the Lord Shall Go Forth*. Edited by Carol L. Meyers and M. O'Connor. Winona Lake, Ind.: Eisenbrauns, 1983.

Kuchner, Fred Carl. "Emphases in Malachi and Modern Thought." In *The Law and the Prophets: Old Testament Studies Prepared in Honor of Oswald T. Allis*, pp. 482–93. Edited by John Skilton. Philadelphia: Presbyterian and Reformed, 1974.

McKenzie, Steven L., and Howard N. Wallace. "Covenant Themes in Malachi." CBQ 45 (1984):549–63.

Mitchell, Hinckley G.; John Merlin Powis Smith; and Julius A. Bewer. *A Critical and Exegetical Commentary on Haggai, Zechariah, Malachi and Jonah*. ICC. New York: Scribner's, 1912.

Radday, Yehuda T., and Moshe A. Pollatschek, "Vocabulary Richness in Post-Exilic Prophetic Books." ZAW 92 (1980):333–46.

Smith, John Merlin Powis. *A Critical and Exegetical Commentary on the Book of Malachi*. ICC. New York: Scribner's, 1912.

Swetnam, James. "Malachi 1,11: An Interpretation." CBQ 31 (1969): 200–9.

Torrey, C. C. "The Prophecy of 'Malachi.' " JBL 17 (1898):1–15.

INDEX OF SUBJECTS
AND PERSONS

Abiathar, 186
Abijah, 127
Abraham, 120
Accession year, 281
Acrostic, 218–20
Ahaz, 19, 126, 128, 134, 137, 139, 154, 217
Ahijah of Shiloh, 21
Akitu festival, 221
Alexander the Great, 317
Allegory, 232, 330–31
Alliteration, 108, 220
Amaziah of Bethel, 13, 22, 72, 74, 76, 81
Amaziah, King, 126, 256
Ammon, oracles against, 199, 244, 256
Amon, 166
Amos, 12, 41, 55–83, 103, 120, 135, 173, 271, 331
Anathoth, 186 n.2
Antichrist, 289, 296
Antiochus IV Epiphanes, 289, 296
Apocalypse, 235–36, 290, 292, 311–12, 331
Arabia, oracles against, 141
Aramaic, 281, 285–87, 289
Artaxerxes I, 278
Asshur, fall of, 163, 193
Asshur-uballit, 217
Asshurbanipal, 167, 171, 217, 218
Assonance, 220
Assyria, oracles against, 139
Astyages, 277
Autobiography, 31

Baalism, 17, 21, 22, 26, 78, 81, 87, 98, 166, 210
Babylon, oracles against, 140, 199, 200
Babylon/Babylonians, 114, 138–39, 146, 148, 150, 195, 217, 285
Babylonian Chronicle, 200, 217, 282
Balak, 105, 120
Baruch, 33, 190, 192, 202, 203
Bel and the Dragon, 176
Belshazzar, 281, 283, 284, 292, 294–95
Biography, 31, 201–2

Call, prophetic, 133–34
Cambyses, 277, 302, 303
Carchemish, Battle of, 164, 182, 194, 199, 282
Chaldeans, 138, 163, 177, 178, 179, 180, 200, 228, 295
Chananiah ben Hezekiah, 239
Chiasm, 302
Child sacrifice, 116, 151 n. 68, 209
Christ, 296, 298
Chronicler, 127, 165, 193
Confessions of Jeremiah, 189, 204
Covenant, Abrahamic, 92
Criticism
    form, 66, 94, 95, 117, 189
    tradition, 107, 109
Cult, 113
Cyrus, 12, 136, 139, 145–48, 149, 150, 151, 152, 154, 156, 157, 277, 283, 284 n.18, 285, 289, 291, 292, 294, 296, 297, 298, 301, 302, 303, 310
    decree of, 12, 297, 301, 310

Damascus, oracles against 199
Daniel, 167, 279–300
Daniel of Ugarit, 280, 280 n.1
Darius I, 277, 279, 284, 292, 296, 335
Darius the Mede, 284–85, 292, 294, 296
David, 24, 44, 137, 157
Davidic dynasty, 15, 75, 82, 97, 113,
    305
Day of the Lord, 18, 69, 76, 82, 169,
    172, 238, 241, 243, 246, 254, 257,
    258, 259, 260, 262, 267, 268, 271–72,
    312, 324, 327, 331, 332–33, 342
Dead Sea Scrolls. *See* Qumran
Deutero-Zechariah, 313
Divination, 14, 27

Edom, oracles against, 141, 199,
    256–57
Edom/Edomites, 38, 70, 72, 78, 141,
    149, 187
Egypt, oracles against, 140, 199, 223,
    246
Elam, oracles against, 199, 256
Elders, 228, 228 n. 1, 330
Elders of the land, 104
Eli, 186
Elijah, 21, 22, 25, 45, 48, 337,
    342
Elisha, 15, 21, 45, 52
Elkosh, 216
Esau, 256, 262
Eschatology, prophetic, 109, 110,
    145–56, 239–41, 327
Ethiopia, oracles against, 140
Exile, 23, 35, 96, 114, 146, 147, 148,
    149, 263, 267, 271–72, 312
Exodus, 22, 79, 116, 178
    new, 120
Ezekiel, 73, 99, 131, 164, 227–53, 279,
    321–22
Ezra, 278, 297, 338

Gedaliah, 320
Genesis Apocryphon, 287
Greek Empire, 295
Gubaru, 285, 294

Habakkuk, 164, 174–84, 224
Haggai, 277, 301–9
Hagiographa, 263
Hananiah, 26
Hazor, oracles against, 199
Hezekiah, 18, 106, 107, 128, 144,
    146–47, 163, 166
    reform of, 77, 113, 127
Hilkiah, 187
History, 120–21
Holiness, 307, 322
Holiness Code, 231
Hophra, Pharaoh, 201, 244
Hosea, 84–102, 103, 122, 127, 131, 335
Hoshea, 86
Huldah, 235
Hymns, 74–75

Iddo, 127
Idolatry, 23, 121–23, 151, 183–84, 197
Immanuel, 126, 134–37, 157
Irony, 81, 114
Isaiah, 88, 121, 141, 125–59, 215, 218
Isaiah Apocalypse, 142
Israel, oracles against, 140

Jacob, 255, 261
Jehoahaz, 163, 193–94
Jehoiachin, 164, 193–94, 234
Jehoiakim, 163, 189, 194, 199
Jehoiakim
    "fourth year," 281
    "third year," 281–83
Jehonadab, 21
Jehu, 127
Jeremiah, 33, 131, 146, 163–64,
    185–213, 256, 297
Jeroboam I, 15, 55
Jeroboam II, 39, 41, 59, 60, 73, 86
Jerusalem
    fall of, 18, 112, 229, 256, 260, 264,
    267, 271
    oracles against, 141
Jeshua (Joshua), 302, 304, 306, 319
Job, 255, 263
Joel, 278, 324–34

Jonah, 41–54
Josiah, 163, 166, 192–93
Josiah, reform of, 168–69, 280
Justice, 19, 24–25, 80, 116, 183, 261–62

Kedar, oracles against, 199
Kingdom of God, 227, 310, 321, 322–23
Kittim, 182
Knowledge of God, 93, 100

Lamentations, 254, 260, 263–73
Liturgy, 220
Love, Yahweh's, 335, 342

Maccabean Period, 115, 286
Magic, sympathetic, 63
Malachi, 278, 335–43
Manasseh, 18, 151, 164, 167, 169, 176, 182
Mari, 14, 32
Masoretes, 145, 219, 327
Masoretic text, 87
Mechilta, 230
Medes, 108, 193, 217, 285, 289
Medo-Persian Empire, 285
Megillot, Five, 263
Merodach-baladan, 108, 114, 127, 138, 146, 163
Messenger speech, 65, 132
Messiah/Messianic Age, 137, 140, 153, 156, 157, 240, 295, 315
Micah, 75, 88, 103–24
Micaiah, son of Imlah, 16, 31, 103
Moab, oracles against, 139–40, 199, 256
Monarchy, 15, 308
Moresheth-Gath, 104, 107
Moses/Mosaic law, 19, 55, 135, 148, 199, 227, 280, 337, 342

Nabataeans, 265, 339, 342
Nabonidus, 277, 283–84, 285
Nabopolassar, 163, 174, 217
Nahum, 215–26
Nathan, 16, 21

Nebo (Nabu), 51
Nebuchadnezzar, 12, 141, 164, 186, 194, 195, 199, 207, 239, 277, 281, 282, 283, 284
Neco, Pharaoh, 163, 164, 246
Nehemiah, 116, 159, 256, 278, 297, 329
Neo-Assyrian Period, 12, 39–40, 82, 126, 134–35, 150, 174, 182, 188, 193, 217, 218, 221
Neo-Babylonian Period, 12, 106, 114, 150–51, 163–64, 175, 180–81, 288, 295
New Year's festival, 72, 112, 178, 261
Nineveh, 46–48
fall of, 163, 168, 171, 193, 215, 216
Nonaccession year, 281

Obadiah, 164, 254–62, 328
Oppression, social, 24–25
Oracles against the nations. *See* oracles, national
Oracles
judgment, 109
national, 29–30, 63–68, 137–41, 185–86, 199–201, 215, 223–24, 256–57
prophetic, 28–30
salvation, 109

Palistrophe, 93
Parallelism, 303
Paranomasia (word play), 70, 108, 220
People of the land, 167, 167 n. 6
Persian Period, 12, 277–78
Persians, 139, 296
Personification, 266
Philistines, oracles against, 128, 139, 199
Poetry, 31
Prediction, 20, 30, 34, 151–52
Priests/priesthood, 17, 121, 227, 228, 272, 307, 308, 310, 331
Prophecy
literary, 15
nonliterary, 15–16
origins of, 13–15

Prophet, call of, 17, 73, 133–34
Prophetic books
  canonization of, 34–36
  composition and literature, 27–34
Prophetic perfect, 215, 215 n. 1
Prophets
  classical, 15, 43, 50
  cult, 56, 58, 220–21, 229, 302,
  324–25
  false, 26–27, 103, 105, 118, 119, 123,
  272, 323–24
  former, 45
  latter, 11, 45
  literary, 22
  major, 11
  Mesopotamian, 224
  minor, 11, 336
  sons of the, 16
Proto-Zechariah, 313
Psalms, imprecatory, 225
Psamtik I, 218
Pseudepigrapha, 147

Qinah, 229
Qumran/Dead Sea Scrolls, 130, 145,
  179, 286–87

Rechabites, 191, 201
Rehoboam, 55, 127
Restoration, 238, 258–59
Revelation of John, 311
Righteousness, 19, 23, 122, 145, 243, 279
Roman Empire, 296

Sacrifice, 309, 335
Samaria, fall of, 18, 34, 77, 86, 91,
  104, 106, 127, 254, 290 n. 49
Samuel, 21
Sargon II, 39, 107, 108, 128, 144
Scythians, 168–69, 196 n. 12
Second Isaiah, 145
Seder Olam, 176 n. 4
Sennacherib, 39, 52, 106, 107, 109, 113,
  114, 127, 128, 131, 144, 147
Septuagint, 14, 180, 199, 206–7, 262,
  269, 301, 327

Servant Songs, 152–54
Shalmaneser V, 39, 86
Shemaiah, 21, 127
Sheshbazzar, 277, 302
Son of Man, 240, 296
Spirit of the Lord, 320, 324, 333
Suffering Servant, 152–54, 157
Symbolism, prophetic, 88, 190, 231
Syria, oracles against, 140
Syro-Ephraimite Alliance, 86, 96, 107,
  126, 127, 134

Talmud, 239, 254, 263
Targum, 230, 235, 287, 336
Temple, 104, 110, 112, 117, 151, 191,
  197, 227, 228, 238, 240, 249, 270,
  272, 301, 302, 303, 305, 306, 310,
  319, 321, 322, 323, 324, 325, 339, 340
Thebes (No-Amon), 217, 218
Tiglath-pileser III, 39, 59, 82, 85, 134,
  135, 141, 174
Torah, 257, 280
Trito-Zechariah, 313
Twelve, Book of the, 129, 338, 342
Tyre, oracles against, 141, 245–46

Ugbaru, 277
Universalism, 149
Uz, 255
Uzziah, 39, 59, 126, 128, 134, 256

Valley of Jehoshaphat, 324, 326, 332
Visions, 30–31, 70–73, 231–32, 318–20
Vulgate, 263

Wisdom, 175, 255, 279
  theology of, 116
Wrath of God, 225, 268, 271
Writing, 189–90

Zechariah, 35, 129, 277, 302, 310–23
Zedekiah, 185, 191, 198, 200, 201, 270
Zephaniah, 18, 30, 35, 165–73, 258
Zerubbabel, 227, 277, 304, 305, 306,
  308, 319
Zimrilim, King, 14

INDEX OF AUTHORS

Aalder, G. C., 44, 45

Ackroyd, Peter R., 73, 74, 303, 304, 308

Ahlstrom, G. W., 329

Albright, W. F., 13, 178, 182, 234

Alexander, J. A., 151, 154

Allen, Leslie C., 109, 110, 112, 115, 118, 259, 326, 328

Allis, O. T., 151, 154, 220

Alt, A., 86

Anderson, F. I., 87, 88, 92, 93, 95

Anderson, G. W., 122

Anderson, R. T., 127

Archer, Jr., G. L., 90, 151, 166, 182, 259, 287, 288

Baldwin, Joyce G., 285, 288, 293, 296, 303, 314, 319, 338, 340

Baly, Denis, 255

Barton, John, 65, 68, 78

Bentzen, Aage, 63, 138

Bertholet, Alfred, 229

Bewer, J. A., 50, 51, 216, 258, 259, 260, 303, 321, 326

Blank, Sheldon H., 54, 153, 197

Bloomhardt, Paul F. 303

Bright, John, 141, 146, 165, 167, 193, 196, 197

Brinkman, J. A., 146

Brownlee, W. H., 130

Bruce, F. F., 322

Brueggeman, Walter, 58, 93, 95

Budde, Karl, 177, 265

Bullock, C. H., 142, 170, 225, 236, 239, 251, 263, 265

Bush, F. W., 150

Buss, Martin J., 96

Buttenwieser, Moses, 233

Calvin, John, 88, 234

Cannawurf, E., 112

Carley, Keith W., 231, 251

Carlson, E. L., 104, 110

Carroll, R. P., 246

Cashdan, Eli, 301

Caspari, P. C., 259

Charles, R. H., 286

Childs, Brevard S., 44, 50, 75, 170, 179, 315, 317, 336

Clements, R. E., 50, 150

Cooke, G. A., 240

Copass, B. A., 104, 110

Coxan, Peter W., 287

Craghan, John F., 14

Credner, K. A., 328

Cripps, Richard S., 59

Davidson, A. B., 90, 191, 194, 203, 206, 234, 249

Day, John, 280 n.1

Delitzsch, Franz, 145, 146, 154

Dentan, Robert C., 337, 338

DeVries, S. J., 219

Di Lella, A. A., 294

Dougherty, R. P., 283

Dressler, Harold H. P., 280

Driver, S. R., 61, 66, 73, 110, 150, 218, 270, 287, 326, 328, 329

Duhm, Bernhard, 182

Dumbrell, W. J., 322, 335, 342

Eaton, J. H., 182
Eichrodt, W., 233, 238
Eiselen, F. C., 86
Eissfeldt, Otto, 61, 96, 109, 110, 115, 146, 167, 168, 197, 204, 205, 206, 207, 220, 265, 302, 314, 317, 330
Ellison, H. L., 245
Engnell, I., 127

Feinberg, C. L., 233, 245
Fisch, S., 239
Fohrer, Georg, 52, 61, 89, 92, 95, 96, 99, 106, 110, 116, 176, 177, 182, 220, 314
Fosbroke, Hughell E. W., 61, 73, 76, 77
Freedman, D. N., 87, 88, 92, 93, 95, 230
Freehof, Solomon B., 137

Galling, Kurt, 229
Gileadi, Avraham, 130
Glueck, Nelson, 255, 256
Goldman, S., 259
Gordis, Robert, 90, 91, 266, 268, 270
Gottwald, Norman K., 67, 137, 168, 263, 264, 265, 266, 270
Gray, G. B., 129, 133, 139, 140, 142
Greenberg, Moshe, 30, 229, 234, 235
Guillaume, Alfred, 14
Gunkel, Hermann, 117, 218, 265

Haldar, Alfred, 221
Hallo, W. W., 127, 144
Hammershaimb, E., 116
Hanson, Paul D., 142
Harper, W. R., 59, 61, 79, 87, 92, 96, 97
Harrison, R. K., 45, 48, 59, 61, 75, 85, 86, 96, 97, 110, 150, 151, 168, 179, 182, 198, 203, 235, 271, 301, 315, 317
Hartman, Louis F., 294
Haupt, Paul, 220
Hayes, John H., 14, 63
Heaton, E. W., 289
Herntrich, Volkmar, 230

Heschel, Abraham, 9, 25
Hill, Andrew E., 339
Hillers, Delbert R., 264, 265, 269, 270
Hoelscher, Gustav, 229
Holladay, J., 43
Hornblower, W. H., 271
Howie, Carl G., 76, 82, 229, 231
Hubbard, D. A., 150
Huffmon, H. B., 26, 101
Humbert, Paul, 220
Hyatt, J. P., 30, 73, 76, 122, 197

Irwin, W. A., 229

Jerome, 296, 298
Josephus, Flavius, 152, 245, 282, 283

Kaiser, Otto, 127, 133, 137, 139, 141, 142
Kapelrud, Arvid S., 56, 57, 58, 67, 76, 112, 117, 324, 329
Kaufmann, Yehezkel, 23, 43, 51, 57, 87, 88, 142, 182, 183, 193, 236, 312
Keil, C. F., 45, 52, 61, 94, 108, 111, 166, 168, 170, 180, 182, 216, 218, 283, 289, 319, 326, 338
Kimchi, David, 46, 88, 126, 153, 176, 235
Kirkpatrick, A. F., 328, 331
Kissane, Edward J., 145, 146, 147, 148, 151
Kitchen, K. A., 72, 287
Koch, Klaus, 13, 319

Ladd, George Eldon, 312
Laetsch, Theodore, 225
LaSor, William S., 150
Lehrman, S. M., 166, 182, 218
Leupold, H. C., 139, 141, 286, 287, 289, 296, 315
Lindblom, J., 24, 90, 135, 137, 142, 176, 237
Lods, Adolph, 85

Mackay, Cameron, 322

McKeating, Henry, 91
McKenzie, John L., 100, 150
Macloskie, G., 48
Maier, Walter A., 218, 221
Maimonides, Moses, 88
Malamat, Abraham, 14, 237
Margalioth, Rachel, 151
Mason, Rex A., 315
Mauchline, John, 86, 97
May, H. G., 205
Mays, James Luther, 92, 100, 104, 108, 109, 111
Meek, T. J., 13, 14
Millar, W. R., 142
Mitchell, H. G., 50, 153, 303, 321
Moldenke, H. N. and A., 56
Moran, William L., 14
Morgenstern, J., 24, 60, 72, 74, 77
Motyer, J. A., 69, 77, 135
Mowinckel, S., 87, 150, 178, 204
Muilenberg, James, 151

Naegelsbach, C. W. E., 268, 270
Nielsen, Eduard, 33, 113
North, Christopher R., 153
North, Robert, 311

Oesterley, W. O. E., 110, 115, 153, 230
Olmstead, A.T., 284, 285
Overholt, Thomas, 26

Perowne, T. T., 45
Pfeiffer, 85, 89, 96, 204, 229, 259, 291, 309, 330
Pollatschek, Moshe A., 338
Pusey, E. B., 93, 168, 170, 183, 259, 315, 317, 338

Radday, Yehuda T., 338
Rashi, 126
Reicke, Bo, 117
Robertson, Edward, 21
Robinson, H. W., 89, 153
Robinson, T. H., 100, 108, 110, 115, 230, 258

Rowley, H. H., 89, 91, 146, 153, 196, 229, 284, 286, 291
Rudolph, W., 99

Schoville, Keith N., 67
Scott, R. B. Y., 139, 140
Sellers, Ovid R., 331
Sellin, Ernst, 52, 61, 89, 92, 95, 96, 99, 106, 110, 116, 176, 177, 182, 220, 314
Skinner, John, 233
Smith, G. A., 44, 45, 50, 52, 86, 96, 97, 109, 110, 112, 167, 168, 175, 177, 178, 216, 260, 314, 325 n.3, 329, 342
Smith, J. M. P., 50, 91, 109, 110, 115, 167, 216, 219, 220, 223, 303, 321, 326, 336
Smith, James, 230
Smith, L. P., 169
Smith, Ralph L., 176
Snaith, Norman H., 16, 87, 89, 97
Soggin, J. Alberto, 74
Stade, Bernard, 109
Stephenson, F. R., 330 n. 17
Swetnam, James, 340

Taylor, Jr., C. L., 179, 180, 246, 249
Thiele, Edwin R., 59, 281, 328
Thomas, D. W., 308
Thompson, John A., 186, 200, 204, 205, 258, 259, 260, 326, 330
Torrey, C. C., 145, 150, 182, 339
Treves, Marco, 330

van der Woude, A. S., 123
Vawter, Bruce, 104, 115
von Orelli, C., 132, 140, 141
von Rad, Gerhard, 293
Vriezen, T. C., 111

Waltke, B. K., 168
Walton, John, 43, 47, 48, 147
Ward, W. H., 176, 180, 216, 326
Watts, J. D. W., 30, 58, 60, 72, 74, 75, 77, 168, 176, 182, 255, 259, 260, 261

Weiser, Artur, 61, 76, 109, 110, 177, 223, 258

Wenham, G. J., 93

Westermann, Claus, 28, 29, 94, 336

Wevers, John W., 30, 233

Whitcomb, Jr., John C., 284

Whiting, John D., 325 n.3, 330

Whybray, R. N., 153

Widengren, Geo, 29, 33

Wildberger, Hans, 111

Willis, John T., 117

Wilson, Ambrose John, 48

Wilson, Robert Dick, 281

Wilson, Robert R., 234

Wiseman, D. J., 45, 46, 47, 51, 199, 200, 217, 246, 282, 283, 285

Wolf, Herbert M., 137

Wolfe, Rolland E., 106, 109

Wolff, H. W., 59, 63, 65, 66, 69, 73, 74, 76, 86, 92, 95, 105, 326

Yamauchi, Edwin M., 285, 288

Young, E. J., 136, 140, 141, 142, 143, 146, 150, 206, 281, 283, 289, 295, 296, 297, 298, 315

Zimmerli, Walther, 232

Zimmermann, Frank, 286

INDEX OF SCRIPTURE

OLD TESTAMENT

DEUTERONOMY
18:22   26
21:15–17   89
28   24, 55

1 SAMUEL
8:11–18   24
9:8   16
10:5–13   16

2 SAMUEL
7:17   16
12   55

1 KINGS
13   136
13:18   16
21   55
22   103, 223
22:13–23   16

2 KINGS
14:25   41
15:19–20   39
19   146–47
18:13–20:19   107
21–25   186
24:1   283

EZRA
4:5–7   284

PSALMS
138, 146–49   301

ISAIAH
1–12   131–37
2:2–4   110
6   17, 133–34
6:1   126
6:8   147
7   34–37
7:14   135, 156
8:16   32, 33, 127, 131, 136, 81, 92, 160
9   137
13–23   137–41
20   88
24–27   141–43, 290
28–33   143–45
28:12   25, 155
33, 34   130
34–35   130, 145–46
36–39   146–47
37–38   127
37–39   31
40–66   147–54
40:6   147

JEREMIAH
1–25   196–99
2:11   209
2:13   208
2:32   209
20:9   19
26   103–4
26–29   201

26:18	104, 106, 279
27	30
27–29	26
27:2–4	185
28	204
29	191
30–31	199
31:31–34	20, 199, 210–11
32–45	201–2
46–51	199–201
49:14–16	259, 259 n. 15
51:59–64	30, 200
52	202–3

LAMENTATIONS

1:1–2	272

EZEKIEL

1–24	238, 239–43
1:1	234–35
25–32	243–46
33–48	238, 246–49
38–39	290, 292
40–48	248–49

DANIEL

1:1	281–83
1–6	291–92
2	295
2, 7–12	292, 312
7	295–96
8	296
9	296–98
9:2	286, 279
10–12	298

HOSEA

1	46
1–3	88–93
1:9	99
1:9–10	120
2	92
2:7	78
4–14	93–96
8:12	19
11:1	98
12:13	19

JOEL

1:1—2:17	331–32
2:18—3:21	332

AMOS

2:9–12	22
3:7	14
3:8	19
5:18–20	42, 254, 268
5:19	41, 268
6:1	41
7	17
7:10–17	73–74
7:14–15	13, 73
7:15	19, 42
9:7	79
9:11–15	75–76

OBADIAH

1–5	259

MICAH

1–3	108–11
4–5	111–15
4:1–4	111–14
6–7	115–17
6:8	116, 122

NAHUM

1	218–20
1:7–8	224

HABAKKUK

1–2	179
1:2–4	176–77
2:2–3	177–78
3	178–79, 181

ZEPHANIAH

3:18–20	170

HAGGAI

1:1–15	305–6
2:1–9	306–7
2:10–19	307
2:20–23	307–8

ZECHARIAH

1:1–6	317
1:7–6:15	318–20
7:1–8:23	320
9–14	292

MALACHI

1:6–2:9	339–40
1:1, 2–5	339
2:10–16	340–41
2:17–3:5	340
3:6–12	341
3:13–4:3	341
4:4–6	342

NEW TESTAMENT

MATTHEW

2:5–6	121
12:39–41	45

LUKE

11:29–30	45
11:51	311

1 PETER

1:12	121